Humble Women, Powerful Nuns

KRISTIEN SUENENS

Humble Women Powerful Nuns

A Female Struggle for Autonomy in a Men's Church

LEUVEN UNIVERSITY PRESS

This book appears in the peer-reviewed series
KADOC Studies on Religion, Culture & Society

EDITORIAL BOARD

Timothy Brittain-Catlin, University of Cambridge
James Chappel, Duke University
Kim Christiaens, KADOC - KU Leuven
Wilhelm Damberg, Ruhr-Universität Bochum
Jean-Dominique Durand, Université Lyon
James C. Kennedy, University College Utrecht
Rupert Klieber, Universität Wien
Mathijs Lamberigts, KU Leuven
Peter Jan Margry, Meertens Instituut / Universiteit van Amsterdam
Francisca Metzger, Pädagogische Hochschule Luzern
Madalena Meyer-Resende, Universidade Nova de Lisboa
Anne Morelli, Université Libre de Bruxelles
Silvia Mostaccio, Université catholique de Louvain
Patrick Pasture, KU Leuven
Isabelle Saint-Martin, EPHE Sorbonne I Paris
Joachim Schmiedl, Philosophisch-Theologische Hochschule Vallendar
J.T. (Thijl) Sunier, VU Amsterdam
Steven Van Hecke, KU Leuven

Cover: Wilhelmina Telghuys and Father Petrus Bogaerts among the first sisters of the congregation at the occasion of the first profession ceremony in December 1866.
[Photograph – 1866 – ADHH, 255]

© 2020 Leuven University Press/Presses universitaires de Louvain/Universitaire Pers Leuven, Minderbroedersstraat 4, B-3000 Leuven (Belgium)

All rights reserved. Except in those cases expressly determined by law, no part of this publication may be multiplied, saved in an automated data file or made public in any way whatsoever without the express prior written consent of the publishers.

ISBN 978 94 6270 227 1
eISBN 978 94 6166 327 6
D/2020/1869/51
https://doi.org/10.11116/9789461663276
NUR 704

CONTENTS

Introduction   9

PART I
RELIGIOUS REVIVAL, ROMANTICISM AND FEMALE ACTION   39
IN A POST-REVOLUTIONARY AGE: FOUR YOUNG WOMEN
(CA. 1820-CA. 1860)

'Foremothers', Revolutions and Revival (ca. 1820-ca. 1848)   42
The female pioneers of the revival   43
Ambiguous images of women   48
Aut maritus, aut murus? Between marriage and the convent   66

Female Religious Entrepreneurship on the Offensive   74
(ca. 1848-ca. 1860)
Religious education: the female voice of the revival   76
The need for male support   79
Enterprising and discursive mechanisms   81
Social and political tensions and female agency   94

The Spiritual Dialectic of Revival Devotion   102
"L'eucharistie peut sauver le monde"   104
A plurality of devotional practices and ascetic self-denial   108
A passion paradigm   112
Female saints as role models   116

PART II
FEMALE AGENCY AT A TURNING POINT: FOUR CONGREGATION   121
FOUNDERS (1857-1867)

Between Longing and Coercion: Spiritual Partnerships   124
"Une religieuse, c'est une paroisse": frustration and appreciation   127
Jesuits: irresistible and unavoidable   139

Soulmates and Rivals: The Power(lessness) of Female Alliances — 146
The convent as a place of refuge — 148
An alternative family unit: ambiguous female bonding on a micro level — 153
"Autel contre autel": the limits of a wider female coalition — 157

Mechelen and Rome: Normative Identity and Ecclesiastical Positioning — 162
Sterckx's pragmatic policy — 164
Basic feminine inspiration — 171
Male implementation — 175
Containing the revival: the struggle with the contemplative legacy — 183
The crowning accomplishment: a Roman approval — 189

PART III
FEMALE ENTREPRENEURSHIP AND LEADERSHIP IN AN ULTRAMONTANE CHURCH: FOUR CONVENT SUPERIORS (CA. 1865-CA. 1885) — 195

Between Dream and Reality: Charisma and Numbers — 198
The story behind two typical congregations — 203
"Les Dames illusionnées": ambitions and criticism — 208

Convents and Castles: An Uneasy Alliance — 218
In the grip of ultramontane elites — 220
A forced turn to the countryside — 226
"Au comble du bonheur": women for women — 231
The female alliance challenged — 234

Crusading in a Convent Habit — 238
A modern apostolate, conservative ideas — 240
Female agency, the European culture wars and the missionary drive — 246
The inevitability of the crusade: the School War (1879-1884) — 253
The challenge of social Catholicism — 256
Victims and religious entrepreneurs: the spiritual dynamics of ultramontanism — 264

"Pas assez femme"? Female Leadership in Women's Convents — 270
"Une hostie vivante": institutionalised self-denial — 272
Internal power balances — 278
Lay sisters: women among women — 281

"Domina ista valde facunda est" 286
Female Leadership in a Male Church
A double-voiced 'conventualisation' 288
Gender, power and freedom of conscience: the confessor issue 293
Roman feminism? 301

Epilogue 308
The Shaping of Perceptions
Fanny Kestre: an active "femme forte", a spiritual "âme simple" 310
Antoinette Cornet: between oblivion and rediscovery 315
Anna de Meeûs: "trop robuste pour être sainte" 318
Wilhelmina Telghuys: always independent 324

Conclusion 329
A Study in Ambiguity

Timeline 344

Bibliography 347

Index of names 377

Colophon 381

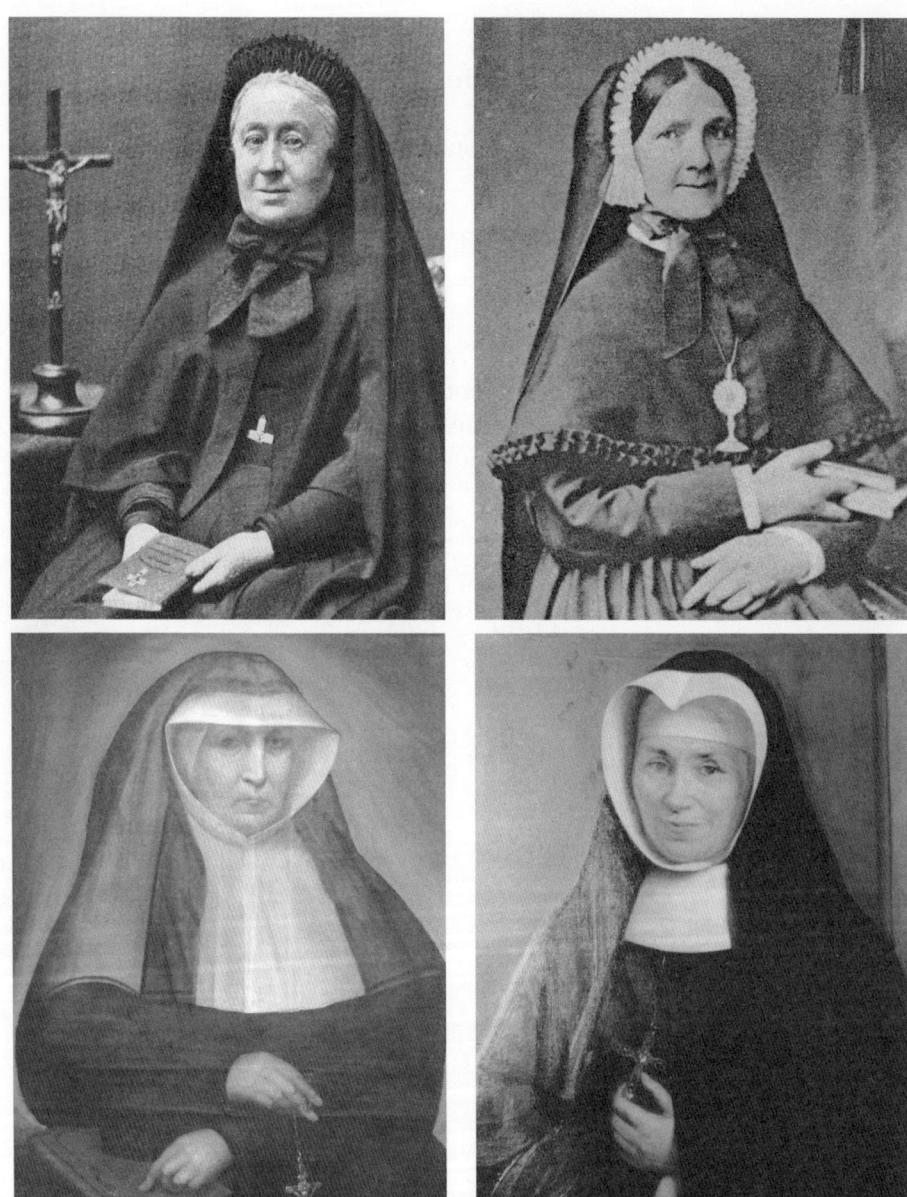

Anna de Meeûs (1823-1904).
[Mortuary Card – 1904 – ARE]

Fanny Kestre (1824-1882).
[Mortuary Card – 1882 – ADSJ]

Antoinette Cornet (1820-1886).
[Painting – ca. 1885 – *Soeurs du S. Cœur de Marie,* La Hulpe]

Wilhelmina Telghuys (1824-1907).
[Painting – S.d. – Collection *Dienstmaagden H. Harten*, Antwerp]

INTRODUCTION

In December 1866, seven religious women posed for a photograph with their confessor. The picture, taken in Antwerp in the early years of commercial photography, captured the official start of their religious life as Servants of the Sacred Hearts of Jesus and Mary. Seven of them, wearing a virgin white veil, had become convent novices. The female founder and superior of the community, Wilhelmina Telghuys, had just taken religious vows and was the only one allowed to wear the full black habit of a professed nun. Gently smiling, she looked away from the camera and seemed to have found her place next to the self-confident and proud male co-founder, Father Petrus Bogaerts. The traditional setting of the picture – a dominant male cleric surrounded by humble women religious – was a stereotypical illustration of gender relations within the Roman Catholic Church of the nineteenth century. The story behind it, however, was far more nuanced and exiting. As a charismatic, socially committed and entrepreneurial young woman, Telghuys was the real driving force behind the project of a religious congregation. Using and at the same time by-passing her position as a devout and obedient woman of the Church, she gradually extended her influence and her autonomy. The humble woman on the picture became a powerful nun and convent superior.

From that perspective, the cover picture of this publication points to a paradox that fundamentally shaped the world of female religious in the Catholic Church: controlled by patriarchal dominance and bounded by religious vows on the one hand, empowered by their status, spiritual inspiration and apostolic importance to act autonomously on the other. Despite a manifest and spectacular growth in the nineteenth and early twentieth centuries, convent life – and especially female convent life – has remained a *terra incognita* for a long time. The female protagonists of this impressive phenomenon remained hidden for a long time behind a curtain of historiographical neglect and religious modesty. Only in recent decades gender and religious historians revealed parts of this fascinating religious landscape. By drawing a critical biographical and comparative group portrait of four female founders of active religious congregations in mid-nineteenth-century Belgium, this study wants to open new perspectives on the gender relationships in nineteenth-century convent life. An analysis of the life stories of Wilhelmina Telghuys and three of her colleagues will unveil the specific opportunities, obstacles and mechanisms that underpinned the intriguing interaction between suppression and autonomy inside and outside Belgian convent walls.

Exploring a *terra incognita*: a historiographical survey

Only in the last quarter of the twentieth century did historians make concerted efforts to intensively explore the universe of nineteenth-century religiously inspired women. The contours of a hidden world of female spirituality, agency and community life were unveiled, within the framework of mutually interwoven historiographical domains: the social, political and cultural history of the early 'revivalist' and the later 'ultramontane' nineteenth-century Church in relation to post-revolutionary society, religious history and women and gender studies.

Romantic revivalism and militant ultramontanism: Church and society

For a long time, research on the nineteenth century was dominated by the idea of continuous and general secularisation. Starting in the 1980s, however, interest grew in religion as an important emotional, cultural and social factor in society after the French Revolution.[1] This inspired an historiographical focus on the nineteenth-century Romantic religious revival as an important socio-cultural development and a countermovement to the secularising and ration-

---

1   For a historiographical overview, see: McLeod, "Weibliche Frömmigkeit", 141; Idem, "New Perspectives", 137-138; Pasture, "Beyond the Feminization Thesis", 7-33; Van Osselaer and Buerman, "Feminization Thesis", 497-498.

alising tendencies of the revolutionary age.² International studies identified the Catholic religious revival as a powerful phenomenon of religious intensification that fostered an increase in popular religious events and devotional exercises, pious and socio-religious associations and religious personnel. Though there is no consensus in international literature about the revival's chronological boundaries, most indications point to its roots in the Napoleonic period, after which it matured in most countries in the second third of the nineteenth century.³ On the one hand it fostered an affective, emotional and repentant piety, often displayed in extra-sacerdotal engagements such as pilgrimages, processions and semi-official devotional activities. This religiosity was inspired by medieval and Tridentine legacies and was fuelled by a new interest in popular devotions, which in the eighteenth century had to a large extent been discredited by rigorist Jansenist influences and the rationalism of the Enlightenment.⁴ On the other hand, the revivalist mentality also strongly emphasised an activist piety and an apostolic engagement in society, that owed much to the example of the Catholic Reformation and to the Enlightenment ideal of social utility. This emphasis was an important stimulus for a 'renaissance of charity', which was closely related to the socio-economic and political developments of the time.⁵

After the Belgian independence in 1830, the revivalist mentality and activities were stimulated by the liberties afforded by the new Belgian Constitution (1831) and the enormous social needs of the new state. By pragmatically embracing the far-reaching constitutional liberties, revivalist Catholics wanted to restore the important position of faith and the Catholic Church in society. With social services and education relying heavily on private initiative, the undeveloped structures of the young Belgian state gave additional opportunities to religiously inspired people to develop their own plans.⁶

2   The revival has been analysed for a broad spectrum of countries and denominations. For a general introduction, see: McLeod, *Religion and People*; Jarlert (ed.), *Piety and Modernity*. For revivalist Catholicism, see: Fleckenstein and Schmiedl (eds.), *Ultramontanismus*; Blackbourn, "The Catholic Church in Europe", 780-786. For France: Cholvy and Hilaire, *Histoire religieuse*; Gibson, *A Social History*; Price, *Religious Renewal*. For the USA, Britain and Ireland: Dolan, *Catholic Revivalism*; Brown, *The Death of Christian Britain*; Heimann, *Catholic Devotion*; Larkin, "The Devotional Revolution in Ireland". For the Netherlands: Monteiro, Rooijakers and Rosendaal (eds.), *De dynamiek van religie en cultuur*. For Germany: Sperber, *Popular Catholicism*; Anderson, "The Limits of Secularization"; Blaschke, "Das 19. Jahrhundert". For Belgium: De Maeyer and Hellemans, "Katholiek reveil"; 61-63; Viaene, *Belgium and the Holy See*.
3   About the chronological debate, see: Clark, "The New Catholicism", 16-18.
4   Although some analyses also point to eighteenth-century precedents for the revival's focus on a popular and emotional piety. For an overview, see: Clark, "The New Catholicism", 15.
5   On the international and multidenominational relationship between the revival, the socio-economic context and the 'renaissance of charity', see: Van Molle, "Comparing religious perspectives", 20-21.
6   Viaene, *Belgium and the Holy See*, 177; Moeys, *Subsidiary Social Provision*.

From 1848 onwards, the pragmatic revivalist confidence in the modern state was undermined by the threat of revolutionary movements throughout Europe and by radicalising anticlerical liberals in Belgium. These developments paralleled the crystallisation of intransigent ultramontanism within Belgian Catholicism. As Belgian historians have pointed out, Belgian ultramontane Catholicism was a complex political and religious movement.[7] It combined an anti-liberal, anti-revolutionary and sometimes theocratically inspired traditionalism with a strong focus on popular, demonstrative piety and the promotion of devotional and charitable associations. In its rejection of the autonomy of the civil state and its belief in the primacy of clerical – and especially Roman – authority, it echoed the opposition of eighteenth-century ultramontanism to the growing dominance of the civil authorities over ancient church prerogatives.

In its mid-century intransigent version, Belgian ultramontanism radicalised and problematised the pragmatic acceptance of the modern state that had characterised revivalist Catholicism. Even though important differences existed between fundamentalist and moderate ultramontanism, its intransigence generally nurtured a siege mentality towards the secular world as well as a militant Catholic opposition to liberal politics. The radicalising anti-liberal Roman politics of the 1860s, the proclamation of papal infallibility by the First Vatican Council (1870), the Paris Commune of 1871 and the escalation of the Roman question after the Franco-Prussian War (1871) caused a mixture of fear, resentment and combativeness. This evolution has already been extensively analysed in the case of the international scene and with regard to French Catholicism.[8] Belgian historians have thoroughly researched prominent lay nineteenth-century ultramontane Catholics, such as Joseph de Hemptinne or Arthur Verhaegen, and their role in the 'culture wars' of the second half of the nineteenth century. Special attention was given to the social importance of their engagement in the ultramontane movement.[9]

Women, gender and religion

Until late into the twentieth century, research into the interaction of women and religion suffered from serious neglect in several historiographical traditions, due to what some historians call a 'double blind spot'.[10] On the one hand, religion was considered to be unimportant in the dominant secularisa-

---

7   Lamberts (ed.), *De kruistocht tegen het liberalisme*; Viaene, *Belgium and the Holy See*, 37-111; Idem, "Katholisches Reveil".
8   Lamberts, *The Struggle with Leviathan*, 147-175. For France: Burton, *Holy Tears, Holy Blood*; Harrison, *Romantic Catholics*.
9   Lamberts, "Joseph de Hemptinne"; De Maeyer, *De rode baron*; Deferme, *Uit de ketens van de vrijheid*, 253; Gérin, "Sociaal-katholicisme".
10 Buerman and Van Osselaer, "De feminisering van religie", 5; Duriez, "Introduction", 14-15.

tion narrative. On the other hand, it was hazardous for women's emancipation from the point of view of the early feminist or women's studies research of the 1960s and 1970s and the gender studies that grew out of it in the 1980s. With regard to church history, women suffered from serious neglect as well. Until the 1960s and 1970s church historians focussed nearly exclusively on the institutional developments of the male-dominated Church and on hagiographies of saints and prominent church figures. The historical spirit changed in the last quarter of the twentieth century. Social, cultural and anthropological shifts in historical research created an opening for the study of everyday life, mystical experiences, religiously inspired practices and habits and the history of the masses. In these areas, women and the meaning of religious experience came into their own, bringing both topics to the historian's attention.[11]

The advent of gender studies in the 1980s, defining gender as the social and cultural construction of male and female identities and relationships, simultaneously paved the way for research into complex mechanisms of power, and the norms, symbols, representations and practices behind it. Following the call of gender studies pioneer Scott to apply gender as a historical category, historians started to focus on male-female relationships as a way of understanding historical developments.[12] From the 1990s onwards, gender historians pointed to the importance of religion as a crucial aspect in gendered power relationships and constructions of femininity and masculinity.[13] Conversely, religious historians intensified and diversified their implementation of gender as a thematic focus and methodological tool.[14]

Of great importance for the historiographical recognition of the powerful relationship between women and religion was the advent of the feminisation thesis and the related discussion about the separate spheres of private and public life as analytical frameworks for the nineteenth-century history of the Church, women and society.[15] From a Catholic perspective, the thesis posited the existence of different social and religious developments in the nineteenth

---

11 Brown speaks of the "power of discursive Christianity" in Britain, whereas Turin focuses on "une étude des caractère ou des sentiments" in France: Brown, *The Death of Christian Britain*, 12; Turin, *Femmes et religieuses*, 9. The feminist literary critic Showalter 'discovered' the religiously inspired, albeit disguised, female activism of Florence Nightingale: "Like other gifted women of her generation, she translated intellectual and vocational drives into the language of religion, the only system that could justify them." Showalter, "Florence Nightingale's Feminist Complaint", 397.
12 Scott, "Gender: A Useful Category"; Perrot, "Pouvoir des hommes".
13 King, "Religion and Gender"; Blaschke, "Das 19. Jahrhundert". For an overview, see: Van Osselaer, *The Pious Sex*, 12-14.
14 Albrecht, Bühler-Dietrich and Strzelczyk (eds.), *Glaube und Geschlecht*; Della Sudda and von Tippelskirch, "Nouvelles approches"; Brejon de Lavergnée and Della Sudda (eds.), *Genre et christianisme*; Lux-Sterritt and Mangion (eds.), *Gender, Catholicism and Spirituality*; Morgan and De Vries (eds.), *Women, Gender and Religious Cultures*.
15 For a thorough historiographical introduction to both theories, see Pasture, "Beyond the Feminization Thesis"; Van Osselaer and Buerman, "Feminization Thesis".

century: the feminisation of religious worshippers, which created a striking discrepancy between large numbers of pious women and an increasing group of secularised men who were indifferent, even hostile to the Church; the feminisation of religious personnel due to the spectacular and unprecedented success of female religious life, with Catholic nuns outnumbering male religious as well as secular priests; the feminisation of Catholic charity, mirrored in the thousands of well-to-do Catholic '*dames d'œuvres*' who engaged in initiatives for the poor, the sick and the destitute; and the feminisation of Catholic piety, which predicated a shift from a pre-revolutionary '*pastorale de la peur*' to a nineteenth-century soft, passionate and affectionate '*pastorale de la cœur*'.[16]

The feminisation thesis at once supported and contradicted the simultaneously developed thesis about the separate spheres. This thesis assumed that nineteenth-century industrialising bourgeois society had pushed women within the private boundaries of the home and the family, making the public domain of politics and economics an exclusively male sphere. Endorsed by the image of a feminised religion and the preponderance of devout women, a private sphere of female religiosity, modesty and domesticity was opposed to a public sphere of male rationality, competitiveness and power. The strong presence of pious women in the public terrain of charitable work and the activities of large numbers of female religious in education, health care and the social services were serious indications, however, that even the boundaries of the sharply gender-divided society of the nineteenth century were diffuse and overlapping.[17]

Recent historiography has put both the feminisation and the separate spheres theories into a broader perspective, especially by criticising their exclusive focus on female religiosity and by reviving interest in masculine forms of nineteenth-century piety and religious action.[18] Some authors have also pointed to the continuing discrepancy between a feminising religious base and a persistent and dominant male clerical hierarchy.[19]

---

16   Analyses of different, though not necessarily all aspects of this thesis can be found in: McLeod, "Weibliche Frömmigkeit"; Brown, *The Death of Christian Britain*; Cholvy and Hilaire, *Histoire religieuse*; Langlois, "Feminisation du catholicisme"; Abrams, *The Making of Modern Woman*; Busch, "Die Feminisierung der Frömmigkeit"; Burton, *Holy Tears*; De Maeyer, "Les dames d'œuvres"; Viaene, *Belgium and the Holy See*; Ford, *Divided Houses*; Luddy, *Women and Philanthropy*.

17   Abrams, *The Making of Modern Woman*, 34-41; Ford, *Divided Houses*, 8-9; Brown, *The Death of Christian Britain*, 42; Bock, *Women in European History*, 84-108; Fuchs, *Women in Nineteenth-Century Europe*, 2-3; McMillan, *France and Women*, 53-54.

18   Pasture, "Beyond the Feminization Thesis", 20-26; King, "Religion and Gender", 76-77; Ford, "Religion and Popular Culture", 152-175; De Maeyer, "Les hommes d'œuvres", 185-204; Fouilloux, "Femmes et catholicisme"; Brejon de Lavergnée, "Le genre du philanthrope"; Idem, "Making the Charitable Man"; Rousseau, "Vingt ans d'histoire religieuse"; Werner (ed.), *Christian Masculinity*; Van Osselaer, *The Pious Sex*, 237-240.

19   Schneider, "Feminisierung der Religion", 130-141.

Women religious

The developments and paradoxes that characterised the historiography about women and religion are mirrored in very similar ways in the scholarly research about nineteenth- and twentieth-century female convent life. The cultural turn, together with the advent of the feminisation thesis and the development of women's and gender studies decisively spurred pioneering surveys about the post-revolutionary history of women religious.[20] Two perspectives dominated the first wave of these scholarly publications. First, from a 'feminisation' perspective, there was a strong focus on a quantitative analysis and explanation of the exceptionally strong growth of women's active congregations during the nineteenth century. Second, the focus was largely on religious life as being the cradle of women's self-development and agency. In his monumental study of French female religious congregations, Langlois, for example, stipulated clearly that: "ces congrégations doivent faire appel à des femmes d'action. Elles leur offrent des postes de responsabilité où elles pourront faire preuve d'initiative et d'esprit d'entreprise, même si elles sont contrôlées par le clergé (...)."[21]

In the 1990s Dutch historians and theologians opened up an interesting new avenue of research, focusing on discourse analysis and on the use by women religious of 'double-voiced' mechanisms of appropriation and expropriation of gender conventions.[22] Their research reflected a general shift in different domains of women's history, where, under the influence of the 'linguistic' turn of poststructuralism, textual analysis and research into different layers of meaning and interpretation became important methodological tools. The pioneering studies of the 1970s and 1980s had made religious women 'visible' in the historical narratives of Church history and in women's and gender studies. In the 1990s, the focus shifted from this 'contribution' history to more intense research into the social, cultural, political and economic significance of women religious and their evolving position in the wider narrative of women's emancipation. Mechanisms of female power, agency and identity in relation to existing gender models and conventions were analysed in the framework of their apostolates and their emotional relationships both within and outside the convent walls.

On a collective level, interest grew in the motives and strategies that determined the creation of congregational structures of governance as female, transregional and even transnational power structures in relation to a male-

---

20 These pioneering studies include: Alkemade, *Vrouwen XIX*; Van Heijst, *Zusters, vrouwen van de wereld*; Ewens, *The Role of the Nun*; O'Brien, "Terra Incognita"; Clear, *Nuns in Nineteenth-Century Ireland*; Langlois, *Le catholicisme au féminin*; Turin, *Femmes et religieuses*; Rocca, *Donne religiose*.
21 Langlois, *Le catholicisme au féminin*, 642.
22 On the development of the 'double-voiced' concept, see infra.

dominated Church.[23] On a biographical level, the ideas, goals and tactics of individual female religious were illuminated, especially in the first generation of scholarly biographies of female congregation founders. These biographies had a double merit. On the one hand, they replaced the hagiographical tradition in writing about female religious and saints. On the other hand, they unveiled the characteristics of female initiative in the foundation processes of religious congregations, which had been wiped out of history for a long time both by a disproportionate attention to male (co-)founders and protagonists as by the convent tradition of modesty and self-denial.[24]

Women (religious) in Belgian historical research

Scholarly research into the history of women in nineteenth- and twentieth-century Belgium mirrored the moderate and non-revolutionary progress of Belgian women's emancipation. Despite the liberal Constitution of 1831, Belgian women were confined to the strong patriarchal structures of the Napoleonic civil code. Only in the second half of the century did liberal and later Catholic initiatives promote better and further education for women. Access to university education and the professions was gradually granted from the 1880s onwards. The first women's emancipation organisations were founded in the 1890s and the first women in the public service were appointed in 1893. Voting rights in local elections followed in 1920 and only in 1948 – as a result of complex political pull and push factors – for national elections.[25]

At the end of the 1960s, inspired by the climate of emancipation at the time, Belgian scholars took their first steps in exploring women's history.[26] Given the long neglect and in line with international historiographical tendencies, the focus was initially on 'rehabilitation' or 'celebratory' history. Feminist biographies of female 'heroines' or prominent figures in the eman-

23 Studies exploring the variety of themes have been published in the form of general scholarly surveys, including: McNamara, *Sisters in Arms*; Werner (ed.), *Nuns and Sisters*; Raughter (ed.), *Religious Women*; Meiwes, *Arbeiterinnen des Herrn*; Smyth, *Changing habits*; Wall, *Unlikely Entrepreneurs*; Walsh, *Roman Catholic Nuns*; Fitzgerald, *Habits of Compassion*; Van Heijst, Derks and Monteiro, *Ex Caritate*; Mangion, *Contested identities*.
24 Some examples: Langlois, *Catholicisme, religieuses et société* and Cholvy (ed.), *La religion et les femmes* (both with biographical articles about several French nineteenth-century female congregation founders); Langlois, *Le désir du sacerdoce*; Kilroy, *Madeleine Sophie Barat*; Stogdon, "A Journey with Thérèse Couderc"; Lecuir-Nemo, *Anne-Marie Javouhey*; Schraut, *Antonia Werr*; Bari, "Pauline von Mallinckrodt"; Lancaster, *Cornelia Connelly*; Hamer, *Elizabeth Prout*; Mangion, "Why would you have me live upon a gridiron?"; Polet, *De weg van Adélaïde*.
25 Inspiring scholarly overviews of women's history and emancipation in Belgium are to be found in: Deneckere, "Droits de l'homme, ook voor vrouwen", 607-624 and Gubin, "Du politique au politique".
26 For historiographical analyses, see: Eijt, "Women's History"; Christens, "Verkend verleden"; De Metsenaere, "Veel geschiedenis"; Gubin, "Histoire des femmes".

cipation movement were intended to take women out of the shadows of history into a new era of 'herstory'.[27] Almost simultaneously, socio-economic, political, juridical and pedagogical research on women set out to reveal the suppressive structures and stereotypes of a patriarchal society. In the margins of this research, religion, though a seldom used angle of research in Belgium, was identified by some contemporary Belgian feminist scholars as a major structure of suppression.[28]

In the 1980s the field of women's history was broadened to include more intensive research into different and specific domains of women's life. Although the studies often had geographically and thematically limited perspectives, the new research did put the dominant discourse of women's confinement in the private sphere to the test of scholarly analysis. The results of research into the history of women with regard to labour, education and organisational life pointed to contradictions between the rhetorically uncontested ideal of women in the home and the reality of class and economic determinations, new initiatives in women's education and the social activities of women. Most of these historiographical fields of interest were further explored in the last years of the twentieth century and into the new millennium. Following the renewed interest in micro-history and biographies, which will be further discussed, historians also published new biographical studies about Belgian women. Prominent women were still the focus of attention, but in contrast with earlier research, most of the new work on the history of Belgian women had a more explicit and in-depth conceptual, contextual and gendered perspective. With regard to nineteenth-century women's history, this is especially the case for recent scholarly research on feminist protagonists, women in literature, art and science, the history of the female psyche and body, and the latest Belgian research into the feminisation thesis.[29]

This last topic is indicative of the renewed interest in the history of women, gender and religion in Belgium. Until the end of the twentieth century, Bel-

27 For example: Gérin, "Louise Van den Plas"; Keymolen, "Isala Van Diest"; Van Praag, "Emilie Claeys"; De Bueger and Van Lierde, "Marie Popelin".
28 See, for example Aubenas' theory that the stronger and earlier feminist agitation in Flanders is related to the greater suppression of women by ecclesiastical structures in this region: Aubenas-Bastie, "1968-1978: Dix ans de féminisme", 321.
29 Some examples: Gubin, "Femmes et l'art"; Creusen, *Femmes artistes*; Michaux, "Femmes de lettres belges"; Brogniez, "Poétesses belges"; Vandenbussche, "Peripheral autonomy"; Idem, *Het veld der verbeelding*; Wils, "Science, an Ally of Feminism?"; Vandenbussche et al., "Virginie Loveling"; Verschaffel, "Vrouwenrollen"; Vanpaemel, "Laissons aux hommes"; Wils (ed.), *Het lichaam*; Van Osselaer, De Smaele and Wils (eds.), *Sign or Symptom*. Contextually embedded biographies or biographical notices of nineteenth-century Belgian women include: Christens and Hansen, "Vrouwen en onderwijs"; Gubin and Piette, *Isabelle Gatti de Gamond*; Keymolen, *Victoire Cappe*; Reymenants, *Marie Elisabeth Belpaire*; Brems, "Ik hoop dat gij braaf zijt"; Carlier, "Emilie Claeys"; Wiertz, *Adellijk en artistiek*. Short biographical notices are also to be found in Gubin et al. (eds.), *Dictionnaire des femmes belges*.

gian research into the multifaceted nineteenth-century relationship between gender and religion had a three-pronged, but overall moderate output. First, sociological and statistical studies from the 1960s onwards, partly triggered by the contemporaneous decline in vocations and religious practice, pointed to changes in church attendance and religious personnel since the post-revolutionary period.[30] Second, the issue of women, Church and religion surfaced in the late 1970s in the margins of the historiography about the late nineteenth-century Catholic women's movements as well as in a few studies about Catholic theories and practices relating to marriage and the family.[31]

Third, in the slipstream of the statistical and sociological studies, the first limited – that is, confined to specific dioceses or regions – historical surveys of female religious institutes appeared.[32] These contributions were followed by the first scholarly monographies of individual congregations. Paul Wynants was a pioneer with his doctoral dissertation about the *Sœurs de la Providence* (Sisters of Providence) of Namur, one of Belgium's largest teaching congregations.[33] In his study, as well as in two later articles about the 'feminine condition' and governmental structures in women's convents, Wynants indicated that religious life for women was a socially accepted alternative to marriage and motherhood with modest possibilities for agency and self-fulfilment, although within the framework of a male-dominated and often suppressive Catholic hierarchy.[34]

While leaving some findings open for further research, Wynants' studies paved the way for intensive historical research on women's religious institutes from the 1990s onwards. Research conducted by KADOC-KU Leuven resulted in a series of monographs about active, mainly Flanders-based con-

---

30 On the statistics for secular and regular clergy: Boudens, "De mannelijke religieuzen"; Art, "De evolutie van het aantal mannelijke roepingen"; Collard, "L'étude sociologique"; Dingemans, *Les instituts religieux*; Tihon, "Les religieuses"; Wynants, *Religieuses*; Hostie, *Leven en dood van de religieuze instituten*; Mertens, "Vrouwelijke religieuze roepingen"; 'T Serstevens, *Le recrutement et l'origine sociale*.

31 On the Catholic women's movement and Christian feminism in Belgium, see: De Weerdt, *En de vrouwen*, 105; Keymolen and Coenen, *Stap voor stap*, esp. 26-41; and on its key nineteenth-century protagonists: Keymolen, *Victoire Cappe*; Reymenants, *Marie Elisabeth Belpaire*. On the Catholic women workers' movement: De Decker, *Vormingswerk in vrouwenhanden*; Osaer et al., "De christelijke arbeidersvrouwen-beweging". On the relationship between church, women and the family, see: Gevers, "Gezin, religie en moderniteit"; Servais, "The Church and the Family"; De Maeyer, "Relatie en huwelijk in de Moderne Tijd".

32 Art, *Kerkelijke structuur*, 33-84; Boudens, "De vrouwelijke religieuzen"; Jacobus, "De vrouwelijke religieuzen".

33 Wynants, *Les Sœurs de la Providence*. On the first master theses focussing on female religious institutes, see: Wynants, "Les instituts féminins", 46.

34 Wynants and Hanoteau, "La condition féminine"; Wynants, "Le gouvernement"; Wynants and Paret, "Les religieuses de vie active".

gregations.³⁵ The nature of these studies determined the predominant institutional perspective of the research. Even within this framework gender issues and questions about the relationship between women and religion were increasingly raised. Research into government structures, apostolic activities and internal and external power relationships resulted, on the one hand, in pioneering insights about the potential of Belgian convent life for women's agency and development: "They got opportunities as women that they could never have had within the still influential and widespread nineteenth-century bourgeois world view".³⁶ On the other hand, the studies also pointed to the inescapability of the patriarchal structures of the Catholic Church.³⁷

The paradoxical tension between suppression and autonomy was addressed in most of the monographs, raising interesting questions for further research: "Did this mean that the Church's interaction with this congregation was patronising, or did it rather point to some unwanted female resistance?"³⁸ Whereas the institutional point of view of most of these studies had the merit of highlighting the tension, it did not allow in-depth research into individual motivation, or into the strategies and challenges of female convent life that could lead to a more nuanced understanding of the paradoxical situation. Where the attempt was made, for instance in studies by Christens, Timmermans and Strobbe, researchers were confronted by a fundamental lack of personal and individual sources, echoing a general historiographical frustration about the scarcity of ego-documents in convent archives.³⁹

In recent Belgian historiography on nineteenth- and twentieth-century female religious, only three studies put gender analysis at the centre of their research. In 2003 Dujardin presented gender as a promising category for (especially twentieth-century) mission history. Unfortunately, her pioneering study

35 Christens, *100 jaar Heilig-Hartinstituut*; Segers, *150 jaar Zusters van het Heilig Hart*; Dhaene and Dhaene, *Sint-Jozef Kortenberg*; Vanderstraeten and Preneel, *175 jaar Zusters van de Christelijke Scholen*; Segers, *Zusters in het Wit*; Timmermans, *Het Convent van Betlehem*; Suenens and De Staercke, *Eén van hart en één van ziel*; Strobbe and Suenens, *Zusters Kindsheid Jesu*.
36 "Als vrouwen kregen zij kansen die zij binnen de wijdverspreide en nog lang doorwerkende 19de-eeuwse burgerlijke opvattingen niet zouden kunnen realiseren." See: Timmermans, *Het Convent van Betlehem*, 460.
37 Lacroix, *La vie à Saint-André*, II, 861; Califice and Janssen, *Le feu sur la terre*; Dhaene and Dhaene, *Sint-Jozef Kortenberg*, 294-295; Deneckere, *Het Gentse Sint-Vincentiusziekenhuis*, 28-29; Cocriamont, "Soigner les corps et les âmes".
38 "Betekent dit dat de interactie van de kerk met deze congregatie er een was van absolute bevoogding, of wijst dit juist op enige ongewenste vrouwelijke weerstand?", in: Christens, *100 jaar Heilig-Hartinstituut*, 366. Similar questions in: Deneckere, *Het Gentse Sint-Vincentiusziekenhuis*, 28-29.
39 Timmermans, *Het Convent van Betlehem*, 460; Strobbe and Suenens, *Zusters Kindsheid Jesu*, 76. For international historiographical discussions about the scarcity of ego-documents in convent archives: Suenens and Marcelis, "Vrouwelijke religieuzen", 844-846; Luddy, "Convent archives as sources", 98-115; Thompson, "Women, Feminism and New Religious History", 138-140; Eijt, *Religieuze vrouwen*, 22; Turin, *Femmes et religieuses*, 9-10.

was not followed by new innovative research into Belgian female missionary congregations. The only exception was Christens's study on Belgian sisters in Africa, which clearly showed that women's missionary work was more than an appendix to male action.[40] In 2008 Viaene examined the interesting story of the *Dames de Saint-André* from Tournai and their conflicts with the Belgian and Roman authorities, stressing important links between the 'modern' and female face of the nineteenth-century revival and the ambiguous dynamics of Roman politics.[41] In 2012, Marcélis published a thorough and detailed study, based on her doctoral dissertation on the nineteenth- and twentieth-century history of Belgian enclosed nuns (Carmelites and Poor Clares) in the Namur region. She highlighted the gendered structure of intra- and extra-mural cooperation between male clerics, lay women and contemplative women religious.[42]

Scholarly biographies of individual Belgian women religious are scarce. Important work has been done on Justine Desbille (1801-1866), founder of the *Sœurs de l'Enfant Jésus* (Sisters of the Infant Jesus) of Nivelles, on Julie Billiart (1751-1816), the early nineteenth-century French founder of the *Sœurs de Notre Dame* (Sisters of Notre Dame) of Namur, and her closest assistant, Françoise Blin de Bourdon (1756-1838).[43] Collections of letters and spiritual writings by another pioneering nineteenth-century female founder, Agathe Verhelle (1789-1838) of the *Dames de l'Instruction Chrétienne* (Ladies of Christian Instruction), were also recently published, but these did not offer any detailed scholarly research on social, religious or gender roles and positions.[44] For other Belgian female founders there are only older and less scholarly biographies, if any.[45]

Research into the history of Belgian women's religious institutes and their impact on gender models also surfaced indirectly in studies about the development of professions for women in education, health care and charitable work.[46] Equally interesting is the research into the economic and entrepre-

---

40   Dujardin, "Gender: een beloftevolle invalshoek"; Christens, *Terra incognita*.
41   Viaene, "The Second Sex".
42   Marcélis, *Femmes cloîtrées des temps contemporaines*.
43   Hanoteau, *Une grande nivelloise*. See for a general overview of all publications on Billiart: Henneau, "Récit de vie", 235-236.
44   *Les écrits spirituels de Mère Agathe Verhelle*.
45   Some examples: Pietromarchi, *Mère Marie-Thérèse Haze*; Pignal, *Si Jansénius avait su*; Suau, *La mère Marie de Jésus*; Duhamelet, *Mère Marie-Xavier Voirin*; De Meulemeester, *Mère Agnes de Jésus*.
46   Depaepe, Devroede and Simon (eds.), *Geen trede meer om op te staan*; Depaepe, Lauwers and Simon, "De feminisering van het leerkrachtenkorps"; Hellinckx, Simon and Depaepe, *The Forgotten Contribution*; Christens and Suenens, "L'enseignement comme vocation et projet"; Van Molle and Jacques, "De verpleegkundigen"; De Maeyer and Deferme, "Vrouwelijke religieuzen"; De Maeyer, "Les dames d'œuvres"; Viaene, *Belgium and the Holy See*, 188-191; Van Dijck and Suenens, "La Belgique Charitable".

neurial potential of female religious institutes.⁴⁷ In the past decade innovative Belgian research has also been conducted into constructions of femininity and masculinity in the Catholic Church. These studies provide us for the first time with a nuanced understanding of the Belgian position in the feminisation narrative, confirming signs of the feminisation of religious personnel and church attendance, which is counterbalanced however by important forms of masculine religiosity and religiously inspired charitable, political and social action by men. Although the focus is mainly on Catholic lay people, analyses of female religious as heroines or role models and insights about the link between charitable work and female agency provide new and promising frameworks for assessing the historical role of female religious as well.⁴⁸

A group portrait of four religious women

This study presents a detailed and comparative analysis of four Belgian female congregation founders in the nineteenth century. Selected for their exceptionally rich, but largely unexplored documentary heritage, the case studies offered coherent as well as diverse subjects for research.

Anna de Meeûs (1823-1904) was born into a wealthy, upper-class family from Brussels and founded in 1857 the semi-contemplative *Institut de l'Adoration Perpétuelle* (Institute of Perpetual Adoration), situated in the heart of Brussels. The congregation combined a special devotion for the Blessed Sacrament with apostolate activities in religious education, retreat work and the promotion of the Eucharistic devotion by means of an international pious association. Hardly a couple of hundred meters away from the Brussels convent of de Meeûs, a similar semi-contemplative Eucharistic congregation was founded by Fanny Kestre (1824-1882), a lower middle-class woman from the capital. Her congregation of *Dames de Sainte-Julienne – Apostolines du Très Saint Sacrement* (Ladies of Saint Julienne, Apostles of the Most Blessed Sacrament) was also focussing on religious education and retreat work. Antoinette Cornet (1820-1886), a middle-class woman from the Walloon town of Walcourt, first entered the teaching congregation of the *Sœurs du Saint Cœur de Marie* (Sisters of the Sacred Heart of Mary) in Alsemberg. Later on, in 1863, she founded her own teaching congregation, also named the *Sœurs du Saint Cœur de Marie*, in the village of La Hulpe, south of Brussels. Born into a wealthy Dutch-Belgian and Protestant-Catholic family of textile and maritime merchants, the above-mentioned Wilhelmina Telghuys (1824-1907) founded in 1866 the *Dienstmaagden van de Heilige Harten van Jezus en Maria* (Servants of

---

47   Heyrman, "La culture d'entreprise", 303; Van Dijck, "From workhouse to convent".
48   Van Osselaer, *The Pious Sex*, 155-158; Art and Buerman, "Is de katholieke man wel een echte vent?".

the Sacred Hearts of Jesus and Mary). Based in the city of Antwerp, this congregation focussed on general education, care and education for orphans and destitute children and hosted a semi-industrial laundry business in nearby Kontich.

All of them operated in comparable frameworks. On the one hand, the similar geographical (Archdiocese of Mechelen) and chronological (mid-nineteenth century) boundaries of the case studies constituted a preliminary basis for comparison, a preamble to the comparative national and international framing mentioned above. On the other hand, there was still enough variation in the selection (social and geographical background, spiritual and apostolic predilections, local, national or international expansion, social networks, etc.) to perform a differentiated analysis.

An ambiguous social niche: research hypothesis and double-voiced methodology

Central perspective of this critical group portrait of four Belgian female congregation founders of the late revival, is the following research hypothesis: the specific cultural and religious context of the nineteenth century and the socio-economic and political Belgian framework offered opportunities for this group of leading women religious to realise spiritual, apostolic and personal goals and to develop strategies that enabled them to create a unique social niche of female autonomy, entrepreneurship and power in the male-dominated Church and society of the time.

Three levels of analysis

The central research hypothesis is analysed and tested on three different levels. At the first level is a biographical analysis of the four women's life stories, focusing on three interwoven elements: their characters, their ideas, motives and ambitions, and their social background and network. Second and analogously, the analysis is conducted on the level of the historical context from four main angles: the radical socio-economic transformations in combination with political and legal preconditions; the religious and cultural perspective of the revival and emerging ultramontanism; church structures and clerical relationships; and the predominant gender patterns of nineteenth-century bourgeois society. Interactions between both analyses will illuminate the strategies employed by these women in responding to the context-defined challenges and opportunities. This offers a better understanding of their accomplishments and failures within the socio-economic, political, cultural, religious and gender contexts.

The evaluation of the central research hypothesis will be solid and relevant only if the micro-study of these four women is firmly embedded in a wider perspective. This comparative perspective is the third level of my research. Accordingly, it is crucial that the group portrait is compared with scholarly biographies and studies of nineteenth-century female religious, both in Belgium (insofar as is allowed by the historiography) and abroad. Where possible, for example with regard to normative texts and mechanisms of the foundation process, comparisons will also be made with male religious, especially non-clerical institutes of religious brothers. I also intend to confront the ideas, strategies and agency of the female congregation founders with biographical studies of Belgian lay women, although well-documented and intimate accounts are often limited to exceptional or prominent women artists, scientists, travellers or pioneers of the emancipation movement.

RESEARCH DIAGRAM

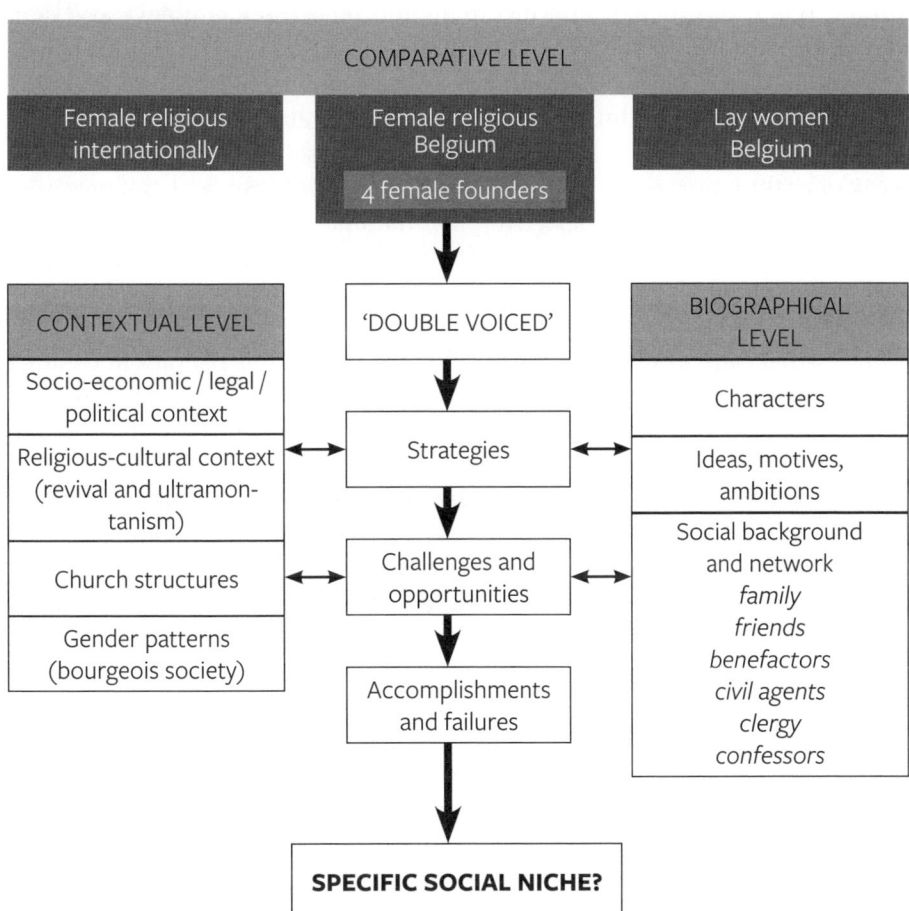

The comparison on the level of ideas and discourse, accomplishments (and failures) and broad social relevance will further determine, refine and evaluate the contextual factors and mechanisms, strategies and networks. This approach is crucial in order to ascertain whether the four women in my research were exceptions on the national and international scene or not. It is also crucial to determine the 'intersectional' impact of gender, class, wealth and clerical status (lay/religious) on the chances for or obstacles to development. Equally, the comparative perspective will help to evaluate the role of the specific Belgian context as a challenge and/or opportunity for the creation of a unique social niche of female agency and influence.

The muted and the dominant: double-voiced discourse

The key methodological concept to be used in the analysis of the three levels is the 'double-voiced' approach, already mentioned in the historiographical survey. Dutch theologians and historians introduced the double-voiced concept in the historiography of female religious to refer to the layered discourse and ambiguous position of female religious in nineteenth-century society.[49] The research of the feminist literary critic Showalter was the main source of inspiration for the Dutch scholars. Showalter herself was influenced by the work of anthropologists.[50] However, the double-voiced concept can be traced back to a much broader perspective, the fundamental characteristic of which is "the fact that duality is almost always connected in one way or another with the outsider status".[51] Ambiguity and paradox are inherent in the identity of all marginalised groups under the hegemony of white, male, western society, whether these are women, people of colour or indigenous peoples in colonial empires.

Influenced by the linguistic turn of poststructuralism, Showalter stressed the potential of multi-layered discourse analysis. In order to exist and survive, women had no choice but to express themselves in the dominant language of men, often confirming female docility, passivity and subordination. However women did integrate echoes of another, sometimes opposing "muted voice" of female agency into their apparently conformist writings: "women's writing is

---

49 Van Heijst and Derks, "Godsvrucht en Gender", 25-32; Eijt, *Religieuze vrouwen*, 35-36; Derks, "Vrouwen, confessionalisering en biografie", 127; Derks and Monteiro, "Met wijsheid opent zij haar mond", 9-26. In Belgian historiography on religiously inspired women, the concept double voiced was applied in: Willems, *Maria Baers* and Delhaye, "Vliegen en stelen", 21-23.
50 Showalter, "Feminist Criticism in the Wilderness", 199-205. Elaborated and annotated in: Idem, "Introduction - The Rise of Gender", 4-5.
51 Brownley, *Deferrals of Domain*, 109. Brownley makes a critical survey of the concept in relation to its theoretical ties and points to the use of the double-voiced concept in literary criticism and in ethnic and colonial history.

a 'double-voiced discourse' that always embodies the social, literary, and cultural heritages of both the muted and the dominant".[52] The feminist critic's job is to discover this muted voice, to see "meaning in what has previously been empty space" by looking for "gaps, silences [and] a capacity to read between the lines".[53]

Showalter's double-voiced concept of women apparently endorsing the dominant discourse but implicitly challenging or by-passing also bears similarities to the theories of the 'performative' turn in gender studies. Coined by the gender theorist Butler – 'gender is not what we are, but what we do or perform' – a performance analysis of the acts, physical expressions and writings of women brought new insights into mechanisms of gender agency and subjectivity.[54] From this perspective, 'passive' or 'muted' acts and expressions, like maladies, modesty, silence, penance, fasting and so on, were examined as important elements creating one's gender, rather than being just a passive reflection of the dominant cultural codes. Butler also introduced the 'paradox of subjectivation' in gender research, stressing that the very codes, structures and processes that cause women's subordination also create possibilities for female agency. These theories echoes Scott's classic definition of women's and gender studies as a domain of inescapable paradoxes.[55] It also illustrates the doubts of historians of gender and religion about representing women's emancipation as a linear, uninterrupted and progressive movement towards success. Instead, they emphasise that religion was not only or not primarily a means for achieving women's development, but was a goal in its own right.[56] These topics are also related to the complexity and diversity of the terminology of the women's emancipation process. Different or overlapping meanings are often attributed to terms such as 'agency', 'emancipation', 'the women's movement' and 'feminism', making it difficult to position religiously inspired women within this narrative. Butler already argued for a broader interpretation of the concept 'agency', not or not only as a synonym for actions opposing or transforming structures and relations of domination, but as the ability to act or perform, consciously or not, within the boundaries of these traditional structures.[57] The double-voiced approach has its place within this reconceptualization of agency as a product of power relations rather than a conscious

---

52 Showalter, "Feminist Criticism in the Wilderness", 201.
53 Idem, "Literary Criticism", 435, also paraphrased by: Harvey, *Ventriloquized Voices*, 20.
54 Butler, *Gender Trouble*, 25; Wils, "Inleiding", 13.
55 Scott, *Only Paradoxes to offer*, 1-2, 13-14. Applied to women and religion, see: De Vries, "More than Paradoxes to Offer", 188.
56 Morgan, "Rethinking Religion in Gender History", 113-124; De Groot and Morgan, "Beyond the 'Religious turn'", 395-421; Apetrei, *Women, Feminism and Religion*, 36; Lux-Steritt and Mangion (eds.), *Gender, Catholicism and Spirituality*; Sprows Cummings, *New Women of the Old Faith*.
57 Butler, *Bodies that matter*, 15.

and intended act of a supressed subject against opposing structures and relations.

If concepts like emancipation, feminism and the women's movement are understood in the framework of an explicit, voluntary and teleological female struggle for total independence and equality, they are very anachronistic terms to use in the context of the nineteenth century. Gender constructions at that time were determined by gender difference and interdependence. Even most of the early feminists in the nineteenth century used a 'relational' discourse, to use Offen's concept, that did not challenge the notion of fundamental differences between the sexes and accepted the idea of different but complementary responsibilities for men and women.[58] At the end of the twentieth century the Dutch historians Van Drenth and De Haan came up with a useful and nuanced scale for measuring women's social development. They did not focus on a linear and teleological emancipation, but took evolutions in women's agency and power, especially 'caring power', as the determining factor. Analysing the ideas and activities of nineteenth-century philanthropic women, Van Drenth and De Haan distinguished between women's activism (women becoming involved in society), women's movement (women becoming involved on behalf of other women) and feminism (women fighting for equal political and social rights).[59]

A double-voiced reading of texts, contexts and networks

In this study, I define the double-voiced concept in terms of the ability of the four women to dedicate and submit themselves to the ruling and often male-dominated social, cultural, religious and clerical structures on the one hand and the ways they were able – consciously or not – to create spaces for female agency within these traditional power structures on the other. An additional question will be if this agency also resulted in counterbalancing these submissive structures with opportunities for successful entrepreneurship, autonomy and prestige. Through a thorough discourse analysis of the ego-documents of the four women, 'looking for gaps' and 'reading between the lines' is exactly what I intend to do. A detailed discourse analysis and 'close reading' of some crucial excerpts should make it possible to discern the double-voiced character of their writings. An analysis of the specific vocabulary of appropriation and expropriation, suppression and autonomy, forms of address and titles, opening and closing sentences can reveal often implicit mechanisms of negotiation, persuasion and even blackmail. By analysing the writings of the four protagonists of my study, I hope to highlight the potential and the limits

---

58   Offen, "Defining Feminism", 135-149; Van Molle, "De nieuwe vrouwenbeweging in Vlaanderen", 371-381.
59   Van Drenth and De Haan, *The Rise of Caring Power*, 167.

of the interaction between the dominant and muted voices with regard to the specific characteristics of nineteenth-century revival and ultramontane piety, charitable or apostolic action and male-dominated church structures.

Research on religiously inspired women has already shown that female double-voiced discourse and the paradox of suppression and autonomy was not peculiar to Catholicism, nor was it exclusive to the nineteenth century. In her analysis of the nineteenth-century English educational activist Emily Davis (1830-1921), Green points to the "forked tongue" of her research subject and her "ambiguous ideological valence – apparently orthodox in its vocabulary, potentially radical in its implications". Davis referred to both feminist literature as well as Saint Paul – "no supporter of women's intellectual emancipation" – to defend her battle for women's higher education.[60] In her study on Teresa of Avila, Weber speaks of the "double bind" in the writings of the female reformer and saint: "Teresa's rhetoric of feminine subordination – all the paradoxes, the self-depreciation, the feigned ignorance and incompetence, the deliberate obfuscation and ironic humor – produced the desired perlocutionary effect".[61] Female agency in relation to the rhetoric of humility was also discussed in the case study of seventeenth-century Brussels Visitandines.[62] Monteiro describes the religious language of seventeenth-century Dutch lay religious virgins or 'kloppen' as "more than just the jargon of suffering and obedience (...)", but also an incentive "for what their vigour with God and the fellow men could result in".[63] Vanderputten interpreted the 'reformatory corporality' of medieval nuns both as a factor of modest female agency and as a gateway to male suppression and recently analysed the ambiguity of their position between oppression and self-determination.[64] With regard to research on the role of women in the contemporary Islam, Mahmood analysed religiously inspired women in the Egyptian Islamic revival as the 'docile agents', combining both docility and religious agency.[65] Kandiyoti explained strategies of women 'bargaining with patriarchy' for women in Africa, Asia and the Middle East. A concept that was also used by sociologist Ebaugh in her studies on twentieth-century American female religious.[66]

If so many parallels can be found, in what way did the specific context of the revival and the 'culture wars' shape new possibilities for female agency?

60 Green, *Educating Women*, 1-2.
61 Weber, *Teresa of Avila*, 159.
62 Wang, "Neither ex officio nor ex gratia".
63 My translation of: "meer dan enkel een jargon van lijdzaamheid en gehoorzaamheid" and "van wat hun daadkracht bij God en hun naasten zou kunnen bewerken". See: Monteiro, *Geestelijke maagden*, 350.
64 Vanderputten, "Reformatorische lichamelijkheid", 478. For an interesting overview of new research on gender ambiguities in the medieval monastic world, see: Idem, *Dark Age Nunneries*, 6-8.
65 See: Mahmood, "Feminist Theory" and Idem, *Politics of Piety*.
66 Kandiyoti, "Bargaining with patriarchy"; Ebaugh, "Patriarchal bargains".

To what extent was the typical devotion of the nineteenth century – passionate (penitence and suffering), affective and often categorised as typically feminine – a means for female congregation founders to achieve personal development, fulfilment and power? To what extent could their work in feminine areas such as (religious) education, care for orphans and vulnerable women, and the production of liturgical vestments and objects offer them a place in the re-Christianisation movement of the Catholic Church and the socio-economic and cultural fabric of the time? Could and did they intent to transform the essentially submissive aspects of bourgeois gender patterns into powerful tools to strengthen their own positions and fulfil their goals? Were there loopholes in the masculine clerical and social system that allowed them to challenge existing gender boundaries?

Analysis should also specify the role of the social and family networks within their accomplishments (and failures). Family members, friends, male co-founders, confessors, aristocratic and upper bourgeois benefactors, confidants among the clerical authorities, all could pave the way for their actions and ambitions. However, these partners – driven by their own ideas about the restoration of Catholic society, about gender and cultural patterns or about the relief of socio-economic needs – could equally well constitute obstacles to female engagement and self-determination. On the subject of their male spiritual advisers, this study aims to analyse the characteristics, tensions and hierarchy of their gender relationships. Finally, by analysing their relations with lay women benefactors and friends, I aim to examine possible patterns of rivalry, competition, cooperation and bonding. It is also my objective to position both groups on a comparative scale of female agency and autonomy.

The benefits and challenges of a biographical group portrait

After decades of neglect during the supremacy of the *'histoire totale'* of the French *Annales* School and the German *Gesellschaftgeschichte*, biographical studies regained scholarly popularity in the final quarter of the twentieth century. Eventually, the biographical method was also rediscovered by historians of religion.[67] A biographical approach – described by Derks as "pointing the way to a plurality of interpretations" – offers important opportunities for first-hand and intimate contact with the four protagonists of my study.[68] The choice to draw a group portrait broadened the perspective of the individual micro-study, without losing the advantages of an individual approach. However, some methodological challenges have to be taken in account.

---

67 Le Goff, "After Annales, the life as history", 394-405; De Baar, Kuiper and Renders, "Inleiding", 11.
68 "Wegwijzer naar meerduidigheid", Derks, "Vrouwen, confessionalisering en biografie", 110.

Biographical sources and methodology

The four case studies underpin the perception of the female convent world as an age-old *terra incognita*. Antoinette Cornet was quickly forgotten after her death in 1886, reflecting the fate of many other female congregation founders. Anna de Meeûs, Fanny Kestre and Wilhelmina Telghuys received a good deal of attention from contemporary observers and supporters, but their legacy lost splendour when their congregations lost vitality in the second half of the twentieth century. The biographies and the contemporary perception history of de Meeûs, Kestre, Cornet and Telghuys will be examined in further detail in the epilogue at the end of my study. Apart from my own preliminary research, recent studies concerning the four women and their congregations are very scarce.[69] Anna de Meeûs and her congregation were examined briefly by Italian historians in connection with the Italian convent foundations. The Belgian convents of her congregation in Ghent and Liège were more thoroughly researched.[70] She herself figured briefly as one of those "strong-willed women (...) manipulating their confessors with a determination that sent shivers down the spine of their bishops" in the already mentioned studies of Viaene and Paret and Wynants.[71] A paper about the life of Fanny Kestre and her fascinating gender relations with Archbishop Dechamps was presented by De Maeyer at the 2004 RELINS conference on 'Religious Institutes and the Roman Factor in Western Europe'.[72] A short biographical study of Wilhelmina Telghuys was part of a recent publication on the history of the congregation's 'Mère Jeanne' school and the reconversion of the convent buildings in Antwerp.[73]

The key sources for the research were the four congregations' archives. Largely unexplored, the archives offered an exceptional wealth of ego-documents and enabled a thorough research into interpersonal and gender relationships. Collections of letters have been preserved for all four founders, as well as spiritual or autobiographical notes outlining their spiritual and apostolic motives, strategies and goals, and identifying the characteristics and importance of social and family networks. Since theorists of the biographical method have often pointed to the dangers of the narrow, personal perspective of ego-documents, an important benefit of the four selected case studies was

---

69 Preliminary and partial research results have been published concerning the relationship between Anna de Meeûs and the Brussels Jesuits (Suenens, "'Pères spirituels' en 'Dames illusionées'), her spiritual entrepreneurship (Idem, "Apostolische actie en spirituele passie"), and concerning the Ignatian character of the congregations of de Meeûs, Cornet and Telghuys (Idem, "Jésuites et congregations féminines").

70 Torcivia, "Il Can. F. Russo"; Tagliaferri, *Anna de Meeûs*; Moons, *Historische evolutie*; Godinas-Thys, "Les sœurs du Saint-Sacrement".

71 Viaene, *Belgium and the Holy See*, 188-189; Paret and Wynants, "La noblesse belge", 512.

72 De Maeyer, "Fanny Kestre and Victor Dechamps", unpublished. For information about the international research forum RELINS, see: www.relins.eu.

73 Scheerlinck, *Mère Jeanne*.

the availability of parallel accounts and documents of other actors from their social network. Keeping in mind that "different accounts could relay different truths, about the same events and persons", these accounts were a necessary link between the personal lives and the social context in which they were embedded.[74]

First, ego-documents from fellow female religious in their immediate entourage threw light on how the ideas and actions of the female founders were perceived as well as on the personal motives and goals of the first-generation sisters. Ego-documents were confronted with other archival documents such as normative texts (rules, constitutions, books of customs), chronicles or annals, reports of internal boards and meetings and membership registers. Economic sources from the convent archives – mainly accounts of receipts and expenditures, notarial deeds and annual financial reports – were used to qualify and illustrate the entrepreneurial capacities and challenges of the four female founders and their institutes. However, most Belgian religious institutes had no legal or corporate personality until the 1920's and made ample use of obscure and semi-legal constructions to administer their finances and properties. Coherent or complete economic sources, therefore, are lacking and seriously complicated an exhaustive examination of this topic.[75]

Second, given the importance of gender relationships and social networks in this research, the availability of well-documented archives of other prominent actors in the lives of the four women was also an important benefit: family archives, the archives of their main benefactors and the papers of male clergy and regulars (Jesuits and Redemptorists in particular). Third, research in these ecclesiastical archives was equally important, as it was indispensable for studying the position of women in the Church and for evaluating how their roles were viewed by the men at the top. The well-preserved archives of the Archdiocese of Mechelen were the main source of information, but the archives of other Belgian and foreign dioceses with which the female founders interacted were examined as well. Research was also conducted in the archives of the parishes where the convents were founded, but these seldom provided much information. The exempt (pontifical) status of Anna de Meeûs' and Fanny Kestre's congregations necessitated research in the Vatican Archives.

Despite the variety and richness of the source material and the contextual and comparative framework of my research, inescapable shortcomings are inherent to the biographical approach. The highly paradoxical position as women in nineteenth-century society was not only the most important perspective of my research, but also the most confusing. It's a perfect illustration of Virginia Woolf's struggle with the 'granite and rainbow' challenges of bio-

---

74 Long, *Telling women's lives*, 2.
75 For detailed information about this source issue, see: Van Dijck and De Maeyer (eds.), *The Economics of Providence*.

graphical writing. What gives personal colour and emotion to historical 'facts' and the massive structures of the contextual framework is often intangible and impossible to describe without interpretational 'impurity'.⁷⁶

The problem of representativeness

Some important remarks remain regarding the general representativeness of the selection inspired by the availability of sources. A short overview of the general panorama of women's convents in nineteenth-century Belgium might be helpful. New research, based on the most recent and accurate sources available, estimates that 183 new female religious institutes were founded in Belgium between 1800 and 1899.⁷⁷ This number includes both totally new initiatives as well as institutes that were re-established after decades of dissolution. Institutes with a pre-revolutionary history which remained active – officially or clandestinely – during the revolutionary years into the nineteenth century were not included since they had no distinct (re-)founders. Forty-four of the 183 new institutes were monasteries or abbeys with an exclusive monastic or contemplative purpose, and a majority of 139 were newly founded active institutes. Using four criteria – foundation date, geographical base, geographical expansion and apostolic identity – an attempt is made to situate the four selected congregations within the larger group of nineteenth-century Belgian active institutes for women. Other criteria of distinction – spiritual identity, membership statistics, class and social ranking – would have been interesting as well, but could not be identified adequately for all 139 institutes. These topics will be analysed in the corpus of this study, using the data and statistics of individual institutes that were available for research.

First, with regard to the foundation date, all four congregations in my research originated between 1850 and 1870, being part of the substantial group (28%) of institutes that were created in the last decades of the revival. Later analysis will show that a foundation date in the 'late' revival period determined the identity of the institutes, which combined obvious revivalist characteristics as well as the above-mentioned influences of the crucial political, religious, cultural and socio-economic changes of the second half of the century.

76 Gualtieri, "The Impossible Art", 349-361.
77 The data are based on different sources. Wynants, *Religieuses*, provides crucial information concerning female religious life in Wallonia, the largest part of the diocese of Tournai excepted. Concise information for the diocese of Tournai can be found in: Matte, "Les religieuses". Luyten, "Limburg voor Christus", presents statistics for the province of Limburg, while data for the dioceses of Bruges and Ghent are available in Art, *Kerkelijke structuur*, 33-35 and Boudens, "De diocesane clerus en de religieuzen". All this information has been supplemented with information from the ODIS database and the series of diocesan annuals. Comprehensiveness was the aim, but could not be fully guaranteed due to the heterogeneity of some sources and the limited reliability of others (i.e. diocesan annuals).

Second, all four of the selected case studies were situated in the Archdiocese of Mechelen-Brussels. This choice was not an accidental decision. The framework of the archdiocese presented important benefits. The nineteenth-century archdiocese covered a large, central and bicultural (Flemish and Walloon) part of the country (roughly corresponding with the nineteenth-century provinces of Brabant and Antwerp). It presented an interesting diversity of rural areas, small provincial towns and large cities such as metropolitan Brussels and cosmopolitan Antwerp. A serious advantage was that both the nineteenth-century general history of the archdiocese and the major nineteenth-century archbishops are well documented.[78] Moreover, several of the above-mentioned scholarly monographs of KADOC concern congregations within the archdiocese, reinforcing the regional comparative perspective. Finally, in the Belgian landscape of convent life, the archdiocese held an important position. Almost one in three (29%) new institutes in nineteenth-century Belgium were founded in the archdiocese. Only the Diocese of Bruges had more nineteenth-century foundations. In the Flemish dioceses and in the archdiocese, there was an overall majority of small and local institutes, representing two thirds

FOUNDATION PERIOD AND MOTHERHOUSES OF NEWLY FOUNDED OR RE-ESTABLISHED FEMALE APOSTOLIC RELIGIOUS INSTITUTES IN BELGIUM (1800-1899) - (100% = 139 INSTITUTES)

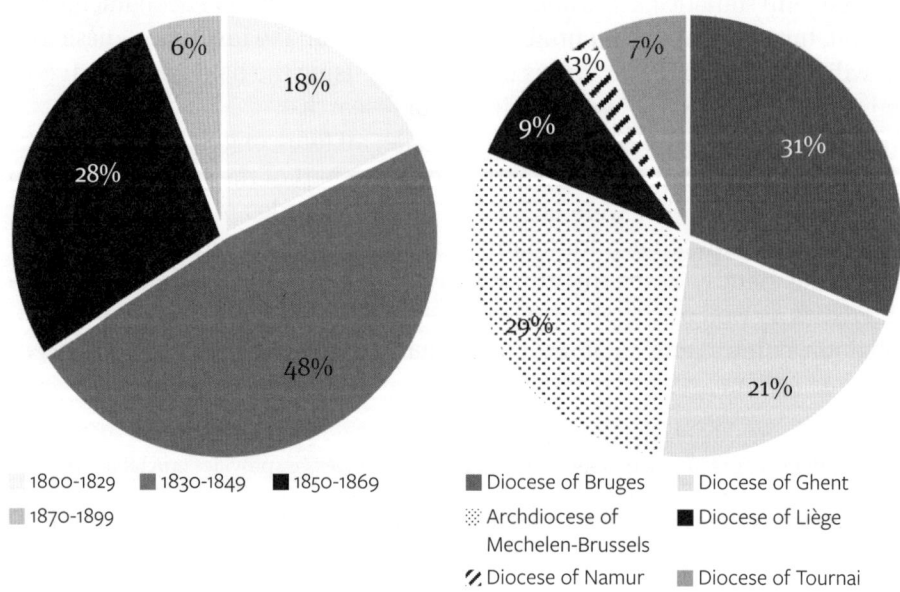

---

78 Viaene, "De ontplooiing van een 'vrije' kerk"; De Maeyer, "De wending van de kerk naar het volk"; Idem, "Een kerk in de moderniteit"; Simon, *Le Cardinal Sterckx et son temps*; Becque, *Le Cardinal Dechamps*.

EXPANSION AND APOSTOLATE OF NEWLY FOUNDED OR RE-ESTABLISHED
FEMALE APOSTOLIC RELIGIOUS INSTITUTES IN BELGIUM (1800-1899)
(100% = 139 INSTITUTES)

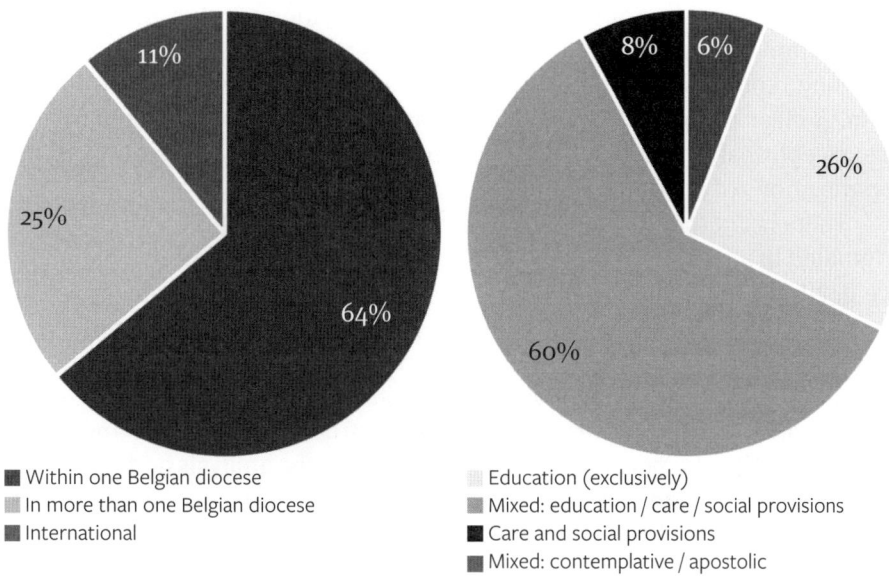

■ Within one Belgian diocese
▦ In more than one Belgian diocese
■ International

▨ Education (exclusively)
■ Mixed: education / care / social provisions
■ Care and social provisions
■ Mixed: contemplative / apostolic

(64%) of the new congregations with convents in only one diocese. In the French-speaking areas, on the contrary, the female religious landscape was dominated by a limited number of large congregations, often present in several dioceses.

Third, within the group of the four selected institutes, the congregations of Cornet, Telghuys and Kestre belonged to the dominant group of relatively small or medium-sized congregations. A difference has to be made however between Telghuys' institute on the one hand and the congregations of Cornet and Kestre on the other. Telghuys's congregation had a distinct Antwerp character and resembled many other Flemish congregations with a narrow geographical focus. Although small also, the institutes of Cornet and Kestre had convents in more than one diocese. They belonged to the 25% of female congregations with a somewhat broader geographical base. Only de Meeûs' institute expanded from its Brussels origins beyond the national borders. Belonging to a small (11%) group of Belgian female institutes with foreign convents in the nineteenth century, it offers opportunities for a fascinating study of international relationships, tensions and opportunities.

Fourth, in terms of social or 'apostolate' activities, Cornet's institute represents the 25% of new nineteenth-century female apostolic institutes with an exclusive focus on education, one of the key characteristics of post-revolutionary convent life. Focusing on education, orphans and socially vulnerable women, Telghuys' congregation belonged to the largest group of congregations that combined educational activities with an apostolate in health care or other social services. The Eucharistic congregations of de Meeûs and Kestre were part of a small group (6%) of new congregations with a double focus on contemplative life and religiously inspired social action. We must consider that they represented a minority in nineteenth-century convent life in Belgium. A clear comparative perspective has to highlight the consequences of this exceptional position for the main research questions in relation to the congregations of the dominant active type.

There is another discrepancy in the selection. Three of the four institutes originated in an urban context, whereas more than half of the new Belgian active institutes for women in the nineteenth century had a rural background.[79] Moreover, the La Hulpe congregation of Cornet, in the green hinterland of Brussels, had important connections with the urban context as well. This specific urban contextual framework was crucial for many aspects such as social networks, funding, accessibility to power structures, apostolic and social identity etc. These aspects have to be considered in the analysis and have to be compared with existing accounts of the situation in rural congregations, with their own typical problems and opportunities for female agency.

Structure and language

Given the biographical approach of the research, this study is structured around a chronological-thematic outline, based on the rhythm of the life stories of the four protagonists. The first part focuses on the early decades of the revival (ca. 1830-1855) with the four women's youth, adolescence and their first social and religious activities as the main perspective. After analysing the impact of the French Revolution on Catholic minds and actions and the interactions with various gender constructions and relationships, special attention is given to different possibilities for female social and religious agency during the revival and the shift to a conservative mentality after 1848. Finally, an analysis is made of the spiritual background of the four women, with reference to the post-revolutionary discourse of penance and restitution and the supposed 'feminine' nature of revival piety.

The second part deals with the vocations and the foundation history of the four women and their congregations during the final decades of the revival (ca. 1855-ca. 1869), which were marked by intensifying cultural and political tensions and growing ultramontane militancy. Concerning the religious vocations of the four women and their spiritual partnerships with male clerics, the

---

79   74 out of 139 institutes had a rural background, whereas 65 had urban origins.

focus is on analysing complementary and conflicting clerical and emotional gender roles in a turbulent era. Women's attraction or aversion to convent life in the specific context of mid-nineteenth-century society is further examined with regard to other women involved in the foundation processes. The interaction of the women religious with local and general church politics and their role in formalising the foundation process is placed within the framework of the overall consolidation of the congregational model for female convent life and the ongoing struggle with monastic prestige and heritage.

The third part further analyses the consolidation and expansion of the foundation initiatives and the development of the four women as congregation superiors, against the background of the 'culture wars' and dominant ultramontanism (ca. 1870-ca. 1885). After examining the recruitment and expansion strategies of the female superiors, an analysis is made of the benefits and difficulties that emerged from their ambiguous and gendered relationships with fundamentalist, opportunistic or strong-minded benefactors. The strengths and the limitations of their own contribution to the ultramontane cause of the 1870s and 1880s are examined, keeping in mind the tension between their modern apostolate and expansion strategies and the conservative social, spiritual and gender outlook of the ultramontane crusade. Finally, an assessment is made of the opportunities and obstacles facing female autonomy and agency in the light of the internal power structures of the congregations as well as the specific politics and strategies of the ultramontane Church.

The main narrative of this research ends with the trajectory of their common experiences in the mid-1880s and the death of Kestre (+1882) and Cornet (+1886). Still, the later developments in their congregations, as well as the last decades in the lives of de Meeûs and Telghuys are briefly analysed in an Epilogue. Against the background of social, religious and clerical developments, the epilogue also focuses on the perception of the four female founders inside and outside their congregations.

Finally, a brief word about the language issue in this study. Most of the sources examined for this research were either in French or in Dutch. I decided not to translate the French quotations cited in this study in order to offer the reader a sense of the typical discourse and climate of the nineteenth-century religious world. For the convenience of the reader, and because many of the Dutch-language sources were actually in Flemish with dialect expressions, Dutch/Flemish quotations are translated into English. However, the original quotations are cited in the footnotes. The names of institutes, organisations and places will not be translated, except in those cases where an English version is common. The English translation of each institute or organisation will be given, however, every time an institute or organisation is mentioned for the first time. For places, streets and parishes in Brussels, the French name is used, although the city had a much more distinct Flemish character in the nineteenth century than it has today. However, since the world of de Meeûs and Kestre, our two protagonists in Brussels, was an exclusively French one, I considered it legitimate to use their language as a template.

Acknowledgements

The present publication is an adapted version of my PhD-dissertation, successfully defended in October 2018 at KU Leuven. I sincerely thank my supervisor, Jan De Maeyer, for his encouragements, enthusiasm and incredibly extensive historical expertise as well as a joined fascination with this 'terra incognita' of nineteenth-century female religious life. I also owe much to the chair and members of my examination jury, Brigitte Meijns, Matthieu Brejon de Lavergnée, Leo Kenis, Carmen Mangion, Marit Monteiro and Magaly Rodríguez García and their constructive as well as challenging remarks, encouraging me to fine-tune my research results into this reworked publication. I was very fortunate to be advised by other specialists as well. Claude Langlois, brilliant pioneer as well as the French authority in the history of women religious, commented on and further inspired my research on the occasion of my doctoral seminar. Leen Van Molle repeatedly offered essential expertise to correctly frame the research questions within the context of women and gender history, but was equally well a discreet and much-appreciated supporter. I also thank the Research Foundation – Flanders (FWO) for granting me a special scholarship to complete the redaction of my dissertation.

It is impossible to imagine a more inspiring environment for research into the world of female religious than KADOC-KU Leuven. Nowhere else could I have had the opportunity to explore my research field in a more thorough and facilitating way. Many thanks Honorary Director Jan De Maeyer and Director Kim Christiaens for giving me the opportunity to conduct my research. I owe much to Let Smets and Patricia Quaghebeur for finding every book and archive dossier I needed; to Sabine Van Reybroeck, Luc Schokkaert and Bernadette Costermans for solving many practical issues, and for very nice chats as well; to Godfried Kwanten and Carine Dujardin for a shared interest in the world of religious archives and libraries; to Jo Luyten, for his astonishing knowledge of Jesuit heritage and the hidden pearls he discovered for me. I'm grateful to Roeland Hermans, Joris Colla and Katrien Weyns, my 'contemporaries', and to Karim Ettourki and Lore Lievens, my officemates, for shared experiences, coffee breaks and encouragement; and to Peter Heyrman, who was an experienced and benevolent guide into the machinery and vocabulary of scholarly research. Many thanks also to Luc Vints, Alexis Vermeylen and Lieve Claes, for their assistance and expertise during the publication project and to Maria Kelly, for her careful translation.

I also owe much to the expertise of many archivists 'in the field', who willingly offered me access to often unknown material. Sister Renata Crauwels in Antwerp, Sister Noëlle Hausman in La Hulpe and Sister Maria in Rome, with full confidence and enthusiasm, allowed me to carry out my research in their convent archives. My special thanks go to Gerrit Vanden Bosch of the Archives of the Archdiocese of Mechelen-Brussels for sharing his profound knowledge of the history and heritage of the archdiocese.

Many thanks also to my family and friends for their support and encouragements. I'm incredibly grateful to be a mother of two fantastic children who, by just being themselves, made my day, every day. Thanks to Hannelore, for being such a lively, enthusiastic and helping person and for always being my big little girl. Thanks to Thomas for just being the sweetest and most thoughtful boy in the entire world. No words can describe how much Jan has meant for me on this journey. I could not have imagined a more careful, witty, encouraging and supporting husband. Thank you for being my soulmate, a fellow historian and a passionate lover of books.

PART I

RELIGIOUS REVIVAL, ROMANTICISM AND FEMALE ACTION IN A POST-REVOLUTIONARY AGE: FOUR YOUNG WOMEN (CA. 1820-CA. 1860)

> (...) à répandre autour d'elles les bienfaits de l'éducation qu'elles avaient reçue, stimulait leur désir de faire un peu de bien, et leur indiquait, comme but digne de leur foi et de leur dévotion en ce temps des calomnies et outrages, entre autre, le soin de l'église et des pauvres de leur paroisse.
> ARE, *Chroniques, II. La Voie*, 10.

Paris, 1841. In the exclusive and internationally renowned boarding school of the *Dames du Sacré-Cœur* (Religious of the Sacred Heart), the '*maîtresse-générale*', Madame d'Avenas, gave this impassioned and self-confident end-of-year address to her departing pupils. Madame Aimée de Guillin d'Avenas (1804-1871) had a meteoric career in the French congregation founded by Sophie Barat (1779-1865). Intelligent, somewhat flamboyant, and with a certain aristocratic elegance, she had become head of the Paris boarding school of the congregation in the elegant Byron Hotel in 1835. However, given her sharp tongue and close involvement with Parisian high society, she was not beyond reproach. She had struggled intensely with the trauma of the French Revolution and the loss of the monastic traditions of the *Ancien Régime*.[1] Her congregation, founded on the cusp between two centuries and two eras, was nevertheless one of the flag-bearers of the 'modern' congregational model that would dominate in the nineteenth century.

The passionate, missionary zeal of Madame d'Avenas, with her dual focus on the needs of the Church and of society, moulded a new generation of Catholic women. They were the prototypical Romantic, religiously inspired women of the Catholic revival of the first half of the nineteenth century. Though tormented and confused by the revolution's upheavals and by advancing religious ignorance and apostasy, the post-revolutionary *tabula rasa* also stimulated them to engage in a future-oriented revival movement. However, they believed above all in the superiority of the Catholic faith as the foundation of society, with charitable work and atonement as the driver of a moral, religious and ecclesiastical restoration.

The portrait of Madame d'Avenas against the background of her time sets the tone for this first part, which offers a biographical and contextual portrait of four Belgian religiously and socially engaged young women during the nineteenth-century revival. Chapter 1 brings together the results of an exploration into the post-revolutionary world of women's religious and social action. The second chapter focuses on the consolidation of the socio-religious activities of the four women against the background of the transformation of the Roman-

---

[1] Kilroy, *Madeleine Sophie Barat*, 394-395.

tic revival into a more militant variant between 1848 and 1860 and within the framework of dominant clerical and gender relationships. The third chapter will investigate the way in which the devotion of the revival determined their spiritual development as religious women in the Church and society of the mid-nineteenth century.

Between 1820 and 1904, the 'Hotel Byron' in central Paris was home to the prestigious boarding school of the *Dames du Sacré-Cœur*. The young Belgian woman Anna de Meeûs was inspired here by her religious teachers to partake in a socially and religiously engaged life as a '*dame d'œuvres*'.
[Postcard – ca. 1901 – Private collection]

'FOREMOTHERS', REVOLUTIONS AND REVIVAL (CA. 1820-CA. 1848)

The female pioneers of the revival

In the midst of the international community of aristocratic and upper bourgeois young women in the Byron Hotel in Paris, a slight seventeen-year old girl was deeply touched by the words of Madame d'Avenas. Anna de Meeûs (°1823), the oldest daughter of the affluent Belgian governor of the *Société Générale*, Ferdinand de Meeûs, had arrived in the Paris boarding school only a year before.[1] However, she had a poor health and was forced to return home. In the green surroundings of the château of Argenteuil, just outside Brussels, she recovered her strength. At the same time, she developed an interest in religious and social engagement that was inspired by the ideas of her former teacher, d'Avenas.

Anna's contemporaries Fanny Kestre (°1824) and Antoinette Cornet (°1820), two other future congregation founders, were also motivated by a generation of post-revolutionary religious women in their convent boarding schools. Kestre, who came from the Belgian border town of Chimay, went to the boarding school of the *Dames du Sacré-Cœur* in the Northern French town of Charleville – just like her French mother and her older sisters, Félicie and

---

[1] Anna was the daughter of Ferdinand de Meeûs (1798-1861) and Anne Meeûs (1797-1874). She had ten brothers and sisters: Ferdinand François (1825-1916), Henri (1826-1913), Julien (1827-1867), Joseph (1829-1910), Marie-Louise (1831-1865), Marie-Hortense (1833-1859), Eugène (1834-1915), Anatole (1836-1855), Henriette (1838-1907) and Paul (1841-1922).

Although the boarding schools of Kestre in Charleville and Cornet in Pesche did not have the prestige of de Meeûs' institute in Paris, they did offer the same environment of post-revolutionary trauma, mixed with a militant desire for retribution. Above: the boarding school of the *Dames du Sacré-Cœur* in Charleville, after the forced departure of the sisters due to French anticlerical legislation at the beginning of the twentieth century. Below: the modest buildings of the convent and boarding school in Pesche in the 1870s, decades after Cornet stayed there in even more humble circumstances.
[Postcard – After 1904 – Private collection]
[Drawing – [After 1872] – *L' École Normale de Pesche. 1869-1969* (S.l.: s.n., 1970), 30]

Sidonie.[2] The institution in Charleville had for long been run by mainly upper-class Belgian sisters from the French congregation of the *Dames de la Providence* (Ladies of Providence). Though less prestigious than the Paris boarding school of de Meeûs, it produced its own share of socially engaged Catholic women.[3] Moreover, when Fanny Kestre stayed there in the late 1830s, the institute was in full transition, having been taken over only a few years before by Barat's congregation of the *Dames du Sacré-Cœur*.[4]

Antoinette Cornet was the oldest of five children from a butcher's family in Walcourt, a provincial town in Namur.[5] Although the exact chronology of her school career is not clear it is certain that she was sent by her parents to the boarding school of the *Filles de Marie* (Daughters of Mary) in nearby Pesche. Appropriate to her middle-class background the institute in Pesche was a modest school, founded in 1820 by a young religious community that was recognized by diocesan authorities in 1835.[6] The simple school building in Pesche seemed small in comparison with the majestic buildings in Charleville and completely paled into insignificance in comparison with the Parisian grandeur of the Hotel Byron. Still there were striking parallels. First, many of the sisters in Pesche had received their education with the sisters in Charleville. Second they were also imbued with the characteristic discourse, world view and role models of the Paris and Charleville convent schools.

In the nineteenth century, many girls from the well-to-do bourgeoisie and the aristocracy were safely stowed away in strict and enclosed convent boarding schools. Although some of these schools had already built up a solid educational reputation by the first half of the nineteenth century, there was no escaping the puritan, hierarchical and highly religious message that was conveyed there. Women were primarily educated to be decent and pious Christian wives and mothers.[7] Still, the young girls' longings for excitement and drama could find some satisfaction in the stories of a generation of religious women with horrific memories of the French Revolution. The "*calomnies et outrages*" of Madame d'Avenas mirrored the experiences of her founder Barat, who fifty years after the Revolution still became petrified on hearing the Marseillaise. They also echoed the history of the convent in Charleville where the original

2   Fanny was the daughter of Louis Kestre (1792-1851) and Angélique Leclercq (1792-1869). She had three sisters: Félicie (1820-1866), Sidonie (1822-1859) and Marie (1834-1902).
3   On this, see Leon Dehon's letter about his mother: ARSC: Letter of Leon Dehon (s.d.).
4   ADSJ, 1.1: *Dossier franciscae ab eucharistia Kestre*; Baunard, *Histoire de Madame Barat*, II, 100-101.
5   Antoinette was the daughter of François Cornet (1789-1851) and Marie-Antoinette De Spineto (1793-1860), a housewife. She had two sisters, Ermeline (1822-1900) and Crisaline (1827-1893) and two brothers, Charles (1823-1825) and Omer (1825-1900).
6   ASCMLH, A.3.8: Biography Mère Gonzague; AFMP: *Le cahier de Sœur Joseph*, 5-6, 18.
7   Rogers, *Les bourgeoises*, 199, 210; De Vroede, "The Catholic Boarding Schools", 313-337; Christens and Suenens, "L'enseignement comme vocation", 151-154; Gubin and Piette, *Emma, Louise et Marie*, 27-28; Piette, "Un réseau informel", 157-159.

community of sisters never totally recovered from the dissolution and expropriation of the revolutionary period, a situation that had opened the way to the takeover by the *Dames du Sacré-Cœur*. And the words also described the experiences of the founders in Pesche, who shuddered as they recalled the persecutions "qu'un gouvernement intrus faisait à tous ceux qui professaient la religion catholique".[8]

Other pioneers of early nineteenth-century Belgian convent life shared in the traumatic legacy as well. The personal history of Cicercule Paridaens (1769-1838), a nun who had been expelled under the French regime, became a prominent theme in the foundation history of her new religious congregation, the *Dochters van Maria* (Daughters of Mary) of Leuven (1805). With a feeling for romantic drama, Marie-Thérèse Haze (1782-1876) from Liège, translated the exile, death and deprivation that befell her family in the revolutionary years into the name and spirituality of her congregation of *Filles de la Croix* (Daughters of the Cross), which she founded in 1832.[9]

The French Revolution, and above all its consequences, became a dominant driving force in the lives of de Meeûs, Kestre and Cornet. Moreover, as young adolescents, they were confronted with personal traumatic experiences related to the revolutionary turmoil of the Belgian independence in 1830, ending the short-lived existence of the United Kingdom of the Netherlands (1815-1830). When only six years old, Anna de Meeûs had been terrified when angry "émeutes" destroyed the stately home of her parents at the Schaerbeek Gate in Brussels. Her father, a prominent member of the Brussels banking and commercial world, and his young family paid the price for his role as mediator between the Belgian revolutionaries and the Dutch regime.[10] Fanny Kestre moved from Chimay to Brussels in 1843, following her father's bankruptcy. The Kestre family belonged to the Catholic commercial bourgeoisie in Chimay. The "*sérieux revers de fortune*" of the family, caused according to Kestre by the economic turbulence after Belgian independence, meant a considerable social downgrading. Her father found a new job as a civil servant in the capital, but he never recovered from the economic drama and suffered from depression for the rest of his life.[11]

The Belgian revolution also gave the life of another future founder a decisive turn. Wilhelmina Telghuys (1824) spent her youngest years in the rapidly growing Belgian industrial town of Verviers. Her father Hendrik Telghuys, a

8 AFMP: *Le cahier de Sœur Joseph*, 1.
9 Baunard, *Histoire de Madame Barat*, II, 99-100; Kiroy, *Madeleine Sophie Barat*, 18-19; ADML, 3: Spiritual lectures by Mère Marie Thérèse (1817-1820); Hümmeler, *In hoc signo vinces*, 9-17.
10 ARE, *Lettres divers*: Anna de Meeûs to Boone (23 Oct. 1857); ARE, *Chroniques, II. Souvenirs de famille*, 3-4; Brion and Moreau, *De Generale Maatschappij*, 28-34; Thonissen, *Vie du Comte Ferdinand de Meeûs*, 11-12.
11 *La Révérende mère Fanny*, 9-11; ACGC: Birth certificate Fanny Kestre; ADSJ, 1.1: *Dossier franciscae ab eucharistia Kestre*; ADSJ, 1.6: Sidonie Kestre to Kestre (18 Feb. 1851).

Dutch Protestant textile merchant, and her mother Maria-Anna De Smedt, an upper-class Catholic from Brussels, had an elegant house in the textile district of Hodimont. The district was also home to a substantial English community, from which the first teacher for Wilhelmina and her five older sisters and brother was recruited. Later, her sister Isabella (1815) took over that task. Educated by lay women, Wilhelmina ended up in a different educational environment than that of the boarding-school girls.[12]

Verviers did not escape the socio-economic consequences of Belgium's rapid industrialisation in the first half of the nineteenth century. The demise of cottage industries in the surrounding villages and the increasing proletarianisation of factory workers in the city had already provoked social disturbances in the 1820s.[13] Increasing anti-Dutch resentment aggravated the discontent, making Verviers an unsafe place for the Dutch-Belgian Telghuys family. Hendrik Telghuys fled with his business and his family to Antwerp. With his Dutch mercantile spirit, he succeeded in transforming his textile business into the prominent shipbroking firm of Telghuys & Co., profiting from the ongoing transformation of Antwerp from a textile centre to a commercial port city.[14]

Her father's successful economic transition gave Wilhelmina's family access to the Antwerp *beau monde*. She and her siblings, like her mother baptised Catholics, became acquainted with the Catholic Teichmann family. The very wealthy Teichmanns bore witness to a remarkable cross-pollination between their prominent presence in the salons of the Antwerp high society and their explicitly religious commitment to the poor who were excluded from the balls, theatres and concerts of the upper classes.[15] Wilhelmina became attached to the *mater familias*, Marie-Antoinette Teichmann-Cooppal, whom she affectionately called her "seconde mère". It was an implicit criticism of her own mother, who, though intelligent and distinguished, was rather rational and emotionally 'cold'. The daughter, Constance Teichmann (1824-1896), drew Wilhelmina into a dynamic world of female *caritas*. Just like the sisters in the boarding schools of Kestre, de Meeûs and Cornet, the Teichmanns were true 'foremothers' for Telghuys, role models for developing a distinct female com-

12 Wilhelmina was the daughter of Hendrik Telghuys (1772-1858) and Maria-Anna De Smedt (1784-1865). She was the youngest of six children: Isabella (1815-1879), Marie-Louise (1817-1907), Marie-Hubertine (1818-1891), Pauline (1821-1887) and Henri (1822-1904). ADHH, 22: Genealogy; RAAnd, Civil Registry of Verviers, 1069365-1070447.
13 Lejaer, "Histoire de la ville", 76, 172-177; De Smaele, *Rechts Vlaanderen*, 322-323.
14 ADHH, 16: Verest Manuscript; Lejaer, "Histoire de la ville de Verviers", 172-177; De Smedt, "Zilt succes", 133-135.
15 The Teichmann-Cooppal family coupled the political influence of the father, Théodore Teichmann (1788-1867), governor of Antwerp between 1842 and 1862, with the economic power of the family of the mother, Marie Cooppal (1799-1867), which had a gunpowder factory in Wetteren. On the Teichmann family, see: Christens and Hansen, "Vrouwen en onderwijs", 61-62; Van Molle, "Constance Teichmann", 524-525; Belpaire, *Constance Teichmann*.

mitment.[16] Unlike the religious in Paris, Charleville and Pesche, the Teichmanns were living proof that this ideal could also be realised on a parallel lay path.[17] Constance Teichmann, who remained celibate all her life, was a key figure in the Antwerp literary and musical scene. As founder of the Children's Hospital Louise Marie in 1846, as a nurse during various cholera epidemics and on the battlefields of the Franco-Prussian war, she became the Florence Nightingale of Belgium and was remembered as the 'Angel of Antwerp'.

Ambiguous images of women

The specific contours of these female role models become fully visible only against the background of both the evolving image of women and the burgeoning religious revival of the first half of the nineteenth century. The revolutionary period had not only occasioned trauma for Catholics but also offered opportunities for women's initiatives. The Church's structures were totally dismantled during the Revolution and could only be partly rebuilt during the Napoleonic regime under strict state supervision. Clerics were deeply mistrusted by the civil authorities and a section of the public. Muzzled and sometimes persecuted, they struggled to perform their ministry. Within that ecclesiastical vacuum lay opportunities for women.[18] As an adolescent, Anna de Meeûs had greatly admired Adelaïde de Cicé (1749-1818), founder of the French congregation of the *Filles du Cœur de Marie* (Daughters of the Heart of Mary).[19] During the Revolution, de Cicé had arranged hiding places in Paris for refractory priests. Later, this model of "vierges et martyres qui préfèrent verser leur sang (...)" was one of the key features in the identity of the religious institute that was founded by de Cicé and her male co-founder.[20]

In the Belgian regions as well, women supported male clerics in difficulties. During the Napoleonic and Dutch regimes, Circercule Paridaens hid former Jesuits in an annex of her Leuven convent.[21] Elisabeth de Robiano (1773-1864), Baroness of Gijzegem near the city of Aalst and founder of a local Vincentian sister congregation, provided sanctuary for the priests of the

16 Since the 1990s, the historiography on women and religion has highlighted the influence of the motives and experiences of 'foremothers' in the Christian tradition on female religious participation and agency: Børresen and Vogt, *Women's Studies*; King, "Religion and gender", 78.
17 ADHH, 253: *Annales des Servantes des Sacrés-Cœurs*; Belpaire, *De families Teichmann en Belpaire*, 11.
18 Curtis, "Charitable Ladies", 125-133; Chopelin, "Une affaire des femmes", 176.
19 ARE, *Lettres divers*: de Meeûs to Boone (22 May 1851).
20 Rayez, "Retour aux sources", 277. Cicé founded the society of the *Filles du Cœur de Marie* together with the ex-Jesuit, Pierre-Joseph de Clorivière (1735-1820) at the height of the revolution in 1790.
21 Pignal, *Si Jansénius avait su*, 69-101; Suenens and Luyten, "Jesuits as Promoters".

After revolutionary upheavals forced the Telghuys family to move from Verviers to Antwerp, Wilhelmina Telghuys was introduced to the Antwerp high society. Portrayed here as a distinguished young woman in the 1840s, she joined the cultural and charitable circles around the Teichmann family.
[Painting – 1840s – Collection *Dienstmaagden H. Harten*, Antwerp]

dissolved Society in her château. She also supported them financially. In 1832, the general of the restored Jesuit order respectfully called her one of the founders of the Belgian Jesuit province.[22] Other women organised clandestine Masses and religious education. Julie Billiart (1751-1816), founder of the *Sœurs de Notre-Dame* (Sisters of Our Lady) in Amiens and later Namur, owed much of her authority to the successful catechetical activities she had developed as a laywoman in the aftermath of the Revolution. Together with Barat she became one of the most influential female congregation founders of the early nineteenth century.[23]

Reparation and atonement

During the revolutionary period an interesting dialectic arose between the weak political position of women on the one hand and their considerable contribution to the survival of a besieged Church on the other. It was a relationship that provided a lifeline to the struggling Church, and at the same time opened the way for women's agency and recognition.[24] The interaction between female weakness and female power received powerful and paradoxical dimensions in the passionate penance and 'reparation' or atonement discourse that took hold of Catholicism soon after the Revolution. As many aspects of nineteenth-century Catholicism, the spirituality of 'reparation' was not a novelty. Medieval mystics saw their ascetic life of fasting, suffering and adoration as a participation in Christ's suffering and a reparation for their sins and the sins of others. From the Counter Reformation onwards, penance and atonement became a retribution for apostasy, religious indifference and eventually the rationalism of the Enlightenment.[25] The horror at the outrages of the Revolution strongly intensified this desire for atonement, with one crucial novelty: a strong focus on social action. The willingness of individuals to sacrifice themselves gave every Catholic the opportunity to participate in a collective action of atonement for Christ and his Church. Women, who according to many – not least themselves – were naturally called to self-sacrifice, found a powerful mode of self-expression in a wide variety of penitential practices. Recent historical research pointed out that as '*réparatrices*' they were able to turn the submissive and passive characteristics of the female role model into

---

22 AZVG, 1.1.4.11.1: Roothaan to Lecandèle de Gijzegem (3 Dec. 1832); Pirson, *Elisabeth de Robiano*, 63-69.
23 Henneau, "Récit de vie", 239.
24 De Giorgio, "La bonne catholique", 171.
25 Bynum, "Women mystics"; Mulder-Bakker, *Lives of the Anchoresses*, 87-88; Caspers, "Eerherstel".

publicly recognised activities.²⁶ Sophie Barat, for example, clearly expressed the social and 'active' power of this atonement discourse as the fundament of her education apostolate: "Si nous avions de jeunes élèves que nous formions à l'esprit d'adoration et de réparation, que ce serait différent. Je voyais des centaines, des milliers d'adoratrices (...). Il faut nous vouer à l'éducation de la jeunesse; refaire dans les âmes les fondements solides d'une foi vive (...), y combattre les traces du jansénisme qui a amené l'impiété."²⁷

However, while the discourse of penance and atonement created opportunities for women, it also confirmed the social and ecclesiastical view of them as being called to self-denial and suffering. Constance Teichmann wrote in her diary in 1845: "Since the autumn I have at times such horrible feelings about the souls that are lost (...). I welcome these feelings, especially on Shrove Tuesday, and I wish that this feelings were even more fierce so as to wipe away, if possible, something of the indifference with which people insulted God in those days."²⁸ As such, the dialectic between female weakness and ambition in the context of these post-revolutionary religious women is, in my view, an interesting prelude to the complex double-voiced discourse that were used by the four female founders in this study.

The double ambiguity also marked the bourgeois ideal of female domesticity, which became dominant in the nineteenth century. The civil law of the Napoleonic period had legalised the subordination of women to their male relatives. The French Revolution had not translated its discourse of equality into gender equality; on the contrary, sexual differences and gender awareness were definitively embedded in the law. Landes even referred to this "cultural inscription of gender in social life" as being one of the most important legacies of the Revolution.²⁹ This fundamental inequality was also inscribed in Belgian law, despite the country's liberal constitution. In the 1830s, a small, progressive group of Brussels middle-class women were attracted by the proto-feminist ideas of some utopian socialist movements, but in general a consensus about the woman's role as wife and mother in service of the family dominated all levels of the ideological spectrum.³⁰ Yet, precisely within this ideal of domesticity, a more positive image of the woman took shape as well:

26 Viaene, *Belgium and the Holy See*, 186-189; Busch, "Die Feminisierung der Frömmigkeit", 209; Kane, "'She Offered Herself Up'", 87-91; Burton, *Holy Tears*, XVI-XVII. See also pp. 112-116.
27 Cited in: Kilroy, *Madeleine Sophie Barat*, 457, n. 53.
28 "Sedert den herfst ondervind ik soms zulke akelige gevoelens over het verloren gaan der zielen, (...). Ik heet die gevoelens welkom, vooral in den vastenavondtijd en ik zou willen dat dit gevoel nog wreeder ware om, als het mogelijk is, iets uit te boeten van de onverschilligheid waarmede de menschen God in die dagen beleedigen": entry in the diary of Constance Teichmann (26 Jan. 1845), cited in: Belpaire, *Constance Teichmann*, 31-32.
29 Landes, *Women and the Public Sphere*, 170-171.
30 Moors, "Drempels van de droom", 32-33; Gubin, *Choisir l'histoire des femmes*, 162-163; Gubin and Piette, *Emma, Louise et Marie*, 17-24; Van de Putte, *Partnerkeuze*, 54-55.

the woman as the angel of the household, a moral beacon in the home at a time of decadence and unrest in the outside world.

This image of the woman was not necessarily progressive. After all, it was also based on the idea of women's intellectual and physical incapacity to compete in the public arena. However, the ideal of the angel in the house did offer a conceptual framework for recognising the value of women.[31] The liberal-minded Flemish writer Jeanette Delcroix praised the female protagonists of her novel as "two pious, brave, courageous, lovable creatures" and of one character she wrote: "you have never been praised for your clever mind, but who will ever know the treasures that your heart contains".[32] Even ultra-conservative Catholic nineteenth-century thinkers like the then widely-read Joseph de Maistre thought that "Elles [women] peuvent même prétendre au sublime, mais au sublime féminin. Chaque être doit se tenir à sa place, et ne pas affecter d'autres perfections que celles qui lui appartiennent".[33]

Religion played a highly prominent role in the paradigm shift. On the one hand it sanctioned gender inequality as part of the divine plan. On the other hand religion was both a legitimation and a language for female agency. The Jesuit Jean-Baptiste Boone (1794-1871), the future spiritual director of Anna de Meeûs and Fanny Kestre, was an influential conservative opinion-maker of the first half of the nineteenth century. He characterised this ambiguous relation between religion and the Christian woman thus: "Qu'elle soit disposée à suivre toutes les inclinations raisonnables de son mari, c'est un devoir; mais qu'elle ait aussi assez de force pour résister, quand il s'agit de participer à ses désordres (…); qu'elle ait assez de conscience pour ne pas négliger ses devoirs religieux".[34] Religion could offer the woman a framework for personal development within the contours of the discourse on the angel of the house, but not necessarily within the boundaries of the household.

In the following paragraphs, I want to argue that the model of the angel in the house was indeed problematic from multiple perspectives. The rhetoric supported the public and private spheres theory, which for decades helped shape the historiography of the nineteenth century. In recent historiography, however, the absolute claims of this model have increasingly come in for criticism. The nineteenth-century boundaries between the public, masculine sphere and the private, female domain have been given a more relative and

---

31 McMillan, *France and Women*, 97; Mills, "Negotiating the Divide", 32-34; Curtis, "Charitable Ladies", 133-137, 153-156.
32 "twee vrome, brave, moedige, liefderyke wezens (…) Nooit werd gy geroemd om uwen schranderen geest, maer wie zal ooit de schatten kennen die uw hart bevat": Delcroix, *Fernandina en Frederika*, 130. On Jeanette Delcroix (1826-1897), see: Van Gemert, "A Witty Pioneer", 548-549.
33 De Maistre (1743-1821) to his daughter Constance (1808), cited in *Lettres et opuscules inédits*, I, 144.
34 Boone, *Des devoirs de la femme chrétienne*, 34-35.

diffuse character.³⁵ It has already been shown that disruptive political changes provided religiously engaged women with opportunities to play a significant role. The narratives of Kestre, de Meeûs and Telghuys provide opportunities to examine if the characteristics of specific social environments, socio-economic necessity, new convent models as well as the religious ideas of the revival created loopholes in existing gender boundaries that can further challenge the double spheres theory.

The angel in the house? Alternative social environments

Although the bourgeois domestic ideal gained influence in the first half of the nineteenth century, a stay-at-home wife was not economically viable for many middle-class families, and even less so for the majority of working-class families.³⁶ After the move to Brussels, Fanny Kestre's father Louis, for example, was partially dependent on "les peines et les embarras du commerce" of his wife Angelique Leclercq to repay his business debts.³⁷ Shortly after their arrival in 1843, she started her own lingerie shop in the neighbourhood of the *Saint-Gudule* Church. The shop, in which Fanny Kestre together with her sisters Félicie and Marie also helped out, was necessary to balance the household budget. Angelique and her daughters were part of a large group of working women in Brussels. Known for its dynamic retail trade, the capital's economy was characterised by a large number of female boutique owners.³⁸ Forced for economic or other reasons to work outside the home, they could count on a certain amount of public understanding even in the context of the new bourgeois values, and especially when their commercial activities were in line with what was seen as a female, domestic environment. Over 98% of Brussels boutiques were then run by women, although most of them struggled to survive.³⁹

Apart from pressing socio-economic needs, there were opportunities for female action outside the domestic sphere in some high-bourgeois and artistic circles too. In the socio-cultural network around the Teichmann and Telghuys families, women derived their influence and prestige, not from their exemplary role as housewives, but from their artistic talent, their organisational

---

35   Van Osselaer, "Religion, Family and Domesticity", 7-25; Abrams, *The Making of Modern Women*, 1-20; Fuchs and Thompson, *Women in Nineteenth-Century Europe*, 177-180; Mills, "Negotiating the Divide", 30-31; Harrison, *Romantic Catholics*, 295.
36   Gubin, *Choisir l'histoire des femmes*, 174-175; Keymolen, *Vrouwenarbeid in België*, 11; Van Molle, "Zakenvrouwen of vrouwenzaken?", 38-39.
37   Louis Kestre to Fanny Kestre (31 Dec. 1843), cited in *La Révérende Mère Fanny de l'Eucharistie*, 11.
38   Gubin calculated that in 1842 46% of Brussels women had jobs, a significant proportion of which were in the artisan or commercial clothing sectors. Gubin, "La grande ville", 84-85.
39   Van Molle, "Zakenvrouwen of vrouwenzaken?", 35-36; Gubin, "La grande ville", 85.

and charitable achievements and – not least – from the female provenance of the family fortune.⁴⁰ There even was room for romantic love stories. Isabella Telghuys, sister and teacher of Wilhelmina, was a talented painter. While a student at the Antwerp Art Academy, she succumbed to the charms of her teacher, Nicaise De Keyser (1813-1886), at that time a well-known painter in the Romantic school. The two married in 1840 and travelled around Europe to art cities and exhibitions. In Antwerp they hosted an artistic salon, where the Teichmanns were regular guests. Isabella Telghuys and her husband were later among the most generous benefactors of Wilhelmina's charitable projects and her congregation.⁴¹ Still, although artistic and charitable activities created opportunities outside the context of the family and the home, the prevailing bourgeois gender conventions were rarely questioned. Like the female shopkeepers discussed above, historical research into Belgian female artists, authors and (amateur) scientists has convincingly shown that these women also largely conformed to a female role model. Many women artists and writers, like Isabella Telghuys for example, cut back on their own artistic work after marriage.⁴²

Like the Telghuys family in Antwerp, the de Meeûs family lived in an upper-class environment. The great ancestral fortune of both spouses was built up through trade, financial and property speculation. As the young governor of the *Société Générale*, Ferdinand was a prominent figure in the young Belgian state. He turned out to be a brilliant director and an opportunistic investor. Under his management the *Société Générale* developed into the most important financial, commercial and industrial holding in the country.⁴³ His château in Argenteuil became a meeting place for the well-to-do Catholic circles of Brussels. In this environment, the foundations were laid for the important social network from which Anna de Meeûs would derive much of her future power and influence. It was also a favourable setting for female projects, but again within well-regulated gender lines. Women gathered in the salons to launch charitable activities, while the men discussed current affairs in the billiard room. Vincenzo Pecci (1810-1903), later Pope Leo XIII, was a frequent guest in Argenteuil while papal nuncio to Belgium in the years 1843-1846. He and Anna de Meeûs met several times in the château's dining room. As was often the case in the elite Catholic circles of that time, the nuncio even attempted to

---

40 Christens, "Vrouwen en onderwijs", 61-62; Van Molle, "Constance Teichmann", 524-525.
41 ADHH, 58: Mère Jeanne to Schoofs (13 Nov. 1873); ADHH, 69: Report (19 Jan. 1899); Belpaire, *De families Teichmann en Belpaire*, 50-51.
42 Creusen, *Femmes artistes*, 142-149, 200; Michaux, "Femmes de lettres belges", 33; Schenkeveld-Van der Dussen, Porteman, and Couttenier, "Inleiding", 11; Vanpaemel, "Laissons aux hommes les recherches savantes", 182.
43 Meuwissen, *Les grandes fortunes*, 123-126; Brion and Moreau, *De Generale Maatschappij*, 28-34.

In 1846 Fanny Geefs, one of the few professional female painters in Belgium, portrayed the de Meeûs family. Above left is pictured the first château of Argenteuil, a year before it was destroyed by a catastrophic fire. Anna de Meeûs is second from the left.
[Painting – 1846 – Private collection]

arrange a marriage for her – in vain, as turned out later.⁴⁴ Still, he became an important friend who many years later did not fail to support Anna's institute and charities from within the Vatican. Young, female artists also had contact with the de Meeûs family. The château housed a large art collection. In 1846 the Irish-Belgian painter, Fanny Geefs (1807-1883), who at the time was one of the few professional female artists in Belgium, painted a portrait of the de Meeûs family.⁴⁵ Her portrait of the de Meeûs family also depicted the original château of Argenteuil, which in 1847 was destroyed by fire. The new luxurious building that was erected in the 1850s was an even more illustrious reflection of the family's elite reputation than the château where Anna had spent a large part of her childhood.⁴⁶

Initially, the de Meeûs couple did not send their eldest daughter Anna to a convent boarding school. Like many other well-to-do families in Brussels,

44   ARE, *Souvenirs de Famille, La Vocation*, 25.
45   Van Cauwenberge, "Femmes artistes en Belgique", 14-15.
46   Meuwissen, *Les grandes fortunes*, 125; Verwilghen, *Le mythe d'Argenteuil*, 72.

they opted instead for the boarding school run by Zoé Parent (1804-1887) on the *Rue Isabelle* in the heart of Brussels. Although Parent agreed that religious instruction was important for the education of girls, the boarding school she founded in 1830 did not have the overriding confessional character of convent schools. Moreover, Parent frequented the liberal circles around the pedagogue and *avant-la-lettre* feminist, Zoé de Gamond (1806-1854), with whom she enthusiastically shared the progressive ideas of utopian socialists. In 1836, she married Constantin Heger, a liberal-minded teacher at the Brussels Atheneum.[47] Unusually, in terms of the bourgeois conventions that prevailed at the time, she continued to run the boarding school after her marriage, although it became known as the *Pensionnat Heger*.[48]

The precise years of Anna de Meeûs' stay in Parent's boarding school are not known. It is certain however that she entered the prestigious institute of the *Dames du Sacré-Cœur* in Paris in 1840. Anna maintained lasting contact with the Heger-Parent family, and one of the family's daughters later became one of the benefactors of her congregation.[49] Most likely the main reason for the change in schools lay in the changing social status of the de Meeûs family. Much more than the *Pensionnat Heger*, the Paris convent school appealed to the standing of the aristocracy, to which the 'de' Meeûs family was elevated in 1836.[50]

The angel in the house? The challenge of the congregational model

Not only did female shopkeepers, artists and boarding school directors have an ambiguous relationship with the ideal of the woman in the home, female active religious had so as well. First, the concept of religiously inspired community life for women was in itself a source of controversy. In countries with a non-Catholic majority, England and the Netherlands for example, the status of female religious in the first half of the nineteenth century was often problematic. In Protestant circles, the female ideal of the caring wife and mother was even more dominant than among Catholics, and religious community life for women was not a socially accepted 'third way'. Although female celibacy emerged in Anglican and Protestant sisterhoods, and although some proto-

---

47 Heger, *Héger 1700-2000*, 32-36; Depage, *La vie d'Antoine Depage*, 31-40. On the circle around Zoé de Gamond, see: Gubin, "Politics and anticlericalism", 123.
48 The Heger boarding school has a famous place in the history of English literature. In 1842-1843 the Brontë sisters stayed in the *Pensionnat Heger*. Charlotte Brontë (1816-1855) even fell in love with Constantin Heger. Her painful experiences of unrequited love found expression in two of her later novels, *Villette* (1853) and *The Professor* (1857), which also offer very negative views of Catholicism and mid-nineteenth-century Brussels. Sellars, *Charlotte Brontë*, 38-51.
49 ARE, *Cahier Propriétés-Maisons*: Loan of Mlle Heger (20 July 1878).
50 ARE, *Chroniques, II. Souvenirs de famille*, 5-7.

feminist Protestant women expressed their admiration for the autonomy of Catholic convent superiors, much scepticism and mockery remained. A whole literary tradition of Gothic novels flourished in England and identified nuns with sexual indulgence, masochism and a lust for power.[51] The view of female religious as imperfect women sometimes received dramatic and highly mediatised proportions. In the mid-nineteenth century, the American-English congregation founder, Cornelia Connelly (1809-1879) was reviled by Protestant public opinion because she had abandoned her husband and children for the convent, even though a much more complex story lay hidden behind the family drama.[52]

In the Catholic tradition, convent life offered women a respected alternative to marriage and motherhood, although it was limited for a long time to the strict boundaries of the enclosed monastic model. This kind of religious life for women with solemn, irrevocable vows and a *'mort civile'* to the secular world had been tightly regulated in terms of strict – papal – enclosure ever since the sixteenth-century Council of Trent. It was in many ways as rigid as the nineteenth-century bourgeois gender concepts.[53]. Attempts had already been made in the seventeenth century to free women's convents from complete enclosure, the flexible and successful structure of the Jesuit order being an important source of inspiration. The reaction of the highest ecclesiastical authority to these attempts varied, but was by no means positive. The *'jésuitesses'* of Mary Ward were excommunicated and disbanded because their model of 'wandering nuns' contradicted "their weak sex and character, ... female modesty and especially ... maidenly reserve".[54] The Ursulines and the Visitation Sisters were obliged to introduce enclosure, even though it was contrary to their original identity. The *Filles de Charité* (Daughters of Charity) of Vincent de Paul were recognised, but had to content themselves with the canonically inferior designation of *'filles dévôtes'*.[55] Notwithstanding the second-rate clerical status of these religious women, they laid the seeds for the success of the congregational model in the late eighteenth and nineteenth century, as will be clearly shown later in the case of Belgium.

Religious sister congregations, with an active apostolate in the world, simple vows and partial or no enclosure, challenged the ideal of the angel in

51 Eijt, *Religieuze vrouwen*, 166-167; Van Heijst, Derks and Monteiro, *Ex Caritate*, 314-315; Mumm, *Stolen Daughters*, 3-11; Mangion, "Women, Religious Ministry", 79; O'Brien, *Leaving God for God*, 57.
52 O'Brien, "With a Mother's Imagination", 202-205.
53 Medioli, "The Dimensions of the Cloister", 165-180; Liebowitz, "Virgins in the Service of Christ", 139-141.
54 Quotation from the papal Bull of Suppression (1631) of Ward's institute, cited and translated in: Cotter, *The General Chapter*, 27.
55 Liebowitz, "Virgins in the Service of Christ", 140-145; Caffiero, *Religione e modernità*, 121-123; Brejon de Lavergnée, *Histoire des Filles de la Charité*, 201-225; Monteiro, *Geestelijke maagden*, 29-33.

the house in more fundamental ways than did the old monastic model. They were also controversial because of the strong position of female superior generals. Powerful, leading sisters were not a nineteenth-century novelty. Medieval and early modern women's convents had their share of abbesses whose influence went beyond the papal *clausura*. Unlike pioneering congregation superiors such as Barat, Billiart or de Cicé who headed international networks of monasteries, the power of abbesses was usually restricted to a limited number of monasteries. Moreover, it was closely connected with their often aristocratic origins. By comparison, the founders in the post-revolutionary period – when the age-old privileges of the nobility and the Church were no more – had more the profile of self-made women, although a well-to-do background still was an important element of success.[56]

The innovative nature of the position of female congregation superiors could be measured by the sharp resistance they often faced. At the time that Anna de Meeûs was living in the cocoon of her Paris boarding school, the congregation of the *Dames du Sacré-Cœur* of founder-superior Barat, for example, was struck by a severe crisis. Ambitious local superiors with abbess ambitions, including Aimée d'Avenas, French bishops with little appreciation for Barat's centralisation efforts and Jesuits from Rome with their own agenda, gnawed away at the founder's position.[57] Her fellow founder, Julie Billiart, fled from Amiens in 1809 to escape the interference of the diocesan clergy. Grievances about her authoritarian personality were mixed in with comments on the essence of the centralised congregational model. Billiart's closest companion, Françoise Blin de Bourdon, made the significant comment, "si chaque diocèse se met en devoir de nous gouverner à sa façon, cela ne laissera pas que de faire une belle musique".[58]

Billiart eventually found a home in future Belgium, with the support of Bishop Pisani of Namur.[59] But also in this context, female religious superiors were controversial. Discontent about Pisani's pro-Napoleonic attitude, for example, affected the reputation of his protégé Billiart, who was criticised for her independent position and course of action. The situation even encouraged resentment among her own sisters.[60] In the Archdiocese of Mechelen, Archbishop Sterckx, at the end of the 1840s obliged Justine Desbille (1801-1866),

56 Wynants, "Le gouvernement", 82-90; Friedlander, "Les pouvoirs de la supérieure", 246-247; Venarde, *Women's Monasticism*, 124-125; Langlois, *Le catholicisme au féminin*, 273-283.
57 Serra, "Madeleine-Sophie Barat", 276-277; Luirard, "Les pouvoirs de la supérieure générale", 318.
58 Blin de Bourdon to Sister Anastasie van Jumet (27 Sept. 1815), cited in Henneau, "Récit de vie", 245.
59 The Frenchman Charles-François-Joseph Pisani de la Gaude (1743-1826) was bishop of Namur from 1804. He saw great potential in the services of the active congregations for the rebuilding of his diocese. Murphy, *Julie Billiart*, 100-102.
60 Ibidem, 180-184.

founder of the *Sœurs de l'Enfant-Jésus* (Sisters of the Infant Jesus) of Nivelles, to give up the convent she had founded in England. He argued that it was "moralement impossible qu'une femme gouverne bien d'autres maisons".[61] Large congregations, which were difficult to manage, and that were led by powerful female superiors, could not easily be brought under diocesan jurisdiction and control. Still, criticism or attacks by diocesan authorities seldom caused a Belgian congregation to disintegrate completely. A decisive reason for their relative invulnerability was the other essential aspect of the nineteenth-century sister congregations: their 'apostolic' involvement in education, care and in the broad sector of social services.

The angel in the house? The stimulating environment of 'dames d'œuvres'

Social engagement was a distinct feature of post-revolutionary Catholicism. Since the Church had been deprived of its political power, nineteenth-century revival Catholics wanted to give religion a new place in modern society through charitable projects and 'social' piety. Members of the charitable association of Saint Vincent de Paul, which was founded in 1833 in France by a group of Catholic students around Frédéric Ozanam (1813-1853) and Emmanuel Bailly (1794-1861) and rapidly expanded internationally, became the flag-bearers of this new movement.[62] On the one hand, they gave a Catholic interpretation to the eighteenth-century humanistic and social utility discourse of the Enlightenment philosophers. This discourse had been the basis of the actions of Enlightened rulers like Joseph II (1780-1790) against contemplative – and therefore socially 'useless' – monastic communities, but it had also influenced nineteenth-century Catholics. On the other hand, the Vincentians, and in their footsteps, many 'Romantic Catholics', saw spontaneous and religiously inspired charitable action as the basis for social harmony and community formation. It was an antidote to individualism, and to the rationalist social theories of the Enlightenment.[63]

If the Vincentian society created the mould for the charitable foundations of the revival, then the Breton aristocrat Chateaubriand (1768-1848) supplied it with a Romantic manifesto. In his *Génié du Christianisme* (1802) he was lyrical about the power of Catholicism to heal heart, soul and society. As the

---

61 Engelbertus Sterckx (1792-1867) was archbishop of Mechelen between 1832 and 1867. On his policy towards Justine Desbille, see: AAM, CF, File of the Sœurs de l'Enfant-Jésus de Nivelles: Sœur Marie-Thérèse to the archbishop (23 May 1850). About his policy, see also: Viaene, "De ontplooiing van een 'vrije' kerk", 73 and part II.
62 Brejon de Lavergnée, *La Société de Saint-Vincent de Paul*, 500.
63 The term "Romantic Catholics" is used by Carol Harrison in her work on a generation of Catholic men and women living in the first years of the nineteenth century, with optimistic beliefs in the possibilities for faith and the Church in post-revolutionary society: Harrison, *Romantic Catholics*, 202-206.

Constance Teichmann (1824-1896) was an important figure in Catholic charity of mid-century Antwerp. Known as the 'Angel of Antwerp', she introduced Wilhelmina Telghuys in a world of a socially and religiously engaged elite of *'dames d'œuvres'*.
[Mortuary Card – 1896 – Private collection]

'*rêveur de Combourg*', he wrote the charter for the sacramental, devotional and emotional religiosity of the revival. Old popular devotions, fuelled by emotional rather than rational or profound theological inspiration, were revived and became a buffer against the intellectualism of the Enlightenment and the inflexibility of Jansenism. The ideal for the future was painted with the brush of the medieval past, with Gothic cathedrals as the architecture of the divine mystery and medieval corporatism as the model for a harmonious society. Even prayer and penance were given a social and Romantic dimension within the framework of the revival. The religious foremothers of the early nineteenth century were poised here at a turning point. Cicercule Paridaens, with her rigorous eighteenth-century morality, still saw in convent life a chance to perform individual penance for the salvation of her own doomed soul, whereas the aforementioned Barat included personal penance in a broad array of social action and collective reparation.[64] Individual mystical contemplation and physical chastisement as stringent means of salvation were replaced in the nineteenth century by social atonement and collective devotional passion.[65]

The future founders grew up in this dynamic environment of the revival. In the following chapters, I will explain in detail how they sought a synthesis between the revival's ethos of social and charitable action and the devotional and spiritual framework of the time. In this chapter, I would like to examine the genesis of their early social engagement. Like many Belgian and foreign congregation founders, de Meeûs, Kestre and Telghuys started their 'careers' as *dames d'œuvres*.[66] Inspiring figures such as Mère d'Avenas paved the way, while models were also to be found within their own family and circle of friends. Constance Teichmann hated the thought of "being useless in the world, of living and dying without having done anything for humanity, for my country, for religion". Not surprisingly, she drew Wilhelmina Telghuys into an almost incessant round of charitable projects.[67] Herself a rather good singer and "gaie comme un pinson", Telghuys became a member of the *Accord Parfait* and the *Société Orphée*, two cultural associations founded by the Teichmann sisters to collect money for charitable causes. Telghuys also took on voluntary work in an orphanage in the Antwerp suburb of Hoboken, founded in 1856 by Marie-Antoinette Teichmann-Cooppal.[68]

---

64 ADML, 3: Lectures of Mère Marie Thérèse (1817-1820). For the quotation from Barat, see supra, p. 51.
65 Viaene, *Belgium and the Holy See*, 185-203; Pirotte, "Néo-gothique et fantasmes"; Anderson, "The Limits of Secularization", 668; Atkin and Tallett, *Priests, Prelates and People*, 106-108; Clark, "The new Catholicism", 16-18.
66 For parallels, see: Luddy, *Women and Philanthropy*, 24; Mangion, *Contested Identities*, 48-56; Meiwes, *Arbeiterinnen*, 30-38.
67 Belpaire, *Constance Teichmann*, 26.
68 ADHH, 16: Verest Manuscript; Belpaire, *De families Teichmann en Belpaire*, 50-51.

Kestre and de Meeûs became involved in religious and charitable associations as well. Both became members of the *Filles de Marie*, a lay women's congregation attached to the convent of the *Dames du Sacré-Cœur* in the Brussels suburb of Jette. Lay congregations and confraternities experienced an international resurgence during the revival.[69] From the 1820s onwards they were set up also in convent schools and girls' boarding schools. The *Dames du Sacré-Cœur* were pioneers in this field, but pious associations for female pupils were soon introduced in other convent boarding schools too. Historians have emphasised that these associations offered more than a path to excellence for the most devout pupils. They were a powerful tool for the sisters to disseminate their religious worldview and a typical revivalist means for furthering the importance of good works. Moreover, because the associations *intra muros* frequently had counterparts and successors outside the school walls, it was an important gateway to exerting influence in the secular world.[70]

The pious congregations formed an important pillar in the revival's pursuit of a new Christian foundation for society. The *Filles de Marie* in Jette, who were given firm spiritual support by the Brussels Jesuits, started many charitable projects in the capital.[71] These women's confraternities were also a lever for female development. They brought opportunities for action and possibilities of recognition within reach for many *dames d'œuvres*, outside the often restricted atmosphere of their own houses.[72] Although the pious associations were bound to strict clerical supervision, male dominance was not any tighter than it was in nineteenth-century marriages. Moreover, recent research for France and Belgium has highlighted an important emotional stimulus. Van Osselaer interpreted the bond between the female members of the Belgian branch of the Apostolate of Prayer and their male companions both as a sign of benevolent female submission as well as a female strategy to achieve more power and influence. In the context of the Marian pilgrimage site in Lourdes, Harris notes the special bond that could exist between religiously inspired women and their male companions, which enabled them "to talk about religious preoccupations and to confront issues of identity and selfhood, to share with intelligent, educated men problems close to their hearts".[73] Father Jean-Baptiste Boone, one of the architects of the Catholic benevolent foundations

---

69 Viaene, *Belgium and the Holy See*, 180-185; Atkin and Tallett, *Priests, Prelates and People*, 114.
70 Rogers, *Les bourgeoises*, 203-208; Curtis, "Charitable Ladies", 121-156.
71 Poncelet, *La Compagnie de Jésus*, 159.
72 For Belgium, see: De Maeyer, "Les dames d'œuvres"; Hemelsoet, *Liefdadigheid als roeping*. Internationally, there are interesting discussions in: Raughter, "A discreet benevolence"; Luddy, *Women and Philanthropy*; Curtis, "Charitable Ladies" and Mills, "Negotiating the Divide".
73 Van Osselaer, *The Pious Sex*, 230-231; Harris, *Lourdes*, 235; McMillan, "Religion and gender", 63.

of the revival in Brussels, was the authoritarian but charismatic spiritual leader of the *Filles de Marie*. Almost every week he attracted a crowd of admiring *dames d'œuvres* to his passionate spiritual lectures. For many, such as Kestre and de Meeûs, he became a valued spiritual counsellor.[74]

The stimulating bond between female 'pupils' and male 'teachers' was not peculiar to the ecclesiastical scene. It was also noted in artistic circles, for example.[75] Nevertheless, the phenomenon elicited comments about the peculiar alliance between male clerics and women, conspiring against their 'rational' and anticlerical husbands.[76] In French historiography, in particular, it was seen as an expression of the 'Two Frances' concept. Related to the separate spheres theory, this concept envisioned nineteenth-century French society as marked by a dichotomy between two spheres that were increasingly drifting apart: a sentimental and religious, mainly female sphere of life on the one hand and an anticlerical, rational men's world on the other.[77] Recent historiography argues, however, that these conceptualisations were largely indebted to nineteenth-century discourse on the private role of women and anticlerical caricatures of indoctrinated pious women and degenerate priests, a topic that will be more thoroughly analysed in part II.

Moreover, historians have also pointed out that men too played their part in the religious revival movement.[78] Anna's father Ferdinand de Meeûs, for example, turned out to be such an *homme d'œuvre* for whom "la piété la plus austère, jointe à la soumission la plus absolue aux lois de l'Église, peut se concilier, à tous les égards, avec les conceptions audacieuses et les œuvres grandioses de l'industrie moderne".[79] These harmonious words by his nineteenth-century biographer belied the clear field of tension in which post-revolutionary Catholics operated in the public domain. Ferdinand de Meeûs belonged to the group of liberal-Catholics, largely coinciding with Harrison's Romantic Catholics in France, who pragmatically embraced the new Belgian state. He was convinced that the Church should seek its salvation in the liberties of the new Constitution in order to restore its position in society.[80]

De Meeûs supported the political union between Catholics and liberals that took shape in Belgium in the 1830s and 1840 and was also a full-blooded

---

74 ARE, *Cahier des lettres 1*: de Meeûs to Cogels (17 Aug. 1853), de Meeûs to Boone (14 Sept. 1847).
75 See for example: Michaux, "Femmes de lettres", 136.
76 ABSE, 4.2.6. Boone, Jean-Baptiste, 1226: Annotations by Fr. Broeckaert. See also: Atkin and Tallett, *Priests, Prelates and People*, 114; Van Osselaer, *The Pious Sex*, 47-48.
77 Cholvy and Hilaire, *Histoire religieuse*, 176-186; Gibson, *A Social History*, 187-188.
78 Brejon de Lavergnée, "Le genre du philanthrope", 102-103; Harrison, *Romantic Catholics*, 18-19; Van Osselaer, "Religion, Family and Domesticity", 14-15; Idem, *The Pious Sex*, 47-48, 237-240; McMillan, "Religion and Gender", 57-63; Mangion, "The Mixed Life", 169-170.
79 Thonissen, *Vie du Comte Ferdinand de Meeûs*, VII.
80 Harrison, *Romantic Catholics*, 2-3, 6-7. On the complex balancing act of Belgian liberal Catholics, see: Viaene, *Belgium and the Holy See*, 64-99.

Around 1860, Anna de Meeûs' father ordered the construction of an impressive iron, neo-Gothic church on his domain in Argenteuil, symbolising both his Romantic fascination with the medieval past as well as his belief in the compatibility of the Church and modern society.
[Postcard – ca. 1900 – Private collection]

revivalist Catholic. Intellectual and well-read, he liked to refer to the French liberal-Catholic preacher, Jean Baptiste Lacordaire (1802-1861) as support for his views on Catholic participation on the public stage. He was also convinced of Lacordaire's synthesis of sacrifice with social engagement: "le feu de la charité qui consume le vrai chrétien, et qui fait que l'épouse, la mère, l'ami, s'offrent mille fois à Dieu pour le bonheur de l'époux, de l'enfant, de l'ami qui s'écarte de la véritable voie".[81] His business acumen and knowledge of the financial markets enabled him to devise innovative fundraising constructions for the benefit of Catholic charities, mainly schools.[82] The iron neo-Gothic church he had built in the mid-nineteenth century on his domain in Argenteuil was the ultimate synthesis of his belief in industrial progress, his religious commitment and his ambitious entrepreneurship.

The charitable, social engagement of the laity and religious of the revival was not exclusively the product of Romantic religious idealism. Its emergence was equally influenced by the hard realities of the nineteenth century. The industrial revolution, which had passed from England to the continent at the end of the eighteenth century, fundamentally disrupted the existing socio-economic fabric. In regions – such as Belgium – where industrial upheaval sprouted rapidly, the consequences for rural and home industries were catastrophic. Rural flight, uncontrolled urbanisation and population growth went hand in hand with impoverishment, rising crime, famine and epidemics. All of the future female founders of our study were sooner or later confronted with the socio-economic misery of the nineteenth century. In the Teichmanns' children's hospital and orphanage, Telghuys encountered the children of the many unemployed textile factory workers or underpaid dockers. Fearlessly, and much against the wishes of her parents, she wandered through the poor working-class neighbourhoods in the parish of *Sint-Joris* (Saint George) and just outside the city walls in Borgerhout. There she came across the outcasts of the successful economic mutation of Antwerp from industrial centre to commercial port city.[83] Via the *Filles de Marie*, Kestre and de Meeûs discovered the miserable conditions in the impoverished districts of Brussels. With her best friend, Micaela Desmaissières y López (1809-1865), the sister of a Spanish diplomat, de Meeûs undertook charitable missions on the streets of the poor *Marolles* district.[84]

Political instability and the immature structures of the early Belgian state after 1830 prevented the construction of an adequate public welfare system.

---

81 De Meeûs to General Evain (s.d.), cited in: Thonissen, *Vie du Comte Ferdinand de Meeûs*, 169. On Lacordaire, see: Harrison, *Romantic Catholics*, 6-7; Viaene, *Belgium and the Holy See*, 188 and Atkin and Tallett, *Priests, Prelates and People*, 109.
82 Van de Perre, "Catholic fundraising".
83 ADHH, 58: Telghuys to Van den Bergh (9 Feb. 1872). On the socio-economic situation in Antwerp, see: Blondé, Van Dijck and Vrints, "Een probleemstad?", 294-297.
84 ADSJ, 1.3./1: Journal of Kestre, 21 Oct. 1856; ADSJ, 1.5: Notice by Fanny Kestre (1846).

This situation provided a fertile breeding ground for religiously inspired engagement. Operating clandestinely or under strict restrictions during the Napoleonic and Dutch regimes, religious charity was stimulated after 1830 by the constitutional liberties of the Belgian state. According to historian Viaene, within the framework of political unionism and the socio-economic needs of the young state, Catholic welfare initiatives were offered an 'empire by invitation'.[85]

Aut maritus, aut murus? Between marriage and the convent

Conditioned by boarding-school life

The discourse of sacrifice and charity that was passed on in the religious boarding schools fitted in with the Romantic passion and social activism of the revival. However, it did not always fit as seamlessly into the worldly life to which many of the well-off boarding-school students returned after their school days ended. Anna de Meeûs wrote to her confessor, Father Boone, that she became increasingly alienated from the luxurious world of aristocratic balls and "obligations de famille" after her return from Paris.[86] Her experiences were in line with the complaints of other girls from elite backgrounds. Having left their convent boarding schools, they ended up in "le monde banal (…) devant lequel elles se présentent pour la première fois en toilette décolleté", the only goal being to get a suitable husband as soon as possible.[87] Telghuys incurred her parents' anger because she was damaging her reputation with her charity work in the working-class districts. Her mother desperately pointed out that her initiatives and wanderings in the suburbs were seriously compromising her marriage perspectives.[88] In her turn, Anna de Meeûs came in for a lot of misunderstanding from her family when in 1844 she rejected a marriage proposal that had been arranged by Nuncio Pecci. She was very critical of this pressure for aristocratic marriage: "(…) faut-il donc absolument passer toute sa vie à subir toutes ces exigences dont il semblait qu'on ne pouvait pas se dispenser?". But she also feared the dull existence of a spinster: "rester vieille fille m'était encore plus pénible. Je sentais un vif désir de servir Dieu librement et de faire du bien. J'y étais très excitée; je sentais qu'en me mariant, je ne pourrais pas être toute à Lui."[89]

Anna was supported in her reservations about marriage by her confessor Boone. With the permission of this renowned Jesuit she took a private and secret vow of virginity in March 1844.[90] From the point of view of female agency

---

85 Viaene, *Belgium and the Holy See*, 177.
86 ARE, *Lettres divers*: De Meeûs to Boone, 1 Jan. 1851.
87 de Haulleville, *Portraits et silhouettes*, I, 198; Rogers, *Les bourgeoises*, 333-337.
88 ADHH, 253: *Annales des Servantes des Sacré-Cœur*.
89 ARE, *Lettres divers*: de Meeûs to Boone (1 Jan. 1851).
90 Ibidem.

the vow of virginity is a very interesting concept. Although often rooted in the discourse of female self-denial and asceticism – and in particular the voluntary renunciation of marriage and motherhood – the vow also concealed a strikingly 'rebellious' message. Biographies of medieval and early modern women saints and congregation founders often pointed to a parallel between taking a vow of virginity and opposition to imposed marriages.[91] Ruether, for instance, argued for the early medieval Church that: "Women dedicated to asceticism could count on the support of the Church in making decisions against their family's demands that they marry and bear children".[92] Even among the future nineteenth-century congregation founders, a dedication to virginity was often an important step towards personal development and an autonomous life.[93] In the case of de Meeûs it was a form of silent resistance, an act of rebellion against her family that was validated by the clergy. Boone had rather pessimistic, perhaps realistic, views on marriage too. He considered it to be "un joug, une sujétion, une espèce d'esclavage, pardonnez-moi le mot, où l'on renonce à sa liberté".[94]

Similar remarks were made by many nineteenth-century women. Juliette de Robertsart (1824-1900), who came from the same Belgian aristocratic and Catholic milieu as de Meeûs, did not want to sacrifice her freedom, her life as a writer and her adventurous travels for "les maximes du marriage". A short-lived romance with Louis Veuillot (1813-1883), the godfather of French ultramontane and conservative Catholicism, did not change her views.[95] Kestre also spoke about the dangers of marriage, but more in terms of the pain and sadness of motherhood, recalling her mother's lifelong mourning for the early death of her brother Louis, the first and only son of the family. Kestre, too, had taken a vow of virginity at the age of sixteen.[96]

Shocked by the dramatic clash between the enclosed life of boarding school and the sophisticated lay world, many former pupils of elite convent schools found their way to the novitiates of their former boarding-school sisters.[97] Fanny Kestre's older sister, Sidonie, was one of them. She joined the

91 See, for example, the notes on the fourteenth-century Italian founder Angeline de Corbara or the seventeenth-century French founder Jeanne de Cambry in Hélyot, *Dictionnaire*, III, 205-206, 309-310.
92 Ruether, "Mothers of the Church", 72.
93 See, for example: Wenner, "Théodelinde Dubouché", 1743-1745; Wirth, *Don Bosco et les Salesiens*, 178; Champ, *William Bernard Ullathorne*, 101-102.
94 Boone, *Des devoirs de la femme*, 33.
95 Mortier, *Juliette de Robertsart*, 15-16.
96 ADSJ, 1.6: Kestre to Sidonie Kestre (27 Oct. 1846). Louis Kestre was born in Chimay on 5 April 1819, and died there on 6 April 1819. ACC, *Registres de l'Etat Civil*.
97 On this important pattern of recruitment, see: Rogers, "Retrograde or Modern", 154-156; De Vroede, "The Catholic Boarding Schools"; 225-227; Christens and Suenens, "L'enseignement comme vocation", 146-150; Van Heijst, Derks and Monteiro, *Ex Caritate*, 629, 633-634; O'Brien, "Terra Incognita", 119-123.

Dames du Sacré-Cœur in Jette in 1843, shortly after she had left the Charleville boarding school. Following her religious profession, she became an emotional and spiritual support for the family, even after she was transferred to the congregation's convent in Nancy in the late 1840s. She was an especially devoted sister to the wavering Fanny, tempering her ascetic extremes ("tu es sérieuse comme un anachorète") and her melancholy moods ("je crois que c'est un gracieux caprice").[98] Fanny repeatedly stated that her constitution was too frail to endure the demanding life of the novitiate of the *Dames du Sacré-Cœur*. Sidonie tried to convince Fanny that convent life could offer her a peaceful life with opportunities for educational activities. With great difficulty she arranged a meeting for her with the superior general Barat, but in the end Sidonie had to conclude that Fanny was looking for something "plus orageux".[99]

Was the life of an 'ordinary' convent sister not challenging enough for the more restless spirits among the *dames d'œuvres*? Did they seem to be looking for an escape route from the old precept imposed on women: *aut maritus aut murus?*[100] In her turn, Anna de Meeûs oscillated between admiration for convent life and aversion to its harsh, stifling and routine character. Like Fanny Kestre and many other female contemporaries, Anna de Meeûs struggled with her frailty.[101] Her poor health, however, was not the only reason de Meeûs considered herself unsuitable for the "austérités" of the convent. Her letters also hint at her desire for an original project that could not be reconciled with the routine of religious life.[102] Other energetic women of the revival expressed similar views. The Belgian writer Camille du Bourg (1836-1873) had a great deal of respect for the dignity and apostolic achievements of her religious teachers at the boarding school of the *Zusters van de Visitatie* (Sisters of the Visitation) in Ghent, yet still recoiled from "une existence décolorée" in the convent.[103] The French Romantic Catholic women writers portrayed by Harrison chose to present the convent vocation of the main characters in their literary bestsellers as a choice for anonymity and self-denial. The English convert, author and Catholic patron, Lady Georgiana Fullerton (1812-1885), struggled with the longing for a strict, ascetic religious life on the one hand and a passion for literature on the other.[104] So did Belgian writers and contemporaries of Kestre and de Meeûs, such as the liberal-minded but not unreligious Johanna Court-

---

98 ADSJ, 1.6: Sidonie Kestre to Kestre (s.d. and 28 Dec. 1848).
99 ADSJ, 1.6: Sidonie Kestre to Kestre (26 June 1853).
100 Lux-Sterritt and Mangion, "Introduction", 7.
101 Compare, for example, with the founder Julie Billiart, who was bedridden for half her life, or Camille de Bourg mentioned below, who was described by Viaene as the lay equivalent of the 'female martyr'. See: Viaene, *Belgium and the Holy See*, 188.
102 ARE, *Lettres divers*: de Meeûs to Boone (24 Jan. 1847), de Meeûs to Boone (1 Jan. 1851).
103 de Haulleville, *Portraits et silhouettes*, I, 198.
104 Harrison, *Romantic Catholics*, 171-172, 282-284. It concerned *Marguerite à Vingt ans* (1879) by Victorine Monniot (1824-1880) and *Récit d'une sœur* (1866) by Pauline Craven (1808-1891). On the dilemma facing Fullerton, see: Jaeger, "A writer or a religious?", 271-282.

mans (1811-1890), who in her novels questioned the life of "(....) virtuous nuns whose bravery and sacrifice I admired from the first to the last day I lived in the convent. But were all the nuns happy? Happy nuns there were, this I cannot deny, but how small was their number! There I saw more tears flow than the dewdrops my flowers can imbibe".[105]

The story of the average convent sister

And what about Antoinette Cornet? We lost track of her at the end of her boarding-school time in Pesche. It is not clear whether and for how long she returned to her parents' home in Walcourt. In any case, in 1838 she appeared as 'sœur Gonzague' in the register of entrants to the *Sœurs du Saint Cœur de Marie* in Alsemberg, a small village on the outskirts of Brussels. Presumably, Cornet's family had a devout background. Her younger brother Omer (1825-1900) later opted for an ecclesiastical career as a secular priest in the Diocese of Namur. The convent in Alsemberg, which had been founded only in 1833, was in full expansion when Antoinette arrived. An eighteen-year-old, French-speaking novice with a boarding school past would not be denied entry, especially after the congregation had started its own French-speaking boarding school in 1834. On the other hand, an entrance in a new congregation offered Cornet interesting opportunities for a professional and religious career: she was trained as a teacher and just a few years after her profession in 1841, she became the headmistress of the boarding school and member of the general council of the congregation.

For many Catholics, education, and particularly the education of the poor, was the ideal way to re-Christianise and inculcate a sense of morality in large sections of the population. This strategic concern of the Church for the people was also unfolded in other areas such as care for the sick, the aged, orphans and prisoners and an even broader spectrum of social services. Nevertheless, education became the most important feature of the social face of the nineteenth-century Belgian Church. As in other countries with a strong or burgeoning Catholic tradition, educational needs were a powerful engine for the expansion of female convent life.[106] In the centrally located Belgian archdiocese of Mechelen, which included Alsemberg, 23 new apostolic sister con-

---

105 "(...) deugdzame nonnen wier moed en opoffering ik van den eersten tot den laatsten dag dat ik in het klooster woonde heb bewonderd. Maar waren al de nonnen gelukkig? Gelukkige waren er, dit mag ik niet ontkennen; doch hoe gering was haar getal! Daar heb ik meer tranen zien storten dan mijne bloemen dauwdroppelen kunnen zwelgen": Courtmans, *De Gemeente-Onderwijzer*, 141. On Johanna Courtmans (née Berchmans), see: Couttenier, "Bekroond met een keizerlijk geschenk", 860-870.
106 Christens and Suenens, "L'enseignement comme vocation", 138-141; Langlois, *Le catholicisme au féminin*, 323-327; Van Heijst, Derks and Monteiro, *Ex Caritate*, 84-90; Mangion, *Contested Identities*, 124-125; Lannon, *Privilege, Persecution, and Prophecy*, 73.

Antoinette Cornet entered the congregation of *Sœurs du Saint Cœur de Marie* in the small village of Alsemberg in 1838. She quickly made career as the head-mistress of the boarding school. The convent is pictured here on the left in the late nineteenth century, when it was already transferred to a German congregation, in exile because of the *Kulturkampf*.
[Postcard – after 1870 – Collection *Heemkundig Genootschap 'van Witthem'*, Beersel]

gregations were founded between 1800 and 1850, 21 of which focused (either exclusively or partially) on education.[107] Archbishop Sterckx, whose policy was characterised by a pursuit of efficiency and recovery, actively promoted them. The 1842 Law on Primary Education, which he supported, rolled out the red carpet for huge initiatives by the Church. In obliging each municipality to have a primary school, the law created the premise of the aforementioned 'empire by invitation', to which active congregations of sisters (and to a lesser extent of brothers) enthusiastically consented.[108]

In the footsteps of beguines and spiritual daughters

In order to better understand the complexity of the nineteenth-century success story of women's convents and the situation in Alsemberg, we should return once more to the development of the active and congregational convent model. The history of the community in Alsemberg is a very illustrative exam-

107 This calculation is based on the files relating to religious institutes in the archdiocesan archive (AAM), the information in the database www.odis.be, the nineteenth-century yearbooks of the archdiocese and notes about congregations in the work of Tyck, *Notices historiques*. By way of comparison: in the Diocese of Ghent, 26 out of 28 new congregations founded in the (entire) nineteenth century were exclusively or partly involved in education; in the Diocese of Namur, 19 of the 33 founded in the period 1830-1930. See: Christens and Suenens, "L'enseignement comme vocation", 138-141.
108 Viaene, "De ontplooiing van een 'vrije' kerk", 43-44.

ple. The first two sisters in the convent at Alsemberg – including the superior Thérèse Fontaine – came from the beguinage of Nivelles where the beguines had already opened a modest school in the eighteenth century.[109] Through their educational activities, they tried to legitimise themselves in the eyes of the civil authorities, who were increasingly taken by Enlightenment principles about social utility and the perfectibility of human beings.

The Nivelles beguines however also positioned themselves in an even older tradition of teaching beguines and spiritual daughters.[110] Ever since the second half of the seventeenth century, there was a strongly entrenched model in the Southern Netherlands of celibate pious women living together in small, semi-religious communities. They often devoted themselves to the education of the poor and maintained themselves with lacemaking or other forms of needlework. Although they frequently collaborated with the local clergy, some of these women, who often were wealthy widows or daughters from well-to-do families, still managed to acquire an influential position.[111] The communities of 'pious daughters' constituted a fourth, very loosely structured group in the landscape of women's religious life during the *Ancien Régime*, along with the contemplative enclosed convents, the hospital communities in the cities and the first teaching communities of various congregations, including the Ursulines. Thanks to their low profile, the pious daughters managed for a long time to escape the attempts by both Church and civil authorities to institutionalise or control them. From the eighteenth century on, in the border area with France, many of these devout communities modelled themselves on the already mentioned *Filles de Charité* of Vincent de Paul.[112]

As women living independently, without a formal monastic organisation, beguines and groups of pious daughters were at times the target of suspicion or mockery, just like the afore-mentioned *jésuitesses* of the sixteenth and early seventeenth centuries. In the beguinage of Nivelles there was also internal division between a conservative, illiterate group and a group of 'headstrong' school teachers, who evolved more and more towards becoming a congregational organisation. Despite the frictions and opposition, these communities laid a solid foundation for the growth of women's active congregations in the nineteenth century. Nearly a third of the active congregations in the mid-nineteenth-century archdiocese had started out as eighteenth-century com-

---

109 ASCMLH, D.6: *Le dernier béguinage Nivellois*; Hanoteau, *Une grande nivelloise*, 12-21.
110 On the beguinage of Nivelles, see: Majérus, *C'est femmes qu'on dit béguines*, II, 668-684; Hanoteau, "Le dernier Béguinage nivellois", 178-195.
111 See for example: Weemaes, *In het spoor van Anna Piers* and Demeestere, "Leven en werk van Joanna Francisca Amerlinck"; De Meulemeester, *Geschiedenis der Maricolen*; Schmidt, *Agnes Baliques*.
112 De Vroede, *'Kwezels' en 'zusters'*, 251-256; Annaert, "Les filles dévotes", 3-10; Harline, "Actives and contemplatives", 541-567; Delbaere, "Het klooster", 1-20.

munities of beguines or devout women.[113] In the case of the beguines, however, the success of the congregational model seems to have been achieved partly at their expense. There are various stories about beguines moving to the new congregations, while the reverse rarely happened.[114] Despite the lack of a thorough study of the decline of beguinages in Belgium in the nineteenth century – from 1,989 beguines in 1824 to 313 in 1900 – it is sufficiently clear that they could not compete as a religious model with the sister congregations with their efficient organisation, flexible apostolates and possibilities for geographical expansion.[115] However, in the course of their centuries-old existence, beguines certainly made people more tolerant of socially engaged, devout women. Nineteenth-century active religious in Belgium were therefore able to gain respect more quickly than their 'sisters' in countries – such as Ireland or England – where the tradition of beguines or *filles dévotes* was much less developed, if at all.[116]

Father Van Hoylant of Alsemberg asked Archbishop Sterckx in 1833 for "a foundation of spiritual daughters, who will especially serve to provide a good and Christian education".[117] Through the aegis of the beguinage chaplain of Nivelles, Amand Helsen (1787-1841), Van Hoylant was sent Therese Fontaine and a fellow sister in 1833. Disagreements between the sisters in Alsemberg and their superiors in Nivelles eventually led to a rift between them, encouraged by the opportunistic Van Hoylant. He belonged to a pioneering network of priests, inspired by Ignatian spirituality, that had been formed at the beginning of the nineteenth century in the clandestine seminary of Father Jean Devenise in Leuven.[118] With support of his network, Van Hoylant detached his sisters from the Nivelles motherhouse and looked to more stable and Ignatian

113 My own calculation; for sources, see footnote 107.
114 Various (ex-)beguines played a role in the creation of new sister congregations. In addition to the aforementioned foundations issuing from the Nivelles beguinage, other examples in the archdiocese can be noted, such as Antoinette Loos (1803-1874), former beguine and in 1834 founder of the Antwerp *Zusters van het Onbevlekt Hart van Maria* (Daughters of the Immaculate Heart of Mary). The history of the *Zusters van het Convent van Betlehem* (Sisters of the Convent of Bethlehem) of Duffel also is a nice illustration of the way in which beguine life and the model of the spiritual daughters eventually inspired a strong, nineteenth-century congregation. Beguines from Hoogstraten were involved in the foundation of the Dutch congregation of the *Zusters van Liefde* (Sisters of Charity) of Tilburg. On these congregations, see: Hallez, *Uit het leven van Moeder Concordia*; Timmermans, *Het Convent van Bethlehem*; Luyten, *Ja Zonhoven gaat vooruit*.
115 Geybels, "De begijnenbeweging", 136-142; Tihon, "Les religieuses", 32; Majérus, *Ces femmes qu'on dit béguines*, 74-70; De Cant, "Een wereld van onafhankelijke vrouwen", 35-42.
116 Rapley, *The Dévotes*, 6-7, 41; Clear, *Nuns in Nineteenth-Century Ireland*, 78.
117 "eene stigting van geestelijke dogters, die bezonderlijk zullen dienen om een goed en Christelijk onderwijs te verschaffen": AAM, CF, La Hulpe: Van Hoylandt to Sterckx (12 Nov. 1833). Joannes Van Hoylant (1755-1861) was parish priest in Alsemberg from 1820 until his death. See: Meeussen, "Joannes Van Hoylant".
118 About the Devenise network: see: Luyten and Suenens, "'Jesuits' as promotors".

inspired female institutions such as the *Dames du Sacré Cœur* and the *Sœurs de Notre Dame* of Namur as model for his own congregation in Alsemberg. Eventually, he copied parts of the constitutions of the Namur sisters – which were also influenced by members of the Devenise school – for the community in Alsemberg. The introduction of this normative framework in 1838, the year that Antoinette Cornet entered, led to the formal recognition of the Alsemberg community as an independent congregation: the *Sœurs du Saint Cœur de Marie*. Equally important was the congregation's entry into the Ignatian sphere of influence. This would be of great significance for Cornet's future.[119]

Entering a young congregation at an early age meant that Antoinette Cornet joined the first generation of young Belgian women – mainly from lower middle-class, commercial or farming backgrounds – who, from the 1830s, opted for the new teaching congregations in large numbers.[120] Immersed in the revival's discourse of action and the great social needs, she found in the emerging convent community both challenges and opportunities for development. The colourless routine existence, which some of the *dames d'œuvres* in the circles around Kestre, Telghuys and de Meeûs feared, was not her share. Just like Kestre's sister Sidonie, she succeeded in building up a successful career. However, this demanding pioneering role came at a cost. Swallowed up by the apostolate work, Cornet longed for spiritual relief. Moreover, Alsemberg's sister community had failed to consolidate the promising, but still relatively unregulated religious climate of the first half of the nineteenth century. Sterckx had warned Van Hoylant in 1833 that it was risky to work in Alsemberg with inexperienced female religious. He had, however, agreed to this because of the pressing educational needs in Alsemberg and the frequent requests to Van Hoylant for a remedy by parishioners and the municipal authorities.[121] It was the downside of the nineteenth-century apostolic 'empire by invitation', where (educational) needs outstripped supply and both Church and civil authorities looked for a solution in the services of willing and cheap, but often inexperienced religious.[122] The lax recruitment policy, the unstable financial situation and intense internal quarrels brought the congregation to the edge of ruin in the mid-1850s. These factors led Antoinette Cornet to follow the path taken by de Meeûs, Telghuys and Kestre and thus to become a congregation founder after all.

119 AAM, CF, La Hulpe: Helsen to Vrindts (2 Dec. 1834), Vrindts to Sterckx (22 Dec. 1834).
120 Tihon calculated that the number of female religious in Belgium increased from 3,135 (1824) to 8,368 (1846). In the provinces of Brabant and Antwerp, which largely coincided with the archdiocese, the total number of female religious increased from 872 in 1824 to 2,312 in 1846. In 1846 about two thirds of these female religious were active in education. Tihon, "Les religieuses", 32, 40, 42.
121 AAM, CF, La Hulpe: Van Hoylant to Sterckx (18 Dec. 1833), Sterckx to Van Hoylant (24 Dec. 1833).
122 Viaene, "De ontplooiing van een 'vrije' kerk", 73.

After 1848 Anna de Meeûs structured her charitable and spiritual activities into a formal 'work'. Referring to a medieval anti-Semitic Eucharistic legend, she illustrated her social and clerical commitment with the militant motto 'violatae caritatis reparatio' or 'reparation of the violated love'.
[Excerpt of *A la mémoire vénérée de Madame Anna de Meeûs*, Brussels: Polleunis & Ceuterick, 1904]

FEMALE RELIGIOUS ENTREPRENEURSHIP ON THE OFFENSIVE (CA. 1848-CA. 1860)

> Je veux tirer les filles du peuple du bourbier où elles se salissent, les moraliser, les ennoblir, faire d'elles des chrétiennes; en même temps leur apprendre à se servir de leurs mains et de leur doigts, de manière à gagner honnêtement leur vie; leurs donner aussi ce vernis de délicatesse et d'urbanité qui n'est nullement incompatible avec la condition la plus humble; bref, les rendre pieuses, vertueuses, travailleuses, et, par le fait, heureuses ...
> ADHH, 16: Verest Manuscript, 26.

Her wanderings and charity works in the city's suburbs prompted Telghuys to think about more structured and better organised projects on behalf of Antwerp's needy, and particularly vulnerable working-class girls and young women. This evolution was indicative of the social and psychological changes that occurred at the end of the 1840s both in the world of the *dames d'œuvres* and in the wider society. In 1848 the post-revolutionary optimism of the revival was dealt its first major blow. The revolutionary uprisings in Paris and the rest of Europe also awakened a fear of riots in the working-class neighbourhoods of Belgium. Strengthened by the emergence of the first communist and anarchist ideas and Karl Marx' stay in Brussels between 1845 and 1848, the social issue became a dark cloud on the horizon of the ruling classes. Large-scale riots did not break out in Belgium, but the revolutionary threats and social misery provoked a conservative, disciplinary and moralising response that had consequences for religiously inspired social action by women.

This change in mentality also led to a renewed alliance between certain civil and aristocratic circles and the Church, with the latter in the role of guardian of the social order. The Catholic elite, who were active in charitable organisations such as the Vincentian societies, gave their social engagement a more structured, as well as a disciplinary and moralising accent.[1] The relatively spontaneous, voluntary charity work of the early years was exchanged for a more entrepreneurial and militant engagement. These social and psychological transitions, which caused the lives of de Meeûs, Kestre, Telghuys and Cornet to fall into a definitive pattern, form the *leitmotiv* through this second chapter. The obstacles and opportunities that resulted were decisive for the 'coming of age' of the four women in the second half of the 1840s. The young enthusiasts of the early revival became the determined, creative, but sometimes tormented champions of a more assertive Church.

Religious education: the female voice of the revival

In 1848 Kestre joined a group of women who gave catechism lessons in the poor neighbourhood of the *Marolles* district in Brussels. The Belgian capital, by that time, was in full transition from a provincial town into a metropolis with international appeal. Large-scale urban renewal and expansion made the capital the centre of a self-confident, young state. Besides being the political, legal and administrative heart of the country, Brussels also became the home of an aristocratic and upper-bourgeois elite, a commercial centre and a communication hub. This new Brussels took shape in its boulevards, new residential districts and shopping streets on the one hand and in the development of a waterway and railway infrastructure on the other.[2] Not only was Brussels attractive to a national and international elite, it also experienced an influx of inhabitants from the countryside. Fleeing hunger, unemployment and especially the collapsed rural textile industry, they sought salvation in the city. Between 1830 and 1866 the population of the city rose from 100,000 to 150,000 inhabitants. In the rapidly developing Brussels suburbs, the population rose from 40,000 to 140,000 in the same period. The barely industrialised Brussels economy could not deal with this incursion, resulting in widespread structural and seasonal unemployment. In the small city centre, within the boundaries of the pentagon or the historic city walls, population growth led to problems of overpopulation, unhygienic conditions and epidemics.[3]

1   Lamberts, "Het ultramontanisme", 46; Wils, "België in de negentiende eeuw", 22-23; De Maeyer, Heyrman and Quaghebeur, "Een glorierijk verleden", 279; Van Osselaer, "Reform of piety", 108.
2   De Smaele, *Rechts Vlaanderen*, 368-372; Van den Eeckhout, "Brussels", 69-73; De Schaepdrijver, "Trois images", 35.
3   ADSJ, 1.6: Fanny Kestre to Sidonie Kestre (23 Jan. 1849).

Within this social-economic framework Kestre found opportunities for militant action. She quickly became the driving force behind the catechism classes in the Marolles neighbourhood. Female engagement in religious instruction had a long history. Kestre placed herself in an old tradition of religiously inspired women whose catechetical activities gave them both social prestige and opportunities for self-development. The Council of Trent had emphasised the importance of religious instruction in the fight against Protestantism. Even then, it offered women, who played an important role in religious education, a certain amount of leeway for public action. The sixteenth-century Ursulines of Milan, for example, were absolved by Bishop Charles Borromeo from complete enclosure to enable them to carry out their catechetical work outside the convent walls. In the Southern Netherlands also, women were already playing a role in religious instruction during the Counter Reformation. The importance of successful catechetical work at the time of the French Revolution for the further ecclesiastical career of Julie Billiart has already been highlighted. In Belgium, Justine Desbille used her catechetical work as legitimation for the establishment of her own congregation in the 1830s.[4] For the American and English contexts, Dolan and Mangion have shown that women were able to reach a large audience and exert influence through their activities in religious instruction.[5]

Catechism lessons did not require much theological training. The question and answer format of the *Mechelse Catechismus*, the official diocesan catechism, offered clear guidelines that left little space for doctrinal deviation. In the eyes of the ecclesiastical authorities, catechesis was therefore a 'safe' domain to hand over to women, especially because it was related to their role as religious educators in the family. Just as during the Counter Reformation, in the first half of the nineteenth century religious instruction became a weapon in the Church's quest for recovery. For women, it offered a respected opportunity for fulfilment and participation in social and religious development.[6]

If the possibilities for a personal spiritual contribution to the catechetical work were limited, then there was room for organisational pioneering work. In the early 1850s Kestre worked out a structure in which the traditional religious instruction in the Sunday schools was supplemented with afternoon and

---

[4] Liebowitz, "Virgins in the service of Christ", 143; De Vroede, *Religieuses*, 151; Hanoteau, *Une grande nivelloise*, 25-26.

[5] On the parish missions in Belgium: Viaene, *Belgium and the Holy See*, 172-173; Idem, "De ontplooiing van een 'vrije' kerk", 45-55. On the link between the missions and convent vocations, see for example the story of Elisabeth Scheys (1808-1880) who decided to found a religious congregation following a parish mission in Lubbeek. Halflants, *150 jaar Zusters Dominicanessen*, 11-13, 18; Dolan, *Catholic Revivalism*, 193-195; Mangion, *Contested Identities*, 124-125.

[6] Simon, "L'enseignement du catéchisme", 238-241; Quaghebeur, "De Eucharistische Kruistocht", 101-102; Morelli, *Kinderen en hun religieuze opvoeding*, 45-48.

evening classes on weekdays. The lessons were part of the preparation for first communion around the age of twelve, but were also a prelude to continuing religious instruction and religiously inspired leisure activities for older girls. Kestre was driven by a desire for the recovery of a "foi vive". In this she was carrying on the ideas of Romantic Catholics of the early revival who saw in the 'genius' of Christianity the key to the restoration of a harmonious, Christian society in the post-revolutionary period. However, her ideas about catechesis also illustrated the turn to a more organised revival. Offering religious instruction and support from first communion until adolescence was a key feature of the first Catholic attempts to bring the working classes into the Catholic milieu.[7]

Kestre's intention to reach out to a wider public through children was an interesting one. Her ideas echoed the opinions of prominent Catholics – such as Bishop Dupanloup of France – about the importance of religious formation for children: "L'œuvre des Catéchismes, (...) devient plus précieuse et plus importante que jamais dans un siècle irréligieux où l'enfance est l'unique espoir de l'Eglise désolée."[8] In the mid-nineteenth century, Brussels was one of the few places in the archdiocese where '*le siècle irréligieux*' had already set in, both among a radicalising, anticlerical liberal elite and in some secularised working-class neighbourhoods.[9] Moreover, despite an increase in the total number of male clerics in the first half of the nineteenth century, the ecclesiastical system in Brussels was inadequate. In the mid-nineteenth century, one parish in Brussels averaged around 13,000 inhabitants, compared with just under 3,500 in smaller cities such as Leuven and Mechelen. In 1856, only one priest was available on average in Brussels for almost 3,000 inhabitants. Moreover, the clergy was unevenly distributed. The shortage of priests in a number of difficult parishes such as the *Minimes* parish, contrasted with a strong presence of diocesan priests in the more elite parishes and in diocesan colleges.[10]

Entrepreneurial women like Fanny Kestre could benefit from this shortage of priests in the capital. She soon became known as an enthusiastic catechism teacher. Moreover, she relied on extra tools of persuasion by promising hot meals, and distributing bread and awards. Parallel with her own activities in religious instruction, she also focused on the didactic and religious formation of catechism teachers. She brought the women together in a pious as-

---

7   Harrison, *Romantic Catholics*, 20-21, 35-36.
8   Dupanloup, *Manuel des catéchismes*, I. Felix Dupanloup (1802-1878) was a prominent French priest, theologian and political thinker. From the 1840s and later as bishop of Orléans (1849-1878) he was one of the most innovative advocates of catechetical education. On this, see: Gadille, "Grands courants doctrinaux", 132; Gibson, *A Social History*, 167.
9   Witte, "The battle for monasteries", 121; Viaene, "De ontplooiing van een 'vrije' kerk", 89; De Smaele, *Rechts Vlaanderen*, 370-371.
10 Houtart, *Les paroisses de Bruxelles*, 33-58; Viaene, "De ontplooiing van een 'vrije' kerk", 59.

sociation, with weekly prayer evenings and monthly retreats. The association was recognised by Sterckx in 1856 as *l'Association du Seigneur*.[11]

The need for male support

Despite the opportunities for female agency, religious action by women could only survive by conforming to diocesan policies and by accepting male support. Kestre, for example, needed preachers for her retreats for catechism teachers. In 1851, she turned to Father Boone and the Brussels Jesuits for support. With its good reputation in the areas of spiritual guidance and religious education, the Society of Jesus was an obvious choice for Kestre. Nevertheless, given her own charismatic qualities, she also tried to get permission to conduct the retreats herself. The idea was ambitious, but not exceptional. In nineteenth-century France, women religious were already involved in giving retreats. Thérèse Couderc (1805-1885), for example, had been leading the Ignatian Spiritual Exercises since 1826. She also helped found the *Sœurs du Cénacle* (Sisters of the Cenacle) who made women's retreats their mission. In a certain sense they were the successors of the women who had enabled Catholicism to survive underground during the revolution. Others, like Théodelinde Dubouché (1809-1863), founder of the French *Congrégation de l'Adoration Réparatrice* (Congregation of the Adoration of Reparation), were inspired by the 1848 Revolution to re-Christianise the population through retreats.[12] Belgian religious women also ventured into this area. The *Sœurs de l'Enfant Jésus* of Nivelles were already giving religious lectures for female workers in 1846. One of them was even known as '*le petit curé*'.[13]

Kestre's prospects, however, were hindered by her passionate character and her reluctance to accept male support. Kestre regarded her appeal to Boone as a necessary evil. He persuaded her to develop her catechesis and retreat plans with the help of a group of aristocratic *dames d'œuvres* who had gathered around Anna de Meeûs. The women worked in the parish of *Saint-Jacques sur Coudenberg*, outside the old Salazar chapel, in the heart of Brussels. Boone offered Kestre a clerical framework and infrastructure for her work. Sharing the responsibility for her project was a difficult task, however, as was cooperating with the nobles ladies around de Meeûs. Boone was initially impressed by the efficiency and broad approach of Kestre's plans. Despite his authoritarian and conservative nature, he was not hostile to women with a strong socio-religious commitment. Still, a conflict arose between them

---

11 ADSJ, *Dossier franciscae ab eucharistia Kestre*, 2-13; ADSJ, 1.6: Boone to Kestre (26 June 1849, 21 Aug. 1851, March 1853), Kestre to Boone (6 Aug. 1853).
12 Benoist, *Le Sacré-Cœur*, 1341; Stogdon, "Expression of self-surrender", 150; Wenner, *Théodelinde Dubouché*, 1743-1745.
13 Hanoteau, *Une grande Nivelloise*, 102.

after 1854. The disagreement revolved mainly around Kestre's stubbornness and undiplomatic discourse. As will be explained in detail later, it was also exacerbated by Boone's disbelief in her visionary inspiration and her jealousy about his close ties with the elite club around de Meeûs.[14]

In search for more autonomy, Kestre left the group around Boone and de Meeûs in the winter of 1854-1855 and looked for support from the parish priest and dean of the *Saint-Gudule* parish, Ludovic Verhoustraeten (1804-1870).[15] As Boone before him, Verhoustraeten acknowledged the potential of Kestre's plans for improving religious instruction and moralising leisure activities for the girls in his parish. He financed her catechetical work for some years, but soon quarrelled with Kestre about the target group and the recruitment of catechists.[16] The collaboration could have succeeded, but just like many others after him, Verhoustraeten could not deal with Kestre's push for autonomy. Destitute and without male protection, she moved her catechesis work a third time to the parish of *Saint-Josse-ten-Noode*. In 1862 she found accommodation there in a small house on the *Rue de la Charité*.

Kestre's story shows how the nineteenth-century revival, combined with the social and ecclesiastical needs of time, at once created space for female action while also limiting it. Just like Verhoustraeten and Boone, Archbischop Sterckx did not get on with Kestre. His sober management style did not mesh with her unpredictability. Through Verhoustraeten, Sterckx repeatedly tried to embed her projects in the parish structures and urged they be put under the supervision of one of the parish curates. His policy fitted in with general tendencies in the Church. Langlois noted that in France (catechesis) instruction was increasingly entrusted to 'controllable' forces, especially female religious. In Ireland too, church authorities gave preference to convent sisters over lay women.[17] Still, Sterckx was careful not to publicly call Kestre to order, even after she came into conflict first with Boone and then with Verhoustraeten. There was just one reason for this at a time when the revival was becoming more militant: "c'est qu'elle réussit".[18] For a revival bishop like Sterckx, religious ignorance was "la source des maux et des iniquités qui inondent la terre" and religious instruction was an important remedy.[19] In 1861 Kestre and her catechists taught 461 Brussels children and young people before and after

14 ADSJ, 1.6: Boone to Kestre (26 June 1849, 21 Aug. 1851, March 1853, 11 Nov. 1855), Kestre to Boone (6 Aug. 1853)
15 Verhoustraeten, former college president in Mechelen, was parish priest and dean in Brussels between 1853 and 1870. Vanden Bosch, "Ludovicus Verhoustraeten".
16 ADSJ, 1.3./1: Journal of Kestre (1 Nov. 1855, 20 Nov. 1855, 9 Jan. 1856, 3 June 1856); ADSJ, 1.7: Verhoustraeten to Kestre (29 Jan. 1857, 31 May 1855).
17 Langlois, *Le catholicisme au féminin*, 646; Luddy, *Women and Philanthropy*, 24.
18 ADSJ, 1.6: Sterckx to Verhoustraeten (26 March 1857, 17 Nov. 1858), Sterckx to Kestre (25 Sept. 1856, 3 Oct. 1862).
19 Tihon, "Dieu dans les mandements de carême", 666.

their first communion.[20] These were not sophisticated boarding-school girls, but people from the working-class neighbourhoods of the capital who were 'endangered' by religious indifference.

Enterprising and discursive mechanisms

The genesis of a charitable organisation

Anna de Meeûs' experiences seem in many respects the triumphant opposite of the struggling trajectory that Kestre travelled. In 1843 de Meeûs visited the dilapidated church of the village of Ohain, during one of her walks in the immense grounds surrounding the chateau of Argenteuil. Remembering the words of Madame d'Avenas, she promised to help the local parish priest. She convinced her mother to get some old curtains from the attic and sat down with her sisters to turn them into vestments, with the help of one of the chambermaids. Later, she collected money for a silver ciborium from a few cousins and friends. In the years that followed, several churches in the region of Argenteuil and Ohain could count on her help. Initially, the work was limited to a small group of family members and friends. The wave of revolutions in 1848, however, gave the modest charity work of de Meeûs a new impetus. Shortly after the events in Paris, the Brussels winter circuit of aristocratic balls was temporarily cancelled, partly because of the official curfew that had been imposed, but also because of the fear that gripped the elite after the Paris 'proletarian' upheavals.[21] Anna de Meeûs could suddenly call on a larger group of women, looking for some distraction and social contacts. Inspired by the entrepreneurial skills of her father, de Meeûs grasped the opportunity to give her family activities on behalf of rural churches an enhanced scope and a more organised character as the *Œuvre des Églises Pauvres* (Work for Poor Churches).

The revolutionary upheavals of 1848 thus created opportunities in Brussels for new projects by women. Moreover, Paris not only send echoes of the revolution but also inspiring models for female initiative. In the French capital, the vicar general, François-Alexandre de la Bouillerie (1810-1882), had started the *Œuvres des Tabernacles* at the behest of a number of aristocratic

---

20 ADSJ, 1.3./2: Journal of Kestre (18 Oct. 1861). By comparison, at that time the parish of Saint-Gudule had between 22,000 and 25,000 inhabitants. Houtart, *Les paroisses de Bruxelles*, 45.
21 *Les voies de Dieu*, 37-38; ARE, *Chroniques, Chapitre II. La Voie*, 13-17, 25-26; ARE, *Lettres divers*: de Meeûs to Boone (1 Jan. 1851, 29 Jan. 1851).

ladies.²² Material and liturgical assistance to poor churches was the central focus. Elsewhere in France, revolutionary events had also inspired women from well-to-do circles to do something for "des temples dans nos villages, dans nos hameaux éloignés de la cité, qui attristent l'œil par leur nudité; les autels sans ornements, les tabernacles sans splendeur (…)."²³ As will be explained in detail in the next chapter, many of these projects were given a spiritual boost by the revival's rhetoric of penance and devotion to the sacraments. Another striking parallel was the increasing fascination of the Catholic urban elite with the problems and the authenticity of rural life. Both in Paris and in Brussels, Catholics were confronted from 1850 on with a growing liberal anticlericalism. Catholic politicians had difficulty getting a foothold in Brussels, while the liberal party, with Masonic lodges gaining influence in the background, was able to build a strong bastion of power there. Catholics then looked to the quiet and docile countryside as still offering potential for the Church. Material support for poor rural parish churches from a rich Brussels Catholic elite fitted perfectly in this picture.²⁴

Between May 1848 and November 1850, Anna de Meeûs' *Œuvre des Églises Pauvres* delivered liturgical vessels, vestments and saints' statues to 74 rural churches. The requests came from far outside Brabant or the archdiocese. Meanwhile, the group around de Meeûs had risen to 25 women and established headquarters in the above-mentioned Salazar chapel.²⁵ With aristocratic women such as Baroness Marie-Thérèse van der Linden d'Hooghvorst (1783-1859), Viscountess Julie Desmanet de Biesme (1828-1913) and a few daughters from the large family of Count Victor de Robiano among the first members, the fledgling association was a prestigious aristocratic club.²⁶ De Meeûs was

22 The aristocratic de la Bouillerie, the future bishop of Carcassonne (1855-1873) and Bordeaux (1872-1882), was archdeacon and vicar-general of the Archdiocese of Paris from 1844. See: Ricard, *Vie de Mgr. de la Bouillerie*, 130-141.
23 On the *Association en faveur des Eglises Pauvres* founded in Lyon in the 1830s by a number of wealthy ladies, see: Bez, *La ville des aumônes*, 228-299. In Montluçon an association of the same name was founded in the late 1840s by Louise-Thérèse de Montaignac de Chauvance (1820-1885), a pious and socially committed aristocratic lady who had fled from Paris in 1848 and later became a congregation founder. See: Montaignac, *Souvenirs*, 143-157.
24 Tyssens and Witte, *De vrijzinnige traditie*, 21-26; Witte, "The battle for monasteries", 121; De Smaele, *Rechts Vlaanderen*, 257-270. For parallels in France, see: Price, *Religious Renewal*, 190.
25 AAM, File Institut de l'Adoration Perpétuelle, Rapport, Nov. 1850.
26 Marie-Thérèse van der Linden d'Hooghvorst, née d'Argenteau, was married to Joseph van der Linden d'Hooghvorst (1782-1845) and came from the upper echelons of the Catholic aristocracy. Both Desmanet de Biesme (Kruishoutem) as well as the family of Victor de Robiano (1864-1907) came from other corners of the country, but spent the winter months in Brussels. See: RAG, Family Archives of Desmanet de Biesme, 116: Documents relating to the inheritance, and 126: Birth certificate; De Robiano, "La famille des Comtes de Robiano", 7.

called to Mechelen in 1850 by Sterckx to present an account of her activities. Shortly afterwards, her work was given ecclesiastical recognition as the *Association de l'Adoration Perpétuelle du Très-Saint Sacrement et de l'Œuvre des Eglises Pauvres* with Baroness d'Hooghvorst as the first chair and de Meeûs as vice-chair. Sterckx, who approved her firm approach, was persuaded by de Meeûs and Boone to promote the work through diocesan circulars and at Sunday sermons. They also received permission to promote it in other dioceses.

Apart from the initiatives in favour of the poor village churches, de Meeûs' association also focused on promoting the Eucharistic devotion. In the years after its official foundation in 1850 it mobilised the faithful in their thousands all over Belgium for adoration, novenas and processions in honour of the Blessed Sacrament. The pronounced spiritual dimension, which will be analysed in more detail in the next chapter, was important because it fitted in with the morally paternalistic Catholic ideas of the mid-nineteenth century. For example, the West-Flemish canon and Catholic politician, De Haerne, emphatically pointed out that de Meeûs' association "contribue au développement du sentiment religieux et moral (...) et de cette manière, on s'oppose au progrès de la misère, qui prend souvent sa source dans l'absence de ce sentiment."[27]

Boone played an important role in the expansion of the association. Experienced in the socio-religious activities of the revival, he called on all his connections and modern promotional channels to propagate the work of the association. In this way it expanded into a partnership between clerics and women. He urged his fellow Jesuits to promote the association during popular missions and retreats for nuns and priests. Moreover, the Jesuits also convinced many of their female confessees from the upper classes to join the new association.[28] The initial focus on assistance to poor churches was expanded first in Brussels, later in other large cities, to include religious instruction and retreat work. The catechism activities were – as already indicated – largely devised by Fanny Kestre. After her unhappy departure in 1854, the work of religious instruction in Salazar increasingly took on large-scale proportions. Anna de Meeûs' broad social network of aristocratic ladies and influential Jesuits was crucial for the success of her projects. At least as important was her sharp social intelligence and her strong position on the balance sheet of double-voiced discourse.

---

27   De Haerne, *Tableau de la charité chrétienne*, 85-863. In 1858, Désiré de Haerne (1804-1890) published a unique overview of all the Catholic charities in Belgium, a statistical account of the 'active piety' of the revival. On this see: Van Dijck and Suenens, "La Belgique charitable", 171.
28   ASV, NB, *Religiose dell'Adorazione Perpetua*: Boone to Sterckx (29 July 1854).

In search of a double-voiced discourse

In the introduction I have already discussed the historiographical development of the double-voiced concept and its meaning as the interaction between the dominant discourse of female humility and submission on the one hand and the veiled 'muted voice' of female autonomous action on the other. In this section, I would like to analyse the initial steps in this plurivocal discourse of women in their contacts with male partners and authorities and the ambitions and possibilities for self-development that may have resulted from this. In the next chapter, I will focus on the efficacy of nineteenth-century revival piety as a spiritual *lingua franca* for this dialogue.

The support that de Meeûs received from Boone and Sterckx was due in part to this double-voiced discourse. Her letters to the archbishop revealed the use of the dominant gender language, saturated in the rhetoric of submission and gratitude: "Votre Eminence s'est toujours montrée si bienveillante à l'égard de notre association qui lui doit toute l'extension qu'elle a prise par les encouragements et les privilèges dont elle l'a comblée si abondamment". At the same time, however, she implicitly tried to get what she wanted: a diocesan approval for the annual report of her congregation. "Nous désirons comme marque de notre reconnaissance et de notre respect envers votre Eminence de ne pas faire poursuivre l'impression de notre rapport sans l'avoir soumis à son examen". She emphasised the necessity of the request in the typical language of revival activism: "pour répandre de plus en plus l'amour et le dévouement envers le Saint-Sacrement". Anna also humbly, but strategically encouraged Sterckx of reacting to the rivalry of other catechist groups in Brussels, by stressing her emotional ties as his spiritual daughter: "il me parait que c'est un devoir pour moi de confier à Votre Eminence toujours tout ce qui nous pousse comme tout ce qui nous réjouit. Nous devons comme membre de l'institut regarder Votre Eminence comme notre père et agir avec conséquence avec toute simplicité et confiance".[29]

The double-voiced approach of the "très humble et très obéissante servante", as she ended most of her letters to the archbishop, was very successful and became a fixed pattern in her communication with the archbishop. Her submission to Sterckx as her 'clerical father' and her desire to participate in the post-revolutionary struggle of the Church were sincere and an important factor of her spiritual well-being. Her double-voiced discourse, therefore, was not fake or merely strategical. But it did create chances for agency and self-development. Sterckx's approval of the report was done with such conviction it could be used in the association's promotional campaign. With the support of Boone and the archbishop, de Meeûs had also discovered the press to be a powerful and modern promotional channel. From 1850 on, the association

---

29 All citations here: AAM, CF, Salazar: de Meeûs to Sterckx (4 Dec. 1851, 27 June 1858).

Anna de Meeûs' association quickly developed into an international organisation. Making use of her extended social and clerical network and the entrepreneurial skills learned from her father, she promoted her work very intensively. In 1850 she began to publish reports, sold for the benefit of the *Œuvre des Églises Pauvres*, that provided a yearly overview of the activities and statistics of the association.
[Published report – 1851 – KADOC]

published an annual bulletin announcing impressive figures for membership, turnover and distribution. However, de Meeûs' double voiced discourse did not lead to an unconditional *carte blanche* for her projects. In accordance with the dominant gender discourse, Sterckx explicitely emphasised the role of the male protagonist Boone: "je ne puis que l'approuver et remercier Dieu d'avoir bénit si abondamment les efforts de l'excellent Père Boone et de ses zélées coopératrices."[30] Nevertheless, it quickly became clear in the archdiocese who was in control at the headquarters in Salazar. The dominant discourse of humility did not stand in the way of de Meeûs' growing power. Correspondence with the association was sent, not to the chair, Baroness d'Hooghvorst, but to her adjunct, de Meeûs: "c'est elle qui dirige".[31]

Interaction between the dominant language of female humility and the possibilities for female development is also recorded for other nineteenth-century women, both inside and outside the ecclesiastical context. Interesting discourse analysis of French and English congregation founders, such as the aforementioned Thérèse Couderc, Cornelia Connelly and Anne-Marie Javouhey (1779-1851), points to mechanisms of discursive submission to ecclesiastical authorities being used to create and legitimise female agency.[32] Just as in the case of de Meeûs and Kestre, pressing social and ecclesiastical needs were also acknowledged in these contexts as being an additional impetus for accepting and valuing female initiative. Mangion concluded aptly in the case of English women religious: "The language they used often reflected obedience and humility, yet their actions did not preclude exerting their own authority or negotiating with the Catholic hierarchy (...); women religious saw obedience as a means of deciding and collaborating to provide much-needed social services and evangelization".[33] In the case of Dutch founders, Eijt has emphasised their double-voiced discourse of obedience to church authority in combination with attempts to have their own critical voice in the field of the apostolate.[34]

Similar female discursive mechanisms were also detected outside the religious domain. The Dutch botanist Hoola van Nooten (1817-1892), who published her work in Belgium, conformed her publications in the dominant gender language of "les missions qui sont celles de notre sexe (...) la charité dans l'humilité", but at the same time she enthusiastically defended the

30 AAM, CF, Salazar: Sterckx to de Meeûs (11 Nov. 1851).
31 AAM, CF, Salazar: Sterckx to de Meeûs (9 Dec. 1850); ARE, *Cahier de Lettres* 3: Boone to de Meeûs (24 Dec. 1853).
32 Anne-Marie Javouhey was the founder of the *Sœurs de Saint-Joseph of Cluny* (Sisters of Saint-Joseph), see: Lecuir-Nemo, *Anne-Marie Javouhey*, 235; Langlois, *Catholicisme, religieuses et société*, 177-180. On Couderc and Connelly, see: Stogdon, "A Journey with Thérèse Couderc", 216-229; Lancaster, *Cornelia Connelly*, 148-149, 281.
33 Mangion, *Contested Identities*, 213.
34 Eijt, *Religieuze vrouwen*, 35-36, 415.

scientific nature of her research.³⁵ Brogniez has described how nineteenth-century female poets were modest and reserved so as to find favour with male patrons and literary critics.³⁶ This duality was evident also in literary works by nineteenth-century Belgian women. In her essay *Het Meesterschap* (The Mastery) of 1874, Rosalie Loveling (1834-1875), who together with her sister was among the most important nineteenth-century Flemish writers, wrote somewhat daringly: "The woman goes to work in a very clever manner. She seems to consult the man about everything, and succeeds in arranging things in such a way that he believes to the end that everything at home and outside his house is done according to his will". Virginie Loveling (1836-1924) took up these thoughts again in her later novella, *Het Hoofd van 't huis* (The head of the house) (1883).³⁷

However, a double-voiced discourse could not easily thrive in the environment of impetuous souls such as Fanny Kestre. Though sincere and forthright, as a young entrepreneurial woman she was constantly getting into trouble because of her direct way of speaking. The analysis of her personal writings, especially the reports or her visionary experiences, reveal a self-image of "une humble servante" and a "très obéissante fille", in conformity with dominant gender and clerical discourse. But the credibility of this position was undermined by her passionate character and her militant desire to take up a personal role on the clerical scene. In her letters and her journal she pleaded unequivocally for "ma liberté d'action, que je désire faire l'œuvre de Dieu et non pas celle du clergé ou des religieux", a female discourse that was too autonomous to pass the doors of the nineteenth-century male-centred church hierarchy.³⁸ It was the muted voice of the double-voiced discourse sounding louder than the dominant one of female submission and it was unacceptable for clerical authorities. The drama of Kestre's position, as will be shown over and over again, was that her militancy to integrate herself in the reparation movement of the Catholic Church, prevented her from being accepted, leading to only more and often desperate persistence. Archbischop Sterckx, for example, had great difficulty with Kestre's request that her newly found association for female catechesis teachers would be recognised as '*Apostolines*', a name that reflected her strong missionary zeal for her catechesis work, but which Sterckx saw mainly as an expression of her "discours peu modeste".³⁹

35   Foreword by Bertha Hoola van Nooten to her book *Fleurs, fruits et feuillages* (1863), cited in: Vanpaemel, "Laissons aux hommes", 180.
36   Brogniez, "Poétesses belges", 146.
37   The early death of Rosalie Loveling prevented the planned publication of the book. For the quotation from *Het Meesterschap*, see: Couttenier and Musschoot, *Meesterschap in tweevoud*, 56. On the works by Rosalie and Viriginie Loveling mentioned here, see: Stynen, *Rosalie en Virginie*, 95-96, 124-125.
38   ADSJ, 1.3./1: Journal of Kestre (28 March 1856).
39   ASDJ, 1.8: Winnen to Kestre (17 Oct. 1856); ADSJ, 1.6: Sterckx to Kestre (24 April 1856); ADSJ, 1.3./1: Journal of Kestre (3 July 1856).

Dissatisfied by Mechelen's opposition, Kestre wrote the first in a series of lengthy letters to Nuncio Matteo Gonella (1850-1861) in Brussels and to the Holy See. She left Pope Pius IX in no doubt about the importance of her work, and about her own contribution: "il me semble qu'il est question d'une œuvre qui intéresse l'église (...). Je me suis si pressée d'agir pour Notre Seigneur, que je ne peux attendre plus longtemps".[40] She also clearly expressed her longing for independence: "J'aurai voulu aller au bout du monde pour être indépendante et communiquer à l'autorité ecclésiastique loin des Jésuites".[41] Rome and the nuncio did not respond to this bold, but also somewhat naive appeal of a young Belgian woman.

Nevertheless, in appealing to the Holy See, Kestre was not an exception. Her letters coincided with one of the most important evolutions in the nineteenth-century Church: a more prominent role for the papacy and growing adulation of the pope in the international Catholic community. During the revival, the pope's prestige had grown because he was seen by many Romantic Catholics as a beacon of freedom and church unity.[42] The election in 1846 of Pius IX, who as a young cardinal had maintained a relatively benevolent attitude towards the modern world and the Italian nationalists, created high expectations. However, the revolutionary climate of 1848, which forced Pius IX to flee Rome for Sicily, and his difficult position as leader of the Catholic world in the Italian-Austrian conflict hardened his spirit. With his worldly power and personal integrity under threat from Italian revolutionaries, he increasingly came to adopt a very conservative and intransigent position after 1848.[43]

Kestre's letters marked this important turning point. She referred both to the harmonious dreams of the revival – "propager le message de l'amour du Christ parmi le peuple entier" – and to the growing militancy of the ultramontane Church – "défendre avec ferveur Notre S.M. l'Eglise contre les attaques virulentes".[44] In this last aspect particularly, she prefigured other devoted Catholics who supported the pope after 1860 in the reactionary struggle against the modern world. However, she lacked the networks and the financial strength to be heard or to play a role of any significance. The Holy See was much more accessible to combative laymen who could contribute to the precarious financial situation of the pope and the Papal States.[45] Ferdinand de Meeûs, for example, had been a staunch defender of the papal cause since the early 1850s, in his own ambitious style. In 1860 he contributed more than

---

40 ADSJ, 1.5: Kestre to the pope (9 May 1856); ASV, NB, *Religiose dell'Adorazione Perpetua*: Kestre to Gonella (14 March 1857).
41 ASV, NB, *Religiose dell'Adorazione Perpetua*: Kestre to the nuntio (s.d.).
42 Harisson, *Romantic Catholics*, 13; Viaene, "Katolisches reveil", 133.
43 Viaene, "The Roman Question", 139-143; Aubert, *L'église dans le monde moderne*, 66-69.
44 ADSJ, 1.5: Kestre to the pope (9 May 1856).
45 Viaene, "The Roman Question", 143-150; Van Osselaer, "Reform of piety", 116-117.

100,000 francs to a loan for the pope's Zouave army.⁴⁶ His financial support and broad network was also important for the progress of his daughter's work. In 1853, when staying in Rome with her family, Anna succeeded in elevating her association to an arch-association. Her cause was mediated by a family friend and confidant of Pius IX, François-Xavier de Mérode.⁴⁷

The elevation to an arch-association was a typical example of the Roman centralisation strategies: legitimise and control local devotions and initiatives by giving them a papal *placet*.⁴⁸ Less common was the way in which the doors of the Vatican were opened for a young Belgian woman. Viaene estimated that the number of Belgian travellers to Rome before 1860 was barely a few dozen. Although ultramontane tendencies won the pope many Belgian sympathisers, most of them were deterred by the long journey and the cost. *Dames d'œuvres* who still managed to get to Rome seized the opportunity to promote their pious projects. The pope often gave an audience to these highly placed lay women. Among others, de Mauroy, who was involved in founding the abovementioned *Œuvre des Tabernacles* in Paris, started to lobby in Rome for her work. The Belgian Countess Mathilde de Nédonchel (1842-1867), one of the driving forces behind the pious association of the *Garde d'Honneur du Sacré Cœur* (Guard of Honour of the Sacred Heart), sought support in the Vatican as well. Although not unique then, de Meeûs' successful trip to Rome once again marked the difference between her and less highly-placed women as Fanny Kestre.⁴⁹

Without a fortune or a network and unwilling to compromise, Kestre irked too many important figures in her network. Her forwardness also brought her into conflict with possible benefactors. Since 1858 Count Charles de Villermont (1815-1893) had sponsored some of the accommodations for the catechesis classes of Kestre in Saint-Josse-ten-Noode. A wealthy industrialist, politician, publisher and a renowned ultramontane Catholic involved in a variety of pious associations, he could have been Kestre's liaison with a world of influential, rich and devout Catholics.⁵⁰ But then again, things went wrong. In 1859 Kestre provoked a conflict with the Jesuits by accusing Boone of intellectual theft. In her opinion, Boone had stolen her innovative ideas for cateche-

---

46 Thonissen, *Vie du Comte Ferdinand de Meeûs*, 161-162.
47 ABSE, 4.2.6. Boone, Jean-Baptiste, 12467: de Meeûs to Marie Malou (16 March 1856). The bonds of friendship between the de Mérode and the de Meeûs families dated back to the years of Belgian independence. A soldier and priest, de Mérode (1820-1874) was a Belgian prelate in Rome, a secret chamberlain of Pius IX and his military adviser. In 1860 he laid the foundations for the formation of the Zouave army. Viaene, *Belgium and the Holy See*, 490-491; Thonissen, *Vie du Comte Ferdinand de Meeûs*, 184-185.
48 Clark, "The New Catholicism", 18.
49 Viaene, *Belgium and the Holy See*, 240-241; Ricard, *Vie de Mgr. de la Bouillerie*, 131; Baas, *Leven der Gravin Mathilde de Nédonchel*, 238.
50 AFDV, E.11: de Jonghe d'Ardoye to de Villermont (12 May 1865); Simon, "Comte Charles-Antoine de Villermont", 713-715.

sis and retreat work and implemented it in de Meeûs' association in Salazar. There were indeed strong similarities and an analysis of the correspondence between Boone and Kestre in the years between 1849 and 1855 confirms that Boone was aware of all the details of Kestre's plans, although he later denied it. Nevertheless, Kestre's statements were not considered credible. She was ruthlessly criticised for her impertinent discourse and accusations, by Count de Villermont, the Jesuits and eventually also by Archbishop Sterckx. The criticism put Kestre – "cette personne qui ne fait qu' à sa tête, dont les excentricités compromettrez son Eminence" – under heavy pressure to apologise to Boone.[51] After long hesitation and discussion with the women around her, she finally gave in. The conflict left her with a lifelong aversion to the Jesuits and an increasingly irrational suspicion of conspiracy and opposition. Despite her concession, Count de Villermont distanced himself from her and left her, once again, without substantial support.[52]

Female religious entrepreneurship: challenging gender conventions?

While Kestre struggled with her reputation, Anna de Meeûs' association grew spectacularly. In 1851, barely a few months after the official founding of the association, it had 3,000 members spread over local branches in Ghent, Bruges and Antwerp. In 1860 there were around 45,000 members and every Belgian town had its own branch.[53] Further afield, in Bavaria, Austria, Poland and the Netherlands, the seeds of international expansion were sown. In 1860 more than 100,000 liturgical objects were sent to 1,215 churches at home and abroad.[54] In the course of the 1850s the activities of the association also increasingly came into line with the more demonstrative character of the revival. Committees everywhere in the country organised large-scale exhibitions of all the objects that were later to be sent to the parishes. Such exhibitions of women's (handi)work were a tried and tested form of promotion and fundraising, both inside and outside the Catholic world. With her broad social network de Meeûs succeeded in persuading bishops, deans and local notables to make an *acte de présence* and praise the work of the proud *dames d'œuvres*. The exhibitions organised by the central committee in Brussels could even sometimes count on the visit of a prince or princess.[55]

---

51   ADSJ, 1.6: Boone to Kestre (26 June 1849, March 1853), de Villermont to Auchard (20 March 1861).
52   ADSJ: Kestre to Lauwers (12 March 1861).
53   AAM, CF, Salazar: *Rapport de l'Association*, 1851, 3; ARE: *Coup d'œil sur la situation*, 1865, 1. The membership figures are in line with other pious confraternities such as the Apostolate of Prayer and the *Bonden van het Heilig Hart* (Unions of the Sacred Heart). See: Quaghebeur, "De Eucharistische Kruistocht", 108; Van Osselaer, *The Pious Sex*, 118.
54   AAM, CF, Salazar: *Coup d'œil sur la situation*, 1865, 1; *Les Voies de Dieu*, 76.
55   AAM, CF, Salazar: de Meeûs to Vicar-General Corten (ca. 1853).

The success of de Meeûs' association is an argument against an overly strict interpretation of the separate spheres theory. Women were active in their thousands outside the home and contributed to the material and spiritual restoration of the Church. Participation in the association was a route towards getting social and clerical recognition.[56] Those women active at the administrative levels had considerable financial responsibilities. In 1855, the Belgian branches of the *Œuvre des Églises Pauvres* distributed almost 100,000 francs worth of liturgical goods, more than one hundred times the annual wages of the average Belgian worker.[57] In principle, every local committee had a priest as director, who was responsible for offering it spiritual support and maintaining contacts with the diocese. Nevertheless, the leading women of the association themselves negotiated with diocesan authorities about the regional distribution of the objects, with deans about the needs of their parishes and with parish priests about the terms of the donations. Moreover, they often showed they were shrewd businesswomen in their dealings with goldsmiths and fabric merchants.

With the exception of the spiritual counsellor, the boards of the association were exclusively female. From 1852 on, men also could become members of de Meeûs' association. Their numbers in Belgium increased from 23% or 8,220 members in 1858 to 32% or 21,312 members in 1865. They were exclusively involved in spiritual activities and events and had no administrative functions.[58] Although in the minority, men participated in the adoration of the Blessed Sacrament and, thus, did not collectively remain aloof from nineteenth-century devotional life. Moreover, they assumed the role of ordinary 'worshippers' in an association led by women and priests. Since many of the male members were recruited by priests and Jesuits in colleges and existing socio-religious organisations, the association was probably not seen by the men as female-dominated. Still, Anna de Meeûs clearly aimed at promoting a 'masculine' religion as well: "Ne doit-il pas aguerrir le jeune homme contre les tempêtes de son âge, et le former à des vertus mâles et solides? (…)".[59] A mixed membership led by an exclusively female management team was not unique

---

56 Van Osselaer came to similar conclusions with regard to the members of the Apostolate of Prayer. Van Osselaer, *The Pious Sex*, 147. For international parallels, see: Abrams, *The Making of Modern Women*, 34-41; Brejon de Lavergnée, "Le genre du philanthrope", 91-92; Luddy, *Women and Philanthropy*, 23.

57 As a comparison: the *Dames de la Charité* and the Vincentians each distributed about 35,000 francs in alms in Brussels in 1855. In the whole Diocese of Bruges, the Vincentians gave about 53,000 francs to charitable causes, see: De Haerne, *Tableau de la Charité*, 86, 91, 122-123. The *Société Civile de Crédit de la Charité*, the charitable organisation of Anna's father, Ferdinand de Meeûs, disbursed for over 51,000 francs in 1860, see: Van de Perre, "Catholic fundraising", 71-72. For the comparison with workers' income, see: Scholliers, "A Century of Real Industrial Wages", 106-136.

58 *Annales de l'Association*, 1858; 1865.

59 *Rapport de l'Archiassociation* (1854), 5.

in nineteenth-century revival Catholicism and proved that the model of socio-religious action offered opportunities for female development and agency that reached beyond the boundaries of the 'angel in the house' model.[60]

The gendered division of tasks within the association was also reflected in another remarkable male-female relationship. The busy correspondence the female board members maintained with rural parish priests gave witness to their growing prestige. As Van Osselaer has already noted in the case of the female members of the Apostolate of Prayer, a great deal of diplomacy was often required to convince parish priests of the importance of a new confraternity.[61] However, the material help to poor churches gave de Meeûs an extra fillip in gaining acceptance for the devotional projects of her association. Although a tone of humility and a genuine interest in the 'pure' countryside dominated the letters of the female board members of de Meeûs' association, between the lines a different power relationship could be discerned. Many parishes struggled with the loss of income from the funds for perpetual Masses, the endowments for which had been confiscated by the government during the French period. Moreover, since then parish finances were supervised by the municipal authorities. The parish priests had to call on well-to-do benefactors or the "bonnes dames" of the association for extra resources.[62]

Although the development of de Meeûs' association calls for refining existing gender models, important comparative remarks have to be made. The position and possibilities for female autonomous action of the aristocratic ladies around de Meeûs differed from those of pious women from poor or average backgrounds. They were bound more tightly by clerical and masculine constraints than were de Meeûs and her entourage. Colourful anecdotes in nineteenth-century narratives about the foundation of modest rural Flemish congregations illustrate the underlying social and gender differences. In Deftinge, a small village near the Flemish town of Geraardsbergen, the village priest went by horse and cart to 'pick up' shy farmer's daughters to serve in a poor school in his parish. His colleague in the village of Handzame, just moved the community of young pious women working in the local school together with his belongings to his new parish in Pittem. In Wevelgem, like Handzame and Pittem also in rural West-Flanders, the first female teacher of the parochial school was reimbursed for her services with board and lodging at the local priest's house.[63] Although, as I will argue later, the foundation narratives of some rural congregations wrongfully downplayed the impact of the female protagonists of the story, there is a clear relation between social

---

60   Van Osselaer, *The Pious Sex*, 230-231.
61   Ibidem, 122.
62   ARE, *Cahier des Lettres 3*: Benoit to de Meeûs (16 June 1849).
63   Premereur, *Om Christus' Liefde*, 28; Deschout, *De congregatie van de zusters van Maria*, 42-43; Haeyaert, *Iuventus et pauperes*, 19.

background and networks on the one hand and female religious agency on the other.

Moreover, these social differences were also decisive for female agency within de Meeûs' association. With Boone's support, Anna de Meeûs had drawn up a very hierarchical structure for her association, with an important role reserved for the central council in Brussels. The management positions in the association were only accessible for a relatively small group of generous members from the Catholic upper class. These tactics ensured a strong financial base for the association and a list of board members that could have graced an aristocratic address book. However, the largest group of the association's members served under the top layer of its administrators and often under their strict orders. Individual initiative was discouraged and often flatly blocked. There was no question of social interaction or mobility between the aristocratic women at the top and the large middle group of middle-class women. The female board of the association was in that sense more of a hindrance than a stimulus for the development of their own 'subjects'. Along with Van Osselaer, I would therefore like to emphasise that these leading women seemed more concerned with guarding class differences than with questioning or breaking through traditional gender relations.[64]

With regard to this last aspect, the nature of the women's activities in the association should be further elucidated. The embroidery and liturgical workshops of the association were entirely in keeping with nineteenth-century role patterns for women. In contrast to the prominent role and agency of the board members, the large group of women who were sewing, decorating or drawing during the association's meetings, could hardly be seen as a threat to the image of the woman in the home. From that perspective, and despite its rather original combination of praying men and leading ladies, de Meeûs' association did repeat the traditional gender differentiation in other Catholic pious organisations. Again, parallels can be found elsewhere. The artistic activities of women artists were often tolerated precisely because they were compatible with the role of housewife. The above-mentioned Loveling sisters, for example, recited literary works while doing needlework in their living room.[65] The relationship between religious action and female agency or self-fulfilment was marked by many nuances and diffuse boundaries, in which socio-economic differences played a greater role than strict gender conventions. The pious associational life could therefore be seen as both a challenge to and a confirmation of the traditional gender patterns.

---

64 Van Osselaer, *The Pious Sex*, 126, 230-231.
65 Creusen, *Femmes artistes*, 322; Michaux, "Femmes de lettres belges", 33; Schenkeveld-Van der Dussen, "Inleiding", 8-9, 39-40.

Social and political tensions and female agency

'The great social evil': women helping women

Wilhelmina Telghuys also gave her charitable projects a more structured character in the second half of the 1850s. Through the ubiquitous Teichmann family she came into contact with Father Petrus Bogaerts (1803-1877) of the *Sint-Augustinus* (Saint Augustine) parish in Antwerp. Bogaerts was the prototype of the enterprising and militant revival priest. He re-embellished his church, promoted several devotional practices and founded different confraternities, organisations and charities.[66] Concern about the poor living conditions and the moral character of the large population of dockworkers in his parish, especially in the impoverished neighbourhoods around the *Oude Vaartplaats*, inspired him in 1856 to establish a branch of the *Sint-Franciscus-Xaverius Genootschap* (Saint Francis Xavier Fraternity).[67] Bogaerts maintained good contacts with the Jesuits and had his association quickly affiliated with the Archconfraternity of Saint Francis Xavier, which was founded in 1854 by Father van Caloen, a Jesuit priest. Within the framework of the mid-nineteenth century revival, the Xaverian societies shared a common focus on raising moral standards and religious re-education. Urban workers and working-class neighbourhoods had to be converted again through the mediation of 'apostles' from their own classes. Respectable leisure activities, religious processions, evening classes and 'good books' were promoted to keep the regained souls on the right path.[68]

The male converts of the Xavierian society got support from a group of praying female devotees, confirming traditional gender patterns once again.[69] Men 'fearlessly' went out to working-class districts, trying to reconcile the most hostile souls with the Church. Repentance was a crucial element in their path towards a better, or at least a more decent life. Women offered support in a 'feminine' way, by praying and supplying food and clothing packages. Telghuys, however, who became chair of the women's branch in 1858, did not go along with the purely praying or supportive role. She herself went out to recruit men and women in the working-class districts. Moreover, in 1858, separately from Bogaerts' initiatives, she started her own charitable work in a rented house on the *Arenbergstraat*, near the *Oude Vaartplaats*. There she had an office with an emergency night shelter for needy families and she helped

---

66 Bogaerts was parish priest of the *Sint-Augustinus* parish from 1843 until his death in 1877. Peeters, *L'Église de Saint-Augustin*, 204-228; ADHH, 253: *Annales de Servantes des sacrés-cœurs*.
67 ADHH, 16: Verest Manuscript, 18-19; Peeters, *L'Église de Saint-*Augustin, 249.
68 On the origin and mission of the Xavierian societies: Masson, *De aartsbroederschap*, 28-46; Viaene, *Belgium and the Holy See*, 180-181.
69 Masson, *De aartsbroederschap*, 53.

them to find food, work or a house. She made use of her family's social and business networks to generate resources for her work, but always followed an independent course. In the *Arenbergstraat* she was "parfaitement libre" in her charitable engagements, "ce que m'eut été absolument impossible dans ma famille".[70] After the death of her father in 1858, everything but an ardent supporter of her charitable initiatives, she embarked on a new venture. In 1862 she started a rag business in a former inn in Borgerhout, intended to provide work for girls and women who had come down in the world. Shocking her family once again, the initiative flirted with the limits of bourgeois norms of respectability and earned her nothing but incomprehension in well-to-do circles. Even at the Teichmanns, Telghuys' actions caused some commotion.[71]

Her actions were motivated by a strategy of engagement by women for women that was characteristic of nineteenth-century charities.[72] The plan had grown during her youthful wanderings in the working-class districts and been polished with the religious, moralistic and reformist discourse of the mid-nineteenth-century revival, as is clearly illustrated by her words quoted at the beginning of this chapter. The rag business was not very successful, however, and after a few months Telghuys turned it into a laundry and refuge for orphan girls and 'vulnerable' girls from the poor Antwerp neighbourhoods. This was a more acceptable alternative, both symbolically as well as for her family and supporters. Families, benefactors and the municipal social services could send girls to the institute, where they could be prepared for society by prayer, a modest education and the 'purifying' labour of the laundry. She got the idea from some English trading contacts of her brother, who had taken over the Telghuys shipbroker company after the death of her father.

In England and Ireland, shelters, where 'fallen women' (prostitutes, unmarried mothers, deviant girls), needy or socially vulnerable girls and women could stay and learn a profession, had existed from the eighteenth century onwards. In the nineteenth century female religious took over many of the shelters. Some of them were inspired by an older tradition of religious institutes with refuges for female penitents, such as the seventeenth-century French congregation of *Sœurs de Notre-Dame de Charité* (Sisters of Our Lady of Charity). The far-reaching economic transformations of the nineteenth century had forced a lot of women into poverty, promiscuous factory workshops and prostitution, especially in those countries – such as England and Belgium – that had experienced rapid industrialisation. Prostitution, 'the great social evil', and more broadly the moral dangers posed and faced by people in the margins of society inspired charitable as well as disciplinary action. In Ireland, the refuge model evolved into the abusive system of the 'Magdalen Laundries'

---

70 ADHH, 253: *Annales de Servantes des sacrés-cœurs*; ADHH, 16: Verest Manuscript, 18-21.
71 ABA, File Dienstmaagden H. Harten: Bogaerts to Sterckx (7 Nov. 1862).
72 De Maeyer, "Dames d'œuvres", 110; Van Heijst, Derks and Monteiro, *Ex Caritate*, 374-392.

that were run by convent sisters. In England and the United States, the idea of re-education, rehabilitation and reintegration remained intact, even though exploitation was the harsh reality in many places.[73]

With regard to the Belgian situation, Telghuys positioned herself within a double evolution. On the one hand her initiative clearly showed parallels with mid-nineteenth-century public and private initiatives to 'save' poor, delinquent or deviant children by withdrawing them from the corrupting environments they grew up in. Her initiative showed similarities with the public reform institutes to re-educate these children, which were introduced in Belgium by the social reformer Edouard Ducpétiaux.[74] On the other hand, Telghuys did not question in any way the rigid and paternalistic system of confinement, regulation and discipline that characterised Belgian social policies. Although she believed in the possibilities of re-educating and reintegrating vulnerable, displaced and morally deviant girls, further analyses of her institute and policies will highlight her conviction that this could only be achieved by discipline, hard work and strict supervision. Shortly after the foundation of her institute, Telghuys started a collaboration with the social services of the city of Antwerp for the placement and reimbursement of orphans or displaced or deviant girls. This ensured discreet public supervision and a second source of income, in addition to the necessary laundry activities. It aligned her initiative with the nineteenth-century obsession with social, moral and hygienic order.[75]

Telghuys' institution was a 'house of prevention' for female orphans and girls in danger of ending up in prostitution. From that perspective, her initiative also resembled the multitude of 'Providence homes' that emerged in nineteenth-century France. In her care for orphans, she was also inspired by the orphanage of the Teichmann family and the *Mariazusters* (Sisters of Mary) of Waasmunster in Hoboken, where girls received a basic education and a professional training in sewing, embroidery or laundry work and worked in the local laundry and sewing '*ouvroir*' to finance the institutions. The combination was inspired by 'pedagogical' as well as financial concerns. Preparing children for reintegration in society by teaching them social and gender appropriate professions and skills was crucial to the nineteenth-century policy regarding children in institutions. However, the children's labour was also crucial to balance the budget of the institutions, supplementing the subsidies

---

73 Kollar, "Magdalenes and Nuns", 316-320; McCarthy, *Origins of the Magdalene Laundries*, 173-181. On the institutes in Ireland, see especially: Smith, *Ireland's Magdalen Laundries* and Luddy, *Prostitution and Irish Society*, 76-122; Prunty, *Our Lady of Charity*, 95-99.
74 D'hoker et al., *Het kind in de inrichting*, 41-42; Dupont-Bouchat, *De la prison à l'École*, 27-48.
75 De Schaepdrijver, "Reglementering", 490-491; Huberty and Keunings, "La prostitution à Bruxelles", 19-21; Rodríguez García, "Ideas and practices", 136-138; Steverlynck, "La traite des blanches".

and donations from benefactors. As we will see later, this aspect of the "commerce des congregations" would be an important factor in the intensifying tensions between Catholics and liberals.[76]

Telghuys did not accept prostitutes or unmarried mothers in her hospice. She sent repentant prostitutes to the nearby penitential home of the *Zusters van het Heilig Hart van Jezus* (Sisters of the Sacred Heart of Jesus). The home and the congregation had already been established in the 1820s on the initiative of a local woman, Helena Kums-Van Celst (1779-1864). A few years later Van Celst also took over a home for penitent women in Brussels. Together with the *Zusters van Liefde* (Sisters of Charity) in Ghent and Bruges, the *Sœurs du Bon Pasteur* (Sisters of the Good Shepherd), an offshoot of the aforementioned French *Sœurs de Notre-Dame de Charité*, in Mons and Namur and the *Filles de la Croix* in Liège, the Van Celst Institute was a pioneer in the field. Most of these institutions operated in close collaboration with the civil authorities, thereby supporting the political policy in nineteenth-century Belgium designed to regulate and control prostitution and to discipline, confine and re-educate repentant prostitutes.[77] However, despite the recent increase in scholarly interest in the history of marginality in general and prostitution in particular, an in-depth study of the approach of these female congregations to the prostitution problem is still lacking.[78]

As in many institutes for destitute girls and women, life in Telghuys' laundry was difficult. Often there was not enough food and the inexperienced women had to work long hours to get the work done. The laundry was barely profitable in the first few years because it was difficult for Telghuys to build up a customer base. The first young women were sent to Marie-Antoinette Teichmann's institution in Hoboken for training as laundresses. On their return they were put in charge of the laundry, but had difficulty in managing the young group of women efficiently. As a result, the clothes were often badly washed, torn or returned to the customers too late. Though Telghuys spent a large part of her day with the women, she did not herself live in Borgerhout, nor in her

76 On the 'Providence' institutions, see: Mas, "Internat et travail". A general survey about Catholic nineteenth-century orphanages does not exist, but a 1904 publication giving an overview of Belgian charitable organisations confirms the widespread system of orphanages with workshops. See: Vloeberghs, *La Belgique charitable*. On the system of workshops and the revenue from child labour in orphanages, reform institutes and child detention centres: see: D'hoker et al., *Het kind in de inrichting*, 54-55; Dupont-Bouchat, "Criminalité féminine", 78. For parallels in the Netherlands and France: Van Heijst, Derks and Monteiro, *Ex Caritate*, 99; Brejon de Lavergnée, "Congrégations féminines", 96, 99-100, which points out that the French *Filles de Charité* had over 20,000 orphans in their *ouvroirs* in the nineteenth century.
77 Piette, "Maintenir les servantes", 47-48; Van Loon, "Opvattingen", 106-107; De Schaepdrijver, "Reglementering", 490-491; Dupont-Bouchat, "La prostitution urbaine", 109-129.
78 For developments in Belgian historiography: Rodríguez García and Lauro, "Belgian History", 32-36.

In 1863 Telghuys transferred her laundry business from Borgerhout to the centre of Antwerp, and sought refuge and stability within the *Sint-Augustinus* parish. Daily life for the girls under Telghuys' care meant long working days in hot, damp rooms and on the bleaching meadows in the inner courtyard of the building on the *Sint-Jorisvest*.
[Photograph – Before 1893 – ADHH, 219]

office on the *Arenbergstraat*. Even the headstrong Wilhelmina could not defy the prevailing gender and decency standards to that extent. The parental home on the *Mutsaertstraat* remained her home. Under pressure from her family, Telghuys moved the laundry in March 1863 to the *Sint-Jorisvest*, just inside the city walls. It was housed in the former lace school of the Teichmann family, which had collapsed due to the crisis in the Antwerp textile and lace industry.[79]

As a result, Telghuys' institute ended up in Bogaerts' *Sint-Augustinus* parish, near the socially turbulent *Oude Vaartplaats*. With the support of the parish priest, the laundry and orphanage, which became known as the *Sint-Franciscus-Xaveriusinstituut* (Saint Francis Xavier Institute), gained in respectability. In this way Wilhelmina was integrated in the extensive charity network of Bogaerts, which was absolutely essential in providing her with the support she needed after her adventures in Borgerhout. Her experiences there proved it was impossible to carry out a daring project as an autonomous lay woman without the support of a male ally, a broader social network or access to a substantial family fortune. Telghuys was intelligent enough to realise that her position was precarious. By falling back on Bogaerts, her institution flourished, and later, as a respected sister and convent superior, she would make a new stab at ambitious female entrepreneurship.

The pressure of 'les mauvais journaux'

Telghuys' decision to retreat into Bogaerts' sphere of influence and not to completely withdraw from family and social support was also determined by another factor. Just like other charitable institutions for girls 'in moral danger', her *Sint-Franciscus-Xaveriusinstituut* was not beyond reproach. In the early

---

79   ABA, File Dienstmaagden H. Harten: Bogaerts to Sterckx (15 March 1863).

years, rumours about the poor living conditions sporadically trickled through into the liberal press, and intensified when girls ran away from the institute. Their testimonies threw the volatile neighbourhood around her institute into turmoil. Now and then skirmishes occurred at the gates of the institute. Since the polarisation in the political arena was worsening, Bogaerts and Archbishop Sterckx were very alert to negative perceptions of Catholic initiatives.[80] For example, in 1863, the year Telghuys moved her laundry to the centre of Antwerp, the *Zusters van Liefde* in the penitential institute in Bruges were accused of physically abusing one of the women under their care. The superior was detained in prison for several weeks and the case was the subject of furious comment in the press.[81]

By the mid-nineteenth century, the union between Catholics and liberals of the first decades after Belgian independence was over. Radicalisation was now the order of the day on both sides. From the end of the 1840s, the Church's growing influence in the public domain increasingly irritated the liberals, who largely dominated the political stage between 1848 and 1884. The dissatisfaction was mixed with old anticlerical ideas and frustrations about the wealth, parasitic existence and immoral behaviour of the Catholic clergy. In 1857 the last unionist government foundered on a number of ideological issues, including the controversial 'Convent Law'. The law envisaged the construction of a legal framework for donations to private charitable institutions, including religious institutes. Liberals regarded it as a disguised form of funding for monasteries and saw the old spectre of the religious *main-morte* looming.[82]

Anticlerical popular protests in various large and smaller cities were directed against religious institutes and Catholic charities. Although these protests were mostly limited to breaking windows, Catholic outrage about the 'power of the street' grew. Old traumas from the French era surfaced, giving rise to greater caution.[83] Sterckx, who stuck to a moderate course, urged priests and religious not to give cause for provocation or provide any other grist for the liberal mill. Scandals had to be avoided, or in any case kept private. The women in our study also felt the consequences of the political turbulence. For Telghuys it was an extra element in the ecclesiastical and social pressure to conform. For Antoinette Cornet, on the other hand, the polarised ideological climate surprisingly opened up an escape route. At the same time, her story showed the relative nature – at least on the local level – of the tensions on the political front.

80 ABA, File of the Dienstmaagden H. Harten: Bogaerts to Sterckx (15 March 1863, 19 April 1864); ADHH, 253: *Annales de Servantes des sacrés-cœurs*.
81 Rotsaert, "De laatste penitenten", 206-207.
82 See: Van Dijck and De Maeyer, "An Introduction", 7-25; Witte, "The battle of monasteries", 109-114; Deneckere, *Geuzengeweld*, 37-61; Koppen, *De Kloosterkwestie*, 206-247.
83 On the disturbances, see: Van Kalken, *Commotions populaires*, 41-48; Koppen, *De Kloosterkwestie*, 219-222.

As already noted, in the 1850s Cornet's congregation in Alsemberg experienced the repercussions of unwisely consolidated pioneering initiatives, financial troubles and internal tensions. Later Cornet described it as "l'esprit de division régnait dans cette maison, donc plus de charité, plus de soumission, plus de droiture; mais intrigue sur intrigue, cabale, défiance (...) et des scandales si public que nous étions honteuses de nous dire d'A. [Alsemberg]".[84] The dependent convents that were founded in Waterloo (1851) and in La Hulpe (1857) became refuges for sisters who were dissatisfied in Alsemberg or unwilling to stay there. The stories of sisters who left the congregation alarmed family members, parish priests from the area and finally also the archbishop in Mechelen.[85] Cornet appealed for help in the summer of 1859 and asked Sterckx for permission to leave Alsemberg: "dans ma position présente, je ne puis faire un bien réel pour les autres, ni pour moi un vrai progrès dans la perfection".[86] Worried about the scandals "qui ne feront qu'augmenter si les mauvais journaux commencent à s'amuser", Sterckx intervened.[87] Liberal commentators, who were increasingly virulent in their criticism of the 'sanctimonious' and backward countryside, would have a field-day with the chaos in Alsemberg.[88]

Mechelen implemented stricter rules for contacts between the sisters and the outside world and tightened the supervision of recruitment. Cornet and some other dissatisfied sisters were given permission to move to the annex in La Hulpe in September 1859. For Cornet, who became the local superior there, the pressure of ideological tensions had steered her own trajectory in the right direction. Moreover, the tensions between liberals and Catholics in La Hulpe – as in many other rural areas – were not as high as expected.[89] By 1857, the liberal-minded municipal administration of La Hulpe had granted the sisters' school a subsidy. Pragmatic considerations about the sound, flexible and inexpensive education of the sisters took precedence over ideological principles: "Cette école offre à La Hulpe toutes les garanties désirables et présente moins d'inconvénient que si elle était appelée à être dirigée par une institutrice diplômée".[90] Although living conditions in La Hulpe were initially poor, Cornet got a new lease of life there. The girls' school of the sisters soon had 75 pupils, and shortly after her arrival, she also started a new boarding

84 ASCMLH: *Notice autobiographique*, 4.
85 AAM, CF, La Hulpe: Petit (curate in Braine-l'Alleud) to Vicar General Lauwers (20 March 1859), parish priest of Woutersbrakel to Sterckx (3 May 1859).
86 ASCMLH, A.2: Cornet to Sterckx (25 June 1859).
87 AAM, CF, La Hulpe: parish priest of Woutersbrakel to Sterckx (3 May 1859).
88 Concerning the liberal perception of nineteenth-century rural and Catholic Flanders, see: De Smaele, *Rechts Vlaanderen*, 312-317.
89 This is in line with findings for the situation in West Flanders, where the ideological struggle in the 1850s and 1860s did not prevent female religious from remaining active in the public education or care sector. Van Dijck and Suenens, "La Belgique charitable", 175-178.
90 AR-LLN, Archives of the municipality of La Hulpe, 12: Lord Mayor Mathieu to the school inspector (4 April 1857).

school. As her educational activities grew, so did her authority and self-confidence. She began to put pressure on the ties that connected her to Alsemberg and repeatedly stressed that "la mort la plus cruelle me paraît mille fois préférable au retour".[91] Eventually, Archbishop Sterckx would give in and allow her to be a congregation founder herself. Cornet, for that reason, profited both from the 'empire of invitation' offered to congregations in the young Belgian state as well as the pressure of increasing ideological tensions.

---

91   ASCMLH, A.2: Cornet to Sterckx (25 June 1859).

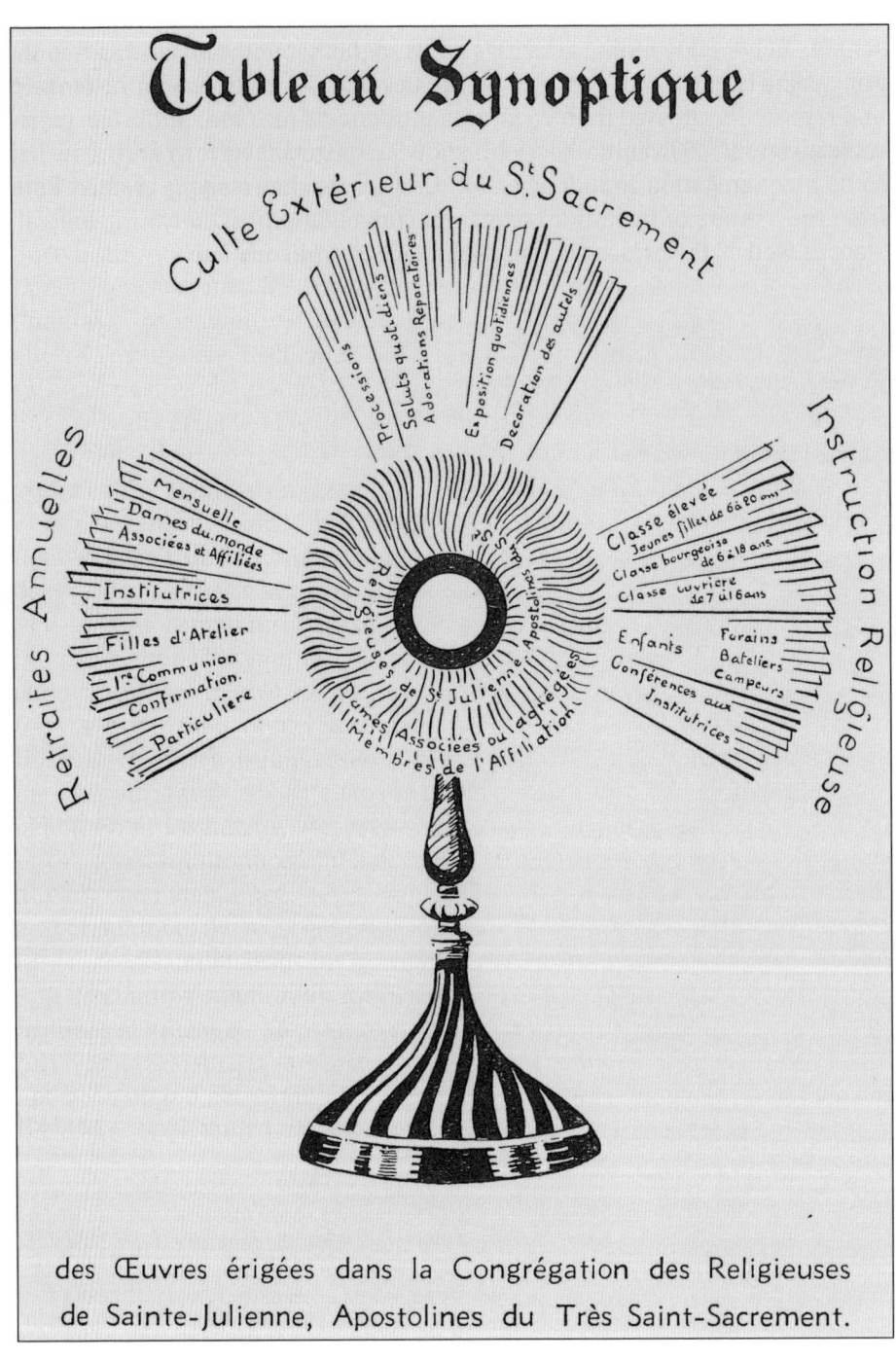

Inspired by her visions, Kestre was already using the symbol of a radiant monstrance in the 1850s to present her religious and apostolic project. As an expression of her Eucharistic and Christocentric spirituality and her revival activism, this project would be realised only in 1867.
[Printed drawing – S.d. – ADSJ]

THE SPIRITUAL DIALECTIC OF REVIVAL DEVOTION

> De tout temps j'avais compris qu'il y a des âmes intérieures dans le monde, âmes de prière qui doivent éprouver un besoin insupprimable d'union avec Dieu pour le mieux connaître et surtout aussi pour mieux entrer dans les desseins et j'ose presque dire dans les désirs insatiables que N.S. éprouve dans le St. Sacrement de se communiquer aux âmes et d'en trouver qui le secondent dans son amour pour les hommes.
>
> ADSJ, 1.3./3: Kestre to Dechamps, (s.d.).

Historians have often interpreted the transition from eighteenth-century religious practice to the nineteenth-century revival as an evolution from a 'religion of fear' to a 'religion of the heart'. Rigoristic and Jansenist tendencies gave Catholicism prior to the French Revolution a stricter face than the Romantic and emotional life of faith that prevailed after the turn of the century. Revival piety had a popular character, was passionate and penitent, and aimed at demonstrative action rather than profound introspection or theological discussion.[1] Kestre's passionate intention to attend to the love and '*désires insatiables*' of Christ was a striking illustration of the affective spiritual discourse of the nineteenth century. In the context of the feminisation thesis, some historians have pointed to a feminisation of nineteenth-century devotion, which was dominated by an affective relationship with the body

---

1 Gadille, "Grands courants doctrinaux", 123-125; Cholvy and Hilaire, *Histoire religieuse*, 20-22, 79-89; Viaene, *Belgium and the Holy See*, 186-187.

and heart of Christ and symbolised by the growing popularity of Mary.[2] Other researchers, however, have highlighted nuances or elements of continuation rather than spiritual paradigm changes. Research into the nineteenth-century discourse in French religious boarding schools, apocalyptic Marian apparitions, the parish missions or Belgian diocesan circulars has shown that the image of a punishing God or the fear of eternal damnation remained intact even after the revolutionary period.[3] Analyses of devotions labelled as typically 'feminine', such as the adoration of the Sacred Heart, revealed that these devotional forms could also have an exceptionally masculine and militant appeal.[4] In this chapter I will examine how the possibilities for development of the four women in my study were affected by the spirituality of the revival, both in its predominantly Romantic and reparative characteristics of the first half of the century and its more aggressive and disciplinary variant of the 1850s. Of essential importance is the role of the specific and double-voiced religious language of their time and the way in which it enabled or prevented women from achieving and justifying their own ideas, ambitions and strategies.

"L'eucharistie peut sauver le monde"

When Anna de Meeûs encountered the *Œuvre des Tabernacles* of de la Bouillerie in 1848, not only did she find inspiration for her work for poor churches, she was also deeply impressed by the growing devotion to the Blessed Sacrament that was associated with it in France. Above all, the *Association de l'Adoration nocturne*, which was promoted by de la Bouillerie in Paris, particularly appealed to her imagination.[5] The practice of nocturnal adoration originated in Rome and was introduced to Paris, not coincidentally, in the revolutionary year 1848. Encouraged by "*la passion espagnole*" of her Belgian-Spanish friend Desmaissières, de Meeûs joined the association and was assigned a monthly hour of nightly worship.[6] The genesis of de Meeûs' religious framework to a great extent also characterised the spiritual foundations of the

---

2 Busch, "Die Feminisierung der Frömmigkeit", 203-204; Van Osselaer and Buerman, "Feminization Thesis", 505-508; Pasture, "Beyond the Feminization Thesis", 8-12.
3 Gibson, *A Social History*, 244-254; Langlois, "La conjoncture mariale", 37-38; Viaene, "De ontplooiing van een 'vrije' kerk", 44-55; Tihon, "Dieu dans les mandements de carême", 661-678.
4 McMillan, "Religion and Gender", 59-62; Van Osselaer, *The Pious Sex*, 237-240; Menozzi, *Sacro Cuore*.
5 Ricard, *Vie de Mgr de la Bouillerie*, 130-141.
6 ARE, *Chronique. Chapter III. La Vocation*, 27.

revival. Southern – especially Italian and French – influences largely gave the revival a passionate, devotional and demonstrative religiosity.[7]

Consequently, and with reason, revival devotion was often called 'ultramontane' – from over the mountains.[8] I would prefer to reserve the term 'ultramontanism' for the later evolution in the nineteenth-century Church and nineteenth-century spirituality, which will come to the fore in parts II and III of this book. After 1860, 'ultramontane' became a synonym for a tormented and anti-modern siege mentality in Catholicism which, under the motto '*omnia instaurare in Christo*', simultaneously envisaged a militant re-Christianisation of society. It differed from the more open mentality of the early revival, but nonetheless built on Romantic emotions and the emphasis on penitence of the first half of the nineteenth century.[9]

Devotion to the Blessed Sacrament became the spiritual foundation of de Meeus' *Œuvre des Églises pauvres*. By analogy with the parish missions, her discourse had a strong proselytising message. She encouraged her association's members "à relever et à encourager, dans les paroisses, toutes les saintes pratiques instituées en l'honneur du S. Sacrement, enfin à exercer une influence salutaire".[10] Just like the sisters in the convent boarding schools and the early nineteenth-century founders of religious institutes, de Meeûs was imbued with a desire for penance and reparation. Eucharistic devotion became the most important expression of this. Upset by the revolutionary threat from Paris, de Meeûs wrote about the events of 1848: "On a tant besoin de réparation pour les erreurs du temps. Seulement la ferveur de l'Eucharistie peut sauver le monde".[11]

Her fascination with the Blessed Sacrament was neither new nor exceptional. Since the Middle Ages there had been a special bond between Eucharistic devotion and religious women, based on both the identification of women with Christ's sacrifice and the possibilities that the devotion offered for female religious agency outside the established lines of celebrating Mass. Through veneration of the Eucharist, a female alternative to the sacerdotal role of the priest took shape.[12] Eucharistic devotion also intensified during the Counter Reformation, largely linked to a call for atonement for the Protestant rebellion in general, and in particular, the Protestant denial of the real presence of Christ in the Eucharist. Eucharistic devotion became a prominent theme

7   On influences in Belgium, see: Viaene, *Belgium and the Holy See*, 271. On international parallels, see Cholvy and Hilaire, *Histoire religieuse*, 154-165; Heimann, *Catholic Devotion*, 30-37; Aubert, *L'Église dans le monde moderne*, 130; Gibson, *A Social History*, 256-257.
8   See for example: Priesching, "Grundzüge", 77; Heimann, *Catholic Devotion*, 9-10.
9   On the evolution of the concept of 'ultramontanism' in the context of the Belgian Church, see: Lamberts (ed.), "Het ultramontanisme".
10 *Rapport de l'Association* (1852), 3.
11 ARE, *Cahier des lettres 3*: de Meeûs to anonymous (13 Nov. 1848).
12 Bynum, *Holy Feast*, 26; Mulder-Bakker, *Lives of the Anchoresses*, 78-116; Caspers, "Eerherstel", 101-106.

in the French spiritual school, one of the most important Counter Reformation movements, and inspired many religious women.[13] In 1652 Cathérine de Bar (1614-1698), for instance, founded the *Bénédictines du Saint Sacrement* in Paris, which focused on atoning for the victimisation of Christ. Endowed with a strong personality, great perseverance and a talent for writing, she became one of the few female voices in the religious and ecclesiastical debates of her time.[14]

The nineteenth-century Church's struggle with the legacy of the French Revolution paralleled the Church's response to the sixteenth-century Reformation. During the revival there was a resurgence of Eucharistic devotion in response to new upheavals, and again religious women played an important role in this. Théodelinde Dubouché, for example, shocked by the strongly anticlerical-inspired revolutionary events of 1848, founded a Eucharistic confraternity and congregation in Paris to do penance for the sins of her fellow citizens.[15] Other French founders of congregations and colleagues in Italy, Spain and Germany followed the same spiritual path with a parallel discourse. Theresia Bonzel (1830-1905), the German founder of the *Arme Franziskanerinnen von der Ewigen Anbetung* (Poor Franciscan Sisters of the Perpetual Adoration), saw convent life as a spiritual mission, "(...) their adoration should be an atonement for the innumerable insults to the Eucharistic suffering that the silent sufferer must endure in the sacrament of love".[16] Most of the nineteenth-century Eucharistic congregations combined contemplative adoration of the Blessed Sacrament with an active engagement in religious instruction or retreat work.[17] In England, the attraction of the post-revolutionary reparation and Eucharistic discourse seemed to have been less of a motive for congregation founders. The focus was put more intensely on their roles as pioneers and missionaries in a Protestant world.[18] Still, Eucharistic piety as a means of atonement was not totally absent from the English Catholic scene. Mother Mary Clare Knight (+1860), the 'refounder' of the Benedictines of the Blessed Sacrament of Cannington and Colwich, for example, established perpetual adoration in their convent in the 1830s and it achieved an influential reputation as a renowned retreat centre. But, like many other convent founda-

---

13 Cognet, *La spiritualité moderne*, I, 358, 462.
14 Andral, "Mechtilde du Saint-Sacrement", 1621-1637.
15 Wenner, "Théodelinde Dubouché", 1743-1745.
16 "indem ihrer Anbetung Sühne sein soll für die unzähligen Beleidigungen, für die eucharistischen Leiden, die der stille Dulder im Sakramente der Liebe ertragen muss". Hardick, *He Leads, I Follow*, 20.
17 Other examples are Marie-Eugénie Milleret (1817-1898), founder of the French *Religieuses de l'Assomption* (Religious of the Assumption) and Gertrude Comensoli (1847-1903), founder of the Italian *Suore Sacramentine* (Sacramentine Sisters) of Bergamo, see: Donnet, "Marie-Eugénie de Jésus", 555-557 and *Un'anima Eucaristica*, 74.
18 Mangion, *Contested Identities*, 120-123.

tions in England, Knight's convent had a distinct French character as well as a traumatic experience caused by the French Revolution.[19]

In Anna de Meeûs' circle, Desmaissières and Kestre were also attracted to the devotion to the Blessed Sacrament. Desmaissières would found her own Eucharistic congregation after she returned to Spain.[20] Kestre claimed to be divinely inspired. She had already written about her visions on the organisation of her catechesis work in letters from the early 1850s. These became increasingly passionate on the subject of the Eucharist, culminating in 1853 in a sensual and almost mystical discourse: "Méditant sur les qualités d'épouse de N.S. et cherchant à me les appliquer pour les pratiquer je dis: Seigneur, faites que le fruit de notre union soit des âmes et donnez m'en les moyens, aussitôt je suis recueillie, puis je vois un vase de sang couler dans la bouche d'une femme, puis sortir par le cœur, en dessous se trouvaient des âmes qui recevaient l'infusion du sang de N.S. Je fus confirmée que la vie eucharistique de N.S. devra être le modèle (...)."[21] She also used the symbol of a radiant monstrance as blueprint for the organisation of her future congregation. The revival did not produce mystics with the fame of some medieval beguines or nuns. Nineteenth-century piety was focused on atonement and less on contemplative introspection.[22] Yet the story of Kestre's visions – like that of other women inspired by the Eucharistic devotion – shows that the visual language of the revival was embedded in a rich spiritual legacy.[23]

In its emotional and sensual tone, Eucharistic worship reflected the essence of the revival and its popular dimension. And yet it also had an ambiguous relationship with it. The adoration of the Eucharist was more elitist than it was popular. Ever since the Counter Reformation, devotion to the Blessed Sacrament was often the preserve of the high-born or educated faithful. In the nineteenth century, this exclusive connotation continued. Théodelinde Dubouché was the daughter of an important public servant and was a talented and trained painter. The Belgian baroness and founder of the *Société de Marie Réparatrice* (Society of Mary Reparatrix), Emilie d'Oultremont (1818-1878), was a member of one of Belgium's most important noble families.[24] Even Eucharistic congregations devoted to poverty were headed by wealthy, intel-

---

19 The community in Colwich was originally based in Paris and had to flee France due to the Revolution in 1795. See: Champ, *William Bernard Ullathorne*, 212-213.
20 Garcia Iglesias, "Institutos religiosos", 525.
21 ADSJ, 1.5: Kestre to the Holy See, 1856.
22 On this, see: Viaene, *Belgium and the Holy See*, 197; Aubert, *L'Église dans le monde moderne*, 130.
23 Dubouché, for example, had visions about the bleeding heart of Christ becoming one with hers and calling her to found a Eucharistic congregation, see: Wenner, "Théodelinde Dubouché", 1743-1745.
24 Suau, *La mère Marie de Jésus*, 12.

lectual women.²⁵ Belgian lay women, such as the aforementioned Countess de Nédonchel, also emphasised the exalted character of the devotion to the Blessed Sacrament.²⁶

This exclusivist character perfectly suited the noble ladies around Anna de Meeûs – "par nos positions sociales plus aptes que d'autres à travailler à la vigne du Bon Maître" – but presented the middle-class Fanny Kestre with a considerable challenge.²⁷ Some of the criticism she received as a visionary was provoked by her ambitious plan to make her own of the 'difficult' devotion to the Blessed Sacrament. Whereas opponents of nineteenth-century religiosity were often denigrating about the sentimental and extroverted veneration of the Sacred Heart or the Marian devotion, the 'more serious' and somewhat abstract contemplation of the Blessed Sacrament was often treated with respect. De Meeûs was also convinced "que l'adoration perpétuelle du Très St Sacrement est peu comprise, qu'elle ne parle pas à toutes les âmes, parce que c'est une œuvre trop intérieure, et que généralement l'on s'attache de préférence aux œuvres qui ont plus d'éclat et d'entraînement extérieur".²⁸ The particularity of the devotion to the Blessed Sacrament can as such be an illustration of what McLeod has called the successful Catholic strategy of offering a devotional model both for the masses and for the elite.²⁹ However, the continuation of the stories of de Meeûs and Kestre will show that the complex legacy of the Eucharistic inspired identity was not always easy to manage.

A plurality of devotional practices and ascetic self-denial

In response to eighteenth-century rigour and to turbulent social developments, the Catholicism of the revival sought strength and consolation in an intense experience of the sacraments. Moreover, they were no longer seen as a reward for perfection, but as encouragement on the way to it.³⁰ In the context of the Eucharistic devotion, this thinking led to the renewed popularity of frequent communion, which from a rigoristic and Jansenist perspective was seen as an abuse. Both Kestre and de Meeûs had an obsessive desire to receive communion frequently: "n'est-ce pas après la communion fervente que l'âme dans ses entretiens avec N.S. exposé s'éclaire, se fortifie et prend des résolutions?"³¹

25 See, for instance, the aforementioned Theresia Bonzel, the wealthy German woman who co-founded the *Arme Franziskanerinnen von der Ewigen Anbetung*. See: Meiwes, *Arbeiterinnen des Herrn*, 106-108.
26 Baas, *Leven der Gravin Mathilde de Nédonchel*, 165, 209.
27 ARE, *Chronique. III*: de Meeûs to de Jonghe (1857).
28 ARE, *Chronique IV*, 1864.
29 McLeod, *Religion and the People*, 47; Caspers and Magry, *Het Mirakel*, 173-174.
30 Gibson, *A Social History*, 256-259; Viaene, *Belgium and the Holy See*, 197-198.
31 ADSJ. 1.3./3: Kestre to Dechamps (18 Sept. 1870).

It was a *Leitmotiv* in the lives of many nineteenth-century religious women. The aforementioned Julie Billiart received communion daily from the age of twenty. Other founders such as Emilie d'Oultremont or Caroline Lenferna de Laresle (1824-1900) described it as their greatest spiritual desire.[32] However, the desire for frequent communion had caused a sharp gender tension between religious women and their male confessors ever since medieval times. For women religious the Eucharistic devotion created opportunities for frequent and close contact with their divine bridegroom and was a sign of religious perfection, while their male confessors often worried about the dangers of the excess and 'hysteria' in women's passion for Christ.[33]

This field of tension persisted into the nineteenth century. Although male religious institutes such as the Jesuits and the Oblates actively promoted frequent communion, it remained a sensitive subject for many clerics. Not until the beginning of the twentieth century and the pontificate of the 'Communion Pope' Pius X was Jansenist rigidity completely erased.[34] Nineteenth-century women like Kestre and de Meeûs with their desire for "une intime et fréquente rencontre avec N.S." were following in the footsteps of medieval religious, but also added their own revivalist touch. Campaigning for frequent communion became an active commitment to deepening their faith.[35] Within her association, de Meeûs made the promotion of communion an important goal, with an interesting gender variation. Initiatives that had been successful with male members, whom many saw as resistant to the practice of frequent communion, were triumphantly announced in the association's publications. Prominent church figures, such as the nuncio, were invited to lend their support, explicitly with the intention of persuading more men to go to communion.[36]

Frequent communion was also important for Antoinette Cornet and Wilhelmina Telghuys in their pursuit of a greater "ferveur religieuse". If we look more closely at the spiritual trajectory of the four women, there are even more parallels to be drawn. If the stories of Kestre and de Meeûs illustrated the resurgence of Eucharistic devotion, then the spiritual path of Cornet and Telghuys led to two other devotions that were central to the revival: the devotions to the Sacred Heart and to Mary. The devotion to the Sacred Heart was as strongly embedded as the Eucharistic worship in the affective dimension and

---

32   *Life of the Venerable Servant of God*, 13; Suau, *La mère Marie de Jésus*, 22-23; Dubois, *Notice biographique*, 92-93. See also: Mangion, *Contested Identities*, 31 and Brejon de Lavergnée, *Histoire des Filles de la Charité*, 371. There are also examples of lay women who longed for frequent communion: see: De Maeyer, *De rode baron*, 44.
33   McNamara, *Sisters in Arms*, 346; Bynum, *Holy Feast*, 227-229.
34   Gibson, *A Social History*, 257-259; Kilroy, *Madeleine Sophie Barat*, 163-1167. With regard to the pontificate of Pius X (1903-1914), see: Quaghebeur, "De Eucharistische Kruistocht", 98-106.
35   ABSE, 4.2.6. Boone, Jean-Baptiste, 12467: de Meeûs to Marie Malou (3 Jan. 1853); ADSJ, 1.6: Boone to Kestre (26 June 1849).
36   ARE, *Chronique. VIII. Vers la profession*, 129-132.

in the penance and reparation discourse of revival spirituality. Even before the Sacred Heart became the banner of a militant ultramontane crusade in the second half of the nineteenth century, the wounded, bleeding and loving heart of Christ was already exerting a powerful attraction and a strong call to action.[37] At the beginning of the nineteenth century, Barat, for example, wrote that "we become holy ourselves by taking the divine Heart of Jesus as our model, trying as far as we are able to unite ourselves to his feelings and innermost dispositions; and at the same time we dedicate ourselves to extending and promoting the knowledge and love of his divine Heart".[38]

Equally characteristic was the way in which devotions were amalgamated, diversified and extended into a wide range of means to attract and engage believers. Cornet, for example, brought both the devotion to the Sacred Heart and to Mary with her from Alsemberg to La Hulpe. She proved herself to be a master of the typical eclectic spiritual language of the revival: "(...) les grâces obtenues par l'intercession de la Ste Vierge jusqu'à la protection des Sts Anges sans parler de la miséricorde [du] Cœur de Jésus dans le St Sacrement qui, a été pour nous ce que fut l'arche dans la maison d'Obededon". The reference to the Old Testament again illustrated the longing of nineteenth-century believers to valorise the Blessed Sacrament and at the same time to preserve and protect it from greater calamity.[39]

International research has already highlighted the diversity of the revival's devotions and its influence on the resurgence of nineteenth-century convent life.[40] Nowhere did this diverse character come to the surface more strongly than in the popular devotion to Mary, the most polymorphic figure of Catholicism. Even before the actual 'century of Mary' began with the proclamation of the dogma of the Immaculate Conception (1854), the Romantic Catholics of the revival had already embraced the figure of Mary. Marian devotion reflected the soft and affective face of revival piety, while at the same time being adaptable to the dominant discourse of suffering, penance and reparation.[41] Cornet emphasised the traditional role of Mary as mediator. Her affinity with the Sacred Heart of Mary, however decisive in the naming of the congregation in Alsemberg and her own future institute, remained otherwise vague and generalised. Telghuys was particularly attracted to a special aspect of Marian devotion: the veneration of Our Lady of the Seven Sorrows. Her de-

---

37 Gadille, "Grands courants doctrinaux", 125; Cholvy and Hilaire, *Histoire religieuse*, 167-476; Van Osselaer, *The Pious Sex*, 99-106; Idem, "Reform of Piety", 110.
38 Kilroy, *Madeleine Sophie Barat*, 97.
39 ASCMLH: *Notice autobiographique*, 1. Obed-Edom was an Old Testament figure, to whose house David brought the Ark of the Covenant for safekeeping for a while, with numerous blessings bestowed on the house as a result.
40 Viaene, *Belgium and the Holy See*, 195-200; Mangion, *Contested Identities*, 178-179; Langlois, *Le catholicisme au féminin*, 175-201.
41 Di Stefano and Ramon Solans, "Introduction", 6-12.

votion to Mary was embedded in the age-old Marian traditions of Antwerp, but Telghuys was also susceptible to the sentimental and apologetic discourse developed by Alphonsus Liguori (1696-1787) in the eighteenth century.[42]

Liguori, the founder of the Redemptorists, was one of those popular Italian voices that had been carried across the Alps by the spiritual currents emanating from southern Europe. In the nineteenth century, his popular writings gave an important boost to Eucharistic and Marian devotion. In Belgium as elsewhere, his *Visite al SS. Sacramento* (1751) was translated and distributed during the Redemptorist parish missions. His publications were also recommended by the Jesuits as edifying literature for their *Filles de Marie*. It is not impossible that de Meeûs and Kestre were introduced to Eucharistic devotion in this way, although they never explicitly referred to his work.[43] Telghuys did, and she adopted the French translation of his work *Le glorie di Maria* (1760), with a well-known passage about the seven sorrows as the starting point for her spiritual thinking. Marian devotion provided a permanent source of inspiration for her active engagement: "Enseigner et moraliser les filles, comme notre Mère, notre Patronne et notre Maîtresse".[44] Telghuys also linked her personal devotion to penance and atonement for "l'énormité de l'outrage (…) à la Majesté divine". Finally, her veneration of Mary was adapted to the emotional and sensual discourse of the revival: "comme votre tendre mère, si dévouée et courageuse dans ses douleurs, j'essuie par baisers les larmes que mes péchés vous ont causés".[45]

In this way, even Marian devotion was linked with the essentially Christocentric character of nineteenth-century spirituality. From that perspective, the life and suffering of Christ were both a subject of veneration as well as an ideal. The emphasis on the human figure of Christ and his sacrifice inspired a passionate discourse of asceticism, personal self-denial and self-sacrifice in imitation of Jesus. Anna de Meeûs wrote to one of her friends that "(…) pour arriver à cette véritable vie en N.S. il faut être bien des fois brisé et anéanti".[46] Desmaissières called her Eucharistic congregation in Spain the "Adoratrices Esclavas del Santísimo Sacramento". The Italian founder of a Eucharistic congregation, Gertrude Comensoli, claimed that she was "willing to do and suffer whatever he wants from me. I hope that the good Jesus will help me with his

---

42 ADHH, 1: First Communion card, and 10: Notebook of Mère Jeanne.
43 De Meulemeester, *Influences ascétiques*, 9-32. Ligurian influence was widespread in Belgium, both among lay people as well as among active and contemplative religious, see: Vanderstraeten, *175 jaar Zusters der Christelijke Scholen*, 138-141; Marcélis, *Femmes cloîtrées*, 664. Liguori also had a significant impact on nineteenth-century devotion internationally: Anderson, "The Limits of Secularization", 656; Mills, "Negotiating the Divide", 42; de Giorgio, "La bonne catholique", 186.
44 ABA, File Dienstmaagden H. Harten: Bogaerts to Sterckx (3 Feb. 1862).
45 ADHH, 13: *Les châtiments du péché*, and 41: Notes by Jan Bergen, Meditations of Mère Jeanne.
46 ARE, *Cahier des lettres 1*: de Meeûs to de Biesme (24 July 1853).

grace to completely destroy my strong self-love and to achieve the total deconstruction of myself for the divine glory."⁴⁷

Despite various spiritual preferences, the emphasis on asceticism, detachment and self-renunciation was also important in the stories of the other women in our study. Cornet justified her cry for help to leave Alsemberg with her desire for a stricter and ascetic convent life according to the model of Christ. She also cherished the extreme poverty of the first sister community in La Hulpe: "c'est touchant de voir le dévouement de nos Sœurs, qui se sacrifient avec tant de zèle (...)".⁴⁸ Telghuys was of a similar mind when she expressed her desire to live in the poor quarters of the *Sint-Franciscus-Xaveriusinstituut*, despite her family's resistance, "pour me détacher de tout confort mondain et pour m'anéantir et me soumettre au pouvoir divin".⁴⁹ Often there were allusions to the strong but popular language of Rodriguez' *Pratique de la perfection chrétienne*.⁵⁰ Reading the rules of Rodriguez on submitting to the divine will inspired one of Kestre's visions about forming a congregation "des apostolines, humblement prosternées aux pieds de Notre Seigneur, souffrantes pour son amour, dévouées à Lui défendre."⁵¹

A passion paradigm

Kestre's words illustrate what the theologian Annelies van Heijst in the context of Dutch religious women has called the 'passion paradigm' of the nineteenth century.⁵² Action was the motto of revival Catholics, but the spiritual touchstone was 'a passion for the Passion' – referring both to the ubiquitous focus on suffering, ascetism and penance as well as the passionate experiences associated with it. In my view, Kestre's words also reflected the interesting dialectic between female suffering and humility on the one hand and female agency on the other that took shape within the passion paradigm. Building on the discourse of the post-revolutionary *foremothers*, the atonement spirituality of the revival offered new opportunities for female fulfilment, though also

47 "disposta a fare e a soffrire qualunque cosa vorrà da me. Spero che il bon Gesù con la sua grazia mi aiuterà a far morire interamente il molto mio amor proprio ed arrivare allo spogliamento totale di me stessa per la divina gloria": *Un'anima Eucaristica*, 74.
48 ASCMLH, A.2: Cornet to Sterckx (28 Aug. 1861).
49 ADHH, 253: *Annales des Servantes des Sacrés-Cœurs*.
50 *La Pratique de la perfection chrétienne* was based on the spiritual notes of the Spanish Jesuit, Brother Alphonso de Rodriguez (1532-1617). They were written in practical and simple language, but with an emphasis on humiliation, renunciation of one's own will and total submission to God. For these reasons they were considered suitable for a female audience and were included in many Catholic (convent) libraries. For other examples, see: Van Heijst, Derks and Monteiro, *Ex Caritate*, 540; Marcélis, *Femmes cloîtrées*, 658.
51 ADSJ, 1.5: Kestre to the Holy See (1856).
52 Van Heijst, "Het passie-paradigma", 17-33.

new obstacles. The religious language of suffering and penance could offer women spiritual well-being as their desire for a closer bond with Christ and an imitation of his passion was fulfilled. In some cases it could also become a double-voiced metaphor for recognition and autonomy. In less favourable conditions, however, it became a new straitjacket that reinforced the dominant expectation of female sacrifice, humility and self-denial.

Religious women were deeply inspired by the memory of their first communion. They luxuriated in a romantic passion, remembering the day when they strode through the church "à Lui rencontrer pour la première fois".[53] Their experiences were expressed in the affective language of many contemporary women for whom first communion was their earliest encounter with their divine bridegroom. It was a rite of initiation in a world of girlish adoration and purity, commemorated in lace-edged 'holy pictures' as a one-way ticket to an angelic future. As such, the practice of first communion confirmed the traditional roles of nineteenth-century gender discourse.[54] Yet, the first communion ceremony and discourse could hide a form of double-voiced subversion, or at least a subversion that might be attributed to it later. The passionate adoration for a divine beloved was not free from the dialectic between female submission and autonomy. On the one hand, they committed their selves tot their heavenly groom in a romantic act of total submission. On the other hand, first communion was more than girlish adoration. For Kestre and de Meeûs it was also a first step on "la voie libre", as they called it in their journals and letters.[55] In this sense it was a prelude to their private vows of virginity as a form of resistance to the family pressure to marry. Telghuys, who never took a vow before entering the convent, cherished the memory of her first communion as the beginning of her struggle to choose her own way of life.[56]

In reconstructing the stories of their lives, Kestre, de Meeûs and Telghuys used the religious language of the sacraments or rituals in order to escape the compelling bourgeois gender patterns of marriage and motherhood and to legitimise that escape route. In stories about other congregation founders also, first communion is confirmed to have been a crucial moment in the formation of a religious vocation. Teresia Bonzel defended herself against her mother's coercing her to marry with the first communion motto, "Er führt, ich gehe". The inspiration of first communion led Dubouché, "indépendante, orgueilleuse, mais dévouée et généreuse", to a vow of virginity and a convent voca-

---

53 ADSJ, 1.6: Kestre to Busine (18 Nov. 1857).
54 Harrison, *Romantic Catholics*, 20-21; Rogers, *Les bourgeoises*, 203; Smith, *Ladies of the Leisure Class*, 100-101.
55 ADSJ, 1.3./1: Journal of Kestre (21 Nov. 1856); ARE, *Cahier des lettres 3*: Kestre to Boone (17 March 1853).
56 ADSJ, 1.6: Kestre to Sidonie Kestre (23 Jan. 1849); ARE, *Cahiers des lettres 3*: de Meeûs to Boone (23 Feb. 1851); ABA, File Dienstmaagden H. Harten: Telghuys to Sterckx (25 Jan. 1862).

tion. Fitzgerald has pointed to the power of this religious language for American sisters: "Catholic nuns used a legitimating language that drew from their culture and theology to argue for increased power in the public sphere".[57]

Opportunities for female agency lay also in identifying with Christ's suffering and self-sacrifice. Anna de Meeûs perfected her double-voiced discourse with the religious language of the passion paradigm. Her requests for support, approval or recognition were couched in the language of a subordination: "(...) pour m'attirer à N.S. envers lequel, malgré tant de grâces, je suis ingrate".[58] But it gained her and her compatriots the respect of male clerics as "enfants d'élite et de prédilection de Jésus".[59] Telghuys emphasised that her desire to leave the parental home as a single woman was motivated by her longing "pour m'anéantir". Cornet used her weakness and suffering to successfully justify her desire for independence from Alsemberg: "Je viens d'apprendre qu'Alsemberg sollicite encore mon retour: dans l'effroi et la peine qui m'empêchent de dormir, je suis allée me prosterner aux pieds du Divin Sauveur (...), je viens vous supplier de n'y pas consentir. (...) Mon expérience de plus de 20 ans a assez prouvé non seulement mon impuissance à y faire un bien réel, mais encore le danger où mon salut serait exposé avec une santé faible et une tête épuisée qui ne saurait plus supporter tout ce train (...)."[60]

Cornet's argument also reflected the ambiguous nineteenth-century attitude to the female physique. Kestre and de Meeûs invoked their fragile health to prove their unfitness for traditional convent life, while at the same time creating space for their own innovative projects. On the other hand, the allegedly fragile body of the woman was a source of distrust and ridicule and an argument for her safe confinement within the domestic sphere. The boredom and cramped nature of that life pushed many women into a vicious circle of ailments, fainting and general malaise. For many nineteenth-century angels in the house "ill-health became a way of life".[61] Just as easily, the vulnerable woman could become the chosen framework within which suffering for Christ could take shape, giving rise to female heroism and martyrdom. Even Kestre could in that way use the dominant discourse on women's frailty to create space for recognition and development. "Dans mes courts instants passés auprès de N.S., je pense que cette maladie est une leçon, une expiation, et une préservation. Jamais on n'a autant travaillé à éteindre la foi dans les cœurs et à arrêter la connaissance de la Religion, à étouffer le règne de J.C. dans les cœurs! La maladie enlève généralement plus d'enfants et de jeunes filles pieuses que de personnes âgées ou d'un autre sexe. Dieu ne semble-t-Il

---

57 Hardick, *He Leads, I Follow*, 20; Wenner, "Théodelinde Dubouché", 1743-1745; Fitzgerald, *Habits of Compassion*, 28.
58 ARE, *Extraits traitant de l'origine*: de Meeûs to Boone (1 Jan. 1851).
59 ARE, *Extraits traitant de l'origine*: Boone to de Meeûs (9 Aug. 1855).
60 ASCMLH, A.2: Cornet to Sterckx (28 Aug. 1861).
61 Abrams, *The Making of Modern Women*, 20-29; Smith, *Changing Lives*, 198.

pas dire en les frappant: ce sont là des anges d'expiation qui seront privés d'un avenir funeste."[62]

Again her strategy shows interesting parallels with older examples. In her pioneering study on medieval religious women, Bynum discussed the mechanisms by which the body of the woman and her predetermined destiny to suffer could be a source for development, recognition and fulfilment, even within a discourse of vulnerability and weakness.[63] More recently, La Rocca unveiled similar links between the seventeenth-century devotion to the 'humble' childhood of Jesus and the possibilities for agency and fulfilment for its female devotees.[64] However, Bynum also pointed out that this religious gender language of suffering and physicality confirmed women in a stereotypical role. For the nineteenth-century women in this study too, the ambiguity of the passion paradigm did not bring about a fundamental adjustment in gender conventions. If weakness, suffering or humility could create a platform and legitimacy for agency, these mechanisms also enforced the image of female frailty and modesty. This was also clear in the case of Kestre's visions, which were criticised by the Brussels clergy and the Jesuits as the outcome of the irrational imagination of "cette femme illusionnée".[65] Only a few female followers and her future confessor Dechamps showed some appreciation for her intuitions concerning the divine.

The revival was open to women's supernatural or mystical experiences, but within the boundaries of existing clerical and gender models. In times of social and political turbulence, supernatural apparitions were both a source of images of apocalyptic doom and an appeal for social and religious commitment.[66] In 1833 Marie-Thérèse Haze spoke of a vision of a flying cross and took it as inspiration for the foundation of the *Filles de la Croix* of Liège. In 1830, the French *Fille de la Charité*, Cathérine Labouré, experienced visions of Mary that led to the wide-spread devotion to '*la médaille miraculeuse*'. To protect herself from the nearby liberal university, Anna de Meeûs placed in the Salazar garden a statue of Our Lady of La Salette – a weeping Mary, displeased by religious apostasy, who was said to have appeared to some French shepherd children in 1846.[67] However, visions or intense spiritual experiences were accepted only if they took place in a humble setting or in a context of clear male supervision. In her study about nineteenth-century spiritual female writers in France, Dauzet described this as a "mystique bien tempérée: une mystique

---

62 ADSJ, 1.3./3: Kestre to Dechamps (1859).
63 Bynum, *Holy Feast*, 26-30.
64 La Rocca, "L'Enfant Jésus et les femmes", 35.
65 ADSJ, *Cahier 37.1*: de Villermont to Auchard (20 March 1861).
66 Viaene, *Belgium and the Holy See*, 199; Langlois, "La conjoncture mariale", 37-38; Van Osselaer, "Introduction", 13-14; Kselman, *Miracles and Prophecies*, 102-106.
67 Pietromarchi, *Mère Marie-Thérèse*, 52; Gibson, *A Social History*, 145-146; ARE, *Chronique, XXIV. Maison-Mère*, 248.

bien équilibrée ou réglée, bien surveillée, cadrée par un savoir dogmatique et une vérification ecclésiale".[68] For example, the name of Labouré as the visionary behind the popular miraculous medal remained unknown for years. Kestre's openness about her visions did not measure up to this expectation of humility.[69]

Female saints as role models

Even when, after one of her many setbacks, Kestre exclaimed "je ne peux pas renoncer à une œuvre pour laquelle j'ai souffert le martyr pour plus de dix ans", the discourse of humility was turned against her: "Ste Thérèse se plaisait à répéter que Dieu ne bâtit que sur le néant, et c'est pourquoi elle ne cessa de s'anéantir".[70] The reprimand came from Father Edouard Busine, a Belgian Redemptorist who, from the mid-1850s, was Kestre's spiritual counsellor, and will be discussed further below. His reference to Teresa of Avila was not without significance. The sixteenth-century Carmelite was a role model for nineteenth-century religious women. While Mary was by far the most popular source of inspiration and legitimacy for women's action and passion, Teresa of Avila was one of her crown princesses. She was chosen by many congregation founders as their patron and was at the top of the devotional calendar of the four women in this study. As already stated, devotion to a varied and colourful array of saints was part of the diversity of revival spirituality[71] The devotion to Teresa of Avila was rooted in and surrounded by an aura of sincere female admiration. Anna de Meeûs wrote about: "(...) la séraphique Thérèse, malgré d'autres tempêtes infernales, embrassa la primitive observance avec ses héroïques novices".[72] Teresa had great spiritual authority. As a strict monastic reformer, she answered to the penance and reparation ideal of the revival. She was equally valued in the nineteenth century because she combined the contemplative life of a Carmelite nun with an active and successful life as a convent founder. Unlike the medieval women in Bynum's study whose agency rested almost exclusively on their own suffering relationship with the

---

68 Dauzet, *La mystique bien tempérée*, 17.
69 O'Brien, *Leaving God for God*, 207; Bouflet and Boutry, *Un signe dans le ciel*, 165; Kselman, *Miracles and Prophecies*, 32. The Italian historian Caffiero very powerfully expresses this ambiguity: "La profezia della donne non deborda più dai limiti imposti, non ribalta i ruoli sessuali, 'controdiscorso' femminile, ma esprime l'adesione e l'interiorizzazione da parte della donne della norme e dei discorsi maschili e della categorie che fondano la loro subordinazione." Caffiero, *Religione e modernità*, 179.
70 ADSJ. 1.6: Kestre to Busine (23 Oct. 1858), Busine to Kestre (1 Nov. 1858).
71 Lux-Steritt and Mangion, "Introduction", 14; Sprows Cummings, *New Woman*, 55, 97; Hümmeler, *In hoc signo vinces*, 99. On the veneration of saints during the revival: Viaene, *Belgium and the Holy See*, 195; Atkin and Tallett, *Priests, Prelates and People*, 182-184.
72 ARE, *Chronique. VII. La Croix*, 70.

divine, Teresa of Avila appealed to the spirit of the revival because her prestige was also derived from her actions outside her own convent cell. Moreover, as a woman she managed to hold her own among the prominent male figures of the Counter-Reformation Church, although she too used a highly double-voiced discourse of humility and obedience.[73]

The Counter Reformation as the cradle of women's apostolic convent life and women's commitment to the restoration of the Church also returned in the devotion to another female saint, Jeanne-Françoise de Chantal (1572-1641), who together with Francis de Sales, founded the Visitation Order. As a woman at the head of one of the apostolic institutes that were regarded as pioneers of non-monastic convent life for women, de Chantal was an inspiring figure for de Meeûs, Telghuys and Kestre. Although the active character of her institute was greatly scaled back under ecclesiastical pressure, de Chantal continued to be admired for her commitment to the weak and the poor. Telghuys made her "la patronne de mes œuvres charitables", later chose Jeanne-Françoise as her religious name and wore a relic of de Chantal around her neck throughout her life. Kestre repeatedly referred to de Chantal's humility and obedience in an attempt to gain recognition for her own visions in the mid-1850s: "j'ai lu et relu mme de Chantal qui m'a fait grand bien par son jugement, droiture, simplicité et obéissance à ce qu'elle croyait la volonté de Dieu". In this respect she illustrated the positive influence that role models of women saints could have on the framework for evaluating nineteenth-century women. As has already been noted, the resurgence of the devotion to Mary, and subsequently to figures such as Teresa of Avila and Jeanne de Chantal, was interpreted by several historians as an important catalyst in the nineteenth-century rehabilitation of the woman as the pure and moral guardian of society and an important link in passing on the divine message.[74]

The recognition of female saints also inspired a reassessment of forgotten religious women, such as the medieval saint Juliana of Cornillon or Louise de Marillac, the seventeenth-century co-founder of Vincent de Paul's *Filles de Charité*, whose canonisation was set in motion in the nineteenth century.[75] At the same time, the popularity of these female role models also confirmed female stereotypes, both positive and negative. The nineteenth-century *Filles de Charité*, for example, praised above all the humility of their female founder: "Si elle n'est pas canonisée, c'est saint Vincent qui ne le veut pas ni aucune Fille de la Charité pour nous maintenir dans l'humilité".[76] Kestre's aforementioned attempt to legitimise her own spiritual ideas by referring to de Chantal

---

73 Weber, *Teresa of Avila*, 46-48.
74 Cholvy and Hilaire, *Histoire religieuse*, 176-186; Ford, *Divided Houses*, 107; Abrams, *The Making of Modern Women*, 34-41.
75 On the rediscovery of Louise de Marillac (1591-1660): O'Brien, *Leaving God for God*, 47-48; Brejon de Lavergnée, "Du mythe des origines", 27-33.
76 Cited in Brejon de Lavergnée, "Du mythe des origines", 32.

was fiercely fended off by Father Busine: "Mais ne mettez pas de secrets où il n'y en a pas: c'est une faiblesse de femme, et il faut être homme comme S.J. de Chantal".[77]

Busine's statement associated femininity with weakness and unnecessary secrecy, while de Chantal's boldness and intelligence were seen as masculine qualities. This was a discursive and narrative phenomenon, frequently evident in the context of religious or holy women, which did not help broaden the existing image of women. As a gender language, religion offered opportunities to women to go beyond their own sex and become legitimate exceptions, but it did not in any way change the underlying stereotypes. Dominica Van der Stichele (1816-1887), the founder of a congregation of Dominican Sisters in Bruges, was described by her biographer as a woman with "a big and generous heart, a truly masculine willpower".[78] Similar observations were also recorded in artistic circles. Women artists with unusual qualities were often labelled as masculine or unwomanly. An early twentieth-century Belgian male art critic summarised it thus: "Until recently, painting women could be divided into two categories: those who were not women and those who were not painters."[79] Female development was possible only within the framework of the dominant gender language, both within and outside the framework of the Church and religion.

The admiration for Jeanne-Françoise de Chantal also expressed another desire. De Meeûs wrote to Boone in the summer of 1851: "(...) j'enviais surtout le bonheur de Sainte Chantal d'avoir trouvé quelqu'un qui comprit si bien les besoins de son âme".[80] The male companion of de Chantal, Francis de Sales was, just like Liguori, a promotor of the 'religion of the heart' on to which the nineteenth-century revival was later grafted.[81] With regard to gender views, he was convinced of the close bond between women, "le sexe dévot", and religion. At the same time, he was a child of his time, and shared the view that the female sex "veut être conduit et jamais, en aucun entreprise, il ne réussit que par la soumission".[82] Yet, his charisma made him an exceptional spiritual guide who still spoke to the imagination of the nineteenth century. This tension between female submission on the one hand and fulfilment and recogni-

---

77 ADSJ, 1.6: Kestre to Busine (16 March 1855), Busine to Kestre (4 April 1855).
78 "een groot en edelmoedig hart, een echt mannelijke wilskrascht (sic)". Cited in: Suenens, "Dominica Van der Stichele", 13.
79 "Tot voor kort konden de schilderende vrouwen worden ondergebracht in twee categorieën: zij die geen vrouwen waren en zij die geen schilders waren." Remark by the Belgian art critic Gustave Vanzijpe in 1903, cited in the biography of the painter Henriette Ronner-Knip (1821-1909): Kraaij, *Henriette Ronner-Knip*, 9.
80 ARE, *Extraits traitant de l'origine*: de Meeûs to Boone (29 July 1851).
81 de Giorgio, "La bonne catholique", 193; Van Osselaer, *The Pious Sex*, 42; Cognet, *La Spiritualité Moderne*, 274-277; Bluyssen, "Naar het model van Franciscus van Sales", 111-116.
82 De Sales to the abbess of the Benedictines in Montmartre, cited in: Friedlander, "Les pouvoirs de la supérieure", 243. See also: Ford, *Divided Houses*, 18-19.

tion in spiritual partnerships on the other hand also determined the relationships of the four future founders with their own male spiritual confessors. In the next section, extensive attention will be given to this, because the spiritual partnerships formed an essential part of each woman's trajectory towards a religious vocation and a religious foundation.

PART II

FEMALE AGENCY AT A TURNING POINT: FOUR CONGREGATION FOUNDERS (1857-1867)

> C'était le 5 juillet. C'est en ce jour que, dans la plus grand secret, eut lieu, au cœur de Bruxelles, la fondation de l'Institut, par la prise de possession de son saint asile et l'installation des premières novices.
>
> ARE, *Annales, X. La terre promise.*

The foundation of the *Institut de l'Adoration Perpétuelle* of Anna de Meeûs in the summer of 1857 took place without any celebration or publicity. Circumstances were not favourable to enter *"la terre promise"* of convent life. At the end of May of that year, the political tensions surrounding the Convent Law had given rise to street protests and the vandalising of some Brussels convents.[1] The fear was that the rumour of a new religious foundation would rekindle unrest. The foundation faced other difficulties as well. The aristocratic families of de Meeûs' companions, Léopoldine de Robiano, Caroline Cogels, Zoé de Jonghe and Julie Desmanet de Biesme, reacted with mixed feelings to their daughters choosing a religious institution without a pedigree, ignoring other, more prestigious alternatives.[2] The secular clergy in Brussels distrusted the opening of a new convent chapel and the hold that influential Jesuits had on the young community. Existing congregations or women with similar plans feared the competition from an extra player in the contest for ecclesiastical support, benefactors and novices.

Post-1850 congregation founders, including the four women of our study, found themselves at a turning point. The decade in which the four foundations took place began in 1857 with the agitation around the Convent Law. It ended in 1867 with the Third Congress of Mechelen, which called for the mobilisation of the Catholic world against liberal anticlericalism, but which also witnessed sharp differences between liberal-Catholic defenders of "l'église libre dans l'état libre" and a growing group of ultramontane Catholics. The latter felt threatened by anticlericalism and sought refuge in a rejection of the modern world and in a militant struggle for the restoration of a society built on religious foundations. In the meantime, decisions in Rome reinforced the polarisation and created the framework for growing adulation of the pope, militancy and intransigence. In 1864, with his encyclical *Quanta Cura* and the accompanying *Syllabus Errorum*, Pius IX issued the manifesto of an ultramon-

---

1 Van Kalken, *Commotions populaires*, 41-42; Deneckere, *Geuzengeweld*, 37-61; Koppen, *De Kloosterkwestie*, 58-61.
2 Zoé de Jonghe (1814-1875), after 1857 'de Jonghe d'Ardoye', came from an aristocratic Catholic family whose main residence was in Ardooie. Her father Auguste-Charles (1783-1868) was a member of the National Congress and later became a senator in the Catholic right-wing party.

tane struggle against the liberal foundations of post-revolutionary society. The harmonious thoughts of the revival had to make way for the crusade of the so-called 'Zouave ultramontanism'.[3]

In this context, the four founders struggled with new motives, old prejudices and rigid gender patterns that presented both opportunities and obstacles. This section focuses on each of the four women's trajectory to founding an actual congregation. In the first two chapters, the *dramatis personae* in the foundation process are presented through an analysis of the spiritual partnerships of the women with the male actors and the forging of female alliances, with special attention paid to the interesting mechanisms of double-voiced affection, dominance and rivalry. In the third chapter, I will examine the role of the female founders against the background of changing diocesan and Roman church politics.

---

3   Lamberts, "Het ultramontanisme", 49-51; Aubert, *L'Église dans le monde moderne*, 42-49; Harrison, *Romantic Catholics*, 238-239; Viaene, "A Pope's Dilemma", 250-251.

Jesuit Aloysius Legrelle (1818-1883) was in charge of several Jesuit colleges and residences in Belgium during the nineteenth century. An expert in the organisation and regulation of female convent life, he became an advisor to both Antoinette Cornet and Wilhelmina Telghuys.
[Photograph – S.d. – KADOC]

BETWEEN LONGING AND COERCION

SPIRITUAL PARTNERSHIPS

When Virginia Woolf, writing about the art of biography, referred to the difficult symbiosis between 'the rainbow and the granite', she probably did not have a religious vocation in mind.[1] Still there are few elements that are so determinative and at the same time so 'rainbow-like intangible' as the longing for a metaphysical, divine point of reference. Wilhelmina Telghuys, while working in her *Sint-Franciscus-Xaveriusinstituut* in 1863, felt for the first time "que je n'agissais pas par moi-même, et qu'un esprit qui ne m'appartenait pas, conduisait tout mon être".[2] In 1851 de Meeûs also sensed she was being "fortement poussée par Dieu. (...) Ces pensées me revenant sans cesse (...) je crus que pour mettre ma conscience à l'aise, le mieux était d'écrire au p. Boone".[3] Although neither experienced the passionate visions of Kestre, a divine call was undoubtedly given a place in their lives. As for many others, a religious vocation was intangible and confusing, arousing both fascination and disbelief. Their demanding involvement in apostolate work in an ideologically polarised society and their uncertainty about their definitive life choices had already created a desire for moral support. The struggle with a religious calling intensified that feeling. The pressure of dominant gender and clerical patterns was ubiquitous and pushed the women towards a priest-di-

---

1 On Woolf's theme in relation to the intangibility of a religious vocation, see: Lancaster, *Cornelia Connelly*, 247-248.
2 ADHH, 253: *Annales des Servantes des Sacrés-Cœurs*, 65.
3 ARE, *Extraits pour perpétuer le souvenir* (1851).

rector. In their quest for a spiritual confidant, longing and coercion competed for a leading role.

Telghuys, Kestre, de Meeûs and Cornet chose their own male allies, often after an arduous process of trial and error. In this respect, their foundation narratives show strong parallels with recent international historical research on female founders. These studies analyse the formation of spiritual partnerships from a complementary and not an exclusively male hierarchical perspective.[4] Although the male allies had their own agendas and tried, in varying degrees of domination, to link them to the women's motives, the stories of the four women in this study did not become copies of traditional, very male-tinted foundation narratives. Priests were often given the leading role in these narratives, limiting the part played by the 'pious daughters' under their care to one of amenable docility.[5] Sometimes, as in the case of the already mentioned rural congregations in West- and East-Flanders, this script was very plausible. However, exclusive attention to male entrepreneurial drive could also wrongly assume the absence of substantial female input. A typical example of this approach is the long list of priest founders mentioned in Boudens' article about female convent life in the Diocese of Bruges. Male founders were acknowledged, while the influential role of female founders such as Agatha Lagae (1799-1864) in Heule or Annette Serweytens (1822-1888) in Bruges were neglected. Lagae initiated, financed and developed the congregation of the *Zusters van Liefde* (Sisters of Charity) in her home village, while Serweytens conceived the original plan – analysed further on in this study – of a religious institute for both active and contemplative sisters.[6] Together with the foundation narratives presented here, these examples can be an argument against allowing the gender balance to be tilted too far to the male side. Women with strong charismatic, elitist or apostolic credentials continually fluctuated between admiration and scepticism, autonomy and submission.

---

[4] Eijt, *Gesticht door stichtsters*, 177-178; Rocca "Les jésuites", 136; Mangion, *Contested Identities*, 159; McGuinness, "Why Relationships Matter", 221-230.

[5] See for example: De Meulemeester, *Geschiedenis der Zusters van St.-Vincentius te Deinze*, 14-16. The Redemptorist Maurits De Meulemeester (1879-1961), historian of his institute, was very active as the author of monographs about female religious institutes. It is to his credit that this historical '*terra incognita*' got some attention in the mid-twentieth century. De Meulemeester generally documented his research well, but - probably partly because of the scarcity of source material about female protagonists - he focused mainly on the role of male founders.

[6] Boudens, "De parochiepastoors", 423-424. On Lagae and Serwetyens, see: Maes et al., "150 jaar Klooster", 1-48; Rotsaert, "Annette Serweytens", 131-142.

"Une religieuse, c'est une paroisse": frustration and appreciation

The emotional quest for stability

From her difficult social position on the edge of bourgeois decency, Telghuys found a refuge in Father Bogaerts and in the *Sint-Augustinus* parish in 1862-1863. On the apostolate level, it was a fruitful alliance. Telghuys not only engaged in the parish's Xaverian Society, she also participated in local catechesis and youth work. In return, Bogaerts offered her patronage and a socially acceptable label for her laundry and orphanage as well as access to his social network. The spiritual and emotional rapprochement between the two, which ultimately formed the basis for the foundation of the congregation, followed a similar pattern. Continuing pressure and criticism from her bourgeois milieu and her family did not leave even a free-spirited woman like Telghuys unaffected. Until the death of her mother in 1865, however, her desire to please them remained. Nevertheless, as becomes clear from some of her intimate, personal writings and prayers, her hunger for family affection clashed with her growing appreciation for the passion paradigm of the revival: "que je suis encore méprisable, Seigneur, (...) je me plais pour plaire aux autres créatures plutôt que de m'élever vers Vous en me servant de leurs mépris comme marchepieds pour arriver à Vous".[7] Bogaerts helped Telghuys to deal with her experiences, both her attachment to her family as well as her divine inspiration: "C'est aux sages conseils et aux soins paternels de ce Saint homme, que je dois les lumières que Dieu daigna m'accorder pour me faire sortir de la vie inutile que je menais. Je m'abandonnais aveuglement à sa direction, et il ne m'est jamais arrivé de douter un instant de la prudence de ses avis. Je crois m'avoir jamais eu à me reprocher de lui avoir désobéi."[8]

Telghuys probably recorded this last remark after Bogaerts' death in 1877, so it carries a certain tinge of retrospective melancholy. Still, it illustrated the ambiguous and double-voiced position of women religious in the nineteenth-century Church, also described in international literature. As Mangion and Eijt point out in their history of English religious and Dutch semi-religious women or Marcélis concerning Belgian contemplative sisters, many religious considered spiritual support to be a privilege and the accompanying obedience a duty. It becomes clear, however, that this promised obedience did not necessarily imply a lack of female agency.[9]

---

7 ADHH, 41: Notes of Jan Bergen, note by Telghuys, À la plus grande gloire de Dieu.
8 ADHH, 16: Verest Manuscript, 15.
9 Mangion, *Contested identities*, 213-214; Eijt, "Leeuw en lam", 38-39; Marcélis, *Femmes cloîtrées*, 331.

In early-twentieth-century accounts on the relationship between Bogaerts and Telghuys was stated that he withheld her from unwise or 'rash' actions; a stereotypical, but very common representation. The influential Cardinal Wiseman (1802-1865), though an ardent promoter of female convent life in England, spoke of regulating "le fragile figlie di Eva" when discussing the role of male clerics in the context of a convent foundation.[10] In accounts on Belgian congregation founders like Voirin, Haze or d'Oultremont, women had to be restrained or 'broken' by their confessors in their spiritual passions or their apostolic hubris, which were labelled as "une extravagance, une folie".[11] To a large extent, this characterisation naturally followed the stereotypical gender patterns of that time. Viaene has already pointed out that the average nineteenth-century Belgian village parish priest did not think very highly of the extremely devout women or 'kwezels' in his parish.[12] McNamara called it "the clergyman's burden": the priest's fear of women's seductiveness and irrationality, mixed with doubts about his own spiritual qualities.[13]

Bogaerts' role too reflected some of these presumptions, as did the setting of the photograph on the cover of this book. He was deterred not so much by her spiritual passions – in this Telghuys was quite moderate – as by her adventurous behaviour. Despite her avowed obedience, a conflict broke out with Bogaerts in 1864 about her decision to purchase a commercial property on the *Sint-Jorisvest*.[14] Without financial reserves and a laundry business that was not yet generating a sufficient income, she got herself into a risky agreement with the owner about monthly repayments. Although Telghuys relied on the 'economy of providence', which often was the basis of heroic but at the same time reckless religious entrepreneurship, she was severely rebuked by Bogaerts for "cette imprudence des femmes".[15]

The male fear of autonomous and divinely inspired women had already affected the life of Fanny Kestre in the 1850s. Disappointed in both the Jesuits and the Brussels clergy, in the second half of the 1850s she looked to the Redemptorists for support. The Congregation of the Most Holy Redeemer established its first house in Belgium in 1831 and then quickly took up a position on the barricades of the Belgian revival Church with its pastoral focus on popular missions, retreats and confraternities. The Redemptorists had been in Brus-

---

10 Lancaster, *Cornelia Connelly*, 246.
11 Duhamelet, *Mère Marie-Xavier Voirin*, 84, 123; Pietromarchi, *Mère Marie-Thérèse Haze*, 39; Suau, *La mère Marie de Jésus*, 20-21.
12 Viaene, "De ontplooiing van een 'vrije' kerk", 60.
13 McNamara, *Sisters in Arms*, 220. Similar conclusions in: Kane, "She offered herself up", 106 and Scaraffia, "Christianity has liberated her", 255-256.
14 This was the former laundry '*De Jonge Handboog*', which Telghuys bought in 1864 for 85,000 francs. ADHH, 109: Notarial acts; ADHH, 253: *Annales des Servantes des Sacrés-Cœurs*, 56-57.
15 ABA, File Dienstmaagden H. Harten: Bogaerts to Sterckx (17 Nov. 1864). See also: Van Dijck (ed.), *Economics of Providence*.

sels since 1841, but only really gained a foothold in the capital when in 1849 they accepted responsibility for the *Saint-Joseph* church, located in the elitist *Léopold* district. The district had been conceived by Ferdinand de Meeûs and was part of the urbanisation plans of mid-nineteenth-century Brussels.[16]

Kestre initially came into contact with the aforementioned Redemptorist, Edouard Busine (1818-1888), who came from the Chimay region of Kestre's family. Like many of his colleagues, Busine was an energetic preacher, but his letters reveal him to have been an affable man with a genuine concern for Kestre's problems. Without actually encouraging her, he offered a listening ear for her visionary inspirations.[17] He became Kestre's main advisor in her catechesis and retreat work. With his support, she decided in 1856 to leave her parents' home and move into a room near the premises of her apostolates, first in Brussels, then in Saint-Josse-ten-Noode. Kestre saw it as the start of her novitiate 'in the world', based on the blueprint of a convent life revealed to her by God.[18] However, both Kestre and Busine had seriously underestimated the rigidity of the reigning gender patterns. Even though single women were not unusual in nineteenth-century Brussels, they were an anomaly in the bourgeois discourse of motherhood and family. Church and society were quite intolerant of the single, relatively poor, but enterprising Kestre "qui est ni particulière, ni religieuse".[19]

Her visions and her desperate desire to monopolise Busine fully for her own spiritual and apostolate needs gave critics additional arguments against her. Her fiercest opponents, in particular the Brussels secular clergy around Dean Verhoustraeten, quickly set their sights on Busine. Gossip about overly intimate ties between him and Kestre reached the Belgian provincial and finally the general of the Redemptorists in Rome. In 1859-1860 Busine was ordered to detach himself from his protégée and to concentrate fully on his preaching mission.[20] Kestre, as usual, resisted passionately and clung to Busine, who was completely distraught. The provincial, Kockerols, however, responded rather ironically: "Vous ignorez peut-être, Mademoiselle, que dans un ordre religieux les sujets n'ont pas le droit de contrarier les décisions des supérieurs?"[21]

As provincial of the Redemptorists, Kockerols had to deal with the deepening ideological tensions of the second half of the nineteenth century. The

16 De Meulemeester, *De Belgische Redemptoristenprovincie*, 11; Becque, *Le Cardinal Dechamps*, I, 320-321. On the *Léopold* district, see: Leroy, "Quand l'aristocratie".
17 ADSJ, 1.3./1: Journal of Kestre (8 May 1856); ADSJ, 1.6: Kestre to Busine (20 Sept. 1856).
18 ADSJ, 1.3./1: Journal of Kestre (30 Jan. 1856).
19 ADSJ, 1.6: Kestre to Aertssens (parish priest of Saint-Josse-ten-Noode) (5 Sept. 1864); Gubin, *Choisir l'histoire des femmes*, 148-149.
20 ADSJ, 1.6: Van Achter to Kestre (6 April 1859 and s.d.), Kestre to Leloucher (11 Dec. 1859).
21 ADSJ: Kockerols to Kestre (8 Jan. 1860). Jean Kockerols (1823-1894) was provincial of the Belgian Redemptorists from 1857 to 1874 and from 1880 to 1893. See: De Meulemeester, *De Belgische Redemptoristenprovincie*, 17; Art, "Documents", 357-358.

Jean Kockerols (1823-1894) (left), the strict provincial of the Belgian Redemptorists was a fierce critic of Kestre's visionary and unconventional behaviour and forbade his fathers to have close contact with her. Not all of them followed his directions, however. His fellow Redemptorist and future archbishop of Mechelen, Victor Dechamps (1810-1883) (right), showed more affinity for passionate religious women and was Kestre's spiritual director for more than a quarter of century.
[Photographs – S.d. – KADOC]

growing anticlericalism among liberal radicals targeted the clergy and their avid proselytism of 'vulnerable' children and women. In accordance with the already mentioned separate spheres discourse, liberal newspapers of the 1850s and 1860s fiercely complained about parish priests who had female confessees in their power and influenced family life and the voting behaviour of their husbands.[22] During the same period, for example, Father Bogaerts was involved in the sensational Kohrsch affair. Together with his friend, the Jesuit Philippe Schoofs, he was accused of having converted a Protestant girl, Anna Bella Kohrsch, against the will of her guardian. Bogaerts was also suspected of having helped her to 'escape' from her family, after which she went into hiding in French and Belgian convents for months. The two priests were acquitted

22 On Belgian liberal criticism of the influence of parish priests in the confessional, see for example: *L'Indépendance Belge* (10 June 1852, 2; 13 Dec. 1857, 2); Koppen, *De Kloosterkwestie*, 128-131; Morelli, "Les thèmes de la caricature".

by the correctional court of Ghent and were subsequently hailed as heroes by the Catholic community in Antwerp. It was one of those highly publicised cases of the second half of the nineteenth century with religious in the leading role and Catholics and liberals diametrically opposed to each other.[23]

In this context, the ecclesiastical authorities counselled priests to be more cautious and detached in the confessional.[24] Kockerols, with his reputation as a strict and authoritarian provincial, also strongly emphasised the sanctity of his priests as "the first weapon of the warrior for Christ" on the barricades of the revival.[25] Writing to Marie-Barbe Maus-Poncelet (1789-1873), one of Kestre's catechesis collaborators and a trusted confidant, the provincial made no effort to conceal the true nature of Busine's departure: "c'est un devoir de conscience pour moi de ne pas exposer mes Pères au ridicule qui touche sur votre œuvre (...) de nature à nous compromettre devant le public et devant les autorités ecclésiastiques les plus respectables, et nous avons, en ce temps malheureux surtout, besoin à toute notre réputation".[26]

Anticlerical pressure, strict gender patterns and clerical caution were in this way sometimes detrimental to the spiritual needs and spiritual originality of religious women. They also discouraged the often sincere efforts of individual priests in the field. After the painful separation between Kestre and Busine, Father Van Achter offered Kestre an apology in his place: "Quant à la règle de St. Alph. [Alphonse], elle nous défend toute espèce de direction de couvent ou d'un institut quelconque; c'est sans doute à cause de ce paragraphe que les supérieurs en ont décidé de la sorte. *Pardonnez-moi*".[27] Van Achter paved the way for an illustrious colleague, Victor Dechamps (1810-1883), who paid little attention to the prohibitions of his founder Alphonsus or the restrictions of Kockerols. As a charismatic shepherd of souls, he was the opposite of his strict provincial. His spiritual relationship with Kestre would last for a quarter of a century and will be fully analysed in the following chapters. Dechamps, nonetheless, sometimes also complained about the complex aspects of spiritual guidance: "St. François de Sales (je crois que c'est lui) disait qu'une religieuse, était une paroisse".[28]

---

23   See: ABSE, 4.2.6. Schoofs Philippe, 15738: *Le Procès Anna-Bella Kohrsch*. Years later in 1876, Bogaerts was denied an appointment in the Order of Leopold by the liberal Antwerp mayor Léopold De Wael (1872-1892) because of his involvement in the Kohrsch affair. See: RAA, Archive of the Province of Antwerp, series N, 146/76: De Wael to the Antwerp provincial governor (29 April 1876).
24   Van Osselaer, *The Pious Sex*, 47-48.
25   ADSJ, 1.6: Kockerols to Kestre (8 Jan. 1860); Art, "Documents", 357-358.
26   ADSJ. 1.6: Kockerols to Maus (24 Aug. 1861).
27   ADSJ, 1.6: Van Achter to Kestre (6 April 1859). Felix Van Achter (1819-1862), initially a priest in the Diocese of Ghent, was professed a Redemptorist in 1850. See: Laurent, "Felix Van Achter".
28   ACSSR-NB, 1496: Dechamps to Fanny Kestre (1 May 1867). On the mutual antipathy between Dechamps and Kockerols, see: Art, "Documents", 357-358.

The Jesuits in the entourage of de Meeûs and Boone had reservations too about closely collaborating with female religious: "une œuvre qui exige le concours des femmes, on ne fera rien de stable que l'on n'a pas eu le bonheur de rencontre une âme bien tempérée".[29] Moreover, they referred – just as Van Achter had in the case of the Redemptorists – to the incompatibility of the 'curia monialium' with the constitutions of the Society of Jesus. In the sixteenth century, the founder Ignatius had explicitly forbidden close relationships between Jesuits and female religious. According to Ignatius, such close involvement had devastating consequences for the flexible deployment of members in the apostolate that was so characteristic of the order.[30] Yet, whether rhetorical or real, male reservations about religious women did not prevent the emergence of a framework of appreciation and a space for complementary and close relationships. International literature has already pointed out that medieval and early-modern spiritual partnerships between religious women and men could also be a source of mutual inspiration.[31] This pattern returned in the nineteenth century. In enclosed convents intense spiritual ties existed between spiritual mothers who prayed and collected alms for their spiritual priest-sons in the world.[32] Dauzet and Müller showed that in nineteenth-century France nuns and sisters as well as Catholic lay women could inspire their spiritual directors.[33] Moreover, founders of typical nineteenth-century Catholic priest societies, such as Eymard, d'Alzon and Dehon, were inspired by the reparative devotions or the suffering discourse of female religious.[34]

An emotional Redemptorist and a tempted Jesuit

The earliest contacts between Dechamps and Kestre dated from the second half of the 1850s, shortly after Dechamps' mandate as provincial (1851-1854) of the Belgian Redemptorists had ended. In the meantime, he had become a prominent figure in the Belgian Church and in his congregation, as well as a close friend of Pope Pius IX. Together with his brother Adolphe (1807-1875), a Catholic-inspired member of parliament and minister in a number of unionist governments, he embodied the social success of his originally modest *Hainaut* family. Both brothers propagated the liberal-Catholic belief in the possi-

29 ABSE, 4.2.3. Jean-Baptiste Boone, 1226: Notes of Father Joseph Broeckaert, 5.
30 O'Malley, *The first Jesuits*, 335-345; Suenens, "Jésuites", 249-270.
31 Griffiths and Hotchin, *Women and Men*, 5-6; Monteiro, *Geestelijke maagden*, 345-346.
32 Marcélis, *Femmes cloitrées*, 452-454; Rotsaert, "Annette Serweytens", 131-142.
33 Dauzet, *La mystique bien tempérée*, 18-22; Muller, *Au plus près des âmes*, 336-337.
34 Pierre Eymard (1811-1868), founder of the Congregation of the Blessed Sacrament, was inspired by the Eucharistic spirituality of the already mentioned Theodelinde Dubouché. The correspondence between Emmanuel d'Alzon (1810-1880), founder of the Assumptionists, and Milleret, founder of the *Sœurs de l'Assomption*, reads like a spiritual love story. Dehon was fascinated by the suffering spirituality of the *Servantes du Sacré-Cœur*. See: Harris, *Lourdes*, 226-236; Ledure, *Le Père Léon Dehon*, 173.

bility of reconciling religion and progress. Victor Dechamps' decision to enter the Redemptorists in 1835, following earlier seminary studies in Tournai, was consistent with his dynamic revival spirit. He was an emotional orator and an influential opinion maker, with an audience at the royal court and in the upper-class Catholic salons of the capital. After entering the Redemptorists he appealed to his social network to encourage high-born ladies from the Brussels *Léopold* district to become involved in charitable work.[35]

While Dechamps' great prestige opened doors for him to the aristocratic châteaux, his troubled and poetic spirit gave him a deep affinity with Romantic soulmates. He oscillated between a keen awareness of his ecclesiastical dignity on the one hand – certainly after his appointment as bishop of Namur in 1865 and archbishop of Mechelen in 1867 – and a deep emotional empathy on the other. In dealing with women who struggled with their existential choices and religiosity, his sensitivity often bested his usual elitist reserve. As confessor to the royal children in Laeken, he tried to help the impetuous Princess Charlotte (1840-1927) in the mid-1850s through a crisis of faith. He maintained an emotional correspondence with Camille du Bourg, the above-mentioned Catholic writer who struggled with her literary ambitions and her deteriorating health, and died young. At the end of the 1860s he was impressed by the visions and stigmata of the Walloon working-class girl Louise Lateau (1850-1883) and defended her against critics and sceptics.[36] Dechamps also showed goodwill towards passionate, but poorly supported foreign women religious. He helped both the French founder of the *Consolatrices du Cœur de Jésus* (Comforters of the Heart of Jesus), Jeanne-Françoise Bel (1843-1922) and her compatriot, Marie Deluil-Martiny (1841-1884), founder of the *Filles du Sacré Cœur de Jésus* (Daughters of the Sacred Heart of Jesus), to find a home in Belgium.[37]

Dechamps' affinity with Lateau and Bel, women with visions, stigmata and ecstasies, resembled his spiritual relationship with Kestre. Unlike Verhoustraeten, Sterckx or Kockerols, he allowed the nineteenth-century revival's appreciation for and admiration of miracles and mystical experiences to take precedence over the distrust of the female nature. In his dealings with Kestre, who 'claimed' Deschamps in the early 1860s as her regular spiritual director, he showed both his paternalism and his vulnerability. Kestre had not learned anything from the unfortunate affair with Busine and bombarded Dechamps with letters, cards and requests for personal contact. Dechamps advocated patience and moderation with humour and irony: "vous m'êtes une occasion de pratiquer la condescendance si recommandée par St. f. de Sales,

---

35 For a good profile of Dechamps, see: Viaene, "De ontplooiing van een 'vrije' kerk", 40-42. For a detailed, if somewhat apologetic biography, see: Becque, *Le Cardinal Dechamps*.
36 de Haulleville, *Portraits et silhouettes*, I, 233-239; Becque, *Le Cardinal Dechamps*, II, 101-111; Van Osselaer, "The 'Affair of the Photographs'", 798.
37 *Une âme réparatrice*, 133-134; Becque, *Le Cardinal Dechamps*, II, 141-142.

mais elle aussi doit avoir ses limites".[38] He could also show his sensitive side. Mutual criticisms about a lack of respect, commitment or perseverance were many, although they also created a curious space for openness and intimacy. In her letters with Dechamps, Kestre sincerely tried to integrate her passionate desire for support and comfort within traditional gender and clerical roles: "Ne suis-je pas votre fille, couverte de votre manteau de protection (...)?". But once again, when Dechamps did not immediately attend to her needs, some impertinence slipped in: "Est-ce ainsi que St François de Sales a agi avec Ste Chantal et cependant vous avez promis pour moi, d'être ce qu'il a été pour elle".[39] Fortunately, Dechamps had a much greater sensibility for female worries and desires than Sterckx. He protested *pro forma* against Kestre's tone, but generally accepted Kestre's attention not without pleasure.

Often, their correspondence became a shared lamentation about their poor health – as much an obsession for Dechamps as for the swooning women of popular imagination – and their hectic but lonely lives: "Puis, à certaines heures, le soir surtout, quand je sens le besoin de débander l'arc, c'est-à-dire de reposer la tête, je n'aurai plus personne, je serai seul (...). Priez pour moi".[40] The tone of complaint intensified when Dechamps was unexpectedly appointed bishop of Namur by Pope Pius IX in 1865, and when Kestre contracted cholera in 1866, following a visit to one of her ill catechism pupils. However, the essence of their affinity lay in their shared belief in Kestre's divine inspirations. Dechamps was impressed by her discourse of suffering and atonement and was also the first to listen to her plans for a congregation.[41] It was no coincidence that Dechamps, who was very susceptible to the Romantic nostalgia of the revival, introduced Juliana of Cornillon as a model for Kestre. As has already been mentioned, devotion to this thirteenth-century religious, hermit and promoter of the feast of Corpus Christi, was revived in the nineteenth century and was enthusiastically advocated by Dechamps.[42]

Dechamps' admiration for both the visionary experiences and the misfortunes of Julienne's life inspired him to sympathise with Kestre's longing for full religious status, a safe space in which she could shape her spiritual and apostolic ambitions.[43] Initially he advised her to adhere to her lay status, "libre d'aller et de venir, afin que la maison de Bruxelles subsiste et prospère".[44]

38 ADSJ, 1.4: Dechamps to Kestre (20 Oct. 1870).
39 ADSJ, 1.3./3: Kestre to Dechamps (ca. 1860).
40 ADSJ, 1.4: Dechamps to Kestre (19 Nov. 1865).
41 ACSSR-NB, 1496: Dechamps to Kestre (14 Feb. 1866).
42 ACSSR-NB, 1496: Dechamps to Kestre (6 Oct. 1866, 10 Feb. 1867). On Julienne of Cornillion, see: Mulder-Bakker, *Lives of the Anchoresses*, 79-111. In 1845 Dechamps published a brochure about the feast of Corpus Christi and Juliana of Cornillon. ACSSR-NB, 1496: Printer's proofs *Culte de Sainte-Julienne*.
43 ADSJ, 1.3./3: Kestre to Dechamps, (s.d. (ca. 1867), 29 June 1859); ADSJ, 1.4: Dechamps to Kestre (1 Oct. 1867).
44 ADSJ, 1.4: Dechamps to Kestre (14 Oct. 1866).

Jean-Baptiste Boone (1794-1871) was one of the most eminent members of the Society of Jesus in Belgium. He re-established the Jesuits in Brussels and was a renowned preacher, spiritual adviser and pamphleteer. Despite his authoritarian attitude, he admired and valued women's religious engagement and played a decisive role in the development of Anna de Meeûs and her congregation.
[Photograph – ca. 1870 – KADOC]

Here again, Dechamps showed himself to be a child of the revival, with an appreciation for the benefits of lay initiative and action in the world. Only after his appointment as bishop of Namur would the foundation of Kestre's convent take shape.

In Antwerp, Bogaerts also supported Telghuys' growing desire for a religious life. On the one hand, he was impressed by her strong commitment to the Xaverian society and to the catechesis and youth work in his parish. On the other hand, he also confirmed Telghuys in a traditional female role and an affective and repentant piety as the "épouse de Jésus Christ, qui attend encore de vous des larmes de compassion pour son cœur surtout qui souffre de la perte de tant d'âmes".[45] In Brussels, Jean-Baptiste Boone became the fatherly Francis de Sales figure for which de Meeûs longed. However, the relationship of de Meeûs and Boone cannot be reduced to one of female doubt and male consolation. Even Boone, with his long track record as a spiritual director, was impressed by de Meeûs' ardour for the Blessed Sacrament and her youthful energy. Boone was in his late fifties and after a rich life as founder, preacher, pamphleteer and confessor, he seemed ready for a period of spiritual reflection: "Cependant le surcroit d'occupations extérieures me rendait souvent négligent".[46] But, there was more going on. In the spring of 1853, in an unusually intimate letter to the dying general of the Jesuits, Jan Roothaan, he recounted his struggle with "des très violentes tentations contre la pureté".[47] Boone gave no further details about the nature of the temptation and stressed that he had never given in to the temptations. Deeply affected by his feelings, however, he searched for some spiritual balance.

His meeting with Anna de Meeûs and her request for support had aroused mixed feelings in him. On the one hand he feared he would relapse into his old temptations. On the other hand, her charities and her devotion to the Eucharist gave him a new purpose in life: "Cette bonne œuvre réveille donc la dévotion de mon enfance, de ma jeunesse et de mon scolasticat. Je reviens en quelque sorte à moi! Je suis triste d'y avoir pensé si tard (...)".[48] Boone and de Meeûs quickly reached a consensus on the foundation of a new religious institute devoted to Eucharistic adoration. Equally important was the intention to give the *Œuvre des Églises Pauvres* a more solid structure. The rapid expansion in the 1850s meant that the association could not continue to be run solely on volunteer work by lay women. Co-ordinating the association therefore became

---

45 ADHH, 28: Sermons of Bogaerts.
46 ABSE, 4.2.6. Jean-Baptiste Boone, 1223: Commentary by Father De Buck.
47 Ibidem. The date of the letter is not clear. At the end of his life, Boone dated a copy to 15 July 1853, but that is impossible given the fact that Roothaan had already died on 8 May 1853. The original of the letter was never found. Father Victor De Buck (1817-1876) quotes the letter almost entirely in his commentary on Boone's life. He confirmed that the letter was indeed answered by the dying Roothaan, in the form of a short blessing.
48 Ibidem.

the main objective of new congregation, which saw the light of day in the difficult circumstances of 1857.[49]

Bogaerts and Telghuys also wanted to anchor their apostolates in a stable religious institute: he saw the potential for giving structural support to his parish work, while she was searching for a stable structure for her fragile laundry project. Moreover, after the loss of her mother, Telghuys had to handle her affairs from the dubious position of a single lay woman. In spite of the prejudices outlined above against the restrictions imposed by convent life on the individual, its collective strength and esteemed status appealed to committed religious women. Internationally, this attractive feature of convent life has been repeatedly highlighted. Where lay initiatives ran up against bourgeois, material and gender boundaries, religious life provided women with prestige, stability and possibilities for personal development.[50]

Moreover, because of the strongly gendered spiritual partnerships, female religious had more bargaining power than non-ordained religious men. The nineteenth century witnessed an increase not only in the number of women's congregations but also of active religious congregations of brothers. In their social engagement, organisational structure and humility towards the clergy, they were very similar to the congregations of sisters. However, the emotional relationships between priests and religious women rarely found a parallel among men, with the result that the brothers were deprived of the chance to gain more prestige or room for fulfilment through the gendered interaction of appreciation and temptation. For the brothers, the relation with priest-confessors was reduced to its clerical essence: the dominating and unyielding hierarchy between clergy and non-clergy.[51]

While many *dames d'œuvres* entered religious life in order to develop their apostolic engagement, it was not an attractive option for upper-class *hommes d'œuvres* to opt for the humble status of a religious brother. Social and clerical patterns were sometimes more rigid than gender relations.

However, there was no question of any fundamental change. Appreciation and admiration by male clerics did not preclude adherence to the prevailing gender or clerical views. Since her appointment in 1859 as superior of the community of sisters in La Hulpe, Antoinette Cornet – *Mère Gonzague* – had

---

49 ARE, *Chronique. V. Vers l'institut religieux*, 46-49.
50 Luddy, *Women and Philanthropy*, 24; Mangion, *Contested Identities*, 88; O'Brien, "Religious Life for Women", 121-122.
51 Scholarly surveys examining the social and clerical position of nineteenth-century brother congregations are scarce. Exceptions are the publications of Van Vugt on the Netherlands and O'Donoghue on the English-speaking world. They both extensively emphasised the low social and subordinate clerical status of religious brothers. See: Van Vugt, *Broeders*, 51-54, 158; O'Donoghue, *Catholic Teaching Brothers*, 39-55. There are similar findings for Belgium in monographs and articles; see: Stockman, *Broeders in actie*, 133-134; Suenens, "Glorieux", 81-86; Hermans, *Scheppers*, 27; Wouters, *Broeders*, 27-61.

built up a good relationship with the local parish priest, Jean-Baptiste Chevalier (1810-1899). He urged the city council and his parishioners to support the sisters and their school.[52] Material help was welcome for the first group of sisters, who lacked food, furniture and heating.[53] In 1861-1862 Chevalier increasingly presented himself as a protector and spokesperson for the sisters in their continual conflicts with the motherhouse in Alsemberg, especially in financial matters.[54] As long as Alsemberg remained a threat to her hard-won autonomy in La Hulpe, Cornet resorted to Chevalier and the submissive tone of the dominant gender discourse: "soumettre toutes mes difficultés, à Monsieur le Curé et qu'ainsi je ne pouvais me perdre".[55] It became clear however that she had paid a price for the partnership with Chevalier. Gradually the sisters became a group of parish workers. With Chevalier being increasingly consulted by Mechelen about "vos religieuses", Cornet risked disappearing into the background.[56]

The same happened in Antwerp, where Telghuys also experienced pressure from Bogaerts. He did not see her refuge and laundry work for orphans and girls as her most important field of action, and wanted to channel her efforts towards his own parish work: Sunday schools, leisure activities for girls, catechism classes and distributing alms for the neighbourhood's poor. In a blatantly dominant male discourse, he made a request to Telghuys and her first companions in the summer of 1866: "Maintenant, mesdemoiselles, (...), je viens vous demander si vous voulez vous dévouer à notre paroisse, me seconder dans les œuvres qui y sont établies et vous mettre sous ma directoire?".[57] Moreover, Bogaerts was not afraid to impose his personal spiritual preferences on Telghuys. As parish priest of *Sint-Augustinus*, the ancient monastic church of the Antwerp Augustinians, he became fascinated by the spirituality of the patron saint and his order.[58]

Dechamps too occasionally called Kestre to order with remarks that highlighted both her inferiority and female fragility. He often advised against reading complex spiritual writings, even though they were written by female role models. For example, *Le château de l'*âme by Teresa of Avila was suitable only for "âmes plus saintes que vous".[59] When Kestre wanted to impose a stricter schedule and a more intense prayer regime on herself, he tempered her am-

---

52 Wautrecht and Pandor, *La Hulpe*, 88-91.
53 ASCMLH: *Notice chronologique*, 2, 4-5.
54 AAM, CF, La Hulpe: Chevalier to Sterckx (19 March 1861), Chevalier to Vicar-General Lauwers (18 April 1861).
55 ASCMLH, A.2: Cornet to Lauwers (1 Sept. 1860).
56 AAM, CF, La Hulpe: Lauwers to Chevalier (26 Sept. 1862).
57 ADHH, 16: Verest Manuscript, 63; ABA, File of the Dienstmaagden H. Harten: Bogaerts to Sterckx (26 Nov. 1866).
58 Bogaerts, *Levensschets*; Peeters, *L'Église de Saint-Augustin*, 208.
59 ADSJ, 1.4: Dechamps to Kestre (14 Oct. 1866).

bitions by reminding her of her poor health.⁶⁰ It was an approach that Dechamps also used with other female confessees. For example, he counselled Camille du Bourg, who in the early 1870s succumbed to a deep spiritual crisis, to pray a lot, read the lives of the saints and not ask too many questions: "Les bonnes lectures de l'âme ne sont pas une étude, mais un repos".⁶¹ Such recommendations indicate that even the tolerant Dechamps aligned with those aforementioned clerics who felt called upon to curb '*le fragile figlie di Eva*' and to protect them from themselves. There were also echoes of the '*mystique de l'ordinaire*' which, according to Marcélis, typified the dominant spirituality of nineteenth-century enclosed convents in Belgium and did not testify to much confidence in the originality of female spirituality either.⁶²

It is equally significant that Kestre needed a strong figure like Dechamps to get her projects back on track and to reassure benefactors. Thanks to his support, her catechesis, retreat and prayer activities in Saint-Josse-ten-Noode flourished once again. Count de Villermont renewed his offer of aid at Dechamps' request. After his appointment as bishop of Namur, Dechamps brought Kestre to the seat of his diocese. In the suburb of Salzinnes, the place where Juliana of Cornillon had spent her final years, he allowed her to finally complete her plans for a convent. Very indicative for the power relations between them is that the name selected for the congregation in 1867 was not the contested *Apostolines du Saint-Sacrement*, which was proposed by Kestre, but Dechamps' choice of *Dames de Sainte-Julienne*. At the end of the foundation process, Dechamps, not without a certain vanity, explicitly claimed: "C'est moi que Dieu veut bien employer pour vous aider, c'est donc chez moi qu'il faudra s'établir."⁶³

Jesuits: irresistible and unavoidable

A strong link in the turbulent relationship between Kestre and Dechamps was his support in her unremitting struggle against de Meeûs and the Jesuits. Dechamps was not a fanatic opponent of the Society of Jesus. He worked with them from time to time and regularly pointed out to Kestre their great contributions to the Church's struggle against religious ignorance and indifference. But there was always a latent rivalry between the Redemptorists and the Jesuits, the two most important male religious institutes of the revival in Belgium.⁶⁴ Dechamps confirmed to benefactors and to Archbishop Sterckx

60   ADSJ, 1.4: Dechamps to Kestre (30 Nov. 1865, 9 Dec. 1865, 2 Dec. 1866).
61   Dechamps to du Bourg (s.d.), cited in de Haulleville, *Portraits et silhouettes*, I, 231.
62   Marcélis, *Femmes cloîtrées*, 664.
63   ADSJ, 1.4: Dechamps to Kestre (25 Jan. 1868).
64   Becque, *Le Cardinal Dechamps*, II, 111-112; ADSJ, 1.5: Dechamps to Kestre (3 Jan. 1869); ADSJ, 1.6: Kockerols to Kestre (4 Jan. 1861).

the legitimacy of Kestre's complaints about obstruction from the camp of de Meeûs and Boone: "L'opposition faite à l'œuvre par Salazard (sic) ou plutôt par le R.P. B. (...). Son Eminence sait mieux que personne que cette opposition fut constante et vive".[65] Despite her deep-rooted aversion to the Jesuits, Kestre nevertheless envied de Meeûs for the strength and power she could draw from her relations with the Society. It was an asset that de Meeûs made use of very strategically.

Spiritual expertise

In the first half of the nineteenth century, the Jesuits had acquired a strong position in the archdiocese as founders of convents and spiritual directors. The Society had recovered quickly after its official re-establishment in Belgium in 1832 and had acquired an influential position within the Belgian Catholic elite through its education activities, its pioneering role in many religious associations and its traditional spiritual guidance.[66] Just like the Redemptorists, but in contrast to other exempt male religious orders, Jesuits were not subject to the supervision of an apostolic visitator in the decades after Belgian independence. The appointment of that secular 'watchdog' was a concession by Rome to Archbishop Sterckx's distrust of the exempt male orders. In dealing with the Jesuits, he vacillated between appreciation for their spiritual expertise and their vibrant apostolic work on the one hand and his above-mentioned reservations about the rapid growth of their educational network on the other hand.[67]

The Jesuits' spiritual expertise also made them an important resource for the increasing number of female religious institutes in search of guidance. Apart from Bruges, where relations with the bishop were difficult, the Jesuits were prominent in all dioceses as advisors to convents. In Ghent they were even explicitly engaged in the diocese's convent policy under the episcopacy of Delebecque (1838-1864). In the archdiocese, their strong position was related to the aforementioned Ignatian network around Devenise and the impact of several Jesuits who left their mark as writers of convent constitutions, networkers and spiritual directors.[68]

The success of the collaboration between women's religious institutes and the Jesuits was not an exclusively Belgian phenomenon. International re-

---

65 ADSJ, *Cahier 37.1*: Dechamps to Sterckx (15 March 1861).
66 Lindeijer, Luyten and Suenens, "The Quick Downfall". On the role of the Jesuits as spiritual directors of the Catholic elite, see: Suenens, "L'École du Grand Chrétien", 374.
67 Viaene, *Belgium and the Holy See*, 411-415.
68 Luyten and Suenens, "'Jesuits' as promoter". Long before he came in contact with de Meeûs and Kestre, Boone had also been the spiritual director of the superior of the Poor Clares in Bruges, Julie Berlaymont (1799-1871) and had lobbied successfully for a Poor Clare foundation in Brussels. ABSE, 2.4.6. Jean-Baptiste Boone, 1217: Letters to the Poor Clares.

search has shown that the Jesuits' active charisma, their institutional model and their aura of indestructibility and resilience appealed to women with a similar inspiration in many local settings.[69] Anna de Meeûs did everything to associate herself as closely as possible with Boone and the Jesuits. She tried to persuade the Jesuits to agree to be permanent confessors to her emerging community and to be permanent spiritual directors of the association. Her intentions made the future congregation and association spiritually very dependent on the priests of the Society. For de Meeûs it was the logical completion of her cooperation with the Jesuits in exchange for their protection of her projects and their prestige.[70] The situation, however, was in conflict with canon law, which reserved the appointment of confessors and spiritual directors for diocesan authorities, wanted to guarantee both the sisters' freedom of conscience and diocesan autonomy. As with the Redemptorists, de Meeûs' request could not be reconciled with the aforementioned prohibitions concerning the *curia monialium* in the constitutions of the Jesuits either.

Reinvigorated by his renewed enthusiasm and admiration, Boone felt flattered by de Meeûs' intentions. His fellow Jesuits had less sympathy for the intense way in which Boone looked after de Meeûs. They feared her influence and authoritarian character and doubted the sincerity of her religious calling.[71] Boone's friend and confrere, the Bollandist Victor De Buck (1817-1876), was particularly worried about her effect on Boone's spiritual doubts and temptations.[72] Archbischop Sterckx acted cautiously. On the one hand, he thought of the idea of a permanent Jesuit director as: "(…) excellent, en soi, et cela peut avoir lieu dans mon diocèse. Je tiens même à ce que cela soit ainsi". Sterckx was well aware of the strength of the society's network and expertise to foster the congregation as well as de Meeûs' association. On the other hand, Sterckx was apprehensive about problems when expanding to other dioceses, where the contradictions with canon law and the Jesuit constitutions would certainly cause difficulties.[73] Nevertheless, both Sterckx and Boone's superiors eventually agreed to de Meeûs' request, hoping in this way to keep some control over the strong expansion of her association. The exclusive spiritual guidance of the Jesuits was later formally embedded in the constitutions of de Meeûs' congregation. The seeds for future conflict were already sown then, but for the time being the cooperation with the Jesuits reaped only benefits for de Meeûs.

---

69 Mostaccio et al. (eds.), *Échelles de pouvoirs*.
70 ABSE, 4.2.6. Jean-Baptiste Boone, 12467: de Meeûs to Marie Malou (July 1854).
71 ABSE, 1226: Notes of Fr. Joseph Broeckaert, 3-4; ASV, NB, *Religiose dell'Adorazione Perpetua*: "*Courte relation*".
72 ABSE, 4.2.6. Jean-Baptiste Boone, 1226: Notes of Fr. Broeckaert; 1232: Notes Father De Buck.
73 AAM, CF, Salazar: Sterckx to Boone (5 Nov. 1855).

Networking and recruitment

Even before the actual foundation, de Meeûs acquired access to the Jesuits' network of penitents and benefactors. Caroline Cogels, among others, came into contact with de Meeûs through the Antwerp Jesuits.[74] The Salazar Chapel and the adjacent mansion, where the association had its headquarters, was offered for sale in 1849 by the owners, the Visitation Sisters. Anna de Meeûs convinced the president of her association, Baroness d'Hooghvorst, to buy the property. Boone especially insisted that Salazar become the centre of de Meeûs' initiatives. As a place with a rich Eucharistic tradition, Salazar appealed to his revivalist nostalgia, just as Salzinnes had appealed to Dechamps. The classical Salazar Chapel, on the corner of the *Rue des Sols* and the *Rue des Douze Apôtres*, was erected in the eighteenth century on the presumed site of a Brussels synagogue where, according to a medieval legend, communion hosts were dishonoured by Jews. The story of the Brussels communion hosts, which had miraculously started to bleed after having been desecrated, formed the basis of a centuries-long cult of the *Saint-Sacrement de Miracle* (Blessed Sacrament of the Miracle) in the capital. Eucharistic processions and confraternities became a distinct feature of the devotional life in Brussels, though they also formed the basis of a sad tradition of racism against Jews.[75]

It was significant that after the foundation, de Meeûs chose as symbol of her congregation a chalice with the pierced hosts, inscribed with the motto '*Violatae Caritatis Reparatio*'. Identifying with the medieval legend gave an extra legitimacy to de Meeûs' initiative. The devotion to the *Saint-Sacrement de Miracle* revived after Belgian independence, becoming both a national symbol for the young state and an illustration of the renewed popularity of devotions that had been suppressed by the Enlightenment and the French Revolution. Anna de Meeûs succeeded in translating the source of spiritual inspiration introduced by Boone into a militant 'brand' for her congregation. She thus found a perfect symbiosis between a humble identification with the victimhood of Christ and a leading role in the revival's appeal for reparation.

The mansion next to the chapel, where in 1857 the first community of sisters took up residence, came into the hands of Count de la Serna. Pierre-Ferdinand de la Serna (1806-1887) was one of the oldest supporters of the Jesu-

---

74 ARE, *Cahier des lettres 1*: de Meeûs to Cogels (17 Aug. 1857).
75 Dequeker, *Het sacrament van mirakel*. The name 'Salazar' was taken from the Spanish knight Louis de Velasco de Salazar who had his residence next to the chapel in the sixteenth and seventeenth centuries. In the nineteenth century it came into the hands of the Visitation Sisters. Terwecoren, *Salazar ou la chapelle*, 427-444.

its in Brussels.⁷⁶ Cooperating with influential mediators and wealthy proxies was of crucial importance in the nineteenth-century political climate. As in other countries struggling with the division between Church and state, Belgian convents were juridically vulnerable.⁷⁷ Until 1921, religious communities could acquire a legal personality only under very specific conditions. Most congregations, however, remained without a formal legal status so they had to resort to somewhat dubious legal technicalities in order to acquire property. Most of the congregations relied on proxies, intermediaries such as de la Serna who, though closely affiliated with the Jesuits, did not have any overly obvious ties with de Meeûs and her companions that would arouse suspicion among anticlerical opponents.

Cornet and Telghuys also reaped the fruits of an association with the Jesuits during the founding process. Cornet was increasingly at loggerheads with Father Chevalier. The village priest was very committed to the girls' school in his village, which was served by Cornet's sisters. He was less positively disposed towards her boarding school, for fear that the sisters would eventually withdraw from his village school. Cornet, indeed, was fully committed to expanding the boarding school. Starting a boarding school in order to finance education for the poor and the material needs of religious institutions was a proven economic strategy in many teaching congregations in the nineteenth century. The 'empire by invitation' had offered religious institutes ample opportunities to make themselves useful in the social domain, but did not grant them financial security.⁷⁸ The village school in La Hulpe especially attracted children from poor families. Of the 75 pupils around 1860, only 20 were not destitute, and the municipal subsidy was not enough to cover all the costs.⁷⁹ Cornet wanted her boarding school to be a financial reservoir for the poor village school. However, as Chevalier rightly suspected, her plans reached further. She preferred to develop her convent community into an institution of respected boarding school teachers rather than an institute focusing exclusively on educating the poor.⁸⁰

It should come as no surprise that Cornet's preference for education brought her to the Jesuits. She had known them as confessors in the convent

---

76 ARE, *Chronique, IV. L'Association naissante*, 37-39; ASV, NB, *Religiose dell'Adorazione Perpetua*: Letter de la Serna (29 Oct. 1855). Pierre-Ferdinand, Count de la Serna-Santander, originally belonged to the Spanish nobility, but was naturalised in 1839. He was active in the Walloon coal sector. See: Dusausoit, "Les jésuites et l'argent", 258-259.
77 For international comparisons, see the articles in: De Maeyer, Leplae and Schmiedl (eds.), *Religious Institutes*; Van Dijck and De Maeyer (eds.), *The Economics of Providence*; for Belgium in particular, see: Stevens, "Les associations religieuses".
78 Christens and Suenens, "L'enseignement comme vocation et projet", 153.
79 AR-LLN, Archives of the Municipality of La Hulpe, 116: Register of council meetings (13 Aug. 1859); ASCMLH: *Notice Chronologique*, 4.
80 ASCMLH, A.2: Cornet to Sterckx (11 June 1861); AAM, CF, La Hulpe: Chevalier to Lauwers (26 Aug. 1862), Sterckx to Chevalier (30 June 1866).

of Alsemberg. In the early 1860s, she contacted Father Aloysius Legrelle (1818-1883).[81] Legrelle was appointed superior of the Jesuits in Leuven in 1862. He had both a wide erudition in the field of women's religious life and years of experience as a spiritual director. He studied the rules and analysed the history of some Jesuit-affiliated women's congregations, such as the *Dames du Sacré-Cœur* and the *Religieuses de l'Instruction Chrétienne*. Although he did not always judge female religious positively, Cornet held him in the highest esteem.[82] Legrelle helped her to come to terms with the demons of her difficult past in Alsemberg: "ce qui a paru le [le démon] faire déloger pour ainsi dire entièrement ce faut la visite du Bon Père Legrelle".[83] Legrelle supported Cornet in her difficulties with parish priest Chevalier and helped her to find benefactors. He was a descendant of a very wealthy Antwerp aristocratic banking family and put Cornet in touch with Viscountess Marie Vilain XIIII, an aristocratic lady from among his family's circle of acquaintances, who will be portrayed in detail further on. Together with other Jesuits he also sent a number of possible postulants to Cornet, even though most of them did not meet her demanding ascetic standards.[84] Her many reasons for associating with the Jesuits once again underlined the power of the Society. Systematically and successfully, she urged the archbishop to replace her secular confessors with Jesuits.[85] She gained autonomy for herself from the alliance, but again – and willingly this time – she ceded ground. Cornet was not only looking for autonomy or independence. She also longed for companionship and expressed a desire for lasting support in exchange of her submission and obedience: "mes péchés, mes inconséquences en vous écrivant trop naïvement, sans charité peut être, avec orgueil (...) je suis prête à toutes les humiliations et les réparations pourvu que vous continuiez à nous aider".[86]

Wilhelmina Telghuys was the only founder who did not herself initiate contact with the Jesuits. Members of the Society were already part of Bogaerts' network. The above-mentioned Father Philippe Schoofs (1803-1878) was a childhood friend of Bogaerts and had stood by his side during the Kohrsch process. In Antwerp he was known as an inspiring mission preacher and a

---

81 Legrelle, who joined the Jesuits in 1841, was the socius of the provincial between 1853 and 1880. In 1860 he became rector of the college in Namur, and in 1862 he became rector in Leuven. In 1870 he was transferred to Liège and subsequently ended his career as rector of the college in Antwerp. ASCMLH, 4.1: Aloysius Legrelle, *Précis Historiques*, 1883, 246.
82 In a review of Baunard's biography of Sophie Barat, published in 1876, Legrelle stated bluntly that the true founders of the *Dames du Sacré-Cœur* were the *Pères de la Foi* around Father Varin and not Barat. See: ABSE, 4.2.6. Legrelle Aloysius, 14487: Note Baunard.
83 ASCMLH: *Notice chronologique*, 6.
84 Ibidem, 35-37.
85 AAM, CF, La Hulpe: Cornet to Sterckx (30 May 1866).
86 ASCMLH, A.2: Cornet to Legrelle (14 July 1873).

respected spiritual director for the upper classes.[87] Schoofs was asked by Bogaerts to provide spiritual guidance to Telghuys and the first group of women who joined her in her charitable work. This small community would form the basis of Telghuys' future congregation. Schoofs confirmed the women in their humble role of victims: "(…) Lui reconnaissant notre indignité, notre néant, offrons Lui notre jeunesse, notre santé, notre volonté, notre vie même afin qu'Il agisse selon son bon vouloir". At the same time he created opportunities for self-improvement: "non seulement donner notre âme mais la rendre parfaite, elle doit nous aider à déraciner tous nos vices, toutes nos imperfections pour faire place aux vertus qui formeront l'esprit de notre maison qui sera peut-être un jour appelée à des grandes choses."[88]

Schoofs' sacrificial spirit fitted closely with Telghuys' own affective, Christocentric piety. With the arrival of the Jesuits, the discourse of female suffering became closely linked to the thriving devotion to the Sacred Heart, which the Jesuits had ardently promoted since the Counter Reformation. Although there were obvious similarities in spiritual tone, the Sacred Heart devotion worked to the detriment of Telghuys' specific devotion to Our Lady of the Seven Sorrows, which disappeared from the range of her future congregation's devotional panorama for many years. Her personal writings do not make clear if she embraced the new spiritual direction whole-hearted or if she only strategically accepted it in order to guarantee male support. Perhaps it was a double-voiced combination of both. In a letter to Schoofs in 1872, she herself humbly asked for promotion of a passionate Sacred Heart devotion, but linked it at the same time to her own Marial inspiration: "Je vous prie de nous communiquer quelque chose de cet amour brûlant pour le S. Cœur qui perçoit toujours dans vos instructions si propres à ranimer notre dévotion languissante; nous en avons la confiance que la Ste Vierge vous inspira de venir voir ses pauvres servantes."[89] The double inspiration finally culminated in the naming of Telghuys' congregation as the *Dienstmaagden van de Heilige Harten van Jezus en Maria*, instead of Telghuys' own preference for *Zusters van het Sint-Franciscus-Xaveriusinstituut* (Sisters of the Saint-Francis-Xaverius institute). This encapsulation by her male clerical allies, both in terms of the spirit and the name, was the price she paid for the consolidation and legitimation of her female initiative.

---

87 Schoofs was also the author of various spiritual publications. see: ABSE, 4.2.6. Schoofs, Philippe, 14944: Personalia.
88 Ibidem.
89 ADHH, 58: De Beukelaer to Schoofs (30 April 1872).

Léopoldine de Robiano, like many of de Meeûs' friends and recruits, came from an important aristocratic family. Tormented by family grief, she found a soulmate in Anna de Meeûs. Later, de Robiano became superior of the convents in Brussels and Rome and general assistant of the congregation.
[Painting – S.d. – *Het Instituut van de Gedurige Aanbidding* (Brussels: Bulens, 1957)]

SOULMATES AND RIVALS

THE POWER(LESSNESS) OF FEMALE ALLIANCES

> Madame de Meeûs, noble et riche, avait à ses côtés la fille du comte de Robiano de Marchin, près de Huy, et la fille du baron Cogels, toutes deux nobles et riches; (...) Quelle ambition humaine pouvaient avoir ces femmes d'élite en s'envieillissant dans un institut religieux pour y partager la vie cachée et l'Hôte divin des tabernacles?
> ARE, *Chroniques, Chapitre XIV. Les débuts de l'institut.*

During the foundation process, a special role was reserved for the first female supporters and companions of the four founders. Formed in the intimacy of a circle of friends, catechism class or sewing circle, the emergence of female alliances was more difficult to trace than the partnerships with male clergy. Nonetheless, their close relationships revealed even more of the motives, obstacles and strategies that were associated with religious vocations and associations of women in the mid-nineteenth century than did their interactions with men. This chapter focuses on the mechanisms that determined female bonding in and around new congregations of sisters, as well as the way in which the female alliances in turn affected the success or difficulty of the foundation process. Within this context, it is also interesting to find out whether female bonding could have an effect on women's agency at the micro and macro levels and on the way women positioned themselves in relation to male control. In short, the narratives of the first female companions of the four founders – not all of them "noble et riche", but quite different from the majority of their colleagues in the wealth of sources we have about them –

offer the prospect of a nuanced answer to the question posed by the chronicler of de Meeûs' congregation.

The convent as a place of refuge

From the end of the 1850s, Kestre received support and comfort from Louisa Auchard de Saint-Laurent (1804-1880), a friend who was twenty years her senior. They shared a history of sorrow, humiliation and setback. Kestre's companion was born Louisa Carless to a wealthy London family. By her own account, she was sent as a teenager by her parents from cold England to relatives in British India because of her poor health – presumably the result of a chronic heart condition.[1] In India she came to admire the work of Catholic missionaries. After the death of her parents, she fell in love with a self-proclaimed French aristocrat who was on tour in India, Baron Jean-Louis Auchard de Saint-Laurent (1810-1871). In truth, Auchard was a deeply indebted '*chatelain*' from the region of Paris, who – probably attracted by her rich inheritance – married Louisa in an Anglican ceremony in 1845 at his Belgian country residence near Opont. For several years the couple frequented the Parisian aristocratic salons, but the marriage soon ran aground. Louisa was abandoned by her husband and retired to the house in Opont.[2] She was attracted by the 'warm' Catholicism of the revival and planned to return to India as a lay missionary. In 1857 she was baptised and moved to Brussels. Through her confessor, Father Busine, she came into contact with Kestre and volunteered in Kestre's expanding catechesis apostolate while waiting to leave for India. Both women soon became friends. Kestre eventually persuaded Louisa – who officially was still married and therefore was addressed as "Madame Auchard" – to shelve her missionary dream and stay in Brussels.[3]

Auchard quickly turned into a stable force in Kestre's entourage. She supported Kestre financially, by paying part of the rent of the rooms for catechism classes. Several times she also had to put out the fires caused by Kestre's rashness. With her endearing English accent and friendly manner, she had quickly turned into a mother figure, both for Kestre and for the children in the catechism classes.[4] In 1865 they both went to reside in the same house and started a regulated life as pious women. Religious community life gave Auchard a future in which she could realise her spiritual and apostolic ambi-

1   ADSJ, 4.3: Biographical note by Mère Louisa du St. Sacrement.
2   Masson, *Napoléon et son fils*, 99.
3   It is not clear whether the Anglican marriage between Louisa and Jean-Louis was ever dissolved. In 1869 Jean-Louis Auchard entered into a Catholic marriage with a new spouse. ADSJ, 4.3: Biographical note by Mère Louisa du St. Sacrement.
4   ADSJ, 1.3./2: Journal of Kestre (8 Jan. 1859, 13 Jan. 1859, 12 July 1861); ADSJ, 1.7: Burgeon, dean of Tournai, to Kestre (13 Jan. 1862, 15 Aug. 1862).

tions, but at least as important was the opportunity it gave her for individual recovery "après les affronts, les peines et le désespoir".[5]

The story of Auchard's life adds extra colour to the already richly varied array of women's motives for entering a convent in the nineteenth century. With her missionary drive and appreciation for the affective language of Catholic piety, she fitted in perfectly with the spirit of the revival. Her story also reflected the motives of numerous other nineteenth-century Anglican converts who, often inspired by the Oxford Movement in the Church of England, found their way to Catholicism.[6] In seeking consolation for her own intense personal traumas, Auchard was also responding to the timeless and universal appeal of the cloister as a safe haven. In the case of Irish female religious and French teaching sisters, Luddy, Raftery and Rogers maintained that convent life offered a way out of difficult family situations, setbacks and pressing social and gender conventions. Walsh, in her turn, considered the desire to escape the stifling atmosphere of the middle class to be an important motive for English women to enter convent life. Finally, a study on nineteenth- and twentieth-century Dutch active sisters gives evidence of women who fled to the convent because they did not meet the physical ideals of the secular world.[7]

Nineteenth-century Belgian observers and present-day historians also pointed to a religious vocation as being something for "les grandes infortunés": a refuge for unhappy, traumatised or not particularly beautiful or charming women who could not succeed in the 'real' world and who were in part victims of the surplus of women in the nineteenth-century Belgian marriage market.[8] Zénobie Vermeersch (1816-1872), a Flemish congregation founder, turned to convent life in 1859, after her parents refused her permission to marry the husband of her choice. In her diary, Teichmann partly attributed her persistent, but never acknowledged desire for convent life to her dull physical appearance: "It is true that no one ever courted me in the slightest way, I say it in all humility: it must be that I am not very charming".[9]

Of course, it is difficult to objectively judge the 'charm' of the four women in our study. Portraits of Kestre, de Meeûs and Telghuys show young women

5   ADSJ, *Cahier 37.1*: Auchard to Kestre (20 May 1865).
6   Compare, for example, with the stories of the English congregation founders, Elizabeth Hayes (1823-1894) and Fanny Taylor (1832-1900), both converts from Anglicanism who were attracted by the mobilising power and rituals of the revival. See: Shaw, *Elizabeth Hayes*, 10-13; O'Brien, "Religious Life", 115-117.
7   Raftery, "Rebels", 735; Luddy, *Women and Philanthropy*, 34; Rogers, "Retrograde", 155; Walsh, *Roman Catholic Nuns*, 153-155; Van Heijst, Derks and Monteiro, *Ex Caritate*, 635.
8   Viaene, "De ontplooiing van een 'vrije' kerk", 71; de Haulleville, *Portraits et silhouettes*, I, 216.
9   "Waar is het dat niemand mij ooit op de geringste wijze het hof maakte, ik zeg het in alle ootmoedigheid: het is te gelooven dat ik weinig bekoorlijk ben": entry in Teichmann's diary (9 July 1846), in Belpaire, *Constance Teichmann*, 37; Ameeuw, *De Zusters van de H. Gehoorzaamheid*, 13-14.

who were not unattractive, and the stern, but confident look of Cornet in the portrait of her as superior does not give the impression of a woman betrayed by nature either. The sources never referred to their appearance or an unhappy love life as a factor in their choosing convent life. The personal documents of women in the founders' entourage do offer the opportunity to look for other motives that may have played a role. Léopoldine de Robiano, de Meeûs' most loyal companion, lost her mother Louise de Namur d'Helzée (1812-1848) at the age of 15, shortly after the birth of her youngest brother Eugène, the tenth child in the de Robiano family. Her father, Victor, remarried in 1851 and five half-brothers and sisters were born in the family. Léopoldine suffered from the dramatic changes and found comfort with Anna de Meeûs during the winter months in the family's townhouse in Brussels.[10]

In 1855 de Meeûs was also mourning the loss of her younger brother Anatole (°1836). When in 1859 she lost her sister Marie-Hortense (°1833) as well, a chink of doubt appeared in the de Meeûs's penitential armour: "un sacrifice en plus, espérons-nous, chère Léopoldine, que Dieu sera reconnaissant".[11] Both women were on the same emotional wavelength, and de Meeûs quickly planned Leopoldine's 'escape route' and the path to their vocation. She encouraged Léopoldine to seek support from her grandmother and from her grandaunt, the above-mentioned Baroness Elisabeth de Robiano, who were well disposed towards her vocation. The women acted as a counterweight to her initially reluctant father.[12] Later, Léopoldine and Anna de Meeûs also orchestrated the entrance of Léopoldine's sisters Eugénie (°1837) and Victorine (°1832), who had also been affected by the loss of her mother.[13]

In one of her letters to de Meeûs, Eugénie recounted the sad motives for her grief-inspired choice of the religious life, referring to the convent as a place "où je peux porter le deuil; où la mort ne peut plus me toucher, où je n'ai plus personne à perdre".[14] The young woman wanted to escape the vulnerability of nineteenth-century life, a motivation that was not unique. With regard to Belgian contemplative religious Marcélis emphasised the difficulty of dealing with the loss of a loved one as a motive for entering.[15] The revival's discourse of suffering, penance, detachment and rehabilitation as the spiritual

10 de Robiano, "La famille", 7-9; ARE, *Cahier des lettres 3*: Léopoldine de Robiano to de Meeûs (8 May 1855).
11 ARE, *Cahier des lettres 3*: de Meeûs to Léopoldine de Robiano (20 April 1859); ARE, *Chronique, VIII. La Croix*, 76.
12 ARE, *Cahier des lettres 1*: de Meeûs to Léopoldine de Robiano (July 1854, Sept. 1854).
13 Eugénie entered in 1858, Victorine in 1863. ARE, *Cahier des lettres 1*: de Meeûs to Eugénie de Robiano (2 Nov. 1858, 29 Nov. 1858); *Nos Sœurs au Ciel*, Biographical note of Eugénie de l'Enfant Jésus.
14 ARE, *Cahier des lettres 3*: Eugénie de Robiano to de Meeûs (3 Dec. 1858).
15 Marcélis, *Femmes cloîtrées*, 155-163. Compare also Arnold, *Le corps et l'âme*, 168-170.

framework of nineteenth-century convent life appealed to wounded souls. As Harris convincingly argued in the context of the *dolorisme* that dominated nineteenth-century Lourdes, this spiritual discourse offered hope for salvation and women's personal development. Analysing the story of the French congregation founder, Antoinette Fage (1824-1883), a contemporary of Kestre and de Meeûs, Harris showed how she used the suffering discourse of the revival as a means of turning her youthful traumas, disabilities and psychological suffering into a charisma of dynamism and strength, which had a great appeal for her 'followers'.[16] However, the focus on suffering and penance also had a tormented downside of emotional escapism, in which human affection was sublimated in exclusive dedication to Christ. Adèle Delvigne (1846-1909), the future Sister Adèle du Sacré Cœur, wrote to Kestre in connection with the death of her sister Félicie Kestre in 1866: "Que l'amour de N.S. peut effacer le chagrin d'amour humain".[17] A similar discourse of suppressed sadness is to be heard in "la mort, toujours la mort, la vie religieuse sans liens, ni affections humaines est si douce, (...) il n'y a que N.S. à aimer".[18]

Yet, the dream of emotional detachment turned out to be largely utopian. Cornet's experience in Alsemberg showed that life in the convent could be as emotionally turbulent and threatening as that in the outside world. Family ties and worries reached across convent walls, and illness and death were as unavoidable inside as outside. Moreover, family considerations proved to be just as powerful an obstacle to entering the convent as a motivation. Despite the enthusiasm for religion in the nineteenth century, more than one young woman in her longing for convent life was hindered by her family's opposition, which was often linked to her role as an indispensable companion or surrogate mother in the family. Telghuys witnessed the religious vocation of her friend Teichmann being vetoed by her family, who didn't want their daughter's cheerfulness to be hidden "under the cowl of a humble hospital nun".[19] The well-known Ghent *dame d'œuvre* Marie de Hemptinne (1818-1846) could not enter the convent because as the daughter in a motherless family she was irreplaceable.[20] Anna de Meeûs was also attached to family life in Argenteuil. She turned away from the aristocratic balls and courtship rituals, but loved the daily life of the family. Fanny Kestre, following the death of her father in 1851, declared that the care for her mother and sisters was an additional ar-

16   Harris, *Lourdes*, 236-344.
17   ADSJ, *Cahier 37.1*: Delvigne to Kestre (25 July 1866).
18   ARE, *Cahier des lettres 3*: Anonymous to de Meeûs (4 May 1863).
19   Belpaire, *Constance Teichmann*, 40.
20   Marie de Hemptinne, the daughter of the wealthy Ghent textile manufacturer Joseph de Hemptinne, founded numerous Catholic charitable initiatives. Like Constance Teichmann, she became a well-known figure. After her early death in 1846, her reputation for humility and self-sacrifice was celebrated in brochures and pamphlets. See: *Notice nécrologique*, 19; Hemelsoet, *Liefdadigheid als roeping*, 265.

The English Anglican convert Louisa Auchard (née Carless) became Kestre's first female companion. Hurt by a broken marriage, she found consolation in Catholicism and energy in the missionary zeal of the revival.
[Photograph – s.d. – Collection *Archivio Storico della Casa Generalizia delle Religiose di Gesù – Maria*, Rome]

Hortense Pieraerts was Telghuys' first companion. Both felt a desire for the religious life, but were restrained by family duties or concerns. Eventually Telghuys would enter the convent after the death of her mother in 1865. Pieraerts followed soon, but only after her mother was accepted as a boarder too.
[Photograph – S.d. – ADHH, 204]

gument for not answering Sidonie's insistence to join her in the convent of Nancy. There are similar stories of the ambiguous relationship between family attachment and religious calling in the case of nineteenth-century German and French religious and Belgian contemplatives.[21]

And also in the case of Telghuys, interesting family related mechanisms were apparent. Telghuys finally moved to the *Sint-Franciscus-Xaveriusinstituut* in 1865 after the death of her mother. She was joined in the spring of 1866 by Hortense Pieraerts, daughter of a wealthy Catholic family in Antwerp and member of one of Bogaerts' pious associations.[22] Other female companions joined the two women soon after. The path that eventually led Pieraerts to the convent illustrates the full complexity of the emotional and familial fac-

---

21 Meiwes, *Arbeiterinnen*, 98-113; Curtis, *Civilizing Habits*, 104-106; Marcélis, *Femmes cloîtrées*, 652.
22 Pieraerts was the sister of Constant Pieraerts (1835-1887), rector of the university of Leuven. ADHH, 40: Obituary Sr. Augustine.

tors that determined the attractiveness of the religious life. Pieraerts, who took charge of her ill mother's care after the death of her father became seriously ill herself in the winter of 1865-1866. Telghuys had her cared for and restored to health in the *Sint-Franciscus-Xaveriusinstituut*. During this stay, Pieraerts developed a longing for a convent existence, again as a comforting safe haven for worldly troubles. For the sake of convenience, Pieraerts' mother also moved to the institute and was accepted as a paying 'boarder'. It was a honourable solution for what Bogaerts called her "devoirs de la piété filiale".[23]

The survival of congregations had often necessitated taking a tolerant attitude to special family relationships. The aforementioned Antwerp penitential institute of the *Zusters van het Heilig Hart van Jezus* was founded in 1824 by a widow, Helena Van Celst and her daughter Sophie (1803-1878), who succeeded as superior after her mother's death. In the 1830s, Justine Desbille left the beguinage of Nivelles to set up her own convent community together with her mother. In the end, her mother did not enter, but did contribute to the catechesis project of the congregation. By 1854 the aforementioned Belgian widow Emilie d'Oultremont had formed a convent community of *Réparatrices* in Paris. Two of her daughters would enter the congregation as well. In the context of the pioneer churches of Canada and the United States, there are similar stories about widows looking to combine their being mothers with their role as founders of women's convents.[24]

An alternative family unit: ambiguous female bonding on a micro level

The structures of convent life showed striking parallels with those of the bourgeois family. Mangion and Alkemade argued convincingly that the initial success of English and Dutch female convent life in the nineteenth century was due to the convent being presented as an alternative family unit.[25] The affective and at the same time complementary relations between Kestre and Auchard, Telghuys and Pieraerts, and de Meeûs and Léopoldine de Robiano were crucial for the success of the foundation process. On a micro level, female solidarity under the protective umbrella of religious life offered possibilities for women's self-development. The process revealed an interesting cross-fertilisation between the attraction of convent life and the emergence of female bonding or bonds of womanhood. These latter concepts have been used by historians in the English-speaking world to describe the positive mechanisms

---

23 ADHH, 16: Verest Manuscript, 34.
24 Grégoire, *Rosalie Cadron-Jetté*, 72-74; O'Donnell, "Elizabeth Seton", 1-17.
25 Mangion, *Contested Identities*, 88; Alkemade, *Vrouwen XIX*, 105-113.

of socialisation and appreciation that could result from religious and charitable initiatives by (lay) women.[26]

The literature about convent life also refers to the importance of this female bonding between early companions. Barat improved the internal cohesion in her first religious community by encouraging her companions to talk about their lives and revolutionary traumas in the evening around the fire. The initial relationship between Billiart and Blin de Bourdon was one of intense friendship and shared grief. Curtis sketched a touching picture of the way in which the French founder Emilie de Vialar (1797-1856), a non-enclosed, active religious whose first initiatives came in for fierce criticism, was supported by her childhood friend, the French Catholic writer Eugénie de Guerin (1805-1848).[27] Relinde Meiwes pointed to the decisive role of female bonding among German bourgeois women involved in charitable work, who later became founders, but also admitted that "female participation here remained in the dark".[28]

This lack of sources is also evident in Belgian stories of female bonding. There is very little correspondence between female companions at the beginning of convent life, not only because it was not preserved, but because often there wasn't any. To a certain extent this also pointed to an important social distinction. Many modest religious communities were brought together by male founders, without the women's prior knowledge. The first six sisters of the *Zusters Kindsheid Jesu* of Ghent, for example, were recruited in 1836 from East Flanders, Antwerp and Brabant by the male founders, Canon Triest and Canon De Decker. They met each other for the first time within the convent walls. The first sisters of the *Zusters van Sint-Vincentius* (Sisters of Saint Vincent) of Opwijk were chosen by the priest-founder from different regions and different social backgrounds. Female bonding on the model of Kestre, de Meeûs or Telghuys was far more difficult in these situations.[29]

For the four founders of our narrative, female bonding clearly offered added value in the initial phase. Even the experienced Antoinette Cornet leaned on her emotional companions, first in Alsemberg and later in La Hulpe. Sister Des Anges (°1827) and Sister Marie (°1832), who entered Alsemberg at the beginning of the 1850s, joined Cornet in rebelling against the irregulari-

---

26 On early nineteenth-century sisterhoods in the USA, see: Cott, *The Bonds of womanhood*.
27 Kilroy, *Madeleine Sophie Barat*, 59; Murphy, *Julie Billiart*, 39; Curtis, *Civilizing Habits*, 102-108.
28 Meiwes, *Arbeiterinnen*, 38-40.
29 Strobbe and Suenens, *Zusters Kindsheid Jesu*, 16; Verschuere, *Hoe zij groeide*, 24-26.

ties in Alsemberg.³⁰ It is quite likely that both sisters, who came from well-off families in Groningen and Brussels, had been pupils in the boarding school in Alsemberg while Cornet was a teacher there. Lists of pupils have not been preserved, but the superior of Alsemberg, Thérèse Fontaine alluded to their history. Irritated about the combined front of Cornet and her supporters, Fontaine denounced the ingratitude of these sisters, "les plus opiniâtres", who owed their schooling to the congregation but had now opted for Cornet.³¹

The process of female bonding often followed the standard affective models of the family. Auchard and Telghuys accepted the role of the caring mother, while Cornet fell back on the attachment of her young fellow sisters, and on their shared dislike of Alsemberg. Relations between de Meeûs and de Robiano initially had the stamp of a shared sisterly grief. However, describing convent life as "a close approximation [of family life] with none of the disadvantages" as Smith did in her pioneering work on the bourgeois women, seems to be an overstatement.³² Together with the affective and caring functions, patterns of control and power also trickled from ordinary family life into the convents and the women's alliances.

Anna de Meeûs turned out to be a particularly devoted, but also meddlesome '*mater familias*' and did not shy away from exerting paternal-style domination. She consoled, advised and directed, usually with good intentions and based on her own spiritual convictions, but often in a pedantic tone. "On n'est du reste pas ici-bas pour jouir, il faut apprendre à jouir dans la souffrance", she wrote to a very ill Caroline Cogels in 1862.³³ She could be generous, yet also very harsh, especially towards vulnerable persons. Cogels, who strongly doubted her convent vocation because of her poor health, was reproachfully reminded of "combien vous savez peu vous renoncer", while the equally fragile Julie Desmanet de Biesme was not spared either: "Si j'ai donc été froide à votre égard, c'est bien contre mon cœur, mais pour vous indiquer vos incapacités".³⁴ Eugénie de Robiano, sulking because she was not allowed to join de Meeûs on a trip to Rome in 1863 to lobby for papal approbation, was told that "quand l'amour propre s'en mêle, le découragement se fait sentir".³⁵

---

30 Respectively Anna 'Annette' de San (Sister Des Anges), born in 1827 (though 1830 is sometimes given as the date) in an originally Flemish Catholic family in Groningen, and Sylvie Poodts (Sister Marie) from Brussels. Their exact entrance dates are not available given the very incomplete data in the Alsemberg register of entrants. See: ASCMLH: *Notice chronologique*, 1; ASCMH: *Livre des professions*. Through research in the civil registry of Alsemberg, a number of details could be traced and are listed in: Vastiau, "De bewoners", 66.
31 AAM, CF, La Hulpe: Fontaine to Sterckx (s.d.).
32 Smith, *Ladies of the Leisure Class*, 115.
33 ARE, *Cahier des lettres 1*: De Meeûs to Cogels (19 July 1862).
34 ARE: de Meeûs to Desmanet de Biesme (26 July 1852); *Cahier des lettres 3*: de Meeûs to Desmanet de Biesme (19 Sept. 1856).
35 ARE: de Meeûs to Cogels (15 May 1863), de Meeûs to Eugénie de Robiano (7 April 1863).

Anna de Meeûs also put her supporters under financial pressure. After Cogels had decided to leave the convent, she was urged to continue supporting the *Œuvre des Églises Pauvres*: "il me semble que vous ne devez pas non plus croire qu'il faille y être complètement indifférent, car l'esprit de l'Institut veut qu'on se donne soi-même à Dieu avec tout ce que l'on possède."[36]

Only her best friend Léopoldine de Robiano and the motherly Zoé de Jonghe seemed to have escaped her needling. Though she was by far the youngest in the first group of five pioneers, Léopoldine was put in charge of the convent in Brussels in 1863 while de Meeûs was in Rome. Zoé de Jonghe, who was about 15 years older than the other women, became de Meeûs' right hand at the head of the association.[37] The combination of the busy schedule of prayer and apostolic activities and de Meeûs' severe character created a strong core in Salazar, but also frightened off several candidates. Julie Desmanet de Biesme, who like Caroline Cogels left de congregation after a few years, noted that she had not only been physically unsuitable for the demanding regime in Salazar, but also had found de Meeûs' harshness difficult to accept.[38]

In La Hulpe, Antoinette Cornet evolved along a parallel route into becoming a concerned, albeit rigid mother. The miserable living conditions of her first community of sisters and boarding-school students, though cherished by Cornet as an opportunity for penance and purification, tested and damaged the process of community formation. Only the most hardened but also loyal and complementary characters remained. As will be explained in the next chapter, Cornet was inspired by the convent life of the *Sœurs de Notre-Dame* of Namur, which had a particularly strict reputation in the mid-nineteenth-century Belgian religious landscape.[39]

In the meantime, Cornet received permission from Sterckx to bring another companion, who had remained behind in Alsemberg, to La Hulpe to help meet its educational needs. Sister Augustine (1833-1894) was an energetic soul, often repeating: "Si j'avais été un garçon, je me serais fait missionnaire". She shared Cornet's ascetic attitude and the same time provided the community with additional teaching experience and a keen interest in economic matters. She would become an important link in Cornet's expansion ambi-

---

36 ARE, *Cahier des lettres 1*: de Meeûs to Cogels (15 June 1862).
37 ABSE, 4.2.6. Boone, 1251: de Jonghe to du Chêne (9 Feb. 1856, 2 March 1858).
38 ABSE, 4.2.6. Boone, 1251: Desmanet de Biesme to Boone (5 Sept. 1869); AEL, Fonds de Montpellier, 16, File Institut de l'Adoration Perpétuelle: Desmanet de Biesme to de Montpellier (26 June 1870), Desmanet de Biesme to de Meeûs (24 June 1870).
39 ASCMLH, A.2: Cornet to Sterckx (11 June 1861). The superior of the congregation in Namur recorded in 1850 that "La congrégation méritait déjà la réputation qu'on lui a faite, surtout dans les Flandres, d'être difficile pour recevoir et surtout pour conserver les sujets. Plaise à Dieu qu'on ne se relâche pas sur ce point." Mère Marie-Xavier Voirin, cited in De Smedt, *Mgr. Kinet*, 285.

tions.⁴⁰ The group of four – Cornet and Sisters Des Anges, Marie and Augustine – formed the core group of pioneers in La Hulpe. Their alliance, forged by resentment, poverty and determination, was crucial for the survival of the community. However, it also caused a lasting rivalry with their fellow sisters in Alsemberg. Moreover, the obsession with asceticism and rehabilitation already contained the seeds for future conflicts that would eventually destroy the strong female bonding of the pioneer group.⁴¹

Kestre's close friendship with Auchard also had its downside. Some confessors – including a number of Redemptorists – discouraged their confidants from joining the small community because they distrusted the two, somewhat peculiar, women. Father Jan Looijaard (1814-1895), a close collaborator of Dechamps, warned Kestre about the prejudices against her: "certes, vous n'avez rien de mondain, mais on se demande si c'est vraiment un couvent, ou plutôt une curiosité de deux femmes exaltées."⁴² Jesuit confessors shared in the gender stereotyping of their Redemptorist colleagues. Though they were the most important suppliers of vocations in the start-up period of de Meeûs' congregation, they also pointed to the "comportement dominateur de la supérieure et son petit clan d'âmes d'élite" as being a significant obstacle for them to encourage new candidates to join the Salazar community.⁴³ As Buerman and Van Osselaer have already pointed out in the case of lay women's initiatives, the mechanisms of female community formation and socialisation thus remained firmly under the aegis of male approbation and appreciation.⁴⁴

"Autel contre autel": the limits of a wider female coalition

At the micro level, female bonding was important, though not free of conflict or criticism. On a wider level, female coalitions were even more complicated. Traditional gender relations were never explicitly questioned by the four female founders. Nor did they hesitate to compete with women outside their family unit, imposing the dominant gender discourse on other women. Historians who came to similar conclusions on the basis of international parallels found interesting explanations both in the religious climate of the revival and in women's strategies. Catriona Clear and Kathleen Sprows-Cummings, astonished by the lack of cooperation and rivalry between Irish and American congregation founders, pointed to the role of the overpowering drive for

---

40   Sœur Augustine, Marie Vanderhaegen, was the daughter of a Flemish farmer from Linkebeek. She entered in Alsemberg in 1854. ASCMLH, C.1: *Registre des entrées; Registre des nécrologies*; ASCMLH: *Notice chronologique*, 6.
41   See p. 207.
42   ADSJ, 1.6: Looijaard to Kestre (7 Sept. 1870).
43   ABSE, 4.2.6. Boone, 1226: Notes of Father Broeckaert.
44   Buerman and Van Osselaer, "Feminization thesis", 527-258.

socio-religious action. Passionately impelled by their ambition to bring about a religious recovery, the founders shared a common mission, but often in their ruthless zeal they got enmeshed in harsh competition with one another.[45]

In the crowded convent landscape of the late revival, it was not an easy task for a new congregation to acquire a good position in the market for recruitment and financing.[46] Dechamps, who was bishop of Namur between 1865 and 1867, had to face severe opposition by the clergy and the sister congregations of his episcopal city when preparing the foundation of Kestre's first convent.[47] Anna de Meeûs got involved in a conflict with a former acquaintance. For years she had an intimate friendship with Fanny-Joseph Maes (1825-1869), the daughter of a well-to-do Brussels bourgeois family. Like de Meeûs and Kestre, Maes had been a member of Boone's *Filles de Marie* and was part of the pioneering group that started the catechesis work in Salazar. For a long time, it looked like Maes would join de Meeûs' congregation, but she too had to withdraw at a crucial moment in order to look after her sick mother. During her forced retreat, her Jesuit confessor Joachim Delcourt brought her into contact with the *Filles du Cœur de Marie* (Daughters of the Heart of Mary) in Paris, which she eventually entered after her mother's death in 1863. Anna de Meeûs, who had been continuously pressing Maes to enter her own institute, now felt betrayed. The break was all the more painful because – as the following chapter will show – the very active and loosely structured *Filles du Cœur de Marie* would act as a model for de Meeûs' own congregation. Boone, who did not have particularly good relations with his colleague Delcourt, also shared de Meeûs' displeasure. The rivalry grew when the now professed Maes was sent by her superiors to Brussels in 1865 to set up a new branch of the French institute. From her parental home in Saint-Josse-ten-Noode, barely a few hundred meters from the Salazar convent, Maes trained new novices and laid the foundation for a diverse ministry in education, formation and welfare assistance in the working-class districts of Brussels.[48]

Anna de Meeûs tried to oppose Maes' foundation with a rather ambiguous discourse. She suggested to Archbischop Sterckx that "ces femmes qui n'ont pas de vie communautaire, ni des couvents, ni d'organisation claire"

---

45 Clear, *Nuns in Nineteenth-Century Ireland*, 149-151; Sprows-Cummings, *New Women*, 155.
46 For examples of the competition between Belgian teaching congregations, see Christens and Suenens, "L'enseignement comme vocation", 148-149; Art, *Kerkelijke structuur*, 77.
47 ADSJ, 1.4: Dechamps to Kestre (24 May 1866, 14 Oct. 1866).
48 AFCM-PB: *Historique Bruxelles* (1865-1914); ARE, *Chronique, III. La Vocation*, 28; ABSE, 4.2.6. Boone, 1222: Delcourt-Boone File. Joachim Delcourt (1809-1893) was first a diocesan priest in the diocese of Cambrai and subsequently entered the Belgian Society of Jesus in 1834. He was well-known as a mission preacher and confessor to religious institutes. See: *Précis Historiques*, 1893, 429-432. Delcourt and Boone had already been involved in a conflict in 1863 while acting as confessors to competing devout associations for lay women, see: ABSE, 4.2.6. Boone, 1222: Boone to Sterckx, s.d. (ca. 1863).

could not contribute anything to the religious and charitable world in the capital.[49] Would de Meeûs have noticed that she was using the standard language of distrust of uncontrolled female action, not only because she wanted to conform to it, but also in the interest of her own ambitions? In any case, she illustrated once again that women's double-voiced conformity to the dominant discourse could also hinder female development. In that sense, they became an obstacle to the binding and emancipatory capacity of female action. To use Hobsbawm's words, women "had learned over the generations 'to work the system'", a lesson that could also be turned against their own sex.[50]

By expressing herself in the language of male superiors, de Meeûs could harbour the hope that her request would be heard. Sterckx, however, did not rise to the bait. In his response he pointed to Maes' past as a charitable and devout lay woman and expressed his concern about the devastating consequences of an "autel contre autel" struggle.[51] The use of the dominant gender language against women outside their own group was apparent in other circumstances as well. Kestre dismissed de Meeûs as "cette dame, sans sensibilité féminine", causing Dechamps to remark that "Salazar est pour vous l'objet d'une vraie passion dominante".[52] The mutual rivalry was both assertive and passive. At the end of the 1850s, when Kestre was looking for premises to continue her catechesis work, Anna de Meeûs refused to help her despite the pleas of some mutual acquaintances.[53]

Other congregation founders also strategically 'forgot' the explicit language of female bonding from time to time. Barat, who in the early nineteenth century had herself been involved in a constant struggle with male authorities to consolidate the authentic character of her foundation, reacted coldly and aloofly when her colleague Billiart came into conflict with the bishop of Amiens. A few decades later, Billiart was 'denounced' to the local bishop by her own sisters in Ghent because she had been subversive and had not adequately respected the rule. She in turn referred to the instability and impressionability of her young sisters in Ghent. In the United States, the establishment of daughter houses often led to internal and ethnic-based conflicts when European motherhouses ordered adherence to a strict rule. The European directions were difficult to reconcile with the 'more liberal' character of American society and the pioneering frontier circumstances. During the conflicts, the ideal of female obedience and submission was frequently used as argument to denounce fellow sisters. The same happened in England, where congregation founder Elizabeth Prout was accused of disobedience, decadence

---

49 ARE, *Cahier des lettres 3*: De Meeûs to Sterckx (16 Dec. 1865).
50 Hobsbawm, *The Age of Empire*, 209.
51 ARE, *Cahier des lettres 3*: Sterckx to de Meeûs (23 Dec. 1865).
52 ADSJ, 1.3./3: Kestre to Dechamps (4 Feb. 1866); ADSJ, 1.4: Dechamps to Kestre (8 Aug. 1871).
53 ABML, Section XX, Section F, 1055: Joseph Fabri, Notes.

and disrespect for the rule by her own sisters. Recognition and confirmation by the ecclesiastical and male elite came at a price and sometimes at the expense of other women.[54]

Yet, the story was not exclusively one of struggle and envy. Outside the arena of direct competition there was certainly room for mutual support. Kestre built up good contacts with the Visitandines of Brussels and Lennik over the years.[55] The fellow religious of her deceased sister Sidonie, the *Dames du Sacré-Cœur* of Jette, in their turn, offered a listening ear and lobbied benefactors for support. De Meeûs and her first companions occasionally sought solace from the prioress of the Brussels Carmelite convent in the difficult period prior to the foundation of the congregation.[56] She also maintained good contacts with the Carmelite sister, Mina Lammens, a former member of the association in Ghent. From her enclosed cloister in Charleroi, Lammens solicited the help of the Catholic elite for the expansion of de Meeûs' institute.[57]

Carmelite and Visitandine cloisters had a rich tradition of giving spiritual assistance. From behind their grilles the (semi-)contemplative sisters acted as advocates for their active soulmates, especially those in the more elitist circles. However opposition to or complaints about existing gender relations in the Church and the wider society were only rarely expressed. At the height of Kestre's difficulties with the Brussels clergy, Sister Marie de Chantal of the Visitation convent in Brussels warned her for male interference: "les prêtres peuvent ruiner une œuvre pieuse pour favoriser une autre, essayez à trouver un qui entre dans le plan Divin".[58] The female founders in our study helped other female religious as well. At the same time that de Meeûs was trying to obstruct Maes' foundation in Brussels, she committed herself to helping a number of teaching congregations. Relying on her network and growing prestige as an aristocratic founder, she brought the *Zusters van Liefde* of Ghent to Brussels in the late 1850s to found a school in the new *Léopold* district. Between 1863 and 1866 she searched for a congregation to provide education in the poor neighbourhoods of the city. In the end, the *Sœurs de Notre-Dame* de Namur accepted her invitation to work in the parish of the *Riches Claires* in 1866.[59]

54 Kilroy, *Madeleine Sophie Barat*, 98-99; *Lettres de Sainte Julie Billiart*, VI, no 340: Billiart to Le Surre (July 1814); Murhpy, *Julie Billiart*, 181; Ewens, "Removing the Veil", 266; Idem, *The Role of the Nun*, 75-77; Thompson, "Women, Feminism", 142; Hamer, *Elizabeth Prout*, 148-152.
55 ADSJ, 1.3./1: Journal of Kestre (18 and 24 March 1856); ADSJ, 1.6: Sr. Alphonse (Lennik) to Kestre (16 Jan. 1877).
56 ADSJ, 1.6: Madame Gouvion to Kestre (4 June 1865, 1 Oct. 1869); ARE, *Cahier des Lettres 1*: de Meeûs to Desmanet de Biesme (24 July 1853).
57 ABG, Poortakker Convent, *Papiers concernant la fondation de Gand*. About Lammens, see also part III.
58 ADSJ, 1.6: Sr. Marie de Chantal Maus to Kestre (26 Jan. 1861).
59 ARE, *Chronique Chapitre XVII: Marthe et Marie*, 178-179; *Chapitre XXIV. Maison-Mère*, 249-251.

In this way, apostolic aspirations promoted cooperation between women. As teaching institutes, however, these congregations obviously did not constitute any direct competition for de Meeûs' own activities. Moreover, they hardly recruited in the elite circles where she went looking for novices.

Another development also seemed to be at play here. It was the determined but increasingly respected "très révérende mère" de Meeûs, who asserted herself in these cases for the benefit of other female institutes. By that time, de Meeûs was an established figure in the convent landscape and could exert her influence in favour of other institutes. This position was the result of the final stage in the foundation process of her congregation: the normative and organisational consolidation.

Engelbert Sterckx, between 1832 and 1867 archbishop of Mechelen, was a lasting ally of the revival's focus on social commitment. In his convent politics the safeguarding and expansion of the apostolate of sister congregations was the major concern.
[Lithograph – 1852 – KADOC]

MECHELEN AND ROME

NORMATIVE IDENTITY AND ECCLESIASTICAL POSITIONING

> Nous vous exhortons, mes très chères filles en Jésus-Christ, à regarder cette mesure comme un nouveau bienfait de Dieu et d'en profiter pour votre plus grande perfection. Qu'une étroite union et une sainte émulation pour travailler à la plus grande gloire de Dieu et à l'éducation de la jeunesse chrétienne ne cesse de régner parmi vous, et le Dieu de paix et de charité sera toujours avec vous.
>
> AAM, CF, La Hulpe: Copy of Sterckx's decree (24 April 1863).

Sterckx's decree granting recognition to Cornet's congregation in the spring of 1863 was steeped in the religious and gender language of the time. His emphasis on perfection and unity on the one hand and his focus on the teaching apostolate on the other reflected his concerns with Cornet's difficult foundation history. It also illustrated the typical convent policy of efficiency and social utility of the 'manager-bishop' of Mechelen. Moreover, Sterckx's paternal recommendations to "mes très chères filles" outlined the contours of the clerical and gender discourse and framework within which the female founders had to operate. New social and ecclesiastical needs continued to create opportunities for new initiatives, within the contours of a diocesan policy of control. At the same time, the growing ideological tensions and the increasingly militant Catholic mentality of the period 1857-1867 shaped a new range of social and clerical conditions that both created and inhibited opportunities for female agency.

Sterckx's pragmatic policy

Sterckx was known as a revival bishop with liberal Catholic sympathies and was not an ideological hardliner. The increasingly anticlerical liberal governments that had come to power after the political crisis provoked by the Convent Law, along with the growing drive to mobilise on the Catholic side brought the clerical-liberal conflict more prominently to the forefront. Still, Sterckx remained committed to compromise even in the last decade of his episcopacy (1832-1867).[1] This was not without consequence for his convent policy. He refrained from provoking the liberal side. In the summer of 1857, for example, he urged Boone and de Meeûs to start convent life in Salazar as discreet as possible because of the political tensions aroused by the Convent Law and the specific location of the Salazar convent. Just a stone's throw away from the chapel, in the former palace of the sixteenth-century Cardinal Granvelle, the *Université Libre de Bruxelles* had established its headquarters in 1842. The university was founded in 1834 by Brussels liberals with the support of the Freemasons, as a counterweight to the restored Catholic University of Leuven, and had quickly became the most feared of all anticlerical opponents.[2]

Sterckx was concerned that the new convent could become a popular target for anticlerical students, especially since Father Boone was a fierce critic of the liberal university. Despite repeated solicitations by Boone and de Meeûs, Sterckx refused to make an official appearance in the new convent until most of the unrest had subsided. He did gave permission for the first five novices to receive the habit and for the provisional installation of a tabernacle with the Blessed Sacrament. Anna de Meeûs accepted this decision with modesty and gratitude, but not without reminding Sterckx of his promise in her double-voiced revival discourse: "nous sommes donc heureuses, Monseigneur, et très heureuses des faveurs que vous avez daigné nous accorder et aussi de la promesse que, Votre Eminence, nous fait de réparer en des meilleures circonstances tout ce qui a du (sic) nous être refusé aujourd'hui".[3]

Sterckx and Boone had a peculiar relationship. Ideologically they were complete opposites. Stimulated by his own traumatic experiences in the aftermath of the French Revolution – as a seminarian in Ghent Boone was transported in 1813 to a prison camp because of his opposition against the church politics of Napoleon – Boone had already emerged as a conservative opinion-maker in the 1830s and 1840s. Under a pseudonym he had agitated against Felicité de Lamennais, a French priest who was very popular in Bel-

---

[1] Viaene, "De ontplooiing van een 'vrije' kerk", 44.
[2] Deneckere, *Geuzengeweld*, 33-34.
[3] AAM, CF, Salazar: de Meeûs to Sterckx (5 July 1857, 23 July 1857). See also: ARE, *Relation sur l'entrée*: Van Hemel to the first sisters (4 July 1857); ARE, *Cahier des Lettres 1*: de Meeûs to Cogels (6 July 1857).

gium (1782-1854). Unlike Boone, de Lamennais believed in the potential of modern, post-revolutionary liberties for the progress of the Church and religion.[4] Lamennais inspired the Romantic and liberal-Catholics of the early revival, but his ideas were condemned by the Holy See in 1832. With his controversial index of forbidden books, Boone was a pioneer in the Church's battle against anticlerical literature in the 1840s. In the eyes of liberals and the more progressive Catholics, his actions placed him in the camp of the ultramontane 'rétrogrades'.[5]

Sterckx preferred not to be provocative, but nevertheless he greatly appreciated the merits of Boone. Both men worked very well together in their revival involvements. With his conferences and retreats for secular priests, Boone played an important role from the 1840s onwards in Sterckx's attempts to raise the moral and intellectual level of his priestly corps. His contribution to the Jesuits' popular missions was equally consistent with the pastoral concerns of the archbishop. When Sterckx' dealings with the Jesuits in general became more turbulent as the Society increasingly profiled itself as the champion of militant ultramontanism, Boone continued to be a confidant of the archbishop.[6]

New social needs and Catholic mobilisation

Although Sterckx may have acted cautiously in dealing with the fraught situation in the Salazar chapel and installing the first community of sisters in a tense political context, fundamentally he was pleased by the foundation of a new sister congregation providing religious instruction in the Belgian capital. As in the Flemish dioceses of Ghent and Bruges, there had been a strong increase in new female religious institutes in the archdiocese in the second quarter of the nineteenth century. In Ghent and Bruges, this strong growth gave rise in the mid-nineteenth century to a policy of rationalisation, eventually inhibiting the emergence of new congregations from the 1850s onwards.[7] Archbishop Sterckx, however, continued to approve foundations in the 1860s. His policy took account of the nature and the needs of the large cities in his archdiocese and was inspired by his preference for indigenous and controllable religious institutes.

---

4   ABML, Section XX, Section F, 1055: Joseph Fabri, Notes. On de Lamennais, his connections with Belgium or his popularity in the milieu of revival Catholics, see: Viaene, *Belgium and the Holy See*, 40, 60-61; Harrison, *Romantic Catholics*, 6-7, 22-23.
5   Dusausoit, "Portraits", 315-319; Simon, *Lettres de Pecci*, 45-46; Brouwers, "Jean-Baptiste Boone", 143.
6   ABSE, 4.2.6. Boone, 1242: Register of conferences; Simon, *Le Cardinal Sterckx*, II, 37-38, 59, 166, 254, 257.
7   Art, *Kerkelijke structuur*, 63-34; Jacobus, "De vrouwelijke religieuzen", 427.

Brussels and Antwerp, the two major cities of the archdiocese, had a significant number of female religious within their boundaries by the middle of the century. But there still were many new needs to attend to. The importance of female religious institutes, such as the one of de Meeûs, offering religious instruction to assist the overburdened clergy has already been mentioned. Sterckx also counted on female religious to care for the disabled and prisoners, to provide homes for the neglected elderly, poor orphans and girls, and to offer shelter to women 'endangered' in urban workplaces, brothels or working-class neighbourhoods. Extending religious and material support to people on the margins of society was, as already indicated, an important concern in a post-1848 society that was preoccupied with order and control. In the 1860s various congregations from outside the archdiocese were approached for specific projects in the cities. In Antwerp – as in Brussels and Leuven – this included the French *Petites Sœurs des Pauvres* (Little Sisters of the Poor) who in 1863 took responsibility for the care of the needy elderly. In Leuven (1864) and Brussels (1873) the aforementioned French *Sœurs du Bon Pasteur* were asked to take on

WOMEN'S RELIGIOUS INSTITUTES IN FOUR BELGIAN DIOCESES (1800-1890)*

Foundation Date	Archdiocese			Bruges			Ghent			Namur		
	A	C	T	A	C	T	A	C	T	A	C	T
AR-institutes	40	5	45	33	8	42	21	6	27	2	0	2
1800-1830	9	1	10	9	1	10	13	0	13	1	0	1
1831-1860	31	8	39	54	3	57	19	10	29	3	1	4
1831-1845	10	5	15	41	3	44	14	5	19	2	1	3
1846-1860	21	3	24	13	0	13	5	5	10	1	0	1
1861-1890	9	3	11	2	3	5	2	1	3	1	3	4

(A = active; C=contemplative; T=total; AR-institutes include women's religious institutes that were founded before 1800 and that survived both the French and Dutch regimes, either clandestinely or otherwise.)

* Basic data were taken from the following sources: *Annuaire Ecclésiastique de l'Archevêché* of 1860 and 1891 for the archdiocese; *Almanach der Bisdommen Brugge en Gent* of 1860; *Almanach voor het Bisdom Brugge* of 1891; Art, *Kerkelijke structuur*, 33-35; the list of priest-founders in Boudens, *De parochiepriesters*, 423-424 for the dioceses of Bruges and Ghent and Baix, *Le Diocèse de Namur*, 122-165, for the diocese of Namur. All data were supplemented and corrected with data from the ODIS database. There are no homogenous datasets available for the dioceses of Liège and Tournai. For the Limburg section of the diocese of Liège, Jo Luyten's analysis shows that no single institute from the *Ancien Régime* succeeded in being successful in the nineteenth century. There were only eleven new autonomous foundations in the nineteenth century: six active congregations or priories and five contemplative institutes. See: Luyten, "Limburg voor Christus", 38, 44.

the care of prostitutes and vulnerable women. The *Sœurs de la Providence* of Champion became active in the prisons of Leuven (1869) and Mechelen (1874), after previous assignments in Antwerp (1838) and Forest (1840).[8]

Inexpensive, efficient and expected to be morally armed against bad influences, female religious were considered to be a desirable workforce, not only in the eyes of the ecclesiastical authorities, but also the civil authorities. Even in an age of ideological polarisation, the 'empire by invitation' of the Belgian state and its predominant focus on subsidising private initiative was not dismantled. This especially held true for female religious, who, in sensitive sectors such as the prison system, proved to be indispensable. Moreover, just as in the revolutionary period, women appeared to be more acceptable to civil authorities than male religious. The *Broeders van Onze-Lieve-Vrouw van Barmhartighed* (Brothers of Our Lady of Mercy) of Mechelen, for example, were dismissed as prison workers by the liberal authorities in 1850.[9]

Driven by his concerns for new social needs in the urban context, Sterckx was also well disposed towards Telghuys' initiatives for destitute girls and women in Antwerp. The issue featured prominently on the agenda of the Catholic Congresses of Mechelen, which debated about Catholic mobilisation and social positioning in a time of political tension. During several congress sessions, the deployment of religious institutes to provide religious and moral support for the poor and the working classes was welcomed and approved. The Second Congress of Mechelen in 1864 pushed for the provision of better religious and moral support to 'save' vulnerable women and girls in promiscuous factories. It was precisely the group that Telghuys was targeting with her association.[10] In the 'difficult' parish of Bogaerts in Antwerp, with its impoverished and volatile community of dockers, she manned the ecclesiastical barricades against secularisation and moral derailment. Non-surprisingly, she quickly gained diocesan approval, all the more so because she was 'safely' guided by Bogaerts. At the end of 1866 Sterckx gave permission for the profession of Telghuys and for her first companions to start their novitiate as *Dienstmaagden van de Heilige Harten*. Sterckx underscored his appreciation for Bogaerts by immediately appointing him as religious director of the congregation.[11]

However, Sterckx's goodwill towards new convent foundations also had its limits. Even after Dechamps had taken Kestre under his wing, Sterckx could not bring himself to see a worthy congregation founder in the

---

8   Suenens, "Congregatie van de Sœurs de Notre Dame"; Torfs, *Nieuwe geschiedenis van Antwerpen*, II, 413, 442.
9   Dupont-Bouchat, *De la prison à l'école*, 185-189; Viaene, *Belgium and the Holy See*, 175; Hermans, *Scheppers*, 24-25. On the continuing public-private partnership in the post-unionism period, see: Moeys, *Subsidiary Social Provision*, 213-259.
10 *Assemblée Générale des catholiques*, 1864, II, 108-109.
11 ABA, File Dienstmaagden van de H. Harten: Bogaerts to Sterckx (26 Nov. 1866), Bogaerts to Dechamps (12 Aug. 1874); ADHH, 33: Chronicles.

Wilhelmina Telghuys – Mère Jeanne – sitting among her first companions shortly before Archbishop Sterckx granted them permission to start religious community life at the end of 1866. Hortense Pieraerts is standing first from the left, Coleta De Beukelaer (Sister Vincent), who would become Telghuys first assistant superior, is standing in the middle.
[Photograph – 1866 – ADHH, 255]

unpredictable and blunt visionary. As a cautious liberal-Catholic prelate and a nineteenth-century male figure of authority, he was once again dismayed by her behaviour when in a speech at a prize-giving ceremony for her catechism pupils in February 1858 Kestre herself appeared on stage. She lashed out at the anticlericalism of the Convent Law: "Grand nombre de personnes, lors des tristes événements du mois de Mai dernier, ont été étonnées de la promptitude avec laquelle s'est opérée en Belgique le bouleversement général dans les idées religieuses. Quinze jours de fables et de calomnies ont suffi pour égarer l'esprit de nos populations, et pour leur faire perdre le respect dû à la propriété, à la vertu et à l'église."[12] Kestre spoke on the occasion because the Redemptorist Busine had been banned by his superiors from speaking there.

12 ASV, NB, *Religiose dell'Adorazione Perpetua*: "*Courte relation*": *Allocution de Mlle Fanny Kestre* (1858); ADSJ, 1.6: Sterckx to Kestre (24 Feb. 1858).

For Sterckx, Kestre's performance was proof of her uncontrolled militancy. She had not only pointed the finger at anticlerical opponents, but had also come out strongly against the parenting of middle- and upper-class Catholics who were unable to keep their daughters away from "un atmosphère corrompu et enchanteur". Her fervour illustrated both the discourse of burgeoning ultramontanism and the increasing tensions among Catholics. A growing group of extremely devout and equally militant ultramontanes criticised the pragmatic and – in their eyes – lax approach of moderate Catholics, the political (Catholic) right and some bishops towards the policies of the liberal government and the modern world. Just like Kestre, they did not hesitate to denounce moderate or liberal-Catholics who were looking for a *modus vivendi* with the modern world.

These internal ideological contradictions also characterised the Congresses of Mechelen. Initially liberal-Catholic in inspiration, the congresses developed into a platform for ultramontane Catholics to promote their influential ultramontane network of devotional associations, social organisations and press organs. After 1864 ultramontane forces felt empowered by Rome's reactionary policy rejecting modern society, which dominated after *Quanta Cura* and the *Syllabus errorum*.[13] However, unlike wealthy male Catholic radicals, such as those in the Ghent ultramontane milieu that will be discussed in Part III, Kestre lacked both the fortune and the network to exercise any effective influence in the ecclesiastical arena. Moreover, in contrast to his outspoken ultramontane colleagues in Ghent, Bruges or Liège, Sterckx had little affinity with such radicalising discourse. Even her confessor Dechamps, hesitating between the liberal-Catholic views of his youth and of his brother on the one hand and the reactionary ideas of his friend Pius IX on the other, was more in favour of Kestre's impetuous and nostalgic spirituality than of her radical social statements. It is also revealing that Sterckx did not protest in 1867 when Dechamps 'took' Kestre away with him to establish a convent in Namur, insisting only that her apostolic activities in Brussels be continued.[14]

Divide and conquer: small and local institutes

Sterckx' policy in favour of new religious institutes that would address new ecclesiastical and social needs in itself cannot completely explain the sustained *temps de fondations* in the archdiocese. After all, religious institutes were also encouraged in other dioceses to work for new target groups and problems. Another explanation has to be found for Sterckx' continued enthusiasm for new institutes. The Cornet case might offer some clarification. Catholic educational

---

13   Lamberts, "Het ultramontanisme", 47-48; De Maeyer, *De rode baron*, 67; Witte, "The Battle for Monasteries", 115-116; Harrison, *Romantic Catholics*, 25-26.
14   ADSJ, 1.4: Dechamps to Kestre (24 May 1866, 12 Nov. 1866).

needs in La Hulpe and the threat of new conflicts and reputational damage in Alsemberg had convinced Sterckx to allow Cornet to move to La Hulpe in 1859. The rapid expansion of the apostolate in La Hulpe and the persistent bitterness towards Alsemberg then paved the way for a formal separation in 1863. Nevertheless, behind these seemingly smooth developments lay some interesting ecclesiastical and female intrigues and a strategic use of double voiced discourse. In 1860, Superior Fontaine in Alsemberg had been enfeebled by a number of strokes and wanted to summon Cornet back to Alsemberg to appoint her as assistant superior. Her letters to the archdiocese were those of a vulnerable and fragile superior, humbly begging the archbishop and Vicar-General Lauwers to send Cornet back to support her.[15] However, in her internal correspondence with fellow sisters she also admitted that it would be easier in this way to keep Cornet in line. Sterckx and Lauwers gave permission for the transfer of Cornet, but were confronted subsequently with a similar strategy by Cornet herself. She also played up the excuse of her weak physical and spiritual health to prevent her being forced back to Alsemberg and eventually succeeded in convincing Mechelen to confirm her as superior in La Hulpe.[16]

Four years of conflicts followed between the mother house in Alsemberg, the community in La Hulpe and another daughter house in Waterloo, quarrelling about a separation of convents, members and means. In 1863, the three communities were stretched to a breaking point. The sisters from Waterloo and La Hulpe did not agree on the distribution of resources proposed by Alsemberg. Given all the uncertainty, some sisters threatened to leave and to demand their dowries back. The apostolic work in the three communities suffered from a lack of resources and people. It was only then that Sterckx intervened and obliged the women to reach a compromise. The superiors in Alsemberg dropped their claim to the convent buildings in La Hulpe, while Cornet and her fellow sisters gave up their demand for the restitution of their dowries and trousseaus. Eventually the communities went their separate ways. In 1863 Antoinette Cornet became the first superior of the new congregation of the *Sœurs du Saint Coeur de Marie* of La Hulpe.

Although Sterckx's decision had led to the creation of three small and financially shaky institutes, it was still compatible with his diocesan convent policy. As has already been noted, Sterckx feared the concentration of power inherent to the rapid growth of the congregational model, with influential (female) superiors empowered to supervise a network of daughter houses and

---

15   Jean-Baptiste Lauwers (1811-1878) was appointed vicar-general by Sterckx in 1855, see: Meeussen, "Joannes-Baptista Lauwers".
16   AAM, CF, La Hulpe: Sr. Marie-Louise (Alsemberg) to Lauwers (10 May 1860), Lauwers to Fontaine (22 Aug. 1860), Cornet to Lauwers (1 Oct. 1860).

apostolic institutes.[17] Since the 1840s, Sterckx decided to split up several larger sister congregations that were expanding and confirmed the independence of local convents from their former motherhouses. Of the 30 active institutes that were established after 1846, at least 19 were the result of a separation from an existing institute.[18] Sterckx created his own '*temps des séparations*' in his archdiocese, similar to the diocesan policy that Langlois outlined for a number of French dioceses in the mid-nineteenth century.[19]

Basic feminine inspiration

Sterckx's policy regarding approbation closely interfered with the normative frameworks into which the new congregations were integrated. On the surface this process had all the appearance of a male arrangement. However, contrary to what the final versions of the rules, constitutions, statutes, etc. suggested, women definitely played a role in editing normative documents. To some extent their input was erased from history, sometimes even with the strategic assent of the female founders themselves. In accordance with the gender conventions of the times, this aspect of the foundation narrative was subsequently rewritten as a traditional chronicle of male normative mastery. Nevertheless, basic female inspiration was never completely swept under the rug. The emotional interplay of the spiritual partnerships, alternating between admiration and control, and the double-voiced discourse of some women kept the door open for female influence.

In all four cases, women created the first normative framework. Telghuys, de Meeûs and Kestre personally wrote down the first guidelines for their institutes. Cornet brought both experience and constitutions with her from her time in Alsemberg. In 1850, at Boone's request, Anna de Meeûs collected her ideas and ambitions for a future convent foundation. She dreamed of an institute for women from the social elite, dedicated to the adoration of the Blessed Sacrament. In order to create space for the apostolate to flourish and contacts with "les personnes du monde" to continue, de Meeûs, like the Jesuits, wanted to drop the Divine Office and the religious habit. At the same time she also emphasised her preference for intensive meditation, adoration and radical self-denial as alternatives to the Office and physical penance.[20] These last desires were not always easy to reconcile with the wide and flexible apos-

---

17   As illustration, see his pronouncement in connection with the international expansion of the *Sœurs de l'Enfant Jésus* of Nivelles, mentioned on pp. 58-59.
18   See for example the separation of several branches of the Annuntiate Sisters of Veltem and Ranst or the Daughters of Saint-Joseph in his diocese: Suenens and Kwanten, "Zusters voor de klas", 5; De Meulemeester, *De Congregatie van de Dochters van de H. Jozef*, 29-53.
19   Langlois, *Le catholicisme au féminin*, 257-261.
20   ARE, *Extraits pour perpétuer*: de Meeûs to Boone (13 Sept. 1850).

tolic ambitions of her congregation, but were in keeping with the sacramental, affective and basic ascetic inspiration of the revival. De Meeûs longed for "une sainte union et familiarité avec N.S.; faire ses délices de demeurer près du Tabernacle et y faire tous ses exercices; apprendre la mortification intérieure, que je sens être si nécessaire pour arriver à gouter Dieu".[21]

Wilhelmina Telghuys also had her own ideas about convent life. Her outline of 18 provisions was probably drawn up in 1865 and was the basic regulatory document of the first group of sisters. Afterwards, every reference to the text disappeared until the beginning of the twentieth century, when the sisters themselves wrote about it in a report to the archdiocese. The original manuscript was lost during the bombing of the convent in the Second World War, so only some fragments of Telghuys' text cited in a manuscript by Father Verest (1907) are preserved. The focus lay on the apostolate for "des filles que la divine providence nous enverra, pour effacer en elles le souvenir corrupteur du monde dans lequel elles vivaient".[22]

Telghuys' basic text was replaced in 1866 by new, official constitutions edited by Bogaerts and Schoofs and thus did not become the normative basis for the later congregation. The clerical prestige of the two men was a factor here, but Telghuys' own naïve ideas also militated against her. In her own foreword she deviated too far from the dominant discourse of humility: "j'écris ce règlement, m'abandonnant totalement à Son inspiration (...), qu'elles [the sisters] y soient si attachées qu'elles considèrent la moindre infidélité comme une désobéissance directe à la personne de Jésus Christ, par qui je leur transmets ces ordres". Her double-voiced discourse of total submission to Christ on the one hand and an implicit path towards personal prestige on the other was too much of a challenge to existing clerical and gender patterns. The reference to her text being divinely inspired was difficult for Bogaerts and Schoofs to accept and made it unsuitable, in their eyes, as a normative foundation for a new congregation.[23]

This presented a striking similarity with the ambitions, plans and discourse of her Brussels fellow founder, Kestre. The convent blueprint that Fanny Kestre drew up on the basis of her visions focused mainly on the structure of the institute as a kind of mystical entity.[24] The details varied somewhat, but the essence of her ideas was based on a complex four-part structure. As was the case for many nineteenth-century congregations – including those of Cornet, Telghuys and de Meeûs – she retained the traditional distinction between lay and choir sisters, which will be explained later. By analogy with the monastic model, the choir sisters in Kestre's plans had a purely contemplative

---

21 ARE, *Extraits pour perpétuer*: de Meeûs to Boone (13 Sept. 1850).
22 ADHH, 16: Verest Manuscript, 66-68.
23 Ibidem, 66-67.
24 ASV, NB, *Religiose dell'Adoratione Perpetua*: Kestre to Gonella (s.d.).

task and were not – in contrast with most active congregations – involved in apostolate work. They prayed the Divine Office and were subject to enclosure. The lay sisters dealt with household tasks only. Kestre's attachment to the monastic legacy however was hard to reconcile with the importance of her catechesis, procession and retreat apostolates. She tried to solve this difficult span by introducing two extra branches: the internal and external third order.

The external third order, based on the model of the secular Oblates or secular groups associated with (male) religious institutes, consisted of lay women, "pieuses, mais pas faites pour les austérités de la vie conventuelle" who were to take care of the apostolic tasks.[25] It was unusual for nineteenth-century active sister congregations to have a secular third order or '*co-associées*' under their wing. However, there are parallels to be drawn with other Eucharistic congregations. The above-mentioned Théodelinde Dubouché, who founded a French Eucharistic congregation in 1848, attached a lay institute to her congregation.[26] Boone and de Meeûs also founded a group of secular '*dames co-associées*', who were "des excellentes personnes qui ne sont pas appelées à la vie religieuse ou qui sont empêchées de l'embrasser présentement et qui désirent cependant vivre pieusement".[27] All of these Eucharistic congregations had difficulties in combining the intensity of frequent adoration with apostolate work. Pious supporters 'in the world', preferably with money and influence, were welcomed, and strengthened the material and spiritual base of the congregations outside the convent walls. Some of the associates eventually decided to enter convent life, making the third order attractive as well from the recruitment point of view.[28]

There were other motives as well. The initiative to found third orders often came from enterprising founders, aiming to lead their own sisters as well as lay women in the world. It was typical of the persistent influence of the revival that both Kestre and de Meeûs wanted to continue to encourage lay people to become religiously involved. However, it was precisely this female ambition to provide guidance to a broader group of women that provoked criticism. Even the mild Dechamps was not completely in favour of Kestre's plans: "vous devriez gouverner un couvent, pas la société".[29]

Dechamps repeated his misgivings when Kestre introduced an even more problematic proposal: an internal third order. Although never quite clearly defined, it was conceived as a group of religious with temporary vows, who would not be bound to enclosure or to praying the Divine Office. They would oversee the apostolate work together with the members of the external third

25 ADSJ, 8.1.5: Kestre to the pope (s.d. and 19 July 1856, 8 May 1857).
26 Wenner, "Théodelinde Dubouché", 1743-1745.
27 The *co-associées* of the *Institut de l'Adoration Perpétuelle* started simultaneously in 1857 with a congregation and had seven aspirants. ARE, *Chronique, XIII. Vers la profession*, 128.
28 ARE, *Nos Sœurs du Ciel*: Biographical note by Sr. Elisabeth de la Sainte-Famille.
29 ADSJ, 1.3./3: Kestre to Dechamps (9 Oct. 1869).

order. The most pious members of the internal order could eventually enter the elite group of choir sisters. Kestre was partly inspired by the initiative of her contemporary Annette Serweytens (1822-1888) in Bruges, where a strictly separate contemplative order and an active sister community formed one institute.[30]

Although Kestre herself never explicitly made the link, her ideas also bore vague similarities with the structure of the Visitandines, with whom she had close contact and whose founders she admired. Francis de Sales introduced a third category of religious into his institute after the Visitandines had evolved under ecclesiastical pressure into a semi-monastic foundation. By creating a new category of sisters, de Sales hoped to retain the possibility of offering a future in the institute to those women who did not feel called to a strictly contemplative life – sisters with poor health or widows.[31] Kestre's plan put more emphasis on the availability of her internal third order for apostolate work, but, like de Sales, she clearly regarded it as a third category of sisters alongside the choir and lay sisters. Kestre, who had always declared that she was not accepted by the de Meeûs' community in Salazar because she could not bring a fortune with her, explicitly stated that there were no financial requirements for the choir and lay sisters in her congregation.[32] For the members of the internal third order, however, Kestre required sufficient financial means. Their special position thus came at a price and was intended as Kestre's link with the upper middle classes.[33]

Apart from an extremely complex structure, with a number of elements that were difficult to justify canonically, Kestre's plan contained other peculiar details. There was an unusually long novitiate of seven years, with moments of transition linked to particular ages, whether symbolic or otherwise: a vow of chastity at 26 years, chastity and obedience at 28, three temporary vows at 30 and finally the permanent vows for the choir sisters at 33, symbolic for a death to the world at the age Christ was crucified. Her visions also inspired her to create an original but complicated habit. The colour of the sisters' scapulars had to change in accordance with the liturgical calendar and would therefore be predominantly green, but sometimes also red, purple, or white. Religious institutes were often extremely inventive in coming up with original habits. White, black, blue and even red scapulars were not uncommon. However, Kestre's idea of changing colours in accordance with the liturgical year was ex-

---

30   ADSJ, 1.4: Kestre to Dechamps (1867). Serweytens founded a contemplative community in 1849 and attached an active community to it in 1859. Until 1897 they formed one institute under the leadership of one superior general. Rotsaert, "Annette Serweytens".
31   Maridet, "Les Visitandines", 304.
32   ADSJ, 1.6: Kestre to Boone (8 March 1855).
33   ADSJ, 1.4: Dechamps to Kestre (27 Sept. 1870); ADSJ, 1.5: Kestre to Pius IX (s.d. and 19 July 1856, 8 May 1857).

ceptional and seems to suggest a certain desire for a kind of sacerdotal dignity. However, for the record, she did not make that link herself.[34]

Although the concrete output varied, Telghuys, de Meeûs and Kestre all wanted to contribute to a specific identity for their future institutes. From this perspective, again, their narratives differed from the model in congregations with a lower social profile. There, the normative process was often exclusively in the hands of the priest-founders, generally inspired by the initiatives of colleagues in neighbouring parishes. The patchwork of Vincentian foundations in West and East Flanders, for example, was largely passed on from one parish priest to another.[35] Moreover, the foundation process of the congregations of Telghuys, de Meeûs and Kestre also contrasted with the pattern in congregations of brothers. Van Vugt emphasised in the case of Dutch brother congregations that the role of 'founder' was rarely if ever reserved for a brother. In Belgium as well, it was virtually impossible for the first brothers, who were often lower-class and poorly educated, to exert an impact on the foundation process. The priest-founders usually played the leading role. They were either prominent figures, who were well connected with the diocesan curia and the civil authorities, such as the aforementioned canon of Ghent, Petrus-Jozef Triest (1760-1836), or the Mechelen canon, Victor Scheppers (1802-1877). Or they were idealistic clerics, such as Stefaan Glorieux in Ronse (1802-1872), who could kindle the enthusiasm of young, naive brothers for their plans, but also dragged them into reckless ventures. Only in a second phase some brother superiors were able to claim a role for themselves.[36]

Male implementation

Following the rebuilding of the church's structures after 1830 and the beginning of the process of diocesan patronage, the original identity of the pioneer institutes was consolidated and at the same time cast in a tighter mould of diocesan rules or recommended models. Unlike his colleagues in Bruges and Ghent, Sterckx did not opt for a diocesan rule, but he did aim to streamline the rich variety of female convent life in his archdiocese.[37] Through a careful strategy of promoting models and cross-references, the result nevertheless was a

---

34 ADSJ, 1.5: Kestre to Pius IX (n.d. and 19 July 1856, 8 May 1857).
35 For examples, see: Art, *Kerkelijke structuur*, 50, 64-65; Jacobus, "De vrouwelijke religieuzen", 427-428; Vanderstraeten and Preneel, *175 jaar Zusters van de Christelijke Scholen*, 50-51.
36 Van Vugt, *Broeders*, 53-54; Stockmans, *Liefde in Actie*, 102, 116; Hermans, *Scheppers*, 24; Suenens, "Glorieux", 68-74.
37 Diocesan convent rules were enacted in Bruges and Ghent in 1851 and 1856 respectively. Jacobus, "De vrouwelijke religieuzen", 427; Art, *Kerkelijke structuur*, 68.

diocesan streamlining in practice, albeit not limited to one text or source of inspiration.

An Ignatian genealogy

Cornet brought constitutions with her from Alsemberg that were largely a copy of the documents of the *Sœurs de Notre Dame* of Namur, edited by the French *Pères de la Foi*, Julie Billiart and Françoise Blin de Bourdon. The *Pères de la Foi* – often called 'Jesuits in disguise' because they modelled their late eighteenth-century institute closely on the then suppressed Society of Jesus – gave Billiart's institute a clear Ignatian profile.[38] Like many other women's religious institutes which imitated the normative framework of the Jesuits, the *Sœurs de Notre Dame* did not take the actual Ignatian constitutions as a starting point, but were inspired by a number of documents derived from them. Intensive use was made of the *Sommaire* and the *Examen général* of the constitutions of Ignatius, the *Règles communes*, the *Règles particulières* and the *Règles de Modestie*. All of them were texts in the Ignatian tradition that gave a more concrete interpretation of the Jesuit constitutions. The *Sommaire* and the different sets of rules offered ready-made provisions for convent life. At the same time, the essence of the Ignatian spirit and model – searching for God in everything, absolute obedience to superiors, a keen spirit of spiritual self-examination and a tight and efficient hierarchical structure, coupled with considerable apostolic flexibility – remained intact.[39]

It was an exceptionally attractive combination for many nineteenth-century active congregations of sisters, especially the teaching institutes. The intellectual lustre and '*l'art du discernement*' of the Society represented a very different ideal than, for example, the intellectually very modest profile of nineteenth-century congregations active in health care, often of Vincentian or Augustinian inspiration.[40] Still, the choice of secondary Ignatian documents also reflected a persistent distrust of the female spirit, a legacy of the age-old fear of autonomous *jésuitesses*. For some men, not in the least some Jesuits themselves, the Ignatian constitutions were "trop universels ou trop relevés et propre à faire dévoyer une congrégation des femmes".[41] The remark was made by General Roothaan in alerting his colleague, Father Jennesseaux, to the risks of implementing the 'full' Jesuit constitutions in the Belgian congregation of the *Dames de Saint-André* of Tournai.

---

38 Luyten and Suenens, "'Jesuit' as promoters".
39 Ganss, *The Constitutions*, 46-47, 85; Clancy, *An introduction to Jesuit Life*, 64-65; Suenens, "Jésuites et congrégations féminines", 256-260; Mostaccio et al., "Introduction", I-XIX.
40 Compare for example with the 'childlike' virtues prescribed for the *Zusters Kindsheid Jesu* of Ghent or the repetitive rosaries for the barely literate sisters in the hospital in Boom: Strobbe and Suenens, *Zusters Kindsheid Jesu*, 23-25; Segers, *Zusters in het Wit*, 65.
41 Roothaan to Jennesseaux (1852), cited in: Lacroix, "L'influence ignatienne", 102.

The much more detailed and practical provisions drawn from the secondary Ignatian normative documents found their way into the constitutions of Alsemberg through the constitutions of the Namur sisters. They also formed the initial normative basis of the community in La Hulpe. After the formal approval of her congregation in 1863, Cornet approached Father Legrelle, requesting that he draw up new constitutions. Legrelle broadened the normative horizon and sought additional inspiration in the constitutions of the *Dames du Sacré-Cœur* (Barat) and the *Dochters van Maria* (Paridaens) of Leuven. The choice was not accidental. From his own research into the history of women's religious institutes, Legrelle was familiar with the congregation of Sophie Barat, which in the second half of the nineteenth century was still an influential model for women's congregations based on Ignatian principles. As rector of the Jesuit college in Leuven, he had contact with the Paridaens convent, where some of his colleagues were working as confessors and spiritual counsellors. The Paridaens sisters could also fall back on an Ignatian-inspired rule as well as on the special appreciation of Sterckx, who recommended their constitutions as a model in his archdiocese.[42]

Legrelle amalgamated the texts of Alsemberg, Paridaens and the *Dames du Sacré-Cœur* into constitutions for Cornet's congregation. It provided the new congregation with a strong hierarchical structure, with considerable power vested in the superior general and a strong focus on absolute obedience and the renunciation of the individual will and senses. Detailed provisions for each function regulated both the internal life of the convent and the teaching tasks down to the most minute detail. Although Cornet was occasionally asked to review the finished chapters, there are few traces of her input in the editing of Legrelle's constitutions. However, there are no indications that she did not agree with his work; on the contrary, she frequently complimented him and minimised her own role "par crainte de vous être importune".[43] The constitutions were not completed before Sterckx's death. They were officially confirmed by his successor Dechamps only in 1869.[44]

A decade before Legrelle edited the constitutions of Cornet's congregation, Boone had already given Anna de Meeûs' *Institut de l'Adoration Perpétuelle* an Ignatian spiritual and organisational basis. Just as Legrelle in La Hulpe, Boone relied on normative documents from the Jesuit tradition as well as on the examples of existing Ignatian female religious institutes. The essence of the constitutions of de Meeûs' congregation was taken almost *verbatim* from those of the aforementioned French society of the *Filles du Cœur de Marie*. This society was an outsider in the landscape of women's religious life. Pro-

---

42   *Constitutions des Sœurs de Notre-Dame*; ASCMH, *Constitutions*; ASCMLH, A.2: Cornet to Sterckx (11 June 1861), Cornet to Legrelle (28 Dec. 1863), D.1.B: *Constitutions*.
43   ASCMLH, A.2: Cornet to Legrelle (28 Dec. 1863).
44   ASCMLH, A.2: Legrelle to Cornet (29 Jan. 1869).

foundly inspired by the Jesuits, they renounced not only enclosure but also the habit and community life. Founded by Father de Clorivière and de Meeûs' role model, Adelaïde de Cicé, this institute based its regulations largely on the *Sommaire* of the Jesuit constitutions.[45] Boone also took the descriptions of the various functions from the *Règles Particulières* and wrote an introductory chapter describing in particular the Eucharistic and mixed active-contemplative character of the institute.

But de Meeûs played her role as well. Despite his authoritarian and conservative character, Boone had greater sympathy for de Meeûs' desires and inspiration than many of his colleagues. He informed Sterckx in 1857 that, "Je mis la dernière main aux règles, toujours aidé par des lumières que je dirais instinctives de Mlle A. de M".[46] Although he significantly labelled her input as an 'instinct' and not as a rational or well-considered plan, Boone did implement de Meeûs' ideas into the definitive framework of the congregation. It helped, of course, that her preferences fitted easily within the contours of Boone's Ignatian world. In order to maximise the flexibility required for the apostolate work of de Meeûs' congregation, Boone sacrificed the Divine Office. Following the *Filles du Cœur de Marie*, he also excluded the traditional habit, religious names and enclosure from the *Institut de l'Adoration Perpétuelle* "afin de faciliter ainsi leurs rapports avec le prochain, et leur coopération active aux bonnes œuvres".[47]

Anna de Meeûs' sisters would wear a simple black habit, resembling the clothes of lay women in mourning. They retained their first names, sometimes with the addition of a devotional element. Anna de Meeûs, for instance, became *Anna du Saint-Sacrement*. However, in communicating with the outside world, these convent names were never used. The sisters of the *Institut de l'Adoration Perpétuelle* always signed with their full civil names, as was prescribed in the constitutions. The absence of a number of crucial aspects of traditional convent life was a decisive element in the identity of the new congregation. The same was true for the elitist nature of the institute which was conceived by de Meeûs, but strongly accentuated by Boone. Explicit conditions or amounts for a dowry were not laid down, but the stipulation in the constitutions that "on demande aussi ordinairement de la fortune, comme moyen pour faire le bien, selon l'esprit de l'Institut" was more than clear.[48]

---

45 *Instructions propres aux filles du cœur de Marie*. Polet, *De weg*, 308-320.
46 ABSE, 4.2.6. Boone, 1231: Boone to Sterckx (s.d., ca. 1857).
47 ARE, *Règles et Constitutions*, 24; ARE, *Extraits pour perpétuer le souvenir*: de Meeûs to Boone (13 Sept. 1850).
48 ARE, *Règles et Constitutions*, 32.

Identity and tonality

The last constitutions approved during Sterckx's episcopate were drawn up by Bogaerts and Schoofs in 1866 for the *Dienstmaagden van de Heilige Harten*. Schoofs and Bogaerts redirected the exclusive focus of Telghuys' original text on the care of orphan girls and women 'in danger' to a much broader range of mainly parochial apostolates. As has already been mentioned, on the spiritual level, the devotion to the Sacred Hearts of Jesus and Mary was foregrounded and Telghuys' preference for Our Lady of the Seven Sorrows overruled. But above all, the new constitutions drowned in the typical exuberance of nineteenth-century devotion: "Morning prayer is to be said, consisting of the Our Father, the Hail Mary, the twelve articles of faith, the Ten Commandments of God, the five commandments of the Holy Church, the exercises of faith, hope, love and repentance; prayer is to be concluded with an invocation to the Sacred Hearts of Jesus and Mary, St. Joseph, St. Francis Xavier, St. Augustine, the Guardian Angel, all the Angels and Saints".[49]

The normative transformation of Telghuys' initiative is a good illustration of the ambiguity that was hidden in the identity mechanisms of nineteenth-century convent life. Under pressure from the unprecedented expansion of convents, it was vital for new institutes to emphasise their uniqueness. This led to a great diversity in naming, devotional focus and religious habits, although the majority of the apostolic congregations were grafted onto existing Vincentian, Augustinian, Marian, Franciscan or Ignatian models. There were not only sisters, but also little sisters, ladies, daughters, servants and religious. The Sisters of Mary existed next to the Sisters of Our Lady, Sisters of the Sacred Heart of Mary, Sisters of the Immaculate Conception, Sisters of Our Lady of the Seven Sorrows, Sisters of Our Lady of Perpetual Succour, Sisters of Our Lady of the Presentation, Sisters of Our Lady of the Visitation, Sisters of Our Lady of Mercy and Sisters of Mary Mediatrix.

The shaping of an identity was an ambiguous process, influenced by multiple factors and actors. Telghuys hardly referred to the Sacred Heart devotion or the official name of her congregation, but did place an imposing sculpture in the convent garden in the 1870's to please one of her benefactors. It is indicative of the naming of revival congregations – rich and diverse in devotional references, but rarely profoundly spiritual – that Telghuys would have to be reminded years later by Archbishop Dechamps to use the official name

---

49 "men leest er het morgengebed bestaande uit den Vader ons, den Wees gegroet, de twaalf artikelen des geloofs, de tien geboden van God, de vijf geboden van de heilige kerk, de oefeningen van geloof, hoop, liefde en berouw; men sluit met de aanroeping van de heilige Harten van Jezus en Maria, van den H. Joseph, den H. Franciscus Xaverius, den H. Augustinus, den H. Engel bewaarder, alle Engelen en Heiligen." ADHH, 44: *Regels en Constitutien*, 63-64.

The prominent Sacred Heart sculpture in the garden of Telghuys' convent in Antwerp was a material expression of the new devotional framework that was created by her male advisors. However, the spiritual focus was less important for the identity of her institute than the apostolate activities for destitute girls and women, gathered here for the twentieth anniversary of the congregation in 1886.
[Photograph – 1886 – ADHH, 255]

of her congregation instead of the more common *Zusters van het Sint-Franciscus-Xaveriusinstituut*.[50] However, she was not the only one. Apart from Telghuys' *Dienstmaagden van de Heilige Harten*, Antwerp in 1875 was home to the aforementioned *Zusters van het Heilig Hart van Maria* and the *Zusters van het Heilig Hart van Jezus* as well as to the French *Filles du Sacré-Cœur de Jesu* who settled in Berchem. None of these congregations were well known by their official title; they were instead referred to as the 'Sisters of the Paardenmarkt', the 'Van Celst Sisters' and the 'Basilica Sisters' respectively.

For Telghuys, identifying with her own apostolic institution was therefore the most efficient way to profile her institute, regardless of the new spiritual accents introduced by Schoofs. Cornet followed a similar path. Her *Sœurs du Saint Cœur de Marie* were known as *Sœurs de Marie*, *Filles de Marie* or simply as the '*sœurs du pensionnat*'. Inconsistency and confusion were widespread, both in Belgium and abroad. Research has confirmed similar superficial relations between naming, identity and spirituality in nineteenth-century France and the Netherlands. In English congregations, there seemed to have been a stronger connection between naming, identity and spirituality. Narratives of

50 ADHH, 47: Explanatory note of Father Legrelle.

founders such as Connelly and Fanny Taylor (1832-1900) point to the importance of the personalities and spiritual ambitions of certain female converts and congregation founders, eager to profile their congregations against the background of a non-Catholic majority and their own non-Catholic past.[51]

In Belgium, even the ecclesiastical authorities in Mechelen were not able to make much sense of all the diversity and willingly joined in the use of unofficial but clearer alternatives. De Meeûs' sisters, for example, were usually referred to as 'Ladies of Salazar'. Equally significant – and painfully ironic – was that even in Rome Fanny Kestre was confused with her rival Anna de Meeûs and both were classified together under the title *Religiose dell'Adorazione Perpetua*.[52]

While Telghuys might have had a complex attitude towards the official name and devotions of her congregation, she fully embraced the Ignatian governing structure and spirit that Schoofs laid down in the constitutions of 1867. The chapters on the governing functions and the vows were very similar to those in the constitutions of other Ignatian congregations such as the one in La Hulpe, the *Dames du Sacré-Cœur* and the *Sœurs de Notre-Dame* of Namur. Telghuys' own claims to divine inspiration were erased, but were echoed at the same time in the hierarchical structure and the strong position reserved for the superior general, "so that people do not regard the person of the superior as a human being, subject to miseries and flaws, but as Christ himself".[53] Provisions on obedience and the submission of one's own will were tightened, including the provision that every sister should be "like an old man's staff, or even a corpse that can be moved back and forth without resistance".[54]

This last provision was an almost iconic maxim from the Jesuit constitutions which had found its way into the constitutions of many Ignatian-inspired congregations in the nineteenth century. The emphasis on total obedience as the foundation of religious community life was of course deeply rooted in all monastic traditions and was therefore not in any way surprising. In the context of nineteenth-century Christocentric devotion, this theme was boosted by the focus on self-denial and self-negation after the example of Jesus, which has been discussed above.[55] What is interesting, however, is the search for differences in tonality. The Ignatian *'perinde ac si cadaver essent'* was almost

---

51 Langlois, *Le catholicisme au féminin*, 175-201; Van Heijst, Derks and Monteiro, *Ex Caritate*, 41-57; Mangion, *Contested Identities*, 178-179; O'Brien, "With a Mother's Imagination", 205-208. On Fanny Taylor, founder of the Poor Servants of the Mother of God, see Part III.
52 ASV, NB, *Religiose dell'Adorazione Perpetua: Allocution de Mlle Fanny Kestre* (1858).
53 "dat men den persoon van de Overste niet aanziet eenen mensch, onderworpen aan ellenden en gebreken, maar Christus zelf". ADHH, 44: *Regel en Constitutiën*, 49.
54 "als de stok van eenen ouden man, of gelijk een dood lichaam welke zich zonder tegenstand overal heen en weer laten trekken". ADHH, 44: *Regel en Constitutiën*, 49.
55 Turin, *Femmes et religieuses*, 128; Adelman, "Empowerment", 145; Mangion, *Contested Identities*, 213-214; Meiwes, *Arbeiterinnen*, 63-66; Raftery, "Rebels", 737-743.

literally copied in the constitutions of Bogaerts and Schoofs and in the normative texts of Boone.[56] In the constitutions of La Hulpe, it had been replaced by a slightly more mildly worded "obéissance aveugle", again in imitation of the *Dames du Sacré-Cœur*.[57]

The Ignatian emphasis on total obedience in the normative plan of Telghuys' congregation was tempered by the tone of Bogaerts' Augustinian inspiration. On the one hand, a number of monastic features such as choir prayer and the Friday chapter of faults were included in the constitutions. On the other hand, there was the strong emphasis on the '*cor unum*', the sense of community with and love for one's fellow sisters and the needy. The Augustinian influence somewhat softened the Ignatian basic layer of the constitutions; something Telghuys was eager to emphasise in order to attract new recruits: "nous suivons la règle de St. Augustin avec l'esprit doux de St. François de Sales et les sœurs s'efforcent de pratiquer la charité et la plus grande simplicité entre elles".[58]

The softer and more tolerant Salesian inspiration of the Augustinian rule was evident in the provisions concerning the lay sisters who were explicitly identified as equal members of the congregation. The equality was partly rhetorical, because the lay sisters did not have a voice in the election chapter. Apart from this, however, her congregation had the same rules, spiritual exercises and daily schedule for both choir and lay sisters. In the congregations of Cornet and de Meeûs, as in many other Ignatian congregations, this was clearly different. As will become clear later, lay sisters had a second rank status, in total submission to the choir sisters.[59]

The difference in tonality was also apparent in the regulations concerning the so-called '*manifestation de conscience*'. In some religious institutes members were expected to consult regularly with their superiors about matters of conscience, such as temptations, feelings and thoughts. The practice was taken from the Ignatian tradition and introduced in the regulations of a limited group of female religious institutes including the above-mentioned *Filles du Cœur de Marie*, the *Sœurs de l'Enfant Jésus* of Nivelles, the *Dames du Sacré-Cœur*, the *Dames de Saint-André* of Tournai and the congregations of de Meeûs and Telghuys.[60] The introduction of the *manifestation* in the constitutions underscored their position as powerful superiors and the confidence of Boone, Bogaerts and Schoofs in their leadership qualities. However, the *manifestation* was difficult to reconcile with the Church's growing concern for the freedom of conscience and confession of women religious. In most congre-

56 ARA, *Règles additionnelles*, 17-18.
57 ASCMLH, D.B.1, *Constitutions*, 11: *Constitutions et Règles de la Société du Sacré-Cœur*, 39.
58 ADHH, 58: Telghuys to the parish priest of *Sint-Macarius* in Ghent (1 March 1875).
59 For an extensive analysis of the difference between choir and lay sisters, see pp. 281-285.
60 ARE, *Règles et Constitutions*, 27; ADHH, 44: *Regels en Constitutiën*; Sadoux and Gervais, *La vie religieuse*, 329; Lacroix, "L'influence ignacienne", 88-107.

gations the sisters confessed to an ordinary confessor once or twice a week, and they could go to a special confessor four times a year, in order to ensure freedom of conscience. The same situation prevailed in the institutes of our four founders. In its convent policy of the second half of the nineteenth century, the Holy See increasingly emphasised its preference for the practice of regular confession with a recognised (male) confessor in women's convents, instead of the *manifestation de conscience* to a female superior. In 1890 Rome would even completely ban the practice in women's institutes.[61]

This decision unveiled an important gender issue. An intimate talk about conscience between Jesuits and a male priest-superior was one thing, but the same openness between women religious and their female superiors was something else. Distrust of women's theological ignorance and their suspected emotional and volatile nature also cropped up in this debate.[62] Father Legrelle, for example, noted in his research about the normative history of female religious institutes that the *Sœurs de Notre Dame* of Namur, at Rome's behest, had already deleted the *manifestation* from the rule around 1850. Legrelle supported Rome's view that it was not the task of the female superiors but of the confessors to be concerned about the conscience of women religious and "leurs passions et leurs inclinations".[63] He therefore did not introduce the practice of the *manifestation* in the constitutions of Cornet's congregation in La Hulpe.[64]

Containing the revival: the struggle with the contemplative legacy

It is striking that the most emotional and turbulent spiritual partnership in this study resulted in a very sober and practical outline for a constitution. Dechamps, who had become archbishop of Mechelen in 1867 in succession to Sterckx, had hardly any time to edit a convent rule that translated Fanny Kestre's ambitious ideas. He was overburdened by his duties and by the preparations and sessions of the First Vatican Council (1869-1870). It did not help either that Kestre refused to cooperate with anyone else but Dechamps himself and ignored his staff or the priests appointed by him to help her. The concise rule that he eventually completed in 1870 reflected the essence of her desires, stripped of the most peculiar components of her visionary promptings.[65]

The rule of the *Dames de Sainte-Julienne*, in manuscript barely 8 chapters and 27 pages, was limited to an outline of the congregation's structure. Spiritu-

61 On the evolution of this, see: Mac Avoy, "Ouverture de conscience", 1070-1076.
62 Rocca, *Donne religiose*, 88-89; Idem, "Les Jésuites", 142-147.
63 ABSE, 4.2.6. Legrelle, 14490: *Règles des Sœurs de Notre-Dame*.
64 ASCMLH, *Constitutions*, 25.
65 ADSJ, 1.4: Dechamps to Kestre (28 Feb. 1869, Aug. 1869, 16 Jan. 1870).

al reflections, digressions about sources of inspiration or precise details about daily life were not included. Dechamps himself declared that stipulations regarding the interpretation of the vows, the religious virtues and practical tasks had to wait until after the council.[66] The text proposed a mixed contemplative-active congregation focusing on religious instruction and adoration of the Blessed Sacrament. The combination resembled that of Salazar, but with enclosed choir sisters it had a more strongly contemplative character. Dechamps replaced Kestre's ideas about a long and age-related formation trajectory with the usual two-year novitiate. Thirty-three years was retained as the minimum age for taking a fourth vow of devotion to the Blessed Sacrament. Dechamps quietly replaced Kestre's proposal for a multi-coloured habit with "l'habit des dames du monde en deuil, mais des dames pieuses et sans vanité", again following the example of de Meeûs. As in the *Institut de l'Adoration Perpétuelle* convent names were a copy of the sister's civil names, with the addition of a devotional specification. Fanny Kestre became *Fanny de l'Eucharistie*.

Despite the fundamental changes, there were no signs of protest from Kestre's side. Her only little act of 'rebellion' was mentioning the name *Apostolines* on the title page of the manuscript of the rule. Dechamps did not protest, although the name had been criticised in the past for a lack of modesty. Surprisingly, he also showed a lot of understanding for some of her other ideas, the complex organisational structure in particular. Although he was pessimistic about its success, he allowed the internal and external third order to be started as an experiment.[67]

On other points, the normative framework of the *Dames de Sainte-Julienne* was completely in line with the mainstream convent model. Despite the presence of contemplative choir sisters, much emphasis was placed on the work of the apostolate, as well as on the strong position of the superior general. The *manifestation de conscience* was not included. Like Legrelle, Dechamps was a clear opponent of the practice and, as will be shown later, he made confession with recognised confessors one of the core points of his convent policy. His belief in Kestre's qualities as superior was enshrined in the constitutions in a different way. In contrast to de Meeûs and Cornet and Telghuys, who had been appointed for renewable periods of nine and three years respectively, Kestre was the only one of the four founders to be appointed for life.[68] Although the practice of appointing a superior for life occurred in other nineteenth-century congregations, it was also a continuation of a monastic tradition. It is unclear whether Kestre explicitly pushed for this 'abbess statute' or whether it was Dechamps' idea. At Kestre's request, Dechamps did include some other monastic elements in the rule such as the Divine Office and the chapter of faults.

---

66   ADSJ, *Premières Règles de l'Institut*; ADSJ, 1.4: Dechamps to Kestre (28 Feb. 1869).
67   ADSJ, 1.4: Dechamps to Kestre (9 Dec. 1865, 28 Feb. 1869, 1 Oct. 1870, 17 Oct. 1870).
68   ADSJ, *Premières Règles de l'Institut*.

It is a striking fact that the successful nineteenth-century active congregation model never completely detached itself from the monastic legacy of the *Ancien Régime*. Though all four of the institutes examined in this study were congregations with a clear apostolic focus, limited or no enclosure and simple vows, the monastic model remained very influential. In the second half of the nineteenth century the model of a mixed active-contemplative religious life for women even gained in popularity. The typical active convent template of the revival was contained in a semi-monastic model. The mixed congregations of Kestre and de Meeûs were interesting examples of this evolution.

It cannot be a coincidence that in Brussels, in a period of barely ten years, three congregations emerged with a mixed active and contemplative profile that was clearly drawn up by women founders. In addition to the congregation of de Meeûs and that of Kestre, which strictly speaking was founded in Namur but had clear Brussels roots, Henriette Lauwers (1836-1895) founded the *Sœurs de Notre-Dame de VII Douleurs* (Sisters of Our Lady of the Seven Sorrows) in Brussels in 1857. Lauwers' congregation, which was founded with the support of Father Jean-Philippe Winnen (1818-1900), combined a focus on health care for the poor with a strong contemplative orientation.[69] Winnen saw the potential in the dual character of Lauwers' plans: "Tant de jeunes personnes ont le goût d'une vie de prière et n'ont point la santé nécessaire pour embrasser une vie cloîtrée; tant d'autres n'ont point de goût pour la vie de Sœur hospitalière ou Sœur de Saint-Vincent de Paul...".[70]

Similar initiatives also took shape in other dioceses and abroad. Tihon's figures show that the number of women religious in Belgium who belonged to a mixed contemplative-active institute rose from 10% of the total number in 1856 to almost 20% in 1880, while the share of purely contemplative sisters continued to fluctuate around 6%.[71] In Germany, in the early 1860s, two communities of Franciscan sisters were formed which combined contemplative devotion to the Blessed Sacrament or the Sacred Heart with the care of orphans and the sick. Almost simultaneously with de Meeûs' congregation, the mixed active-contemplative foundation of the *Religieuses de Marie-Réparatrice* was established in Strasbourg, on the initiative of the afore-mentioned Belgian aristocrat, Emilie d'Oultremont. On the other side of the social spectrum, in Montferrand-le-Château in France, the *Dominicaines de Béthanie* were founded, consisting of ex-prisoners and ex-prostitutes who combined the Dominican contemplative life with the care of women in difficulty. Belgian and English active Dominican sisters also pursued this form of 'mixed life', attracted by the prayer life and the prestige of the Dominican second order. In the Netherlands,

---

69 Winnen was a curate in *Saint-Gudule* parish between 1848 and 1868, and subsequently parish priest in Uccle. See: Meeussen, "Jean-Philippe Winnen".
70 Cited in: De Meulemeester, *Mère Agnès de Jésus*, 25.
71 Tihon, "Les religieuses", 40.

there is the interesting story of the Franciscan sisters of Oirschot trying to link up with their contemplative past as Penitents-Recollectines by re-introducing strict enclosure.[72]

In a certain manner, this longing for a semi-monastic convent life illustrates the transition of the (European) Catholic Church from the revival to a more ultramontane mode. It is striking that in the same period American female religious, in a true 'revivalist' spirit, claimed their right to make the opposite transition: from the strict second order of Dominicans, for example, to the more flexible third order to enable them to adapt more fully to the needs of the local church.[73]

This 'monastic turn' of the late 1850s and the 1860s, in contrast with the post-1870 'conventualisation' policies of church authorities, which will be discussed in Part III, came to a considerable extent from the women religious themselves. In my opinion, it can be seen first as a reaction to the revival's dominant emphasis on apostolic involvement. The strong social commitment of women religious was often at the expense of the life of prayer. While director of the boarding school in Alsemberg, Cornet, for example, came to experience spiritual difficulties and longed for religious fervour. Kestre wanted her select group of choir sisters to be exclusively reserved for Christ. There are testimonies of other nineteenth-century sisters who, because of their busy apostolate work, had to neglect part of their religious life and experienced a lack of spiritual intensity.[74] Once again, models from the past were recalled. Co-founder Winnen of the *Religieuses de Notre Dame de VII Douleurs* saw "la ressemblance de ces projets avec ceux de saint François de Sales (...) une vie de prière, jointe à des œuvres extérieures de charité corporelle et spirituelle".[75] The contemplative-active character of the Visitation order was an important source of inspiration. De Sales' spiritual originality lay partly in the way in which he had made the monastic pursuit of religious perfection into an ideal for a much wider audience.[76]

Second, the monastic turn can also be linked to the fledgling ultramontane siege mentality. As will be explained in more detail in a later section, the 'culture wars' of the second half of the nineteenth century generated not only a militant Catholic mobilisation, but also a fear and rejection of secular society. Some religious communities increasingly felt the need to isolate themselves from a sinful world. In 1850, the Augustinian canonesses in the Belgian city of Turnhout asked Archbishop Sterckx for permission to erect grilles in their

---

72 Meiwes, *Arbeiterinnen*, 106-108; de Gensac, *Présentation*, 106; Lelong, *Les dominicaines*; Suenens, "Dominica Van der Stichele", 13; Mangion, "'The Mixed Life'", 165-179; Monteiro, *Vroomheid in veelvoud*, 46-57.
73 Murray, "The Least Qualified", 59-62.
74 Mangion, "The Mixed Life", 170-171; Segers, *Zusters in het Wit*, 64-65.
75 Cited in: De Meulemeester, *Mère Agnès de Jésus*, 25.
76 Cognet, *La spiritualité moderne*, 275-281.

parlours, even though they remained fully committed to their teaching apostolate. In 1855 they attempted to establish a contemplative branch of the order in Meerhout. The Bruges Dominican Sisters, who struggled with anticlerical opposition to their apostolate, wanted to withdraw as monastic nuns within the 'safe haven' of enclosure.[77] In the hours of private prayer and the intimate seclusion of "la pureté du S. Sacrement", Anna de Meeûs prayed for support against "les menaces du démon" outside her convent gates.[78] Kestre also combined a militant desire to re-Christianise society with a monastic dream: "Être des vraies religieuses, avec la clôture papale".[79]

However, reconnecting with the traditional monastic model was not easy. The revivalist Bishop Sterckx initially refused the request of the Turnhout sisters and gave permission only in 1858 under continuous and persistent pressure from them. Dechamps also warned Kestre about the practical implications of her dream: "Comment, par exemple vous gouvernerez de la clôture un ordre apostolique?"[80] In contrast to Sterckx, Dechamps deeply appreciated the contemplative life. Within his own Ligurian family he was familiar with the contemplative communities of Redemptorist Sisters. A few years after his appointment as archbishop, he played a crucial role in the foundation of the above-mentioned *Filles du Sacré Cœur de Jésus*, an originally French contemplative community that assumed responsibility for the new *Heilig-Hartbasiliek* (Sacred Heart Basilica) in Berchem (near Antwerp).[81] He was critical, however, of Kestre's fascination with the monastic world and finally forced her to accept a more realistic version of the plan she had designed: a select group of contemplative sisters, but without strict papal enclosure. Dechamps also tempered her plans for a semi-active congregation with papal enclosure because of canon law objections: "C'est une idée fausse, née d'inexpérience, et aussi, il faut bien vous le dire, de l'ignorance de la discipline canonique".[82]

Dechamps' remark not only confirmed Kestre in her submissive position as a woman without canonical experience, it also alluded to a third reason for the attraction of the monastic model. The strong expansion of the congregational model in the nineteenth century had not led to canonical validation. Under canon law only institutes with solemn vows and papal enclosure were fully recognised as religious. Congregation sisters with simple vows had to content themselves with a canonical second-rate status until the beginning of the twentieth century, even though – as will be explained further on – some kind of papal approbation was possible. This was not without consequence for the social prestige of female religious institutes. For example, vocations

77 Faes and Jacobs, *333 jaar Heilig Graf*, 92-93; Suenens, "Dominica Van der Stichele", 9-10.
78 ARE, *Chronique, X. La terre promise*, 98-99.
79 ADSJ. 1.6: Kestre to Sr. Alphonse (25 Sept. 1875).
80 Faes and Jacobs, *333 jaar Heilig Graf*, 92-93; ADSJ. 1.4: Dechamps to Kestre (27 Nov. 1867).
81 Becque, *Le Cardinal Dechamps*, II, 141-142.
82 ADSJ, 1.4: Dechamps to Kestre (27 Nov. 1867, 28 Feb. 1869, 15 Nov. 1870).

among aristocratic women – in Belgium as well as abroad – were still largely channelled towards monastic or contemplative communities. The *Dames du Sacré-Cœur* were a significant exception. For the rest, communities of Carmelites, Canonesses, Visitation and Redemptorist Sisters were particularly popular.[83] At the end of the nineteenth century, the founding of the Benedictine Abbey of Maredret in Belgium even provided Belgian aristocratic Catholic circles with an establishment that equalled the aristocratic '*Stifter*' of the *Ancien Régime*.

The difficulty in maintaining a balance between the flexibility of the apostolate and the prestige of the contemplative life also characterised the story of de Meeûs' *Institut de l'Adoration Perpétuelle*. Several elite candidates (and their families) were put off by the diffuse, semi-active and semi-contemplative identity of de Meeus' institute. The aforementioned Mina Lammens, a woman from an affluent Ghent bourgeois background and one of the first and most fervent supporters of de Meeûs, chose to enter the Carmelites in 1863.[84] The family of Léopoldine de Robiano distrusted the absence of a habit and the Divine Office. The congregation, on the one hand, wrestled with an image of extreme exigence, derived from the strong focus on meditative prayer in combination with the many apostolate tasks. On the other hand, rumours about lax enclosure rules, alternative novitiate trajectories or dispensations for family visits gave rise to doubts about the normative orthodoxy of the institute. Parental concerns and the struggle to retain an aristocratic lifestyle and privileges complicated matters even more. The parents of Caroline Cogels criticised the flexible provisions concerning enclosure, but at the same time they pushed for a milder regime and a 'novitiate in the world' because of the weak health of their own daughter. Julie Desmanet de Biesme had doubts about her vocation in a community without enclosure, but that didn't restrain her from asking permission to be cared for by a servant in the convent during a period of illness.[85]

A similar balancing act marked other elite foundations as well. Emilie d'Oultremont had to defend herself as both a founder and a widowed mother. She was criticised as a religious for maintaining contact with her family and for allowing two of her daughters to enter her own congregation. By introducing a semi-monastic way of life and a particularly majestic blue and white

---

83 Paret and Wynants, "La noblesse belge", 507; Marcélis, *Femmes cloîtrées*, 116, 122-123. On international parallels, see: Langlois, *Le catholicisme au féminin*, 611-620; Goujon, "Gender", 69; McNamara, *Sisters in Arms*, 602.

84 ABG, Poortakker, *Relation de l'organisation de l'œuvre*; De Maeyer, *De rode baron*, 110-111; *Notice sur la vie et la mort*, 12, 20-21.

85 ARE, *Cahier des Lettres 1*: de Meeûs to Desmanet de Biesme (17 July 1854), de Meeûs to Cogels (21 Aug. 1858); ARE, *Chronique, XIII. Vers la Profession*, 130, and *XIV. Les débuts de l'institut*, 145-146; ABSE, 4.2.6. Boone, 1220: Boone to de Meeûs (10 Sept. 1858, 2 Nov. 1858); AAM, CF, Salazar: Cogels to Sterckx (1 May 1862).

habit, she tried to meet some elite demands. More important, however, for the survival of her institute was the support of the Jesuits and the ecclesiastical authorities.[86] This was also an indispensable factor in determining the consolidation of de Meeûs' congregation. Sterckx showed significantly more patience and tolerance towards the noble ladies in Salazar than towards the humble Kestre. Officially he was annoyed by the 'novitiate in the world' of some novices of Anna de Meeûs, but he never forbade or prevented it.[87] De Meeûs' powerful social and clerical network was equally decisive when she unrolled her plans in the early 1860s to apply to Rome for papal approbation of her *Institut de l'Adoration Perpétuelle*.

The crowning accomplishment: a Roman approval

Some of the active communities that strove for a more contemplative ideal in the mid-nineteenth century had an additional motive. Their pursuit of a monastic life was not only driven by a desire for a more intense prayer life, but also enclosed a strategy for achieving clerical legitimacy and greater autonomy, supported by a double-voiced discourse. By stressing their sincere wishes for monastic seclusion and isolation, promoted by clerical authorities as a fundamental principal of female religious life, some women religious implicitly created space for greater autonomy and independence. The Bruges Dominican Sisters, for example, aspired to the status of second-order nuns partly to escape the diocesan control of Bishop Malou. As full religious members of an exempt order, they would be able to appeal to the support of the Dominicans. Malou, however, refused to allow his own jurisdiction to be undermined in this way.[88] The aforementioned Dutch Franciscan Sisters of Oirschot were also involved in a long battle to recover their papal status, against the will of the local bishop, but with the support of the male Franciscans.[89] The stories illustrate the opportunities and obstacles for female agency and autonomy that could arise from the intriguing power balances within the nineteenth-century Church.

The rapid growth of de Meeûs' association continued throughout the second half of the nineteenth century. However, foreign expansion required adjustments to the existing organisational structure. Within Belgium, the status of an archconfraternity gave ample scope for action. Beyond the borders, Anna de Meeûs had to take account of other power relations, jurisdictional problems and local religious customs. The position of the institute as head

---

86 SUAU, *La Mère Marie de Jésus*, 87-111.
87 ABML, Section XX, Section F, 1055: Joseph Fabri: Notes.
88 Suenens, "Dominica Van der Stichele", 9-10.
89 Monteiro, *Vroomheid in veelvoud*, 46-57.

of the association and guardian of its international uniformity was thus jeopardised. Boone and de Meeûs saw a solution in a provisional recognition of the congregation by Rome, as a first step towards getting a pontifical statute. Although a genuine canonical recognition was not possible for religious institutes with simple vows, alternatives were available. The Roman curia, impressed by the success of the congregational model, offered the possibility for some kind of Roman support in the form of a papal approval of the constitutions or the institute or by means of a papal 'laudatory decree'. Boone and de Meeûs were inspired by other Belgian examples. Together with several French congregations, Belgian female congregations were in the first half of the nineteenth century among the first non-monastic religious institutes to receive a Roman approval.[90]

This is illustrative of the Franco-Belgian phalanx of the renewal of religious life in the nineteenth century. In the southern Catholic countries, the congregational model had expanded more slowly. In Italy, for example, 115 new female religious institutes emerged between 1800 and 1860 against at least 140 in the much smaller Belgium in the same period. In 1856 there were nearly 25 female religious per 10,000 inhabitants in Belgium, whereas Italy counted 19.4 sisters per 10,000 inhabitants in 1861. Around 1880, as a result of the restrictions imposed on religious life in the aftermath of the Italian unification, the figures differed even more: nearly 36 in Belgium, against 9.9 in Italy.[91] In Spain, the expansion of convent life was hindered by state restrictions until the last quarter of the nineteenth century, and within clerical circles there was a lasting suspicion of '*congregaciones modernas*' led by female superiors general.[92]

It was not until the 1850s that the energetic secretary of the Roman Congregation of Bishops and Regulars, Bizzarri, started compiling the different forms of papal approval into a formal recognition process. His *Methodus*, officially published in 1863, stipulated a graduated trajectory with a first approbation and a laudatory decree preceding a provisional and finally a definitive recognition of the constitutions and the institute. Within a few years, the administration in Rome was inundated with requests for recognition. Between 1862 and 1865 74 congregations of religious with simple vows acquired pon-

90   Callahan, *The Centralization*, 44-45; Jarrell, *Legal Structures*, 305-306. Other Belgian female congregations who had received a Roman approval were: the *Zusters van Liefde* of Ghent (1816), the *Religieuzen van het Christelijk Onderwijs* of Ghent (1827), the *Sœurs de Notre Dame* of Namur (1844), the *Filles de la Croix* of Liège (1845) and the *Sœurs de la Providence of Champion* (1858). For an overview of the first congregations receiving an approval or laudatory decree by Rome, see: Bizzarri, *Collectanea*, 861-866.
91   Scaraffia, "Christianity Has Liberated Her", 261-263; Rocca, *Donne religiose*, 49-50; Idem, "Le nuove fondazioni", 117-118.
92   Garcia Iglesias, *Institutos religiosos*, 503. About the state restrictions in Spain, see: Lannon, *Privilege*, 59-61.

tifical approval.⁹³ The road was long and unpredictable, but the benefits were alluring. Recognition by Rome did not grant them the status of monastic nuns, but it did protect congregations against excessive diocesan intervention and created opportunities for international expansion.

The request for papal approval of the *Institut de l'Adoration Perpétuelle* confronted Archbishop Sterckx with the new Roman procedures for the first time. He realised that approbation by Rome could promote the expansion of the association, with its seat in his archdiocese. Sterckx successfully asked the other Belgian bishops for references as well. These recommendations were not without importance, since de Meeûs' congregation was still in its early days. At the beginning of 1863, when the first concrete plans for papal recognition were drawn up, the institute had existed for only six years and had barely eleven members. It was not a strong vantage point from which to enter the back rooms of the unpredictable Roman bureaucracy. The experienced Bollandist, the Jesuit Victor De Buck, wrote the supplication to the pope. Well aware of the small scale and the newness of the institute, he opted for a significant ultramontane discourse to divert attention: "La Belgique, bien éloignée de Rome, mais ne se laissant surpasser par aucune nation en dévouement à l'Eglise romaine (...)".⁹⁴

Boone left for Rome in February 1863. He presented his case before the Congregation for Bishops and Regulars, supported by the Belgian general of the Jesuits, Petrus Beckx (1795-1887), who had succeeded Roothaan in 1853. Anna de Meeûs joined him in April. Together with her mother and with sister Gabriëlle Baesen she stayed in a small apartment in the Palazzo Pamphili on the Piazza Navona.⁹⁵ Opinions are divided on the how and why of her presence in Rome. Many post-factum sources were biased because of the conflict between de Meeûs and the Jesuits that developed in the late 1860s and will be discussed in Part III. Years after the visit of Boone and de Meeûs to Rome, the Jesuits claimed that she had been a liability, that she could not gain access to the Vatican bureaucracy and that her staying in an unenclosed apartment had given rise to gossip. By contrast, the historiography of the *Institut de l'Adoration Perpétuelle* strongly emphasised that Anna de Meeûs was needed in Rome

---

93 Jarrell, *Legal Structures*, 283-306. Giuseppe Andrea Bizzarri (1802-1877) was attached to the Vatican Congregation of Bishops and Regulars from 1837 onwards: first as under- and pro-secretary, from 1854 as secretary and from 1872 as cardinal-prefect. See: Jadin, "Bizzarri", 49.

94 AAM, CF, Salazar: Boone to Pius IX (s.d., 1863); ABSE, 4.2.6. Boone, 1224: Boone to De Buck (27 May 1863).

95 ABSE, 4.2.6. Boone, 1224: Note by Fr. De Buck. Gabriëlle Baesen (1822-1885) entered the congregation in 1861 and soon became one of de Meeûs' confidents. She later became the first superior of the convent in Ghent, see pp. 220-224.

to rescue the application after Boone's failure to get support from his Roman colleagues and General Beckx.[96]

The reality was far less dramatic than both these versions suggested and pointed rather towards a fruitful cooperation. Authentic travel reports and correspondence from the spring of 1863 show no trace of tension between de Meeûs and the Jesuits. At the most, they expressed frustration about the impenetrability of the Roman bureaucracy. De Meeûs' decision to stay in the prestigious Palazzo Pamphili indeed gave rise to some pejorative remarks by Italian Jesuits. The fact that she had gone to Rome together with her mother, thereby unintentionally highlighting the ambiguous character of her institute, also raised some eyebrows. For the time being, however, these were only incidental remarks. Boone's appreciation for de Meeûs was well-known and, unlike some of her fellow founders, de Meeûs realised that she could not achieve much in Rome without male protection. Some years before, for example, the attempts of the *Dames de Saint-André* of Tournai to get rid of their intrusive bishop through Roman channels failed because of the headstrong actions of their superior.[97] Also, de Meeûs' exceptionally rich family network once again proved its worth in Rome. An appeal was made to François-Xavier de Mérode, who had already lobbied in favour of de Meeûs at the time of the recognition of the association in 1854. Moreover, Anna's mother successfully asked for support of Luigi Ferrari, undersecretary of the Congregation for Extraordinary Ecclesiastical Affairs. Ferrari was an old friend of her late husband Ferdinand and "elle savait qu'il serait heureux de faire quelque chose en mémoire de notre bon père".[98]

The Jesuits also played their part. General Beckx brought the case to the attention of the pope, while de Mérode and Ferrari negotiated behind the scenes. Anna de Meeûs and her mother visited Beckx several times and in the summer of 1863, before returning to Brussels, the family made various financial donations to the Jesuit study house in Rome.[99] At the Congregation of the Bishops and Regulars, the file came into the hands of the French curial prelate Ludovic Chaillot, who as a *consultor* was responsible for French-language constitutions and will be portrayed further on in Part III. His contacts with Boone and de Meeûs were cordial and constructive. He made some remarks about the small membership of her congregation, but still saw sufficient potential in it. Anna de Meeûs wrote to Léopoldine de Robiano on the 4th of May: "on s'étonne, non seulement du bon résultat, mais aussi de la promptitude, il faut

---

96 ARE, *Aperçu Général sur les Rapports de l'Institut avec les SJ. 1er Cahier*.
97 ARE, *Cahier des Lettres 1*: de Meeûs to Léopoldine de Robiano (21 April 1863). For the remarkable story, see: Viaene, "The Second Sex".
98 ARE, *Cahier des lettres 4*: de Meeûs to Léopoldine de Robiano (6 April 1863, 21 April 1863). On Ferrari, see: Boutry, *Souverain et pontife*, 695.
99 ARSI, *Registri Externi Saeculares (1858-1879)*: Beckx to de Meeûs (13 July 1863); ARSI, *Registers Provincia Belgica (1856-1866)*: Beckx to Boone (8 Aug.1863).

être à Rome pour croire que notre affaire marche vite, croyez-le nous sommes au nombre des privilégiées".[100] She was not deceived in her expectations. Finally, on the 20th of May 1863, just three months after Boone's arrival in Rome, the *decretum laudis* was given to the *Institut de l'Adoration Perpétuelle*.

Strong (and wealthy) family networks also offered other female congregation founders a passage into the antechambers of the Holy See. The English Benedictine sisters of Cannington, for example, had already made their way to Rome in the 1830s to plead, with the help of friends and family, their case against the local bishop. The French Emilie de Vialar used family connections to make contact with the nuncio and Roman prelates in 1840 after a conflict with the French bishop of Algiers.[101] In the 1860s, the interventions of Anna's family were characteristic of the specific mechanisms that formed the basis for the expanding ultramontane Church. Pope Pius IX, who from 1859-1860 onwards was threatened in his territorial power and personal integrity by the Italian unification movement, increasingly called on the support of wealthy lay people and the Catholic opinion. The loss of much of the Papal States and the financing of a Zouave army had serious financial consequences for the Vatican treasury, leading Pius IX to look for financial and moral support 'beyond the mountains'. It was no coincidence that the Jesuit De Buck, in his 1863 supplication, referred to the attachment of Belgian Catholics to the pope. The events of 1859-1860 had generated a wave of moral and financial solidarity for the 'prisoner' of the Vatican.[102]

As de Meeûs and Boone were lobbying for papal approbation in Rome in May 1863, the French liberal-Catholic de Montalembert was delivering an impassioned address at the first Congress of Mechelen on "une église libre dans un état libre". His speech captured for the last time the spirit of the revival and the dream of Romantic Catholics to reconcile the Church with modern society. In the coming two decades ultramontane Catholics would dominate the ecclesiastical scene. They created a militant and tensed framework in which the four congregation founders would start a next phase in their convent career. As superior generals they were up for new challenges, balancing once again between docility, agency and power.

---

100 ARE, *Cahier des lettres 4*: de Meeûs to Léopoldine de Robiano (4 May 1863).
101 Champ, *William Bernard Ullathorne*, 213-214; Curtis, *Civilizing Habits*, 121.
102 Lamberts, *Het ultramontanisme*, 49-50; Viaene, "A Pope's dilemma", 250-252.

PART III

FEMALE ENTREPRENEURSHIP AND LEADERSHIP IN AN ULTRAMONTANE CHURCH: FOUR CONVENT SUPERIORS (CA. 1865-CA. 1885)

> Que puis-je hélas! vous dire, aujourd'hui que nous vivons dans un pays barbare? (...) Ici, grâce à Dieu, tout va encore assez bien, jusqu'à ce que peut-être la révolution nous chassera! Il ne faudrait donc pas, chère rév. Mère, être étonné qu'un beau matin nous nous trouvons devant la porte d'une de vos maisons!
>
> ADHH, 183: De Beukelaer to Taylor (12 Sept. 1884).

The ideological tensions between anticlericals and Catholics and among Catholics reached a climax after the mid-1860s. With the fall of the last unionist cabinet following the Convent Law of 1857, liberal governments were in power in Belgium until 1870. Worried about the influence of a Church that had grown considerably and was recruiting widely, liberal policy makers focused more than ever on secularisation and laicisation and on safeguarding the foundations of the liberal state. Under pressure from a growing movement of freethinkers and freemasons, moderate liberals were increasingly being pushed towards a militant anticlericalism, which in turn – as expressed in the dramatic words of Sister Vincent De Beukelaer, Telghuys' assistant, to the English congregation founder Fanny Taylor – raised alarm among Catholics. These developments strengthened ultramontane Catholics in their rejection of the modern, liberal state. The ideological polarisation dominated the societal debate between 1865 and 1885. Political as well as private life became the subject of a fierce verbal battle, which was fought in parliament and in the press, and sometimes also in street skirmishes. Both parties were diametrically opposed to each other and clashed in ideological battles about charity, cemeteries and scholarships. Finally, during the School War (1879-1884), they collided head-on in a divisive conflict about the 'soul of the child'.[1]

With a fearful and rigid siege mentality on the one hand and a chivalrous fighting spirit on the other, ultramontane Catholics pushed for the restoration of a Christian society. The most radical among them even dreamed of one with a theocratic character. Most fundamentalist ultramontanes had nothing but contempt and criticism for the Catholic inspired politicians who came to power between 1870 and 1878 and who sought a *modus vivendi* with modern society. Even moderate ultramontane or vacillating bishops like Kestre's confident Victor Dechamps were attacked. Suspicious of the ultramontane 'orthodoxy' of Catholics in leading positions, ultramontanes preferred to focus on the 'real country'. After the last Congress of Mechelen in 1867, they tightened their grip

---

1   Lamberts, "Het ultramontanisme", 50-52; Witte, "The battle for monasteries", 102-128; Koppen, *De kloosterkwestie*, 118-144.

on Catholic charities and organisations, and after 1875 played an important role in the burgeoning social Catholicism.[2]

Developments and incidents abroad further intensified this Belgian 'culture war' and the internal polarisation in the Church. The French defeat in the Franco-Prussian war and the subsequent Paris Commune of 1871 raised the spectre among Catholics of a disordered, even godless society. Anticlerical measures in France together with the German *Kulturkampf* (1872-1879) reinforced that feeling. In Rome, the secular power of Pope Pius IX came under further pressure from the Italian unification movement. As a martyr in the Vatican he became the leader of the international ultramontane movement and the idol of an entire generation of Catholics. The declaration of papal infallibility at the First Vatican Council (1869-1870) tried to crown him in his new role as moral leader of a world Church, but at the same time strengthened the perception of Catholics as the anti-modern subjects of a foreign ruler.[3]

Within that tumultuous framework, the four women in this study developed into convent superiors and social and religious entrepreneurs. In the following chapters I will explore how they positioned themselves as women, as religious and as female leaders within the dynamics of the national and international ideological struggle. An analysis is made of the ambiguous relations of the four women with often militant Catholic lay people and benefactors, of their apostolic and spiritual entrepreneurship from the double perspective of social and female engagement and anti-modern action, of the way they exercised their leadership within their own convent communities, and in relation to the 'conventualisation' policies of the ecclesiastical authorities in Mechelen and Rome. However, an evaluation of the social and ecclesiastical role of the four superiors can only be done against the background of their religious institutes. The first chapter then focuses on the consolidation and expansion of their congregations in the first decades after the foundation.

---

2   Lamberts, "Catholic Congresses", 214-219; Idem, "Het ultramontanisme", 49-56.
3   Viaene, "The Roman Question", 143-175; Clark, "The New Catholicism", 21-23.

Internal recruitment from among boarding-school pupils was an important recruitment mechanism for teaching congregations. Cornet recruited one out of five of her sisters from the devout members of the Marian congregation in her school, pictured here in the last quarter of the nineteenth century before the Lourdes grotto in the garden of the school.
[Postcard – ca. 1890 – Collection *Sœurs du S. Cœur de Marie*, La Hulpe]

BETWEEN DREAM AND REALITY

CHARISMA AND NUMBERS

In another letter to Fanny Taylor, Sister Vincent was not very optimistic about her congregation's recruitment: "Nous avons en ce moment 11 novices dont 4 novices de chœur, ce qui est beaucoup pour nous, car ici les postulantes ne pleuvent pas comme chez vous et surtout ce ne soit pas toujours de bonnes qui se présentent. La semaine passée nous avons encore refusé 3 postulantes de chœur dont l'une était prétentieuse, l'autre avait un caractère désagréable et la 3ᵉ ne savait pas obéir."[1] At first sight, however, her views did not correspond with the congregation's statistics. The institute was one of the fastest growing religious institutes in the city of Antwerp, reflecting the rapid growth of Belgian female convent life at the time. Both in Belgium and in the archdiocese, the numbers of female convents and of sisters almost doubled in the last third of the nineteenth century. The '*temps des fondations*' of the first half of the century segued into a period of intrinsic expansion. The number of sisters in Belgium rose from about 9,000 around 1850 to more than 30,000 at the end of the century, representing in 1900 more than 46 nuns and sisters per 10,000 inhabitants. Small Belgium was – even in absolute numbers – one of the centres of female convent life.[2]

1 ADHH, 185: Sr. Vincent to Taylor (20 July 1882).
2 Statistics according to Tihon, "Les religieuses", 32, 42, 45. At the turn of the nineteenth and twentieth centuries there were almost 130,000 female religious in France, 40,251 (1901) in Italy, 40,030 in Spain, 50,000 (1908) in Germany, 8,000 (1901) in Ireland, 10,000 in England and Wales and 40,000 in the USA. See, respectively: Langlois, "Les effectifs", 53; Martina, "Italia", 230-231; Miranda Garcia, *Religión y clero*, 257-258; Anderson, "The Limits of Secularization", 653; O'Brien, "A Survey of Research", 109-110; Mangion, *Contested Identities*, 1; Radford Ruether, "Catholic Women", 21. For further international statistical parallels, see Mangion, *Contested Identities*, 46-47.

The number of convent communities in the archdiocese rose from 162 in 1866 to over 500 in 1900 and the numbers of sisters from nearly 4,000 to over 9,000. In contrast to De Beukelaer's perception, vocations were 'raining down' not only in England but in Belgium as well.[3] Still, despite the growing numbers, De Beukelaer voiced an interesting and repeated concern. The rhythm of the recruiting and the quality of the recruits did not always meet the wishes and objectives of the leading sisters or the demands of the growing apostolate. As will be analysed further on, bridging the gap between dream and reality was not always easy.

Moreover, regional differences persisted. In the nineteenth century, the congregations of Kestre, Cornet and Telghuys belonged to the large group of institutes – found mainly in Flanders – with fewer than 50 members and only a few daughter houses.[4] Until the twentieth century this kind of relatively small congregations was dominant in the northern part of the country, where only a small minority of congregations counted more than 100 members.[5] In the period 1857-1885, de Meeûs' institute grew into an international institute, with 112 sisters in seven convents in the mid-1880s. Despite this expansion, and to the frustration of Superior General de Meeûs, the congregation could not compete with some rapidly growing institutes in Wallonia, where large and supra-regional teaching institutes remained dominant. The membership of the *Sœurs de la Providence* of Champion reached the 1,000 mark in 1885-1886, while the *Filles de Marie* of Pesche – Cornet's old school sisters – had almost 400 in the same period.[6]

---

[3] O'Brien notes the robust growth of women's convents in England and Wales in the second half of the nineteenth century, with about 10,000 religious and 549 convents around the turn of the century. O'Brien, "A Survey of Research", 109-110.

[4] Unless otherwise stated, all the statistics and data included in this chapter with respect to the members of the four congregations come from the institute's entrance registers. See: ADHH, 73: Register of Members; ARE, *Registre des members*; ADSJ, *Registre Religieuses de Chœur*; *Registre Sœurs*; ASCMLH, C.1: *Registre des entrées*. Data concerning the social background of the sisters could not be traced via the entrance registers. For this reason, incidental information from chronicles and correspondence was combined with research in the civil registries (birth certificates). In this way, the social background of at least half of the sisters who entered up to the mid-1880s could be traced for each of the four congregations, with a representative spread of geographical origin, date of entry and type (choir or lay sisters).

[5] Art, *Kerkelijke structuur*, 41-43; Fauconnier, *Vrouwenkloosters*, 168-169; Jacobus, *De vrouwelijke religieuze roepingen*, 30-38; Becque, *Le Cardinal Deschamps*, II, 141-148.

[6] Wynants, *Les Sœurs de la Providence*, 305-306.

WOMEN RELIGIOUS (1800-1900)*

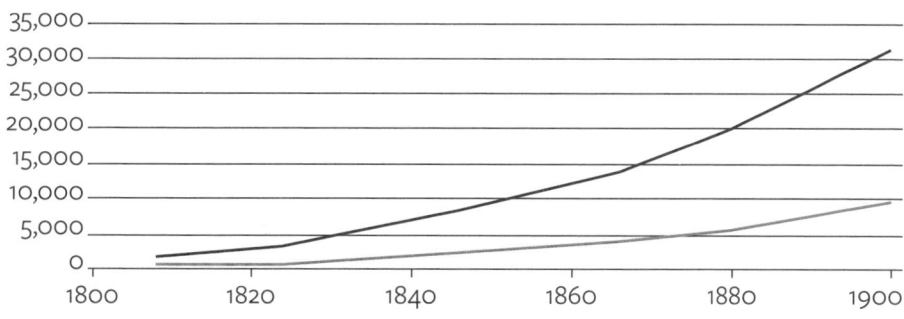

— Belgium
— Antwerp and Brabant (approx. Archdiocese)

WOMEN'S CONVENTS (1800-1900)*

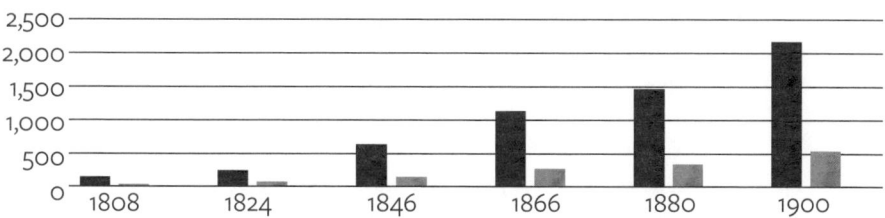

— Belgium
— Antwerp and Brabant (approx. Archdiocese)

* Tihon, *Les religieuses*, 32, 42, 45.

MEMBER STATISTICS (1857-1885)

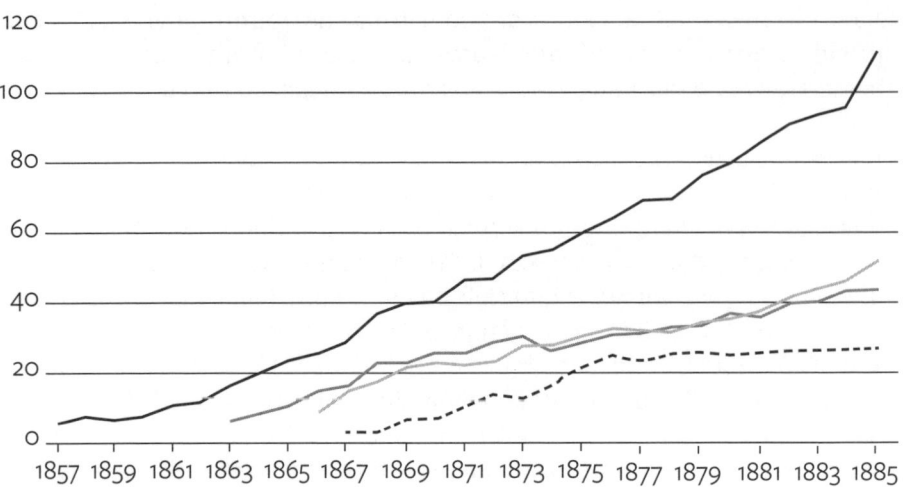

— Institut de l'Adoration Perpétuelle (de Meeûs)
— Sœurs du S. Cœur de Marie (Cornet)
— Dienstmaagden van de H. Harten (Telghuys)
--- Dames de Sainte-Julienne (Kestre)

DAUGHTER HOUSES FOUNDED (AND DISSOLVED) IN THE PERIOD 1857-1886

Institut de l'Adoration Perpétuelle (de Meeûs)	Sœurs du S. Cœur de Marie (Cornet)	Dienstmaagden van de H. Harten (Telghuys)	Dames de Sainte-Julienne (Kestre)
1857: Brussels	1863-1867: La Hulpe	1865: Antwerp	1867: Brussels
1864: Ghent	1866-1886: Bazel	1872-1875: Wuustwezel	1867-1879: Namur
1866: Liège	1867-1873: Steendorp	1875: Kontich	
1866: Maastricht/ Rotterdam	1867: Maleizen	1886: Kontich Rozenhof	
1870: Watermael	1883: Dieupart		
1878: Rome			
1879: Manchester			

The story behind two typical congregations

Marked by a steady growth, Telghuys and Cornet succeeded in extending their pioneering group of five sisters in the mid-1860s to 51 and 44 sisters respectively in the mid-1880s. Their institutes fitted seamlessly into the apostolic mould of nineteenth-century Belgian convents, which was dominated by active congregations with a teaching apostolate or a mixed focus on education and care.[7] Their position in this densely populated market compelled them to strategically align their apostolate and expansion initiatives. This inevitably had consequences for the recruitment policy.

Telghuys' congregation had a diverse recruitment base. The choir sisters mostly came from the urban middle class in Antwerp, with the Jesuit network of Father Schoofs being an important supplier of recruits.[8] From the 1870s on, the choir sisters were outnumbered by the work or lay sisters who, under the impetus of the growing industrial activities of the congregation, came to account for two thirds of the sister population by 1885.[9] Telghuys' lay sisters came from both urban and rural backgrounds. Networks of rural priests ensured a supply of farmers' daughters, who were recruited mainly from the Kempen region in the Antwerp hinterland, with a few others coming from the southern Netherlands and the province of Brabant. Internal recruitment in the *Sint-Franciscus-Xaveriusinstituut* and through Telghuys' various charities in the Antwerp working-class neighbourhoods ensured an increasingly important second stream of recruits.

Despite the initial egalitarian focus within Telghuys' congregation, the choir sisters or '*sœurs*' increasingly pulled the strings in the institute. They managed the large group of work sisters, who were simply addressed with the Flemish '*zusters*'. As elsewhere in Flanders, the social segregation of the second half of the nineteenth century entailed a linguistic divide as well. This

---

7   In 1866 both categories accounted for around 70% of the number of religious and about 77% of the number of convents. On the dominance of active congregations, see: Christens and Suenens, "L'enseignement comme vocation et project", 139; Tihon, "Les religieuses", 39-42.
8   ADHH, 58: Telghuys to De Mol (29 Sept. 1873), Telghuys to Timmerman (31 May 1873); ADHH, 69: Report (18 Aug. 1876).
9   The distinction between choir and lay sisters came from the monastic tradition in which women's monastic communities were divided into a select group of solemnly professed nuns, who devoted themselves exclusively to the Divine Office, and lay sisters who performed manual labour and did not participate in the Divine Office. The distinction was a copy of the situation in the male institutes, corresponding to the difference between priests or choir monks and non-clerical lay brothers. Women religious, of course, never had a priestly statute, which makes the distinction between choir and lay sisters somewhat misleading. The term 'work sisters' is therefore a better alternative, although the terms lay sisters, as well as '*sœurs converses*' or '*sœurs coadjutrices*' were widespread. See: O'Brien, "Lay Sisters", 453-463; Langois, *Le catholicisme au féminin*, 624; Monteiro, *Vroomheid in veelvoud*, 70.

was a legacy of Telghuys' background in the elite, French-speaking bourgeoisie of Antwerp, which, despite her social commitment and Dutch blood, partially determined the profile of the congregation. Telghuys resolutely refused to accept choir sisters who were not fluent in French. Yet, most of the apostolate work – in the orphanage, the parish associations and the schools – was carried on in the Flemish vernacular. Only the professional courses that were set up in 1874 were given partly in French.[10]

Moreover, the growing social distinction in Telghuys' congregation was clearly reflected in the changing financial demands of the institute. The constitutions of 1866 stipulated a sum of 2,500 francs as a dowry for a choir sister. Work sisters paid 1,000 francs, which in the second half of the nineteenth century was two to three hundred francs above the average annual wage of most Belgian factory workers.[11] The amounts were in line with the financial provisions in other congregations that recruited from the lower middle classes. The constitutions of Cornet's congregation, for example, which were based on the provisions of the *Sœurs de Notre-Dame* of Namur, stipulated an amount of 1,500 francs for the choir sisters and 400 francs for the lay sisters, plus an additional sum on profession.[12]

In 1878 new provisions were implemented in the constitutions of the *Dienstmaagden*, requiring 4,000 francs for a choir sister and 500 francs for a work sister. While the work sisters were intensively engaged in the industrial laundry activities, the choir sisters were expected to have more training and intellectual skills to support the expanding teaching apostolate of the congregation. However, the financial requirements were not particularly strict. On the one hand, just as in other congregations, Telghuys was often prepared to compromise if sisters were not in a position to come up with the required amount. Other talents, such as a robust constitution, skills in laundry or needlework, diplomas or teaching experience were then deemed a necessity.[13] On the other hand, affluent families were sometimes asked for more.

---

10   ADHH, 58: Telghuys to Peeters (7 May 1872) and 69: Reports (6 Nov. 1881).
11   ADHH, 44: *Regel en Constitutiën*; Scholliers, "A Century of Real Industrial Wages", 106-136.
12   See: ASCMLH, C.1: *Constitutions*. A further comparison: among the *Zusters van de Christelijke Scholen* of Vorselaar, the *Annonciaden* of Berchem and the *Sœurs de la Providence* of Champion, the dowry fluctuated between 1,000 and 2,000. See: Vanderstraeten and Preneel, *175 jaar Zusters Christelijke Scholen*, 126; Preneel, *Sint-Joanna in Berchem*, 29; Wynants, *Sœurs de la Providence*, 79-81. The centrally imposed rule of the Diocese of Ghent stipulated a dowry of 1,000 francs in 1854, but in the 1870s and 1880s the *Apostolinnen*, the Visitation Sisters, the *Jozefienen* and the *Zusters Kindsheid Jesu* of Ghent (for their choir sisters) all asked for an amount of approximately 2,000 francs. See: Fauconnier, *Vrouwenkloosters*, 182-183; Strobbe and Suenens, *Zusters Kindsheid Jesu*, 75.
13   ADHH, 45: *Constituties*; ADHH, 58: Telghuys to Peeters (18 May 1872), Telghuys to Blomme (3 March 1875), Telghuys to Bruson (29 Jan. 1876), Telghuys to De Weerdt (5 Sept. 1876). Similar conclusions have been made in the case of the *Sœurs de Notre-Dame* of Namur and the *Sœurs de Sainte-Marie* of Namur. See: t'Serstevens, *Le recrutement*, 203, 209.

CHOIR AND LAY SISTERS (1867-1885)*

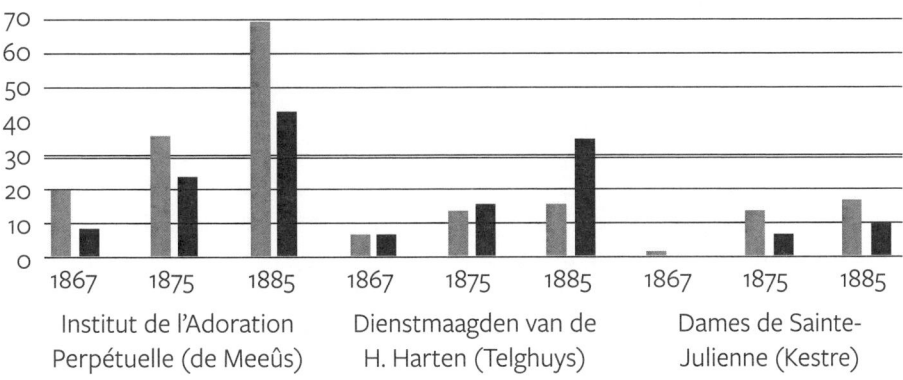

- Choir sisters
- Lay sisters

* The entrance register of the *Sœurs du Saint-Cœur de Marie* (Cornet) did not make a formal distinction between choir and lay sisters.

Telghuys' recruitment partly depended on networks of priests, but she also relied on her own charisma. '*Mère Jeanne*' Telghuys became a well-known figure in the Antwerp working-class districts. Many turned to her in times of need and some even took the step to enter convent life. As will be discussed further on, even the hard work and humble status of the lay sisters was a tempting future perspective for many girls from impoverished backgrounds. This enabled Telghuys to attract 76 postulants between 1866 and 1886. The aforementioned remarks of Sister Vincent De Beukelaer about the difficulties of recruitment was then mostly a reflection of her own vision of the congregation. She was alarmed that the slow increase in the number of choir sisters would jeopardise the educational activities of the institute. More than Telghuys, she was worried about the intellectual level of the congregation, regretting that the industrial laundry activities were determining the congregation's social profile.[14]

Despite the high entrance numbers, Telghuys' congregation did not experience a spectacular growth. In the period noted above, almost a third – 23 out of 76 – of the entrants left, all before the conclusion of the novitiate. The figures for those leaving in the period 1866-1885 were considerably higher

---

14 ADHH, 183: De Beukelaer to Taylor (20 July 1882).

than in the congregations of the other three founders.[15] Moreover, in contrast to the developments noted in other congregations, the number of departures increased rather than decreased over time.[16] In the entrance register, "manque de vocation" was the reason Telghuys most often noted, occasionally alternating with "d'une constitution trop fragile". The work in the laundry was demanding and suitable only for sisters with a robust constitution. Telghuys was very strict in that respect. As already became clear from the words of Sister De Beukelaer, sisters who were too young, too stubborn or too frail were not accepted or were sent on elsewhere. Telghuys' resolute recruitment policy probably contributed to the fact that the *Dienstmaagden* were generally relatively healthy and, despite the hard work, there was no excessive mortality among the young sisters. In 30 years, only two sisters under 30 died. This was strikingly different in congregations with a more tolerant entrance policy. The nineteenth-century *Zusters van de Christelijke Scholen* of Vorselaar, for example, felt compelled to set up their own tuberculosis sanatorium because so many of their sisters, often very young and overworked, fell victim to the disease.[17]

In the first two decades after her foundation, Cornet, like Telghuys, seemed to be doing a competent job at the level of recruitment. She too, had clear principles in mind. Cornet wanted to do everything possible to expand her boarding school. She targeted an affluent middle-class public of shopkeepers, civil servants and well-to-do farmers in and around Brussels.[18] With 54 entrances and an increase to 44 sisters between 1863 and 1885, her congregation experienced a relatively constant growth. Cornet's congregation attracted recruits from socially homogeneous, but geographically very diverse milieus. Most of the sisters came from middle-class and more affluent farming backgrounds. Many came from Brussels, but also from the rural regions of Brabant, Antwerp, Namur, Luxembourg and Hainaut, as well as West-Flanders and the Netherlands. As in other congregations, family ties between sisters played a role. Another important explanation for this geographical dispersion is to be found in the mechanisms of internal recruitment from among the geographically diverse population of boarding-school pupils. In the nineteenth century, Belgian boarding-school education held a strong attraction for many English,

15 Compare the 30% figure for departures from Telghuys' congregation, with approximately 20% from de Meeûs', 21% at Kestre's and barely 13% at Cornet's (although this is probably an underestimation - see infra). Many comparable statistics on departures in the nineteenth century are not available because not all congregations kept statistics on the demographic trend. Wynants does provide consistent figures for the *Sœurs de la Providence* of Champion (slightly more than 11% departures) and the *Filles de Marie* of Pesche (over 7% departures), both well below the figures for the *Dienstmaagden*. See: Wynants, *Les Sœurs de la Providence*, 305-306.
16 Wynants, *Les Sœurs de la Providence*, 86; Langlois, *Le catholicisme au féminin*, 552-553.
17 Vanderstraeten and Preneel, *175 jaar Zusters der Christelijke Scholen*, 144.
18 ASCMLH, F.3.B: *Prospectus*.

Dutch, German and East European families who sought a decent, secured and French-speaking education for their daughters. Official pupil registers for the boarding school were not preserved, but existing membership lists of internal pious associations or congregations in the school indicate that at least one out of five postulants in the congregation was a former pupil and '*congréganiste*'. Once again the pious associations in the convents and boarding schools were important for the prestige and the recruitment of nineteenth-century congregations.[19]

Behind the façade of steady growth, however, conflicts lay hidden. Although the entrance register mentioned only two sisters leaving in the aforementioned period, the correspondence of Cornet, Legrelle and the church authorities noted a higher turnover.[20] This is supported by information from the civil registers, which mention various unknown names that do not appear in the entrance register.[21] Further research made clear that several other sisters left the congregation in the period 1863-1882. Especially in the winter of 1873, the congregation was hit by an important crisis. In the thriving boarding school of the congregation a severe epidemic of scarlet fever broke out. Four pupils died and the school was temporarily closed. In addition, two years in a row the congregation lost a young sister to "des crachements de sang", probably as a result of tuberculosis. In the midst of this crisis, opposition grew among some novices, and the novice mistress Sister Des Anges blamed Cornet for an overly ascetic and rigid policy and a dominant focus on her teaching ambitions. Cornet was not impressed by the criticism and was convinced instead that "l'esprit d'ambition se glissa dans cette âme".[22] The crisis ultimately resulted in the departure of Sister Des Anges, together with some of her novices. Cornet's strict and uncompromising attitude and her boarding school plans became a threat for the future of her congregation.

19 ASCMLH, Registres of the *Congrégation de la Très Sainte Vierge* and the *Archiconfrérie Saint-François-Xavier*. See for parallels, t'Serstevens, *Le recrutement*, 149; De Vroede, "The Catholic Boarding Schools", 315; Christens and Suenens, "L'enseignement comme vocation", 153-154.
20 AAM, CF, La Hulpe: Lauwers to Cornet (5 May 1868), Legrelle to Lauwers (27 April 1868), De Molder to Cornet (10 May 1874); ASCMLH, *Notices autobiographiques*, 9-11.
21 ARLLN, Archive of the Municipality of La Hulpe, 51-53: Population registers (1847-1867, 1867-1880); RAL, Archive of the Municipality of Overijse, 10702: Lists and states of inhabitants (1882-1885) and 10703: Changes of residence (1849-1896).
22 AAM, CF: De Molder to Legrelle (20 Oct. 1874); ASCMLH, *Notice chronologique*, 41-42; ASCMLH, *Notice autobiographique*, 10-11; RAL, Archive of the Municipality of Overijse, 10703: Changes of residence (1849-1896).

"Les Dames illusionnées": ambitions and criticism

It does not come as a surprise that of the four women in our research, the ambitious and opportunistic Anna de Meeûs went in search of new vocations with the greatest diligence. She worried about the modest take-off of her congregation. However, there was nothing unusual about the demographic development of the institute. Ten years after the foundation, the congregation had 25 sisters. By comparison, ten years after their official foundation, the congregations of Cornet and Telghuys had respectively 23 (early 1873) and 29 (early 1876) members. Kestre's congregation also got off to an apparently average start, with 24 sisters after ten years (early 1877) of existence. However, recruitment initially did not keep pace with either de Meeûs' or Kestre's ambitions and expectations, giving rise to internal frustrations and external criticism of their female 'illusions' and the ambiguous identity of their congregations.

Challenges of an elite institute

The initial plan for de Meeûs' institute was modest. Boone had always seen the *Institut de l'Adoration Perpétuelle* as a small and elitist institute.[23] Of the 22 women who were accepted as choir novices in the first 10 years, 13 had an aristocratic title. Others, such as de Druaerts from Brussels, the daughter of a Wavre notary, Maria Lagasse (1839-1914), or Félicité Cawet (1830-1859) from "une des familles les plus opulentes du Luxembourg belge", were recruited from the affluent Catholic bourgeoisie.[24] Only the lay sisters of the congregation – about a third of the average membership – reflected with their farming and middle-class backgrounds the social profile of the average Belgian congregation. An interesting but not unusual detail is that quite a few lay sisters in Salazar had worked as domestic servants in the houses and castles of the elite milieus from which the choir sisters were recruited. Occasionally, their entrance was even sponsored by their former employers.[25] The social relations of the outside world were thus copied inside the convent walls of Salazar.

In the initial decade the Belgian capital was the epicentre of de Meeûs' recruitment network. Fourteen Brussels sisters are listed in the entrance register of the congregation out of a total of 32 choir and lay novices. Although many of the aristocratic novices born in Brussels also had a *pied-à-terre* in the

---

23 ARE, *Extraits pour perpétuer le souvenir*: Boone to de Meeûs (1851); ABME, 4.2.6. Boone, 1231: Spiritual testament of Boone.
24 ARE, *Chronique, XIV. Les débuts*, 141.
25 For example, the Dutch lay sister, Wilhelmina Maartens (1825-1903), first was a servant with the Flemish-Dutch couple De Bruyn-Serruys, benefactors of de Meeûs' congregation in Rotterdam. De Bruyn paid her dowry on her entrance in 1868. ARE, *Nos Sœurs du Ciel – Premier Cahier*: Sr. Marthe de l'Immaculée Conception. Wynants noted similar examples for the *Sœurs de la Providence* of Champion; see: Wynants, *Les Sœurs de la Providence*, 58.

Flemish or Walloon countryside, Salazar clearly started out as a select group of pious women from the metropolitan elite. Moreover, novices from Ghent, Bruges and Hasselt often came into contact with de Meeûs' congregation during their time in the elite boarding schools in Brussels. Some girls from the highly regarded Brussels boarding school of the Augustinian Canonesses of Berlaymont, for example, where a branch of the de Meeûs' *Œuvre des Églises Pauvres* was established, found their way to Salazar.[26]

The constitutions did not stipulate exact requirements about the dowries asked in de Meeûs' *Institut de l'Adoration Perpétuelle*. The loose-lipped Kestre let drop to Dechamps in 1870 that Salazar demanded a dowry of "au moins 20,000 franc". That was without doubt an exceptionally high amount, although one to be regarded with some suspicion given Kestre's bias against Salazar.[27] Compared to the annual allowances granted to married children in some well-to-do families, a once-off, even if large, convent dowry was at first sight a good deal.[28] However, the financial requirements in Salazar were not limited to the usual '*dote*'. In the constitutions, continuing contributions were also considered a precondition for entry. In the family archives of the Casier family – a prominent nineteenth-century ultramontane Catholic family from Ghent – an interesting correspondence between Cécile Leirens (1865-1913), who entered de Meeûs' congregation in 1889, and her parents illustrates the financial pressure that was put by de Meeûs on the families of her wealthy novices. "Lors de mon entrée ici vous avez eu la bonté d'écrire à Mme de Meeûs, que (…) dans toutes les questions de fortune vous me traiteriez toujours comme vos autres enfants. (…) Vous avez accédé, Papa et vous, chère Maman, a ce désir de mes supérieures et avant de faire profession, maintenant que je suis encore libre de mes actes, j'aime à vous rappeler ces promesses que vous avez faites à Mme de Meeûs et grâce auxquelles on m'a reçu dans l'Institut."[29]

The money contributed by the novices was the congregation's main source of income. Together with donations from benefactors, the dowries had to finance the ambitious plans of de Meeûs. The young congregation invested heavily in the construction of a neo-Gothic church and the renovation of

---

26 ARE, *Nos Sœurs du Ciel – Premier Cahier*: Sœur Gabrielle du Cœur de Jésus, Sœur Marie Alphonse du St. Redempteur, Sr. Léocardie de la Croix, Sr. Eugénie de la Croix. For the link with Berlaymont, see: Schyrgens, *Berlaymont*, 235.
27 ADSJ, 1.3./3: Kestre to Dechamps (24 Feb. 1870). Marcélis and Fauconnier mention amounts of between 5,000 and 10,000 francs for the Carmelites who also recruited from among equally high social ranks. Marcelis, *Femmes cloîtrées*, 250; Fauconnier, *Vrouwenkloosters*, 191. In 1860, the elite *Dames Réparatrices* of d'Oultremont asked for 15,000 francs for their choir sisters in Liège. AEL, Fonds de Montpellier, 16. File Réparatrices: Sr. Marie de St. Norbert to de Montpellier (s.d.).
28 De Maeyer, for example, mentions a sum of 6,000 francs, plus board and lodging for the young, Catholic bourgeois Verhaegen-Lammens couple in 1872; see: De Maeyer, *De rode baron*, 86-89.
29 AFC, 652: Cécile Leirens to her mother (19 May 1892).

The eighteenth-century Salazar chapel was situated in central Brussels on the corner of the *Rue des Sols* and the *Rue des Douzes Apôtres*, next to the Gothic convent church that was built by Boone and de Meeûs in de late 1850s.
[Postcard – ca. 1900 – Private collection]

the Salazar Hotel so as to be able to accept more people for retreats, services and other religious events. With the support of the de Meeûs and de Robiano families and of Baroness d'Hooghvorst, chairwoman of the association, a neo-Gothic 'église expiatoire' was completed in 1858 next to the existing Salazar chapel. The convent complex with the new neo-Gothic church and the old Salazar chapel with its medieval past were not only important for the development of the apostolate, they also were expected to alter the ambiguous profile of the congregation. The *Institut de l'Adoration Perpétuelle* presented itself as an elite institute, but continued to struggle with its diffuse identity. This also had consequences for recruitment.

The existing recruit networks of the institute proved to work well in the first decade. Jesuit confessors pointed at least ten of their confessees in the direction of de Meeûs' congregation. Boone was the most successful 'recruiter', but other Jesuits also sent women to Salazar. Other candidates came into contact with the institute through the apostolates. Following the example of de Meeûs, they first committed themselves as *dames d'œuvres* before making the transition to religious life. Nevertheless, the institute's membership base did not keep pace with the rapid geographical expansion that she had embarked on. With the foundations in Ghent (1864), Liège and Maastricht (1866), which will be analysed in the next chapter, de Meeûs imposed a weighty burden on her young institute. At the end of 1867, the management and apostolate tasks in the four convents rested on the shoulders of only 14 professed choir sisters. Compact communities of three or four sisters, serving schools and care institutions in small villages, were not unusual in nineteenth-century Belgium. This was untenable, however, in de Meeûs' urban, semi-active and semi-contemplative foundations, which had a diverse apostolate, combined with intensive worship activities. Other Brussels elite communities, like the canonesses of Berlaymont or the *Dames du Sacré-Cœur* in Jette had over 40 and 70 inhabitants respectively, arousing de Meeûs' frustration about her own numbers.[30]

She was also provoked by the exceptionally rapid international expansion of the *Société de Marie Réparatrice* of her aristocratic contemporary, Emilie d'Oultremont. Only thirteen years after their foundation in 1857, the *Dames Réparatrices*, who shared the active-contemplative profile of de Meeûs' congregation, had more than 300 sisters and 9 houses in 6 countries.[31] Blinded by the competition, de Meeûs did not see the obvious differences between the aforementioned institutes and her own congregation. The *Dames du Sacré-Cœur*, the canonesses of Berlaymont and the *Société de Marie Réparatrice* indeed recruited to some extent in the same elitist environments as Salazar.

---

30 *Annuaire ecclésiastique*, 1860, 56, 59; ARE, *Cahier des lettres 3*: de Meeûs to Boone (14 June 1863).
31 de Gensac, *Présentation historique*, 150; ARE, *Cahier des lettres 3*: de Meeûs to Boone (3 Jan. 1864); ABSE, 4.2.6. Boone, 1264: Report of Father De Buck.

However, they had access to a more diverse recruitment base thanks to their prestigious boarding schools or – in the case of d'Oultremont – their pioneering missions abroad.[32] De Meeûs also continued to resent the rapid success of the *Filles du Cœur de Marie* of her old friend Fanny Maes and the support she was given by the Jesuits in Brussels.

Boone rightly tried to convince de Meeûs that she was overestimating the potential of recruiting in the elite Catholic milieu. Some of his colleagues started mocking the ambitions of the "Dames illusionnées" of Salazar. They advised her to reconcile herself to the idea of a high-quality, but quantitatively modest congregation.[33] Most foundations with an elitist recruitment base indeed had a similar growth in their first decade as the *Institut de l'Adoration Perpétuelle*.[34] Still, de Meeûs' discomfort about the recruitment statistics was also prompted by testimonies of her own sisters. At least five choir sisters who entered in the first decade had vacillated until the last moment between entering Salazar or one of the 'real' enclosed communities of the Carmelites or Poor Clares.[35] With her usual strategic insight, de Meeûs was able to convince a few of the undecideds. She made, for example, a number of well-chosen references to the Carmelite Teresa of Avila, "qui, du reste, a vécu d'une vie toute apostolique, et qui (...) sacrifiait toute sa contemplation du moment qu'il s'agissait de donner à J.C. un tabernacle de plus".[36] However, for other high-born women with a contemplative vocation, the Salazar profile did not sufficiently meet their monastic desires. Moreover, the absence of enclosure and a religious habit also deterred more apostolate-oriented candidates. There is, for example, the story of the German Baroness Thérèse von Wüllenweber (1833-1907). She came into contact with the *Institut de l'Adoration Perpétuelle* through a Belgian cousin in the mid-1860s and eventually made a retreat in Salazar. Anna de Meeûs convinced her in 1868 to enter with the promise that a German convent foundation would be planned in Bavaria. Wüllenweber, however, left in 1870. In her memoirs she praised the sisters of Salazar, but she eventually ran up against the controversial and worldly character of the congregation: "the foundresses were very pious and very distinguished ladies, however (...) they met opposition and (...) had no convent habit".[37] In 1889, she eventually became the first

---

32 Suau, *La Mère Marie de Jésus*, 222.
33 ABSE, 4.2.6. Boone, 1226: Notes of Father Broeckaert.
34 Many nineteenth-century convents of Visitandines and Carmelites in Belgium, for example, counted between 20 and 30 members. See: *Annuaire ecclésiastique*, 1860, 56, 60; Marcelis, *Femmes cloîtrées*, 131-132.
35 ARE, *Nos Sœurs du Ciel – Premier Cahier*: Sœur Gabrielle du Cœur de Jésus, Sr. Amélie du Sacré-Cœur de Jésus, Sr. Clémence de l'Enfant Jésus.
36 ARE, *Cahier des Lettres 1*: de Meeûs to a candidate (18 Oct. 1866).
37 "die Gründerinnen waren sehr fromm und sehr vornehme Damen jedoch (...) Sie hatten Widerspruch und (...) keine Klostertracht". My thanks to Sr. Ulrike Musick (SDS), archivist of the Austrian province of the Salvatorian Sisters, for the excerpts from the memoirs of Theresia von Wüllenweber. For more information, see: Musick, *Therese von Wüllenweber*.

The 'secular' habit of the members of the *Institut de l'Adoration Perpétuelle* (pictured on the left are sisters of the convent of Ghent) was intented to facilitate contacts with the world, but it also deterred many potential candidates from entering the congregation. Thérèse Wüllenweber (1833-1907) (on the right), after leaving de Meeûs' congregation for this reason, became superior of a new congregation with a traditional black and white convent habit.
[Photograph – S.d. – Collection Religieuses de l'Eucharistie, Watermael]
[Photograph – S.d. – Collection Sisters of the Divine Savior, Vienna]

superior of a congregation of Salvatorian teaching and missionary sisters in Rome, with a clear active profile and a traditional black habit.

Wüllenweber came to her conclusions based on her own experience. Other women were warned by their male confessors. In an unsigned report in the archive of the Belgian nunciature, the essential problem was laid bare: "Quel est le directeur prudent qui oserait conseiller facilement un tel genre de vie à une jeune femme?"[38] The report was drafted in the context of the conflict that developed between de Meeûs and the Jesuits after 1867 and was – according to similar documents in the diocesan archives in Liège – probably written by Théodore de Montpellier (1807-1879), an ardent supporter of the Jesuits, and from 1852 onwards bishop of Liège.[39] Once again, Anna de Meeûs paid a price for the diffuse character of her congregation.

Everything changed in 1872, when the constitutions of de Meeûs' institute were definitively approved by Pius IX. As will be seen in the final chapter of this study, it was a hard-won victory over her former critics. Having definitively acquired a pontifical status, the *Institut de l'Adoration Perpétuelle*

---

38 ASV, NB, *Religiose dell'Adorazione Perpetua: Courte relation* (s.d.).
39 AEL, Fonds de Montpellier, 16, File l'Institut de l'Adoration Perpétuelle: *Mémoire sur l'Institut des religieuses de Salazar*.

ascended to another level. At a time when Cornet, Kestre and Telghuys were struggling with the various problems of a beginning, small-scale institute, de Meeûs built hers into a middle-sized and international congregation. In the second and third decades after the foundation, 175 sisters joined the institute and membership increased from 29 in 1867 to 117 in 1886. In the first decade after the foundation of de Meeûs' congregation, no single foreign woman entered, despite the considerable international expansion of de Meeûs' association. Twenty years later, however, a completely different picture emerged. Between 1867 and 1886, at least a third – 57 out of 175 – of the new novices in Salazar was of foreign origin, with Italian (21), Dutch (19) and German (8) sisters especially represented. They were attracted by the presence of the congregation in the Netherlands (from 1866) and in Rome (from 1878), but also by the strong growth of the association in Munich and Palermo, among other places. With the geographic shift, the predominantly aristocratic profile of the congregation also changed. The Brussels baronesses and countesses were succeeded by the daughters of 'manufacturers' from Rotterdam, doctors from the Rhineland, Sicilian lawyers or Liège army officers. They gave the institute a more diverse, though still highly affluent base.

Challenges of a precarious institute

At the end of the 1870s, de Meeûs had surpassed Kestre in every aspect. The continuous struggle for people and resources would not be settled in Kestre's favour. Still, her congregation got off to a promising start. In 1869, she attracted the daughter of a Brussels baker, Albertine Flasselaerts (°1838) to her congregation. Flasselaerts was a typical example of the kind of middle-class women who formed the majority of the choir sisters in the *Dames de Sainte-Julienne*. Almost simultaneously, Théodore Gravez (1867-1883), who had succeeded Dechamps as bishop of Namur, sent two cousins from the distinguished Gérard family of Namur to Kestre's congregation. Kestre initially had doubts about the vocation of Alix Lalieu-Gérard (°1841) and Adèle Delvigne-Gérard (°1846). However, with fathers active in the brewing and mining industries and as notaries, they were an exceptionally good 'catch' for her congregation.[40] The family was prepared to provide a substantial dowry "de quelques milliers de francs", an amount that in general was beyond the reach of the other *Dames de Sainte-Julienne*.[41] Kestre, however, feared the bishop of Namur would interfere too much in her recruitment policy. Moreover, she was worried that the epicentre of her congregation and its apostolate activities would shift too

---

40 ADSJ, 1.3./3: Kestre to Dechamps (29 April 1868) and 1.6: Looijaard to Kestre (11 Dec. 1868).
41 A financial report of 1874 gave a figure of 13,656 francs as the earnings from dowries. Out of a total of 12 sisters (late 1873), this is barely more than 1,000 francs per person. ADSJ, *Rapport de l'Etat général de l'Institut* (1874).

much from Brussels to Namur. The foundation in Namur was 'arranged' by Dechamps in 1867 with the intention of rescuing Kestre from her difficult situation in Brussels, but she herself had little affinity with Namur and continued to focus on her work in the capital.

Under pressure from Gravez and Dechamps, Lalieu and Delvigne eventually entered, quickly won Kestre's approval and together with Flasselaerts and Auchard formed the administrative core of the congregation.[42] After the prosperous start in 1869 however, recruitment became extremely difficult. Only seven candidates – four choir and three lay sisters – entered between 1870 and 1874. Kestre had to divide her little group of sisters between the Namur convent of Salzinnes and the house on the *Rue de la Charité* in Brussels. She also struggled with identity issues. Some of the candidates – and their confessors – mistakenly believed that the convent in Salzinnes was a daughter house of Salazar and that their apostolates belonged to de Meeûs' association.[43] To some extent, they were also confronted with the same prejudices. The Oratorian Pététot, who came to Brussels several times to promote Kestre's apostolate, pointed a finger to "votre costume qui assurément n'a rien de mondain, mais qui n'a pas non plus un caractère religieux". In his view, this dissuaded potential candidates from choosing her institute.[44]

Equally persistent were the rumours about Kestre and Auchard as two eccentrics and the stories about the poor conditions in their convents. While de Meeûs built an impressive infrastructure in Brussels, Kestre had to make do in Brussels and Namur with a few simple rented houses. Pététot also commented on this: "votre maison n'a rien qui annonce une communauté. Elle ressemble à l'extérieur et à l'intérieur aux maisons laïques dont elle est entourée".[45] He recommended some simple interventions – crosses on the doors, some holy images – to give her houses the appearance of a convent. However, Kestre did not have the means to carry out major renovation work and was overwhelmed with other, more acute problems. The damp and chilly rooms in her houses affected the health of the few young people she was able to attract. For example, Alix Lalieu, like Kestre and Louisa Auchard, was laid low every winter by severe coughing and fever, while Albertine Flasselaerts contracted typhus in Namur. The hard-working lay sisters also suffered. Between 1874 and 1877 three lay sister-postulants left the convent in Brussels because of ill-health.[46]

42 ADSJ, 1.3./3: Kestre to Dechamps (21 Nov. 1869); 1.4: Dechamps to Kestre (6 June 1874), Lalieu to Dechamps (s.d.).
43 ADSJ, 1.3./3: Kestre to Dechamps (ca. 1869).
44 ADSJ, 1.7: Pététot to Kestre (29 Oct. 1873). Pierre Pététot (1801-1888) was responsible for the restoration of the Oratorians in France in 1852. Together with Dechamps he was among Kestre's most trusted advisers. On Pététot, see: Boureau, *L'Oratoire*, 70-73.
45 ADSJ, 1.7: Pététot to Kestre (29 Oct. 1873).
46 ADSJ, 1.3./3: Kestre to Dechamps (10 April 1869, Oct. 1869, 21 Nov. 1869).

At times Kestre did not know which way to turn. In her frequent and emotional correspondence with Dechamps, the faltering recruitment was a constant concern, but one that was met with little empathy. Dechamps wrote harsh words: "Voilà bientôt 5 ans que Ste Julienne m'a aidé à vous constituer canoniquement à Salzinnes, et je ne parviens pas à m'expliquer qu'elle n'a pas obtenu, pour son institut plus de deux vocations! Deux vocations en cinq ans... N'y a-t-il pas, chez vous, quelque chose qui explique cette stérilité frappante de la grâce?" This was the downside of Dechamps' passion and romantic belief in divine visions and divine providence. If Kestre's institute were truly a work of God, it would flourish; if not, "De quoi N.S.J.C. n'est-il donc pas content (...)?".[47]

Fanny Kestre was impetuous, stubborn and struggled with the ideal of female humility, but she could not be accused of a lack of piety, commitment or perseverance. In that sense, Dechamps' accusations were unjust, but his judgements were affected by some of her other failures. In 1870, he had allowed her ambitious plans to found an external and internal third order to go through on a trial basis. However, as he had predicted, they did not attract any vocations and after a few years were replaced by an ordinary lay association for devout ladies and catechists. Moreover, his warnings about an overly contemplative profile soon proved to be well-founded. In the early years of the congregation, some of the teachers in the catechesis apostolate were inspired by the charism of Kestre and felt attracted to convent life. They were put off, however, by the strict contemplative regime of the choir sisters in her congregation and decided not to enter. In that respect, Kestre once again had to deal with the same problems as de Meeûs.[48]

Dechamps would have done his own volatile nature an injustice if, despite his sharp criticism, he had not continued to work behind the scenes for his protégée's institute. In 1874 he gave enthusiastic sermons in the cathedral of Namur and the church of *Saint-Gudule* in Brussels on behalf of the congregation. His sermons were later printed and distributed as a promotional brochure for Kestre's institute.[49] In the meantime the lay association had also modestly prospered. By 1874 it had spread across the five Belgian dioceses and had 347 members, some of whom entered the congregation. The combination of lay involvement and episcopal promotion led to several years of growth. Fifteen new postulants entered between 1874 and 1876, broadening the geographical recruitment base considerably. While the first sisters came mainly from Namur, Brussels and the surrounding villages, in the mid-1870s the congregation also attracted postulants from Antwerp, Liège, West Flanders,

---

47   ADSJ, 1.4: Dechamps to Kestre (28 Sept. 1872).
48   ADSJ, 1.3./3: Kestre to Dechamps (18 Nov. 1875); 1.4: Dechamps to Kestre (28 Feb. 1869, 17 Oct. 1870).
49   ADSJ, 1.4: Dechamps to Kestre (1 June 1874, 6 June 1874).

Northern France and the Netherlands. At the end of 1876 the *Dames de Sainte-Julienne* had 23 sisters, eleven more than three years before. However, the effects of Dechamps' promotional campaign were not long-lasting. After 1877, the old problems resurfaced and the growth rate stagnated once more. In 1882, fifteen years after the foundation, the *Dames de Sainte-Julienne* had 26 sisters.

To realise her ambitious boarding school plans, Cornet (above, with the constitutions in her hand) called on the support of the rich Vicountess Marie Vilain XIIII (below, on the right). The aristocratic lady sponsored the construction of a new convent in Maleizen, but in turn maneuvered herself into an important position within the congregation.
[Photograph – before 1883 – Collection *Sœurs du S. Cœur de Marie*, La Hulpe]

CONVENTS AND CASTLES

AN UNEASY ALLIANCE

> vous ne connaissez pas encore assez Mademoiselle; quand elle a fort grondé, il faut faire comme les poules quand elles sont mouillées: elles secouent l'eau et elles vont plus loin.
>
> <div align="right">ASCMLH, <i>Notice chronologique</i>, 48.</div>

Founding a religious congregation not only required (wo)manpower, but financial power as well. This necessity often drove congregation founders towards the wealthy Catholic elite of the country. But – as the quotation of sister Augustine of Cornet's congregation illustrates – cooperating with wealthy Catholic '*Mademoiselles*' was not always easy and often meant dealing with eccentric, stubborn or even dictatorial benefactors. Moreover, in the tense ideological landscape of the culture war of the period 1865-1885 it could also put congregation superiors at the mercy of lay religious fanatics; radical ultramontanes, eager to use their money and influence to restore a Christian society.

From this perspective, it is interesting to examine the situation of post-1850 congregation founders in Belgium in the light of conclusions from the international literature. First, historians focusing on countries where the Catholic population was not in the majority or which had not experienced an expansion of convents similar to that in Belgium have attributed part of the influence of female superiors to their 'power to refuse'.[1] The demand for sisters

---

1 Mangion, *Contested identities*, 228-229; Van Heijst, Derks and Monteiro, *Ex Caritate*, 84-90; Meiwes, "Katholische Frauenkongregationen", 46; Ewens, *The Role of the Nun*, 69.

was greater than the supply, resulting in their superiors having a strong negotiating position. Second, in discussing the situation in post-unification Italy, where the juridical possibilities for convents to own properties was very limited, Scaraffia has made the interesting suggestion that because of the lack of certainty about patrimonial rights, nineteenth-century superiors of convents were forced to develop a strong spirit of entrepreneurship, pragmatism and inventiveness.[2]

In the grip of ultramontane elites

The 'neo-Gothic' network in Ghent

Mina Lammens, the vice-chairwoman of the Ghent *Association de l'Adoration Perpétuelle*, who was planning to enter the strict Carmelite monastery in Charleroi, approached Anna de Meeûs in 1863 about a possible convent foundation in Ghent. Lammens put her in contact with the Ghent cotton industrialist, Joseph de Hemptinne (1822-1909).[3] The de Hemptinne and Lammens families constituted the core of a radical and influential ultramontane lay network in Ghent. With their uncompromising anti-liberal mindset and militant religious zeal, they had few equals in Belgium. They started a conservative and intransigent journal *Le Bien Public*, as opposition to the moderate Catholic *Journal de Bruxelles*. Gathered in mysterious societies, idolising the symbolism of medieval crusaders and knights, they devised strategies for the restoration of a theocratic society under the leadership of the pope. The network sent its sons to the Zouave army and had strong ties with the 'Black International', a secret international organisation directed from the Vatican. They were at the heart of the Belgian branch of the popular Saint Peter's Pence, which was started in 1859 to raise money for their long-suffering idol in Rome. Contacts with the Eternal City were thus close and influential.[4]

The joint initiative of Lammens and de Hemptinne to have the *Dames de l'Adoration Perpétuelle* set up a convent in Ghent was in keeping with both their penitential, ultramontane piety and their strong commitment to Catholic organisations. Ultramontane Catholics strengthened their hold on Catholic social and charitable organisations in the second half of the nineteenth century.[5] In the 1850s and 1860s Lammens was an important figure in Catholic charities in Ghent, as was the already-mentioned Marie de Hemptinne, Joseph's sister. Joseph de Hemptinne and Jules Lammens (1822-1908), Mina's brother, played

2   Scaraffia, "Fondatrici", 479-794.
3   ABG, Poortakker, *Abrégé des Annales* (1863-1864); *Papiers concernant la fondation*.
4   Lamberts, "Joseph de Hemptinne"; Idem, "L'internationale noire"; De Maeyer, *De rode baron*, 89-90.
5   Lamberts, "Het ultramontanisme", 48-49.

a prominent role in the Ghent Vincentians. De Meeûs' congregation appealed to the Ghent network for two reasons. The focus on religious formation fitted in well with their plans to reinstate the Catholic people as a buffer against secularisation and anticlericalism. Moreover, the first Roman approval of the *Institut de l'Adoration Perpétuelle* in 1863 gave de Hemptinne confidence in de Meeûs' Catholic orthodoxy. The obsession of the Ghent ultramontane network with restoring Christian society became very concrete when in 1863 de Hemptinne bought the buildings of the former Poortakker beguinage from the liberal city council of Ghent "afin qu'ils ne fussent pas spoliés".[6] Like many other religious institutes, Poortakker had been secularised during the French regime at the turn of the eighteenth and nineteenth centuries. Lammens and de Hemptinne wanted to restore its religious character by offering it as a convent to de Meeûs.

The 'rescue' of Poortakker came at a cost. Joseph de Hemptinne bought it for 105,000 francs and then leased it to de Meeûs at a rent of almost 4,000 francs a year.[7] In the years that followed, de Hemptinne continued to give financial support to Poortakker. The poor beguine houses into which the first five sisters moved in May 1864 were refurbished with his money. The foundation in Ghent satisfied de Meeûs' ambition to expand, but at the same time pushed her into a relationship of subordination in which many superiors of beginning congregations found themselves. Most nineteenth-century religious institutes were dependent for their success on a solid financial boost from the social elite – with the accompanying demands and whims.[8] Anna de Meeûs' institute was anchored in the upper echelons of society, but the material input of the small pioneer group was nonetheless insufficient to finance all her ambitions. This concern gave rise to a second motive for the new foundation: she hoped to tap into a fertile source of vocations in Ghent.[9] The foundation in Ghent weighed heavily on the limited human resources of the young congregation. The convent was led in 1864 by Gabriëlle Baesen (1821-1885), an unexperienced superior who had taken vows only a year before.

Lammens and de Hemptinne urged de Meeûs and Baesen to work on quickly developing and extending the apostolate. The focus should be on catechism and retreat activities for children and "des personnes moralement vulnérables" from the working classes.[10] The same mix of paternalistic concern and religious-ethical protectionism also determined de Hemptinne's commitment to the Ghent Vincentians and later inspired him in the 1880s to support

6   ABG, Poortakker, *Papiers concernant la fondation, Notice Lammens*.
7   ABG, Poortakker, *Actes Jules Lammens* (8 Oct. 1863, 8 Sept. 1864).
8   Compare with Wynants, *Les Sœurs de la Providence*, 37; Vanderstraeten and Preneel, *175 jaar Christelijke Scholen*, 71-75; Strobbe and Suenens, *Zusters Kindsheid Jesu*, 51-53, 98.
9   ARE, *Cahier des Lettres 3*: Boone to de Meeûs (2 March 1864).
10 ABG, Poortakker, *Abrégé des Annales*, 1864.

the working-class retreats of the Jesuits.[11] Anna de Meeûs, however, had different priorities. In the first instance, she wanted to concentrate on further promoting her association and the adoration activities in the provisionally renovated convent chapel. From 1865 on she was supported in her plans by the newly appointed Bishop Bracq. He considered the elite profile of the new community of sisters as being a serious obstacle to the development of a socially differentiated catechesis apostolate. In the first years after the foundation, the small sister community of de Meeûs did not have any sister who could speak Flemish. For this reason, he favoured the expansion of the association and the devout activities of de Meeûs' institute over the development of a catechesis apostolate. Bracq also stood up for the clergy in Ghent. Less plagued by a shortage of priests than their colleagues in Brussels, the parish priests in Ghent did not want to relinquish responsibility for the religious education of their parishioners. The catechism activities of the congregation in Ghent thus started very modestly, with pupils from the Poortakker neighbourhood only.[12]

Even the headstrong de Meeûs found it difficult to develop her own policy in Ghent. Superior Baesen was overwhelmed by the well-organised network of Lammens and de Hemptinne. Pressure was put on her to urge de Meeûs to provide more 'staff' – a revealing term – for the convent in Ghent. The energetic wife of Joseph de Hemptinne, Pauline Gonthyn (1825-1870), imposed herself on the Ghent branch of the *Œuvre des Églises Pauvres*. In exchange for her generous donations, she demanded that neo-Gothic be the house style of the Poortakker workshops. This was not without significance. Although not exclusively linked to (ultramontane) Catholicism, the neo-Gothic style became the epitome of ultramontane artistic orthodoxy in the nineteenth century.[13] Anna de Meeûs tried to convince Gonthyn of "l'impossibilité d'adopter le gothique et toutes ses idées de perfection" in all aspects of their work. She was afraid the medieval Gothic style would scare of potential association members, catechism pupils or retreat participants. But in the end, de Meeûs had no choice but to accept the preferences of her benefactors. She depended on the network for financial support and also had acquired family ties with the de Hemptinne family.[14]

11 De Maeyer, Heyrman and Quaghebeur, "Een glorierijk verleden", 279.
12 ABG, Poortakker, *Abrégé des Annales*, 1864-1865; ARE, *Cahier des Lettres 3*: Bracq to de Meeûs (25 Oct. 1865), de Meeûs to Boone (7 March 1864). In 1884, Houtart estimated there were about 16,000 inhabitants per parish in Brussels, compared with 8,300 in Ghent. Houtart, *Les paroisses*, 43-44.
13 De Maeyer, *De rode baron*, 103-105; Pirotte, "Néo-gothique", 255-262.
14 ARE, *Cahier des lettres 3*: Gonthyn to de Meeûs (15 May 1865); ABG, Poortakker, *Abrégé des Annales*, 1864-1865. In 1875 Paul de Hemptinne, son of Joseph, married Idalie de Meeûs (1852-1921), the daughter of Anna de Meeûs' brother Ferdinand. In the second half of the nineteenth century, the de Meeûs family had capitalised on its newly acquired aristocratic status with an impressive list of sons- and daughters-in-law from older Belgian and French noble families. See: AFJDH, 2.3.2.8.3: Anna de Meeûs to Idalie de Meeûs (1 Nov. 1869), Anna de Meeûs to Paul de Hemptinne (8 Dec. 1882).

With the support of an ultramontane network of benefactors, de Meeûs was able to build a convent and chapel in the city of Ghent in the 1870s. In return she had to accept the neo-Gothic preferences and the interference of a conservative, ultramontane elite.
[Postcard – S.d. – Private collection]

From the end of the 1860s onwards, plans were made to replace the old Poortakker buildings with a new building, financed almost entirely by de Hemptinne. The engineer and architect Arthur Verhaegen, who was married to Mina Lammens' niece, drew up the plans. In close consultation with Jean-Baptiste Bethune, his mentor and godfather of Belgian neo-Gothic, a complete neo-Gothic project was realised in the 1870s, including a chapel, a convent and apostolate buildings. Initially, Anna de Meeûs had her doubts about the attractiveness of this medieval shrine: "Est-ce que ces bâtiments vont appeler aux enfants ou les dames de l'Association qui ont ni l'esprit de foi exclusive, ni le goût de mr. de Hemptinne?"[15] She pushed for a number of small adjustments, but following mediation by Mina's brother Jules, she finally gave her approval.[16] It was the *modus vivendi* de Meeûs was forced to accept in Ghent.

Family support in Liège

Barely two years after the opening of the convent in Ghent, de Meeûs also sent sisters to Liège. The project for a foundation in Liège was realised with the support of de Meeûs' Jesuit network. Frederic Bossaert (1804-1867), rector of the Jesuit college in Liège, brought Anna de Meeûs into contact with Bishop de Montpellier who wanted to stimulate devotion to the Blessed Sacrament in his episcopal city. Plans were made for the takeover of the 'Hotel Spirlet' in the *Hors Château* district, which until then was in the hands of the *Sœurs de Notre Dame* of Namur. A conflict arose, however, between the Namur sisters and Anna de Meeûs. Together with her brother and spokesman, Henri de Meeûs (1826-1913), she complained about the takeover price of 111,000 francs, which she considered to be much too high. Henri was a prominent figure in the Liège industrial and banking world and a benefactor of many religious associations and charities. Later he would also become involved in the anti-socialist labour movement. His influence and financial strength were crucial for his sister's project, since in Liège too complex power relations and spheres of influence existed between religious, wealthy lay people and the diocesan authorities. The *Sœurs de Notre Dame*, supported by the Liège Jesuits, refused to lower their price. Anna and Henri accused them of chasing profits at the expense of another religious institute. Bishop de Montpellier tried to mediate, but was shocked by Anna de Meeûs' assertiveness. It shaped the negative image, already mentioned, that he formed of her and would also determine his

---

15 ARE, *Cahier des Lettres 3*: de Meeûs to Léopoldine de Robiano (14 Sept. 1872). About Bethune, see: De Maeyer, *De rode baron*, 97-98.
16 ARE, *Cahier des Lettres 3*: de Meeûs to Maria Lammens (14 April 1873). On this, see also: De Maeyer, *De rode baron*, 111.

rigid attitude in the dossier concerning the definitive Roman recognition of de Meeûs' congregation a decade later.[17]

Nevertheless, he gave his blessing for the erection of a convent, not in the *Hotel Spirlet*, but next to the church of *Saint-Anne* which had been bought by Henri de Meeûs. Just like the Poortakker beguinage in Ghent, the former monastic church of the Augustinians on *Boulevard d'Avroye* was rescued in this way from secularisation and decline through the intervention of wealthy lay people. At the same time, Henri de Meeûs' financial support served as collateral for the foundation plans of his sister. The family would invest a total of over 200,000 francs in Liège over a period of several years for the restoration of the chapel and premises for the sisters and the apostolate activities. To the frustration of de Meeûs, the diocese's contribution to the costs, which de Montpellier had promised would amount to 68,000 francs, was not paid until 1875.[18] In addition, as in Ghent, resentment grew among the Liège clergy about the catechetical plans of de Meeûs' sister community which they saw as a threat to their own parish catechesis ministry. The struggle for children, lay workers and benefactors for this work, combined with the limited capacity of the small sister community in Liège, made it difficult to develop a proper apostolate in the city.

Kestre's unequal struggle for autonomy

Though operating in a smaller network than de Meeûs, Kestre too was quickly confronted both with the militant ambitions of benefactors as well as the underlying internal tensions of the nineteenth-century Church. At the end of the 1860s, Dechamps drove the financially and socially vulnerable Kestre into the arms of Antoine 'Tony' Baron Del Marmol (1832-1904), an aristocratic mining engineer from Salzinnes, and his wife Marie de Dorlodot (1835-1882).[19] Baron Del Marmol had already proved to be a generous benefactor to the Redemptorists and was now urged by Dechamps to support Kestre as well. After Dechamps's appointment as archbishop of Mechelen, Kestre was left with few supporters in Namur and could indeed use some extra backing.[20]

Antoine Del Marmol was a typical devout and combative ultramontane, but without the pronounced extremism of de Hemptinne. Together with

17 AEL, Fonds de Montpellier, 17/9. *Sœurs de Notre-Dame. Affaire Salazar/de Spirlet*: Henri de Meeûs to de Montpellier (2 Oct. 1864), Bossaert to de Montpellier (23 Oct. 1864); ABSE, 4.2.6. Boone, 1227: De Montpellier to Bossaert (1 Sept. 1863, 14 Nov. 1864, 12 Nov. 1864).
18 AAM, CF, Salazar: Notice de Meeûs (July 1875); Godinas-Thys, "Les sœurs du Saint-Sacrement", 137-160.
19 ACSSR-NB, 1496: Dechamps to Kestre (25 Sept. 1866); ADSJ, *Cahier 37.1*: Dechamps to de Villermont (15 March 1861); Becque, *Le Cardinal Dechamps*, II, 134; De Maeyer and Wynants (eds.), *De Vincentianen*, 341.
20 ADSJ, 1.6: Leloucher to Kestre (25 Jan. 1870).

Gravez, the outspoken ultramontane bishop of Namur, he tried to reclaim the impoverished and secularised Salzinnes neighbourhood for the Church.[21] He was a director of the Vincentians, the Franciscan lay order and the confraternity of Sainte-Julienne founded by Dechamps in Namur. He supported the local Catholic school and had a neo-Romanesque – and not a neo-Gothic – parish church and presbytery built in 1880 at his own expense. Later he donated the building to the local church council, thereby earning a pontifical appointment as '*Cameriere di spada e cappa*'.[22]

In 1871, at Dechamps's request, the Del Marmol couple bought the two rented houses on the *Rue de la Charité* that together formed the Brussels convent of Kestre's congregation. They also sponsored Kestre's catechesis efforts in Salzinnes. The baroness became active as a patron of the liturgical vestments workshop of Kestre's lay association in Salzinnes and financed promotional leaflets for the institute and the apostolate. In 1873 the baroness also proposed to buy the house that Kestre's community rented in Salzinnes to help the sisters in their work.[23] Kestre held off. Just as in the case of the novices that were suggested by Bishop Gravez, she feared having to accept greater interference by the baroness in return for the favour. However, under pressure from an ironic Dechamps – "vous pensez tout faire vous-même?" – she finally succumbed.[24] Antoine Del Marmol bought the houses in 1875 for 50,000 francs. The generosity of the Del Marmol couple freed Kestre from many of her material worries, but saddled her independent spirit with an uneasy sense of being patronised and controlled.[25]

A forced turn to the countryside

Kestre's fears were not unfounded, as would later turn out. In the second half of the 1870s she clashed fiercely with the Del Marmols. Cornet and Telghuys also felt the pressure of demanding benefactors. Much more than Kestre, however, they both would develop the necessity-driven entrepreneurial capacities and strategies that Scaraffia analysed with regard to their Italian counterparts. Nonetheless, they also experienced the very oppressive downside of their dependence on a lay-religious alliance.

By mediation of Father Legrelle, Cornet started a cooperation with Vicountess Marie Vilain XIIII (1811-1883). Both in name and in fact, the

21 On Gravez as an ultramontane, see: Lamberts, "Het ultramontanisme", 49-53.
22 Del Marmol, *Notice généalogique*.
23 ADSJ, 1.3./3: Kestre to Dechamps (8 April 1873); 1.4; Dechamps to Kestre (13 Nov. 1871); 1.7: Del Marmol-Dorlodot to Kestre (12 Aug. 1873); ACSSR-NB, 1496: Dechamps to Kestre (1875).
24 ADSJ, 1.4: Dechamps to Kestre (3 March 1874).
25 ADSJ, 1.3./3: Kestre to Dechamps (8 April 1873, 16 April 1873); ACSSR-NB, 1496: Dechamps to Kestre (1875).

Vilain XIIII family was a peculiar Belgian aristocratic family. Big landowners with industrial and financial interests, they were not exclusively identifiable with the traditional Belgian landed aristocracy, nor with the new emerging class of nineteenth-century rich industrialists. The male family members played an important role in local and national politics and successfully survived the various regime changes of the later eighteenth and nineteenth centuries. Marie's brothers, Charles (1803-1878) and Alfred (1810-1886), were moderate Catholic politicians. Their father, Philippe (1778-1856), was a buyer of 'black goods' – ecclesiastical property that was confiscated and sold by the French regime – but later on reinvented himself as a leader of the Belgian Catholic nobility.[26]

Marie Vilain XIIII remained unmarried and lived in a mansion near the family castle in Bazel, a small village in East Flanders, between Sint-Niklaas and Antwerp. She totally devoted herself to a life of charitable works. She inherited the patronage of the local Catholic girls' school founded by her father and also sponsored a local hospital and the foundation of the Poor Clare convent in nearby Lokeren. In the mid-1860s, she wanted to start schools in the villages of Steendorp and Rupelmonde, where she was an important landowner.[27] Her stubborn and authoritarian character, however, repeatedly antagonised the sister congregations she had invited as teachers: the *Zusters van Sint-Vincentius* of Gijzegem and the *Annonciaden* of Ranst successively withdrew from the school in Bazel. She flouted diocesan directives that tried to push her in a more cooperative direction, thereby increasingly annoying Bishop Bracq of Ghent.[28]

Encouraged by Legrelle, Cornet decided to join forces with Marie Vilain XIIII, despite strong warnings from the diocesan authorities in Mechelen and Ghent about her stubborn character. Cornet was left with little choice. She had to find a benefactor to enable her to realise her ambitious plans for a new boarding school. Fed up with the continuous interference of parish priest Chevalier and the poor living conditions in La Hulpe, she was thinking of relocating her convent. In 1865 she wanted to buy a three-hectare site in Maleizen, a small Flemish village next to La Hulpe. Marie Vilain XIIII agreed to give Cornet financial support in exchange for sisters to serve her East Flemish schools. In March 1866, barely a month after the first meeting, the first three sisters left for Bazel. In September 1867, on the impatient insistence of Vilain XIIII, a second delegation went to work in Steendorp. For Cornet, there was no such thing as the 'power to refuse' mentioned in international literature, but rather a compulsion to accept new convent foundations, having been forced into this

---

26 On the Vilain XIIII family, see: Francois, "Philippe Vilain XIIII"; Snauwaert and De Wilde, *Het kasteel van Wissekerke*.
27 ASCMLH, F2.6: Copies Fund Vilain XIII, 5535; AFV, 539-540: *Basel. Écoles*.
28 ABG, Fonds Bracq, 2.3.1.3: Van Hemel to Bracq (4 June 1865); AFV, 539-540: *Basel. Écoles*.

position by her own entrepreneurial boarding-school plans. Cornet sacrificed all her Flemish-speaking sisters to the rural schools of Vilain XIIII. The diocesan authorities in Ghent and Mechelen tried to persuade her otherwise, but ultimately admitted that "la comtesse offre tant d'argent, qu'aucune supérieure dans sa position pourrait le refuser".[29]

In 1866-1867, Marie Vilain XIIII donated 60,000 francs for the acquisition of the domain in Maleizen and the construction of convent and school buildings. From a comparative female perspective, it is important to note that Marie Vilain XIIII, as an unmarried and childless aristocrat, could freely dispose of her fortune, a privilege reserved to only a very small minority of women in the nineteenth century. Drawing primarily on income from her extensive property, she was a textbook example of the last wave of important funding of religious initiatives by the old landed aristocracy in the period 1865-1885. Afterwards, the dramatic School War of the mid-1880s, economic upheavals, the crisis in Belgian agriculture, better financing provisions for Catholic initiatives and a *'fatiguer de donner'* among the elite other opportunities had to be searched.[30]

Telghuys too benefited from pious Catholics with large fortunes, although she was not dependent on the traditional landed aristocracy. Like de Meeûs, Telghuys looked to her own social milieu for funds and got support from bourgeois families in the Antwerp shipping and banking businesses. Unlike de Meeûs' network in Ghent, this was not one of radical ultramontanes with a clear political agenda. Telghuys' entourage was dominated by less extremist Catholics, who believed more in the guiding and moral strength of Catholicism. They did not play a leading role in the national ultramontane organisations, but nonetheless contributed to the Catholic cause on a more modest and personal level. In a sense, Telghuys' benefactors bore some resemblance to Harrison's cosmopolitan Romantic Catholics from the first half of the nineteenth century, and also to figures from countries where the extreme ultramontanism of de Hemptinne attracted fewer followers. The two great patrons of English Catholic charities for example, Lady Georgiana Fullerton (1812-1885) and Lady Herbert (1822-1911), threw themselves into helping local religious communities as generously as did Belgian benefactors. At the same time, they kept an open mind on the world, became involved in the political and intellectual salon culture, maintained contacts with politicians and lived in the cosmopolitan milieu of women writers.[31]

There are some, but not many, equally influential Belgian equivalents. Pauline Delehaye (1819-1880) was a niece of Josse Delehaye, the Catho-

29 ABG, Fonds Bracq, 2.3.1.3: File of Vilain XIIII (1865-1866).
30 Wynants, *Les Sœurs de la Providence*, 139, 293; Van Molle, *Ieder voor allen*, 22-30.
31 On Fullerton, see: Harrison, *Romantic Catholics*, 184-1864; Shaw, *Elizabeth Hayes*, 62-63; de Giorgio, "La bonne catholique", 178. On Herbert, see: O'Neil, *Cardinal Herbert Vaughan*, 158-167. Herbert will return later in the English adventures of Anna de Meeûs.

lic mayor of Ghent from 1854 to 1857, and the wife of Edouard Ducpétiaux, philantropist, reformer of the prison system and the liberal-Catholic initiator of the first Mechelen congresses. Delehaye played a pivotal role in a network of Catholic charitable organisations.[32] Using her husband's contacts, she also became involved in promoting the Brussels branch of the *Œuvre des Églises Pauvres*, thereby proving that the pragmatic de Meeûs did not rely exclusively on ultramontane circles. The aforementioned aristocratic traveller and writer, Juliette de Robertsart, based her patronage of Catholic charities on her ultramontane inspiration.[33] Like Fullerton and Herbert, however, she kept in touch with the world. Some time later, Marie Elisabeth Belpaire (1853-1948) emerged from the culture-loving milieu of the Teichmanns in Antwerp as a Catholic writer and an important figure in Catholic girls' education and the Catholic publishing world. Just like her contemporaries Anna Boch (1848-1936) and Marie de Villermont (1848-1939), she combined her artistic aspirations with a deep commitment to Catholic charitable work. Anna Boch was a painter and ideologically had a rather neutral profile, but she did support Catholic good works. Marie de Villermont, also a painter, was the daughter of Count Charles, the aforementioned benefactor and critic of Kestre in Brussels. Though from a radical ultramontane family, she developed a broad and tolerant world view. She was the engine behind a number of local Catholic women's groups and committed herself to Catholic works and Catholic organisations.[34]

Telghuys could rely on women with a comparable disposition. She received donations from her old childhood friends in the affluent Antwerp business world and Bogaerts' parish associations: Ludovica Delehaye and Adelaïde Havenith-Fuchs. Thanks in part to their support, a neo-Gothic chapel was erected in 1870 on the grounds behind the *Sint-Franciscus-Xaveriusinstituut* in Antwerp, replacing the small prayer room that the sisters had to make do with until then. In return for their generous support, Ludovica Delehaye (1834-1928) and her husband Laurent asked Telghuys in 1870 to open a school on their estate in Wuustwezel.[35] Like Cornet, Telghuys had other apostolic priorities than providing education in rural areas. For two years she had doubts about the project in Wuustwezel. Finally, she gave in to the pressure of Bogaerts and her friend Ludovica. Laurent Delehaye offered Telghuys and her sisters free housing in the hamlet that bordered on his estate, along with

---

32 de Haulleville, *Portraits*, II, 232.
33 Dupont-Bouchat, "Pauline Delehaye", 172-173; Mortier, *Juliette de Robertsart*.
34 Reymenants, *Marie Elisabeth Belpaire*; Puissant, "Boch, Anna", 62-63; Wiertz, "Une femme complète".
35 Ludovica Delehaye was married to Laurent Delehaye (1827-1889), a shipowner and insurer in the maritime sector. The couple lived in Antwerp, but from the end of the 1850s they had a second home in Wuustwezel in the Kempen countryside, where Delehaye ran an experimental farm on their Sterbos estate. Cuyvers, *Geschiedenis van Sterbos*, 32-33.

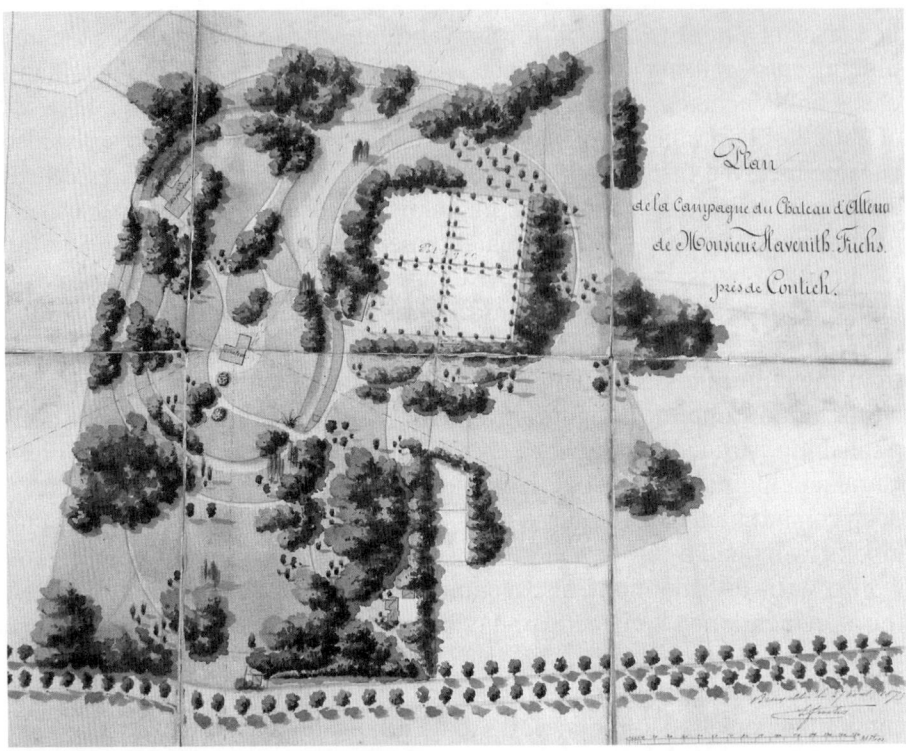

Collaboration with the Antwerp Catholic bourgeois elite gave Telghuys the opportunity to move her laundry activities to a large estate in rural Kontich with ponds and meadows to facilitate the expansion of her laundry business, but it also compelled her to accept directives of her benefactors.
[Plan – 1873 – ADHH, 251]

the maintenance costs for the school and convent buildings, a chapel and an annual allowance of 3,400 francs.

In order to meet the wishes of her benefactors, Telghuys sent two of her sisters on a course to the renowned teacher training school of the Ursulines in Onze-Lieve-Vrouw-Waver in the spring of 1872. Finally, in July 1872, the first four sisters of the congregation settled in Wuustwezel.[36] Though struggling with the somewhat enforced character of the project, Telghuys quickly regained her entrepreneurial spirit. Barely a year after the foundation, she persuaded Delehaye to set up a farm next to the convent in Wuustwezel, which would supply fresh products to her sisters and the residents of the Antwerp foundation. As was the case with Cornet, the 'compulsion to accept' was as closely related to the entrepreneurial ambitions of the female superior as it was the consequence of her difficult alliance with lay benefactors.[37]

36 ADHH, 40: Obituary; 58: Telghuys to the superior of the Ursulines (12 April 1872 and 15 May 1872); 69: Report (18 Oct. 1873).
37 ADHH, 58: Telghuys to Delehaye (14 Oct. 1873); 69: Report (30 March 1873, 10 Sept. 1873).

This became even more clear in the case of the new foundation in Kontich. Adelaïde Havenith-Fuchs (1832-1905) was a wealthy *dame d'œuvres* involved in the networks of Bogaerts and the Teichmann family.[38] In 1874 she proposed to sell her fifteen-hectare estate and castle, 'Altena', in Kontich to Telghuys' congregation. Unlike the foundation in Wuustwezel, Telghuys saw the immediate potential of this proposal.[39] A possible move of the laundry and the orphanage to Kontich would relieve the overcrowded Antwerp institution. In Kontich there was room for a semi-industrial development of her profitable *'blanchisserie'*. Moreover, this would create a more respectable image for the Antwerp convent, which was important in attracting sufficient resources and choir novices. In September 1875 20 sisters and 70 orphans left the Antwerp house for the Altena Castle in Kontich. With the help of loans, support from her two unmarried sisters and some of the families of the choir sisters, Telghuys had amassed the 150,000 francs that Havenith-Fuchs was asking for her estate. It was a considerable amount, but her business sense was reassured by the fact that "chacun nous dit que c'est un peu au-delà de la moitié de la valeur".[40] Part of the costs could also be recuperated because some rooms of the castle were sublet again to Adelaïde Havenith-Fuchs.[41]

"Au comble du bonheur": women for women

Nevertheless, the relationship between Telghuys and her friend Aldelaïde Havenith-Fuchs was much less unilateral than appeared at first. Further investigation revealed that Havenith-Fuchs was in financial difficulties following the death of her husband and the financial recklessness of some of her sons. The country house in Kontich and the family estate in Mortsel were sold well below the market price to pay off the family's debts.[42] Telghuys profited from this. However, she also wanted to help an old friend in need. This was further proof that female bonding between prominent women inside and outside the convent walls remained intact after the foundation period. The original network of *dames d'œuvres* continued to underpin a female space of development and solidarity. It gave women religious both material support and social legitima-

---

38 Adelaïde Fuchs came from an affluent Antwerp banking family and became the second wife of Charles Havenith (1820-1874), who was involved in maritime trade in the port of Antwerp; see: Mercier, *Prins Diamant*, 194; ADHH, 4: Nieuwland to Telghuys (31 Oct. 1870).
39 ADHH, 58: Telghuys to Havenith-Fuchs (7 Aug. 1874), Telghuys to De Molder (28 Sept. 1874); 69: Report (24 and 25 Sept. 1874).
40 ADHH, 58: Telghuys to De Molder (3 Oct. 1874).
41 ADHH, 69: Reports (30 Dec. 1874, 20 April 1875, 5 May 1875).
42 This is suggested by a number of legal judgements as well as the arguments used by the Ministry for Foreign Affairs for its initial refusal of a diplomatic mission to one of Havenith's sons. See: *Jurisprudence de la Port d'Anvers*, 1874, I, 14; Coolsaet, Dujardin and Roosens, *Buitenlandse zaken*, 75.

tion, while providing lay women with social relevance and a workforce for their charities. Moreover, support, motivation and power were mutually exchanged. Internationally, historians have pointed to the importance of this permanent cross-fertilisation between lay women and religious in various contexts.[43]

Ludovica Delehaye could also count on the support of Telghuys. Delehaye used to get lonely during the summer months in the domain in Wuustwezel, while her husband was busy managing the estate and the model farm. According to a mutual friend, Ludovica was "au comble du bonheur" when Telghuys in 1872 consented to the school project in Sterbos. She could now carry on her work as an urban *dame d'œuvres* in her country home.[44] Female alliances also emerged in Ghent and Salzinnes. Despite her initial restraint, Kestre got along well with Baroness Marie-Thérèse Del Marmol-de Dorlodot. Kestre's project offered Dorlodot the chance to escape "la vie vide du château" and Kestre was able to talk to the baroness about her problems in Brussels. De Dorlodot was actively involved in setting up a fundraising campaign for the benefit of Kestre's Brussels convent.[45]

Although irritated by the meddling and neo-Gothic obsessions of Pauline de Hemptinne-Gonthyn, de Meeûs had close ties with other women in the Ghent ultramontane network. Her close relationship with Mina Lammens has already been mentioned. With Emilie van Outryve-d'Ydewalle (1826-1894), the wife of the architect Bethune who was a member of the Ghent branch of de Meeûs' association, she gossiped and 'cocooned' like a schoolgirl. Like Anna de Meeûs, Emilie van Outryve-d'Ydewalle was an enterprising woman, managing the artistic business of her husband.[46] Emilie also confided to de Meeûs in 1864 that her then fifteen-year-old daughter Marie-Antoinette (°1849) was thinking of entering the convent of Poortakker. A year later she urged her husband to use his connections in English artistic circles to get the *Œuvre des Églises Pauvres* off the ground across the Channel. Although neither 'project' was brought to a successful conclusion, both women remained friends.[47]

The ultramontane women's network in Ghent generated a new stream of recruits with the entrances of the choir sisters Louise Rogiers (°1845), Clara Van Crombrugghe (°1844) and especially Marie Lammens (°1848), Mina's

---

43 Eijt, *Religieuze vrouwen*, 189-190, 194; Van Heijst and Derks, "Godsvrucht en gender", 36-37; Luddy, "Possessed of fine properties", 230-237; McNamara, *Sisters in Arms*, 619.
44 ADHH, 4: Nieuwland to Telghuys (31 Oct. 1870); 58: Telghuys to De Molder (2 Sept. 1872).
45 ADSJ, 1.8: de Dorlodot to Kestre (12 Aug. 1873); ADSJ, *Livre des fondateurs* (1874).
46 De Maeyer, *De rode baron*, 129, 575; Wiertz, *Adellijk*, 91-139.
47 ABG, Poortakker, *Abrégé des Annales*, 1864-1865; ARE, *Cahier des lettres 3*: de Meeûs to van Outryve (14 March 1864, 29 May 1865). Bethune's English connections came, primarily, from his contact with the deceased English neo-Gothic pioneer, the architect A.W.N. Pugin. On Bethune and Pugin, see: Maury, "The True Disciple".

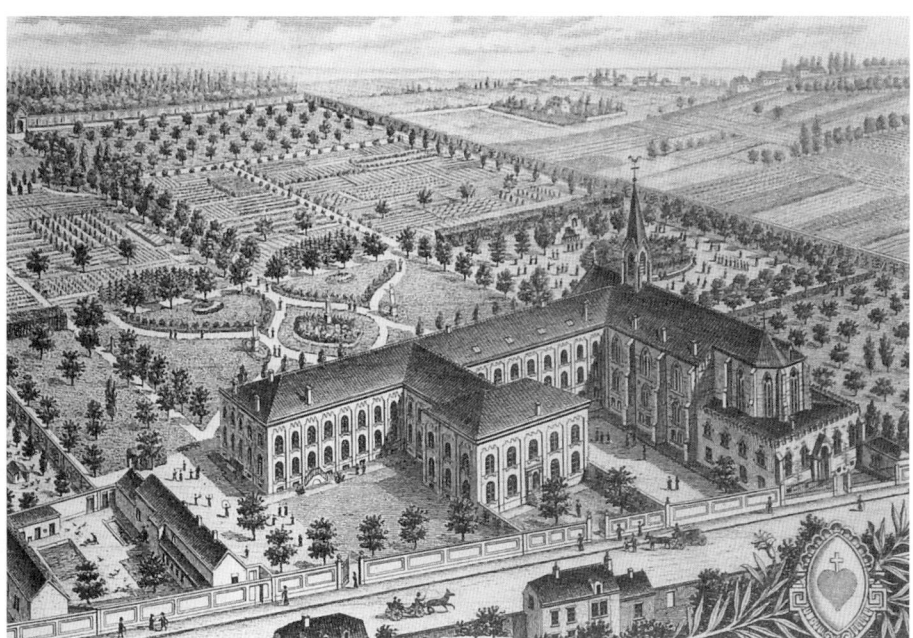

In the late 1860s and in the 1870s Cornet's new boarding school and convent were constructed in Maleizen, a Flemish village in the leafy environment south of Brussels. Prospectuses with idealised drawings and advertisements in Catholic newspapers had to attract daughters from civil servants, shopkeepers and well-to-do farmers.
[Prospectus – S.d. – Collection *Sœurs du S. Cœur de Marie*, La Hulpe]

niece.[48] At first glance then, Marcélis' conclusion regarding the Belgian Poor Clares and Carmelites seems confirmed: "les femmes laïques approvisionnent les couvents en argent (et en enfants)".[49] However, the cases of our four superiors indicate that the female alliance went beyond emotional and material support. Lay women involved in apostolate work and religious sisters sometimes felt empowered to enter male territory in 'tandem'. Marie Vilain XIIII and Antoinette Cornet together drew up the plans for a convent and neo-Gothic church in Maleizen in 1866. The young Brussels architect Almain de Hase finished off the project and also supervised its construction. Despite the peculiar personality of Vilain XIIII, the consultation with Cornet about the building

---

48 Louise Rogiers was a confessee of the Jesuits in Ghent, but was encouraged by Emilie van Outryve-d'Ydewalle to enter. Clara Van Crombrugghe was steered into the association and later the congregation by Marquise de Courtebourne; see: ARE, *Cahier des Lettres 3*: Rogiers to de Meeûs (30 Aug. 1864); de Courtebourne to de Meeûs (15 May 1866).
49 Marcelis, *Femmes cloîtrées*, 646.

plans was surprisingly open.⁵⁰ Still, there is no doubt that the viscountess, while making use of Cornet's dependency and position as a religious woman, was ultimately in control. She carried on the correspondence with the architect and she made the final decisions, even if some luxurious aspects – like the marble floors of the convent for example – were in contradiction with Cornet's ascetic principles.

With the completion of the neo-Gothic convent church in 1879-1880, an imposing building complex was created in Maleizen, the result of Cornet's ambitious plans and Vilain XIIII's generosity. The unmarried, rich viscountess was able to carry on where many married *dames d'œuvres* had to give up. In Ghent, the wives of de Hemptinne and Bethune were not involved in the negotiations about building plans or the management of the patrimony, despite Emilie van Outryve-d'Ydewalle's important role in her husband's company. In Wuustwezel, Ludovica Delehaye did not enter into the negotiations about the construction of the school or the operation of the farm demanded by Telghuys. In each case, their spouses did the talking. Even Havenith-Fuchs was represented by her sons whenever contracts or loans were discussed. By contrast, the four congregation superiors were always involved in 'male' affairs.

The absence of an official male director – or, in the case of Bogaerts, his old age and poor health – in their congregations certainly was of importance here. It gave them access to a position that was different from that of many other congregation superiors, who were forced to conform much more than de Meeûs, Kestre, Cornet and even Telghuys to male authority in matters relating to financial and property management. It would be wrong, however, to conclude that the four women in our narrative totally escaped control or interference. Male patronising as well as the ambitions of their lay female allies hampered their agency as female religious.

The female alliance challenged

In Wuustwezel and in Kontich, Telghuys' growing self-confidence as a superior and entrepreneur clashed over time with her benefactors' own needs and ambitions. Barely a few months after the foundation in Wuustwezel, Telghuys complained to Bogaerts that Ludovica Delehaye was overbearing towards the sisters in Wuustwezel. She checked the teaching activities and barged into the sisters' quarters at every opportunity. Telghuys informed the diocesan author-

---

50 Constant Almain De Hase (1840-1891) had a diverse portfolio of civic and religious buildings in Brussels. His style was eclectic, from the neo-Baroque presbytery of the *Finistère* church in Brussels to the neo-Gothic church, with an adjoining neo-Romanesque building for the Franciscans in Schaerbeek (1868-1886). See the concise obituary of Almain in *L'Émulation*, 1891, 48.

ities in Mechelen and had already spoken – behind Delehaye's back – with Vicar-General De Molder in 1873 about a possible departure. She declared that her sisters were in danger of losing their seclusion from worldly interference. In her letters, Telghuys completely conformed herself to the dominant clerical discourse and policy of enclosure – one of the consequences of the 'conventualisation' of female convent life that will be analysed further on. Doing so, she created room for manoeuvring and acquired a diocesan fiat for her plans. She withdrew her sisters from Wuustwezel in 1875 and transferred them to the newly founded institute in Kontich.[51]

In Kontich the resident former chatelaine, Adelaïde Havenith-Fuchs, caused similar problems as in Wuustwezel. As early as 1875, Telghuys had a dividing wall erected on the grounds so her sisters could escape the curious scrutiny of Havenith-Fuchs. The latter, in her turn, tried to use her good relationship with her personal confessor Bogaerts to gain control of the finances of the laundry in Kontich. Hoping that Bogaerts would order Telghuys to obey him, she prepared a virtual takeover of the laundry management. Although Telghuys had become secure enough to block the manoeuvre, it is striking once again to discover that female allies continued to use male and clerical supremacy in order to get the upper hand over other women – including even friends. Telghuys depended on Havenith's rental income to pay off her burdensome loans. She also derived part of her social legitimacy from the eminent position of the Havenith family in Kontich. Given the precarious nature of the apostolate in Kontich, that support was not unimportant.[52] The problem eventually resolved itself after the death of Bogaerts in 1877 and the decision of Havenith-Fuchs to move to Antwerp that same year. She continued to support Telghuys' congregation until her death in 1905.[53]

Telghuys managed to withstand the pressure of her benefactors thanks to her equal social position and networks. Moreover, she also took advantage of the financial autonomy that the lucrative laundry activities in Kontich offered her congregation. These were important assets. Writing about the Irish context, Luddy pointed to the fact that the chances of success and the closeness of the alliances between female religious and laity were heavily dependent on the social (in)equality of the partners.[54] Belgian historiography also noted that

---

51 ADHH, 58: Telghuys to De Molder (8 April 1875), Telghuys to Dechamps (21 May 1875).
52 ADHH, Reports (30 Oct. 1875, 14 Feb. 1876, 11 April 1877); ABA, File Dienstmaagden H. Harten: Telghuys to De Molder (12 Nov. 1875).
53 ADHH, Reports (5 Aug. 1877, 14 Jan. 1887); 4. Laurent Delehaye to Telghuys (27 Oct. 1883).
54 Luddy, "Possessed of fine properties", 230-237.

an unequal social standing was detrimental in the long term to the alliance between female religious and female benefactors.[55]

While Telghuys eventually took advantage of her autonomous position, Cornet and Kestre were forced into an unequal relationship with their benefactors. Marie Vilain XIIII was a generous patron in Maleizen, but she drove Cornet's sisters in Bazel and Steendorp into "une pénible servitude". The viscountess soon proved deserving of her stubborn reputation. She controlled the sisters and ordered them around in a downright humiliating and authoritarian way. Convent premises and classrooms were subjected to unexpected inspections and all lesson plans had to be approved by the viscountess. She introduced an ascetic and severe regime. Each broken piece of crockery or every tear in a habit had to be accounted for.[56] New sisters on arriving had to present themselves for 'inspection' at her house. Marie Vilain XIIII did not hesitate to reprimand the sisters before the eyes of their pupils, inspiring Sr. Augustine to the quotation mentioned at the introduction of this chapter.

Though Cornet was the superior of the sisters in name, she had no other choice but to leave the *de facto* control of her sisters to Vilain XIIII.[57] From the end of the 1860s, when not enough Flemish-speaking professed sisters were available, novices were sent to East Flanders to meet her constant demand for new school sisters. The exploitation in Bazel and Steendorp and Cornet's unwillingness to put an end to it, was one of the reasons for the conflict with Sister Des Anges that eventually caused her departure.[58] The tensions dragged on for two decades. Even the death of Marie Vilain XIIII in 1883 brought no solution. During the heyday of the School War, it would have been unacceptable for Cornet to withdraw her sisters from a Catholic school. It is noteworthy, however, that just a few months after Cornet's death in 1886, her successor put an end to the East Flemish apostolate of the congregation.

Kestre was less inclined to compromise in order to safeguard the material basis of her congregation. Her friendship with Marie-Thérèse Del Marmol-de Dorlodot waned according as the baroness increasingly pushed to expand and supervise the convent, the devotional activities and the apostolate in Salzinnes. This had a reverse effect on Kestre, who further distanced herself from the foundation in Namur and started writing about a possible withdrawal of her sisters. She first refused to respond to Del Marmol's request for more sis-

---

55 See for example the dominance of aristocratic benefactors over the *Zusters van de Christelijke Scholen* of Vorselaar or the *Sœurs de la Providence* of Namur: Vanderstraeten and Preneel, *175 jaar Zusters van de Christelijke Scholen*, 69-72; Wynants, *Les Sœurs de la Providence*, 37. Similar conclusions have been made for the diocese of Ghent and for the Poor Clare communities. See: Art, *Kerkelijke structuur*, 81-84; Marcelis, *Femmes cloîtrées*, 259.
56 ASCMLH, *Notice chronologique*, 44-57.
57 ASCMLH, *Notice chronologique*: Cornet to Vilain XIIII (13 June 1867, 15 June 1867); ASCMLH, F.2/1: Notes and receipts of Vilain XIIII.
58 AAM, CH, La Hulpe: De Molder to Legrelle (20 Oct. 1874).

ters to be sent to Namur. Despite the wishes of Archbishop Dechamps and Bishop Gravez of Namur, she also left her controversial local superior in place. However, there were various signs that the moody Mother Albertine (Flasselaerts) was unsuitable for the leading position and put off potential novices and benefactors.[59]

Displeased by so much ingratitude and stubbornness, the Del Marmol couple, with the support of Bishop Gravez, went on the offensive. The Bishop of Namur did not get along very well with Kestre. He left Dechamps in no doubt about his feelings: "Quel esprit! Ou plutôt quelle déraison! On a tout à craindre avec une tête pareille".[60] In the heat of the battle, it was no longer Baroness Del Marmol but her husband who intervened. In the autumn of 1877 he threatened to sell all the properties in Brussels and to cancel all financial support if Kestre were to close the Salzinnes foundation. Persistent as ever, Kestre did withdraw her sisters from Salzinnes in May 1879. Antoine Del Marmol carried out his threat and put the convent in Brussels up for sale, but at Dechamps' request, he gave Kestre six months respite to find another owner.[61]

In spite of everything, the archbishop again jumped into the breach for Kestre and together they started a new fundraising campaign. Thanks to the militant climate of the School War, they quickly found a buyer for the Brussels convent and a new benefactor in the very devout and very rich Princess Eléonore-Ursule d'Arenberg (1845-1919). Once again, Dechamps was sensitive to the fate of female religious who asked for his protection.[62] Thanks to him, Kestre was able to safeguard her ambitions and independence, though at a price. Plans for the construction of a 'real' convent and an accompanying chapel had to be put on the long finger. On her death in 1882, Kestre, whose militant religious fervour was unsurpassed, was the only one of the four superiors without a neo-Gothic convent chapel as a status symbol of their religious success.

59   ADSJ, 1.3./3: Kestre to Dechamps (21 Nov. 1869); 1.4. Dechamps to Kestre (24 Feb. 1875); AAM, CF, *Dames Sainte-Julienne*: Dechamps to Kestre (15 July and 30 Sept. 1877).
60   AAM, CF, *Dames Sainte-Julienne*: Gravez to Dechamps (12 Oct. 1877).
61   ADSJ, 1.8: Del Marmol to Dechamps (16 March and 6 April 1879).
62   About the Princess d'Arenberg, see: Goujon, "Gender", 73-74; ADSJ, 1.3./3: Kestre to Dechamps (7 March 1880).

Cornet was one of the pioneers in the modernisation of Catholic girls' education. In the 1860s she extended her boarding-school curriculum with 'modern' courses in languages, bookkeeping and stenography, but with the 'anti-modern' intention to mould a generation of well-educated wives and mothers as buffers against the religious indifference of secular society.
[Postcard – ca. 1890 – Collection *Sœurs du S. Cœur de Marie*, La Hulpe]

CRUSADING IN A CONVENT HABIT

> Une pieuse phalange organisée pour l'apostolat au sein d'une grande cité; s'armant de foi et de charité pour combattre l'ignorance qui méconnait Jésus-Christ et l'indifférence qui se dérobe à son amour, puissant la vaillance de l'action dans la contemplation du tabernacle, au sauvetage des âmes.
>
> *Congrès des Œuvres Eucharistiques*, 283.

In 1881, Fanny Kestre, with the support of the ultramontane Jesuit Charles Verbeke, drew up the main points for a promotional brochure about the *Dames de Sainte-Julienne*. The leaflet was to be presented a month later at the first international Eucharistic Congress in Lille.[1] As can be gleaned from the militant tone of the text, the discourse of the first Eucharistic Congress, a genuine ultramontane mass event, reflected the crusading rhetoric of a Catholic Church into combat mode. The slogan of the congress, the pursuit of a *royaume social du Christ*, revealed the continuing rejection of the modern world in favour of a Christian society in which religion was to be given a central position.[2]

---

1 Lamberts, "Catholic Congresses", 217-220; Langlois, "Les congrès eucharistiques". In the 1880s Jesuit Charles Verbeke (1833-1889) was (vice-)president of the Belgian umbrella organisation of Catholic social and charity organisations (*Verbond der Volkswerken*) and member of the organisation committee of the Eucharistic Congresses. See: De Maeyer, "De Belgische Volksbond", 25.
2 Aubert, *L'Église dans le monde moderne*, 133-135; Menozzi, *Sacro Cuore*, 171-294; Viaene, "A pope's dilemma", 250-253.

This chapter will show how the ecclesiastical crusade had a double effect on the narratives of Kestre, de Meeûs, Telghuys and Cornet: challenging on the one hand, frightening and peremptory on the other. Opportunities awaited the religious superiors if they could succeed in responding to the changing emphases of 'ultramontanisation' and the struggle between liberals and Catholics. Moreover, after the 1870s, the nascent workers' issue created extra challenges for socially-minded and enterprising religious women, within the contours of an ultramontane *économie chrétienne*. At the same time, it was difficult to escape the marching orders of a militantly organised Church. Personal, social and spiritual ambitions sometimes clashed with the growing tendencies to centralisation as well as rigid gender and clerical patterns.

A modern apostolate, conservative ideas

As already mentioned in the introduction to this third part, the spectre of a new anticlerical revolution haunted Catholic minds at the height of the Belgian culture war between Catholics and liberals. Fears of liberal agitation mingled with worries about the 'red threat', certainly after the workers' rage during the Paris Commune of 1871 had exposed a revolutionary and virulent anticlericalism. Congregation founders, clerics and lay Catholics expressed a growing unease.[3] Telghuys, for example, was worried about the growing liberal agitation against the economic or profit-making activities of religious institutes.[4] The liberal complaints about convent 'industries' were widespread and criticised laundries as well as the popular model of convent work schools. The children in these institutions, who were from modest or poor backgrounds, were given a cursory education, but were also employed in the production of cheap textiles or lace to supplement their family's budget as well as that of the school. The outrage of liberals about unfair competition and financial enrichment based on child labour clashed with Catholic counter-arguments about supporting disadvantaged families. The conflicts illustrated the continuing sensitivity of nineteenth-century liberals to the growing wealth of the religious institutes and the opaque mechanisms by which this was accumulated.[5] In France, there were rumours about '*le fameux milliard des congrégations*'.[6] In

---

[3] De Maeyer, "La Belgique", 363; Vanderstraeten and Preneel, *175 jaar Zusters van de Christelijke Scholen*, 113-114; Wynants, *Les Sœurs de la Providence*, 293.
[4] ADHH, 69: Reports (23 June 1872, 9 Nov. 1876).
[5] Koppen, *De Kloosterkwestie*, 308-317; Van Dijck, "From workhouse to convent", 176; De Clerck, De Graeve and Simon, "Dag Meester", 63-67.
[6] Langlois, *Le catholicisme au féminin*, 344-352.

Belgium, discussions, allegations and law suits concerning clerical 'inheritance chasing' were a recurring theme.[7]

The vast convent complexes that were constructed all over the country were also a source of liberal irritation. When Cornet gave up the girls' school in La Hulpe in 1866 to erect a boarding school in Maleizen, liberal newspapers criticised her opportunism and megalomania as well as the substandard quality of the sisters' education in the village school.[8] In the autumn of 1865, the liberal municipal council of La Hulpe withdrew its subsidy from Cornet's school and decided to set up its own state school for girls.[9] For several years, the liberal municipal council had been sympathetic to the sisters. Around 1865 however, the climate had changed and the opposition against the sisters intensified. Wanting to escape both the meddling by Father Chevalier and the "persécutions des libéraux" in La Hulpe, Cornet looked for a new home in Maleizen.[10]

Liberal criticism and harassment generated a twofold dynamic among the four superiors. On the one hand they cultivated their aversion to the modern, secular world and continued to cherish a desire for a protected, 'pure' Catholic society. On the other hand, growing Catholic self-confidence and reactions to anticlerical, liberal actions encouraged demonstrative and public expressions of piety, modern forms of evangelisation and innovative apostolic initiatives. Various historians have pointed to the paradox of this 'anti-modern crusade with modern means' in which also de Meeûs, Kestre, Cornet and Telghuys navigated a path between originality, modern entrepreneurship and a conservative view of women and society.[11]

While preparing and establishing the new foundations in Wuustwezel and Kontich, Telghuys focused on the development of her Antwerp institution as well. She was driven by a resolute desire to fight against secularisation and religious indifference, especially after a liberal city council came to power in Antwerp in 1872. First, the capacity of the orphanage was extended to prevent young girls from ending up in the 'wicked' and 'godless' state institutions. Second, there was less interaction with the city's (liberal) public charitable boards, which had been placing orphans in the *Sint-Franciscus-Xaveriusinstituut* ever since its foundation. Even more prominent was her struggle against "les ateliers sans Dieu ou les femmes sont en contact avec des personnes perverties".[12] In 1874, she came up with the idea of starting 'safe'

---

7   Koppen, *De Kloosterkwestie*, 76-88; Suenens, "Het proces De Buck"; Viaene, *Belgium and the Holy See*, 438-439; Heyrman, "La culture d'entreprise ", 308-309.
8   *Journal de Liège* (7 Feb. 1865); *L'Indépendance Belge* (11 Nov. 1865).
9   ARLLN, *Archive of the Municipality of La Hulpe*, 5: Report (18 Aug. 1865).
10 ASCMLH, *Notice autobiographique*, 8; A.2: Cornet to Sterckx (11 June 1865).
11 Busch, *Katholische Frömmigkeit*; Curtis, *Educating the Faithful*, 63-65; Ford, "Religion", 165-167; Blackbourn, "The Catholic Church", 780; Clark, "The New Catholicism", 45.
12 ADHH, 253: *Annales*.

sewing, ironing and clothing courses and workshops for girls and women. In a way it is tempting to discern a desire for both social and female emancipation in her intention to create these workshops. Nevertheless, some nuance is in order. With her vocational training courses for older girls, Telghuys was indeed among the first female religious to start taking initiatives in this area. She was inspired by lay initiatives. In 1875, for example, the Catholic secondary vocational school *Anna Bijns* was established in Antwerp. It was a project of the network around the aforementioned Marie-Elisabeth Belpaire, intended to provide better education for girls. Belpaire, who was a niece of Constance Teichmann and no stranger to Telghuys, reacted against the 'pernicious' influence of pioneering liberal school projects.[13] Ten years earlier a liberal network around Isabelle Gatti de Gamond (1839-1905), daughter of the aforementioned Zoé de Gamond, founded the first secondary vocational school for girls in Brussels. This was followed in 1873 by a similar initiative in Antwerp, the *École professionnelle de filles*.[14]

The foundation of this school had not escaped Telghuys' notice either. In 1874, together with Fanny Draveman (1842-1894), the lay director she had recruited for the day school that was linked to her workshops, she contemplated "l'érection d'une école moyenne catholique pour former des mères chrétiennes (...) vu les ravages que font les mauvaises écoles".[15] Like Belpaire, she wanted to foster women's development, but without questioning the traditional female gender role or its moral and religious Catholic content.[16] The project, however, would never get off the ground. Unlike Belpaire, a relatively independent lay woman, Telghuys' plans were vetoed by the Antwerp deacon Sacré and the diocesan authorities in Mechelen. Telghuys' male superiors thought that the rough neighbourhood around the *Sint-Jorisvest* would frighten off parents from sending their girls to the school. They were also wary of possible competition with the secondary school in the nearby *Institut Saint-Joseph* of the *Dochters van Maria* (Paridaens).[17] Unable to oppose her male superiors, Telghuys then concentrated on further developing her vocational workshops, which she also introduced in Kontich. Only after her death in 1907 was the Antwerp workshop and school transformed into a fully-fledged secondary trade school for girls.

Cornet also saw the modernisation of her educational apostolate as a weapon in the fight against secularisation, although she maintained a moderate tone. Most of the nineteenth-century convent boarding schools had for long focused on '*une formation désintéressée*' of devout and respectable wives

13 Reymenants, *Marie-Elisabeth Belpaire*, 32-33; ADHH, 4: Belpaire to Telghuys (18 July 1882).
14 De Weerdt, *En de Vrouwen*, 42; Groessens, "Laïcité, anticléricalisme", 504.
15 ADHH, 69: Reports (11 Aug. 1874).
16 Reymenants, *Marie-Elisabeth Belpaire*, 32.
17 ABA, File Dienstmaagden van de H. Harten: Bogaerts to Sterckx (12 Aug. 1874), Sacré to Lauwers (13 Oct. 1874).

and mothers. In the last quarter of the nineteenth century, criticism of the poor quality of their education and the aforementioned liberal school initiatives led to the curriculum being changed and expanded.[18] Cornet made her boarding school in Maleizen into one of the pioneers in this evolution. To accommodate the growing group of daughters of shopkeepers, businessmen and civil servants, she added 'useful' subjects such as bookkeeping, letter-writing and languages to the curriculum. Cornet promoted this 'modernisation' by an intensive advertising campaign in the *Journal de Bruxelles*, the newspaper of the Brussels Catholic middle class. The professional skills were combined with extensive training in housekeeping, as would later become the norm in the many schools of housecraft that arose in the last quarter of the nineteenth century. The importance of this (occupational) training in housekeeping for women's education and development has been interpreted in a variety of ways in the historiography. Both in Belgium and in the Netherlands, historians have focused on the emancipatory power of these training models which offered Catholic girls hope for a more promising future. At the same time, the focus on housecraft hampered the evolution of girls' education in a more intellectual direction, and for that reason came in for feminist-inspired criticism from the end of the nineteenth century. [19]

At the Mechelen congresses of the 1860s, there had already been a call for the better education of girls so as to make them more competent as mothers and spouses in their fight against the moral decay and the secularisation of modern society. There was no mention of more public or professional autonomy for women at the Mechelen congresses, but channels were opened to foster women's personal development through education. Convent superiors found their own modern means to implement this new, but essentially conservative ecclesiastical policy.[20] In 1863, Melanie Van Biervliet (1813-1892), co-founder and superior of the *Zusters van de Heilige Familie* (Sisters of the Holy Family) in Tielt, published a pedagogical handbook for boarding schools. By current standards, the discourse was cringingly conservative, both in its view of the submissive role of the woman and the stereotypes about the limited intellectual abilities of girls.[21] Yet in the 1860s and 1870s it did not differ fundamentally from gender views in general. In her research on nineteenth-century female writers, Keymolen showed that non-Catholic women such as Gatti de Gamond also paid lip service in their educational views to existing bourgeois gender

18 De Vroede, "The Catholic Boarding Schools", 321-332; Christens and Suenens, "L'enseignement comme projet", 154.
19 Van Heijst, Derks and Monteiro, *Ex Caritate*, 68; Christens and Suenens, "L'enseignement comme projet", 154.
20 De Buck, *De l'état religieux en Belgique*, 273-304; De Vroede, "The Catholic Boarding Schools", 326-327; Hoegaerts and Van Osselaer, "Corps et moralité", 442.
21 Van Biervliet, *De l'éducation*. On Melanie Van Biervliet, see: De Vroede, "The Catholic Boarding Schools", 326; Keymolen, "Beroepsarbeid", 17-31.

patterns. The first liberal vocational schools were promoted with the argument that they gave women the opportunity to earn money, but from within the safe context of the home.[22]

In line with the Mechelen congresses, Van Biervliet also called for better education for girls in order to make the woman the family's moral guardian, financial overseer and teacher. This traditional objective was also partly in line with the discourse on the role of women and the importance of education for women that was to be heard in liberal and later socialist circles. Women were responsible for making their households stable, efficient and respectable havens, attractive enough to save their husbands from decadence and misery. The final outcome of the Catholic and liberal ideals, however, was totally different. Better Catholic education had to make women more effective teachers of the faith and buffers against the anticlerical influences of modern society. By contrast, a high-quality liberal or neutral education aimed to help women break free from what was seen as the Church's indoctrination. Armed against superstition, they could then flourish as freethinking mothers and wives, confident in the progress of modernity.[23]

This approach was seen by some historians as an expression of a 'relational approach' or a feminine strategy "to present the amelioration of the position of women as being in the interest of men".[24] There are obvious parallels with some strategical outcomes of the double-voiced discourse. The plea for better education for women gained legitimacy by its being presented as a way of fulfilling male political, ideological or social ambitions, while at the same time confirming traditional gender patterns of the domestic role of women. Only in the last quarter of the nineteenth century did that vision change, first in liberal circles, and then in the early twentieth century in Catholic circles as well.[25]

In the meantime, Anna de Meeûs was active on a larger scale. In the early 1860s, she had already built up a well-developed, tightly structured and energetically promoted organisation with her Eucharistic association and *Œuvre des Églises Pauvres*. After Belgium, the Netherlands, Bavaria and Austria, the organisation also gained a foothold in Poland, the United States, Constantinople, Italy, Spain and England. Only in France was the development of the association hampered by the strong presence of other Eucharistic congregations.[26] Belgium nevertheless continued to be the centre, with over 150,000 members in the mid-1880s, over 100,000 francs of income annually and almost 23,000

22 Keymolen, "Beroepsarbeid", 40-43.
23 Gubin, *Choisir l'histoire des femmes*, 162-163; Gubin and Piette, *Emma, Louise et Marie*, 28-31.
24 Wils, "Science", 419-424. On the relational approach, Wils cites Offen, "Defining feminism", 39-56.
25 Keymolen, *Victoire Cappe*, 61-63.
26 ARE, *Cahier des lettres 3*: de Meeûs to Léopoldine de Robiano (8 Feb. 1872).

liturgical objects distributed. In the space of 15 years, de Meeûs' association generated more than 1.5 million francs. However, while the numbers sound impressive, they must be seen in context. Other religious projects generated much more income. In the city of Liège alone, the Vincentian associations had more than 50,000 francs in income in 1876. The association of the *Dames de Charité* distributed over 36,000 francs in alms to the poor in Brussels in 1866. The immensely popular Saint Peter's Pence, which was started in 1859 in ultramontane circles to financially support the embattled Pius IX, raised almost 1.5 million francs in the parishes of the city of Ghent alone between 1860 and 1885.[27]

As the daughter of a top banker and entrepreneur, she understood the power of numbers and published detailed statistics of the Belgian branch of her association every year. Information on the international expansion, however, is much more fragmented and incomplete. Anna de Meeûs was frequently annoyed by the tardy reporting of foreign associations. In addition to Belgium, in the 1870s and 1880s the archconfraternity had solid strongholds in Munich (8,260 members in 1882), England (10,917 members in 1882-1883), the Netherlands (9,005 members in 1884) and the Austro-Hungarian Empire (at least 87,000 members in 1882).[28] All together, the total membership around 1885 was probably somewhere between 250,000 and 300,000 members. The general statistics were in line with those for other archconfraternities with a predominantly spiritual purpose, such as the Belgian branch of the *Aartsbroederschap van O.L.V. van het Heilig Hart* (Archconfraternity of Our Lady of the Sacred Heart), which was coordinated by the Norbertines of Averbode.[29] However, the figures for de Meeûs' association exceeded those for the popular Apostolate of Prayer of the Jesuits, which had 100,000 registrations in 1884, or for the Xavierians, who had more than 80,000 members at the beginning of the twentieth century.[30]

While the statistical report of her association might not have been exceptional, in her decades-long role as a prominent female coordinator of an international and pontifically approved pious organisation de Meeûs did not have many equals. There were indeed other women who played an important role as founders or promoters of Catholic associations, but their efforts were often on a smaller scale, more anonymous or of shorter duration than the impact of de Meeûs. For example, the Visitandines of Bourg, and Sister Marie du Sacré-Cœur Bernaud in particular, were the driving force behind the archconfraternity of the *Garde d'Honneur du Sacré-Cœur*, which had 4,360 affiliated

27 Gérin, "La Société de Saint-Vincent de Paul à Liège", 333; *Assemblée Générale des Catholiques*, 1867, 400; De Smaele, "Determinanten", 151.
28 *Annales de l'Association*, (1883), 430-448; (1885), 27; (1885), 70.
29 209,239 members in 1885-1886, see: Gevers and Vuurstaek, "Mariadevotie", 80.
30 Van Osselaer, *The Pious Sex*, 118; Poncelet, *La Compagnie de Jésus*, 170.

BELGIAN MEMBERS OF THE ARCHI-ASSOCIATION DE L'ADORATION
PERPÉTUELLE (1860-1890)*

	Women	Men	Founding members	Total
1860	39,317	10,925	4,392	54,634
1865	66,071	21,312	6,057	93,440
1870	87,762	33,198	6,643	127,603
1880	103,337	39,061	6,858	149,256
1890	114,882	47,401	5,865	168,148

*Annales de l'Association, 1860-1885.

associations in 1883. However, the founding sisters mainly operated out of public view, from behind the grilles of their enclosed cloister. Pauline Jaricot (1799-1862), coordinator of the Propagation of the Faith, had to give up her position under pressure from male clerics. Emilie Tamisier (1843-1910) played a key role in the organisation of the Eucharistic Congresses, but remained largely anonymous and gained recognition only after her death.[31]

Female agency, the European culture wars and the missionary drive

In 1872, the aforementioned French Oratorian Pététot, visiting Brussels to assist refugee victims of the Franco-Prussian war, preached in *Saint-Gudule* on behalf of Kestre's apostolates. Kestre met him after she had made a financial contribution to the charity for prisoners of war run by the French Oratorians. She herself had scarcely enough means to survive, but in her own naïve way and on a small scale she tried to play a role on the international stage. In her contacts with the French Oratorians, Kestre benefited from the ultramontane prestige of the Belgian Church and Dechamps' leading role in the debate about

---

31 Marie du Cœur de Jésus (1825-1903) was a prominent figure in a French and Tournai network of religious and active women. In 1863 she herself helped found an international association, the *Garde d'Honneur du Sacré-Cœur*. See: Langlois, *Thérèse de Lisieux*, 39-42. About Jaricot and Tamisier, see: Vial, "Jaricot", 170-171; Langlois, "Les congrès eucharistiques".

papal infallibility, which Pététot supported.³² In the first half of the nineteenth century, the Belgian revival Church had gained the respect of French and international Romantic Catholics for the way in which it had been able to use '*la liberté comme en Belgique*' to its own advantage. That liberal-Catholic admiration had given way in the third quarter of the century to a perception of the Belgian Church as one of the model students in the ultramontane class.³³ This international prestige offered opportunities for superiors of women's religious congregations. Kestre and her apostolates benefited from Pététot's praise. In turn, her retreats and association meetings provided the French priest with a forum to seek moral and financial backing for the precarious position of his own institute and the French Church in the wake of the fiasco of the Franco-Prussian war.³⁴

The exchange evokes memories of the important role played by female religious in the dismantled Church of the revolutionary period. De Meeûs also proved to be a worthy successor to those early nineteenth-century predecessors. A few years before the arrival of Pététot she had managed to snare another charismatic French preacher. In 1858 she convinced Pierre-Julien Eymard, founder of the *Pères du Saint-Sacrement*, to give a few retreat lectures in the Salazar Chapel.³⁵ From 1864 on, de Meeûs was urging Eymard to open a branch of his congregation in Brussels. She wanted the fathers to assume the ministry of the Salazar chapel, counted on their commitment to expose the Blessed Sacrament every day and, alternating with the sisters, to engage in the Perpetual Adoration. Eymard initially held off because he had other projects in mind and did not have enough personnel to attend to all the requests. Anna de Meeûs, however, played a double ace. She tempted the priests with very attractive material conditions and with the important position of her association, leading Eymard to believe that "par cette fondation, nous aurions toute la Belgique; que, par moyen de leurs associations répandues partout, toutes les villes de la Belgique nous étaient ouvertes".³⁶

In 1865 the first community of the *Pères du Saint-Sacrement* was established in the apartments next to the Salazar Chapel. The foundation was a symbiosis of de Meeûs' growing prestige as a congregation superior, her long-term history as a *dame d'œuvres* and, given her family background, her predestined role as a generous patron. Endowed with such talents, women

---

32 Dechamps had defended papal infallibility, along with other topics, against Gratry, the French liberal-Catholic fellow brother of Pététot. Pététot had chosen Dechamps' side in the discussion. See: ADSJ, 1.3./3: Kestre to Dechamps (6 Nov. 1871); Becque, *Le Cardinal Dechamps*, II, 186-202.
33 Viaene, "Nineteenth-Century Catholic Internationalism", 97; De Maeyer, "La Belgique", 373-374.
34 ADSJ, 1.7: Pététot to Kestre (18 Nov. 1871).
35 Eymard to de Meeûs (11 July 1858), in: Stalmans, *Les fondations*, 4.
36 Eymard to Leroyer (22 Sept. 1864), in: Eymard, *Briefe*, no 1437.

religious in the apostolate field could transcend their traditional role as 'assistants to the clergy', especially when male initiatives were at an early stage or in difficulty. International literature shows that the culture wars also created agency opportunities for female religious in other countries. Around the famous *Sacre-Cœur* Basilica in Montmartre, for example, developed an influential network of women religious. The basilica was the symbol of the anti-revolutionary, ultramontane movement of penance and rehabilitation that had started in France after the traumatic losses in the Franco-Prussian War. Among others, the *Dames du Cénacle* of Thérèse Couderc and the *Dames Réparatrices* of Emilie d'Oultremont were approached by the church hierarchy to organise retreats and devotions and to coordinate penitential confraternities.[37] Meiwes pointed to the unexpected, positive consequences of the *Kulturkampf* for the agency of women religious in (and outside) Germany. First, some women's teaching congregations that had fled Germany for other countries – including Belgium – found new inspiration and developed greater self-confidence. Both proved to be essential on their return in successfully consolidating the re-establishment of their congregations and in building a new future. Second, the nursing congregations that were not expelled from Germany were given more opportunities for autonomous action. They escaped the strict control of the church hierarchy that had been muzzled for years by the civil authorities.[38]

A niche for highly esteemed female action also opened up in another area with international branches: the missions. In the third quarter of the nineteenth century, both de Meeûs and Kestre broadened their associations' liturgical apostolates to include the needs of the Catholic missionary movement. Liturgical vessels and vestments, as well as rosary beads, devotional prints and compact altars were sent to missions all over the world, often in collaboration with the Jesuits and the Redemptorists.[39] In this way, the two congregation superiors participated in the growing nineteenth-century fascination of Catholics with overseas territories. The longing for adventure and the idea of the purity of Creation became merged in the missionary movement with a zeal to convert and to make reparation for the sins of the 'old continent'.[40] While Kestre's efforts remained modest and fragmented, de Meeûs' missionary work developed into an efficient and large-scale machine. In 1885, the Belgian branch of de Meeûs' association sent more than 6,400 objects to mission countries worldwide.[41]

---

37 Benoist, *Le Sacré-Cœur des femmes*, 1335-1427.
38 Meiwes, *Arbeiterinnen*, 301-306.
39 ADSJ, 1.6: Kestre to Father Van Opstal (Picpus) (11 Sept. 1877), Pététot to Kestre (22 July 1876); ARE, *Chronique, XVI. Nouvelles Œuvres*, 166-168.
40 Vints, "Komt en haalt ons", 34-36; Viaene, *Belgium and the Holy See*, 191-195.
41 *Annales de l'Association*, 1885; *Collection de Précis Historiques*, 1866, 533.

Women's input in the nineteenth-century mission movement followed well-established gender models: men did the converting and braved danger, women took on the supportive, nursing and teaching tasks.[42] Yet it was also a source of female influence. With her work for the missions embedded within her association, de Meeûs offered a broad group of women access to participation in a global missionary movement. Moreover, she made the male missionary institutes dependent on the material support of her association. Kestre too gained prestige from her service to the missions. In 1881, shortly after the promotional campaign at the Lille Eucharistic Congress, she was asked by the French Jesuits to establish a convent in northern France. In their request they expressed their gratitude for the liturgical vessels that were sent by her to the Jesuit mission in Maduré in India. Kestre did not accept the offer. She rightly argued that she had too few sisters, but privately she also attributed her refusal to her deep-rooted fear of a close collaboration with the Jesuits.[43] Her past traumas remained an obstacle to the expansion of her institute.

As usual, Anna de Meeûs took up the opportunities for internationalisation with a greater degree of opportunism and entrepreneurship. After a short-lived convent foundation in Maastricht failed in 1865 because of a lack of resources and decent housing, the *Institut de l'Adoration Perpétuelle* established its first foreign convent in Rotterdam in 1866. Setting up a foundation in predominantly Protestant Holland was not without risk. The founding of the diocese of Haarlem only a decade before in 1853 had led to considerable anti-papal protest and Protestant fear of burgeoning Dutch ultramontane Catholicism was a constant feature.[44] Following the success of the Rotterdam branch of de Meeûs' association, both the local Jesuits and the wealthy Dutch-Belgian benefactor couple De Bruyn-Serruys insisted on a convent being established to facilitate further expansion.[45] The bishop of Haarlem, Gerardus Wilmer (1861-1877), was less enthusiastic. Although he was an ardent support of Eucharistic piety too, he feared the impact of a new convent church on the limited resources of the Catholic community in Rotterdam. He might also have had his doubts about the 'Roman' character of de Meeûs' institute, then on

---

42 Dujardin, "Gender", 296-299.
43 ADSJ, 1.3./3: Kestre to Dechamps (21 Nov. 1881); 1.6: Kieckens SJ to Kestre (17 Nov. 1881).
44 Margry and te Velde, "Contested rituals", 136-137; Voets, *Bewaar het toevertrouwde pand*, 17.
45 ANSI, 3.7. Van Gulick, 11345: Boone to Van Gulick SJ (18 April 1865); NADH, ABR, 1687: Wilmer to parish clergy (5 April 1866). The West Flemish Caroline Serruys (1819-1876), who had met de Meeûs during a retreat in Salazar, was married to Henri de Bruyn (1814-1888), a wine merchant in Rotterdam. The family belonged to one of the most prominent Catholic families in the city. Caroline's brother, Léonce Serruys (1829-1895), had entered the Jesuits. See: NADH, ABR, 1686: Beckx to Serruys (17 Nov. 1872); ARE, *Chronique, XXV. Rotterdam*, 255-256.

the verge of receiving provisional pontifical recognition. As a rather cautious bishop, Wilmer's experiences with Rome's authority were ambiguous, and this could also have explained his reluctance to consent to the establishment of a congregation that might challenge his diocesan jurisdiction.[46]

In that sense, an ultramontane identity was not always an asset. Once again however, the strength of de Meeûs' network and her strategic insight became apparent when she successfully convinced Archbischop Sterckx to change Wilmer's mind. On de Meeûs' instructions, Sterckx stressed the wide range of the sisters' apostolate as being an important weapon in the missionary offensive. Just as the arrival of Pététot in the 1870s was indicative of the growing, albeit ambiguous ultramontane prestige of the Belgian Church, so Sterckx's arguments emphasised the strength of the Belgian religious institutes from the revival period, which played a major role in the structural and normative development of Dutch convents in the nineteenth century.[47] They also confirm the argument put forward by Viaene and Langlois that the religious institutes themselves were one of the modern means by which the nineteenth-century Church tried to expand its territory and influence.[48]

Just as in the Netherlands, the association also paved the way for a convent foundation in England, although its introduction was initially rather difficult. In 1878, following the success of her association, Anna de Meeûs had made plans to set up a branch of the association in London. She did not receive permission, however, of the archbishop of Westminster, Cardinal Manning. On the one hand he praised the 'Altar Society' of de Meeûs and her *Œuvre des Églises Pauvres*, which for many years had organised the supply of liturgical objects to mission priests in the British Isles. On the other hand, like his Dutch colleague, he pointed to the fact that the Catholic community in his country had insufficient people and resources to support such a demanding charity. In the second half of the nineteenth century, the young English Catholic Church, which had acquired an official structure only in 1851 after having been dormant for centuries, was to a large extent a community of workers and poor Irish immigrants.[49]

Manning and de Meeûs met in Rome, shortly before the cardinal retreated to the conclave that would eventually elect Pope Leo XIII. Anna de Meeûs was there to consult with the Roman curia regarding the expansion of her associa-

---

46 NADH, ABR, 1687: Sterckx to Wilmer (13 Jan. 1866), Wilmer to Sterckx (9 March 1866); ARE, *Cahier des Lettres 3*: de Meeûs to Sterckx (8 Jan. 1866); Voets, *Bewaar het toevertrouwde pand*, 106-107. On Wilmer and his difficult relationship with Rome in the case of the canonisation of the Gorinchem martyrs, see: De Valk, *Roomser dan de paus*, 157-172. On his promotion of the Eucharistic cult, see: Caspers and Magry, *Het Mirakel*, 166.
47 Van Heijst, Derks and Monteiro, *Ex Caritate*, 558-561.
48 Langlois, *Le Catholicisme au féminin*, 634-648; Viaene, "The Second Sex", 449-450.
49 Aubert, *L'Église dans le monde moderne*, 222-236; O'Neil, *Cardinal Herbert Vaughan*, 211.

tion.⁵⁰ During the 1870s and 1880s, Rome increasingly strengthened its position as the centre of a world Church and a meeting place for the Catholic elite. The newly elected Pope Leo XIII, in particular, would be one of the important architects and moral anchor points of the Roman stronghold.⁵¹ It is no coincidence that on his initiative Anna de Meeûs made contact with some wealthy English Catholic converts in the spring of 1879. The network around the aforementioned London aristocrat, Lady Herbert, had given English Catholicism a financial boost in the 1870s and was willing to support de Meeûs' cause as well.⁵² Herbert and Manning recommended de Meeûs to Herbert Vaughan, bishop of Salford (Manchester). Unlike Manning and Herbert, Vaughan was not a convert, but a descendant of an old Catholic aristocratic recusant family. For de Meeûs he proved to be the right man in the right place. Educated by the Jesuits of Brugelette in Hainault and superior of a large number of Belgian missionary priests in his diocese, he was familiar with Belgian potential. The Belgian Xavierians and the Liège *Filles de la Croix* were already active in Manchester, early birds in the flight of dozens of Belgian congregations across the Channel in the second half of the nineteenth century.⁵³

In 1879 Vaughan gave his permission for the establishment of the association and a convent of de Meeûs' 'Altar Society'. Lady Herbert financed the project. Once again, de Meeûs' strong entrepreneurial spirit was evident in the English operation. In the months between the meeting with Herbert in Rome and the foundation in Manchester she quickly learned English. From Bethune's wife she learned about "les mœurs anglaises".⁵⁴ The aristocratic Vaughan was impressed by de Meeûs' entreprise skills: "she is working, walking and talking with an energy and strength of body which has completely put poor Miss Hanmer hors de combat".⁵⁵ In the English mission Church, she also seemed less inhibited by the strict gender limitations, as witnessed by the important role that Vaughan had in mind for the sisters: "I hope that they will accomplish a great work of Faith and Love in this large population by the rekindling of Faith and devotion among the people. I see a large field of the most valuable spiritual work opening out before them. The people are here, but direction and guidance and superintendence are needed such as the nuns can give. I have formed a very favourable opinion of the Mother General."⁵⁶

---

50   ARE, *Racontes des visites (Rome 1878)*, Cahier 2.
51   Viaene, "A pope's dilemma", 250-253.
52   Vaughan to Herbert (31 Aug. 1880), published in: Shane, *Letters*, 320-321; ARE, *Chronique, XXXI. Fondation en Angleterre*, 324-326.
53   O'Neil, *Cardinal Herbert Vaughan*, 213-217, 276.
54   ARE, *Chronique, XXXI. Fondation en Angleterre*, 326.
55   Vaughan to Herbert (12 Oct. 1879), in: Shane, *Letters*, 311. Miss Hanmer was one of the local members of the association.
56   Vaughan to Herbert (19 Oct. 1879), in: Ibidem, 312.

However, despite the promising start, de Meeûs would run up against a lack of enthusiasm and financial means among the Catholic population in Manchester, which largely consisted of impoverished Irish workers. In 1887, in search of vocations and resources, the sisters moved to London, closer to the wealthy circles around Lady Herbert. They purchased a large building plot at the Nightingale Square in the suburb of Balham, south of the London city centre. The association flourished here, although the development of the institute was still hindered by the elite character of de Meeûs' congregation.[57] Most of the native English congregations had a more modest recruitment base and devoted themselves more fully to the education and social advancement of Catholic working-class girls than did the institute of de Meeûs.[58]

Just as de Meeûs found English benefactors for the expansion of her institute, English congregations equally looked for Belgian support. The aforementioned English convert and congregation founder Fanny Taylor, for example, owed her close relationship with Telghuys and De Beukelaer to her visits to Antwerp in 1869 and 1870. After assembling a group of religious women in London, she stayed in Telghuys' *Sint-Franciscus-Xaveriusinstituut* in order to study the operation of the orphanage and the laundry.[59] Brought together by the contacts between the London and Antwerp Jesuits, both women remained friends for life. With the support of the socially sensitive Manning, Taylor eventually founded her own congregation in 1872, the Poor Servants of the Mother of God. The archbishop was clearly more enthusiastic about Taylor's focus on the working class and the large group of poor Irish immigrants than he was about de Meeûs' elite ladies. The congregations of Taylor and Telghuys shared a name as well as a very similar apostolate, including the laundry industries. By supporting Taylor, Telghuys and De Beukelaer participated in their modest way in the missionary drive, which aimed at "l'extension du royaume de Jésus Christ par toute la terre et la conversion de tant de malheureux que l'erreur ou le vice éloignent de leur fin dernière".[60]

---

57 ARE, *Chronique, XXXI. Fondation en Angleterre*, 327.
58 O'Brien, "Terra incognita", 115-117.
59 ADHH, 16: Verest Manuscript, 114-120; 58: Telghuys to Taylor (22 July 1870). On Frances 'Fanny' Taylor, see: Mangion, "Developing Alliances", 207-208; O'Brien, "Taylor", 40.
60 ADHH, 183: De Beukelaer to Taylor (31 Dec. 1883).

The inevitability of the crusade: the School War (1879-1884)

In the meantime, "l'erreur ou le vice" was inextricably linked in the minds of Telghuys and De Beukelaer to the situation in their own country. The School War of 1879-1884 was the culmination of the nineteenth-century ideological struggle between Belgian liberals and Catholics and of the Church's struggle with post-revolution modern society. The conflict was provoked by the decision of the liberal government, which assumed office in 1878, to laicise state education, resulting in the formation of a massive Catholic front. Where in prior decades rivalry between ultramontanes and liberal Catholics had weakened the Catholic cause, from 1878 onwards a more united approach was taken. The Belgian bishops ignored Leo XIII's counsel of moderation and went head-on against the policy of the liberal government in the struggle for the 'soul of the child'. Every parish priest was instructed to establish a Catholic school, committees of Catholic lay people were formed to finance the schools, while religious institutes were solicited to serve them. Catholic parents and teachers who remained loyal to the state school system were threatened with excommunication. The massive mobilisation and radical opinions determined both the success of the Catholic struggle – the definitive unfolding of a Catholic educational network in Belgium and a Catholic electoral victory in 1884 – as well as its inevitability.[61]

Motivated by Archbishop Dechamps, de Meeûs started a Catholic girls' school next to the novitiate that her institute had built in the Brussels suburb of Watermael in the late 1860s.[62] Looking for sisters to serve the school, she eventually convinced the *Annonciaden* of the West-Flemish Diksmuide to send teachers.[63] De Meeûs took on the role of many Catholic benefactors and local parish priests who went in search of religious school staff during the School War. As an employer, she was in a different position than the many convent superiors who were overwhelmed by requests to take part in the Catholic battle for education. Cornet was one of them. With the completion of her boarding school, she had realised her most important ambition. The further expansion of the Maleizen institute, as well as the demanding involvement with Vilain XIIII in East Flanders left little room for other projects. In the 1860s and early 1870s she refused several requests from village parish priests to establish girls' schools.[64]

In 1883 a new request came to take over a Catholic school in Sougné in Liège, a village in the municipality of Aywaille. The school had been founded

---

61 Viaene, "De ontplooiing van een 'vrije' kerk, 98-99; Becque, *Le Cardinal Dechamps*, II, 326; Hellemans, *Strijd om de moderniteit*, 99-104.
62 On the convent in Watermael, see pp. 295-296.
63 ARE, *Chronique, XXXVIII. La Providence de Watermael*, 434.
64 ASCMLH, *Notice Chronologique*, 64.

at the start of the School War for the children of Sougné and neighbouring Dieupart by the local aristocratic de Theux de Montjardin family. Initially the *Zusters van Sint-Vincentius* of Gijzegem assumed responsibility for the operation of the school. When they left, Father Mizet, parish priest of Sougné and a former confessor of one of the sisters in Cornet's congregation, turned in desperation to Maleizen. He offered the Cornet 700 francs per year per sister.[65] The figures once again point to the low cost of hiring religious as being a key factor in the strong demand for teaching sisters. Cornet received 2,800 francs annually for her community of four sisters while in the same period, Telghuys had to apply for a subsidy of 11,000 francs for the reimbursement of four lay employees in her new school.[66]

In Sougné, Cornet's sisters had in more than one respect ended up in a Catholic outpost and it soon became clear why the Gijzegem sisters had left. Aywaille was one of the rural villages where the School War degenerated into a skirmish between liberals and Catholics marked by verbal violence, bullying and blackmail. Even before the arrival of Cornet's sisters, scurrilous anticlerical pamphlets – "le curé de Dieupart a quatre femmes et moi je n'en ai qu'une" – circulated. The priests in turn refused the sacraments to teachers who would not resign from the municipal school or to parents who sent their children to state institutions. Such were the conventional weapons in the battle for the soul of the child.[67] The sisters had to deal with harassment from liberal youths in the neighbourhood. The remote location of the school, isolated between the villages of Aywaille and Sougné, made the building an easy prey for burglars and vandals. In 1885, Cornet had to ask the archbishop for permission to allow her sisters to testify in court against a local gang of thieves that had targeted the convent.[68]

The School War also obliged Telghuys to become involved in primary school activities. In 1878 she started a free school for the girls of the *Sint-Augustinus* parish next to her convent. Shortly afterwards, at the request of parish priest De Molder – the successor to Bogaerts who died in 1877 – a boys' school was added.[69] Telghuys started the project with her usual pioneering and enterprising spirit. She had some renovations carried out on the buildings and acquired buildings next to the convent to expand her activities. Together with Fanny Draveman, the director of her vocational classes, she also hired (expensive) lay teachers for the new school.[70]

65 ASCMLH, F.7. Aywaille, 3: *Les écoles catholiques*.
66 ADHH, 130: Chronicle of the school (29 Aug. 1879).
67 *L'Écho du Parlement* (1 Nov. 1880); *Le Bien Public* (8 Nov. 1880).
68 ASCMLH, F.4. Dieupart: Cornet to Goossens (4 Dec. 1885).
69 ADHH, 58: Telghuys to the Catholic School Committee (25 Sept. 1877).
70 ADHH, 69: Report (3 Sept. 1883).

However, Telghuys was overwhelmed by the success of Catholic mobilisation. In the space of one year, the number of pupils in the new school rose from 180 to 900. She did not have enough trained choir sisters to provide education, while her lay sisters were concentrated in the laundry in Kontich. Expenses for personnel and renovations weighed heavily on the congregation's budget. For the first time since the foundation, Telghuys found herself in severe financial difficulties and she had no choice but to take action.[71] She had become the victim of her own unbridled zeal, but also came under pressure from the parish priest and ecclesiastical authorities. Other congregations experienced similar developments, leading Wynants to take a pessimistic view of the freedom of action the teaching religious had by comparison with the male actors: "Ce sont eux qui orientent l'activité des religieuses, en définissant le besoin social à combler". The aforementioned 'power to refuse' was partly eroded when the Church was in combat mode.[72]

However, some remarks have to be made. After all, female religious also had their own motives and ambitions. Telghuys, for example, had difficulty with the supervision of the lay administrators of the Antwerp Catholic School Committee, founded to finance the new Catholic schools that emerged during the School War. She also was increasingly annoyed by the interference of Father De Molder and Draveman in her school policy. Both insisted on professionalisation and advised Telghuys to allow her teaching sisters to take part in the pedagogical courses organised by the School Committee. Telghuys refused categorically and isolated herself completely. At the end of 1879 she got rid of the boys' school by handing it over to the parish clergy, although she continued to provide some classrooms. She also decided that the remaining girls would be taught by her own sisters and a minimum of lay teachers. Subsidies from the School Committee were refused in order to escape their inspections and their quality control. As was the case in her decision to withdraw her sisters from Wuustwezel, Telghuys once again invoked a double-voiced discourse of obedience to ecclesiastical authorities to justify her strategy. She made clear that it was not desirable for the moral health of her sisters to teach older boys. By using the arguments of clerical authorities, focusing, as will be explained in the next chapter, on containing and isolating female convent life, she paradoxically tried to defend her own autonomy.[73]

Her rigid attitude towards the parish priest and director De Molder was particularly daring. Felix De Molder (1824-1894) was a priest with a long service record. As a former director of the *Colomma* boarding school in Mechelen

---

71 ADHH, 130: Chronicle of the School (1 Oct. 1879, 31 Oct. 1879); 69: Report (11 Aug.1881).
72 Wynants, *Les Sœurs de la Providence*, 260. For other examples of congregations overburdened by the needs of the School War, see: Strobbe and Suenens, *Zusters Kindsheid Jesu*, 90; Timmermans, *Convent van Bethlehem*, 229-230.
73 ABA, File Dienstmaagden H. Harten: Telghuys to Dechamps (18 Nov. 1879).

and a diocesan visitator of religious houses, he was familiar with women's convent life.[74] However, Telghuys did not feel inclined to give him the same loyalty she had given the co-founder Bogaerts. Instead, she denounced his 'worldly' influence and the financial pressure he put on the congregation. De Molder was shocked by her stubbornness and intransigence and informed the authorities in Mechelen about "cette Abbesse, qui est en guerre avec tout le monde".[75]

Nevertheless, given the ongoing School War he could not afford to push Telghuys so far that she would also close the girls' school, an option she effectively held in reserve as an implicit threat.[76] This ultimately highlighted how the massive Catholic mobilisation following the School War had a fundamentally ambiguous outcome. On the one hand, female religious were pressured to engage in the war, but were not always equipped to deal with the consequences of the success or the dangers of a position on the ideological 'front'. On the other hand, the 'power to refuse' was generally eroded, but not in all cases. The high demand for school sisters and infrastructure allowed powerful superiors to impose their own conditions. What was essential, however, was that in her fight against De Molder and the Catholic School Committee, Telghuys was supported by an influential male ally, the Jesuit Aloysius Legrelle. Appointed in 1875 as rector of the house in Antwerp, he had exchanged his role as an adviser to Cornet for a position as Telghuys' spiritual counsellor. As will become equally clear in the following chapters, he was an important figure in Telghuys' pursuit of independence.

The challenge of social Catholicism

From within the strong ultramontane societal networks a strong impetus was given to the burgeoning social Catholicism of the 1870s and 1880s. At the end of the 1860s, a democratically and socially inspired reformism, aimed at the emancipation of the working class by developing Catholic organisations, had arisen in progressive Catholic circles. In the 1870s however, the liberal-clerical struggle, in combination with the spectre of the Paris Commune, inspired a stronger belief in control, guidance and moral-religious education as the main condition for the material improvement of the working classes. What had started as a progressive perspective shifted towards a conservative, ultramontane and paternalistic approach, and only towards the end of the century would it again connect up with a more egalitarian vision. Nevertheless, 'ultramontane' social Catholicism paved the way for the Catholic turn to the people, which

---

74 Meeussen, "Felix De Molder".
75 ABA, File Dienstmaagden H. Harten: De Molder to Dechamps (19 March 1880).
76 ADHH, 69: Report (9 April 1880).

was definitively solidified by Leo XIII's encyclical *Rerum Novarum* (1891). It offered opportunities for broader social initiatives, in which enterprising religious women could also play a part.[77]

Missionaries for the working-class child

In 1873, Anna de Meeûs started catechism lessons for bargemen's children in Ghent. Five years before, she had already started a charity to provide catechetical and recreational activities for the children of market vendors and travelling operators of fairground attractions. Her decision was partly motivated by the difficulties she had experienced in developing her usual catechesis apostolate due to the rivalry with the parish priests of Ghent. It also showed de Meeûs' skill in responding to newly emerging needs.[78] A structural Catholic initiative for market and fairground workers emerged in 1868 in the context of the social work of the Antwerp Capuchins. Shortly thereafter, it was introduced in other large Belgian cities like Ghent, where Anna de Meeûs immediately linked it with her catechesis work.[79] In 1870 she also started similar catechism classes in Liège, which were enthusiastically spearheaded by the charismatic Eugénie de Robiano.

Kestre also positioned herself on the social scene. Over the years she had devised an inductive and animated program of religious education and recreation. In addition, she backed up her catechetical work with a system of material rewards such as prizes, free meals and clothing from the workshops of her association. Although little concrete 'pedagogical' material has been preserved, testimonies from her catechists show that she worked with prints, pictures and music.[80] Her *modus operandi* matched with the tradition of using religious images as 'modern' means of religious education that emerged in the 1860s and preceded the illustrated catechisms that gained wide popularity at the end of the nineteenth century.[81]

Although there is no evidence of a direct influence, her approach to catechesis resembled that devised in France by Bishop Dupanloup, a respected speaker at the Mechelen Congresses of the 1860s. He too focused on lively catechism lessons to make children understand the 'mysterious' language of re-

---

77 Wils, "België in de negentiende eeuw", 35-36; Viaene, "De ontplooiing van een 'vrije' kerk", 94-96; De Maeyer, "La Belgique", 372-373, 382.
78 ABG, Poortakker, *Relation de l'organisation de l'Œuvre*.
79 Boedt, *Enkele aspekten*, 55.
80 ADSJ, 1.3./3: Kestre to Dechamps, 30 March 1872; *Notices sur les religieuses. Mme Estelle de la Providence; Mme Louisa Auchard*.
81 On these religious images and illustrated catechism handbooks, see: Saint-Martin, *Voir, savoir, croire*.

ligion and on a system of raffles, rewards and prizes.[82] Kestre also introduced these techniques in her 'perseverance' and Sunday school classes, which were intended for both older working-class girls and young women. In the beginning of the 1880s, Kestre had 50 teachers and 1,500 participants to her catechist and perseverance classes, mainly from the inner city. In a city centre of 180,000 residents, these were not spectacular figures. What was important, however, was that the children were often from the working class where the Church was looking for new strategies to enhance its influence. Gradually Kestre acquired a reputation as a successful 'missionary' for the secularised neighbourhoods of the capital. At the Eucharistic Congress of Lille an appeal was made "à réaliser un système d'instruction religieuse, graduée et complète, pour les jeunes adolescents qui sont rivés à la chaine officielle, et prendre en cela pour modèle le système pratiqué avec tant de succès par les Dames de Sainte-Julienne."[83] In 1875, the Jesuits of Tournai asked Kestre to establish a convent in the middle of the Hainault industrial basin, because they believed in the potential of her catechism courses for the re-evangelisation of the working-class population. Although Kestre did not accept the invitation, the request of the Tournai Jesuits made clear that she had become an important figure in the religious vanguard. Parallels were to be found elsewhere. Brosnan pointed to the respected role of sisters as a link between the Catholic hierarchy and the large group of poor Irish and German immigrants in nineteenth-century Chicago. Mangion noted that English religious drew their authority from their contacts with broad sections of the population. Van Heijst argued for a reassessment of the importance of the nursing activities of nineteenth-century Dutch religious, because through their apostolate they once again brought socially marginalised groups back into the Catholic world.[84]

Female entrepreneurship in a Christian economy

In the second half of the 1870s Telghuys started with remunerative sewing workshops in Kontich and Antwerp for orphans and girls from working-class districts who could not find a respectable job. She also opened a coffee workshop where housewives could earn an income by sorting coffee beans, work that was compatible with their roles as mothers and wives. Together with her aforementioned vocational courses, these initiatives fitted perfectly with the ultramontane aim to create an 'économie chrétienne' within a Christian society. Long before Leo XIII's 1891 encyclical *Rerum Novarum*, European Catholic

---

82 Gadille, "Grands courants doctrinaux", 132; Gibson, *A Social History*, 167; Saint-Martin, *Voir, savoir, croire*, 543-544.
83 *Congrès des Œuvres Eucharistiques*, 287.
84 Brosnan, "Public presence", 481-482; Mangion, *Contested Identities*, 228-229; Van Heijst, *Models*, 369.

thinkers had already developed a Christian third way between liberal capitalism and the class struggle of socialism. They came up with a harmonious and paternalistic economic model, inspired by medieval corporatism and based on cooperation between the social classes on the one hand and an intensely religious formation of all aspects of life on the other. Telghuys' commitment to offer women workers an opportunity for a better future, safely embedded in a trajectory towards re-Christianisation, reflected both objectives of social Catholicism.[85] Almost simultaneously with the sewing workshops she also founded a lay congregation for domestic servants. The initiative aimed at creating a core of pious servants, who under the direction of Telghuys and a local priest, could play an exemplary Christian role in their own milieu and work environment.[86] Again, Telghuys went further and attached a kind of employment agency for female servants to the lay congregation. Through her extensive network in the well-to-do Catholic classes in Antwerp, she tried to find positions as domestic servants for the orphans from her own institution, for unfortunate girls who had been dismissed elsewhere or for the many postulants who left her congregation.

The social reintegration of girls and women from vulnerable social backgrounds through education and placement as domestic servants was a proven strategy, which was also applied, for example, to the care for 'fallen women' by the Good Shepherd Sisters. It was one of the few ways in which these women could be offered an opportunity for an income and a more or less independent existence. This kind of work usually did not free them, however, from submissiveness and did not protect them from the threat of mental, physical and sexual abuse. In the second half of the nineteenth century, the rising bourgeoisie had driven up the demand for domestic staff in Belgium. On all sides, Catholic, liberal, and Protestant, measures were put in place for the protection and moral supervision of this vulnerable group.[87] Along with the Good Shepherd Sisters, the *Filles de la Croix* in Liège and the German Franciscan Sisters of Brussels, Telghuys was part of the first group of female religious to work in this area. An official Catholic organisation for service personnel emerged only at the end of the nineteenth century.[88] Telghuys was not only motivated by an emotional concern for the women's fate. Like her initiatives for female mothers and workers, she also tried to integrate the female servants into a Catholic world. In that sense, she imposed the isolated ultramontane

---

85   Van Molle, "Comparing religious perspectives", 18-19; De Maeyer, *De rode baron*, 220-224.
86   ADHH, 69: Reports (18 March 1873, 12 Feb. 1874); 58: Telghuys to Speéssen (15 May 1873).
87   Gesquière and Van Rompaey, "Het fenomeen dienstpersoneel", 24-29; Piette, "Maintenir les servantes", 47. De Keyser concluded from the censuses that between 1866 and 1900 the number of domestic servants rose from almost 88,000 to more than 121,000. See: De Keyzer, *Madame est servie*, 355.
88   Keymolen and Van Molle, "Feminisme", 167-170; Piette, "Maintenir les servantes", 47-49, 66.

view on new groups of people, much to the frustration of ideologically more neutral initiatives, such as that of the Protestant Brussels bourgeois woman, Adelheid Momm.[89]

The same ambiguity also characterised Telghuys' other social initiatives. From the beginning of the 1870s, she almost systematically bought up all the labourers' cottages around the convent in Antwerp. On the one hand, this purchasing policy was motivated by her desire for isolation, and her desire to shield the convent grounds from unwanted cans. On the other hand, there were apostolate-related reasons also. Some of the houses were repurposed as rooms and apartments for paying boarders, for the employees of her workshops, for orphans and girls who left the laundry in Kontich at the age of 21 or for destitute people who came knocking at the convent door.[90]

The purchase of the properties was financed almost entirely by the laundry activities in Kontich. After the laundry and a large part of the orphanage and home for girls was transferred from Antwerp to Kontich, Telghuys developed a semi-industrial company there. Following the purchase, Havenith's castle was partly dismantled, and then expanded into a factory, equipped with steam washing machines and professional ironing machines. The old castle gardens were transformed into bleaching and drying meadows. Next to the castle, buildings were erected for the service staff and stables for the horses and carriages that transported the laundry. Early financial reports have not been preserved, but around the turn of the century Telghuys' laundry in Kontich had a turnover of almost 200,000 francs a year. This was double the income of de Meeûs' association and well above the income generated by the labour of orphans in other private and state orphanages.[91]

---

[89] In 1882 Momm founded a home in Forest (Brussels) for female servants, motivated by the same moral reflex as Telghuys, but also to offer an alternative for "des maisons de placement catholiques, où l'on favorisait le placement de leurs compagnes catholiques, ou bien où elles étaient parfois sollicitées à changer de religion". Cited in: Piette, "Maintenir les servantes", 57.

[90] ADHH, 58: Telghuys to De Molder (2 Nov. 1872), Telghuys to Korsch (5 May 1874), Telghuys to Chaigneau (23 Nov. 1872); 69: Reports (25 Oct. 1879, 4 Aug. 1882).

[91] ADHH, 69: Report (9 Feb. 1901). The orphanage of the *Zusters van Sint-Vincentius* of Gijzegem in Ronse generated 3,000 to 4,000 francs from the sewing and spinning work of the girls: Vandenberghe, *De opvang*, 61-63. By further comparison, the fees for Cornet's school in Maleizen were 400 francs a year in that period. With a school population of about 120 students, this yielded an income of about 48,000 francs. Around the turn of the century, the *Annuntiaten* of Heverlee ran one of the largest boarding schools in the country, with 1,000 pupils each paying 250 francs a year. With her laundry of 70 orphans, Telghuys therefore generated almost as much income as the large institute in Heverlee. See: Christens, *Honderd jaar Heilig-Hartinstituut*, 102-103. Evidence for a comparison with companies run by lay women is scarce. Piette mentions the clothing store of the Voss sisters in Brussels. With a turnover of 275,000 francs around 1850 it was among the highest patent tax paying companies in the capital; see: Piette, "Belgium's Tradeswomen", 136.

In a certain sense, Telghuys' laundry industry still lay within the contours of gender norms. Laundry activities together with the sewing and fashion industries were among the few sectors where independent female initiative was tolerated.[92] Telghuys was also able to develop her industry with little male interference. The priests in the *Sint-Augustinus* parish knew little about the laundry business and had their own concerns with the clerical-liberal struggle and the social question. Telghuys did donate part of the income from the laundry activities to the parish of *Sint-Augustinus*, a sponsorship she did not hesitate to use as a bargaining tool during moments of conflict.

A growing urban bourgeoisie increased the demand not only for servants but also for a discreet and inexpensive outsourcing of their laundry needs. It created opportunities for female professional activities, but the laundry activities for lay women were rarely more than a poorly paid survival strategy or a supplement to the family budget. The pressure of work was high and manual labour was increasingly being priced out of the market by industrial companies such as the laundry in Kontich. Unlike lay women, communities of sisters across nations and Christian denominations managed to build up their laundries into profitable businesses. They had greater investment opportunities, a broader network and access to a large supply of cheap labour.[93] Telghuys found a market in her own home base, the Antwerp commercial bourgeoisie, and in a number of large Catholic boarding schools and hospitals. She followed new developments in the business very closely and turned out to be a tough negotiator in setting tariffs and in discussing prices and technical specifications with machine suppliers.[94]

There are clear parallels with 'the unlikely entrepreneurs' in convents elsewhere. The American historian Wall used this designation for the powerful female religious in charge of hospitals in the United States. In Belgium as well, despite their often submissive position in hospitals controlled by civil authorities, women at the head of nursing congregations could find possibilities for entrepreneurship and agency. Mother Marie-Rose Carouy (1851-1923) of the Hospital Sisters of Lessines, for example, gained influence, prestige and wealth for her congregation by inventing, distributing and commercialising an antiseptic medicine.[95] Superiors of large educational institutions also had extensive responsibilities in administering their properties and finances and in conceiving their pedagogical and promotional strategies. Like Telghuys, many of them owed their success to a combination of cheap and disciplined

---

92 Van Molle, "Zakenvrouwen", 10-11; Smith, *Changing Lives*, 148.
93 Firth, "Accounting for souls", 200-201; Kollar, "Magdalenes", 316-323; Smith, *Changing Lives*, 148.
94 ADHH, 58: Telghuys to Peeraer (28 Feb. 1871), Telghuys to Torck-Lemay (30 March 1875); 69: Reports (25 Sept. 1881, 19 April 1885).
95 Wall, *Unlikely Entrepreneurs*, 186-191. On Carouy, see: Yernault, "Deux grands 'guérisseurs'", 50-57.

In the 1870s and 1880s Telghuys expanded her laundry in Kontich into a real business. The industrial-scale work, which provided the congregation with a large income and opportunities for property development came at a cost however, paid for by the hard labour of orphans and destitute girls.
[Postcard – S.d. – Collection *Koninklijke Kring voor Heemkunde*, Kontich]

workers, a strong negotiating position and broad knowledge of the market.[96] Telghuys shared their capitalist-like strategies. She protected her specific bleaching process as a trade secret. She refused to help similar initiatives by other congregations without the guarantee of a return on investment. Moreover, she was not afraid to promote the quality of her own industry at the expense of competing laundries.[97]

Telghuys also implemented a tough personnel policy. Twenty domestic servants and work men were employed in Kontich in the nineteenth century, but most of the work was carried out by a group of 70 to 100 girls between 14 and 21 years of age. They worked six days a week without pay, alternating with classes intended to prepare them for work as seamstresses, ironers, domestic servants or self-employed laundry workers. General education was reserved for the younger orphans between 6 and 14 years of age who stayed in Antwerp until a second institute was opened in Kontich in 1886. Family members or the civil authorities did not have to pay any fees for orphans aged 14 and over, on condition that they stayed and worked at the institute until their 21st birthday.

96 Heyrman, "La culture d'entreprise", 303; Wynants, "Le gouvernement", 86-87.
97 ADHH, 69: Reports (11 April 1873, 18 May 1876, 15 July 1876).

The work was heavy and reprimands about torn, stained or tardy laundry were numerous. Telghuys therefore refused to accept orphans or other girls who did not have the physical or mental capacity to keep up with the work. However, there is no evidence of excessive humiliation, sexual abuse or deprivation, such as emerged in the shocking testimonies about the Irish Magdalen Laundries or in the early twentieth-century criticisms of the penitentiary institutes of the Van Celst sisters.[98] Telghuys instructed her sisters to behave like good mothers, provided a 'bourgeois diet' with butter and meat, arranged trips and kept the orphans strictly separated from the male service staff. Orphans with relatives were allowed home visits every three months. At the end of their 'service' in the orphanage, the girls received financial compensation and a trousseau and, as already indicated, they could count on Telghuys' help in finding a job or cheap housing. From the 1870s a future trajectory was also opened up for them as lay sisters in the congregation.[99]

Apart from the industrial-scale work, the strict regime did not differ much from mainstream nineteenth-century practices in other Catholic and state orphanages, prevention institutes or reform schools.[100] Nonetheless, the compulsory work of children and young women, combined with profitable entrepreneurship gives Telghuys' genuine social commitment an ambiguous character. In Antwerp as well, the opportunistic draw-backs of Telghuys' entrepreneurship were evident. The purchase of workers' houses in the area around the *Sint-Jorisvest* to extent the convent domain and to offer cheap housing to Telghuys' protegees was done at the expense of the tenants, often impoverished working-class families. Tenants who refused to move got no mercy and were sometimes forced out with police intervention. From time to time, incidents were reported before the gates of the convent in Antwerp: graffities on the walls accusing the sisters of greed or orphans who ran away with help of people from the neighbourhood. Telghuys' social commitment was seriously challenged, but she was never formally indicted.[101]

---

98 Bossart, *L'industrie*, 81-97. See above, part 1.
99 ADHH, 58: Telghuys to Osy (21 Sept. 1871), Telghuys to Bruson (29 Jan. 1876), Telghuys to Antoninissen (5 Sept. 1876).
100 Vloeberghs, *Belgique Enseignante*, 319-320; Vandenberghe, *De opvang*, 61-64; Veestraeten, *De wezenzorg*, 62; Strobbe and Suenens, *Zusters Kindsheid Jesu*, 111; D'Hoker, *Het kind in de inrichting*, 54-55; Dupont-Bouchat, *La Belgique criminelle*, 470-486.
101 ADHH, 36: Notes regarding patrimony; 58: Telghuys to the police commissioner (6 July 1871).

Victims and religious entrepreneurs: the spiritual dynamics of ultramontanism

Nowhere were the double dynamics of the ultramontane crusade – the formation of a Catholic siege and victim mentality on the one hand, the push for conquest on the other – more evident than in the spiritual discourse of the four superiors. Harrison saw 1870 as the definitive end of Romantic revival Catholicism and the beginning of a tormented, self-fixated and intolerant ultramontanism. An intense victim spirituality as well as different forms of extremely devout piety were provoked by the well-known events of the Franco-Prussian war, the Roman question, and the Paris Commune. Harrison painted a very pessimistic picture of the new Catholic state of mind, which led both insiders and outsiders to identify the beleaguered Church with the supposed vulnerability and helplessness of the female soul.[102]

Though victim spirituality was already apparent in medieval and early modern Catholicism, it clearly thrived as never before in the late nineteenth century, in France as well as in other Catholic regions. Female religious, though not exclusively and certainly not without male counterparts, played a prominent role among its chief supporters.[103] As an addendum to Harrison's pertinent characterisation of the times, I would argue that the spiritual tone of ultramontane piety was pessimistic and unyielding, but not passive. Militant ultramontanism offered opportunities both for women's social enterprises and for spiritual entrepreneurship. In her study of the Sacred Heart devotion in Belgium, Van Osselaer pointed out that the nineteenth-century clerical perception of women was not merely that of the caricature of the extremely devout pious woman but allowed space for '*femmes fortes*'. Langlois, in his study of the classic nineteenth-century 'victim soul', Thérèse de Lisieux, convincingly showed that her victim spirituality was accompanied in the last years of her life by an ardent desire for predication.[104] The narrative of the four superiors also indicates that religious women could gain prestige and power from the apparently submissive victim spirituality.

Inspired by Mary and the martyr in the Vatican

From the beginning of the 1870s Telghuys' position as convent superior was strong enough to allow her to re-enshrine her personal devotion to Our Lady of the Seven Sorrows in her congregation. Of the diverse forms of Marian devotion, that to Mary's sorrows was possibly the one most suited to the victim spirituality of the last third of the nineteenth century. Mary bore her suf-

---

102 Harrison, *Romantic Catholics*, 25-26, 275-278.
103 Manzoni, "Victimale", 540-545.
104 Van Osselaer, *The Pious Sex*, 94-85; Langlois, *Thérèse de Lisieux*.

fering before, during and after the death of her son, and in this way became an ideal model for the ultramontane spirit of suffering. Telghuys transferred this model to her own sisters. Mary had to be their example of unconditional submission to and confidence in God's will and of a readiness for suffering and detachment. Just as Jesus' mother accompanied her son in his darkest hours, the sisters too had to take care of children and women at risk and share their fate as victims of anticlerical and morally dangerous times.[105] Telghuys' Marian victim spirituality perpetuated the spiritual double-voiced discourse that was explained earlier. On the one hand, the call for female submission, detachment and willingness to suffer confirmed the image of the subservient woman, steeped in a repetitive, superficial and undemanding piety. Telghuys had the seven stations of Mary's sorrows installed in the chapel of her convent in Antwerp, and shortly after, repeated daily visits to the stations became a mandatory ritual for all the sisters, orphans and pupils at the *Sint-Franciscus-Xaveriusinstituut*.

On the other hand, the spirituality of victimhood was also a bridge to female spiritual action and development. Telghuys' entrepreneurial qualities and desire to re-Christianise inspired her in 1874 to promote the Marian devotion more widely. She envisioned a book of prayers and meditations dedicated to the devotion to Our Lady of the Seven Sorrows, based on her own lectures and conferences by Father Schoofs. Her brother-in-law, the well-known artist Nicaise De Keyser provided suitable illustrations. The entire process was conceived, coordinated and paid for by Telghuys, although she never showed any ambition to get recognition for it. The publication appeared in 1874 under the title *Les sept stations de Notre-Dame des sept douleurs, méditations et prières par un Prêtre zélateur de cette dévotion*. In 1870, gender roles still implied an unspoken and anonymous female role in the public domain. There is no evidence that Telghuys was explicitly pressured not to put her name on the brochure. It seems to have been her own decision, based on a combination of sincere modesty and a realistic awareness of the possible negative responses to female authorship.[106] Of course, the reluctance to publicly acknowledge or recognise women's skills or realisations was not peculiar to female religious. In the broader artistic and literary world too, women were often expected to be humble and modest enough not to proclaim their own mastery and to see themselves as 'friends of art' rather than as artists.[107]

Where Telghuys found her ideal of spiritual victimhood in Mary, Kestre and de Meeûs mainly looked to the living martyr in the Vatican. From the late 1860s, the adulation of the pope became an integral part of the catechetical and retreat work, as well as an incentive for new religious events and spiritual

105 ADHH, 10: Lecture by Telghuys on Our Lady of the Seven Sorrows (1878).
106 ADHH, 58: Telghuys to Schoofs (27 Sept. 1873, 2 April 1874).
107 Creusen, *Femmes artistes*, 322; De Maeyer, "Des vierges et des manuscrits", 76-77.

entrepreneurship. In 1871, when Pius IX was pushed back inside the walls of the Vatican by the departing French troops and the advancing Italian revolutionaries, Kestre and de Meeûs were swept along on a wave of ultramontane outrage and sympathy.[108] With half an eye always on their rivals' initiatives, both superiors organised prayer vigils, triduums, processions and novenas for the pope. In 1870, Kestre anxiously rallied all her sisters, associate members and catechism pupils for three days of continuous adoration in her provisional convent chapel: "pénétrées de peine en voyant notre St-Père le Pape prisonnier, l'Eglise en souffrance, la paix troublée entre les princes chrétiens, ce qui fait craindre une guerre ou bouleversement général".[109] In 1872 Anna de Meeûs organised a "croisade de prières" so as to contribute, along with the members of her widespread association, to the rescue of the hard-pressed pope: "Dans les temps de calamités actuelles la prière étant le principal moyen pour attirer sur la Sainte Eglise et sur son Chef-vénéré la grande Miséricorde".[110] Unlike the other convent superiors, she had a direct line to Rome and therefore felt a strong emotional connection to the papal cause. The Roman focus of de Meeûs would further intensify in the late 1870s.

Limited ambitions: competition and centralisation

Spiritual entrepreneurship in the second half of the nineteenth century, however, was not a prerogative of women religious. Spiritual victimhood and the longing for the social kingdom of Christ also provided space and inspiration for lay women. In the *Sacré-Cœur* Basilica in Montmartre, lay women strove side by side with religious to do penance and to re-Christianise their country. In Belgium, Van Osselaer has pointed to the significant contribution of women in the organisation of the Apostolate of the Prayer, which in the last quarter of the nineteenth century became increasingly involved in the struggle for and discourse of the restoration of Christ's reign on earth. In the late 1860s, the Belgian lay woman Mathilde de Nédonchel was the driving force behind the Guard of Honour of the Sacred Heart of Jesus in Belgium, the association that was founded in the Visitandine convent in Bourg-en-Bresse in France.[111]

In comparison with these enterprising lay women, religious superiors like de Meeûs and Telghuys could more easily fall back on the 'woman power' of their congregations, their wide-ranging networks and the scope of their

---

108 On the papal question, see: Viaene, "The Roman Question"; Idem, "A Pope's dilemma", 251-252.
109 ADSJ, 1.3./3: Kestre to Dechamps (5 Oct. 1870).
110 ASV, *Archivio S. Congregazione Vescovi et regolari – Positiones Monialium*, 16275: de Meeûs to Pius IX (12 April 1872).
111 Benoist, *Le Sacré-Cœur*, 1335-1427; Van Osselaer, *The Pious Sex*, 106-110; Baas, *Leven der Gravin Mathilde de Nédonchel*, 220.

apostolates. It is telling that in 1867 de Nédonchel only barely avoided a 'hostile takeover' by de Meeûs. The male director of the Guard of Honour had suggested that the confraternity would have more opportunities for development if it were brought under the wings of de Meeûs' stable association and congregation. Only de Nédonchel's determination and the support of other religious communities, the *Sœurs Réparatrices* of d'Oultremont in Tournai in particular, could ensure an independent existence.[112]

These incidents reveal the complex relationship between religious and lay women, as well as the competition between the religious institutes themselves. The constant factor in the comparison between the spiritual entrepreneurship of lay women and that of female religious, however, was the inescapability of the dominant male voice. After all, female spiritual engagement driven by the spirituality of victimhood was not unanimously welcomed. Liberals gloated over what they considered to be female idolatry and exaggerated piety.[113] There was also criticism from the Catholic, even the clerical side. Women's spiritual role in the ultramontane crusade, unlike their role in the social apostolates, remained problematic. Both de Meeûs and Kestre were faced with criticism from the parish clergy about their uncontrollable desire for spiritual initiative. The quick succession of religious events in their associations and convent chapels lured both believers and income away from the parish. The clergy's frustrations echoed long-standing issues between seculars and regulars, but were also exacerbated by the intensified ultramontane devotional zeal. The criticism was mixed with gender prejudices as well. The Jesuit Provincial Goethals, displeased with the multitude of de Meeûs' spiritual initiatives, considered writing to Archbishop Dechamps about "la ferveur, surtout chez les femmes, ne les préserve pas toujours de tendances (...) exagérées, me serait-il permis d'ajouter?".[114] The passage was later deleted, but pointed to the persistent male and clerical distrust of spiritually overzealous women. The Dutch bishop Wilmer was also annoyed by the ceaseless spiritual entrepreneurial spirit of de Meeûs sisters: "leur esprit ne connait pas de repos".[115]

Like many other teaching sisters, Cornet focused her spiritual entrepreneurship on her school activities. In 1865, with the support of the Jesuits, she set up a Marian congregation in her boarding school, not only as an extra incentive for her most devout pupils, but also as her contribution to the formation of a new generation of engaged Catholic women.[116] Attempts to intensify Eucharistic worship in her boarding school and convent chapel, however, were

112 Baas, *Leven der Gravin Mathilde de Nédonchel*, 210-212.
113 Viaene, *Belgium and the Holy See*, 210-212.
114 ABSE, 4.2.6. Boone, 1235: Matthys-De Buck Report.
115 NADH, ABR, 1686: Wilmer to Nuncio Capri (20 Nov. 1875).
116 ASCMLH, A.2: Cornet to the archbishop (31 March and 18 April 1865).

vetoed by Mechelen. Through the chaplain of the convent chapel, Mechelen sent word that "les religieuses ont parfois l'habitude d'exagérer un peu".[117]

There was also evidence from Ghent, Brussels and Liège that the increasingly intensive adoration initiatives of de Meeûs and Kestre appealed to an extremely pious but limited audience. The straightforward provincial of the Redemptorists, Kockerols, among others, expressed his displeasure at the uncontrolled proliferation and diversity of the different Eucharistic devotions. In the run-up to the First Vatican Council, he argued together with Cattani, the nuncio in Belgium between 1868 and 1875, for tighter regulation and a restriction of "une certaine religiosité vague, nuageuse, sentimentale, efféminée, incapable de produire des actes un peu solides et de conduire à l'abnégation et à la mortification chrétiennes".[118] Even the 'serious' Eucharistic devotion was then subject to gender-inspired criticism about the superficial character of female devotion often associated with the Sacred Heart or Marian piety. Female religious, as already stated, compelled respect because they were an important link between the clerical elite and the Catholic people. When they did not fulfil that role, or did so only for a limited public, their position was quickly undermined, especially when they ventured into the exclusive territory of the male clergy.

Female religious were also confronted with the centralising forces within the ultramontane Catholic Church. The *Pères du Saint Sacrement*, who thanks to the generosity of de Meeûs had been able to settle in Brussels in the mid-1860s, increasingly criticised "les usages antiliturgiques" and "les usages gallicans belges" of the sisters. They strove for a stricter implementation of the Roman rite, with the use of the correct liturgical colours, the correct altar arrangements and better priestly supervision.[119] The male religious of Eymard also were becoming increasingly dissatisfied about their dependence on de Meeûs. They felt inhibited by the sisters' initiatives and the surfeit of activities in the Salazar chapel. For these reasons they opened a second Brussels house in the *Léopold* district in 1867. The benefactor of the new convent, Clarisse de Tomasz de Bossière, combined the generosity and piety of de Meeûs with a much more docile character. Eymard was relieved, "car il vaut mieux être chez Soi; et si jamais les Dames de l'Adoration de la rue des Sols nous

---

117 AAM, CF, La Hulpe: Casters to Lauwers (29 July 1871), Lauwers to Casters (4 Aug. 1871). Eugène Casters (1840-1901) was a chaplain to the convent chapel in Maleizen between 1868 and 1879.
118 Art, "Documents", 505-508. About Nuncio Giacomo Cattani (1823-1887), see: Simon, *Instructions*, 150.
119 Eymard to de Cuers (6 Feb. 1866), Eymard to Leroyer (6 Feb. 1866, 12 Nov. 1867), cited in: Eymard, *Briefe*, nos 1719, 1718 and 2061; Eymard to de Meeûs (March 1866), Eymard to de Meeûs (21 Nov. 1867), cited in: Stalmans, *Les fondations*, 22, 32-33.

voulaient ailleurs, nous ne serions pas à la rue".[120] Ultramontane tendencies and centralisation by diocesan as well as Roman authorities not only affected the entrepreneurship of female superiors. It had serious consequences as well for their position as female leaders inside and outside the convent walls.

---

120 Eymard to Leroyer (12 Nov. 1867), cited in: Eymard, *Briefe*, 2061.

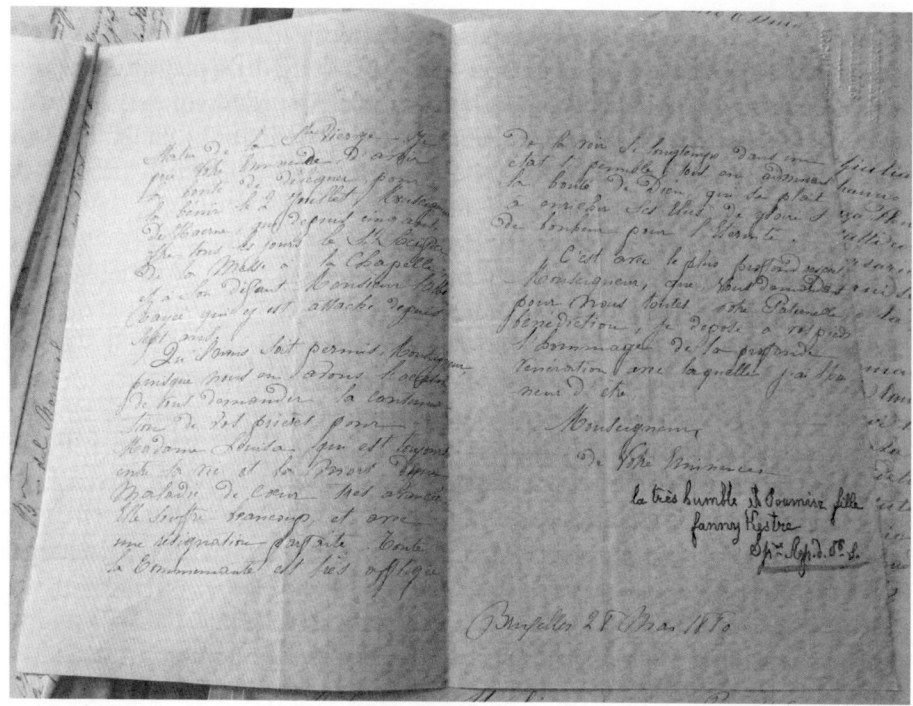

Kestre's charism in her own congregation was partly based on her courageous perseverance, even in times when her health was seriously deteriorating. Struggling with a chronic infection in her arm, writing became difficult. She dictated her letters to Dechamps to another sister, but insisting on signing them herself, stressing her position as a superior, but as a vulnerable and submissive woman as well.
[Letter Kestre to Dechamps – 28 May 1880 – ADSJ, 1.3./3]

"PAS ASSEZ FEMME"?
FEMALE LEADERSHIP IN WOMEN'S CONVENTS

> Vous dirigez vos religieuses d'une manière autoritaire (...). En plus vous oubliez tout ce que j'ai fait pour votre fondation. Vous n'êtes pas assez femme.
> ARE, *Cahier des Lettres 3*: Boone to de Meeûs (27 Aug. 1867)

The previous chapters analysed the development and consolidation of the four congregations and their apostolates against the background of the culture wars and the ultramontane Church. In the last two chapters I would like to discuss in more detail how the four women profiled themselves as superiors during this process. In the first instance, the focus will be on their role within their own communities. In a subsequent chapter, I will examine the possibilities and obstacles that confronted their female leadership with regard to Belgian and Roman ecclesiastical politics.

During the expansion process of the congregations, the original family model came to be put on a more corporative footing. The increase in scale necessitated a different approach. Internally, the transformation was characterised by a process of standardisation and formalisation, with obedience, self-denial and fidelity to the rule being the crucial factors. In essence, this evolution did not deviate from the pattern of consolidation in other congregations and was – as is revealed above in Father Boone's harsh assessment of de Meeûs as an authoritarian and 'unwomanly' superior – seriously affected by gender and clerical power balances. The subtleties and nuances of it, however, were largely determined by the character, charisma and ambitions of the superiors. They shaped the internal 'corporate culture' of the congregations, with styles ranging from lenient leadership to almost dictatorial rule.

"Une hostie vivante": institutionalised self-denial

Antoinette Cornet experienced a turbulent first decade after the foundation, but the success of her boarding school finally paved the way for a definitive consolidation of her institute. The stately and spacious new building in rural Maleizen testified of a new, confident identity. Nonetheless, as superior she continued to give priority to humility and self-denial. These were the anchor points of a policy in which, according to the testimonies of sisters, she was "inexorablement sévère".[1] In her letters she expressed satisfaction with those sisters who were willing to sanctify themselves "par la destruction du vieil homme" and with the fact that "chacune a compris qu'il faut s'humilier en se dévouant".[2] Cornet shared the pessimistic ultramontane view of the sinful human being, but also continued to believe in the redemptive power of sacrifice. Obedience and self-denial were, in her view, the "passe-port pour le ciel", which also kept the earthly convent machine running.[3]

In 1883, Cornet set down her Ignatian focus on the total renunciation of one's own will in a proper manifesto, the *Questionnaire Spirituel*. It was a concise commentary on the rule, in question and answer format just like the *Mechelse Catechismus*. The structure was simple, but the content was an eloquent and powerful expression of Cornet's ideals as a convent superior: "une vierge consacrée à Jésus-Christ a des yeux pour ne point voir les objets créés, des oreilles pour ne point entendre la voix des hommes, une langue pour ne parler qu'à Dieu seul, ou de Lui; des membres pour les sacrifier à la pénitence; de sorte qu'elle peut dire avec l'Apôtre: "je suis attachée à la croix de mon Sauveur et je m'y consume lentement"; elle vit pour mourir à toute heure; c'est une hostie vivante".[4]

Written three years before Cornet's death in 1886, the *Questionnaire Spirituel* was cherished by the congregation as their founder's spiritual testament. However, the work was not original. Further research proves that Cornet based it almost entirely and literally on passages from two Ignatian-inspired texts. The first was a commentary on Ignatius' ideas about self-denial, ascribed to the sixteenth-century Jesuit, Jacques Miron. The second was an early nineteenth-century sermon by the Jesuit preacher Nicholas Tuite MacCarthy. The commentary by Miron, who was known as "un homme (...) ferme, d'une vertu

1 ASCMLH, *Notice Chronologique*, 51-53, 59-60; A.2: Cornet to Goossens (5 Dec. 1885), Sr. Marguerite Verlaine to Sr. Ignace Courrier (26 March 1886).
2 ASCMLH, A.2: Cornet to the sisters in Bazel (21 Feb. 1877).
3 ASCMLH, *Retraite sur la spiritualité*, 71-80.
4 ASCMLH, *Questionnaire spirituel*, 9.

un peu dure", was published in Brussels in 1852 in a work by the Jesuit Bartoli, *Histoire de Saint Ignace de Loyola*. The MacCarthy sermons had already been collected and published in the 1830s.⁵ This new light on the composition of the *Questionnaire* undermines Cornet's internal reputation as an original religious thinker, but underscores her ascetic ideals. It is very significant, for example, that many of the paragraphs in Cornet's *Questionnaire* were derived from MacCarthy's sermon for the profession ceremony of an early nineteenth-century enclosed nun.⁶ Even as the superior of an active congregation, references to the monastic tradition and asceticism remained an important source of inspiration. Cornet's interest in Ignatian literature showed her to be a well-read woman, although within a typical gendered framework. Devoid of access to theological education and works, these women religious resorted to more popularised spiritual reading such as books of sermons, the lives of the saints, or devotional handbooks. Telghuys' Marian prayer book was an illustration of this, as was Cornet's *Questionnaire*. Without circumventing the limits, they were eager to learn and were enthusiastic in their search for spiritual inspiration as well as female role models. In 1877, Cornet received the newly published first biography of the congregation founder Sophie Barat and recommended it to both her own sisters and the dean of Overijse.⁷

Institutionalised self-denial, whether or not expressed in compiling spiritual works, was the basis for the efficiency, flexibility and expansion of the congregation as a business model. Nonetheless, convent superiors were not the only Catholic women who recommended and imposed the model of humility and detachment. Marie-Elisabeth Belpaire, herself active in the Belgian literary, publishing and education world, did not shy away from criticising her colleague, the already-mentioned Virginie Loveling, when in one of her publications she queried the female spirit of sacrifice.⁸ The aforementioned Melanie Van Biervliet, the Catholic promoter of a modernised boarding-school education, accused Isala Van Diest, who in 1884 qualified as Belgium's first woman doctor, of a lack of womanly humility.⁹ It was not even exclusive to

5 In the mid-sixteenth century, the French Jesuit Jacques Miron was provincial of the Portuguese Jesuit province where he antagonised his subordinates with his strictness. See: Bouhours, *La vie de Saint Ignace*, 455. For the passage in Miron, see: Bartoli, *Histoire de Saint Ignace*, II, 14-15, which corresponds to the *Questionnaire Spirituel* of Cornet, questions 8-12. MacCarthy (1769-1833) was a Jesuit of Irish-French descent who became famous in France as a preacher and poet. For the passage from MacCarthy, see: *Sermons du révérend père de Mac Carthy* I, 296-301, which corresponds with the *Questionnaire Spirituel*, questions 15-23.
6 This was a sermon for a profession ceremony in 1819 with the Paris *Bénédictines du Saint-Sacrement*, a congregation of the previously mentioned Mechtilde du Saint-Sacrement. See: *Sermons du révérend père de Mac Carthy*, I, 287.
7 ASCMLH, A.2: Cornet to the sisters in Bazel (21 Feb. 1877).
8 Stynen, *Rosalie en Virginie*, 195.
9 Keymolen, *Beroepsarbeid*, 27.

women. Religious brothers also had to conform to the mantra of humility. In the late 1860s, prominent clerics criticised their ambition to distinguish themselves. Brothers were reprimanded when they wore habits that too closely resembled the priestly soutane or when they called themselves '*messieurs*' and developed a teaching apostolate for the upper classes that was traditionally reserved for priests.[10]

The emphasis on self-renunciation created a body of willing and subordinate sisters, but hampered autonomous development. Of the four congregation superiors, de Meeûs was undoubtedly the one who pushed the focus on self-denial, obedience and total submission the furthest. Her almost dictatorial regime was marked by an obsessive opposition to all forms of deviation or dissent. As in other congregations, the sisters had no control over their own future. Sometimes even an outright culture of fear prevailed. The Ghent sisters, for example, worried about the fate of two fellow sisters who had suddenly been summoned to Brussels by de Meeûs, noted in their daily register that: "cela ne laisse pas de nous émotionner un peu mais comme on dit de prendre des coupons d'aller et retour, cela nous rassure un peu".[11]

Everything in the congregation was regulated and formalised down to the smallest details. Individual initiative was nipped in the bud, but according to the somewhat cynical de Meeûs her approach was necessary to curb the "manie des innovations" of her sisters. The menus for meals in all the houses had to be presented to de Meeûs in advance. Sisters were reprimanded if they bowed too deeply before the Blessed Sacrament. The distance between the knee and the chapel floor was laid down in the board meetings of the congregation. The material culture within the convents was standardised. The convent chapels and churches had largely the same decorations and statues of saints. In every house the curtains had to be made from fabrics designed by Bethune and had to consist of exactly eight folds. Posthumous testimonies from her sisters indicated that de Meeûs was as strict on herself as she was on her sisters. She lived austerely and did not allow herself any material privileges. If she made trips, she did it on foot if possible. If she missed spiritual exercises due to her duties as a superior, she extended her adoration of the Blessed Sacrament as a penance.[12] However, she did create a kind of majestic dignity for herself. The members of the congregation were only allowed to talk to Superior de Meeûs when asked to. The sisters were never to turn their backs on the superior. As in royal circles, they had to walk backwards on leaving de Meeûs' office.[13]

10 Art, "Documents ", 414-145.
11 ABG, Poortakker, Diaries (13 Feb. 1904).
12 ARE, *Chronique, XXXVI. Qualités et vertus*, 392-418.
13 ARE, *Relations des sœurs*; ABG, Poortakker, Meeting of convent superiors (Nov. 1876, Aug. 1879); ADBS, 06290-025 III. Salazar, 007-043.

As already indicated, obedience was the universal basis of nineteenth-century convent life.¹⁴ The same was true for the strong focus on rules and regulations. According to the historian Aubert, the mania for rules had to mask the lack of spiritual and theological depth in women's convent life at the time.¹⁵ I will argue later that the strict adherence to the rule could also open the gates to female autonomy. Still, this does not detract from the fact that Anna de Meeûs was indeed much more of an authoritarian leader and manager than an innovative spiritual figure. Even by nineteenth-century standards, her despotic governance was offensive, provoking internal and external criticism. In 1868, the former sister, Julie Desmanet de Biesme expressed the hope that the arrival of strong confessors would be a way to "empêcher [de Meeûs] de tyranniser ses religieuses".¹⁶ Boone, himself not devoid of an authoritarian character, advised de Meeûs to be milder and less dominant towards her sisters, to be more of a mother and – as already cited – more of a woman. Zoé de Jonghe d'Ardoye, one of the senior sisters in the congregation, left in 1868 because she could no longer stand de Meeûs' pressure, even in matters of conscience.¹⁷ Bishop de Montpellier of Liège also denounced "le caractère impérieux" of de Meeûs towards the sisters of the local convent community in Liège.¹⁸

However, it is important to exercise some restraint here. Both de Meeûs' prominent presence in the ecclesiastical field and her entourage of mature, self-confident aristocratic women made her more vulnerable to criticism. Quite possibly, the dictatorial approach of other female superiors was less immediately obvious. It remained unnoticed in congregations where the less cultivated and lower social profile of the subordinate sisters made it difficult to question the (abuse of) authority by a convent superior. The story of Antonia Schellekens in Arendonk, whose unbearable severity only came to the surface after the break-up of her congregation, is an indication in that direction.¹⁹

Telghuys also grew out to be an authoritarian superior. The smallest mistakes of her sisters – broken dishes, incorrectly worn clothes, false notes while singing in the chapel choir – were punished. Objections to or reservations about decisions by the superior were considered to be a serious violation of the rules. There was no room for doubt or individual initiative in the minutely observed daily life of the convent. Amongst others, choir sister Thérèse (Oeyen), although one of the most experienced sisters in the congregation, was sharply criticised by Telghuys in 1872: "Après votre orgueil qui en effet s'est rendu maître de votre volonté, vous aurez à combattre en premier lieu ce faux esprit d'activité qui vous absorbe. Vous êtes affairée de tout (...). Je

14 See also: Adelman, "Empowerment", 145; Raftery, "Rebels", 736-738.
15 Aubert, *L'Église dans le monde moderne*, 127.
16 Desmanet to Dechamps (22 Nov. 1868), cited in Becque, *Le Cardinal Dechamps*, II, 115.
17 ABSE, 4.2.6. Boone, 1243: de Jonghe d'Ardoye to Boone (29 July 1868).
18 ASV, NB, *Religiose dell'Adorazione: Mémoire de Montpellier* (15 Dec. 1871).
19 Van Hove, *Van Mariadal tot MPI*, 16-17.

The convent culture focusing on obedience, modesty and self-denial introduced by de Meeûs, Cornet and Telghuys could have dramatic outcomes. In 1872 Sister Thérèse Oeyen (1843-1872), who had been severly reprimanded in the past by Telghuys for her curiosity and pride, died at the age of 28 after she had 'penitently' kept silent about her advancing pneumonia.
[Photograph – before 1872 – ADHH, 204]

surprends toujours en vous la préoccupation des choses qui ne vous regardent pas". Once again, self-deprivation and submission were presented as a remedy for mistakes: "tachez de vous vaincre et ne cessez de travailler avant de les avoir tous détruits".[20]

As will be clear further on, Telghuys' discipline was harsh, but she did have an eye on future prospects and a severe reprimand did not stop her from offering opportunities to talented sisters. However, the emphasis on self-denial could also have tragic consequences. Sister Thérèse received Telghuys' admonishing letter while attending a training course at the Ursulines of Onze-Lieve-Vrouw-Waver prior to the foundation of the convent in Wuustwezel. A few weeks later she died of the pneumonia she had contracted in Waver. She had concealed the symptoms from everyone, driven by "son esprit de mortification joint à la crainte de causer de l'embarras".[21] The same Telghuys who had reprimanded her shortly before, now praised her for "son exactitude aux observances et sa grande charité". Driven, no doubt, by both remorse and a sincere exaltation of her suffering and victimhood, she praised Sister Thérèse to Vicar-General De Molder as an "exemple de pénitence, de résignation et de piété".[22]

In suffering and dying even disobedient sisters could then earn a halo. It was a macabre outcome of the nineteenth-century emphasis on self-denial. Yet the same perspective could give rise to a gentler and less oppressive management style. Unlike Telghuys, Cornet and de Meeûs, Kestre did not focus excessively on obedience. Rather, she drew her authority from her own exemplary resignation to suffering, for which her weak health offered ample opportunity. In the mid-1870s, she sustained an affliction in her right arm, an inflamed wound that festered into the bone and never healed. Her functioning was seriously hampered but she continued to devote herself completely to her apostolate. Dechamps responded to Kestre's agony with a mixture of both admiration and irony. On some occasions his words affirmed the legitimacy that some women could derive from their victimhood: "Votre maladie n'est que la voie par laquelle N.S. nous montre la sainteté de vous œuvres".[23] On other occasions he was reserved about the severity of her illnesses: "Vous souffrez, ma fille, mais pas encore pour mourir. La souffrance vous laisse des forces, car il en faut pour écrire 4 pages d'écriture ferrée comme vous venez de le faire."[24]

She also tried to turn her suffering into inspiration for her sisters: "Nous sommes des victimes de N.S., la résignation dans la souffrance est notre force".[25] Kestre immersed her congregation in the victim spirituality of the

20   ADHH, 5: Telghuys to Oeyen (1872).
21   ADHH, 58: Telghuys to the superior of the Ursulines (5 June 1872).
22   ADHH, 58: Telghuys to De Molder (7 June 1872).
23   ADSJ, 1.4: Dechamps to Kestre (20 May 1876).
24   ADSJ, 1.4: Dechamps to Kestre (8 July 1872).
25   ADSJ, 1.8: Kestre to Flasselaerts (18 May 1874).

nineteenth century, but not to the extent of an extreme cultivation of suffering. Ill sisters were encouraged to look after themselves properly so as to be able to continue their work for God. In a letter from Sister Alix, the novice mistress in Brussels, to her fellow sister in Namur, we catch a glimpse of the potential of Kestre's suffering charisma to motivate her fellow-sisters: "comme elle nous montre chaque jour de ne pas capituler, et de nous renforcer dans le renoncement, pour devenir des instruments plus efficaces et autonomes pour le salut des âmes et des épouses nobles de N.S."[26] Renouncing the world was also underlined here, but without the severe tone of Telghuys or de Meeûs. Kestre often had difficulties in using the double-voiced discourse of female modesty and power, but seems to have been more successful than her colleagues in making the paradoxical space between self-denial and self-development that empowered female founders and superiors accessible to her own sisters.

Internal power balances

Despite the obvious suppressive tendencies, convent life also had a modest democratic component. Choir sisters in the four congregations elected their new leader through a secret ballot every three or nine years or after the death of a superior who had been appointed for life. This vote consistently revealed wide support for the incumbent founder-superior. The successive 'election victories' of de Meeûs, Cornet and Telghuys were always almost unanimous, with a maximum of one dissenting vote per election.[27] These observations raise questions about the opportunities for participation, agency and career advancement within the convent walls. In the international literature there is no unanimity about the capacity of convent life to offer chances for social mobility and professional activities to the large group of 'ordinary' sisters. The tenor is moderately positive and puts the emphasis on the modest possibilities for female development within a stable, regulated and secured environment.[28] Some historians, however, point more to the oppressive mechanisms of the emphasis on obedience and self-denial.[29]

26 ADSJ, 1.8: Lalieu to Flasselaerts (22 June 1874).
27 AAM, CF, La Hulpe: Diocesan delegate to the archbishop (6 Oct. 1878, 30 Jan. 1882, 23 Sept. 1885); ARE, *Chronique, XXXVI. Qualités et vertus*, 399; ASV, *Archivio S. Congregazione Vescovi et regolari. Positiones Monialium*, 3390: Dechamps to secretary (ca. 1866); 5729: Goossens to secretary (22 July 1902); ABA, File Dienstmaagden H. Harten: Vervlaet to archbishop (13 Jan. 1881, 25 Feb. 1886), Boon to archbishop (4 April 1889, 11 May 1892, 31 March 1895, 10 March 1898, 28 June 1904).
28 On these conclusions, see: Langlois, *Le catholicisme au féminin*, 642-648; Mangion, *Contested identities*, 194-195; Curtis, *Educating the Faithful*, 49-55, 63-65; Van Heijst, Derks and Monteiro, *Ex Caritate*, 182-187; Alkemade, *Vrouwen XIX*, 258-261.
29 Meiwes, *Arbeiterinnen*, 144-149; Clear, *Nuns*, 88-89; McNamara, *Sisters in Arms*, 616; Boudens, "De vrouwelijke religieuzen", 403-406.

Statistically speaking, in the congregations of Kestre and Telghuys, only one in six professed choir sisters advanced to a management position – local superior, bursary, novice mistress, member of the congregation's council – in the first decades after foundation. In de Meeûs', only one in ten professed choir sisters succeeded in doing this. In the context of the total population of choir and lay sisters, the percentages were considerably lower, at 10%, 7.5% and 6% respectively, since lay sisters were banned from leading positions.[30] This had to do with the profile of the congregations, with a great deal of the power and the membership concentrated in the motherhouse or in a small number of daughter houses. In that sense, the congregations from this study show clear parallels with the organisational structure of religious institutes active in health care. Hospital congregations often consisted of large communities working and living on the same place, with authority in the hands of only a few leading sisters: superiors, hospital directors and ward managers.[31]

This situation curbed the need for any great functional differentiation, such as occurred in larger and more geographically dispersed religious institutes. For large teaching congregations in particular, there were broader career opportunities for a relatively larger group of sisters, even though we lack the statistics to carry out a detailed comparison. Encouraged by the trend towards professionalisation, the teaching congregations could offer their members positions as local supervisors, school principals or class teachers, even though their autonomy within the strongly hierarchical structures of the congregational model was always relative. The story of Fanny Kestre's sister Sidonie as a fulfilled teacher with the *Dames du Sacré-Cœur* supports this conclusion.[32] Better opportunities for development were available also in large congregations without an exclusive educational focus, such as the *Filles de Charité*. O'Brien calculated for the English province of the congregation that 20% of the sisters were able to move into a management position.[33]

The 'middle management' in Telghuys's and Cornet's congregations consisted mainly of school sisters and religious who were responsible for the youth work.[34] However, despite their clear entrepreneurial skills, Cornet and Telghuys were not pioneers in providing professional training opportunities

30 In Telghuys' congregation, there were 6 sisters out of a total of 37 professed choir sisters (16.5%) that were appointed to a management position between the foundation in 1865 and 1885. In Kestre's the ratio was 4 out of 25 (20%) between the foundation in 1869 and the death of Kestre in 1882. Only 10 sisters out of a total of 105 professed sisters (9.5%) were involved in leading positions in de Meeûs' congregation.
31 Dhaene and Dhaene, *Sint-Jozef*, 68-70.
32 Curtis, *Educating the Faithful*, 49-55, 63-65; Van Heijst, Derks and Monteiro, *Ex Caritate*, 182-187; Langlois, *Le catholicisme au féminin*, 642-648; Wynants, *Les Sœurs de la Providence*, 31-33; Strobbe and Suenens, *Zusters Kindsheid Jesu*, 58.
33 O'Brien, *Leaving God for God*, 111.
34 ADHH, 69: Report (17 June 1888); ASCMLH, A.2: Cornet to the sisters in Bazel (21 Feb. 1877), Verlaine to Courrier (26 March 1886).

for their teaching sisters. As has already been pointed out, Telghuys' abhorrence of the secular world increasingly led her to deny her sisters training opportunities outside the convent walls. While in 1872 she had sent two of her sisters for teacher training to the Ursulines of Onze-Lieve-Vrouw-Waver, five years later she refused to give her sisters permission to follow a similar course given by the Antwerp Catholic School Committee.

From then on she relied on a summary in-house training of her teaching sisters, which she herself along with her confidant Sister Vincent provided, even though neither had any demonstrable teaching experience. Although Telghuys was a pioneer in the areas of social work and girls' vocational education, she did not anticipate or follow the professionalisation trends that were apparent in Belgian teaching congregations from the 1860s.[35] Cornet's congregation was not at the forefront of the professionalisation trend either. It was only during the tenure of one of her successors, Mother Marie-Aloysia Willems (1894-1906), that teacher training became customary for boarding-school teachers in Maleizen.[36] In contrast to Telghuys, however, Cornet was able to rely on her own teaching experience and, through her boarding school, she had access to a reservoir of trained teaching sisters. Moreover, she was less hostile to influences from the outside. As has been already mentioned, she was inspired by the pedagogical manuals of Van Biervliet and the *Dames du Sacré-Cœur*. In modernising the curriculum of her boarding school, she consulted the *Broeders van O.L.V. van Barmhartigheid* (Scheppers), who had started vocational education in their boarding school in Alsemberg. With guidance from Brother Philippe, a teacher and later director in Alsemberg, she edited lesson plans for the new courses together with her boarding-school teachers.[37]

The middle management of the congregations of Kestre and de Meeûs consisted not of 'ordinary' school sisters, but catechism teachers, coordinators of the association and retreat organisers. These were challenging functions in themselves, carrying a certain responsibility. Nonetheless, the actual implementation of the tasks depended on the differences between the management culture and the organisational structure, which have been already discussed. Kestre was open to the ideas and respectful of the work of her sisters who were active in the Brussels working-class districts and in catechetical instruction. She implemented new catechetical methods that had been developed and

---

35 Christens and Suenens, "L'enseignement comme vocation", 153-154; Hellinckx, Simon and Depaepe, "The Forgotten Contribution", 34-36.
36 ASCMLH, *Notice chronologique*, 70. Hubertine Willems (1855-1935) entered in 1873 as Sister Aloysia. She became superior between 1894 and 1906 and again between 1917 and 1929.
37 ASCMLH, A.2: Cornet to the sisters in Bazel (21 Feb. 1877). Brother Philippe Sohy (1837-1897), after being a teacher and the director in the *Sint-Victorinstituut* in Alsemberg, in 1890 became superior general of the *Broeders van Scheppers*. On his time in Alsemberg, see: Debremaeker, *Geschiedenis*, 22, 226.

tested on the ground by her sisters.[38] By contrast, the strict hierarchy and obsession with uniformity that characterised de Meeûs' institute left much less room for individual initiative. All the catechism sisters and those responsible for the workshops and retreats had to submit detailed reports to de Meeûs. Sisters who dared to introduce changes in the catechism lessons, order new fabrics for the workshops or offer retreatants beer from bottles rather than from glasses were harshly reproved.[39] An energetic woman like Eugénie de Robiano, who on her own succeeded in generating enthusiasm in Liège for the difficult apostolate among the '*forains*', had to ask de Meeûs' permission for every new step she took. The danger that she would lose herself in "des innovations de l'amour propre" was a constant concern of the superior general.[40]

Lay sisters: women among women

International research has pointed to cases of growing inequality between choir and lay sisters during the consolidation process of the institutes.[41] As the initial family unit of the congregations of Telghuys and de Meeûs came to be replaced by a more corporate model, the lay or work sisters were increasingly oppressed. They never had a voice in the election chapter for choosing the superior general. They depended for everything on the choir sister who supervised them and were pushed back into their own sphere within the convent. This last aspect, especially, intensified as the congregations grew. Anna de Meeûs repeatedly stressed that there should be no contacts between choir and lay sisters without the permission of the superior. She forbade lay sisters to use the spiritual reading of the choir sisters and increasingly restricted their contacts with the outside world.[42]

The same evolution took place in Antwerp. Under the impetus of Father Legrelle, the work sisters were increasingly pushed back into the laundry in Kontich. They had hardly any more rights than the orphans and girls who got shelter there, many of whom were in fact recruited as work sisters. Their habits were made of rougher wool than those of the choir sisters. From 1878 onwards, the work sisters prayed a modest rosary instead of the Divine Office. Apart from a catechism, no spiritual reading was made available to them.

38 ADSJ, 1.3./3: Kestre to Dechamps (2 May 1878); *Religieuses de Chœur, Mme Estelle de la Providence*.
39 ABG, Poortakker, Meetings of convent superiors (Nov. 1876, Oct. 1889); ARE, *Cahier des lettres 3*: de Meeûs to Baesen (4 March 1882).
40 ARE, *Cahier des lettres 1*: de Meeûs to de Robiano (March 1870, 1 Feb. 1872).
41 Monteiro, *Vroomheid*, 70, 121; Luirard, *La Société*, 42-43; Wynants, *Les Sœurs de la Providence*, 33.
42 ABG, Poortakker, Meeting of superiors (juni 1876); ARE, *Cahier des lettres 3*: de Meeûs to Baesen (3 Oct. 1874), de Meeûs to de Limburg-Stirum (7 May 1875).

At a high age Telghuys posed with some of the lay or work sisters of the congregation. Despite the important role of the work sisters in the semi-industrial laundry business, they were inferior to the higher-ranked choir sisters. The difference was clearly expressed in the habit: the work sisters had clothes of rougher wool, with a medallion instead of a cross and without the distinctive heart-shaped veil reserved for the choir sisters.
[Photograph – ca. 1905 – ADHH, 218]

Telghuys also segregated them from the choir sisters in the refectory and the recreation room, seriously altering the initial Augustinian '*cor unum*' of the congregation.[43] In keeping with their isolated position, lay sisters often disappeared from the historical narratives as well. The sources do not reveal much about the position of the lay sisters in Kestre's congregation, for instance. Some concise testimonies from her lay sisters indicated that she treated them with respect and dignity. Yet they played no part in the tasks of the apostolate. When her congregation's constitutions were approved and the plans for a third order, which in Kestre's view was responsible for the external apostolate of the congregation, were abandoned, the apostolate was not passed on to the lay sisters. Kestre chose to ease enclosure for the temporarily professed choir

43 ADHH, 47: Notes Legrelle (1878); 58: Telghuys to Blomme (1 March 1875); 69: Report (22 March 1880).

sisters so that they could deal with the tasks of the apostolate, rather than offer lay sisters greater opportunities for development.[44]

There is not much information about the lay sisters in Cornet's congregation either. In the boarding school in Maleizen a clear distinction was made between the qualified teaching sisters and the lay sisters responsible for manual tasks. As in other teaching congregations, the sisters who were responsible for the household duties in the smaller communities of Bazel, Steendorp and Sougné, were assigned some apostolate tasks, for example in the supervision of the youngest children or in youth work on Sundays.[45] Incidentally, Telghuys and de Meeûs also offered their lay sisters a limited role in the apostolate. Literate lay sisters could give summary catechetical instruction to the orphans or young children. Telghuys also gave her most experienced or adroit lay sisters a role in the practical training in the workshops.[46]

Despite these modest development opportunities, there were few possibilities for social mobility. The barriers that separated the choir and lay sisters were extremely rigid. In the first decades of the existence of the four congregations, there is no known example of a lay sister who made the switch to the elite group of choir sisters. At a certain point Telghuys considered it because of the special abilities of one of her lay novices and the shortage of teaching staff, but in the end the woman in question did not stay in the convent.[47] Here again, distinctions have to be made between the layered congregations of Telghuys and de Meeûs and congregations with a more homogeneous social profile, where possibilities for social mobility were more apparent.[48] On the other hand, there were clear similarities with the situation of lay brothers in priest congregations or monastic orders, who shared the focus on manual tasks and the submissive and second-rate position of their female counterparts. As Monteiro pointed out for the brothers in the Dutch Dominican order, sometimes they were even blamed for being less capable than women in their 'female' occupations in the kitchen, the garden or the laundry.[49]

This points to an ambiguous but rigid gender issue within the convent. As has already been remarked, the distinction between choir and lay sisters reflected the social relations of the wider society, a convent variation on the 'upstairs downstairs' set-up in wealthy households. By maintaining and even

44 ADSJ, *'Notre très chère et vénérée mère'*, testimonies of Sister Eve, Sister Justine.
45 ASCML, *Notice chronologique*, 55-57. For parallels to the *Dames du Sacré-Cœur*, see: Luirard, *La Société*, 41-42.
46 ADHH, 58: Telghuys to Fr. Groesbeek (1887); ARE, *Cahier des lettres 2*: de Meeûs to a novice (4 July 1872).
47 ADHH, 58: Telghuys to De Mol SJ (29 Sept. 1873).
48 For examples, see: Wynants, *Les Sœurs de la Providence*, 32-33; Suenens and De Staercke, *Eén van hart en één van ziel*, 333; Vanderstraeten and Preneel, *175 jaar Zusters der Christelijke Scholen*, 128-129.
49 Monteiro, *Gods predikers*, 94.

emphasising the distinction between work and choir sisters, the female superiors implicitly confirmed the inferiority of what were seen as typically female household tasks. In examining the situation in Irish and English convents, Clear, Mangion and O'Brien concluded that the ideal role of lay sisters in an active congregation was similar to that of women in the bourgeois household: pushed back into their own sphere, subordinate and servile.[50]

In the 1878 constitutions of Telghuys' congregation, analysed in the next chapter, it was emphasised that all lay sisters had the task "de regarder intérieurement toutes les autres comme leur étant supérieures, et de leur porter extérieurement l'honneur et le respect que demande l'état de chacune".[51] In 1875 Anna de Meeûs wrote to a candidate that "les converses ont leur rôle spécifique à faciliter et à honorer les sœurs adoratrices afin que celles-ci puissent se concentrer sur leur apostolat important".[52] Indeed, there are clear parallels with the discourse on the nineteenth-century Catholic ideal of women. The Jesuit François-Xavier Schouppe (1823-1904), for example, who was briefly involved with de Meeûs' association in the early 1870s, wrote in 1881 about the role of the Christian woman: "Cet amour du foyer domestique suppose l'amour de toutes les personnes qui composent la famille: (...) De cet amour naîtra la bonté et l'obligeance à leurs égard, le support de leurs défauts, le zèle pour leur bien spirituel, le soin de tout ce qui regarde leur entretien corporel, une sainte vigilance, une activité infatigable."[53] However, there was one significant and distinct difference. In comparison with the mission of the Catholic (lay) woman, lay sisters were denied the one role that could offer them male and social recognition: the role of the woman as the religious guardian of her relatives and society. In the congregations that role too was a prerogative of the choir sisters.

Still, apart from Kestre, none of the female founders in my research reported a shortage of work sisters. In the mid-1880s, Telghuys even had to reject lay sisters because all the jobs had been filled.[54] Various historians have pointed to the expectation of material and economic security as an important factor in the attractiveness of convent life for women of the poorer classes.[55] Telghuys mentioned this argument in her correspondence with lay sisters. Just

---

50   Clear, *Nuns*, 89-99; Mangion, *Contested Identities*, 208; O'Brien, "Lay sisters", 460.
51   ADHH, 46: *Constitutions 1878*, 35.
52   ARE, *Cahier des lettres 3*: de Meeûs to anonymous (3 Oct. 1875).
53   Schouppe, *La femme*, 20. For a nuanced analysis of the nineteenth-century Catholic image of the woman in relation to her stated domestic tasks, see: Van Osselaer, *The Pious Sex*, 81-83.
54   ADHH, 183: De Beukelaer to Taylor (8 June 1885).
55   Vanderstraeten and Preneel, *175 jaar Zusters der Christelijke Scholen*, 59; Curtis, *Educating the Faithful*, 63-65; Mangion, *Contested Identities*, 68; Clear, *Nuns*, 143; Langlois, *Le catholicisme au féminin*, 643-644; Hoy, *Good Hearts*, 18-20; Viaene, "De ontplooiing van een 'vrije' kerk", 70-71.

as with her orphans, she assured candidates of a 'bourgeois table' and good care in the case of illness or old age. In their recruitment campaigns, Anne de Meeûs and Cornet emphasised the healthy diet, good hygiene and access to fresh air in the convent garden. The fact that Kestre could not attract lay sisters was often contributed to the stories of the poor living conditions in her convents.[56]

She did try to persuade them by offering them respect and dignity. One lay sister of Kestre's congregation, Eve de Saint-Martin (1849-1937), recounted the emotion that overcame her fellow lay sisters when Kestre tried to convince them of their equal role: "Et une de nos sœurs se hasarde de dire que nous ne savons donner à l'institut que notre travail matériel peut-être peu de chose à ses jeux, en comparaison du zèle des religieuses de Chœur dans les œuvres. Très vivement et de tout son cœur Notre Mère nous répond: "Mais que dites-vous là. Mes filles, ne pensez jamais de cette façon-là. Mais qu'est-ce-que je ferais si je ne vous avais pas? Vous êtes aussi nécessaires à l'Institut que les religieuses de chœur et vous avez le même mérite devant Dieu (…)."[57] This issue of dignity would return very prominently when the congregations finally removed the division between choir and lay sisters during the interbellum or in the wake of the Second Vatican Council. Until then it was kept as a distinct feature of their identity.

---

56 ADHH, 58: Telghuys to Peeters (7 May 1872), Telghuys to Father Blomme (1 March 1875); ABG, Poortakker, Meetings of convent superiors (June 1876); ADSJ, 1.3./3: Kestre to Dechamps (27 April 1868, 8 Nov. 1879); 1.4: Dechamps to Kestre (21 Aug. 1869); 1.6: Father Edmond to Kestre (1 April 1873).
57 ADSJ, *Notices 'Notre très chère et vénérée mère', témoignage Sœur Eve*.

The Roman conditions for a new papal approval of de Meeûs' congregation in 1867 included a demand for a more secluded novitiate, isolated from both the world and the professed religious. Facilitated once again by her rich family, de Meeûs was able to meet the new requirement by constructing a convent and novitiate on a large domain of her mother's estate in Watermael, south of Brussels.
[Postcard – ca. 1900 – Private Collection]

"DOMINA ISTA VALDE FACUNDA EST"

FEMALE LEADERSHIP IN A MALE CHURCH

> Une citadelle assurée pour les Religieux, dans laquelle ils trouvent, au milieu des luttes spirituelles, un refuge certain en une complète sécurité.
>
> Dechamps, *Instructions*, 4.

In 1874, Archbishop Dechamps published his *Instructions aux communautés religieuses des femmes*. The work became an important guide for women's convents in his archdiocese, without it being an actual diocesan rule. The *Instructions* were a synthesis of the decisions of the diocesan synods of 1872 and 1873 and some diocesan circulars from the late 1860s and early 1870s.[1] Dechamps' guidelines emphasised convent life as "une citadelle assurée", based on four main principles: segregation and supervision, better education, freedom of conscience and better financial management. Dechamps followed in the footsteps of the Ghent and Bruges bishops who, as already indicated, had already carried out a streamlining of women's convent life in the mid-nineteenth century. The *Instructions* were inspired by the intensifying ultramontane siege mentality, and presented convent life as a shield against a hostile outside world.[2] At the same time Dechamps wanted to counter abuses and difficulties of religious patrimonial management, as well as regulate the contacts with male clerics and improve the limited educational level of women religious, all of which were criticised by liberal and anticlerical opponents.

---

1 *Statuta Dioecesis Mechliniensis*, 1872, 136-148; *Acta secundae synodi dioecesanae*, 1873, 20-25.
2 Art, *Kerkelijke structuur*, 50-52; Wynants, "Le gouvernement", 90-95.

Unlike the spontaneous popularity of 'the mixed life' in the 1850s and 1860s, the isolationist transformation in the 1870s was to large extend imposed from above.

However, the social importance of women religious, their recourse to strategic alliances and Dechamps' sensitivity to female aspirations left room for lasting autonomy. Moreover, loopholes remained available in Rome for influential female religious to escape diocesan clerical control. The factionalism between regulars and seculars on the one hand and the centralisation tendencies of the Roman authorities on the other hand continued to allow space for female agency, legitimised by a double-voiced discourse of submission and allegiance to clerical policy.

A double-voiced 'conventualisation'

Seclusion from the temptations of the outside world was an important aspect in Dechamps' publication. Family visits, contacts in the parlour and freedom to leave the convent were subject to more stringent rules. Where apostolate considerations had led Sterckx to be pragmatic regarding enclosure provisions, Dechamps pushed convent life and apostolate work within a more rigidly defined area. Visiting the sick was tolerated as a necessity, but was tightly regulated, "pour prémunir ces âmes généreuses contre les dangers auxquels les expose quelquefois leur sainte mission, et pour les aider à conserver au milieu du monde, ce véritable esprit religieux".[3] In the field of education, and boarding-school education in particular, both pupils and teachers were strongly encouraged to cut themselves off from the outside world. The concept of what Curtis called the 'classroom as new enclosure' was officially endorsed.[4] Finally, Dechamps, following Rome, insisted that the convent novitiates be isolated more strictly from the world and from the professed sisters as well.[5]

Dechamps' *Instructions* had a pronounced gender component. The separation between the sexes was confirmed in absolute terms. Except in case of emergency, women's convents were forbidden territory for men. Even priests were restricted to the parlour, the confessional and the convent church. Moreover, female religious were no longer allowed to shelter or teach older boys. Even more than before, elements of the monastic tradition became a regulatory principle. Besides the reminders of monastic-like enclosure, this parallel also became evident in Dechamps' reintroduction of the chapter of faults and

---

3 Dechamps, *Instructions*, 38.
4 Curtis, *Educating the Faithful*, 63-71; Segers, *150 jaar Zusters van het Heilig Hart van Maria*, 79-81.
5 Dechamps, *Instructions*, 22-24.

tighter provisions concerning the management of dowries and income. In his *Instructions* Dechamps also reinforced diocesan control by officially implementing an annual canonical visitation by a representative from the diocese. In the course of the 1870s and 1880s, more and more diocesan congregations were assigned a male rector or director.[6]

Dechamps' guidelines fitted within the contours of a general 'conventualisation' of congregational life. French, Belgian and Italian historiography, in particular, makes clear that in the second half of the nineteenth century women's convents ended up in a climate of increasing uniformity, ecclesiastical control and seclusion.[7] As was the case in many other aspects of the clerical policy of the nineteenth century, the tightening of diocesan control was not intended for women's convents only. Brother congregations also were subject to new measures of patronising and control.[8] As Monteiro pointed out clearly for the Dutch Dominicans and Laureys for the Belgian Franciscans, this evolution even had its parallel in male orders.[9] Of course, within these male orders, it was not a measure imposed by diocesan authorities, whereas brothers and female religious did feel the pressure of the clerical hierarchy. The age-old pendulum between the emergence of spontaneous female religious initiative on one side and ecclesiastical containment and paternalism on the other moved in the direction of the latter. The concept of 'conventualisation' had indeed surfaced earlier in the historiography of the Counter Reformation and in the aforementioned actions of the Church against seventeenth-century innovative and non-enclosed female religious life.[10]

Given the stricter ecclesiastical instructions, it was particularly inconvenient for Cornet that her congregation came to experience the serious internal difficulties of the first half of the 1870s that led to the proposal for a new merger with Alsemberg and Waterloo. Remarkably, Cornet also used the new clerical policy to secure her independence. By emphasising the absence of a monastic spirit, obedience and seclusion in Alsemberg, she showed herself an ardent supporter of the stricter diocesan policy. Portraying herself in her letters to the diocesan authorities as "une humble servante" she simultaneously discredited the sisters in Alsemberg: "elles n'ont pas ombre d'esprit religieux et jamais ne sauront obéir parce qu'ordinairement elles contestent les droits

---

6   Idem, 26-28; Vanderstraeten and Preneel, *175 jaar Zusters der Christelijke Scholen*, 76, 134-135; Timmermans, *Het Convent van Bethlehem*, 173; Segers, *150 jaar Zusters van het Heilig Hart van Maria*, 64.
7   Wynants, *Les Sœurs de la Providence*, 38-39; Timmermans, *Het Convent van Bethlehem*, 145; Vanderstraeten and Preneel, *175 jaar Zusters der Christelijke Scholen*, 63; Langlois, *Le catholicisme au féminin*, 85; Rocca, *Donne religiose*, 189.
8   Art, "Documents", 467.
9   Monteiro, *Gods predikers*, 140-144; Laureys, *De Mindere Broeders*, 103-105, 132.
10 See part I and Lux-Sterrit and Mangion, "Introduction", 3-4; Mullet, *The Catholic Reformation*, 106-107.

The conventualisation politics of the clerical authorities stressed the importance of seclusion and isolation from secular society. In the late 1870s Cornet had a large wall built around her convent and school in Maleizen, making it into a 'citadelle assurée' from the world.
[Postcard – ca. 1900 – Collection Sœurs du S. Cœur de Marie, La Hulpe]

de la supériorité". At the same time she sharply castigated her old opponent in La Hulpe, Father Chevalier: "plusieurs personnes scandalisées et indignées nous en ont parlé tout récemment: notez aussi qu'elles [the sisters of Alsemberg] viennent très souvent à la Hulpe dans plusieurs maisons qu'elles savent nous être hostiles, en outre elles sont très liées avec Mr. Le Curé. Sr. Marie Louise y a logé 8 jours pour arranger la procession."[11] By conforming herself enthusiastically to the dominant voice of female seclusion and obedience, she implicitly secured her freedom from both Alsemberg and Chevalier. This double voiced discourse enabled her to turn a policy of conventualisation into one of independence.

To comply to the new diocesan instructions, Cornet gave orders for the building of large wall around her convent complex in Maleizen. Dechamps also encouraged her to organise the novitiate of her congregation in a more stricter manner. On several occasions in the past Cornet had sent novices to help out in the daughter houses in East Flanders. In line with Dechamps' *Instructions*, she cut back on that practice in the mid-1870s. However, she did not fully abandon her policy and continued to use novices in the daughter houses at various times, including at the height of the School War. Moreover, she succeeded once again in bolstering her own ambitions from the perspective of diocesan policy. By referring to ecclesiastical regulations, she could now defend herself more effectively against the demands of her tyrannical benefactor in Bazel. After 1874, she was more firm in refusing the urgent requests of Marie Vilain XIIII to send extra sisters or to shorten the sisters' annual holidays.[12]

11   ASCMLH, A.2: Cornet to Legrelle (15 June [1873]).
12   ASCMLH, *Notice chronologique*, 55-57.

The figure of Father Aloysius Legrelle remained crucial for Cornet's position with regard to the church authorities. Just as during the conflict with Father Chevalier in the 1860s, the Jesuit was also an important buffer between the superior and the diocesan authorities in the following decade. After his transfer in 1870 from the Jesuit residence in Leuven to Liège, contact appeared to have been more difficult for some time. Legrelle's proposal to forward Cornet to another adviser, however, was countered by her emotional response: "maintenant nous aurons des Maîtres seulement mais plus de Père; (...) je suis prête à toutes humiliations et les réparations pourvu que vous continuiez à nous aider de vos conseils".[13] Her supplication had an effect. After his departure from Leuven, Legrelle also successfully lobbied for the independence of the congregation in Maleizen and supported Cornet's accusations against the sisters in Alsemberg.[14]

Like Cornet, Legrelle's discourse focused very strongly on the need for obedience and submission. These were the Ignatian principles par excellence and they formed the anchor points of his vision on female convent life. At the same time, he also supported a strong position for women convent superiors, whom he defended both against dissent from below and against external interference.[15] However, it would be incorrect to see him as a clerical 'feminist'. His zeal for protecting the power of the superior went hand in hand with a strong emphasis on the – rather un-Ignatian – trend to enclosure and isolation. From that perspective, he dared to push female superiors in a more rigid direction than they initially wanted to take themselves. For example, in the conflict with the rebellious novice mistress Sister Des Anges, Legrelle categorically opposed her return, while Cornet sincerely considered accepting the repentant religious back into her community. Eventually, Sister Des Anges would choose for a new future in the beguinage of Turnhout.[16]

Legrelle showed the same equivocation in his dealings with Telghuys. As already noted, in 1877, two years after he was transferred as a Jesuit rector from Liège to Antwerp, Legrelle became Telghuys' counsellor. He accepted the task at Telghuys' express request, succeeding his aging colleague Schoofs (1803-1878) and Bogaerts, who died in 1877. In 1877-1878 he reworked the constitutions of the *Dienstmaagden van de Heilige Harten* in order to adapt them to Dechamps' *Instructions*. Legrelle opted for a strict interpretation of the archbishop's guidelines. Home visits to the poor, one of Telghuys' favourite apostolates, were ended. Despite the fact that no mishaps were reported in the case of Telghuys' congregation, Legrelle, in a commentary on the new 1878 rule,

---

13   ASCMLH, A.2: Cornet to Legrelle (14 July 1873).
14   ABSE, 4.2.6. Legrelle, 14487: De Molder to Legrelle (27 June 1873).
15   ABSE, 4.2.6. Legrelle, 14487: Notes of Legrelle; ASCMLH: Legrelle to Cornet (28 Nov. 1874), cited in *Notice Chronologique*, 41-42.
16   ASCMLH, *Notice Chronologique*, 41: Legrelle to Cornet (28 Nov. 1874).

referred to the 'strong dangers' of the outside world to which such an apostolate would expose the sisters.[17] The rule of 1878 also put an end to male clerics being allowed within the convent walls. The sisters had looked after Bogaerts during his final illness in an apartment within the convent. The practice of directors or chaplains living next to the convent or even in a secluded part of the convent itself was not unusual in Belgium. In the late 1860s, Nuncio Cattani had reported it to Rome as being one of the problems of Belgian convent life.[18] Legrelle clearly indicated that this situation could no longer continue. Contacts with lay people also had to be kept to a minimum and family visits were more strictly regulated. As already indicated, the new constitutions also introduced a stricter division between choir and lay sisters. The interventions by Legrelle thus resulted in a substantial adjustment to the tolerant Augustinian-Salesian inspiration and apostolate of the congregation.[19]

At the same time, Legrelle's constitutions again emphasised total obedience and submission to the superior general more strongly, thereby reinforcing Telghuys' internal position. With Legrelle's support, the emphasis on seclusion and enclosure also proved, paradoxically enough, to enhance her autonomy and room for manoeuvre outside the convent walls. As has already been discussed, Telghuys' isolationism enabled her to successfully oppose the interference of Father De Molder and her lay teachers. At Legrelle's instigation, she used the provisions of her new constitutions and the stricter diocesan policy on contacts with lay people to defend her education policy, which essentially was a quest for autonomy. She also developed a similar strategy towards her demanding and indiscreet benefactors in Wuustwezel and Kontich. Walls were built and hedges planted to ensure "la sainte sollicitude" of the sisters and at the same time protect them from the interference of meddlesome ladies.[20] A double-voiced equivocation lay hidden in her relationship with Father Legrelle as well. She treated him with a dedication and admiration that sometimes embarrassed him: "Merci, ma chère Mère, pour votre sollicitude maternelle, et pour les remèdes que vous m'avez envoyer! (....), mais je vous prie instamment de ne plus jamais m'envoyer un remède, ou un présent quelconque."[21] At the same time she used his influence and erudition to strengthen her own position, causing parish priest De Molder in a letter to Dechamps to describe Legrelle as "le très humble serviteur de la Mère Jeanne, toujours prêt à faire les moindres volontés de la Rév. Mère".[22]

---

17   ADHH, 47: Notes by Legrelle.
18   Art, "Documents", 417-418.
19   ADHH, 47: Explanatory note by Legrelle; 69: Report (10 Dec. 1877).
20   ADHH, 69: Reports (22 April 1873, 20 April 1875).
21   ADHH, 58: Legrelle to Telghuys (25 Oct. 1881).
22   ABA, File of the Dienstmaagden H. Harten: De Molder to Dechamps (19 March 1880).

Dechamps was probably not De Molder's best ally. Despite his strict policy provisions, he remained very sensitive to the needs of his female subjects, Fanny Kestre in particular. For five years he tried to persuade her to allow a diocesan visitator into her community, but she refused access to all priests other than Dechamps. He reacted with his usual somewhat ironic indignation: "vous m'avez dites que vous m'avez toujours obéi, même contre vos vues, je ne me rappelle pas de cela".[23] Very patiently, Dechamps proposed to her one candidate visitator after another, but she wouldn't bend. Like Telghuys, she used the discourse of seclusion of the *Instructions* to preserve her own autonomy: "votre Grandeur a stipulé lui-même que les prêtres ne peuvent pas se faire entrer dans les couvents."[24] The issue was only finally settled after the death of both protagonists in 1882 and 1883.

The focus on adherence to the rules and the embrace of the enclosure process was therefore more than a sign of weakness or a mere substitute for the absence of spiritual and theological depth that Aubert emphasised. The double-voiced use of the new diocesan regulations underscored the authority of Telghuys, Cornet and Kestre. Other historians too have argued that the adherence to rules by female superiors was a paradoxical but successful strategy for creating female autonomy.[25] In addition, responding to the internal power relations within the Church – think of the Jesuit Legrelle and his handling of Father Chevalier in La Hulpe and Father De Molder in Antwerp – or to Dechamps' sensitivity to female desires proved to be equally worthwhile. Unlike, for example, his Ghent and Liège colleagues, Dechamps was not dogmatic in principle and there was usually some negotiating room for double-voiced women. Of all the women in this research, no one would show more mastery in successfully developing all of these strategies than Anna de Meeûs.

Gender, power and freedom of conscience: the confessor issue

Dechamps' *Instructions* focused intensely on regulating confessional practices in convents. Caring for the pious, but 'fragile' female spirit had for long been both a worry and a concern for male Catholic authorities and officials. In the preceding years, the subject had been extensively discussed in some epis-

---

23 ADSJ, 1.4: Dechamps to Kestre (18 March 1878).
24 ADSJ, 1.3./3: Kestre to Dechamps (13 Sept. 1881).
25 Thompson, "Women", 145-146; Liedel, "Indomitable nuns", 471; Monteiro, *Vroomheid in veelvoud*, 57; Ewens, "Women in the convent", 20; Mangion, *Contested Identities*, 227-228.

copal circulars and in diocesan synods.[26] Two common threads ran through the archbishop's motives. First, by rigorously regulating the appointment and freedom of action of ordinary and extraordinary confessors, he confirmed both the tendency towards greater diocesan control and the emphasis on the increasing enclosure of women's convents. Dechamps' strong focus on the relationship between confessors and women religious also surfaced in the diocesan policy of Bracq in Ghent and of de Montpellier in Liège.[27] Second, more than his colleagues, Dechamps also was explicitly concerned about the freedom of conscience of women religious and the autonomy of women superiors. He stressed that female religious had the right – except in the case of serious objections by the superior – to request a confessor other than the usual or special confessor. At the same time, he forbade confessors from interfering or commenting in any way on the administration of the superior general.[28] The subject was also raised during Rome's consultation with the Belgian clergy on the eve of the First Vatican Council. Kockerols, Nuncio Cattani and other prominent clerics pointed to the problem of confessors who exercised too much power and influence in women's convents.[29] The timing of these statements and Dechamps' first pastoral letters on the subject – which appeared at the end of 1868 – suggest that his worries about the issue might have been the result of a large-scale conflict in the archdiocese, with Anna de Meeûs and the Jesuits playing a leading role.

Part II has already pointed out that Anna de Meeûs had explicitly expressed her wish in the 1850s to have the Jesuits as regular confessors and spiritual leaders in her convent. The provision was included in the first constitutions of 1857, but conflicted with the regulations of the Jesuits as well as Rome's policy. In granting the *decretum laudis* in 1863, Consultor Chaillot of the Congregation of Bishops and Regulars expressed reservations about the role of the Jesuits in de Meeûs' congregation, but did not cancel the provisions. In 1867 de Meeûs set in motion the second phase of the procedure for getting a Roman recognition: the preliminary approval of the constitutions. In the spring of 1867, she again left for Rome with her family and some of her sisters to lobby for the case. The now 72-year-old Boone had become too weak to travel with them. However, de Meeûs had other allies to rely on in Rome. Thanks to her mother and her family's generosity to the Pontifical Mission

---

26 See especially Dechamps' pastoral letters about the practice of confession in convents, addressed to confessors (27 Dec. 1868) and to women superiors (27 Dec. 1868, 4 Nov. 1870), published in: *Statuta Dioecesis Mechliniensis*, 1872, 136-148; *Acta Secundae Synodi Dioecesanae*, 1873, 20-25.
27 Art, *Kerkelijke structuur*, 50-52; Daris, *Le diocèse*, 158-159.
28 Dechamps, *Instructions*, 9-12.
29 Art, "Documents", 417-418, 500.

Works and the Saint Peter's Pence, many doors in the Vatican opened once again.[30]

Anna de Meeûs could also count on the continuing benevolence of Chaillot, with whom she had enjoyed a good relationship since 1863. The French curial prelate Ludovic Chaillot was an equally intriguing and mysterious figure. Few details are known about his life and background and yet he was a prominent figure in the Roman curia in the 1850s and 1860s.[31] Born in the early nineteenth century in a bookseller's family in Avignon, he was ordained in Paris in 1830. In 1846 he resurfaced in Rome, where he soon gained a reputation for his excellent knowledge of canon law and church history. He profiled himself as an erudite writer for the French ultramontane camp, fighting against Gallican tendencies and government politics in his homeland. As chief editor of the ultramontane periodicals, *La Correspondance de Rome* (1848-1852) and the *Analecta Juris Pontificii* (1855-ca 1891), he was described as "plus romaine que le Saint-Siège".[32] His radical ideas were welcomed by a section of the French lower clergy, but annoyed the moderate members of the episcopate. Even Pius IX, who forbade his *Correspondance* in 1852, saw him as a vigilante or "*birbante*" and a threat to Rome's relations with the French Church.[33] Nevertheless, because of his intellectual reputation and good relations with the already-mentioned Cardinal Bizzarri, secretary of the Congregation for Bishops and Religious, he succeeded in obtaining an official appointment as consultor for the French speaking religious institutes. He also became a respected confessor and spiritual director of a number of communities of French sisters in Rome.

Thanks to the support of Chaillot and of her Roman network, de Meeûs was granted a Roman *fiat* for a preliminary recognition of the constitutions of her institute only six weeks after her arrival in Rome. The curia did impose some conditions this time. First, the novitiate had to be organised more formally and secluded from the professed religious and the apostolate activities. De Meeûs amply satisfied that requirement. Between 1868 and 1870 she had a novitiate building erected in leafy surroundings on an extensive domain belonging to her mother in Watermael, then a village on the outskirts of Brussels. An orphanage, a convent and a chapel were later added.[34] Second, normative adjustments were required. The constitutions generally had to evince

---

30 ARSI: Beckx to Father De Maeyer (23 Jan. 1872).
31 The most important, though concise, biographical notes on Chaillot can be found in: Maurain, *Le Saint-Siège*, 227-233. Other details in: Palanque, *Catholiques libéraux*, 81-82; Gough, *Paris and Rome*, 138-139; d'Amat, "Chaillot", 177 and in the preface to Rocfer, *Souvenirs*, 1-7.
32 1863 citation from the French Minister of Cults, Rouland, cited in Maurain, *Le Saint-Siège*, 231.
33 Maurain, *Le Saint-Siège*, 228.
34 ARE, *Chronique, XXVI. Rotterdam – Watermael*, 263; AAM, CF, Salazar: Note by de Meeûs (July 1875).

a greater humility: phrases such as "travailler au salut et à la perfection du prochain", had to be replaced by "d'aider selon le faible mesure de leurs moyens au salut et à la perfection du prochain".[35] Rome's recognition came at a price, but de Meeûs was intelligent enough to accept it. In her own reports to her sisters in Brussels she was delighted to present herself as the most humble and grateful of the pope's subjects and to accept the imposed changes to the rule and the structure of the institute with great compliance.[36] Undoubtedly this was in part a strategic submission. Papal recognition compelled modesty in women's discourse and behaviour. But de Meeûs' discourse also revealed a genuine desire to conform to the wishes of her 'sublime chief' in Rome, that exceeded mere strategical purposes.

Kestre had much more difficulty in dealing with the interference of clerical authorities. In 1874, profiting from his post-Vatican I prestige, Dechamps had started lobbying for papal recognition of the *Dames de Sainte-Julienne*. When the *decretum laudis* was received in 1875, Dechamps expected Kestre to be happy with this Roman approval of her small and young institute. Kestre, on the contrary, was furious. She could not understand why the Holy See did not mention her as a founder in the official documents and obliged her to drop the prestigious title of '*Apostolines*'. She was also forced to definitively abandon her ambitious plans for a complicated novitiate trajectory and an internal and external third order. Only the soothing words of Dechamps, pointing out that founders were rarely mentioned by name in a *decretum laudis*, stopped her from rushing to Rome to hold the pope himself to account.[37] She fulminated that "on a ignoré qu'il y eut une pensée Mère, une origine, pour laquelle j'ai tout sacrifié depuis 30 ans et plus".[38]

In some congregations, as was observed by Wynants for example in the case of the *Soeurs de la Providence* of Champion or Monteiro in the case of the Dutch Franciscan Sisters of Oirschot, Rome's interference or approval had an impact on the original profile.[39] In the case of the *Dames de Sainte-Julienne* or the *Institut de l'Adoration Perpétuelle* the congregations' spiritual character or apostolates were not affected. However, the impact on structure was indeed considerable. Kestre's plans lost much of their organisational originality, and in the congregation of Anna de Meeûs an end was put to the strong bond with the Society of Jesus. The Roman decree of 1867 stipulated that all passages in the constitutions referring to the fixed role of the Jesuits as confessors or spiritual directors be deleted. More than the other decisions of 1867, this pro-

35 AAM, CF: Salazar: Boone to Lauwers (6 Feb. 1867).
36 ARE, *Notices historiques*, V. *Decret d'approbation*.
37 ASV, *Archivio S. Congregazione Vescovi et regolari, Positiones monialium*, 28271: *Decretum Laudis* (29 March 1875); ADSJ, 1.3./3: Kestre to Dechamps (12 June 1876); 1.4: Dechamps to Kestre [1875].
38 ADSJ, 1.3./3: Kestre to Dechamps (12 June 1876).
39 Wynants, *Les Sœurs de la Providence*, 38-39; Monteiro, *Vroomheid*, 56.

vision bore Chaillot's stamp. In the course of the 1860s, the Congregation of Bishops and Religious had begun to insist more strongly than before that convent constitutions be brought into line with church regulations.[40] Chaillot had already demonstrated in the *Analecta Juris Pontificii* of the early 1860s that the appointment of regulars as ordinary confessors of sister congregations was contrary to church law and tradition.[41] Presumably under his influence, that policy was taken up by his curial congregation and imposed on various female institutes which, like de Meeûs', had a close spiritual connection with the Jesuits.[42]

Using the Roman regulations as a weapon, de Meeûs wanted to get rid of the Jesuits. Her complaints were many. She was convinced that Boone and his confreres did no longer contribute enough to the recruitment and the promotion of her institute. She also accused the Jesuits of a lack of respect for the Perpetual Adoration activities of the sisters. In general, the strong partnership between Boone and de Meeûs seemed to have reached its limits. The admiration of the energetic but insecure adolescent for the experienced spiritual father had given way to the growing self-confidence of a convent superior, irritated by the criticism, the routine approaches and lack of flexibility of an elderly man. From the mid-1860s onwards, Anna de Meeûs increasingly criticised the inability of the aging Boone to spiritually inspire her sisters and the ladies of the association. De Meeûs' grievances were also confirmed by Julie Desmanet de Biesme, the former religious of Salazar who remained involved in the association's apostolate: "Comment peut-on espérer soutenir pendant plus de 30 ans l'attention d'un même public en prêchant pour toutes les œuvres plusieurs fois par mois? (...) Les réunions des catéchismes étaient devenues insupportables de ce même fait".[43]

In comparison with Boone, Chaillot was full of energy. Charmed by his erudition and charisma, de Meeûs invited him to Brussels in late 1867 to give some lectures to her sisters and association members. Chaillot would make frequent visits to the de Meeûs' headquarters during the next two years, staying in apartments next to the convent. In Salazar he immediately proved himself to be an inspiring spiritual companion. His passionate southern temperament, coupled with a strong personality, was a welcome counterweight to de Meeûs' authoritarian character. However, de Meeûs too was charmed by Chaillot, and gave him access to the sisters' recreation rooms and refectory. Meanwhile, rumours about Chaillot's familiar relations with the sisters and novices

---

40 On this, see: Aubert, *L'Église dans le monde moderne*, 127.
41 [Chaillot], "Confesseurs ", 1290-1297.
42 Rocca, "Les Jésuites", 156-157.
43 ABME, 1055: Joseph Fabri, Notes. See also: ARE, *Annales intimes de l'institut*, II.

alarmed outside supporters of de Meeûs. Julie Demanet de Biesme, among others, complained to Boone about the 'indiscretions' in Salazar.[44]

In the meantime, de Meeûs tried to undermine Boone's position with Chaillot's support. She boldly told Boone he was ready to retire to the Jesuit nursing home in Drongen. Boone felt betrayed, but took the honourable way out by resigning from his position as an ordinary confessor and spiritual counsellor of de Meeûs' institute and congregation in 1868.[45] The Jesuits denounced the disrespectful way in which de Meeûs had got rid of Boone, but canonically speaking they had little ground to protest. Dechamps was concerned about Boone's fate as well, writing to him empathetically that "Il y a longtemps que je me suis dit, à votre occasion, que le Bon Dieu voulait couronner les années de votre vie apostolique par une sorte de passion où rien ne manque: 'eo relicto, discipuli omnes fugerunt'".[46] At the same time, he gave Chaillot permission to hear confessions in Salazar. Moreover, in 1868 and 1869 he published his aforementioned pastoral letters in which he stressed diocesan autonomy in the appointment of confessors, thereby implicitly nipping any possible Jesuit protest in the bud. There were also other motives. Dechamps was convinced that Chaillot was using his time in Brussels to edit a new publication against Gallicanism, and he ignored the first signs indicating that Chaillot might have changed sides.[47] The mysterious Frenchman had indeed thrown off his ultramontane cloak. In opposition to the plans for the declaration of papal infallibility, which caused great turbulence in the Catholic world, he now threw himself with equal fervour into the Gallican battle against Rome. With financial and material support from de Meeûs, who was not aware of the changed content of his writings, Chaillot worked in Brussels on a number of anti-ultramontane and anti-Jesuit publications.[48] Despite warnings from the bishop of Liège, de Montpellier, and Nuncio Cattani, it took the indecisive Dechamps until November 1871 to finally discharge the French dissident.[49] Anna de Meeûs acted more incisively. Once it became clear to her that Chaillot had indeed left the ultramontane camp and that his presence in Salazar was damaging her reputation, she broke off all contact at the be-

---

44 ABSE, 4.2.6. Boone, 1234: de Biesme to Boone (26 Sept. 1868).
45 De Biesme to Dechamps (22 Nov. 1868), cited in: Becque, *Le Cardinal Dechamps*, II, 114; ABME, 1055: Joseph Fabri, Notes; ABSE, 4.2.6. Boone, 1226: *Mémoire Broeckaert*; ARE, *Annales intimes de l'institut*: Boone to de Meeûs (27 Sept. 1868).
46 "And all the disciples forsook him and fled", referring to the passage in Matthew, 26:56. ABSE, 4.2.6. Boone, 1226: *Mémoire Broeckaert*: Dechamps to Boone (16 May 1869).
47 Art, "Documents", 376; Becque, *Le Cardinal Dechamps*, II, 115-116; ASV, NB, *Religiose dell'Adorazione: Courte relation (...) sur Salazar*.
48 These included *Gallia orthodoxa d'après l'autographe de Bossuet* (1869) and articles in his newly founded, Gallican-inspired journal, *L'Avenir Catholique* (1869-1870). See: Maurain, *Le Saint-Siège*, 232 and Gough, *Paris and Rome*, 138-139.
49 Art, "Documents", 376; Becque, *Le Cardinal Dechamps*, II, 122.

ginning of 1870.⁵⁰ Chaillot returned to Paris and eventually to Rome where he continued his scholarly research in the libraries. He died there poor and isolated in 1891.⁵¹

Chaillot had dragged de Meeûs into the Church's factionalism in the run-up to the First Vatican Council. But de Meeûs in turn used Chaillot and the Roman regulations for her own ambitions. Even after his departure nobody could get this genie back in the bottle. Moreover, de Meeûs now had a guarantee of Dechamps's support. Initially, the archbishop avoided an open confrontation with the Jesuits and urged de Meeûs to seek a compromise. However, the conflict escalated after the death of Boone in 1871. Boone had held the post of general director since the foundation of the association in 1848. After his resignation and his death, this role was taken over by his colleague Schouppe, but without Dechamps' official approval. Schouppe was a subtle and moderate man, with a deep appreciation for the social and religious commitment of Catholic women.⁵² In that regard he could have been a capable successor for Boone as head of the association. However, he didn't fit into the plans of de Meeûs and Dechamps.

The archbishop believed that Schouppe had contravened his episcopal privilege to appoint the director of the Brussels headquarters of the association, who was also the general director of the entire association. Irritated by this manoeuvre, Dechamps appointed his Vicar-General De Molder as the new director. The Jesuits could still play a role in the association, but only under the supervision of the diocesan delegate.⁵³ As members of an exempt institution, the Jesuits however, considered it beneath their dignity to subordinate themselves in the association to a diocesan priest.⁵⁴ What followed was an unprecedented stream of public accusations and insinuations, in which the Belgian episcopate, the Belgian and the Roman headquarters of the Jesuits and ultimately Rome itself became involved. The focus was on the future of the association and the final approval of the constitutions of de Meeûs' congregation. The Belgian Jesuits tried to defend their positions in the associa-

---

50 ARE, *Chronique, XXXV. Amour de l'Eglise*, 377-378; ARE, *Cahier des lettres 1*: de Meeûs to de Limburg Stirum (5 Feb. 1870).
51 Maurain, *Le Saint-Siège*, 233; Rocfer, *Souvenirs d'un prélat*, 1-2.
52 In his already cited work on the Christian woman, Schouppe wrote that "la femme est établie par Dieu et par son Christ pour être l'aide de l'homme dans le sens le plus large; son action n'est pas bornée à la famille, elle s'étend à l'Etat et à l'Eglise: elle doit contribuer puissamment à propager la vie chrétienne dans la société toute entière, dans le siècle aussi bien que dans le sanctuaire du cloître". Schouppe, *La femme chrétienne*, 9.
53 ARE, *Notes intimes de l'institut, I* and *II*; ASV, NB, *Religiose dell'Adorazione: Courte relation (...) sur Salazar*; AAM, CF, Salazar: Dechamps to Schouppe (8 Sept. 1871), Goethals to Dechamps (10 Sept. 1871), Schouppe to Dechamps (5 Oct. 1871).
54 ARE, *Notes intimes de l'institut*; ARSI, *Provincia Belgica - Registres (1866-1877)*: Beckx to Goethals (7 April 1871).

tion, with support of Bishop de Montpellier of Liège.⁵⁵ At the end of 1871 he sent the already cited report to Rome in which he made a devastating attack on the institute and unambiguously recommended a change in its leadership. With his report he tried to oppose the definitive recognition of the *Institut de l'Adoration Perpétuelle* – five years after the provisional Roman fiat of 1867. By pointing out that de Meeûs repeatedly appealed to Dechamps to make her grievances known, de Montpellier was also implicitly criticising the archbishop's hesitant approach.⁵⁶

On several occasions, the Jesuit generalate in Rome advised caution. General Beckx wanted to avoid a rupture with Archbishop Dechamps and was also aware of de Meeûs' strong Roman connections. Even after the slip-up with Chaillot, de Meeûs had managed to keep her reputation in Rome intact by constantly seeking new allies. In 1871 she secured the support of Vitteleschi, the new secretary of the Congregation of Bishops and Religious.⁵⁷ Beckx's admonitions to the Belgian Jesuits also expressed his resignation to imminent defeat and his reluctant recognition of de Meeûs as a master tactician: "Domina ista valde facunda est, multa loquitur et cunctas res in suum favorem explicare novit."⁵⁸ In the end de Meeûs got her way on both fronts. Despite fierce opposition from Bishop de Montpellier, the Congregation of Bishops and Regulars definitively recognised de Meeûs' congregation in June 1872. The decree of recognition explicitly emphasised the freedom of conscience of female religious and the jurisdiction of local bishops. The provision in the constitutions about permanent Jesuit confessors was definitively eliminated, causing Anna de Meeûs to telegraph triumphantly from Rome to her sisters in Brussels, "te deum – succès complét". The Congregation for Bishops and Religious did its best to soften the blow for the Jesuits by indicating in the decree that local bishops were free to appoint individual Jesuits as extraordinary confessors or as spiritual directors in the association. The Society's defeat was clear nonetheless. The Jesuits felt they had been treated unfairly, but did not seek any further confrontation. On Beckx's advice, they withdrew from the institute

---

55 ASV, NB, *Religiose dell'Adorazione*: Cattani to Quaglia (13 Jan. 1871). Théodore de Montpellier was bishop of Liège between 1852 and 1879. Like Bishop Malou, who was appointed in Bruges in 1848, his candidacy was supported by the Jesuits. His appointment was part of the conservative appointment policy of Pius IX which also led to the appointment of the ultramontane bishops in Namur (the aforementioned Gravez) and Tournai, see: Viaene, *Belgium and the Holy See*, 555-562.
56 AEL, Fonds de Montpellier, 16. *Dossier Institut de l'Adoration Perpétuelle*: Mémoire de Montpellier (15 Dec. 1871).
57 ARSI, *Provincia Belgica – Registres* (1866-1877): Beckx to Goethals (9 and 14 Dec. 1871, 10 Jan. 1872). The Italian curial prelate Salvatore Nobili Vitelleschi (1818-1875) was appointed secretary only in 1871 but had a long Vatican career behind him. See: Boutry, *Souverain*, 603.
58 "That woman is very fluent, she talks a lot and knows how to explain all things in her favour": ARSI, *Provincia Belgica – Registres* (1866-1877): Beckx to Goethals (23 Jan. 1872).

and most of the branches of the association. Only in places where they had good relationships with the local staff members of the association did members of the Society continue to act as spiritual directors.[59] To be embarrassed in Rome by a woman was not easy for the Jesuits to bear. Despite their official acceptance of Rome's decision, a mocking poem in the Jesuit archives, which was distributed in the Society, left no doubt about the wounded feelings of the Society.

Madame Anna de M… Portrait d'après nature

Etre le directrice	Quelquefois on me blâme
Du clergé séculier	Et je n'en puis rougir,
Un peu réformatrice	Car je sais en mon âme
Du clergé régulier	Que Dieu me fait agir.
En mainte circonstance,	Il me donne sagesse,
Guider l'Episcopat	Lumière et jugement
Voilà bien sans jactance	Je l'en bénis sans cesse
Mon rôle d'ici-bas	J'en parle ouvertement.

ABSE, 4.2.6. Boone, 12467: Letters and notes of de Meeûs.

Roman feminism?

Anna de Meeûs' Roman success was not without precedent. The role of Rome as an arbitrator between religious women and male clerics, regular or secular, has been extensively illustrated in the international literature. In the 1840s, the Italian congregation founder Teresa Vezeri had sent away some of her Jesuit advisers with the support of the Roman Curia. The English Benedictines of Colwich resisted the humiliations of their ecclesiastical superior in the 1830s with support from Rome. Irish and French congregations found an ally in Rome against the omnipotence of the mid-nineteenth-century episcopate. American congregations successfully profited from the late-nineteenth-century power struggle between the Vatican and the American hierarchy to increase their own autonomy.[60]

In Churches with fledgling or limited structures, the emphasis on adherence to the rules was an attractive leverage for both religious women and

59 ARSI, *Provincia Belgica – Registres* (1866-1877): Beckx to Goethals (25 May 1872 and 6 June 1872); ARE, *Annales intimes de l'institut*; Becque, *Le Cardinal Dechamps*, II, 130.
60 Rocca, "Les Jésuites", 136-137; Champ, *William Bernard Ullathorne*, 213-214; Gilbert, *This Restless Prelate*, 111-134. There are other examples in: Mangion, "Women, Religious Ministry", 85; O'Brien, "Religious life", 109. For the Irish and French cases, see: Clear, *Nuns*, 65; Curtis, *Civilizing Habits*, 120-121. For American examples, see: Liedel, "Indomitable nuns", 460-479; Ewens, "Women in the convent", 30-32; Radford, "Catholic women", 23.

Rome. Women religious could thereby remove themselves from the domination of bishops who did not comply with church law while Rome could use it to emphasise the universality of its rules and the supremacy of the Vatican.[61] In established Churches too, such as the French and Belgian, there was an interesting dynamic between Vatican and female aspirations to power in the nineteenth century.[62] Viaene has already pointed out that the Tournai *Dames de Saint-André* in the mid-nineteenth century tried to free themselves from the tyrannical and indiscreet behaviour of their bishop by appealing to Rome. The Roman curia was afraid of the outbreak of a scandal that would give Belgian liberals food for gossip. Rome also saw a perfect opportunity to strengthen its own position, by placing the community in Tournai under the command of Gonella, the nuncio in Belgium between 1850 and 1861.[63] The Tournai sisters also benefited from the support of influential Belgian prelates, like Xavier de Mérode, who has already appeared in the story of de Meeûs.[64] Other congregations also gained from the prestige of Belgian church dignitaries in the Vatican. At the end of the 1860s, a congregation founder from Mauritius, Mère Marie-Augustine Lenferna de Laresle (1824-1900), settled in Brussels. With the support of Dechamps and some Belgian Redemptorists in Rome, she successfully applied for Roman recognition, against the will of the bishop in her home country.[65] Mère Marie-Augustine stayed in Salazar for a few months in 1869-1870, just at the time that de Meeûs was embroiled in her conflict for autonomy and recognition.

Reflecting on all these cases of Rome's support for women religious in their struggle for autonomy, it is tempting to detect a certain 'ultramontane feminism' in Rome's policy towards women's congregations. However, this was far from the truth. Historians such as Rocca, Scaraffia and Viaene have already clearly demonstrated that the pontifical policy aimed first of all at protecting and spreading Rome's supreme authority throughout the Catholic world. The strategic promotion and safeguarding of a relative degree of female autonomy went hand in hand with a permanent and deep-seated Roman distrust of the aforementioned '*fragile figlie di Eva*'.[66] This also was clear in de Meeûs' case. Nuncio Cattani, one of the successors to Gonella, accused de Meeûs of "a natural pride", which was inappropriate in a woman and a harmful example for her followers. Cattani was sceptical about female power and had already expressed his doubts about female congregation superiors

---

61 Liedel, "Indomitable nuns", 464-465.
62 On France, see: Friedlander, "Les pouvoirs", 247; Lecuir-Nemo, *Anne-Marie Javouhay*, 317.
63 Viaene, "The Second Sex". On the policy of Nuncio Matteo Gonella (1811-1870) with regard to religious, see: Simon, *Instructions*, 119-123.
64 Viaene, "The Second Sex", 447-474.
65 Dubois, *Notice biographique*, 42-44.
66 Viaene, "The Second Sex", 472-474; Rocca, "Les jésuites", 157-158; Idem, *Donne religiose*, 81; Scaraffia, "Christianity", 261-263.

in previous correspondence with Rome.⁶⁷ Prefect Quaglia of the Congregation of Bishops and Religious complained to Dechamps about the pressure that de Meeûs, as a woman, exercised on the Vatican.⁶⁸ Even more significant was Rome's policy on the *manifestation de conscience*, which was discussed earlier. In 1872 Rome not only removed the provisions concerning Jesuit confessors from the constitutions of the *Institut de l'Adoration Perpétuelle*, it also deleted the passages about the *manifestation de conscience*, which were fiercely defended by de Meeûs. The Congregation of Bishops and Religious, however, held to the view that women were unfit to discuss problems of conscience with their subordinates.⁶⁹

Anna de Meeûs was not discouraged by this negativity and focused instead on the remaining opportunities. Even before the Roman recognition decree had been fully promulgated, she had already started to consolidate it. Her convent in Rotterdam had ended up in a precarious position. The association members and Bishop Wilmer denounced the constant directives from Brussels. Relations with the Jesuits had soured in the Netherlands as well. The members of the Society, who served their own parish in Rotterdam, were not happy with de Meeûs' over-zealous community, which was taking people and resources away. Moreover, de Meeûs refused to fulfil her contractual financial obligations to the Jesuit parish on which the convent chapel was dependent. By attracting Redemptorists and Dominicans as preachers, she also undermined the position of the Jesuits as directors of the local association and as chaplains of the convent chapel.⁷⁰

The conflict escalated in the spring of 1872 when de Meeûs made use of her impending Roman recognition to broach the Dutch case in the Vatican. Relying on her new constitutions, she tried to bring about a break with the Dutch Jesuits in order to achieve a more independent position.⁷¹ The case was brought before the Propaganda Fide with the support of the generals of the Redemptorists and Dominicans, but it dragged on for more than six years. Both Wilmer and the Jesuits, in the person of Father Joannes Escherich (1817-1891), were amazed at the influence that de Meeûs could exert in Rome: "The pushiness of Madame de Meeûs is insupportable. It seems to me that Monsignor must change position and take measures to maintain the conditions. For a bishop to take a defensive role towards her is too humiliating; she takes ad-

---

67 "una naturale orgoglio": Art, "Documents", 412-415.
68 ASV, NB, *Religiose dell'Adorazione*: Cattani to Quaglia (13 Jan. 1871), Quaglia to Cattani (17 Feb. 1872).
69 Art, "Documents", 414-415.
70 NADH, ABR, 1686: *Geschil betreffende rechten van de kapel*; ANSI, 3.7. Van Gulick, 11347: Wilmer to Escherich and Victorine de Robiano (28 March 1874).
71 NADH, ABR, 1686: *Geschil betreffende rechten van de kapel*.

vantage of this in order to reach her goal, so that every concession makes her stronger".[72]

At the beginning of 1876 the Propaganda Fide decided that de Meeûs' claims were justified on the basis of her new constitutions and her exempt statute. Wilmer was asked to give the convent church an autonomous statute. As members of an institute of pontifical right, the sisters could not be subordinated to a local parish.[73] Concerned about the honour of his parish clergy and the viability of the parochial structures in Rotterdam, Wilmer felt aggrieved. "Has a superior ever shown more impertinence?", he wrote in disbelief to Father Escherich.[74] To Internuncio Capri he denounced the "esprit dominateur" of de Meeûs as an attack on his episcopal authority. The case continued to drag on until after Wilmer's death in 1877. Only in 1878 was an agreement about the autonomous statute of the chapel finally reached between the new Bishop Snickers, the Jesuits and de Meeûs.[75]

In Belgium, Dechamps remained a loyal ally to de Meeûs. Her profuse acknowledgments of his support in the conflict with the Jesuits flattered him as much as Kestre's emotional neediness. The latter was far from happy with Dechamps' role in favour of her rivals in Salazar and sometimes even accused him of betrayal. Her jealousy reached a climax when Dechamps tried to find a solution for de Meeûs' problems with her former benefactors. Count de la Serna had agreed in the 1850s to act as proxy and sponsor of de Meeûs' convent in Brussels. After her conflict with the Jesuits, de la Serna no longer wanted to fulfil that role. He threatened to put the Salazar complex up for sale, but Dechamps counselled patience. Meanwhile, the archbishop found the aforementioned Princess d'Arenberg willing to help the religious of Salazar in their need.[76]

Anna de Meeûs also took advantage of Dechamps' network in Rome. She no longer went to *Borgo San Spirito* for help but now sought support from the generalate of the Redemptorists. In exchange, she had her sisters and the la-

---

72 "Het drijven van Mad. de Meeûs is onverdragelijk. Mij dunkt, monseigneur moest de positie veranderen en positief optreden tot het doen onderhouden der condities: een defensieve rol van een bisschop tegenover haar is te vernederend: zij profiteert hiervan om tot haar doel te komen, zoodat elke toegeevelijkheid haar sterker maakt": NADH, ABR, 1686: Escherich to Wilmer (12 May 1872).
73 NADH, ABR, 1686: Prefect of Propaganda to Wilmer (18 Jan. 1876), Capri to Wilmer (8 Feb. 1876).
74 "Is er een grootere onbeschaamdheid van een superieure mogelijk", NADH, ABR, 1686: Wilmer to Escherich (1 Aug. 1875).
75 ARE, *Suite des racontes des visites. 2ᵉ Cahier* (1878); NADH, ABR, 1686: Escherich to Snickers (13 March 1878), Snickers to Capri (11 March 1878). Giovanni Capri was internuncio in The Hague between 1874 and 1879. Petrus Snickers (1816-1895) was bishop of Haarlem between 1877 and 1883, and subsequently archbishop of Utrecht (1883-1895).
76 ARE, *Cahier propriété maisons*; ASV, NB, *Religiose dell'Adorazione*: de la Serna to Dechamps (14 and 17 Nov. 1871), Dechamps to de la Serna (19 Nov. 1871).

dies of her association promote the devotion to Our Lady of Perpetual Succour, which was coordinated by the Redemptorists.[77] In addition, she had some luck on her side. Pius IX, with whom she already had a privileged relationship thanks to the generous patronage of her family, was succeeded by Pope Leo XIII, the former Belgian nuncio, Vincenzo Pecci, and an old acquaintance of hers. As was discussed in Part I, de Meeûs and Pecci had met each other several times in the salons of the château in Argenteuil, and Pecci had, in vain, tried to arrange a marriage for her. He made this confession to her only in 1878 when they met each other shortly after his election to the Holy See. With his aristocratic reserve, coupled with a great drive and a desire for recognition, Leo XIII got along well with de Meeûs.[78] There were regular audiences in the Vatican, and Leo XIII was always willing to provide de Meeûs with laudatory ecclesiastical references. In the early 1880s he donated some stained-glass windows for the chapel being constructed in Watermael.[79]

Papal support came just at the right moment. After the Roman decision of 1872, the Jesuits had kept a low profile for a long time, but began to 'stir' again in the second half of the 1870s. A number of local councils of the association continued to struggle with the disengagement of the Jesuits and the centralising management style of Salazar. In Turnhout and Antwerp, for example, local ladies from the association again tried to re-establish closer ties with the Society. A displeased Anna de Meeûs complained about this to Beckx in Rome.[80] He responded that the Jesuits did not want to obstruct the association in any way, but added diplomatically that in conscience they could not leave the spiritual needs of the ladies in Antwerp unattended.[81] At the same time, de Meeûs' association had to compete with a local Roman initiative that also focused on providing material support for poor parish churches. It was started in 1859 by a French woman, Caroline de Courballay (1811-1895), who in 1858 had become superior of the Roman *Filles du Cœur de Marie*, the same society that de Meeûs was at odds with in Brussels. Courballay was a match for de Meeûs in many respects. She could fall back on a large group of Roman aristocratic benefactors and, moreover, had a close relationship with Pius IX. She had financially supported him during the Fall of Rome and was known as "la mère des zouaves pontificaux". The local clergy in Rome were also well disposed towards her.[82]

Although the work of de Courballay was supported by prominent Roman prelates such as Cardinal Barnabo and Cardinal Vicar Patrizi, de Meeûs once

77 ARE, *Chronique*, XXX. Rome, 311-314; XL, Epilogue, 465.
78 For a character sketch of Leo XIII, see: Viaene, "Introduction: Reality and image", 11.
79 ARE. *Chronique*, XXXV. Amour de l'Eglise, 379-380.
80 ARSI, *IV. Epistoleres (1872-1883), XIV. Sodalitium Salazar*: de Meeûs to Beckx (15 April 1879, 20 June 1879).
81 ARSI, *X. Registri – Externi Saeculares (1858-1879)*: Beckx to de Meeûs (31 May 1879).
82 Casgrain, *La Société*, III, 82-91.

again was convinced that the Jesuits had a hand in this.[83] Aside from the fact that Patrizi was rumoured to be a puppet of the Jesuits, de Meeûs could not substantiate her accusations.[84] Still, Dechamps and the Roman Redemptorists listened to her. Dechamps raised the issue with Nuncio Vannutelli and together with de Meeûs and the general of the Redemptorists lobbied the new Pope Leo XIII. In 1879 they managed to convince him to integrate Courballay's project in de Meeûs' association. The danger posed by the competition was thus neutralised, although de Meeûs had to give de Courballay a position on the central council of her association.[85] Once again, de Meeûs' broad network along with internal tensions in the Church had a favourable impact on her ambitions.

Leo XIII delegated his confidant Gabriel Boccali (1843-1892) to finalise the matter. Afterwards Boccali continued to be a valuable contact for de Meeûs. The Italian curial prelate was part of the group of confidants that Leo XIII brought with him to Rome from Perugia, the seat of his former bishopric. As auditor and secretary, Boccali handled the correspondence and audiences of Leo XIII. He was part of the unofficial '*gabinetto segreto*' of the pope, through which direct and informal access to Leo XIII could be arranged without the intervention of the unpredictable Vatican bureaucracy.[86] Intriguing research by Lamberts has already shown that secret networks and mysterious intermediaries played a key role behind the scenes in the Vatican in the nineteenth century. It is indicative of the warm relationship between de Meeûs and Leo XIII that she was able to get ready access to him.[87] The close contact with Leo XIII gave a new impetus to her Roman network. In 1878-1879 the pope convinced her to found a convent in Rome and to establish the headquarters of the association there. In doing this, Leo XIII forefronted his centralisation tendencies, but was also giving expression to his view of the devotion to the Blessed Sacrament as the engine for the restoration of the *Règne Social de Christ*.[88] Once again Vatican and female development went hand in hand. De Meeûs' position was not unique. In the same period Leo XIII also persuaded other congregation founders to undertake a foundation in Rome, which benefited

---

83   Casgrain, *La Société*, III, 84-85. Allesandro Barnabo (1801-1874) was prefect of Propaganda Fide between 1856 and 1874. Constantino Patrizi (1798-1876) was cardinal-vicar of Rome between 1841 and 1876.
84   On Patrizi, see: Jankowiak, *La curie romaine*, 310-311.
85   ARE, *Exposé historique*; ASV, NB, *Religiose dell'Adorazione*: Dechamps to Vannutelli (26 May 1878).
86   On Boccali, see: Jankowiak, *La curie romaine*, 444; Levillain, *Le pontificat de Leo XIII*, 122.
87   Lamberts (ed.), *The Black International*.
88   ARE, *Cahier des Lettres 3*: de Meeûs to Leo XIII (15 May 1879). On Leo XIII and his preference for the devotion to the Blessed Sacrament, see: Menozzi, *Sacro Cuore*, 171-294.

both their own expansion and the perception of Rome as the global centre of the Catholic Church.[89]

Although Roman feminism may not have been an issue, there was a strategic commitment by and for women to the benefit of the universal cause of Rome and their own expansion. In the decade after the transfer of the association's headquarters and the foundation of the convent in Rome in 1878-1879, the congregation experienced an influx of almost ten novices per year, whereas in the preceding decade, the balance had fluctuated around five entrances per year. Roman recognition had definitively pushed it towards becoming a medium-sized, international institute and would be decisive for de Meeûs' prestige in the last decades of the nineteenth century.

---

[89] Compare for example with the example of the English congregation founder, Mary Potter (1847-1911), who responded to Leo XIII's request for a foundation in Rome and thereby escaped the growing interference of the bishop of Nottingham. Mangion, *Contested Identities*, 219-220.

After Kestre's death her congregation acquired a more elite profile. It enabled her successor to stabilise and expand the congregation, and finally in the 1880s to construct a neo-Gothic convent and chapel for the motherhouse in Brussels. The changed social status further complicated however the already diffuse identity of the *Dames de Sainte-Julienne*, ultimately hampering a successful future.
[Postcard – ca. 1900 – Collection *Archivio Storico della Casa Generalizia delle Religiose di Gesù – Maria*, Rome]

EPILOGUE

THE SHAPING OF PERCEPTIONS

For sixty years, Cornet, de Meeûs, Telghuys and Kestre followed a parallel trajectory through post-revolutionary trauma, religious revival and intense culture wars. From more than one perspective, the mid-1880s marked the end of the era in which the four congregation founders and superiors had given definitive shape to their lives. First, death put an end to their shared paths. The lives of Fanny Kestre and Antoinette Cornet came to a close in 1882 and 1886. Anna de Meeûs and Wilhelmina Telghuys survived another two decades, into the twentieth century. Second, the deaths of Kestre and Cornet not only completed the group portrait of the four women, they also coincided with a changing *Zeitgeist*: the overriding focus on the ideological struggle shifted towards social issues. The militantly ultramontane crusade remodelled itself into a social movement.

Such changes require a change in perspective. In this epilogue I intend to broaden the focus from a study of the thinking, acting and functioning of de Meeûs, Cornet, Telghuys and Kestre to an analysis of the perceptions that were formed of them. The factors and mechanisms that were decisive for their (posthumous) perception will be investigated against the background of the new social context and the further development of the congregations after 1885. In what way and according to which criteria, gender and other models did their contemporaries and later generations shape the story of their lives and evaluate their legacy? Two constant motifs run through this history of perception: the enduring influence of the revival's ideals of social commitment on the one hand and the struggle with the mould of 'humble saintliness' on the other.

Fanny Kestre: an active "femme forte", a spiritual "âme simple"

On 12 February 1882, after a working meeting with the ladies of her association, Kestre fell prey to a "point pleurétique (...) avec une extrême violence".[1] Already severely weakened by the chronic infection in her arm, it quickly became clear that she would not recover this time. From Mechelen, where Dechamps himself was seriously ill in bed, came a dejected response to the bad news: "Faites faire à votre Mère des actes de conformité à la volonté de Dieu. Je la bénis de toute mon âme, elle et vous toutes".[2] It was the last letter in a correspondence that had spanned almost three decades. Kestre died in the early evening of 3 March 1882, a few weeks before her 58th birthday, while Dechamps' death followed in September 1883. In just a year and a half, the *Dames de Sainte-Julienne* lost both their founder and their most important patron.

A fatal struggle with a complex identity

Immediately after Kestre's death, the emphasis was on the importance of her apostolate and of her innovative catechetical work in particular: "Aujourd'hui les œuvres qu'elle [Kestre] a fait surgir sont aussi florissantes qu'il était permis de l'espérer. (...) Les catéchismes établis dans différentes paroisses moralisent une multitude d'enfants, distribuent d'innombrables secours, font une guerre heureuse à l'ignorance religieuse et ont acquis une popularité méritée."[3] The words were those of the aforementioned Count de Villermont. As we have seen, he was initially a benefactor of Kestre, but later became a harsh critic of her unfortunate attack on the Jesuits in the early 1860s. At the end of her life, however, he expressed admiration for her achievements in the working-class districts of Brussels. His perceptions were emblematic of the evolution that Kestre's image had undergone over a period of thirty years. They also foreshadowed the shifting context and the Church's turn to the people after the end of the School War and the Catholic election victory of 1884.[4] Within the context of this social turn and the integration of the masses and the workers within the ideal of a harmonious, Christian corporatist society, the religious charitable work of Kestre had many strengths. Archbishop Goossens (1884-1906), Dechamps' successor in Mechelen, described her commitment to the

---

1 *La Révérende Mère Fanny*, 281.
2 ADSJ, 1.4: Dechamps to Lalieu (22 Feb. 1882).
3 De Villermont, "Fanny Kestre", in: *Journal de Bruxelles* (8 March 1882).
4 On this, see Lamberts (ed.), *Een kantelend tijdperk*, published on the occasion of the 100th anniversary of Leo XIII's encyclical *Rerum Novarum* (1891), which gave a powerful boost to Catholic social thinking and the Christian workers' movement.

Brussels working class districts in 1892 as "la grande pensée de Mme Kestre".[5] His praise reflected his increasing interest in the social cause after the publication of *Rerum Novarum* (1891), but was also an indication of Kestre's legacy.

Goossens made his statement during a visit to the novitiate of the congregation which was established in 1888 in Cortil in the province of Brabant. The foundation of a separate novitiate together with the erection of a new convent and chapel in Brussels between 1884 and 1886 were a realisation of Kestre's unfulfilled dreams and a result of the strong leadership of her successor, Mère Alix Lalieu (1841-1902). Endowed with a strong negotiating spirit and a more diplomatic character than her predecessor, Lalieu put an end to the poverty-stricken existence of the *Dames de Sainte-Julienne*. The novitiate in Cortil was housed in the former castle of the aristocratic Brou de la Wastinne family. The new chapel of the convent in Brussels was a textbook example of a neo-Gothic *Gesamtkunstwerk*, designed by top architect Joris Helleputte and paid for by the Arenberg family.[6]

The new constitutions of the congregation, which had been drawn up after the definitive papal approbation in 1891, fixed the required dowry for choir sisters at the exceptionally high sum of 20,000 francs.[7] Contrary to Kestre's necessity-driven "amour du pauvre et de la pauvreté", the *Dames de Sainte-Julienne* had evolved into an elite congregation, even before this was confirmed at the turn of the century with the entrance of a number of aristocratic novices.[8] The congregation for the religious instruction of the people now acquired an elite profile. By founding convents in Antwerp (1890) and Namur (1891), Lalieu also moved away from Kestre's exclusive focus on Brussels. Her policy gave the congregation a more secure existence, far from the turbulent waters into which it had often strayed under Kestre's leadership. Around 1900 the institute had grown into an average-sized Belgian congregation with 87 sisters spread over four convents.

Yet this new phase of expansion was again short-lived. During the interwar period, the first signs of a new crisis emerged. The ambiguous identity of the congregation – contemplative adoration of the Blessed Sacrament in combination with a demanding apostolate, reinforced by the difficult spread between a working-class target group and elite recruitment – once again be-

5   ADSJ, *Annales du Noviciat de Cortil* (4 Sept. 1892); Petrus Goossens (1827-1906) was appointed as successor to Dechamps in 1884. See: De Maeyer, "De wending", 102-103.
6   ADSJ, *Vie de Mère Alix*. For a description of the Brussels chapel and the history of its construction, see: Paesmans, "De Julianakapel", 24-34; De Maeyer, Van Molle and Maes, *Joris Helleputte*, II, 255-261. The architect and politician Joris Helleputte (1852-1925), together with the aforementioned Jean-Baptiste Bethune were among the most prominent representatives of the Belgian neo-Gothic school.
7   AAM, CF, *Dames de Sainte-Julienne: Constitutions 1892*.
8   These included, among others, Camille de Hennin de Boussu (1874-1898) and Rita de Thomaz de Bossière (1880-1975). ADSJ, *Registre Religieuses*.

came a problem. Moreover, it could not keep pace with the wide range of social and religious initiatives for youth being offered in the context of the mass movements of Catholic Action. Initiatives such as the *Eucharistische Kruistocht* (Eucharistic Crusade), for example, focused on promoting the Eucharistic devotion to children on a much larger scale. In addition, in the wake of Pius X's communion decrees, large teaching congregations also concentrated on expanding catechetical instruction in their schools.[9] With the competition intensifying, recruitment for the *Dames de Sainte-Julienne* again became difficult. The decreasing numbers of sisters and the diminishing income from dowries forced the closure of the convent in Namur in 1940. The congregation's situation was not exceptional. In contrast to the rapidly growing Flemish congregations, many Walloon and Brussels congregations were already being confronted with a decline in vocations in the first half of the twentieth century.[10] For an average congregation such as the *Dames de Sainte-Julienne*, this negative evolution soon had far-reaching consequences. At Rome's suggestion, the congregation finally merged in 1959 with the teaching congregation of the *Religieuses de Jésus-Marie*, a pontifical institute with French roots. Some sisters remained in Brussels until 1994, when the sale of the convent on the *Rue de la Charité* in Saint-Josse-ten-Noode cut the last link with Kestre's legacy.

"La louange de la femme forte ressort de l'œuvre de ses mains"

Like the obituaries of 1882, the first full biography of Kestre, which was published anonymously in 1897, focused particularly on her apostolic achievements: "Si, d'après l'Ecriture, la louange de la femme forte ressort de l'œuvre de ses mains, les faits que relate cette notice sont le meilleur éloge de Mme Fanny".[11] The biographer's allusion to the well-known verse from the *Book of Proverbs* was not insignificant.[12] Praise for their apostolic work was a common thread in the stream of biographies of congregation founders that appeared in the last quarter of the nineteenth century. From the pioneering apostolate activities of Julie Billiart and Cicercule Paridaens, through the first 'Belgian' congregations of Therese Haze and Justine Desbille to the later achievements of Kestre – and as will be seen – Cornet, de Meeûs and Telghuys, the positive

---

9   Quaghebeur, "De Eucharistische Kruistocht", 112-123.
10 Wynants, *Les Sœurs de la Providence*, 47-49; Tihon, "Les religieuses", 42-43.
11 *La Révérende Mère Fanny*, 282.
12 "Aleph mulierem fortem quis inveniet procul et de ultimis finibus pretium eius": the beginning verses of the proverb in praise of the strong or virtuous woman who distinguishes herself mainly through hard work, entrepreneurial spirit and modesty. See: *Book of Proverbs*, 31, 10-31.

perception of their lives "est toute entière dans les travaux".¹³ The revival's legacy of religiously inspired charitable activity thus provided the founders with a forum for recognition that continued well into the twentieth century.

The biographies of women religious held up an ideal image that was based on an appreciation for their achievements in the apostolate, together with the glorification of passive virtues such as humility, spiritual simplicity or readiness to suffer. If there seemed to be a broad consensus on the first aspect, the perception of the passive virtues was not free of contradiction or camouflage. With her life of adversity and suffering and her hard-won apostolic accomplishments, Kestre fitted nicely into the template: "la pensée que Mme Fanny Kestre avait conçue a dû d'abord être fécondée sous les eaux de la tribulation, prendre racines dans des humiliations de tous genres et germer lentement dans une laborieuse patience".¹⁴ However, comments were far more reserved about the visionary experiences associated with her suffering and work. References to her visions were absent or were only mentioned very briefly, relating to Kestre as a spiritual "âme simple".¹⁵

Still, her charism lived on. Immediately after her death, the first accounts of veneration by former catechism teachers and pupils reached the sisters. Inside the congregation as well, she was remembered for her perseverance and her resignation in suffering and misfortune. The continuing fascination with Kestre led in 1915 to the start of a canonisation procedure, coordinated by the postulator of the Eudists, Father Gabriël Mallet.¹⁶ Kestre was made a Servant of God, canonically one of the first steps towards beatification and canonisation. The file that Mallet drew up in 1915 bore many similarities with the discourse of the biography from 1897. The Eudist again emphasised Kestre's suffering on the one hand and her accomplishments in the apostolate on the other.¹⁷

The same diptych of the socially engaged "femme forte" and the spiritual "âme simple" was also represented in other biographies. Along with her zeal for foundations, Julie Billiart of the *Sœurs de Notre Dame*, for example, was celebrated for her writings "en toute leur simplicité et leur aimable naïveté".¹⁸ Mère Marie-Claire de Jésus of the *Sœurs de Sainte-Marie* of Namur received praise both as co-founder of her institute and for the fact that she had "rien

---

13 Bailly, *Vie de la révérende mère Gertrude*, 10. For other nineteenth-century biographies, see: Baesten, *Vie de la Mère Julie Billiart*; De Ville, *Histoire de la Mère Marie-Thérèse*.
14 *Journal de Bruxelles* (8 March 1882).
15 *La Révérende Mère Fanny*, 18-19.
16 Gabriel Mallet had been the postulator general of the Eudists in Rome since 1895. He was the driving force behind the canonisation dossier of his founder, Jean Eudes. Mallet also became involved in the appeals for canonisation of various female religious. See: *Catalogus ac status causarum*, 1931, 28, 80, 100, 104-105, 135. On Mallet, see: Venard, *Les Eudistes*, 50-53.
17 ADSJ: Mallet, *Beatificationis et canonizationis servae dei Franciscae ab Eucharistia Kestre*.
18 Baesten, *Vie de la Mère Julie Billiart*, VIII.

d'éclatant, rien d'extraordinaire: tout est simplicité, humilité, charité".[19] There were interesting parallels also in the perception of prominent women outside the ecclesiastical sphere. Fanny Geefs, the aforementioned painter who made portraits of the de Meeûs family, among others, was evaluated by a male art critic according to the standard template of female humility: "Prenons le cadre qui renferme la vie d'une femme, et demandons si l'artiste a réussi à bien rendre: piété, amour, douleur".[20] After her death, Rosalie Loveling was considered by male contemporaries to be worthy of taking her place as a female writer 'among men', but at the same time was praised for her abiding humility.

As has been shown on several occasions, Kestre was not disposed to be modest about her spiritual life. She spoke extensively and proudly about her visions, arousing ridicule and disbelief, and causing her divine inspiration to be discreetly tucked away after her death. In that sense, Kestre's story seems to tally with the conclusions of the feminist theologian Johnson, who saw the emphasis on humility, obedience and suffering in the biographies of female saints and religious as an instrument of ecclesiastical control. By constructing an ideal image of the humble Catholic woman, women's value was subjected to a mandatory pre-condition.[21] Posthumous perceptions also showed that while the double-voiced discourse and social initiatives of religious women had created space for female development, they had not significantly changed gender stereotyping, nor the key features of the framework for evaluating women's behaviour and achievements.

Nevertheless, some observations need to be made about this pronounced gender typification in the biographies. References to simplicity, self-denial and suffering, combined with admiration for a strong engagement in religious charitable work were equally characteristic of nineteenth-century or early twentieth-century biographies of male Belgian congregation founders such as Lodewijk Donche (1769-1857), Nicolas Minsart (1769-1837) or Joannes Lambertz (1785-1869).[22] Van Osselaer came to similar conclusions in her analysis of nineteenth- and early twentieth-century biographies of Catholic heroes and heroines. For both men and women, courage and a spirit of sacrifice went hand in hand with humility and obedience, and were also held up as an example to all believers.[23] Recent research into nineteenth- and twentieth-century apparitions and miracles has also highlighted the dangers of an exaggerated gender dualism. Humility, simplicity and submission to ecclesiastical author-

19 Vie de la Révérende Mère Marie Claire de Jésus, 8.
20 Cited in: Creusen, Femmes artistes, 200.
21 Johnson, Friends of God, 152.
22 Respectively founders of the Zusters van de Christelijke Scholen of Vorselaar, the Sœurs de Sainte-Marie of Namur and the Ursulines of Tildonk. See: Bogaerts, Levensbeschrijving, 398; Nicolas-Joseph Minsart, 85; Saintrain, Jean-Corneille-Martin Lambertz, 9. Similar conclusions are to be found in: Art, "Mannen als bruiden", 36-37.
23 Van Osselaer, The Pious Sex, 160-169.

ity were a sine qua non for the recognition of all visionaries, including (the few) males: "More important than gender was the simplicity of the seer".[24]

Taking into account the new perspectives of recent research, then the perception of Kestre is to be viewed, not only in the mould of exclusively female humility, but rather in a template of religious modesty and simplicity that was also applied to religiously inspired men. Still, it was difficult to reconcile this template with Kestre's lived experience: she was not a 'simple' spiritual soul, but a charismatic '*madame*' strongly convinced and inspired by her visions. Presumably this field of tension also played a role in the unsuccessful outcome of her canonisation process. The '*Mme Kestre*' of the laudatory biographical notes focusing on her apostolate achievements differed too much from the sanctified '*Francisca ab Eucharistia*' featured in Mallet's canonisation file. The case finally petered out before the mid-twentieth century, just when the first of a long series of nineteenth-century women founders were beatified or canonised by Rome.[25] A lack of miracles and a lack of resources in the shrinking congregation finally extinguished Kestre's star.

Antoinette Cornet: between oblivion and rediscovery

Even though the perception of Kestre was modelled on standard stereotypes and the canonisation process finally came to nothing, the attention she was given after her death contrasted with the lack of posthumous interest in most nineteenth-century Belgian congregation founders. Antoinette Cornet belonged to that group. There are few details about the circumstances of her death. In her final years she suffered a lot from rheumatism. At the beginning of 1886, her assistant, Sister Marguerite (Verlaine), took over responsibility for the correspondence with the sisters in Bazel and Sougné, presumably because Cornet was no longer able to do so.[26] She died on 14 June 1886 at the age of 66. A short notice in the *Journal de Bruxelles*, mentioning the death of "cette reli-

---

24 Maunder, *Our Lady of Nations*, 53; Van Osselaer, "Sensitive but sane", 132-133; Scheer, "Das Medium", 169-192.
25 These included the aforementioned Barat, canonised in 1925 and Desmaisières, canonised in 1934. The number of beatifications and canonisations of nineteenth-century founders of women's congregations increased sharply in the second half of the twentieth century and especially during the pontificate of John Paul II. At the beginning of the twenty-first century, more than 100 female founders were beatified or canonised and formed the vast majority of canonised nineteenth-century women. For an overview, see: *Martyrologium Romanum*, 2004. Therese Haze, founder of the *Filles de la Croix* of Liège and Emilie d'Oultremont, founder of the *Dames Réparatrices*, who have been already mentioned above several times, are still the only nineteenth-century Belgian female founders to have been canonised, in 1991 and 1997 respectively. Julie Billiart, the French founder of *Sœurs de Notre-Dame* of Namur was canonised in 1969.
26 ASCLH, A.2: Verlaine to Courrier (26 March 1886); *Notice Chronologique*, 66.

Cornet's legacy within her congregation was ambiguous. Her portrait – strikingly larger than the portraits of bishops and clerics that surrounded her – decorated the parlour of the convent in Maleizen for a long time, but details about her personality, her life and her grave disappeared from the collective memory of the sisters.
[Postcard – ca. 1900 – Collection *Sœurs du S. Cœur de Marie*, La Hulpe]

gieuse d'une rare dévouement", was the last public memory of Cornet. When, several months later, the start of the new school year in the boarding school of Maleizen was announced in the same newspaper, her name was not even mentioned.[27]

Reminiscences of the founder within the congregation were ambiguous. Her *Questionnaire Spirituel* was carefully copied by the sisters up until the beginning of the twentieth century. In the special brochure that was published for the 50th anniversary of the congregation in 1913, she was given full credit for the foundation "car l'œuvre de Mère Gonzague a été grande et féconde".[28] As with Kestre, the legacy of Cornet's apostolate determined the way she was perceived. At the same time, most of the references to her as an actual person disappeared, a large portrait in the parlour being the only important iconography left. The 1913 brochure only honoured '*Mère Gonzague*' and did not make any reference to her origin, age or even her official name. Over the years, the memory of her burial place also faded. In the second half of the twentieth century, when the sisters, inspired by the '*ad fontes*' mantra of the Second Vatican Council, literally and figuratively went looking for traces of their founder, no-

27 *Journal de Bruxelles* (16 June 1886, 21 Aug. 1886).
28 *1863-1913. Notice Chronologique*, 13.

body knew exactly where her grave was. It was not until 1980 that her remains were rediscovered during excavations in what appeared to have been the former convent cemetery in Maleizen. By that time, the sisters had already long left. Forced by language regulations in 1960 to close their French-speaking boarding school because it was situated on Flemish territory, the motherhouse of the congregation was transferred back to La Hulpe once again.

After 1886, the congregation in Maleizen largely continued on the path set out by Cornet. The difficult collaboration in Bazel was indeed stopped, but was replaced by new educational activities in Linsmeau in the province of Brabant (1891) and Fumal in the province of Liège (1893). The boarding school in Maleizen consolidated Cornet's focus on the better agricultural and middle-class milieus by adding a second-level agricultural training course in the 1890s. This decision fitted in with Catholic educational and social policy in the interest of the people. The agrarian crisis of the 1880s had put the agricultural sector under great pressure. In order to support farming families, one of the cornerstones of the Catholic model of a corporatist society, church authorities and Catholic governments from 1884 onwards launched initiatives to improve agricultural education.[29]

With 79 members in four convents around 1900, the *Sœurs du Sacré Cœur de Marie* remained an average teaching congregation in the Belgian convent landscape. Cornet had managed to escape strong male control through her aura as a founder, her double-voiced discourse and her opportunistic alliances. Her successors, however, were subjected more to the diocesan supervision that Dechamps had introduced and was continued by Goossens. The first official director of the congregation, Ivan Nolet de Brauwere van Steeland (1849-1903), a diocesan priest with a long track record in Catholic education, had a major impact on the congregation from 1892 onwards.[30] He revamped the curriculum of the boarding school, taught the religious himself and convinced the superior to allow all the teaching sisters be trained at a recognised normal school. In the years after 1886, the congregation had difficulty finding enough vocations, possibly due to the death of the founder and the death soon after in 1888 of her first successor, Verlaine. Nolet's dedication to innovation and better training opportunities for the sisters gave the congregation a second lease of life.[31]

---

29 Van Molle, *Katholieken en landbouw*, 202-203, 331; Christens and Suenens, "L'enseignement comme vocation et projet", 155.
30 Vanderkerken, "Ivan Nolet de Brauwere van Steeland".
31 ASCMLH, *Notice Chronologique*, 70-71; C.1: *Registre des entrées*.

Anna de Meeûs: "trop robuste pour être sainte"

In the meantime, de Meeûs' congregation continued its strong growth and expansion. At the end of the nineteenth century, the congregation had 220 sisters in 11 convents in Belgium and abroad. In Brussels, the death of Kestre in 1882 brought no rapprochement in the rivalry between the *Dames de Sainte-Julienne* and the sisters of Salazar. At the end of the century de Meeûs heard about the plans of the Redemptorist Father Pladys for a biography of Dechamps, in which his close ties with Kestre would be outlined in detail. In Pladys' manuscript – which was never published – Kestre was indeed portrayed as Dechamp's *protégée* and source of inspiration: "La fondatrice (...) que le Père Dechamps vénérait un peu comme une autre Sainte Julienne de Mont-Cornillon".[32] Anna de Meeûs instructed Léopoldine de Robiano to find archival documents that would prove Dechamps had also supported their institute and had lobbied repeatedly in Rome for their recognition.[33] It was a battle for prestige between two sister congregations with prominent female founders. Yet both felt the need to justify themselves as being the successful result of a male prelate's zeal. Humility and obedience may not have been exclusively determined by gender considerations, but clerical, and thus male, support and recognition remained a premise from which there was no escape.

"L'illustre Dame belge"

Barely two years after the publication of the first biography on Kestre, de Meeûs seized the opportunity to counter the perception of her rival. With a special publication for the 50th anniversary of her association, she highlighted the authenticity of her own initiative. It was a first step in constructing a favourable perception of herself. *Les Voies de Dieu. Un Jubilé Eucharistique dans l'Eglise expiatoire du Très Saint Sacrement de Miracle à Bruxelles (1848-1898)* was published in 1899. Although no official author was mentioned, the almost 300-page book had clearly been penned within the convent walls of Salazar. The text bears many similarities with the handwritten annals that were kept in the congregation's archive. Moreover, it was addressed "aux lecteurs de notre revue eucharistique", more specifically the annals of the association that were published by Salazar.[34] If the publication was not written by de Meeûs herself, then certainly one of her closest companions was responsible. Women religious who themselves wrote a history of their institute or the biography of

---

32 ACSSR-NB, 1511: Pladys, *Vie du Cardinal Dechamps*, I, 534.
33 ACSSR-NB, 1497: Léopoldine de Robiano to anonymous (4 Nov. 1899).
34 *Les Voies de Dieu*, XIX.

a founder were not exceptional in the late nineteenth century, although their work, as in the case of *Les Voies de Dieu*, often remained anonymous.[35]

With *Les Voies de Dieu*, de Meeûs created a forum for gaining recognition while she was still alive, even though her discourse continued to refer to the ideal of religious simplicity and the clerical division of roles between an inexperienced woman and a wise man. The complementarity between "la pensée naïve d'Anna de Meeûs" and Boone's "parole éloquente et persuasive", for example, was emphasised.[36] However, the discourse on spiritual humility was countered by an impressive account of her apostolic successes. On the final pages the statistics of the association – which was elevated by Leo XIII in 1895 to the status of a *Prima Primaria* for Eucharistic associations – were presented as the ultimate triumph. At the end of the nineteenth century, there were 279 branches of the association, spread across three continents: from Mosul in present-day Iraq to Lima in Peru, and from San Francisco in the USA to Prague in the Czech Republic. In Belgium, the association was active in around 2,000 parishes and had about 193,000 members.

The anniversary of the association in the summer of 1898 coincided with the international Eucharistic Congress in Brussels. It was again a large-scale Catholic event, with a total of 4,000 attendees spread over the various days and sessions. In the spirit of the Church's turn to the people and the social question, the speeches of the congress strongly emphasised the all-encompassing power of the Eucharist as the anti-revolutionary engine of the *Règne Social de Christ*.[37] The sessions on two of the four days of the congress were held in the church and the Salazar chapel of de Meeûs' convent in Brussels. Anna de Meeûs seized the opportunity to intensively promote her institute and association, with the support of Father Jeroom Van Langermeersch (1850-1911). The Jesuit's involvement is interesting from several perspectives. It was illustrative for the improved late nineteenth-century relations of de Meeûs with the Society of Jesus. It also revealed a link between de Meeûs' association of pious ladies and the burgeoning Catholic women's movement. Van Langermeersch founded the *Ligue des Femmes Chrétiennes de Bruxelles* in 1893, which was a mixed group of workers and upper-class women. In offering religious and professional formation, recreation initiatives and material services, the organisation was responding to the Church's increasing attention to the working classes as well as to the nascent feminism, for which the *Ligue* wanted to be

---

35 Compare, for example, with the biographies on Paridaens (*Cicercule Paridaens*, 1903), Marie Claire de Jésus (*Vie de la Révérende Mère Marie Claire*, 1895) or the monograph – including the biographies of numerous sisters – on the *Dames de Saint-André* of Tournai (*Les Religieuses de Saint-André*, 1908), all written by (anonymous) sisters.
36 *Les Voies de Dieu*, 40.
37 The documents were published in 1899, in the same year as *Les Voies de Dieu*, and gave a complete report of the proceedings of the congress: *XI*e *Congrès Eucharistique International Bruxelles*. See also: Lamberts, "Catholic Congresses", 221-222.

a Christian alternative.[38] Anna de Meeûs and her sisters played no direct role in the *Ligue*, but via Van Langermeersch, who also gave lectures to the sisters and ladies of Salazar, some members of de Meeûs' association became active in his women's movement.

At the congress of 1898, the Jesuit praised his confrere Boone extensively, but at the end of his speech he called on the attendees to give a standing ovation for de Meeûs, "la grande chrétienne dont toutes les œuvres connaissent l'inépuisable générosité et qu'on cette occasion toutes les œuvres semblent acclamer."[39]

During the congress, Leo XIII praised de Meeûs in a *breve* as the founder "digne d'éloges" of the institute, while the cardinal-protector, Vannutelli addressed the public on the subject of "l'illustre Dame belge".[40] So many tributes do call for some explanation. At the Eucharistic Congress, Van Langermeersch's presentation was held at the daily '*Réunion des Dames*' and not during the plenary sessions. Among the female participants were several associate members of the association of de Meeûs. She thus played a largely home game for a well-known audience. Moreover, despite the substantial female representation, the Catholic newspapers barely mentioned the women's meetings, even though they gave extensive coverage to the plenary sessions of the congress. The standing ovation for de Meeûs did not get much response either. Finally, even during the *Réunion des Dames*, the women themselves were not given a forum and their praises were sung exclusively by men. While the "illustre Dame belge" was honoured, she herself did not speak. Again, gender conventions remained unaffected here and women remained in the shadow of men. This was not peculiar to the Catholic congresses of that time. Dupont-Bouchat showed that at non-religiously inspired philanthropic congresses also, such as the *Congrès Internationaux sur la Protection de l'Enfance* in the late nineteenth century, the input of women was limited and was concentrated in the separate sessions for women.[41]

The Catholic press did pay heed to the more than 1,000 members of de Meeûs' association who, after the congress of 1898, participated in the closing procession of the Blessed Sacrament and noted the lavish street decoration done by her sisters and *dames*.[42] Once again the power of numbers and money determined de Meeûs' prestige. During the congress, she gained recognition because of the statistics of her apostolate and her generous sponsorship. Besides the costs of decoration, her congregation also bore a large part of the organisational costs of the congress, which was held in the convent church. The

---

38 On this, see: Osaer et al., "De christelijke arbeidersvrouwenbeweging", 328.
39 *XIe Congrès Eucharistique*, 539.
40 *Les Voies de Dieu*, 219-222, 241.
41 Dupont-Bouchat, "Femmes philanthropes", 83-92.
42 *Journal de Bruxelles* (16 July 1898); *Le Vingtième Siècle* (17 July 1898).

report of the congress issued in 1899 was illustrated with several photographs and sketches of the neo-Gothic expiatory church and the Salazar chapel. In this respect, de Meeûs' marketing campaign had worked well. With the financial support of the Princess d'Arenberg, plans were made for the embellishment of the ancient chapel and the church, which was extended with two neo-Gothic spires. The restoration and construction were only finished after the congress, but gave de Meeûs' Brussels convent complex a new splendour.[43]

A difficult inheritance

The events of 1898 undeniably marked the highpoint of de Meeûs' ecclesiastical career and prestige, but not its end. After the foundation of new convents in Sankt Pölten (Austria) and Palermo (Italy) failed, new foundations in Antwerp (1889), Munich (1894) and - again - Palermo (1896) and the first American house in Washington (1900) confirmed the continuing expansion of the congregation. Anna de Meeûs, now 77 years old, did not dare to make the trip to the USA herself and in September 1900 saw off a number of her sisters, who left from Antwerp for the American 'mission'. However, she continued to traverse Europe with great zeal. After the death of Leo XIII in 1903, she went to Rome for the last time in the spring of 1904 to ask for a papal blessing in a private audience with his successor Pius X. He was the third pope in a row to receive the Belgian woman in the Vatican. During her stay in Rome, de Meeûs felt her strength waning. Presumably she had cancer. On the return trip from Rome she visited her sisters in Munich and Liège, and at the beginning of June finally arrived back in Watermael, deathly ill. She died in the afternoon of Wednesday, June 15th, 1904, aged 81 years.[44]

Anna de Meeûs was buried in the cemetery at Watermael, but very soon after, her sisters and her family asked that her body be transferred to the convent grounds. A chapel with a crypt was built in the garden of the Watermael convent, though the liberal municipal council did not grant permission for the grave to be transferred until 1910. The new tombstone was inscribed with a biblical citation that, just as with Kestre, alluded to the 'strong woman' and her zeal for the apostolate: "Ses Œuvres la loueront".[45] Immediately after her death, her successor, Emma Papeians de Morchoven (1843-1916), published a detailed life story of the founder in the annals of the association. Shortly afterwards, the text was also published in French and Dutch brochures, again with a strong focus on de Meeûs' social and religious work and her promotion of the Eucharistic devotion.

---

43 SAB, Public Works, Construction Permits, 22373: *Parachèvement de l'église Salazar*.
44 *Anna de Meeûs*, 162.
45 ARE, *Chronique. XL. Epilogue*, 459.

Anna de Meeûs' legacy as the *'illustre dame belge'* survived her for half a century. Her commemorative chapel, built as a shrine on the convent grounds in Watermael and visited in 1946 by Archbishop Van Roey of Mechelen, embodied a desire for continual veneration. Despite the emphasis on her personal motto "Tout pour plaire à Dieu, rien pour me satisfaire", her robust character eventually stood in the way of a trajectory to formal sainthood.
[Photograph – 1948 – Collection *Religieuses de l'Eucharistie*]

The perception of de Meeûs' legacy was, however, overshadowed in the years after her death by two more material issues. In the last years of her life she had been upset about the large-scale urbanisation plans of King Leopold II. The old district between the *Mont des Arts* and the *Saint-Gudule* church, where the Salazar complex was located, had to make way for a modern administrative and cultural district and a promenade garden. Anna de Meeûs strongly opposed the plans for expropriation, but her successor could not avert the disaster. The buildings of the motherhouse on the *Rue des Sols*, which had been renovated only some years before, were requisitioned in 1906-1907. In the meantime, the congregation had commissioned the construction of a new convent in the *Léopold* district in Etterbeek, the elite Brussels neighbourhood that de Meeûs' father had initiated in the mid-nineteenth century. The convent complex, very similar to the one in the *Rue des Sols* and with an exact copy of the Salazar chapel, was erected on the *Rue Van Maerlant*, barely two kilometres away from the old Salazar site.[46]

Simultaneously with the expropriation problem, a controversial inheritance issue also affected the public perception of the deceased de Meeûs. Some of de Meeûs' brothers and cousins claimed parts of Anna's family heritage, in particular the convent estate in Watermael, built on land of her mother. Their complaints were found to be unsubstantiated in three court proceedings, but for two years liberal newspapers had a field day with what they saw as a classic example of ecclesiastical greed and underhand strategies. Even some Catholic newspapers referred somewhat ironically to 'Countess de Meeûs' millions'.[47] In the midst of the requisition and inheritance problems, an extensive biography of Anna de Meeûs was not an immediate concern. Only after the First World War did new plans take shape. Initially, the Redemptorist Paulin Lejeune was asked to write it, but it is unclear to what extent he really cooperated in the project.[48] Eventually the work appeared during the Second World War, written by an anonymous sister of the congregation itself.[49] In the preface to the publication, Archbishop Van Roey praised "la femme d'élite qui a joué un rôle considérable dans la vie et l'apostolat catholiques" and put her forward as an example "aux personnes qui cherchent, au milieu du monde à

---

46 ARE, *Plans couvent Rue Van Maerlant*; SAB, Public Works, Construction Permits, 10131: Plans of the convent in Etterbeek. After the departure of the sisters, the convent was converted at the end of the twentieth century into office and library buildings for the European Commission and the European Union. The chapel became an ecumenical place of worship. See: Coomans, "Veel zorgen, weinig zorg", 158.
47 *Het Handelsblad van Antwerpen* (29 Jan. 1907).
48 Paulin Lejeune (1851-1928) was a well-known retreat preacher in Salazar and published various spiritual works and lives of saints; see: ACSSR-NB, 5.3.1. Lejeune, 268: Letters.
49 *Anna de Meeûs, fondatrice de l'Institut des religieuses de l'adoration perpétuelle. 1823-1904. D'après ses écrits et les récits de ses contemporains* (1941).

connaître et à pratiquer la voie de la perfection chrétienne".[50] It proofed once again that the revivalist legacy of active religious engagement in the world survived into the mid-twentieth century.

In spite of de Meeûs' exceptional reputation, plans for a canonisation process were never completed. It was contemplated within the congregation, but "un rédemptoriste nous suggérait que notre Mère était trop 'robuste' pour être sainte."[51] Anna de Meeûs, like Kestre, did not conform to the humble and submissive ideal image of a female saint. Unlike her old rival and other founders of Eucharistic congregations, de Meeûs did not have a history of extreme suffering or martyrdom either. Her old friend, the Spanish congregation founder Desmaisières, died a heroic death in 1865 as a result of her efforts for Spanish cholera victims. She was canonised in 1934. Another contemporary, the French founder Dubouché was mutilated for life after she saved the Blessed Sacrament from a fire. She was declared venerable in 1913. Eucharistic devotion, a humble life of sacrifice and humility, and 'an odour of sanctity' went hand in hand. Anna de Meeûs devoted her whole life to the first, but her self-confidence and her strategies to gain power probably obstructed the image of the second too much, making the third finally unattainable. In that sense, de Meeûs' robustness foundered posthumously on the rigid, idealised images of obedience and sacrifice.

Wilhelmina Telghuys: always independent

After Anna de Meeûs' death in 1904, only Wilhelmina Telghuys remained of the group of four women. At the beginning of the twentieth century, she was the head of a medium-sized Antwerp congregation, with about one hundred sisters and three convents. The branches in Antwerp and Kontich, which together offered shelter or education to about 450 (orphan) girls, were supplemented in 1896 with a convent in Turnhout. Telghuys had only accepted the assignment, which involved running a kindergarten, youth work for girls, catechism classes and a small housecraft school, following repeated requests from local benefactors, the Boone family, and after difficult negotiations with them. Eventually, Telghuys not only succeeded in establishing a thriving third convent, she also found a fertile recruitment ground in Turnhout. Seventeen sisters from the Turnhout region entered the novitiate in Antwerp in the first decade after 1896, more than a fifth of the total number of entrances in that period.[52]

50 *Anna de Meeûs*, 7-8. Jozef Van Roey (1874-1961) became archbishop of Mechelen in 1926, succeeding Archbishop Mercier (1906-1926).
51 ARE, *Chronique 1932-1956*.
52 ADHH, 69: Reports (14 July, 24 July and 8 Sept. 1895, 5 July 1898, 29 Sept. 1899, 20 Feb. 1903).

The growth of the congregation was crowned at the end of the nineteenth century with the construction of a new neo-Gothic convent on the *Sint-Jorisvest* in Antwerp and a neo-Gothic chapel in Kontich. In the meantime, the laundry of the 'soap nuns' in Kontich became well-known in the early twentieth century for its use of a unique bleaching process. Both the construction work and the laundry necessitated that Telghuys and some of her close associates maintain close contact with the outside world.[53] At the same time, the superior kept up an autonomous and isolationist course in Antwerp. Conflicts with the Antwerp Catholic School Committee and the parish clergy of *Sint-Augustinus* flared up repeatedly. More than once, Telghuys 'bought' her freedom by sponsoring parish activities or the boys' school outside the convent complex. In 1907 she took over the parish school of *Sint-Augustinus*, which had fallen into disrepair, but only on the express condition that its management be entrusted exclusively to her sisters.[54] Despite her desire for independence, Telghuys was obliged by the diocesan authorities to revise her reservations about normal school training. Forced by Mechelen, and with a view to extending the housecraft and textile classes in Antwerp, she finally went along with the general trend towards the professionalisation of Catholic education. After nearly three decades of refusal, she again sent sisters to the teacher training institute of the Ursulines in Onze-Lieve-Vrouw-Waver and to housecraft courses in Brussels.[55] With the professionalisation of her vocational sewing, ironing and laundry courses in Antwerp, Telghuys laid the foundation for the future commercial school of the congregation.

In September 1907, Telghuys, who at this stage was almost completely deaf and half blind, had a bad fall. She died a few weeks later, on November 7th at the age of 83. Her funeral procession to the cemetery in Mortsel, where the congregation had a communal plot, attracted hundreds of spectators.[56] Eulogies and obituaries in the Antwerp newspapers focused almost exclusively on her apostolic achievements. Given her prestige as a socially engaged religious, she was remembered more as *Mère Jeanne* than as Wilhelmina Telghuys.[57] Again, biblical proverbs about the "mulierem fortem" endorsed the legacy of the revival. They were repeated by Father Ernest Pauwels in his 1908 biography of Telghuys, published at the request of Telghuys' successor Sœur Vincent De Beukelaer (1907-1910).[58] In comments on this work in the Antwerp

---

53 ADHH, 69: Report (10 Oct. 1907).
54 ADHH, 69: Report (19 June 1907).
55 ADHH, 69: Report (24 Nov. 1897, 19 June 1898, 21 Sept. 1900).
56 The congregation's crypt was later destroyed during the bombing of Mortsel during the Second World War, see: Scheerlinck, *Mère Jeanne*, 22, fn. 14.
57 *Het Handelsblad van Antwerpen* (16 Nov. 1907).
58 Pauwels, *Mère Jeanne*, 158. Ernest Pauwels (1847-1909) was a diocesan priest of the Diocese of Ghent and teacher at the *Sint-Jozefinstituut* in Sint-Niklaas. He was one of the retreat preachers and confessors for Telghuys' congregation.

Wilhelmina Telghuys remained an inspiring figure within her congregation. On the 100th anniversary of her birthday in 1924, the large Antwerp convent community of professed choir sisters, lay sisters, novices and postulants gathered around her portrait.
[Photograph – 1924 – ADHH, 255]

Catholic Press, Telghuys was often mentioned together with her old friend Constance Teichmann, the most famous Catholic *dame d'œuvres* in the city.[59] The decision in the twentieth century to name the above-mentioned '*Mère Jeanne*' commercial school after Telghuys was also testament to her reputation. Women founders whose apostolates carried their name were a rare phenomenon in nineteenth- and early-twentieth-century Belgium.[60]

Just as with Cornet, Kestre, de Meeûs and so many other founders, Telghuys' fame as an active religious persisted. However, she too was hard to fit into the imposed template of humility and obedience. Later projects for a new biography of Telghuys were never completed. Father Jules Verest, the Jesuit who was the regular retreat preacher of the *Dienstmaagden*, provided a second manuscript in the 1920s.[61] Verest based his text largely on the work of Pauwels, but he struggled with Telghuys' stubborn character. He was pressured by the superior Marie-Joseph Dierckx (1910-1950) to conceal Telghuys' conflicts

---

59   *Het Handelsblad van Antwerpen* (28 Nov. 1908).
60   Some examples. In Antwerp there was the aforementioned Van Celst congregation. Cicercule Paridaens lived on in Leuven in her *Paridaensinstituut*. In Ypres, the name of founder Clara Lamotte (1726-1772) was for a long time associated with a local educational institution. In Ghent, the *Crombeeninstituut* of the *Franciscanessen* referred to its seventeenth-century founder, Joanna Francisca Crombeen (1652-1724).
61   Jules Verest (1858-1941) was an experienced author. He published a literature handbook that was widely distributed in Belgium and he was active in debates on Catholic education and the classical humanities, see: Dusausoit, "Les jésuites et l'argent", 258.

with the parish priests of *Sint-Augustinus*, but he protested, "il est contre mon caractère et contre toutes mes habitudes d'altérer ou de dissimuler la vérité".[62] In the end, he did not mention the conflict, but he also refused to give permission for the work to be published. The diocesan priest, Jan Bergen (1883-1963), who became director of the congregation in 1941, made a new attempt in the early 1950s. More than his predecessors, he was interested in the Marian spirituality of Telghuys, presumably because the proposed publication was part of the congregation's plans to have Mère Jeanne be recognised as a Servant of God. However, neither Bergen's plans, nor the fledgling canonisation process got off to a good start. Just as with the perception of de Meeûs, Telghuys' self-confidence and independence probably stood in the way of the ultimate ecclesiastical recognition. Though genuinely impressed by Telghuys' mission, Bergen finally had to conclude with some resignation, "she remains always independent". As with the other founders in our narrative and despite the acknowledgement of her life of religious and social engagement, entrepreneurship and leadership, the ultimate validation of her legacy was finally determined by the spirit of sacrifice, suffering and humility that she had accepted, used and even promoted by her double-voiced clerical and gender discourse.[63]

---

62 ADHH, 18: Verest to Dierckx (15 Aug. 1921). Superior Marie-Joseph (Marie-Colette Dierckx, 1869-1960) was one of the many from Turnhout to enter the congregation. She joined in 1897 and together with Telghuys became one of the leading figures in the history of the Antwerp *Dienstmaagden*.
63 ADHH, 41: Notes of Jan Bergen.

CONCLUSION
A STUDY IN AMBIGUITY

The double-voiced dialectic between submission and autonomy was the prominent feature in the lives of de Meeûs, Kestre, Cornet and Telghuys. Both extremes were alternating poles of a complex field of tension that pervades the centuries-old history of religious women and women religious. The same ambiguous relationship between modesty and power has already been highlighted by the pioneering scholar Bynum Walker in the case of medieval female mystics, and has been forcefully characterised by Weber writing about Teresa of Avila's strategy of "self-depreciation" as one of her "covert strategies of empowerment".[1] The field of tension also influenced the ideas and actions of eighteenth-century religious, who fluctuated "between gratitude and submission on the one hand and a desperate grasp of freedom on the other".[2] In the nineteenth century, the same ambiguity emerged in studies on French women and emerging social Catholicism, religiously inspired Belgian women writers and Anglican activists for the education of women.[3] Last but not least, the tension is also reflected in recent international research on the complex world of nineteenth-century female religious, which was strikingly

---

1   Weber, *Teresa of Avila*, 15.
2   Kirkus, "Yes, my lord", 174.
3   McMillan, "Woman in Social Catholicism", 467; Reymenants, *Marie Elisabeth Belpaire*, 123; Green, *Educating Women*, 1-2.

characterised by Mangion in 2008 as a "paradoxical space" with sisters who were "active agents in manipulating".[4]

The outlines of the paradoxical space in which the four Belgian female founders operated as double-voiced agents have been sketched in the preceding chapters. In this conclusion, those outlines are defined more precisely by focusing on six determinants that were characteristic of the special social niche for female religious that was suggested in the introduction. The analysis of the constant dialectic between female weakness and power in relation to (1) religious and social frameworks, (2) female spirituality, (3) gender relations within the Church, (4) socio-economic determinants, (5) relations between women (6) and the perspective of female emancipation ultimately provides arguments for definitively characterising this niche as a small, elitist, demanding, but above all ambiguous '*hortus conclusus*'.

The 'weaker sex' as a strong social and clerical link

The success or failure of the four founders as enterprising women was to an important extent dependent on their interaction with diverse and radically changing social contexts. Their own lives moved from the committed enthusiasm and sensitive Romanticism of the revival, through the increasing social and ideological tensions of the mid-nineteenth century to the militancy of the culture wars. Inevitably, these three eras also echoed the memory of another historical convulsion. Born in the 1820s, the four women were already a generation away from the French Revolution. Still, through the memories of older family members, acquaintances and, not least, the religious sisters in their convent boarding schools, they were continuously being confronted with the legacy of the Revolution, which was as traumatic as it was appealing. These religious 'foremothers' were a living reminder of the power of the 'weaker' sex as an important social and clerical link. As women in a struggling Church, they assumed a role as guardians and agents of the Catholic faith.

The 'foremothers' had prepared the way for a prominent female share in the religious revival of the second third of the nineteenth century. In the young Belgian state, pressing socio-economic needs, constitutional liberties and the political climate of 'unionism' created a framework for an unprecedented expansion of female convent life. The pronounced commitment of the revival to social engagement, religious atonement and the restoration of a harmonious Christian society gave a decisive boost to Catholic acceptance of apostolic or

---

4   Mangion, *Contested Identities*, 233-235. Similar analyses and characterisations in: Van Heijst and Derks, "Godvrucht en gender", 25-32; Eijt, *Religieuze vrouwen*, 35, 414-145; Sprows Cummings, *New Woman*, 62-63; Stogdon, "Expressions of Self-Surrender", 160; Langlois, *Catholicisme*, 209.

socially active religious women. Within that framework, the frail chatelaine Anna de Meeûs was given chances and incentives for social commitment, Wilhelmina Telghuys could venture away from the path of bourgeois propriety and reserve, while Fanny Kestre escaped from her own depressing family situation. All of them became basic links in a developing social and ecclesiastical system: de Meeûs for the poor rural churches, Telghuys among the impoverished girls and women of Antwerp and Kestre in the secularised working-class areas of Brussels.

Antoinette Cornet joined the fast-growing world of women's teaching congregations, the most typical expression of the revival's cross-fertilisation between female religious engagement and social and clerical demands. However, the active and congregational model of female religious life was not an invention of her time. During the Counter Reformation, communities of socially active *filles dévotes* had already existed throughout Europe. As in the nineteenth century, they grew out of the turmoil of a Church in crisis and were a response to acute socio-economic needs. The Southern Netherlands had a strong tradition of spiritual women, beguines and communities of teaching sisters, which prepared the way for the nineteenth-century founders. Cornet's congregation in Alsemberg, with its roots in both the Ignatian tradition and in the beguinage of Nivelles, was a striking illustration of this.

By mid-century the four women were directing their initial, somewhat naive engagement into more firmly established Catholic charities and religious institutes. Determined and idealistic, they fought a battle to realise their own ambitions, but also had to adjust pragmatically and opportunistically to changing ways of thinking. Seriously affected by the general conservative response to the 1848 wave of revolutions and the ecclesiastical condemnation of the secular and liberal post-revolutionary society in 1864, their role as agents of the faith became institutionalised in an efficient, combative and disciplinarian religious vanguard. Their success, however, required greater conformity to the guidelines and strategies of the church authorities and male supervisors.

This double dynamic of militancy and containment became even more obvious after 1870. The era of European culture wars pushed the founders into the ranks of an ultramontane and anti-modern crusade. At the same time, the siege and victim mentality of a frightened Church led to an increasing 'conventualisation' and a deepening aversion to secular society. Nevertheless, opportunities for autonomy and development could still be found. If the revival had paved the way for the Church's acceptance of active religious, then the ultramontane crusade led to a definitive anchoring of the congregational model as a modern means for an anti-modern cause. In an increasingly centralising Church, that symbiosis between militant clerical strategies and the potential of female religious life led the most influential and wealthiest of the women religious to the centre of the Catholic Church itself, the pontifical curia in Rome.

The role of religious women as guardians and disseminators of the faith was also vindicated by the Church's turn towards the people in the 1880s. Initiatives of the female founders in popular and worker milieus made some of the founders into an important link between the Church and the masses, albeit within unavoidable paternalistic and religious contours. For Telghuys, the Church's growing attention to the social question was a catalyst for her semi-industrial business for women. Kestre was given increasing recognition for her original catechesis work among the working classes, even though this became fully evident only after her death in 1882. During her lifetime, on the contrary, she had mainly experienced the rigidity of clerical control and gender conventions.

In the last quarter of the nineteenth century, all four founders were confronted with conventualisation and stronger clerical supervision. Although these developments could be curbed by a double-voiced discourse or a strategic use of alliances, the pressure became increasingly more compelling. The clerical containment of the dynamic and spontaneous convent life of the revival occurred earlier in countries where it had grown spectacularly, like Belgium and France, or in Italy, where female congregations became the first 'laboratory' for intensifying Roman regularisation. That containment is less apparent in female convent life in more outlying Catholic communities, like England, the Netherlands or the United States. The missionary spirit of these 'young' Churches seemed to have supported the revivalist dynamics longer, until the early twentieth-century changes of *Conditae a Christo* (1900) and the new Code of Canon Law (1917) marked a more significant turning point. For the context of the United States it was even labelled by historian Mary Ewens as 'the Great Repression' of female convent life.[5]

A female spirituality of humble penance and powerful passion

In the slipstream of the apostolic commitment to Church and society, the four women developed an emotional and Christocentric spirituality of penance and atonement. They wanted to 'repair' the humiliation and pain that Christ had suffered because of the apostasy and indifference to religion in the aftermath of the French Revolution. Kestre and de Meeûs based their catechetical and liturgical apostolate on an emotional, affective and penitential adoration of the Eucharist. Telghuys saw in the caring, selfless and suffering figure of

---

5 Radford, "Catholic women", 23-24; Mangion, "Women, Religious Ministry", 86; O'Brien, "Religious life", 123; Ewens, "Removing the Veil", 272-273; Van Heijst, Derks and Monteiro, *Ex Caritate*, 610-611; Eijt, Religieuze vrouwen, 103-106.

Our Lady of the Seven Sorrows a spiritual stimulus for her efforts on behalf of orphan and working-class girls. Cornet, with her ascetic and eclectic spirituality composed of Marian devotion, adoration of the Blessed Sacrament and devotion to the Sacred Heart reflected the boundless emotional religiosity of the time.

In more than one sense, this reparation spirituality seems to confirm the thesis of a feminised – emotional, humble and subservient – nineteenth-century religiosity. Still, this is just one side of the coin. The paradigm of an ardent, active embrace of suffering that these four women all embodied does not at all conform with the traditional image of female passivity. Even the ultramontane victim spirituality, which was a darker and more bitter version of the penance and reparation discourse of the revival, remained above all a call to action. Self-denial, penance and female suffering held together the action and passion ethos of nineteenth-century piety.

By committing themselves to humble penance, the founders created an accepted, respected and stimulating space in which the development and fulfilment of their ambitions and strategies became possible. That paradox was expressed very strikingly in the Eucharistic piety of Kestre and de Meeûs. The devotion to the Blessed Sacrament was penitential and sorrowful, but at the same time prestigious and elitist. It required perseverance in the passive but passionate hours of worship and was at the same time a relatively unregulated terrain that provided opportunities for female agency. In several countries, female founders could benefit from the potential of the Eucharistic devotion to gain spiritual prestige and develop forms of apostolate typically connected with it, such as liturgical workshops, catechesis, retreats and pious lay associations. Some of them, like de Meeûs and the Franco-Belgian Emilie d'Oultremont, used the Eucharistic devotion to advance a powerful agency that reached to distant mission territories as well as into the Vatican itself.

However, there were limits to the emancipating power of the penance discourse. By engaging in a model of suffering and self-denial, female religious put themselves into a straitjacket that could serve as an instrument for male patronage and containment. It confirmed female stereotypes and exposed passionate women to male criticism of "les dames illusionnées", referring both to their excessive devotional practices and their 'illusions' about gaining a more prominent position in the Church. Kestre was distrusted by many for her visions, while for a long time Telghuys had to subordinate her own Marian devotion to the spiritual preferences of her male co-founders. Spiritual entrepreneurship had to happen anonymously and within the 'safe' framework of saintly lives, devotional books and sermons. The women were denied the right to publicly participate in church debates at congresses, prize-givings or retreats. Cornet, de Meeûs and Telghuys were allowed to adopt the pronounced active character and hierarchical structure of the Ignatian model, but they did not gain equal access to the Society's intellectual and spiritual prestige. Both the '*manifestation de conscience*' and a sound theological formation lay beyond their reach. Nineteenth-century emotional and penitential spirituality then offered a path to elevation and prestige, but also to lasting subordination.

A gendered clerical 'Passion Play'

The same duality also manifested itself in the area of clerical and gender relations. The male protagonists in the foundation narratives were inevitable actors on the scene, as authoritarian advisers or as fatherly allies. At the same time they were used as pawns in a chess game of female ambitions. Cornet forced through her request to escape from her hopeless situation in Alsemberg by stressing her weak health and vulnerable state of mind to the church authorities in Mechelen. Kestre and Telghuys acquired protection from unwanted male interference by showing themselves ardent and obedient supporters of Archbishop Dechamps' essentially restrictive policy of conventualisation. Anna de Meeûs submitted herself obediently to Rome and saw herself liberated from Jesuit confessors. Ecclesiastical and human relationships also opened the door to manipulation. The post-revolutionary Church, with its continuous struggle between regular and secular clergy for power, resources and people, offered opportunities for shifting alliances. Cornet and Telghuys set the Jesuit Legrelle up against interfering parish priests. Anna de Meeûs first sought an intimate and fruitful association with the Jesuits, but later broke off all contact. She subsequently used the services of the Redemptorists, the French curial prelate Chaillot and the always obliging Dechamps.

The drama of church affairs was not just a power play, it was also a type of Passion Play and a re-enactment of deep human feelings. Strategical ambitions were certainly at play, but desires for companionship, for genuine submission to a kindred soul or a shared respect for the rules and conventions of the Catholic Church were equally important. This emotional aspect has too often been neglected in traditional institutional histories with their emphasis on organisations, numbers and structures and disappeared from many congregation narratives focused exclusively on the role of the male founder. It was also missed in many feminist critiques on the suppressing characteristics of religion. The stories of the four women in this discourse clearly show that self-fulfilment and agency – if understood, as explained in the introduction, as the capacity for action within structures of docility and submission and not merely as resistance against it – were not only to be found in female power or authority, but also in conformity to Church laws and male superiors and participation in a broader clerical and social project.

The biographical approach used in this study highlighted this male-female interaction and the emotional processes and has proved to be the "signpost pointing the way to a plurality of interpretations" mentioned in the introduction.[6] The unpredictability of personal relationships of affection, respect, envy, manipulation and rivalry were sometimes stronger than the contextual legalities. In the case of these four female founders, this constant field of tension proves that nineteenth-century clerical gender relationships within the convent world cannot be reduced to the traditional image of dominant male founders and obedient female handmaids.

Kestre did not have the subtility of Telghuys or de Meeûs, nor their diversified church networks. However, her vulnerability and naivety, combined with her strong character, appealed to Dechamps' own sensibility. Balancing between the world of Romantic revival Catholics and the divine victims of ultramontanism, Dechamps was attracted to Kestre's supernatural experiences. He found in Kestre not only a spiritual daughter but also a kindred spirit and a source of inspiration. In the same way, the spiritual father-daughter relationship between Boone and de Meeûs did not prevent the Jesuit from being truly impressed by de Meeûs' ideas. She also offered him the chance to have a second career and a *tabula rasa* from previous problems and temptations. Legrelle was critical of female aspirations to power and seriously altered the initial identity of the congregations of Cornet and Telghuys, but at the same time he did not hesitate to defend and formally recognise their autonomy. In that sense, the relativity of the gender relationships in this study is consistent with recent comments on the traditional feminisation thesis, which point to the persistent presence of paradoxical, diffuse and overlapping images of masculinities and feminities in nineteenth-century religious discourse.[7]

This is also confirmed by the very paradoxical relationship of the four female founders with their own role as women and their own femininity. They emphasised their humble and subordinate position towards the male protagonists in the narrative, while at the same time expressing bold ambitions and assuming stubborn characteristics and tactics. As was the case in their spiritual universe, by making humility and weakness distinct aspects of their profiles and strategies, they confirmed traditional gender relationships. When they ventured into the shadowy area of those conventions, the humility they ascribed to themselves was turned against them and they were accused of being "pas assez femme" or "too robust to be saint". Anna de Meeûs was mocked for her dictatorial, 'unwomanly' behaviour and her power ambitions in Rome. The same fate befell Telghuys when she followed an independent, isolationist course in Antwerp. The complexity of maintaining a balance between humility and autonomy surfaced even more in the late nineteenth- and early twen-

6 "Wegwijzer naar meerduidigheid": Derks, "Vrouwen", 110.
7 Van Osselaer, *The Pious Sex*, 237-240; Pasture, "Beyond the feminization thesis", 12-17.

tieth-century perception of the four women. Despite, or perhaps because of their double-voiced discourse and robust actions, their narratives did not fit in easily within the humble model of female sanctity.

Apostolate, class and influential entourages: the levers for female agency

The posthumous perception of the founders not only reflected the ambiguity of female achievement on the one hand and persistent patronising on the other, it also gave an insight into the mechanisms that fuelled the paradox. On the spiritual and clerical scene, the tensions were many, but the social importance of the four women was much less disputed and created genuine opportunities for recognition and initiative. In the apostolate field, gender conventions played in favour of the female founders. Religious formation, liturgical needlework, care and education were fields traditionally identified with women. A framework thus emerged in which female entrepreneurship could take on forms that were original (Kestre's catechesis work), international (de Meeûs' work for poor churches), professional (Cornet's modern boarding-school education) and even semi-industrial (Telghuys' laundry). Moreover, apostolic success was often a buffer against criticism and extreme supervision, from both men and women.

This interaction between success in 'female' apostolic fields, prestige and development was not an exclusively Belgian phenomenon. Studies for France, the Netherlands, and the German and Italian regions show the same link, indicating the great needs of a Church in recovery and of a society in socio-economic transition.[8] Within the unfinished structures of the English and American mission Churches, the same mechanisms allowed for even greater recognition of women's socio-religious initiatives. This was translated into both Vaughan's appreciation for de Meeûs' sisters – "direction and guidance and superintendence are needed such as the nuns can give" – and a greater public and more intellectual role for some English and American congregation founders.[9] Figures such as Fanny Taylor and Elizabeth Hayes, for example, made an important contribution to the Catholic press, different from the anonymous writings of Telghuys, the copy-and-paste fragments of Cornet's *Questionnaire spirituel* and the applauded but passive appearance of de Meeûs at the Eucharistic Congress in Brussels.[10]

---

8   Langlois, *Le catholicisme au féminin*, 634-342; Eijt, *Religieuze vrouwen*, 59; Van Heijst, Derks and Monteiro, *Ex Caritate*, 182-187; Meiwes, *Arbeiterinnen*, 247-268; Rocca, *Donne religiose*, 97-107.
9   Vaughan to Herbert (19 Oct. 1879), published in: Shane, *Lettres*, 312. See also Part III.
10 Shaw, *Elizabeth Hayes*, 62-63; O'Brien, "Taylor", 40. Confirmed also in De Giorgio, "La bonne catholique", 178; Mangion, *Contested Identities*, 120-123.

The great social and ecclesiastical needs of the nineteenth century also highlighted the importance of another factor: the power of money. The founders' chances for autonomous action were directly proportional to their access to financial resources. Cornet was forced into a demanding and demeaning alliance with the rich and ill-tempered noblewoman Marie Vilain XIIII because of her lack of resources and ambitious projects. By contrast, the financial strength of Telguys and de Meeûs opened up many opportunities, especially after the difficult founding years. Telghuys' laundry income shielded her independence from the interference of the parish clergy of *Sint-Augustinus*. Anna de Meeûs made many parish priests of poor rural villages dependent on the liturgical apostolate of her association. A similar service for missionary institutes assured her of the reciprocal services of important male orders and the prestigious rewards of nineteenth-century missionary zeal. Moreover, in the context of the pecuniary troubles of a Roman Church threatened by Italian revolutionaries, the purse of her wealthy family opened up a successful path to international expansion and a quickly granted exempt status.

The financial differences between the four founders paralleled their class differences. The middle-class origins of Cornet and Kestre could not match the urban and elite backgrounds of Telghuys and de Meeûs. A high social class was essential in forming influential social and ecclesiastical relationships. Equally important were the urban networks of *dames d'œuvres* with sufficient resources and time to support the sisters. Among the Antwerp upper bourgeoisie, Telghuys found a clientele for her laundry and employment for the working-class girls in her care. The ties of the de Meeûs family reached deep into elite Catholic circles at home and abroad. These elite bonds constituted the framework of the early *Œuvre des Églises Pauvres*, which Anna de Meeûs expanded into a powerful instrument for further networking and international development. Her unique relationship with Pope Leo XIII himself went back to meetings with him in the salons of her parents' castle in Argenteuil. The elite character of her network was as important as its diversity, which allowed de Meeûs to make the above-mentioned strategic coalition shifts. Kestre, on the other hand, had an influential and respected advocate in Dechamps with whom she was intensely but also exclusively associated. This relationship made her very dependent and allowed few alternative alliances in times of disagreement or conflict.

The class distinctions and the related differences in networks and financial capacity were an international phenomenon. Langlois pointed to the determining influence of class and networking in France on "le degré de liberté dans la fondation elle-même".[11] For the German and Dutch contexts, Meiwes and Eijt stressed the importance of the bourgeois families and finan-

---

11   Langlois, *Le catholicisme au féminin*, 290.

cial resources of female founders in achieving their ambitions.[12] In England, the 'journalists' Hayes and Taylor came from a prosperous middle-class background of Anglican clergymen, with access to the intellectuals of the Oxford Movement. Their progress contrasted sharply with the life stories of founders from a much more modest background who struggled all their lives with "the male Victorian ascendancy" and criticism.[13] A similar contrast was evident in Belgium. Despite Kestre's and Cornet's material problems, all four of the founders in this study had a privileged position by contrast to many founders and superiors of modest rural congregations. By nineteenth-century standards for women, they had all received a solid education and could rely on their experiences as *dames d'œuvres* or – in the case of Cornet – as a boarding-school director. Although specific reference material is scarce, some studies show that it was more difficult for inexperienced, poorly skilled women from the lower social classes to take on a role during the foundation process that was not pre-determined by the male founder.[14] Their network was often limited to a one-sided and subservient relationship with the local parish priest, with no opportunity to take advantage of the prestige and sensitivities of influential clerics as Dechamps, Boone or Legrelle.

Social distinctions were also evident in the policies of the four founders towards their own sisters. The difference between the choir and lay or work sisters clearly paralleled relations in the wider society. Rooted in the discourse of self-denial and obedience, a secure but anonymous and subservient life awaited many of the work sisters. They were given hardly any opportunity to take their own lives in hand and were reduced to the status of female labourers. The ordinary sisters at the bottom of the hierarchy paid the price for the prestige, influence and power which the founders and general superiors derived from the numerical strength and hierarchical structures of their congregations. It is very significant that Kestre, who was probably the most democratic and empathetic of the superiors, was also head of the congregation that had the most difficult and shortest existence of the four religious institutes studied here.

However, from a comparative perspective, these conclusions cannot be simply applied generally. Within the Belgian context, there are clear indications that opportunities for development were more promising in large teaching congregations with an elaborate functional differentiation and in socially more homogenous female religious institutes.[15] In congregations without the distinction between lay and choir sisters, boundaries were more diffuse

12   Meiwes, *Arbeiterinnen*, 38-51; Eijt, *Religieuze vrouwen*, 53-64.
13   Hamer, *Elizabeth Prout*, 125.
14   Vanderstraeten and Preneel, *175 jaar Zusters Christelijke Scholen*, 50-55; Premereur, *Om Christus' Rijk*, 10-15.
15   Wynants, *Les Sœurs de la Providence*, 31-33; Christens, *100 jaar Heilig-Hartinstituut*, 365-367; Strobbe and Suenens, *Zusters Kindsheid Jesu*, 58.

and societal realities and apostolic demands prevailed over social segregation. They were the Belgian equivalent of many institutes in the United States, where the traditional distinction between lay and choir sisters clashed with the egalitarian aspirations of American society or with the focus of native English congregations on the mostly lower-class Catholic community.[16]

A network of *dames d'œuvres*

Another factor linking most middle- and upper-class nineteenth-century founders was their experience as *dames d'œuvres*. The socio-religious commitment of lay women of the revival to various groups of needy people determined the subsequent careers of Kestre, de Meeûs and Telghuys. It provided their future institutes with an apostolic framework, long before there was a distinctive spiritual framework. In addition, their prior history as *dames d'œuvres* laid the foundation for a network of like-minded, religiously inspired women both inside and outside the convent walls. The importance of this female network was not negligible. It provided the founders with benefactors and worldly advocates, with confidantes and with their first fellow sisters. It is probably no coincidence that Cornet, the only one of the four founders without a past as a *dame d'œuvres*, literally and figuratively had to seek far and wide to gain female support. Her limited group of like-minded women consisted exclusively of fellow sisters from Alsemberg and moreover, in the first decade after the founding, was rent by jealousy and personal ambitions.

Indeed, as in the relationships with men, the mutual relations between religiously inspired women were far from straightforward. At the micro level, there was a strong emotional female bonding that transcended the convent walls. The founders derived opportunities from their old networks, but they also offered lay women a platform for development and fulfilment within the structures of their apostolates. However, from an emancipation perspective, the space that was created was again a relative one. Their narratives rarely included talk of forming an explicit female front against male supervision. Driven by their own ambitions and emotions, neither the founders nor the lay women shrank from competing with one another for resources, power and (male) attention. In their zeal to participate in the reparation movement of the revival or the ultramontane crusade, women often tripped over one another and failed to support each other when faced with male critics or opposition.

Moreover, the female founders increasingly tried to guide and control lay women. Both the morally conservative turn of society after 1848 as well as the ultramontane siege mentality contributed to ensuring that female religious became an instrument in the disciplining and guardianship of their own sex.

---

16 Ewens, "Women in the Convent", 19; O'Brien, "Religious Life", 115-117.

Participation in the apostolate of de Meeûs' lay association was possible only under the strict supervision of the sisters and the stifling domination of the superior general. Telghuys offered working-class girls and servants the opportunity to be apostles in their own circles, but only within the pious, respectable and ascetic mould that Telghuys imposed on them. Kestre did not hesitate to lecture mothers from the Catholic elite and middle classes for tolerating their daughters' worldly lifestyles. This hierarchisation between the female founders and Catholic lay women was propped up by the increasing numbers and organisational strength of the convents. The army of willing, flexible and obedient sisters under the founders' command could be used for the benefit but also to the detriment of women. Telghuys thwarted the initiatives of her own lay teachers, while de Meeûs repeatedly attempted to take over pious associations led by lay women.

The female founders differed from most lay women in their circles not only in their numerical strength but also in their changing relationships with men. A comparison with female benefactors repeatedly shows that married women could not escape the dominance of their husbands, even in their socio-religious involvements. The ecclesiastical male control imposed on female congregation founders was not any tighter than was male dominance in marriage or the bourgeois family. Female independence was problematic in every nineteenth-century context, both inside and outside the immediate contours of the Church. An important difference, in my view, is the wealth of opportunities, both strategic and emotional, that female religious derived from their aforementioned ability to change alliances. Married women could not exchange their husbands, had little redress against abusive power, or had to wait for the death or misfortune of their husbands to truly come to the fore. The female founders, by contrast, could use male clerics to escape from the demands of their families or from hopeless personal situations. They also had better or at least multiple chances of meeting kindred spirits.

Analysing the female networks of the four religious, there appears to be just one category of lay women that could equal the female founders in agency and influence. A small group of wealthy, unmarried women from the upper bourgeoisie and the aristocracy could control and expand their socio-religious initiatives, fortunes and relationships with relative autonomy. Constance Teichmann did so in Antwerp, Marie Vilain XIIII in Bazel and Julie Desmanet de Biesme – after a short sojourn in the convent – in de Meeûs' association. Some of them explicitly stated that both marriage and convent life were insuperable obstacles to female accomplishment and fulfilment. Still, they too paid a price for their independence. Social isolation was a constant threat for single women from which the founders escaped because of their religious status. Even Constance Teichmann, who became famous as the 'Angel of Antwerp', worried she would be mocked for being an old spinster. Marie Vilain XIIII ended her days as an isolated woman, who until de final moment of her life antagonised her family by promising a large part of her inheritance to her only confident, her servant.[17]

Female development: a means, not the end

The comparison with lay women indicates that the attitude of the female founders to opportunities for female development was not unequivocally positive. This ambiguity was woven into many of their activities. Their initiatives were often focused on improving the lives of various categories of women: housing and education for orphan girls, formation and material support for girls and women from working-class neighbourhoods, up-to-date boarding-school or vocational education. Sometimes the founders even assumed a pioneering role. Still, in their apostolates the founders' commitment to the cause and doctrine of the Church took precedence over their efforts for female development. Action on behalf of women was for them a means and not an end. They aimed to form better Christian mothers, respectable housewives and pious spouses who would form a buffer against apostasy and religious indifference. In line with prevailing ecclesiastical ideas, this was the key to material and moral improvement. Traditional gender relations, including the discourse of humility and self-denial as being the basis of a Christian life, were promoted and certainly not challenged. The founders' commitment to women's development was not part of a feminist struggle but of an ecclesiastical crusade. This can also be the explanation why some plainly authoritarian and conservative men like Boone still acted as advocates of Catholic women's development.

It remains a difficult exercise to place these four women in the historical narrative about female emancipation, especially since the laden but changing terminology in the field – emancipation, women's movement, feminism, etc. – often leads to additional complexities. In my view, on the nuanced scale of female emancipation used at the end of the twentieth century by the Dutch historians Van Drenth and De Haan, the four women can be placed on the fault line between female activism and the women's movement.[18] They were the midwives of the first phase – the public commitment of women to a broad social target group – and they made modest moves in the direction of the second – the organised commitment of women to women. However, their overpowering focus on the conservative ecclesiastical crusade prevailed over a full and explicit engagement to broaden the role of women in society. In that sense, they were at once friends and enemies of women's development

---

17 AFV, 5570-1: Vandenstaepele to Count Vilain XIIII (30 Dec. 1883, 23 Jan. 1883), Ernalstein to Countess Vilain XIIII (20 Nov. 1883).
18 Van Drenth and De Haan, *The Rise of Caring Power*, 167.

and loyal adepts of the Catholic and bourgeois discourse of the woman as the moral and religious guardian angel of men, children and the family. This validates the warning of contemporary gender and religious historians against depicting female emancipation as a linear and progressive process towards female independence.[19] Feminism, which Van Drenth and De Haan identify as the third phase in the struggle for political and legal equality for women, was not at all among the female founders' ambitions. It was not even part of their mind-sets.

A careful positioning of these four women in the aforementioned second phase of a gender-sensitive women's movement is further complicated by their limited gender consciousness. Explicit remarks about their own femininity or laments about unequal gender relationships between men and women are hardly to be found in their ego documents. With their double-voiced discourse, they indeed cultivated a model of humility, submissiveness and suffering, but without explicitly linking this to their being women. Gender-related comments came almost exclusively from the male protagonists of the story. Even the intimate personal documents in my research only allow for a nuanced attempt to explain the 'gender silence' of the four women religious. First, they confirm the findings in the international literature that nineteenth-century female religious did not problematise the prevailing gender views and were not to be seen as pioneers in a feminist struggle for political and social equality.[20] Second, in my view, the silence can also be seen as an expression of the 'muted voice' of double-voiced discourse. By not explicitly mentioning gender relations, they possibly made room for themselves to occasionally bypass the imposed restrictions. A third explanation for not making male-female relations explicit is also to be found in the warning of contemporary gender theorists and historians that "not all dichotomies must be necessarily binary".[21] Not every form of gender research can be fully accommodated within the tight duality of men and women. Perhaps the mould of humility and submission was not seen as an exclusively female restriction by the female founders. After all, it applied equally to some categories of men. Class distinctions and the clerical dichotomy between clergy and laity constituted equally definitive lines of demarcation as implicit or explicit gender differences. This explains why religious brothers or simple male visionaries, despite their masculinity, were forced into a straitjacket of humility and obedience as well.

---

19 Morgan, "Rethinking Religion", 123-124.
20 Clear, *Nuns*, XIX; Mangion, *Contested Identities*, 2; Brosnan, *Public Presence*, 474; Kane, *Gender Identities*, 122-124.
21 Krylova, "Gender Binary", 322-323. She also expanded on remarks that had been already expressed in the 1990s by Scott in "Fantasy of Feminist History".

The 'hortus conclusus' of a nineteenth-century female religious elite

If, on the basis of this research, definitive contours have to be outlined of the space in which the four nineteenth-century Belgian congregation founders operated, the image emerges of a small social niche, a *hortus conclusus* of exceptional female development. The niche was secluded and elitist, walled in by the persisting gender, social and clerical restrictions which the female founders had to deal with, but also confirmed by their own double-voiced discourse of humility, self-denial and obedience. At the same time, the *hortus conclusus* offered security and an upward perspective, symbolising the opportunities for female development and fulfilment that this exceptional place could offer to the small group of leading female religious who could gain access to it. Those who wanted to enter had to be socially, financially and relationally well positioned, but also had to show a great deal of daring, intelligence and opportunism. A constant alertness was required to forge and change alliances and to discern 'cracks' in the male domination of Church and society – in effect, looking for gaps in the walls of the *hortus conclusus* they had partly constructed themselves.

If the founders as religious women wanted to create a space with power, autonomy and development that was beyond the reach of most lay women and the ordinary sisters, they had to bypass gender conventions of female submissiveness as well as clerical conventions of religious obedience. At the same time, they implicitly institutionalised humility, self-denial, and suffering as a permanent form of discipline for women outside their own small niche. They did so because they believed in it themselves, but also used this ideal of subordination to negatively stereotype other women who were a threat to their own positions and initiatives. The *hortus conclusus* of de Meeûs, Telghuys, Kestre and Cornet was not a harmonious, female Garden of Eden, but a dizzying field of paradoxes, ambiguity and equivocation. Given these findings, the story of the four women – to use the words of James McMillan in characterising French women in social Catholicism – is above all a "study in ambiguity".[22]

---

22 McMillan, "Woman in Social Catholicism", 467.

TIMELINE

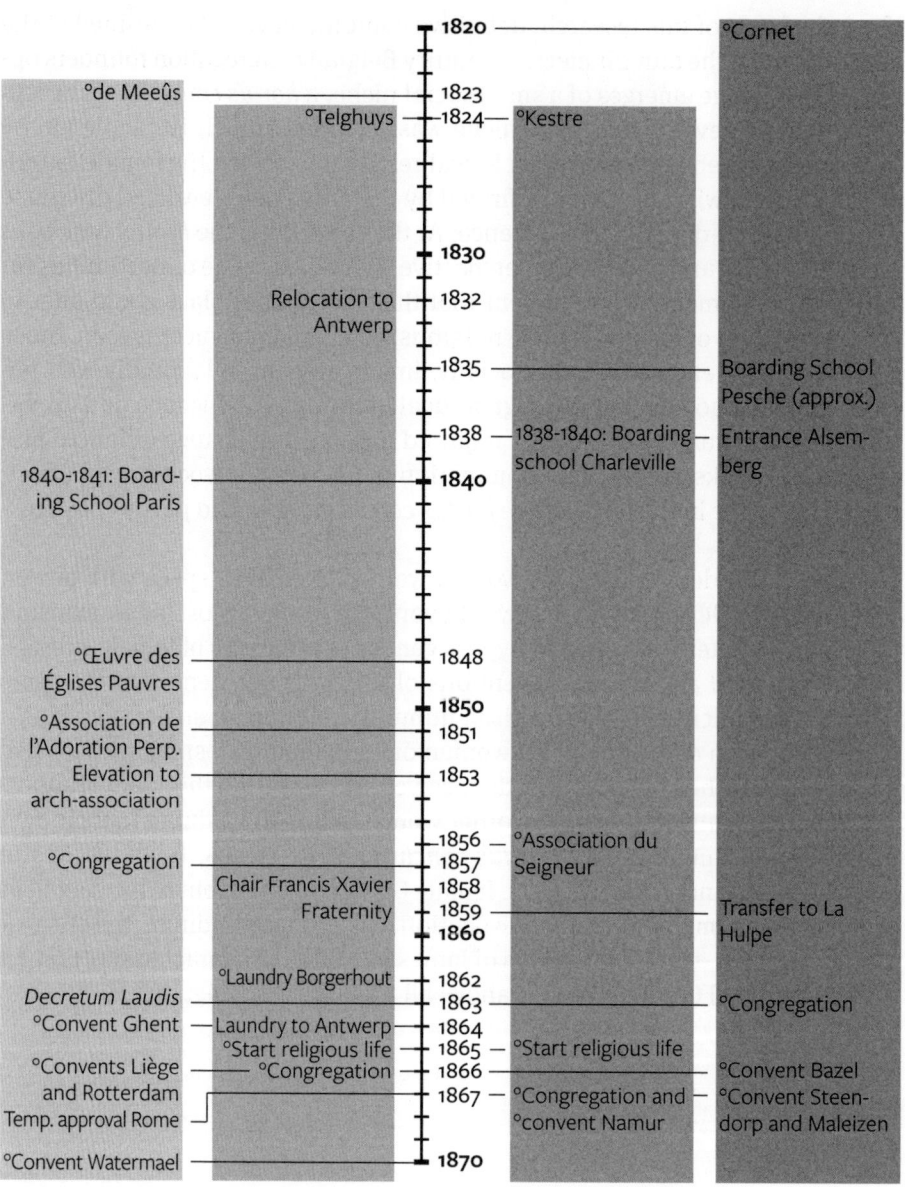

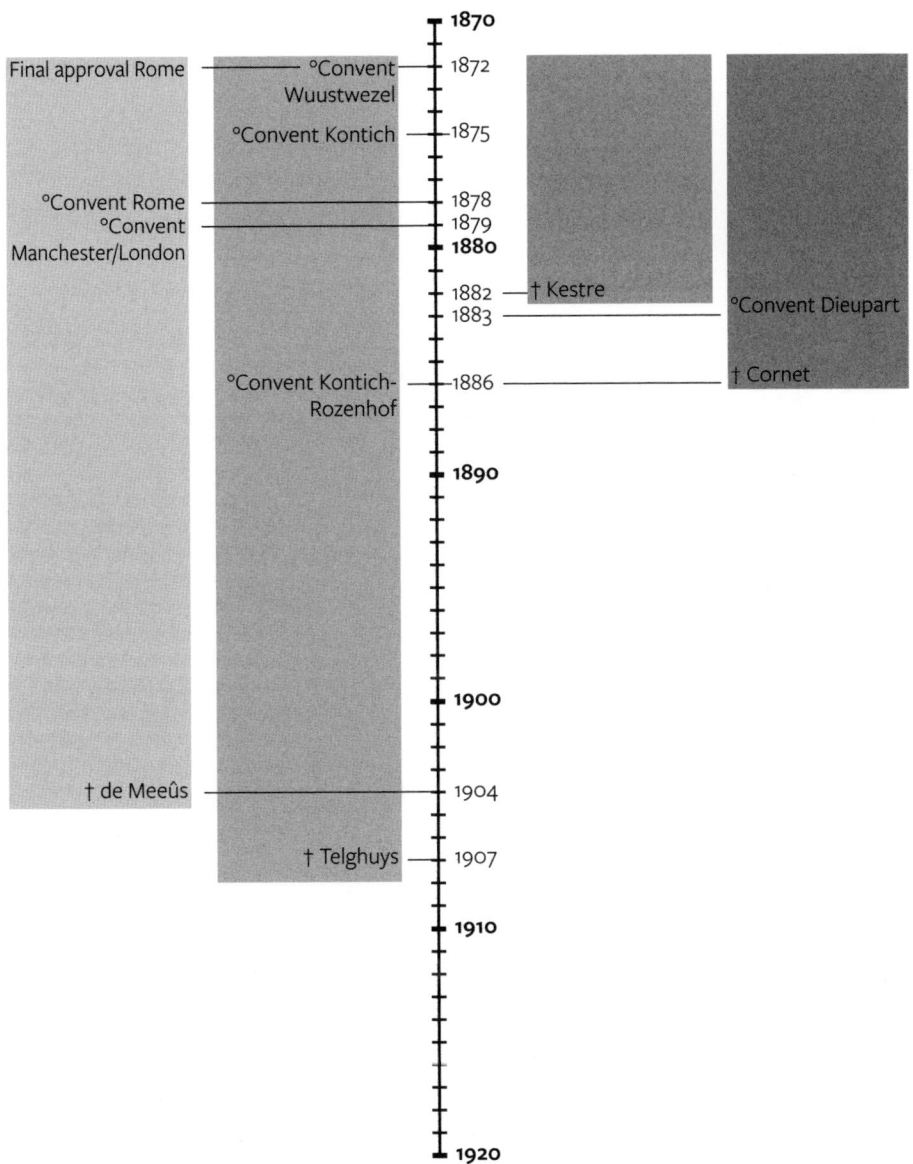

BIBLIOGRAPHY

Abbreviations

AAM	Archives of the Archdiocese of Mechelen-Brussels
ABA	Archives of the Diocese of Antwerp
ABG	Archives of the Diocese of Ghent
ABML	Archives of the Jesuits of the Southern Belgian Province and Luxemburg
ABR	Archives of the Diocese of Rotterdam
ABSE	Archives of the Jesuits of the Flemish Province
ACC	Municipal Archives Chimay
ACGC	Archives of the Genealogic Circle of Chimay, Thiérache and Surroundings
ACSSR-NB	Archives of the Redemptorists – Northern Belgian Province
ADBS	Archives of the de Bethune foundation
ADHH	Archives of the Servants of the Sacred Hearts of Jesus and Mary
ADML	Archives of the Daughters of Mary (Paridaens) of Leuven
ADSJ	Archives of the Ladies of Saint-Julienne
AEL	Archives of the Diocese of Liège
AFC	Family Archives Casier
AFCM-PB	Archives of the Daughters of the Heart of Mary – Belgian Province
AFDV	Family Archives de Villermont
AFJDH	Family Archives Joseph de Hemptinne
AFMP	Archives of the Daughters of Mary of Peche
AFV	Archives Family Vilain XIIII
ANSI	Archives of the Dutch Jesuits
AOFM	Archives of the Franciscans
ARE	Archives of the Religious of the Eucharist
ARLLN	State Archives Louvain-la-Neuve
ARSC	Religious of the Sacred Heart – Archives of France
ARSI	General Archives of the Jesuits
ASCMH	Archives of the Sisters of the Sacred Heart of Mary of Hannut
ASCMLH	Archives of the Sisters of the Sacred Heart of Mary of La Hulpe
ASV	Secret Vatican Archives
AZVC	Archives of the Sisters of the Sacred Heart of Jesus (Van Celst)
AZVG	Archives of the Sisters of Saint-Vincent of Gijzegem
CF	Convent files
NADH	National Archives Den Haag
RAAnd	State Archives Anderlecht
RAAnt	State Archives Antwerp
RAG	State Archives Ghent
RAL	State Archives Leuven
SAA	City Archives Antwerp
SAB	City Archives Brussels

Archives

Congregation archives

Brussels (Watermael)
Archives of the *Religieuses de l'Eucharistie* (ARE) – Anna de Meeûs.

La Hulpe
Archives of the *Sœurs du Saint-Cœur de Marie* of La Hulpe (ASCMLH) – Antoinette Cornet.

Leuven
KADOC-KU Leuven
  Archives of the *Dienstmaagden van de Heilige Harten van Jezus en Maria* of Antwerp (ADHH) - Wilhelmina Telghuys.

Rome
General Archive of the *Congregazione delle Religiose di Gesù-Maria*
  Archives of the *Dames de Sainte-Julienne* (ADSJ) – Fanny Kestre.

Archives of related congregations

Brussels (Saint-Josse-ten-Noode)
Archives of the *Filles du Cœur de Marie* – Belgian Province (AFCM-PB).

Gijzegem
Archive of the *Zusters van Sint-Vincentius, Dienstmaagden der Armen* of Gijzegem (AZVG).

Hannut
Archives of the *Sœurs du Saint-Cœur de Marie* of Hannut (ASCMH).

Leuven
KADOC-KU Leuven
  Archives of the *Dochters van Maria (Paridaens)* of Leuven (ADML).
  Archives of the Dutch Jesuits (ANSI).
  Archives of the Franciscans – Flemish Province Saint-Joseph (AOFM).
  Archives of the Jesuits of the Flemish Province (ABSE).
  Archives of the Jesuits of the Southern Belgian Province and Luxemburg (ABML).
  Archives of the Redemptorists – Northern Belgian Province (ACSSR-NB).
  Archives of the *Zusters van het Heilig Hart van Jezus (Van Celst)* (AZVC).

Pesche
Archives of *Filles de Marie* of Pesche (AFMP).

Poitiers
Religieuses du Sacré-Cœur – Archives of France (ARSC).

Rome
General Archives of the Jesuits (ARSI).

Diocesan and Roman archives

Antwerp
Archive of the Diocese of Antwerp (ABA).

Ghent
Archive of the Diocese of Ghent (ABG).

Liège
Archives of the Diocese of Liège (AEL).

Mechelen
Archives of the Archdiocese of Mechelen-Brussels (AAM)
  Convent Files (CF)
    Sœurs du S. Cœur de Marie, La Hulpe (La Hulpe).
    Institut de l'Adoration Perpétuelle (Salazar).
    Dames de Sainte-Julienne.

Vatican City
Secret Vatican Archives (ASV)
  Archivio della Nunziatura Apostolica in Belgio (NB).
  Archivio S. Congregazione Vescovi et regolari.

Public and family archives

Antwerp
State Archives Antwerp (RAAnt)
  Archief van de Provincie Antwerpen.
City Archives Antwerp (SAA).

Bazel
Family Archives Vilain XIIII (AFV).

Brussels
City Archives Brussels (SAB).

Brussels (Anderlecht)
State Archives Anderlecht (RAAnd)
  Civil Registry of the City of Verviers.

Chimay
Municipal Archives (ACC).
Archives of the *Cercle de Généalogie de Chimay, Thiérache et Alentours* (ACGC).

Ghent
State Archives Ghent (RAG)
  Family Archives Desmanet de Biesme.

Leuven
KADOC-KU Leuven
  Family Archives Casier (AFC).
  Family Archives Joseph de Hemptinne (AFJDH).
  Family Archives de Villermont (AFDV).
State Archives Leuven (RAL)
  Archive of the Municipality of Overijse.

Louvain-la-Neuve
State Archives Louvain-la-Neuve (ARLLN)
  Archives of the Municipality of La Hulpe.

Marke
Archive of the de Bethune Foundation (ADBS).

The Hague
National Archives (NADH)
  Archive of the Diocese of Rotterdam (ABR).

Printed sources

Newspapers

Het Handelsblad van Antwerpen.
Journal de Bruxelles.
Journal de Liège.
Le Bien Public.
L'Écho du Parlement.
Le Vingtième Siècle.
L'Indépendance Belge.

Periodicals

Almanach der bisdommen van Gent en Brugge (1860).
Almanach voor het Bisdom Brugge (1891).
Annales de l'Association de l'adoration perpétuelle et de l'Œuvre des Églises Pauvres (1858-1892).
Annuaire ecclésiastique de l'Archevêché de Malines (1860, 1870, 1891).
Annuaire officiel du clergé de l'archevêché de Malines (1900).
Collection de Précis Historiques et Mélanges religieuses, littéraires et scientifiques (1852-1876).
Jurisprudence du port d'Anvers (1874).
L'Émulation: publication mensuelle de la Société Centrale d'Architecture de Belgique (1891).
Précis Historiques ou Mélanges religieuses, littéraires et scientifiques (1877-1893).
Rapport de l'Archiassociation de l'adoration perpétuelle du très Saint-Sacrement et de l'Œuvre des Églises Pauvres (1850-1864).

Biographical works about the four founders

A la mémoire vénérée de madame Anna de Meeûs, fondatrice de l'Institut religieux de l'Adoration perpétuelle ainsi que de l'Archiassociation de l'Adoration perpétuelle et de l'Œuvre des Églises pauvres. Brussels: s.n., 1904.
Anna de Meeûs, fondatrice de l'Institut des religieuses de l'adoration perpétuelle 1823-1904. Brussels: Desclée de Brouwer, 1942.
De Eerwaarde Moeder Anna De Meeus, stichteres van het Religieuze Instituut der Eeuwigdurende Aanbidding en van de Aartsbroederschap der Eeuwigdurende Aanbidding en van het Liefdewerk der Arme Kerken. Helmond: De Reijdt, 1905.
La révérende mère Fanny de l'Eucharistie (madame Fanny Kestre) fondatrice de l'institut des Dames-de-Sainte-Julienne dites Apostolines du très-saint-Sacrement. Brussels: Société belge de librairie, 1897.
Les voies de Dieu. Un jubilé eucharistique dans l'église expiatoire du Très-Saint-Sacrement de Miracle à Bruxelles: 1848-1898. Bruges: Desclée, De Brouwer, 1898.
Notice extraite de la vie de la révérende Mère Fanny de l'Eucharistie, fondatrice de l'Institut des religieuses de Sainte Julienne, apostolines du Très Saint Sacrement. S.l.: s.n., 1912.
Pauwels, Ernest. Mère Jeanne. Roeselare: De Meester, 1908.
Sous le rayonnement de l'hostie, la révérende mère Fanny de l'eucharistie, fondatrice des religieuses de Sainte Julienne, apostolines du T. S. Sacrement et son œuvre. Brussels: Sifac, 1936.
Van den Gheyn. A la tombe d'Anna de Meeûs, Watermael, 20 septemb. 1948. Ghent: Van Fleteren, 1948.

Other printed sources

XIème Congrès eucharistique international, Bruxelles 13-17 juillet 1898. Brussels: Goemaere, 1899.
Acta secundae synodi dioecesanae. Mechelen: Dessain, 1873.
Assemblée Générale des catholiques en Belgique. Deuxième session à Malines, 29 août–3 septembre 1864. Brussels: Devaux, 1865, 2 vol.
Assemblée Générale des Catholiques en Belgique. Troisième Session à Malines. 2-7 septembre 1867. Brussels: Victor Devaux et Cie, 1868.
Bizzarri, Andrea. Collectanea in usum Secretariae Sacrae Congregationis Episcoporum et Regularium. Rome: Ex Tipographia rev. Camerae Apostolicae, 1863.
Catalogus ac status causarum beatificationis servorum Dei et canonizationis beatorum quae apud Sacram Rituum Congregationem per viam non cultus incedunt. Rome: Typis polyglottis Vaticanis, 1931.
Congrès des œuvres eucharistiques tenu à Lille les 28, 29 et 30 juin 1881. Lille: Lefebvre-Ducrocq, 1882.
Constitutions des Sœurs de Notre-Dame de Namur. Namur: Wesmael-Charlier, 1922.
Constitutions et règles de la Société du Sacré-Cœur de Jésus. Lyon: J.B. Pélagaud et Cie, 1852.
Instructions propres aux Filles du Cœur de Marie tirées du Sommaire des Constitutions de la Compagnie de Jésus. Paris: Charles Douniol, 1856.
Lettres et opuscules inédits du Comte Joseph de Maistre, précédés d'une notice biographique par son fils le comte Rodolphe de Maistre. Paris: A. Vaton, 1851, 2 vol.

Mac Carthy, Nicolas. *Sermons du Révérend Père de Mac Carthy, de la Compagnie de Jésus*. Leuven: Vanlinthout et Vandenzande, 1835.

Martyrologium Romanum. Rome: Typis Vaticanis, 2004.

Stalmans, Frans. *Les fondations du Pères du Sacrement en Belgique*. (1995) [unpublished].

Statuta dioecesis Mechliniensis. In synodo dioecesana anni 1872 promulgata [a] Victore Augusto Isidoro Dechamps [...] quibus insertae sunt additiones a. 1873, 1876 et 1881, ab ejus successore Petro Lamberto Goossens in synodo anni 1892 publicatae. Mechelen: Dessain, 1899.

Internet sources and publications

"Auguste de Jonghe d'Ardoye". *ODIS*. Record last modified date: 12 Nov. 2003. Available from World Wide Web: http://www.odis.be/lnk/PS_27244.

Della Sudda, Magali and von Tippelskirch, Xenia. "Nouvelles approches du fait religieux". *Italie et Méditerranée modernes et contemporaines*, 128 (2016) 2. [Online consultation on 23 May 2018 via http://journals.openedition.org/mefrim/2690].

Eymard. *Briefe und Schriften*. [Online consultation on 17 April 2020 via http://users.libero.it/paul.marsoner/eymard/index.html].

Fouilloux, Étienne. "Femmes et catholicisme dans la France contemporaine". *Clio. Histoire, femmes et sociétés*, 2 (1995). [Online consultation on 22 May 2018 via http://clio.revues.org/498].

La Rocca, Sandra. "L'Enfant Jésus et les femmes au XVIIe siècle: une dévotion émancipatrice". *Clio. Histoire, femmes et sociétés*. [Online consultation on 24 May 2018 via http://journals.openedition.org/clio/57].

Laurent, Theo. "Felix Van Achter". *ODIS*. Record last modified date: 16 Aug. 2010. Available from World Wide Web: http://www.odis.be/lnk/PS_26370.

Mas, Gabriel. "Internat et travail chrétien au milieu du XIXe siècle". In: *Religion et enfermements: XVIIe-XXe siècles*. Rennes: Presses universitaires de Rennes, 2005. [Online consultation on 13 March 2018 via http://books.openedition.org/pur/20389].

Meeussen, Erik. "Felix De Molder". *ODIS*. Record last modified date: 19 March 2015. Available from World Wide Web: http://www.odis.be/lnk/PS_15308.

Meeussen, Erik. "Jean-Philippe Winnen". *ODIS*. Record last modified date: 7 Jan. 2015. Available from World Wide Web: http://www.odis.be/lnk/PS_126171.

Meeussen, Erik. "Joannes Van Hoylant". *ODIS*. Record last modified date: 27 Feb. 2016. Available from World Wide Web: http://www.odis.be/lnk/PS_130582.

Meeussen, Erik. "Joannes-Baptista Lauwers". *ODIS*. Record last modified date: 6 Oct. 2015. Available from World Wide Web: http://www.odis.be/link/PS_14190.

Suenens, Kristien. "Congregatie van de Sœurs de Notre Dame de charité du Bon Pasteur, Angers (1835-heden)". *ODIS*. Record last modified date: 15 Nov. 2011. Available from World Wide Web: http://www.odis.be/lnk/OR_28090.

Vanden Bosch, Gerrit. "Ludovicus Verhoustraeten". *ODIS*. Record last modified date: 31 Aug. 2006. Available from World Wide Web: http://www.odis.be/lnk/PS_70367.

Vanderkerken, Rik. "Ivan Nolet de Brauwere van Steeland". *ODIS*. Record last modified date: 29 June 2007. Available from World Wide Web: http://www.odis.be/lnk/PS_72542.

Literature

1863-1913. Notice chronologique sur la Congrégation des Sœurs du Sacré-Cœur de Marie établie à Malaise-La Hulpe. Brussels: s.n., 1913.

Abrams, Lynn. *The Making of Modern Woman: Europe 1789-1918*. London: Longman, 2002.

Adelman, Sarah M. "Empowerment and Submission: The Political Culture of Catholic Women's Religious Communities in Nineteenth-Century America". *Journal of Women's History*, 23 (2011) 3, 138-161.

Albrecht, Ruth; Bühler-Dietrich, Annette, and Strzelczyk, Florentine (eds.). *Glaube und Geschlecht. Fromme Frauen – Spirituelle Erfahrungen – Religiöse Traditionen*. Cologne: Böhlau Verlag, 2008.

Alkemade, Allegonda J.M. *Vrouwen XIX: geschiedenis van negentien religieuze congregaties, 1800-1850*. 's-Hertogenbosch: Malmberg, 1966.

Ameeuw, Jef. *De Zusters van de H. Gehoorzaamheid, gezeid 'Blauwe Nunnen': kroniek van een kloostergemeenschap (1859-2004)*. Veurne: Pattyn, 2003.

Anderson, Margaret L. "The Limits of Secularization: on the Problem of the Catholic Revival in Nineteenth-Century Germany". *The Historical Journal*, 38 (1995) 3, 647-670.

Andral, Véronique. "Mechtilde du Saint-Sacrement". *Dictionnaire de spiritualité ascétique et mystique, doctrine et histoire*. Paris: Beauchesne, 1980, X, 885-888.

Annaert, Philippe. "Les filles dévotes enseignantes dans le Hainaut et le Tournaisis aux XVIIe et XVIIIe siècle". *De Leiegouw*, 29 (1987) 1-2, 3-9.

Apetrei, $arah. *Women, Feminism and Religion in Early Enlightenment England*. Cambridge: Cambridge University Press, 2010.

Art, Jan. "De evolutie van het aantal mannelijke roepingen in België tussen 1830 en 1975. Basisgegevens en richtingen voor verder onderzoek". *Belgisch Tijdschrift voor Nieuwste Geschiedenis*, 10 (1979) 3, 281-370.

Art, Jan. "Documents concernant la situation de l'Église catholique en Belgique en vue du Concile Vatican I (1869-1870)". *Bulletin de l'Institut Historique Belge de Rome*, 48-49 (1978-1979), 353-563.

Art, Jan. "Mannen als bruiden van de Bruidegom? Enkele verklaringspogingen". In: Marjet Derks, José Eijt and Marit Monteiro (eds.). *Sterven voor de wereld. Een religieus ideaal in meervoud*. Hilversum: Verloren, 1997, 35-47.

Art, Jan. *Kerkelijke structuur en pastorale werking in het bisdom Gent tussen 1830 en 1914*. Kortrijk: UGA, 1977.

Art, Jan and Buerman, Thomas. "Is de katholieke man wel een echte vent? Suggesties voor onderzoek naar mannelijkheid, katholicisme en antiklerikalisme". *Historica*, 30 (2007) 2, 27-29.

Atkin, Nicholas and Tallett, Frank. *Priests, Prelates and People: a History of European Catholicism since 1750*. London: Tauris, 2003.

Aubenas-Bastie, Jacqueline. "68-78: dix ans de féminisme en Belgique". In: Maria A. Macciocchi (ed.). *Les femmes et leurs maîtres*. Paris: Christian Bourgeois, 1978, 309-330.

Aubert, Roger. *Nouvelle histoire de l'Église. 5: L'Église dans le monde moderne: 1848 à nos jours*. Paris: Seuil, 1975.

Baas. *Leven der gravin Mathilde de Nédonchel, dienares Gods*. Ghent: Vander Schelden, 1894.

Baesten, V. *Vie de la mère Julie Billiart: fondatrice de l'Institut des sœurs de Notre-Dame de Namur (1751-1816)*. Tournai: Casterman, 1881.

Bailly, Antoine. *Vie de la révérende mère Gertrude (Melle Justine Desbille), fondatrice de l'Institut des sœurs de l'Enfant-Jésus*. Brussels: Vromant, 1889.

Baix, François and Joset, Camille-Jean. *Le diocèse de Namur (1830-1930)*. Brussels: Vermaut, 1940.

Bari, Barbara. "Pauline von Mallinckrodt und die Gründung ihrer Kongregation Katholische Ordensfrauen als caritative Pioniere des 19 Jahrhunderts". *Westfälische Zeitschrift*, 146 (1996), 287-312.

Bartoli, Danielle. *Histoire de Saint Ignace de Loyola et de l'origine de la compagnie de Jésus*. Brussels: Goemaere, 1852.

Baunard, Louis. *Histoire de Madame Barat*. Paris: Poussielgue, 1876, 2 vol.

Becque, Maurice. *Le cardinal Dechamps*. Leuven: Bibliotheca Alphonsiana, 1956, 2 vol.

Belpaire, Maria E. *De families Teichmann en Belpaire. 1: De tegenzang der liefde*. Antwerp: Buschmann, 1925.

Belpaire, Maria E. *Constance Teichmann*. Antwerp: Leeslust, 1926.

Benoist, Jacques. *Le Sacré-Cœur des femmes. De 1870 à 1860*. Paris: Les Éditions de l'Atelier/ Éditions Ouvrières, 2000.

Bez, Nicolas. *La ville des aumônes. Tableau des œuvres de charité de la ville de Lyon*. Lyon: La Librairie Chrétienne, 1840.

Blackbourn, David. "The Catholic Church in Europe since the French Revolution. A Review Article". *Comparative Studies in Society and History*, 33 (1991) 4, 778-790.

Blaschke, Olaf. "Das 19. Jahrhundert: Ein zweites Konfessionelles Zeitalter?". *Geschichte und Gesellschaft*, 26 (2000), 38-75.

Blondé, Bruno; Van Dijck, Maarten and Vrints, Antoon. "Een probleemstad? Spanningsvelden tussen burgerlijke waarden en sociale realiteiten". In: Inge Bertels, Bert De Munck and Herman Van Goethem (eds.). *Antwerpen. Biografie van een stad*. Antwerp: Meulenhoff/ Manteau, 2010, 277-308.

Bock, Gisela. "Geschichte, Frauengeschichte, Geschlechtergeschichte". *Geschichte und Gesellschaft*, 14 (1988), 364-391.

Bock, Gisela. *Women in European History*. Oxford: Blackwell, 2002.

Boedt, Hendrik. *Enkele aspekten van het foorkramersleven*. Roeselare: School voor Maatschappelijk Dienstbetoon, 1957.

Bogaerts, Petrus. *Levensschets van den grooten mirakeldoender den H. Nicolaus van Tolentinen*. Antwerp: Van Aarsen, 1848.

Bogaerts, Pieter. *Levensbeschrijving van pater Lodewijk Donche, priester des Gezelschaps van Jezus, stichter van de Zusters der christelijke scholen van den heilige Joseph Calasanctius te Vorselaer*. Turnhout: Splichal, 1891.

Boone, Jean-Baptiste. *Des devoirs de la femme chrétienne*. Brussels: H. Goemaere, 1855.

Børresen, Kari E. and Vogt, Kari. *Women's Studies of the Christian and Islamic Traditions: Ancient, Medieval and Renaissance Foremothers*. Dordrecht: Kluwer, 1993.

Boudens, Robrecht. "De mannelijke religieuzen". In: Michel Cloet (ed.). *Het bisdom Gent (1559-1991). Vier eeuwen geschiedenis*. Ghent: Werkgroep De Geschiedenis van het Bisdom Gent, 1991, 394-402.

Boudens, Robrecht. "De vrouwelijke religieuzen". In: Michel Cloet (ed.). *Het bisdom Gent (1559-1991). Vier eeuwen geschiedenis*. Ghent: Werkgroep De Geschiedenis van het Bisdom Gent, 1991, 403-412.

Boudens, Robrecht. "De parochiepriesters en de zielzorg". In: Michel Cloet (ed.). *Het bisdom Brugge: 1559-1994. Bisschoppen, priesters, gelovigen*. Bruges: Westvlaams Verbond van Kringen voor Heemkunde, 1992, 412-424.

Bouflet, Joachim and Boutry, Philippe. *Un signe dans le ciel: les apparitions de la Vierge*. Paris: Grasset, 1997.

Bouhours. *La vie de Saint-Ignace, fondateur de la Compagnie de Jésus*. Liège/Brussels: Duvivier/Lecharlier, 1815.

Boureau, René. *L'Oratoire en France*. Paris: Cerf, 1991.

Boutry, Philippe. *Souverain et pontife: recherches prosopographiques sur la Curie romaine à l'âge de la Restauration (1814-1846)*. Rome: École française de Rome, 2002.

Brejon de Lavergnée, Matthieu. *La Société de Saint-Vincent-de-Paul au XIXe siècle. Un fleuron du catholicisme social*. Paris: Cerf, 2009.

Brejon de Lavergnée, Matthieu. *Histoire des Filles de la Charité. XVIIe-XVIIIe siècle. La rue pour cloître*. Paris: Fayard, 2011.

Brejon de Lavergnée, Matthieu. "Le genre du philanthrope. Pour une histoire sexuée de l'assistance au XIXe siècle". In: Anne Cova and Bruno Dumons (eds.). *Femmes, genre et catholicisme. Nouvelles recherches, nouveau objets (France, XIXe-XXe siècle)*. Lyon: Chrétiens et Sociétés, 2012, 85-103.

Brejon de Lavergnée, Matthieu. "Making the Charitable Man. Catholic Masculinities in Nineteenth-Century France". In: Tine Van Osselaer and Patrick Pasture (eds.). *Christian Homes: Religion, Family and Domesticity in the 19th and 20th Centuries*. Leuven: Leuven University Press, 2014, 83-103.

Brejon de Lavergnée, Matthieu. "Du mythe des origines. Les Filles de la Charité et leurs fondateurs, XVIIe-XXe siècle". In: Matthieu Brejon de Lavergnée (ed.). *Des Filles de la Charité aux Sœurs de Saint-Vincent-de-Paul*. Paris: Honoré Champion, 2016, 19-41.

Brejon de Lavergnée, Matthieu. *Le temps des cornettes. Histoire des Filles de la Charité. XIXe-XXe siècle*. Paris: Fayard, 2018.

Brejon de Lavergnée, Matthieu and Della Sudda, Magali (eds.). *Genre et christianisme: Plaidoyers pour une histoire croisée*. Paris: Beauchesne Éditions, 2015.

Brems, Elke. "'Ik hoop dat gij braaf zijt'. De briefwisseling tussen Hilda Ram en Marie Elisabeth Belpaire, twee intellectuele vrouwen aan het einde van de negentiende eeuw". *Zacht Lawijd*, 11 (2012) 3, 2-23.

Brion, René and Moreau, Jean-Louis. *De Generale Maatschappij van België 1822-1997*. Antwerp: Mercatorfonds, 1998.

Brogniez, Laurence. "Poétesses belges du XIXe siècle: quelques profils perdus". *Sextant*, 17-18 (2002), 131-147.

Brosnan, Kathleen. "Public Presence, Public Silence: Nuns, Bishops, and the Gendered Space of Early Chicago". *The Catholic Historical Review*, 90 (2004) 3, 473-496.

Brouwers, Louis. "Jean-Baptiste Boone. Tambour de l'empereur et tambour de Dieu". In: Alain Deneef et al. (eds.). *Les Jésuites Belges 1542-1992: 450 ans de Compagnie de Jésus dans les Provinces Belgiques*. Brussels: AESM, 1992, 143.

Brown, Callum G. *The Death of Christian Britain: Understanding Secularisation 1800-2000*. London: Routledge, 2001.

Brownley, Martine W. *Deferrals of Domain: Contemporary Women Novelists and the State*. New York: St. Martin's, 2007.

Buerman, Thomas and Van Osselaer, Tine. "De feminisering van religie. Past de internationale these binnen de Belgische context?". *Verslagen van het RUG-centrum voor genderstudies - UGent*, 16 (2007), 5-26.

Burton, Richard. *Holy Tears, Holy Blood: Women, Catholicism, and the Culture of Suffering in France, 1840-1970*. Ithaca: Cornell University Press, 2004.

Busch, Norbert. "Die Feminisierung der Frömmigkeit". In: Irmtraud Götz von Olenhusen (ed.). *Wunderbare Erscheinungen. Frauen und katholische Frömmigkeit im 19. und 20. Jahrhundert*. Paderborn: Schöningh, 1995, 203-219.

Busch, Norbert. *Katholische Frömmigkeit und Moderne: die Sozial- und Mentalitätsgeschichte des Herz-Jesu-Kultus in Deutschland zwischen Kulturkampf und Erstem Weltkrieg*. Gütersloh: Kaiser, 1997.

Butler, Judith P. *Gender Trouble: Feminism and the Subversion of Identity*. New York: Routledge, 1990.

Butler, Judith P. *Bodies That Matter: On the Discursive Limits of "Sex"*. New York: Routledge, 1993.

Bynum, Caroline W. "Women mystics and Eucharistic devotion in the thirteenth century". *Women's Studies*, 11 (1984) 1-2, 179-214.

Bynum, Caroline W. *Holy Feast and Holy Fast: the Religious Significance of Food to Medieval Women*. Berkeley: University of California Press, 1987.

Caffiero, Marina. *Religione et modernità in Italia (secoli XVII-XIX)*. Pisa/Rome: Istituti Editoriali e Poligrafici Internazionali, 2000.

Califice, Isabelle and Janssen, Séverine. *Le feu sur la terre: histoire et spiritualité des religieuses de l'Instruction Chrétienne*. Liège: DIC, 2015.

Callahan, Francis J. *The Centralization of Government in Pontifical Institutes of Women with Simple Vows (from their beginnings till the legislation of Leo XIII)*. Rome: Pontificia Universitas Gregoriana, 1948.

Carlier, Julie. "Emilie Claeys (1855-1943), een adepte van August Bebels 'vrije huwelijk'? Een 'grote' oefening in historische kritiek: het persoonlijke en het politieke in een socialistisch-feministische strijd aan het einde van de 19de eeuw". *Brood & Rozen*, 13 (2008) 3, 5-25.

Casgrain, Henry-Raymond. *La société des filles du cœur de Marie d'après ses annales*. Paris: Devalois, 1899, 3 vol.

Caspers, Charles. "Eerherstel. De belediging van God en de ervaring van tegenslag bij rooms-katholieken, van de twaalfde tot in de twintigste eeuw". In: Marijke Gijswijt-Hofstra and Florike Egmond (eds.). *Of bidden helpt? Tegenslag en cultuur in Europa, circa 1500-2000*. Amsterdam: Amsterdam University Press, 1997, 99-117, 183-188.

Caspers, Charles and Margry, Peter Jan. *Het Mirakel van Amsterdam. Biografie van een betwiste devotie*. Amsterdam: Bert Bakker, 2017.

[Chaillot, Ludovic]. "Confesseurs des religieuses". *Analecta Juris Pontificii*, (1860), 1277-1326.

Champ, Judith. *William Bernard Ullathorne 1806-1889: a Different Kind of Monk*. Leominster: Gracewing, 2006.

Cholvy, Gérard (ed.). *La religion et les femmes*. Montpellier: Centre régional d'histoire des mentalités, 2002.

Cholvy, Gérard and Hilaire, Yves-Marie. *Histoire religieuse de la France contemporaine*. Toulouse: Privat, 1985.

Chopelin, Paul. "Une affaire de femmes? Les résistances laïques à la politique religieuse d'État sous la Révolution française". In: Matthieu Brejon de Lavergnée and Magali Della Sudda (eds.). *Genre et Christianisme. Plaidoyers pour une histoire croisée*. Paris: Beauchesne, 2014, 155-179.

Christens, Ria. *100 jaar Heilig-Hartinstituut Annuntiaten Heverlee: geschiedenis van een school en een congregatie*. Heverlee/Leuven: Annuntiaten/KADOC, 1994.

Christens, Ria. "Verkend verleden. Een kritisch overzicht van de vrouwengeschiedenis 19de-20ste eeuw in België". *Belgisch Tijdschrift voor Nieuwste Geschiedenis*, 27 (1997) 1-2, 5-37.

Christens, Ria. *Terra incognita: 75 jaar annuntiaten in Afrika*. Heverlee: Annuntiaten, 2006.

Christens, Ria and Hansen, Ingrid, "Vrouwen en onderwijs. Isala van Diest (1842-1916), Marie Elisabeth Belpaire (1853-1948) en Marguerite Lefèvre (1894-1967)". In: Dorinda Dekeyser, Luciane Opdeweegh and Oky van der Velden (eds.). *Vrouwenfaam op straatnaam. Vrouwen maken naam*. Leuven/Apeldoorn: Garant, 1999, 52-79.

Christens, Ria and Suenens, Kristien. "L'enseignement comme vocation et projet. Les instituts religieux féminins". In: Jan De Maeyer and Paul Wynants (eds.). *L'enseignement catholique en Belgique. Des identités en évolution, 19e-21e siècles*. Antwerp: Halewijn, 2016, 137-159.

Cicercule Paridaens: mère Marie-Thérèse, fondatrice de la Congrégation des filles de Marie à Louvain. Leuven: Charpentier, 1903.

Clancy, Thomas H. *An Introduction to Jesuit life: The Constitutions and History through 435 Years*. Saint Louis: The Institute of Jesuit Sources, 1976.

Clark, Christopher. "The New Catholicism and the European Culture Wars". In: Christopher Clark and Wolfram Kaiser (eds.). *Culture Wars: Secular-Catholic Conflict in Nineteenth-Century Europe*. Cambridge: Cambridge University Press, 2003, 11-46.

Clark, Emily and Laven, Mary (eds.). *Women and Religion in the Atlantic Age, 1550-1900*. Farnham: Ashgate, 2013.

Clear, Caitriona. *Nuns in Nineteenth-Century Ireland*. Dublin: Gill and Macmillan, 1987.

Cocriamont, Marie. "Soigner les corps et les âmes: les sœurs Augustines des hôpitaux Saint-Jean et Saint-Pierre à Bruxelles au 19e siècle". *Sextant*, 3 (1994-1995), 19-38.

Cognet, Louis. *Histoire de la spiritualité chrétienne. 3.2: La spiritualité moderne. 1: L'essor 1500-1650*. Paris: Aubier, 1966.

Collard, Eugène. "L'étude sociologique des communautés religieuses féminines et de leur recrutement". In: Eugène Collard et al. (eds.). *Sociologie de la vocation religieuse: sociologie des vocations*. Tournai: Casterman, 1958, 208-232.

Coolsaet, Rik; Dujardin, Vincent and Roosens, Claude. *Buitenlandse Zaken in België: geschiedenis van een ministerie, zijn diplomaten en consuls van 1830 tot vandaag*. Tielt: Lannoo, 2014.

Coomans, Thomas. "Veel zorgen, weinig zorg. De lotgevallen van negentiende-eeuwse kerkgebouwen in de twintigste eeuw in België". In: Anna Bergmans et al. (eds.). *Neostijlen in de negentiende eeuw: zorg geboden?* Leuven: Leuven University Press, 2002, 131-160.

Coomans, Thomas and De Maeyer, Jan (eds.). *The Revival of Medieval Illumination: Nineteenth-Century Belgian Manuscripts and Illuminations from a European Perspective*. Leuven: Leuven University Press, 2007.

Cornelis, Mirjam et al. (eds.). *Vrome vrouwen: betekenissen van geloof voor vrouwen in de geschiedenis*. Hilversum: Verloren, 1996.

Cott, Nancy F. *The Bonds of Womanhood: 'Woman's Sphere' in New England, 1780-1835*. New Haven: Yale University Press, 1997.

Cotter, Elizabeth M. *The General Chapter in a Religious Institute. With Particular Reference to IBVM Loreto Branch*. Bern: Peter Lang, 2008.

Courtmans, Johanna. *De Gemeente-Onderwijzer. Romantisch Verhaal door Vrouwe Courtmans (geboren Berchmans)*. Maldegem: Victor de Lille, 1911.

Couttenier, Piet. "Bekroond met een keizerlijk geschenk. Johanna Desideria Courtmans". In: Riet Schenkeveld-Van der Dussen et al. (eds.). *Met en zonder lauwerkrans. Schrijvende vrouwen uit de vroegmoderne tijd 1550-1850: van Anna Bijns tot Elise van Calcar*. Amsterdam: Amsterdam University Press, 1997, 860-870.

Couttenier, Piet and Musschoot, Anne M. *Meesterschap in tweevoud. Novellen en schetsen van Rosalie en Virginie Loveling*. Amsterdam: Amsterdam University Press, 2009.

Creusen, Alexia. *Femmes artistes en Belgique: XIXe et début XXe siècle*. Paris: Harmattan, 2007.

Curtis, Sarah A. *Educating the Faithful: Religion, Schooling, and Society in Nineteenth-Century France*. Ithaca: Cornell University Press, 2000.

Curtis, Sarah A. "Charitable Ladies: Gender, Class and Religion in Mid-Nineteenth-Century Paris". *Past and Present*, 77 (2002) 1, 121-156.

Curtis, Sarah A. *Civilizing Habits: Women Missionaries and the Revival of French Empire*. Oxford: Oxford University Press, 2010.

Cuyvers, John. *Geschiedenis van Sterbos*. Wuustwezel: s.n., 2008.

D'Amat, Romain. "Chaillot, Mgr. Ludovic". In: M. Prevost and Roman D'Amat (eds.). *Dictionnaire de Biographie Française*. Paris: Libraire Letouzey et Ané, 1959, VIII, 177.

Daris, Joseph. *Le diocèse de Liège sous l'épiscopat de Mgr. Théodore De Montpellier 1852 à 1879*. Liège: Demarteau, 1892.

Dauzet, Dominique-Marie. *La mystique bien tempérée. Écriture féminine de l'expérience spirituelle. XIXe-XXe siècle*. Paris: Cerf, 2006.

De Baar, Mirjam; Kuiper, Yme and Renders, Hans. "Inleiding". In: Mirjam de Baar, Yme Kuiper and Hans Renders (eds.). *Biografie & religie. De religieuze factor in de biografie*. Amsterdam: Boom, 2011, 7-17.

Debremaeker, Marcel. *Geschiedenis van het Sint-Victorinstituut en de Scheppersnormaalschool te Alsemberg*. Alsemberg: Koninklijke Oud-Leerlingenbond Sint-Victorinstituut en Scheppers-normaalschool, 1985.

De Buck, Victor. *De l'état religieux en Belgique au XIXe siècle*. Brussels: Greuse, 1864.

De Bueger-Van Lierde, Françoise. "Marie Popelin et les débuts du mouvement féministe belge (1892-1914)". In: Luc Courtois, Jean Pirotte and Françoise Rosart (eds.). *Femmes des années 80. Un siècle de condition féminine en Belgique (1889-1989)*. Louvain-la-Neuve: Academia, 1989, 197-202.

De Cant, Geneviève. "Een wereld van onafhankelijke vrouwen, tussen Kerk en Maatschappij". In: Geneviève De Cant et al. (eds.). *Een wereld van onafhankelijke vrouwen van de 12de eeuw tot heden. De Vlaamse begijnhoven*. Riverside: The Hervé van Caloen Foundation, 2003, 13-42.

Dechamps, Victor. *Instructions adressées aux communautés des religieuses du diocèse de Malines.* Mechelen: H. Dessain, 1874.

De Clerck, Karel; De Graeve, Bie and Simon, Frank. *Dag meester, goedemorgen zuster, goedemiddag juffrouw. Facetten van het volksonderwijs in Vlaanderen (1830-1940).* Tielt: Lannoo, 1984.

De Decker, Annie. *Vormingswerk in vrouwenhanden: de voorgeschiedenis van de Kristelijke Arbeiders Vrouwenbeweging (1892-1924).* Leuven: Acco, 1986.

Deferme, Jo. *Uit de ketens van de vrijheid: het debat over de sociale politiek in België 1886-1914.* Leuven: Leuven University Press, 2007.

de Gensac, Henri. *Présentation historique de la Société de Marie réparatrice (1818-1953).* Rome: Typographie vaticane, 1992.

De Giorgio, Michela. "La bonne Catholique". In: Georges Duby and Michelle Perrot (eds.). *Histoire des femmes en occident. 4: Le XIXe siècle.* Paris: Plon, 1991, 169-197.

De Groot, Joanna and Morgan, Sue. "Beyond the 'Religious Turn'? Past, Present and Future Perspectives in Gender History". *Gender and History*, 25 (2013) 3, 395-421.

De Haerne, Désiré. *Tableau de la charité chrétienne en Belgique ou Relevé des œuvres de bienfaisance dues principalement à l'usage des libertés inscrites dans la constitution belge de 1831.* Brussels: Fonteyn, 1857.

De Haulleville, Prosper. *Portraits et silhouettes: Première série.* Brussels: Lacomblez, 1892.

De Haulleville, Prosper. *Portraits et silhouettes: Deuxième série.* Brussels: Lacomblez, 1893.

De Keyzer, Diane. *Madame est servie: leven in dienst van adel en burgerij (1900-1995).* Leuven: Van Halewyck, 1995.

Delbaere, Jo. "Het klooster der Zusters van Liefde van de H. Vincentius a Paulo te Rumbeke". *Handelingen van de Geschied- en Oudheidkundige Kring van Kortrijk*, 30 (1957-1958), 3-296.

Delcroix, Jeanette. *Fernandina et Frederika of Der vrouwen-peerlen.* Brussels: Greuse, 1860.

Delhaye, Christine. "Vliegen en stelen. Vrouwen en hun relatie tot de cultuur". *Kultuurleven*, 63 (1996) 4, 16-23.

Del Marmol, Tony. *Notice généalogique sur la famille Del Marmol (1394-1968).* Brussels: Librairie Henri Thyssens, 1968.

De Maeyer, Jan. "De Belgische Volksbond en zijn antecedenten". In: Emmanuel Gerard (ed.). *De christelijke arbeidersbeweging in België 1891-1991.* Leuven: Universitaire Pers Leuven, 1991, II, 19-65.

De Maeyer, Jan. *De rode baron: Arthur Verhaegen 1847-1917.* Leuven: Universitaire Pers Leuven, 1994.

De Maeyer, Jan. "Relatie en huwelijk in de Moderne Tijd (ca. 1800-ca. 1950): kerkelijke standpunten en strategieën". In: Roger Burggraeve et al. (eds.). *Levensrituelen. Het huwelijk.* Leuven: Universitaire Pers Leuven, 2000, 31-35.

De Maeyer, Jan. "The Neo-Gothic in Belgium: Architecture of a Catholic Society". In: Jan De Maeyer and Luc Verpoest (eds.). *Gothic Revival: Religion, Architecture and Style in Western Europe. 1815-1914.* Leuven: Leuven University Press, 2000, 19-34.

De Maeyer, Jan. "'Les dames d'œuvres': 19de-eeuwse vrouwen van stand en hun zoektocht naar maatschappelijk engagement". In: Leen Van Molle and Peter Heyrman (eds.). *Vrouwenzaken-zakenvrouwen: facetten van vrouwelijk zelfstandig ondernemerschap in Vlaanderen, 1800-2000.* Ghent/Leuven: Provinciebestuur Oost-Vlaanderen/KADOC, 2001, 108-127.

De Maeyer, Jan. "Les hommes d'œuvres en Belgique (1875-1919/1921): utopistes néo-médiévaux ou hommes politiques". In: Laurence Van Ypersele and Anne-Dolorès Marcélis (eds.). *Rêves de Chrétienté. Réalités du monde. Imaginaires catholiques.* Louvain-la-Neuve/Paris: Cerf, 2001, 185-204.

De Maeyer, Jan. "La Belgique: un élève modèle de l'école ultramontaine". In: Emiel Lamberts (ed.). *The Black International 1870-1878: The Holy See and Militant Catholicism in Europe.* Leuven: Leuven University Press, 2002, 361-385.

De Maeyer, Jan. "Des vierges et des manuscrits dans les châteaux et des abbayes: réalité médiévale ou fiction romantique?". In: Thomas Coomans and Jan De Maeyer (eds.). *The Revival of Medieval Illumination: Nineteenth-Century Belgium Manuscripts and Illuminations from a European Perspective.* Leuven: Leuven University Press, 2007, 63-77.

De Maeyer, Jan. "De wending van de kerk naar het volk". In: Jan De Maeyer et al. (eds.). *Het aartsbisdom Mechelen-Brussel. 450 jaar geschiedenis.* Antwerp: Halewijn, 2009, II, 100-171.

De Maeyer, Jan. "Een kerk in de moderniteit. De kunst van de geleidelijkheid en de beheersing 1860-1920". In: Marcel Gielis et al. (eds.). *In de stroom van de tijd. (4)50 jaar bisdom Antwerpen.* Leuven: Davidsfonds, 2012, 169-194.

De Maeyer, Jan and Deferme, Jo. "Vrouwelijke religieuzen in de openbare en private gezondheidszorg in het België van de negentiende en twintigste eeuw: tussen traditie en moderniteit". In: Liesbeth Labbeke, Vefie Poels and Rob Wolf (eds.). *Bezielde zorg. Verpleging door katholieke religieuzen in Nederland en Vlaanderen (negentiende-twintigste eeuw)*. Hilversum: Verloren, 2008, 10-28.

De Maeyer, Jan and Hellemans, Staf. "Katholiek reveil, katholieke zuilvorming en dagelijks leven". In: Jaak Billiet (ed.). *Tussen bescherming en verovering. Sociologen en historici over zuilvorming*. Leuven: Universitaire Pers Leuven, 1988, 171-200.

De Maeyer, Jan; Heyrman, Peter and Quaghebeur, Patricia. "Een glorierijk verleden: De Vincentianen in Gent (1845-1992)". In: Jan De Maeyer and Paul Wynants (eds.). *De Vincentianen in België. Les Vincentiens en Belgique*. Leuven: Universitaire Pers Leuven, 1992, 279-312.

De Maeyer, Jan; Van Molle, Leen and Maes, Krista. *Joris Helleputte: architect en politicus 1852/1925*. Leuven: Universitaire Pers Leuven, 1998, 2 vol.

Demeestere, Helena. "Leven en werk van Joanna Francisca Amerlinck. 1733-1810". *De Leiegouw*, 40 (1999) 1, 25- 56.

De Metsenaere, Machteld. "Veel geschiedenis, weinig geheugen? Over de belangstelling van Belgische contemporanisten voor de geschiedenis van feminisme en vrouwenbeweging sinds de jaren zeventig". In: Guy Vanthemsche, Machteld De Metsenaere and J.C. Burgelmann (eds.). *De Tuin van Heden. Dertig jaar wetenschappelijk onderzoek over de hedendaagse Belgische samenleving*. Brussels: VUBPress, 2007, 169-208.

De Meulemeester, Maurits. *Geschiedenis der Maricolen: Dendermonde 1663, Gent 1671, Deinze 1816*. Bruges: Houtmond-Cortvriendt, 1911.

De Meulemeester, Maurits. *Influences ascétiques de St-Alphonse de Liguori en Belgique*. Essen: Impr. Saint-Alphonse, 1923.

De Meulemeester, Maurits. *Mère Agnès de Jésus et les Religieuses de Notre-Dame des VII Douleurs*. Brussels: Janssens, Leunis et Havet, 1928.

De Meulemeester, Maurits. *De Belgische Redemptoristenprovincie 1841-1941*. Leuven: Sint-Alfonsusdrukkerij, 1941.

De Meulemeester, Maurits. *De congregatie der Zusters van den H. Vincentius a Paulo te Deinze*. Leuven: Sint-Alfonsusdrukkerij, 1941.

De Meulemeester, Maurits. *De congregatie van de dochters van de H. Jozef te Evere 1855-1955*. Leuven: Sint-Alfonsusdrukkerij, 1955.

Deneckere, Gita. *Het Gentse Sint-Vincentiusziekenhuis: de zusters van liefde J.M. en de ziekenzorg te Gent, 1805 tot heden*. Ghent: Zusters van Liefde van Jezus en Maria, 1997.

Deneckere, Gita. *Geuzengeweld: antiklerikaal straatrumoer in de politieke geschiedenis van België, 1831-1914*. Brussels: VUBPress, 1998.

Deneckere, Gita. "Droits de l'homme, ook voor vrouwen". In: Els Witte (ed.). *Nieuwe Geschiedenis van België 1830-1905*. Tielt: Lannoo, 2005, 607-624.

Depaepe, Marc; De Vroede, Maurits and Simon, Frank (eds.). *Geen trede meer om op te staan: de maatschappelijke positie van onderwijzers en onderwijzeressen tijdens de voorbije eeuw*. Kapellen: Pelckmans, 1993.

Depaepe, Marc; Lauwers, Hilde and Simon, Frank. "De feminisering van het leerkrachtencorps". *Belgisch Tijdschrift voor Filologie en Geschiedenis*, 82 (2004) 4, 969-995.

Depage, Henri. *La vie d'Antoine Depage 1862-1925*. Brussels: La Renaissance du livre, 1956.

Dequeker, Luc. *Het sacrament van mirakel: Jodenhaat in de Middeleeuwen*. Leuven: Davidsfonds, 2000.

Derks, Marjet. "Vrouwen, confessionalisering en biografie. Catharina Alberdingk Thijm of de eigenaardigheid van een karakter". In: Annelies van Heijst and Marjet Derks (eds.). *Terra incognita. Historisch onderzoek naar katholicisme en vrouwelijkheid*. Kampen: Kok, 1994, 109-128.

Derks, Marjet and Monteiro, Marit. "'Met wijsheid opent zij haar mond'. Vroomheid, visie en vrouwelijkheid". In: Mirjam Cornelis, Marjet Derks and Marit Monteiro (eds.). *Vrome vrouwen. Betekenissen van geloof voor vrouwen in de geschiedenis*. Hilversum: Verloren, 1996, 9-26.

de Robiano, Serge. "La famille des Comtes de Robiano, châtelains à Marchin". *Bia Viyèdje. Bulletin du Cercle royal d'Histoire et de Folklore de Marchin*, 11 (1988-1989), 3-10.

De Schaepdrijver, Sophie. "Reglementering van prostitutie, 1844-1877: Opkomst en ondergang van een experiment". *Belgisch Tijdschrift voor Nieuwste Geschiedenis*, 16 (1985) 3-4, 473-506.

De Schaepdrijver, Sophie. "Trois images d'une capitale qui se cherche: Bruxelles, 1850-1914". In: Anne Pingeot and Robert Hoozee (eds.). *Paris-Bruxelles, Bruxelles-Paris. Réalisme, impressionnisme, symbolisme, art nouveau. Les relations artistiques entre la France et la Belgique, 1848-1914*. Paris/Antwerp: Mercator Fonds, 1997, 34-40.

Deschout, Thérèse. *De congregatie van de zusters van Maria van Pittem: ontstaan en uitbreiding tot na de tweede wereldoorlog*. Unpublished PhD thesis, KU Leuven, 1979.

De Smaele, Henk. "Determinanten voor kiesgedrag. Electorale verhouding in een Gentse arbeiderswijk aan de vooravond van de Eerste Wereldoorlog". *Belgisch Tijdschrift voor Nieuwste Geschiedenis*, 27 (1997) 1-2, 135-185.

De Smaele, Henk. *Rechts Vlaanderen: Religie en stemgedrag in negentiende-eeuws België*. Leuven: Leuven University Press, 2009.

De Smedt, Charles. *Mgr J.-B.-Victor Kinet et les origines de la Congrégation des Sœurs de la Providence et de l'Immaculée Conception*. Namur: Wesmael-Charlier, 1899.

De Smedt, Helma; Stabel, Peter and Van Damme, Ilja. "Zilt succes. Functieverschuivingen van een stedelijke autonomie". In: Inge Bertels, Bert De Munck and Herman Van Goethem (eds.). *Biografie van een stad*. Antwerp: Meulenhoff/Manteau, 2010, 109-145.

De Valk, Hans. *Roomser dan de paus? Studies over de betrekkingen tussen de Heilige Stoel en het Nederlands katholicisme. 1815-1840*. Nijmegen: Valkhof Pers, 1998.

de Ville, Théophile. *Histoire de la mère Marie-Thérèse, fondatrice de la congrégation des Filles de la croix, de Liège*. Liège: Dessain, 1887.

De Vries, Jacqueline. "More than Paradoxes to Offer. Feminism, History and Religious Cultures". In: Sue Morgan and Jacqueline de Vries (eds.). *Women, Gender and Religious Cultures in Britain 1800-1940*. Abingdon: Routledge, 2010, 188-210.

De Vroede, Maurits. "The Catholic Boarding Schools for Girls in Belgium before the First World War". In: Heinrich Kanz (ed.). *Bildungsgeschichte als Sozialgeschichte. Festschrift zum 60. Geburtstag von Franz Pöggeler*. Frankfurt: Peter Lang, 1986, 313-337.

De Vroede, Maurits. *'Kwezels' en 'zusters': de geestelijke dochters in de Zuidelijke Nederlanden, 17de en 18de eeuw*. Brussels: Koninklijke Vlaamse Academie, 1994.

De Vroede, Maurits. *Religieuses et béguines enseignantes dans les Pays-Bas Méridionaux et la Principauté de Liège aux XVIIe-XVIIIe siècles*. Leuven: Universitaire Pers Leuven, 1996.

De Weerdt, Denise. *En de vrouwen? Vrouw, vrouwenbeweging en feminisme in België 1830-1960*. Ghent: Masereelfonds, 1980.

Dhaene, Corina and Dhaene, Lieve. *Sint-Jozef Kortenberg: van 'Maison de Santé' tot Universitair Centrum: 145 jaar zorg voor geesteszieken 1850-1995*. Kortenberg/Leuven: Universitair Centrum Sint-Jozef/KADOC, 1995.

D'Hoker, Marc et al. *Het kind in de inrichting. 150 jaar residentiële zorg voor kinderen met psychosociale problemen*. Leuven: Katholieke Universiteit Leuven - Faculteit der Psychologie en Pedagogische Wetenschappen, 1986.

Dingemans, Ludovicus. *Les instituts religieux de Belgique*. Brussels: Centre de recherches socio-religieuses, 1961.

Di Stefano, Roberto and Ramon Solans, Francisco J. "Introduction". In: Roberto Di Stefano and Francisco Javier Ramon Solans (eds.). *Pontifical Mobilization and Nationalism in Europe and America*. Basingstoke: Palgrave Macmillan, 2016, 1-25.

Dolan, Jay P. *Catholic Revivalism: the American Experience, 1830-1900*. Notre Dame: University of Notre Dame Press, 1978.

Donnet, Thérèse. "Marie-Eugénie de Jésus (Anne-Eugénie Milleret)". *Dictionnaire de spiritualité ascétique et mystique, doctrine et histoire*. Paris: Beauchesne, 1980, X, 555-557.

Dubois, Ernest. *Notice biographique sur la révérende mère Marie-Augustine, fondatrice des Sœurs de Charité de Notre-Dame du Bon et Perpétuel Secours*. Rome: Cuggiani, 1901.

Duhamelet, Geneviève. *Mère Marie-Xavier Voirin: fondatrice de la congrégation des Sœurs de la providence et de l'immaculée conception de Champion*. Paris: Desclée de Brouwer, 1953.

Dujardin, Carine. "Gender: een beloftevolle invalshoek voor de studie van missie en zending". *Trajecta*, 12 (2003) 4, 275-306.

Dupanloup, Félix. *Manuel des catéchismes ou recueil de prières, billets, cantiques, avis*. Paris: Flandre, s.d.

Dupont-Bouchat, Marie-Sylvie. "Criminalité féminine – justice masculine. Les femmes devant la justice des hommes en Belgique au 19e siècle. Discours et pratiques". In: Luc Courtois, Jean Pirotte and Françoise Rosart (eds.). *Femmes et pouvoirs. Flux et reflux de l'émancipation féminine depuis un siècle*. Louvain-la-Neuve/Brussels: Collège Erasme/Nauwelaerts, 1992, 74-80.

Dupont-Bouchat, Marie-Sylvie. "La prostitution urbaine. La marginalisée intégrée". In: Éliane Gubin and Jean-Pierre Nandrin (eds.). *La ville et les femmes en Belgique. Histoire et sociologie*. Brussels: FUSL, 1993, 97-129.

Dupont-Bouchat, Marie-Sylvie. *De la prison à l'école. Les pénitenciers pour enfants en Belgique au XIXe siècle (1840-1914)*. Kortrijk: UGA, 1996.

Dupont-Bouchat, Marie-Sylvie. "Femmes philanthropes. Les femmes dans la protection de l'enfance en Belgique". *Sextant*, 13-14 (2000), 81-117.

Dupont-Bouchat, Marie-Sylvie. "Delehaye (Ducpétiaux), Pauline". In: Éliane Gubin et al. (eds.). *Dictionnaire des femmes belges. XIX et XXe siècles*. Brussels: Éditions Racine, 2006, 172-173.

Dupont-Bouchat, Marie-Sylvie. *La Belgique criminelle. Droit, justice, société (XIVe-XXe siècles)*. Louvain-la-Neuve: Presses Universitaires Louvain, 2006.

Duriez, Bruno. "Introduction". In: Bruno Duriez, Olivier Rota and Catherine Vialle (eds.). *Femmes catholiques, femmes engages*. Villeneuve d'Ascq: Septentrion, 2019, 9-21.

Dusausoit, Xavier. "Portraits". In: Bernard Stenuit (ed.). *Les Collèges jésuites de Bruxelles: histoire et pédagogie 1604-1835-1905-2005*. Brussels: Lessius, 2005, 315-330.

Dusausoit, Xavier. *Les jésuites dans la ville: les collèges jésuites et la société belge du XIXe s. (1831-1914)*. Brussels: Le Cri, 2011.

Dusausoit, Xavier. "Les jésuites et l'argent. Fondation et gestion de cinq collèges jésuites belges au XIXe siècle (Alost, Gand, Bruxelles, Mons et Verviers)". In: Maarten Van Dijck and Jan De Maeyer (eds.). *The Economics of Providence: Management, Finances and Patrimony of Religious Orders and Congregations in Europe, 1773-c.1930*. Leuven: Leuven University Press, 2013, 247-265.

Ebaugh, Helen R. "Patriarchal Bargains and Latent Avenues of Social Mobility: Nuns in the Roman Catholic Church". *Gender and Society*, 7 (1994) 3, 400-414.

Eijt, José. "Women's history. The 'take-off' of an important discipline. Developments in the Netherlands and Belgium since 1985". In: N.C.F. van Sas and Els Witte (eds.). *Historical Research in the Low Countries*. The Hague: Nederlands Historisch Genootschap, 1992, 76-88.

Eijt, José. "Gesticht door stichters? Betrokkenheid van vrouwen bij het ontstaan van congregaties". In: Marit Monteiro, Gerard Rooijakkers and Joost Rosendaal (eds.). *De dynamiek van religie en cultuur: geschiedenis van het katholicisme in Nederland*. Kampen: Kok, 1993, 162-181.

Eijt, José. *Religieuze vrouwen: bruid, moeder, zuster: geschiedenis van twee Nederlandse zustercongregaties, 1820-1940*. Hilversum: Verloren, 1995.

Eijt, José. "Leeuw en lam. Jacques van Ginneken en de Vrouwen van Nazareth". In: Marit Monteiro, Peter Nissen and Judith de Raat (eds.). *Steun en toeverlaat. Historische aspecten van geestelijke begeleiding*. Hilversum: Verloren, 1999, 32-56.

Ewens, Mary. *The Role of the Nun in Nineteenth-Century America*. New York: Arno Press, 1978.

Ewens, Mary. "Removing the Veil: the Liberated American Nun". In: Rosemary Ruether and Eleanor McLaughlin (eds.). *Women of Spirit: Female Leadership in the Jewish and Christian Traditions*. New York: Simon and Schuster, 1979, 255-276.

Ewens, Mary. "Women in the Convent". In: Karen Kennelly (ed.). *American Catholic Women: An Historical Exploration*. New York: Macmillan, 1989, 17-47.

Ewens, Mary. *The Role of the Nun in Nineteenth-Century America. Variations on the International Theme*. Thiensville: Caritas Communications, 2014.

Faes, Ilona and Jacobs, Ivo. *333 jaar Heilig Graf Turnhout. 1662/1995*. Turnhout: Heilig-Grafinstituut, 1995.

Fauconnier, Marina. *Vrouwenkloosters in Oost-Vlaanderen tussen 1802 en 1914*. Unpublished master thesis, Universiteit Gent, 1980.

Firth, Joy. "Accounting for Souls: Anglican Sisters and the Economies of Moral Reform in Victorian England". In: Maarten Van Dijck and Jan De Maeyer (eds.). *The Economics of Providence: Management, Finances and Patrimony of Religious orders and Congregations in Europe, 1773-c 1930*. Leuven: Leuven University Press, 2012, 185-204.

Fitzgerald, Maureen. *Habits of Compassion: Irish Catholic Nuns and the Origins of New York's Welfare System, 1830-1920*. Urbana/Chicago: University of Illinois Press, 2006.

Fleckenstein, Gisela and Schmiedl, Joachim (eds.). *Ultramontanismus: Tendenzen der Forschung*. Paderborn: Bonifatius, 2005.

Ford, Caroline. "Religion and Popular Culture in Modern Europe". *The Journal of Modern History*, 65 (1993) 1, 152-175.

Ford, Caroline. *Divided Houses: Religion and Gender in Modern France*. Ithaca: Cornell University Press, 2005.

François, Luc. "Philippe Vilain XIIII (1778-1856), grootgrondbezitter en 'l'homme du parti industriel'". In: Hugo Soly and René Vermeir (eds.). *Beleid en bestuur in de oude Nederlanden: Liber amicorum prof. dr. M. Baelde*. Ghent: RUG. Vakgroep Nieuwe Geschiedenis, 1993, 189-203.

Friedlander, Colette. "Les pouvoirs de la supérieure dans le cloître et dans le monde du concile de Trente à nos jours". In: *Les Religieuses dans le cloître et dans le monde*. Saint-Etienne: Publications de l'Université de Saint-Etienne, 1994, 239-256.

Fuchs, Rachel G. and Thompson, Victoria E. *Women in Nineteenth-Century Europe*. Basingstoke: Palgrave Macmillan, 2004.

Gadille, Jacques. "Grands courants doctrinaux et de spiritualité dans le monde catholique". In: Jacques Gadille and Jean-Marie Mayeur (eds.). *Libéralisme, industrialisation, expansion européenne (1830-1914). (Histoire du Christianisme. Tome XI)*. Paris: Desclée, 1995, 113-136.

Ganss, George E. *The Constitutions of the Society of Jesus*. Saint Louis: Institute of Jesuit Sources, 1970.

Garcia Iglesias, Luis. "Institutos religiosos femeninos de inspiración jesuítica en la España de los siglos XIX y XX". *Estudios Eclesiásticos*, 70 (1995) 275, 501-526.

Gérin, Paul. "Louise Van den Plas et les débuts du Féminisme Chrétien de Belgique". *Belgisch Tijdschrift voor Nieuwste Geschiedenis*, 1 (1969) 2, 254-275.

Gérin, Paul. "Sociaal-katholicisme en christendemocratie (1884-1904)". In: Emmanuel Gerard (ed.). *De christelijke arbeidersbeweging in België 1891-1991*. Leuven: Universitaire Pers Leuven, 1991, 56-113.

Gérin, Paul. "La Société de Saint-Vincent de Paul à Liège (1846-1992)". In: Jan De Maeyer and Paul Wynants (eds.). *De Vincentianen in België. 1842-1992*. Leuven: Universitaire Pers Leuven, 1992, 317-335.

Gevers, Lieve. "Gezin, religie en moderniteit. Visie en strategie van de Belgische bisschoppen (1830-1940)". *Trajecta*, 4 (1995) 2, 103-121.

Gevers, Lieve and Vuurstaek, Anneleen. "Mariadevotie, hefboom voor een uitgeversbedrijf (1877-1914/1973)". In: Rita Ghesquière and Patricia Quaghebeur (eds.). *Averbode, een uitgever apart. 1877-2002*. Leuven/Averbode: Universitaire Pers Leuven/Uitgeverij Averbode, 2002, 70-92.

Geybels, Hans. "De begijnenbeweging na de Franse Revolutie". In: Anton De Preter, Mathijs Lamberigts and Marcel Gielis. *Gelovige en verstandige vrouwen maken geschiedenis. Over begijnen en begijnhoven in context*. Leuven: Halewijn, 2018, 118-154.

Ghesquiere, Ilse and Van Rompaey, Lies. "Het fenomeen dienstpersoneel doorheen de tijd". In: Jan De Maeyer and Lies Van Rompaey (eds.). *Upstairs downstairs. Dienstpersoneel in Vlaanderen 1750-1995*. Ghent: Provinciebestuur Oost-Vlaanderen, 1996, 19-101.

Gibson, Ralph. *A Social History of French Catholicism, 1789-1914*. London: Routledge, 1989.

Godinas-Thys, Anne. "Les sœurs du Saint-Sacrement, de Bruxelles à Liège". *Bulletin de la Société Royale Le Vieux Liège*, 15 (2007) 317, 137-160.

Gough, Austin. *Paris and Rome: The Gallican Church and the Ultramontane Campaign, 1848-1853*. Oxford: Clarendon Press, 1986.

Goujon, Bertrand. "Gender, Family and Religious Identity in Nineteenth-Century Ultramontane Aristocracy". In: Tine Van Osselaer and Patrick Pasture (eds.). *Christian Homes: Religion, Family and Domesticity in the 19th and 20th Centuries*. Leuven: Leuven University Press, 2014, 66-81.

Green, Laura M. *Educating Women: Cultural Conflict and Victorian Literature*. Athens: Ohio University Press, 2001.

Grégoire, Hélène. *Rosalie Cadron-Jetté. A Story of Courage and Compassion*. Montréal: Rosalie-Cadron-Jetté Centre, 2007.

Griffiths, Fiona J. and Hotchin, Julie. "Women and Men in the Medieval Religious Landscape". In: Fiona J. Griffiths and Julie Hotchin (eds.). *Partners in Spirit: Women, Men and Religious Life in Germany, 1100-1500*. Turnhout: Brepols, 2014, 1-45.

Groessens, Baudouin. "Laïcité, anticléricalisme et école catholique au XIXe siècle". In: Jan De Maeyer and Paul Wynants (eds.). *L'enseignement catholique en Belgique. Des identités en évolution, 19e-21e siècles*. Antwerp: Halewijn, 2016, 499-509.

Gualtieri, Elena. "The Impossible Art: Virginia Woolf on Modern Biography". *Cambridge Quarterly*, 29 (2000) 4, 349-361.

Gubin, Éliane. "La grande ville, un lieu féminin. L'exemple de Bruxelles avant 1914". In: Éliane Gubin and Jean-Pierre Nandrin (eds.). *La ville et les femmes en Belgique. Histoire et sociologie*. Brussels: Publications des Facultés universitaires Saint-Louis, 1993, 77-96.

Gubin, Éliane. "Histoire des femmes, histoire de genre". *Sextant*, 2 (1994), 89-103.

Gubin, Éliane. "Du politique au politique. Parcours du féminisme belge (1830-914)". *Belgisch Tijdschrift voor Filologie en Geschiedenis*, 77 (1999) 2, 370-382.

Gubin, Éliane. "Les femmes et l'art. Autour d'une exposition". *Sextant*, 11 (1999), 7-13.

Gubin, Éliane. *Choisir l'histoire des femmes*. Brussels: Éditions de l'Université de Bruxelles, 2007.

Gubin, Éliane. "Politics and Anticlericalism: Belgium". In: James Albisetti, Joyce Goodman and Rebecca Rogers (eds.). *Girl's Secondary Education in the Western World. From the 18th to the 20th Century*. New York: Palgrave MacMillan, 2010, 121-132.

Gubin, Éliane et al. (eds.). *Dictionnaire des femmes belges. XIX et XXe siècles*. Brussels: Éditions Racine, 2006.

Gubin, Éliane and Piette, Valérie. *Emma, Louise et Marie: l'Université de Bruxelles et l'émancipation des femmes (1830-2000)*. Brussels: ULB, 2004.

Gubin, Éliane and Piette, Valérie. *Isabelle Gatti de Gamond: 1839-1905, la passion d'enseigner*. Brussels: GIEF-ULB, 2004.

Haeyaert, Philippe. *Iuventus et pauperes: 150 jaar religieuzen in Wevelgem 1837-1987*. Roeselare: Concordia, 1988.

Hallez, Jan. *Uit het leven van moeder Concordia, 1803-1874, stichteres en overste der Dochters van het Heilig Hart en Onbevlekt Hart van Maria, Antwerpen*. Antwerp: De Branding, 1947.

Hamer, Edna. *Elizabeth Prout (1820-1864), foundress of the Sisters of the Cross and Passion of our Lord Jesus Christ*. Leominster: Gracewing, 2008.

Hanoteau, Marie-Elisabeth. "Le dernier béguinage nivellois (1713-1847)". *Revue d'histoire religieuse du Brabant wallon*, 1 (1987) 4, 178-195.

Hanoteau, Marie-Emilie. *Une grande nivelloise, Mère Gertrude (Justine Desbille), fondatrice des Sœurs de l'Enfant-Jésus de Nivelles, 1801-1866*. Nivelles: Institut de l'Enfant-Jésus, 1985.

Hardick, Lothar. *He Leads, I Follow. The Life of Mother Maria Theresia Bonzel*. S.l.: Our Sunday Visitor, 2018.

Harline, Craig. "Actives and Contemplatives: The Female Religious of the Low Countries before and after Trent". *Catholic Historical Review*, 81 (1995) 4, 541-567.

Harris, Ruth. *Lourdes: Body and Spirit in the Secular Age*. New York: Penguin Books, 1999.

Harrison, Carol. *Romantic Catholics: France's Postrevolutionary Generation in Search of a Modern Faith*. Ithaca: Cornell University Press, 2014.

Harvey, Elizabeth. *Ventriloquized Voices: Feminist Theory and English Renaissance Texts*. London: Routledge, 1992.

Héger, Paul. *Héger 1700-2000. De Charlotte Brontë à l'ULB et de l'ULB à la Communauté européenne*. Brussels: Racine, 2003.

Heimann, Mary. *Catholic Devotion in Victorian England*. Oxford: Clarendon, 1995.

Hellemans, Staf. *Strijd om de moderniteit: sociale bewegingen en verzuiling in Europa sinds 1800*. Leuven: Leuven University Press, 1990.

Hellinckx, Bart; Simon, Frank and Depaepe, Marc. *The Forgotten Contribution of the Teaching Sisters: a Historiographical Essay on the Educational Work of Catholic Women Religious in the 19th and 20th Centuries*. Leuven: Leuven University Press, 2009.

Hélyot, Pierre. *Dictionnaire des ordres religieux ou histoire des ordres monastiques, religieux et militaires et des congrégations séculières de l'un et de l'autre sexe, qui ont été établies jusqu'à présent*. Paris: Petit-Montrouge, 1847-1859, 4 vol.

Hemelsoet, Annelies. *Liefdadigheid als roeping van de dame: het sociaal engagement van de adellijke vrouw in het 19de-eeuwse Gent (1845-1880)*. Unpublished master thesis, Rijksuniversiteit Gent, 2002.

Henneau, Marie-Elisabeth. "Récit de vie d'une sainte en devenir dans le sillage des Pères de la Foi: le portrait de Julie Billiart, fondatrice des Sœurs de Notre-Dame, par sa compagne, Françoise Blin de Bourdon". In: Silvia Mostaccio et al. (eds.). *Échelles de pouvoir, rapports de genre. Femmes, jésuites et modèle ignatien dans le long XIX siècle*. Louvain-la-Neuve: Presses Universitaires de Louvain, 2014, 235-248.

Hermans, An. *Scheppers, onze school: 150 jaar onderwijs aan de Melaan in Mechelen*. Mechelen: Scheppersinstituut, 2002.

Heyrman, Peter. "La culture d'entreprise des écoles catholiques. Les finances et la gestion". In: Jan De Maeyer and Paul Wynants (eds.). *L'enseignement catholique en Belgique. Des identités en évolution, 19e-21e siècles*. Antwerp: Halewijn, 2016, 295-325.

Hobsbawm, Eric. *The Age of Empire. 1875-1914*. London: Cardinal, 1991.

Hoegaerts, Josephine and Van Osselaer, Tine. "Corps et moralité: le genre en classe et dans la cour de récréation". In: Jan De Maeyer and Paul Wynants (eds.). *L'enseignement catholique en Belgique. Des identités en évolution, 19e-21e siècles*. Antwerp: Halewijn, 2016, 437-456.

Hostie, Raymond. *Leven en dood van de religieuze instituten: psychosociologische benadering*. Bruges: Emmaus, 1972.

Houtart, François. *Les paroisses de Bruxelles (1803-1951): législation – délimitation – démographie – équipement*. Louvain: UCL. Institut de recherches économiques et sociales, 1955.

Hoy, Suellen. *Good Hearts. Catholic Sisters in Chicago's Past*. Champaign: University of Illinois Press, 2006.

Huberty, Colette and Keunings, Luc. "La prostitution à Bruxelles au 19e siècle". *Les Cahiers de la Fonderie*, 2 (1987) 2, 3-21.

Hümmeler, Hans. *In hoc signo vinces: in dit teken zult gij overwinnen: leven en werken van moeder Maria Theresia Haze, stichteres van de kongregatie van de Dochters van het kruis, Luik*. Genk: Dochters van het Kruis, 1961.

Jacobus, Anne. "De vrouwelijke religieuze roepingen in het bisdom Brugge 1802-1914". *Handelingen van het Genootschap voor Geschiedenis*, 116 (1979) 1-2, 27-86.

Jacobus, Anne. "De vrouwelijke religieuzen (1834-1914)". In: Michel Cloet (ed.). *Het bisdom Brugge (1559-1984). Bisschoppen, priesters, gelovigen*. Bruges: West-Vlaams Verbond van Kringen voor Heemkunde, 1985, 425-433.

Jadin, L. "Bizzarri (Giuseppe-Andrea)". *Dictionnaire d'Histoire et de Géographie Ecclésiastiques*. Paris, 1937, IX, col. 49.

Jaeger, Kathleen. "A Writer or a Religious? Lady Georgiana Fullerton's Dilemma". In: Peter Clarke and Charlotte Methuen (eds.). *The Church and Literature*. Woodbridge/Rochester: Ecclesiastical History Society/The Boydell Press, 2012, 271-282.

Jankowiak, François. *La Curie romaine de Pie IX à Pie X: le gouvernement central de l'Église et la fin des États pontificaux (1846-1914)*. Rome: École Française de Rome, 2007.

Jankowiak, François and Pettinaroli, Laura. *Les cardinaux entre Cour et Curie. Une élite romaine, 1775-2015*. Rome: École Française de Rome, 2017.

Jarlert, Anders (ed.). *Piety and Modernity*. Leuven: Leuven University Press, 2012.

Jarrell, Lynn. "The Development of Legal Structures for Women Religious between 1500 and 1900: A Study of Selected Institutes of Religious Life for Women". *U.S. Catholic Historian*, 10 (1991/1992) 1-2, 25-35.

Johnson, Elizabeth. *Friends of God and Prophets: A Feminist Theological Reading of the Communion of Saints*. London: SCM, 1998.

Kandiyoti, Deniz. "Bargaining with Patriarchy". *Gender and Society*, 2 (1988) 3, 274-290.

Kane, Paula. "'She Offered Herself Up': The Victim Soul and Victim Spirituality in Catholicism". *Church History*, 71 (2002) 2, 80-119.

Keymolen, Denise. "Isala Van Diest, arts en feministe". *Spiegel Historiael*, 10 (1975) 5, 304-309.

Keymolen, Denise. *Vrouwenarbeid in België van ca. 1860 tot 1914*. Leuven: Acco, 1977.

Keymolen, Denise. *Beroepsarbeid voor vrouwen van betere stand in België omstreeks 1860: een bijdrage tot de mentaliteits- en onderwijsgeschiedenis*. Ghent: RUG. Centrum voor de studie van de historische pedagogiek, 1981.

Keymolen, Denise. *Victoire Cappe (1886-1927): une vie chrétienne, sociale, féministe*. Leuven: Leuven University Press, 2001.

Keymolen, Denise and Coenen, Marie-Thérèse. *Stap voor stap: geschiedenis van de vrouwenemancipatie in België*. Brussels: Kabinet van de Staatssecretaris voor Maatschappelijke Emancipatie, 1991.

Keymolen, Denise and Van Molle, Leen. "Feminisme, vrouwenbeweging en dienstbodenvraagstuk". In: Jan De Maeyer and Lies Van Rompaey (eds.). *Upstairs, downstairs. Dienstpersoneel in Vlaanderen. 1750-1995*. Ghent: Provinciebestuur Oost-Vlaanderen, 1996, 167-175.

Kilroy, Phil. *Madeleine Sophie Barat 1779-1865: a Life*. Cork: Cork University Press, 2000.

King, Ursula (ed.). *Religion and Gender*. Oxford: Blackwell, 1995.

King, Ursula. "Religion and Gender: Embedded Patterns, Interwoven Frameworks". In: Teresa A. Meade and Merry Wiesner-Hanks (eds.). *A Companion to Gender History*. Oxford: Blackwell, 2004, 70-85.

Kirkus, M.G. "'Yes, My Lord': Some Eighteenth and Nineteenth Century Bishops and the Institute of the Blessed Virgin Mary". *Recusant History*, 24 (1998) 2, 171-192.

Kollar, Rene. "Magdalenes and Nuns: Convent Laundries in Late Victorian England". *Episcopal History*, 73 (2004) 3, 309-334.

Koppen, Jimmy. *De Kloosterkwestie. Liberale visies op religieuze instituten, onderwijs en zorg in België, 1830-1921*. Unpublished PhD thesis, Vrije Universiteit Brussel, 2017.

Kraaij, Harry J. *Henriette Ronner-Knip 1821-1909: een virtuoos dierschilderes*. Schiedam: Scriptum, 1998.

Krylova, Anna. "Gender Binary and the Limits of Poststructuralist Method". *Gender & History*, 28 (2016) 2, 307-323.

Kselman, Thomas A. *Miracles and Prophecies in Nineteenth-Century France*. New Brunswick: Rutgers University Press, 1983.

Lacroix, Marie-Thérèse. "L'influence ignatienne sur les constitutions des Sœurs de Saint-André". *Revue d'Histoire Ecclésiastique*, 88 (1993), 88-107.

Lacroix, Marie-Thérèse. *La vie à Saint-André au XIXème siècle (1796-1914)*. Tournai: ARSA, 2007, 2 vol.

Lamberts, Emiel. "Joseph de Hemptinne: een kruisvaarder in redingote". In: Emiel Lamberts (ed.). *De kruistocht tegen het liberalisme. Facetten van het ultramontanisme in België in de 19e eeuw*. Leuven: Universitaire Pers Leuven, 1983, 64-108.

Lamberts, Emiel (ed.). *De kruistocht tegen het liberalisme: facetten van het ultramontanisme in België in de 19e eeuw*. Leuven: Universitaire Pers Leuven, 1984.

Lamberts, Emiel. "Het ultramontanisme in België 1830-1914". In: Emiel Lamberts (ed.). *De kruistocht tegen het liberalisme. Facetten van ultramontanisme in België in de 19de eeuw*. Leuven: Universitaire Pers Leuven, 1984, 38-59.

Lamberts, Emiel (ed.). *Een kantelend tijdperk: de wending van de Kerk naar het volk in Noordwest-Europa (1890-1910)*. Leuven: Universitaire Pers Leuven, 1992.

Lamberts, Emiel. "L'Internationale noire. Une organisation secrète au service du Saint-Siège". In: Emiel Lamberts (ed.). *The Black International 1870-1878: The Holy See and Militant Catholicism in Europe*. Leuven: Leuven University Press, 2002, 15-101.

Lamberts, Emiel. "Catholic Congresses as Amplifiers of International Catholic Opinion". In: Vincent Viaene (ed.). *The Papacy and the New World Order: Vatican Diplomacy, Catholic Opinion and International Politics at the Time of Leo XIII*. Leuven: Leuven University Press, 2005, 213-224.

Lamberts, Emiel. *The Struggle with Leviathan: Social Responses to the Omnipotence of the State, 1815-1965*. Leuven: Leuven University Press, 2016.

Lancaster, Judith. *Cornelia Connelly and her Interpreters*. Oxford: Way Books, 2004.

Landes, Joan B. *Women and the Public Sphere in the Age of the French Revolution*. Ithaca: Cornell University Press, 1996.

Langlois, Claude. "Les effectifs des congrégations féminines au XIXe siècle. De l'enquête statistique à l'histoire quantitative". *Revue d'histoire de l'Eglise de France*, 60 (1974) 164, 39-64.

Langlois, Claude. *Le catholicisme au féminin: les congrégations françaises à supérieure générale au XIXe siècle*. Paris: Éditions du Cerf, 1984.

Langlois, Claude. "Féminisation du catholicisme". In: Jacques Le Goff and René Rémond (eds.). *Histoire de la France religieuse. 3: Du Roi très chrétien à la laïcité républicaine. XVIIIe-XIXe siècles*. Paris: Seuil, 1991, 292-310.

Langlois, Claude. "La conjoncture mariale des années quarante". In: François Angelier and Claude Langlois (eds.). *La Salette. Apocalypse, pèlerinage et littérature (1846-1996). Actes du colloque de l'Institut catholique de Paris (29-30 de novembre de 1996)*. Grenoble: Jerôme Million, 2000, 21-38.

Langlois, Claude. *Le désir du sacerdoce chez Thérèse de Lisieux*. Paris: Salvator, 2002.

Langlois, Claude. "Les congrès eucharistiques. Jalons pour une histoire". In: Claude Langlois and Christian Sorrel (eds.). *Le catholicisme en congrès (XIXe-XXe siècles)*. Lyon: RESEA/LARHRA, 2009, 205-224.

Langlois, Claude. *Catholicisme, religieuses et société: le temps des bonnes sœurs (XIXe siècle)*. Paris: Desclée de Brouwer, 2011.

Langlois, Claude. *Thérèse de Lisieux et la miséricorde*. Paris: Cerf, 2016.

Lannon, Frances. *Privilege, Persecution, and Prophecy: The Catholic Church in Spain. 1875-1975*. Oxford: Clarendon Press, 1987.

Larkin, Emmet. "The Devotional Revolution in Ireland, 1850-1875". *American Historical Review*, 77 (1972) 3, 625-652.

Laureys, Dirk. *De Mindere Broeders van Franciscus. 1842-1991*. Leuven: Minderbroeders/KADOC, 1992.

Lecuir-Nemo, Geneviève. *Anne-Marie Javouhey. Fondatrice de la congrégation des sœurs de Saint-Joseph de Cluny (1779-1851)*. Paris: Karthala, 2001.

Ledure, Yves. *Le père Léon Dehon 1843-1925: entre mystique et catholicisme social*. Paris: Cerf, 2005.

Le Goff, Jacques. "After Annales: The Life as History". *The Times Literary Supplement*, 14-20 April 1989.

Lejaer, Jean. "Histoire de la ville de Verviers. Période hollandaise et Révolution belge de 1830. 1814-1830". *Bulletin de la Société Verviétoise d'Archéologie et d'Histoire*, 7 (1906), 4-320.

Lelong, Maurice. *Les dominicaines des prisons*. Paris: Cerf, 1938.

Leroy, Frédéric. "Quand l'aristocratie et la grande bourgeoisie habitaient le quartier Léopold". *Belgisch Tijdschrift voor Filologie en Geschiedenis*, 88 (2010) 2, 519-540.

Les écrits spirituels de Mère Agathe Verhelle: fondatrice des Religieuses de l'Instruction Chrétienne 1789-1838. S.l.: s.n., s.d.

Les religieuses de Saint-André du XIIIe au XXe siècle. Lille: Société Saint-Augustin, 1908.

Levillain, Philippe. *Le pontificat de Léon XIII: renaissances du Saint-Siège?* Rome: École Française de Rome, 2006.

Liebowitz, Ruth. "Virgins in the Service of Christ: The Dispute over an Active Apostolate for Women during the Counter-Reformation". In: Rosemary Ruether and Eleanor McLaughlin (eds.). *Women of Spirit: Female Leadership in the Jewish and Christian Tradition*. New York: Simon and Schuster, 1979, 131-152.

Liedel, Leslie L. "Indomitable Nuns and an Unruly Bishop: Property Rights and the Grey Nun's Defense against the Arbitrary Use of Diocesan Power in Nineteenth-Century Cleveland". *The Catholic Historical Review*, 86 (2000) 3, 459-479.

Life of the Venerable Servant of God Julie Billiart: Foundress and First Superior General of the Institute of Notre-Dame. London: Art and Book Company, 1898.

Lindeijer, Marc; Luyten, Jo and Suenens, Kristien. "The Quick Downfall and Slow Rise of the Jesuit Order in the Low Countries". In: Marc Lindeijer and Leo Kenis (eds.). *The Survival of the Jesuits in the Low Countries*. Leuven: Leuven University Press, 2019, 13-47.

Long, Judy. *Telling Women's Lives. Subject/Narrator/Reader/Text*. New York: New York University Press, 1999.

Lory, Jacques. *Libéralisme et instruction primaire 1842-1879: introduction à l'étude de la lutte scolaire en Belgique*. Leuven: Bibliothèque de l'Université, 1979.

Luddy, Maria. *Women and Philanthropy in Nineteenth-Century Ireland*. Cambridge: Cambridge University Press, 1995.

Luddy, Maria. "Convent Archives as Sources for Irish History". In: Rosemary Raughter (ed.). *Religious Women and Their History: Breaking the Silence*. Dublin: Irish Academic Press, 2005, 98-115.

Luddy, Maria. *Prostitution and Irish Society, 1800-1940*. Cambridge: Cambridge University Press, 2007.

Luddy, Maria. "'Possessed of fine properties'. Power, Authority and the Funding of Convents in Ireland, 1780-1900". In: Maarten Van Dijck and Jan De Maeyer (eds.). *The Economics of Providence: Management, Finances and Patrimony of Religious Orders and Congregations in Europe, 1773-c 1930*. Leuven: Leuven University Press, 2012, 227-246.

Luirard, Monique. "Les pouvoirs de la supérieure générale de la Société du Sacré-Cœur". In: *Les Religieuses dans le cloître et dans le monde des origines à nos jours*. Saint-Etienne: Publications de l'Université de Saint-Etienne, 1994, 303-327.

Luirard, Monique. *La société du Sacré-Cœur dans le monde de son temps. 1865-2000*. Villeneuve d'Ascq: Presses Universitaires du Septentrion, 2019.

Lux-Sterritt, Laurence and Mangion, Carmen M. "Introduction". In: Laurence Lux-Sterritt and Carmen M. Mangion (eds.). *Gender, Catholicism and Spirituality: Women and the Roman Catholic Church in Britain and Europe, 1200-1900*. New York: Palgrave Macmillan, 2011, 1-17.

Luyten, Jo. *Ja, Zonhoven gaat vooruit, wel niet vlug maar het komt en dat is 't voornaamste: 150 jaar Zusters van Liefde van Onze-Lieve-Vrouw, Moeder van Barmhartigheid (1851-2001)*. Zonhoven: Zusters van Liefde, 2001.

Luyten, Jo. "Limburg voor Christus. Repertorium van kloosters, priorijen en abdijen van vrouwelijke religieuzen in Limburg. 1822-2007". *Limburg - Het Oude Land van Loon*, 87 (2008) 3, 29-95.

Luyten, Jo and Suenens, Kristien. "'Jesuits' as Promoters of Female Religious Congregations in Belgium (c. 1800-1870): Continuity of Discontinuity?". In: Marc Lindeijer and Leo Kenis (eds.). *The Survival of the Jesuits in the Low Countries*. Leuven: Leuven University Press, 2019, 255-277.

Mac Avoy, J. "Ouverture de conscience au supérieur". *Dictionnaire de Spiritualité*. Paris: Beauchesne, 1982, IX, 1070-1076.

Maes, Noël et al. "150 jaar Klooster van de Zusters van Liefde van Heule en zijn stichteres Agatha Lagae". *Heulespiegel*, 8 (1988), 1-48.

Mahmood, Saba. "Feminist Theory, Embodiment, and the Docile Agent: Some Reflections on the Egyptian Islamic Revival". *Cultural Anthropology*, 16 (2001) 2, 202-236.

Mahmood, Saba. *Politics of Piety: The Islamic Revival and the Feminist Subject*. Princeton: Princeton University Press, 2005.

Majérus, Pascal. *Ces femmes qu'on dit béguines... Guide des béguinages de Belgique. Bibliographie et sources d'archives*. Brussels: Archives générales du royaume, 1997.

Mangion, Carmen M. *Contested Identities: Active Women Religious in Nineteenth-Century England and Wales*. London: University of London, 2008.

Mangion, Carmen M. "Women, Religious Ministry and Female Institution Building". In: Sue Morgan and Jacqueline de Vries (eds.). *Women, Gender and Religious Cultures*. Abingdon: Routledge, 2010, 72-93.

Mangion, Carmen M. "'The Mixed Life': Challenging Understandings of Religious Life in Victorian England". In: Laurence Lux-Sterrit and Carmen Mangion (eds.). *Gender, Catholicism and Spirituality: Women and the Roman Catholic Church in Britain and Europe, 1200-1900*. Basingstoke: Palgrave Macmillan, 2011, 165-179.

Mangion, Carmen M. "Developing Alliances. Faith, Philanthropy and Fundraising in Late-Nineteenth-Century St Helens". In: Maarten Van Dijck and Jan De Maeyer (eds.). *The Economics of Providence: Management, Finances and Patrimony of Religious Orders and Congregations in Europe, 1773-c 1930*. Leuven: Leuven University Press, 2012, 205-225.

Mangion, Carmen M. "'Why would you have me live upon a gridiron?'. Pain, Identity and Emotional Communities in Nineteenth-Century English Convent Culture". *19: Interdisciplinary Studies in the Long Nineteenth Century*, 15 (2012), 1-16.

Manzoni, Giuseppe. "Victimale (Spiritualité)". In: *Dictionnaire de Spiritualité*. Paris: Beauchesne, 1994, XVI, 531-545.

Marcélis, Anne-Dolorès. *Femmes cloîtrées des temps contemporains. Vies et histoires de carmélites et de clarisses en Namurois, 1837-2000*. Louvain-la-Neuve: Presses universitaires de Louvain, 2012.

Margry, Peter Jan and Te Velde, Henk. "Contested rituals and the battle for public space: the Netherlands". In: Christopher Clark and Wolfram Kaiser (eds.). *Culture Wars: Secular-Catholic Conflict in Nineteenth-Century Europe*. Cambridge: Cambridge University Press, 2003, 129-151.

Maridet, Estelle. "Les visitandines et la mort. Analyse des abrégés". In: Bernard Dompnier and Dominique Julia (eds.). *Visitation et visitandines aux XVIIe et XVIIIe siècles*. Saint-Étienne: Publications de l'Université de Saint-Étienne, 2001, 301-320.

Martina, Giacomo. "Italia. Gli istituti religiosi in Italia dalla Restaurazione alla fine dell'800". In: Giancarlo Rocca (ed.). *Dizionario degli istituti di perfezione*. Rome: Ed. Paoline, 1978, 217-233.

Masson, Frédéric. *Napoléon et son fils*. Paris: Goupil & Cie, 1904.

Masson, Ignace. *De aartsbroederschap van Sint Franciscus Xaverius in België en voornamelijk in het bisdom Gent (1854-1896)*. Unpublished master thesis, Katholieke Universiteit Leuven, 1966.

Maunder, Chris. *Our Lady of the Nations: Apparitions of Mary in 20th-century Catholic Europe*. Oxford: Oxford University Press, 2016.

Maurain, Jean. *Le Saint-Siège et la France, de décembre 1851 à avril 1853: documents inédits*. Paris: Alcan, 1930.

Maury, Gilles. "The True Disciple. Jean-Baptiste Bethune and A.W.N. Pugin: A Summary of a Complex Relationship". In: Timothy Brittain-Catlin, Jan De Maeyer and Martin Bressani (eds.). *Gothic Revival Worldwide: A.W.N. Pugin's Global Influence*. Leuven: Leuven University Press, 2016, 42-51.

McCarthy, Rebecca Lea. *Origins of the Magdalene Laundries: An Analytical History*. Jefferson/London: McFarland & Company, 2010.

McGuinness, Margaret M. *Called to Serve: A History of Nuns in America*. New York: New York University Press, 2013.

McGuinness, Margaret M. "Why Relationships Matter: Sisters, Bishops, and the History of Catholicism in the United States". *The Catholic Historical Review*, 100 (2014) 2, 219-242.

McLeod, Hugh. *Religion and the People of Western Europe, 1789-1970*. Oxford: Oxford University Press, 1981.

McLeod, Hugh. "Weibliche Frömmigkeit - männlicher Unglaube?: Religion und Kirche im bürgerlichen 19. Jahrhundert". In: Ute Frevert (ed.). *Bürgerinnen und Bürger: Geschlechterverhältnisse im 19. Jahrhundert, zwölf Beiträge*. Göttingen: Vandenhoeck & Ruprecht, 1988, 134-156.

McLeod, Hugh. "New Perspectives on the Religious History of Western and Northern Europe. 1815-1960". *Kyrkohistorisk Arsskrift*, 100 (2000) 1, 135-145.

McMillan, James F. "Women in Social Catholicism in Late Nineteenth and Early Twentieth-Century France". In: W.J. Sheils and Diana Wood (eds.). *Women and the Church*. Oxford: Blackwell, 1990, 467-480.

McMillan, James F. "Religion and Gender in Modern France: Some Reflections". In: Frank Tallet and Nicholas Atkin (eds.). *Religion, Society and Politics in France since 1789*. London: The Hambledon Press, 1991, 55-65.

McMillan, James F. *France and Women 1789-1914: Gender, Society and Politics*. London: Routledge, 2000.

McNamara, Jo A.K. *Sisters in Arms: Catholic Nuns through Two Millenia*. Cambridge: Harvard University Press, 1996.

Medioli, Francesca. "The Dimensions of the Cloister. Enclosure, Constraint and Protection in Seventeenth-Century Italy". In: Anne Jacobson Schutte, Thomas Kuelin and Silvana Seidel Menchi (eds.). *Time, Space and Women's Lives in Early Modern Europe*. Kirksville: Truman State University Press, 2001, 165-180.

Meiwes, Relinde. *Arbeiterinnen des Herrn: katholische Frauenkongregationen im 19. Jahrhundert*. Frankfurt: Campus, 2000.

Meiwes, Relinde. "Katholische Frauenkongregationen und die Krankenpflege im 19. Jahrhundert". *L'homme: Zeitschrift für feministische Geschichtswissenschaft*, 19 (2008) 1, 39-60.

Menozzi, Daniele. *Sacro Cuore: un culto tra devozione interiore e restaurazione cristiana della società*. Rome: Viella, 2001.

Mercier, Vincent. *Prins diamant: het tragische verval van een wereldimperium*. Leuven: Van Halewyck, 2013.

Mertens, Rita. "Vrouwelijke religieuze roepingen tussen 1803 en 1955. Casus: de congregatie van Zomergem en de Zomergemse vrouwelijke religieuzen". *Belgisch Tijdschrift voor Nieuwste Geschiedenis*, 9 (1978) 3-4, 419-479.

Meuwissen, Éric. *Les grandes fortunes du Brabant*. Ottignies: Editions Quorum, 1994.

Michaux, Marianne. "Femmes de lettres belges 1850-1880. Dette idéologique, ruse symbolique". *Sextant*, 6 (1996), 31-52.

Mills, Hazel. "Negotiating the Divide: Women, Philanthropy and the 'Public Sphere' in Nineteenth-Century France". In: Frank Tallet and Nicholas Atkin (eds.). *Religion, Society and Politics in France since 1789*. London: The Hambledon Press, 1991, 23-54.

Miranda García, Soledad. *Religión y clero en la gran novela española del siglo XIX*. Madrid: Pegaso, 1982.

Moeys, Hendrik. *Subsidiary Social Provision before the Welfare State: Political Theory and Social Policy in Nineteenth-Century Belgium*. Unpublished PhD thesis, KU Leuven, 2017.

Montaignac de Chauvance, Louise-Thérèse. *Souvenirs*. Brussels: Vromant, 1931.

Monteiro, Marit. *Geestelijke maagden: het leven tussen klooster en wereld in Noord-Nederland gedurende de zeventiende eeuw*. Hilversum: Verloren, 1996.

Monteiro, Marit. *Vroomheid in veelvoud. Geschiedenis van de Franciscanessen van Oirschot. 1797-1997*. Hilversum: Verloren, 2000.

Monteiro, Marit. *Gods predikers. Dominicanen in Nederland (1795-2000)*. Hilversum: Verloren, 2008.

Monteiro, Marit; Rooijakkers, Gerard and Rosendaal, Joost (eds.). *De dynamiek van religie en cultuur: geschiedenis van het Nederlands katholicisme*. Kampen: Kok, 1993.

Moons, Annelies. *Historische evolutie van de religieuzen der Gedurige Aanbidding in de negentiende eeuw te Gent*. Unpublished master thesis, KU Leuven, 2007.

Moors, Hans. "De drempels van de droom. Vrouwen, vrouwelijkheid en socialisme 1830-1870". In: Denise De Weerdt (ed.). *Begeerte heeft ons aangeraakt. Socialisten, sekse en seksualiteit in België*. Ghent: Provinciebestuur Oost-Vlaanderen, 1999, 17-57.

Morelli, Anne. "Les thèmes de la caricature anticléricale en Belgique au XIXe siècle". In: *De qui se moque-t-on? Caricatures d'hier et d'aujourd'hui, de Rops à Kroll*. Mariemont: Musée Royal de Mariemont, 2001, 13-25.

Morelli, Anne. "Kinderen en hun religieuze opvoeding. 19de-20ste eeuw". In: *Devotie en godsdienstbeleving in de verzamelingen van de Koninklijke Bibliotheek*. Brussels: KBR/ULB, 2005, 39-54.

Morgan, Sue. "Rethinking Religion in Gender History: Historiographical and Methodological Reflections". In: Ursula King and Tina Beattie (eds.). *Gender, Religion and Diversity: Cross-Cultural Perspectives*. London: Continuum, 2004, 113-124.

Morgan, Sue and De Vries, Jacqueline (eds.). *Women, Gender and Religious Cultures in Britain, 1800-1940*. London: Routledge, 2010.

Mortier, Roland. *Juliette de Robersart. Une voyageuse belge oubliée*. Brussels: Le Cri, 2003.

Mostaccio, Silvia et al. "Introduction". In: Silvia Mostaccio et al. (eds.). *Echelles de pouvoir, rapports de genre: femmes, jésuites et modèle ignatien dans le long XIXe siècle*. Louvain-la-Neuve: Presses universitaires de Louvain, 2014, I-XIX.

Mulder-Bakker, Anneke B. *Lives of the Anchoresses: The Rise of the Urban Recluse in Medieval Europe*. Philadelphia: University of Pennsylvania Press, 2005.

Muller, Caroline. *Au plus près des âmes et de corps. Une histoire intime des catholiques au XIXe siècle*. Paris: PUF, 2019.

Mullett, Michael A. *The Catholic Reformation*. London/New York: Routledge, 1999.

Mumm, Susan. *Stolen Daughters, Virgin Mothers: Anglican Sisterhoods in Victorian Britain*. London/New York: Leicester University Press, 1999.

Murray, Cecilia. "The Least Qualified: A Leadership Crisis in the Newburgh Dominicans". *U.S. Catholic Historian*, 29 (2011) 1, 53-71.

Murphy, Roseanne. *Julie Billiart. Woman of Courage: The Story of the Foundress of the Sisters of Notre Dame*. New York: Paulist Press, 1995.

Musick, Ulricke. *Therese von Wüllenweber, Mary of the Apostles: A Short Biography*. S.l.: Sisters of the Divine Savior, 1994.

Nicolas-Joseph Minsart, Dom Jérôme, fondateur de l'Institut des sœurs de Sainte-Marie de Namur 1769-1837. Namur: Impr. et libr. L'Ami de l'Ordre, 1909.

Nihoul, P. *Une âme réparatrice: mère Marie du Cœur de Jésus, fondatrice des Consolatrices du Cœur de Jésus (1843-1926)*. Mons: Godart, 1947.

O'Brien, Susan. "Terra Incognita: The Nun in Nineteenth-Century England". *Past & Present*, 121 (1988) 1, 110-140.

O'Brien, Susan. "Lay Sisters and Good Mothers: Working-Class Women in English Convents, 1840-1910". In: W.J. Sheils and Diana Wood (eds.). *Women in the Church*. Oxford: Blackwell, 1990, 453-465.

O'Brien, Susan. "Religious Life for Women". In: Alan McClelland and Michael Hodgetts (eds.). *From Without the Flaminian Gate: 150 Years of Roman Catholicism in England and Wales. 1850-2000*. London: Darton, Longman & Todd, 1999, 108-141.

O'Brien, Susan. "A Survey of Research and Writing about Roman Catholic Women's Congregations in Great Britain and Ireland (1800-1950)". In: Jan De Maeyer, Sofie Leplae, and Joachim Schmiedl (eds.). *Religious Institutes in Western Europe in the 19th and 20th Centuries: Historiography, Research and Legal Position*. Leuven: Leuven University Press, 2004, 91-115.

O'Brien, Susan. "Taylor, Frances Margaret (Mary Magdalen) (1832-1900)". *Oxford Dictionary of National Biography*. Oxford: Oxford University Press, 2004, 40.

O'Brien, Susan. *Leaving God for God: The Daughters of St Vincent de Paul in Britain, 1847-2017*. London: Darton, Longman & Todd, 2017.

O'Donnell, Catherine. "Elizabeth Seton: Transatlantic Cooperation, Spiritual Struggle, and the Early Republican Church". *U.S. Catholic Historian*, 29 (2011) 1, 1-17.

O'Donoghue, Tom. *Catholic Teaching Brothers: Their Life in the English-Speaking World, 1891-1965*. New York: Palgrave Macmillan, 2012.

Offen, Karen. "Defining Feminism: A Comparative Historical Perspective". *Signs: Journal of Women in Culture and Society*, 14 (1988) 1, 119-157.

O'Malley, John W. *The First Jesuits*. Cambridge: Harvard University Press, 1993.

O'Neil, Robert. *Cardinal Vaughan: A Biography of Herbert Vaughan*. Tunbridge Wells: Burns and Oates, 1995.

Osaer, Antoon et al. "De christelijke arbeidersvrouwenbeweging". In: Emmanuel Gerard (ed.). *De christelijke arbeidersbeweging in België. 1891-1991*. Leuven: Universitaire Pers Leuven, 1991, I, 316-411.

Paesmans, Sabine. "De Julianakapel te Sint-Joost-ten-Node". *Monumenten & Landschappen*, 1 (1982) 5, 24-34.

Palanque, Jean-Remy. *Catholiques libéraux et Gallicans en France face au Concile du Vatican 1867-1870*. Aix-en-Provence: Ophrys, 1962.

Paret, Martine and Wynants, Paul. "La noblesse belge dans les ordres religieux et les congrégations, 1801-1960". *Belgisch Tijdschrift voor Nieuwste Geschiedenis*, 30 (2000) 3-4, 493-539.

Pasture, Patrick. "Beyond the Feminization Thesis: Gendering the History of Christianity in the Nineteenth and Twentieth Centuries". In: Patrick Pasture, Jan Art, and Thomas Buerman (eds.). *Gender and Christianity in Modern Europe: Beyond the Feminization Thesis*. Leuven: Leuven University Press, 2012, 7-33.

Peeters, Ferdinand. *L'Église Saint-Augustin à Anvers*. Antwerp: Veritas, 1930.

Perrot, Michelle. "Pouvoir des hommes, puissances des femmes. L'exemple du 19e siècle". In: Luc Courtois, Jean Pirotte, and Françoise Rosart (eds.). *Femmes et pouvoirs. Flux et reflux de l'émancipation féminine depuis un siècle*. Louvain-la-Neuve/Brussels: Collège Erasme/Nauwelaerts, 1992, 131-143.

Pietromarchi, Maria-Eugénia. *Mère Marie-Thérèse Haze, fondatrice des Filles de la Croix de Liège*. Liège: Soledi, 1948.

Piette, Valérie. "Trajectoires féminines. Les commerçantes à Bruxelles vers 1850". *Sextant*, 5 (1996), 9-46.

Piette, Valérie. "Maintenir les servantes dans le droit chemin. Un engagement des bourgeoises fin-de-siècle". *Sextant*, 10 (1998), 47-74.

Piette, Valérie. "Un réseau informel d'éducation des filles. Pensionnats et institutions privées à Bruxelles 1830-1860". *Sextant*, 13-14 (2000), 149-179.

Piette, Valérie. "Belgium's Tradeswomen". In: Robert Beachy, Béatrice Craig, and Alastair Owens (eds.). *Women, Business and Finance in Nineteenth-Century Europe: Rethinking Separate Spheres*. Oxford: Berg Publishers, 2006, 126-138.

Pignal, Jacques. *Si Jansénius avait su ...: Mère Marie-Thérèse Paridaens, fondatrice de la Congrégation des Filles de Marie*. Toulouse: Prière et Vie, 1967.

Pirotte, Jean. "Néo-gothique et fantasmes de chrétienté du XIXe au XXe siècle". In: Jan De Maeyer and Luc Verpoest (eds.). *Gothic Revival: Religion, Architecture and Style in Western Europe*. Leuven: Leuven University Press, 2000, 255-265.

Pirson, Lutgardis. *Elisabeth de Robiano. Madame Lecandèle de Ghyseghem. 1773-1864*. Averbode: Altiora, 1987.

Polet, Noëla J. *De weg van Adélaïde Marie Champion de Cicé. Een zoektocht van het hart in bewogen tijden (1749-1818)*. Heeswijk: Abdij van Berne, 2019.

Poncelet, Alfred. *La Compagnie de Jésus en Belgique: aperçu historique à l'occasion du 75e anniversaire de l'érection de la Province belge (3 décembre 1832 – 3 décembre 1907)*. Brussels: Bulens, 1907.

Premereur, André. *Om Christus' liefde in Christus' rijk: geschiedenis van de Congregatie van Zusters van de H. Vincentius a Paulo te Deftinge en te Viane*. Deftinge: Geschied- en heemkundige kring Triverius, 2014.

Preneel, Marij. *Sint-Joanna in Berchem, 1848-1998*. Berchem/Leuven: vzw Sint-Joanna Zusters Annonciaden Berchem-Antwerpen/KADOC, 1998.

Price, Roger. *Religious Renewal in France, 1789-1870: The Roman Catholic Church between Catastrophe and Triumph*. London: Palgrave Macmillan, 2018.

Priesching, Nicole. "Grundzüge ultramontaner Frömmigkeit am Beispiel der 'stigmatisierten Jungfrau' Maria von Mörl". In: Gisela Fleckenstein and Joachim Schmiedl. *Ultramontanismus: Tendenzen der Forschung*. Paderborn: Bonifatius, 2005, 77-92.

Prunty, Jacinta. *Our Lady of Charity in Ireland: The monasteries, Magdalen asylums and reformatory schools*. Dublin: Columba Press, 2017.

Puissant, Jean. "Boch, Anna". In: Éliane Gubin et al. (eds.). *Dictionnaire des femmes belges. XIXe et XXe siècles*. Brussels: Éditions Racine, 2006, 62-63.

Quaghebeur, Patricia. "De Eucharistische Kruistocht (1920-1963)". In: Rita Ghesquière and Patricia Quaghebeur (eds.). *Averbode. Een uitgever apart. 1877-2002*. Averbode: Uitgeverij Averbode, 2002, 92-174.

Radford Ruether, Rosemary. "Catholic Women". In: Rosemary Skinner Keller and Rosemary Radford Ruether (eds.). *Our Own Voices: Four Centuries of American Women's Religious Writing*. Louisville/London: Westminster John Knox Press, 1995, 17-60.

Raftery, Deirdre. "Rebels with a cause: obedience, resistance and convent life, 1800-1940". *History of Education*, 42 (2013) 6, 729-744.

Raftery, Deirdre and Smith, Elizabeth (eds.). *Education, Identity and Women Religious 1800-1950: Convents, Classrooms and Colleges*. London: Routledge, 2016.

Rapley, Elizabeth. *The Devotes: Women and Church in Seventeenth-Century France*. Montreal: McGill-Queen's University Press, 1990.

Raughter, Rosemary. "A Discreet Benevolence: Female Philanthropy and the Catholic Resurgence in Eighteenth-Century Ireland". *Women's History Review*, 6 (1997) 4, 465-484.

Raughter, Rosemary. *Religious Women and their History: Breaking the Silence*. Dublin: Irish Academic Press, 2005.

Rayez, André. "Retour aux sources. Clorivière et ses fondations (1790-1792)". *Revue d'histoire de l'Eglise de France*, 56 (1968), 253-279.

Ruether, Rosemary. "Mothers of the Church: Ascetic Women in the Late Patristic Age". In: Rosemary Ruether and Eleanor McLaughlin (eds.). *Women of Spirit: Female Leadership in the Jewish and Christian Traditions*. New York: Simon and Schuster, 1979, 71-98.

Reymenants, Geraldine. *Marie Elisabeth Belpaire: gender en macht in het literaire veld 1900-1940*. Leuven: Leuven University Press, 2013.

Ricard, Antoine. *Vie de Mgr. de la Bouillerie: évêque de Carcassonne, archevêque de Perga, coadjuteur de Bordeaux (1810-1882)*. Brussels: Société Générale de Librairie Catholique, 1887.

Rocca, Giancarlo. "Le nuove fondazioni religiose femminili in Italia dal 1800 al 1860". *Problemi di storia della Chiesa. Dalla restaurazione all'unità d'Italia*. Naples: Edizioni Dehoniane Napoli, 1985, 107-92.

Rocca, Giancarlo. *Donne religiose: contributo a una storia della condizione femminile in Italia nei secoli XIX-XX*. Rome: Ed. Paoline, 1992.

Rocca, Giancarlo. "Les jésuites et les Filles du Sacré-Cœur de Jésus". In: Silvia Mostaccio et al. (eds.). *Echelles de pouvoir, rapports de genre: femmes, jésuites et modèle ignatien dans le long XIXe siècle*. Louvain-la-Neuve: Presses universitaires de Louvain, 2014, 129-176.

Rocfer, Pierre. *Souvenirs d'un Prélat Romain sur Rome et la Cour Pontificale*. Paris: Bureaux de la Revue Britannique, 1895.

Rodríguez García, Magaly. "Ideas and Practices of Prostitution around the World". In: Paul Knepper and Anja Johansen (eds.). *The Oxford Handbook of the History of Crime and Criminal Justice*. Oxford: Oxford University Press, 2016, 132-154.

Rodríguez García, Magaly; Heerma van Voss, Lex, and Van Nederveen Meerkerk, Elise. "Selling Sex in World Cities, 1600s-2000s. An Introduction". In: Magaly Rodríguez García, Lex Heerma van Voss and Elise van Nederveen Meerkerk (eds.). *Selling Sex in the City: A Global History of Prostitution, 1600s-2000s*. Leiden: Brill, 2017, 1-19.

Rodríguez García, Magaly and Lauro, Amandine. "Belgian History and the Making of Marginality and Subalternity". *Belgisch Tijdschrift voor Nieuwste Geschiedenis*, 46 (2016) 1, 10-35.

Rogers, Rebecca. "Retrograde or Modern? Unveiling the Teaching Nun in Nineteenth-Century France". *Social History*, 23 (1998) 2, 146-164.

Rogers, Rebecca. *Les bourgeoises au pensionnat: l'éducation féminine au XIXe siècle*. Rennes: Presses universitaires de Rennes, 2007.

Rotsaert, Koen. "De laatste penitenten in Brugge". *Brugs Ommeland*, 39 (1999) 4, 197-208.

Rotsaert, Koen. "Annette Serweytens en de Dienstmaagden van de Zaligmaker". *Brugs Ommeland*, 40 (2000) 3, 131-142.

Rousseau, Sabine. "Vingt ans d'histoire religieuse des femmes et du genre en France". In: Matthieu Brejon de Lavergnée and Magali Della Sudda. *Genre et Christianisme. Plaidoyers pour une histoire croisée*. Paris: Beauchesne, 2014, 55-71.

Sadoux, Dominique and Gervais, Pierre. *La vie religieuse: premières constitutions des Religieuses de la Société du Sacré-Cœur: texte et commentaire*. Paris: Beauchesne, 1986.

Saint-Martin, Isabelle. *Voir, savoir, croire: catéchismes et pédagogie par l'image au XIXe siècle*. Paris: Champion, 2003.

Saintrain, Henri. *Jean-Corneille-Martin Lambertz curé de Thildonck en Brabant, fondateur de la congrégation des Ursulines dites de Thildonck, mort en odeur de sainteté en 1869*. Tournai: Casterman, 1892.

Scaraffia, Lucetta. "Fondatrici e imprenditrici". In: Emma Fattorini (ed.). *Santi, culti, simboli, nell'età della secolarizzazione (1815-1915)*. Turin: Rosemberg & Sellier, 1997, 479-493.

Scaraffia, Lucetta. "Christianity Has Liberated Her and Placed Her alongside Man in the Family: From 1850 to 1988 (Mulierem Dignitatem)". In: Lucetta Scaraffia and Garbiella Zarri (eds.). *Catholic Religious Life in Italy from Late Antiquity to the Present*. Cambridge: Harvard University Press, 1999, 249-280.

Scheer, Monique. "Das Medium hat ein Geschlecht. Fünf Thesen zum besonderen Verhältnis zwischen Frauen und 'ungemäßer Heiligkeit' aus kulturwissenschaftlicher Sicht". In: Hubert Wolf (ed.). *"Wahre" und "falsche" Heiligkeit. Mystik, Macht und Geschlechterrollen im Katholizismus des 19. Jahrhunderts*. Munich: Oldenbourg Verlag, 2013.

Scheerlinck, Karl. *Mère Jeanne (1824-1907): stichteres van de Zusters dienstmaagden van de Heilige Harten van Jezus en Maria: haar geestelijk en materieel erfgoed*. Antwerp: Zusters dienstmaagden, 2007.

Schenkeveld-Van Der Dussen, Riet et al. (eds.). *Met en zonder lauwerkrans: schrijvende vrouwen uit de vroegmoderne tijd 1550-1850: van Anna Bijns tot Elise van Calcar*. Amsterdam: Amsterdam University Press, 1997.

Schmidt, Rudolf. *Agnes Baliques, Gründerin der Apostelinnen, und ihre (Auto-)Biographie: vom Rechenschaftsbericht zur historischen Quelle*. Unpublished PhD thesis, Universität Köln, 1999.

Scholliers, Peter. "A Century of Real Industrial Wages in Belgium, 1840-1939". In: Peter Scholliers and Vera Zamagni (eds.). *Labour's reward: real wages and economic change in 19th- and 20th-century Europe*. Aldershot: Elgar, 1995, 106-136.

Schouppe, François X. *La femme chrétienne: sa mission, sa formation et sa sauvegarde*. Paris: Société générale de libraire catholique, 1882.

Schraut, Barbara. *Antonia Werr (1813-1868) und die Oberzeller Schwestern: geistliches Profil und sozialer Auftrag einer Frauenkongregation des 19. Jahrhunderts von der Gründung bis zur Gegenwart*. Würzburg: Schöningh, 1995.

Schyrgens, Joseph. *Berlaymont: le cloistre de la reyne de tous les saincts*. Brussels: Dewit, 1928.

Scott, Joan W. "Gender: A Useful Category of Historical Analysis". *The American Historical Review*, 91 (1986) 5, 1053-1075.

Scott, Joan W. *Only Paradoxes to Offer: French Feminists and the Rights of Man*. Cambridge: Harvard University Press, 1996.

Scott, Joan W. *The Fantasy of Feminist Theory*. Durham/London: Duke University Press, 2011.

Segers, Yves. *150 jaar Zusters van het Heilig Hart van Maria van Berlaar: in eenvoud en dienstbaarheid. 1845-1995*. Leuven: KADOC, 1995.

Segers, Yves. *Zusters in het wit. De gasthuiszusters-augustinessen van Boom, 1846-1996. 150 jaar ziekenzorg in de Rupelstreek*. Boom/Leuven: Gasthuiszusters Augustinessen/KADOC, 1996.

Sellars, Jane. *Charlotte Brontë*. London: British Library, 1997.

Serra, Alessandro. "Madeleine-Sophie Barat et la Société du Sacré-Cœur entre Compagnie de Jésus et modèle ignatien". In: Silvia Mostaccio et al. (eds.). *Échelles de pouvoir, rapports de genre. Femmes, jésuites et modèle ignatien dans le long XIXe siècle*. Louvain-la-Neuve: Presses Universitaires de Louvain, 2014, 271-292.

Servais, Paul. "The Church and the Family in Belgium, 1850-1914". *Belgisch Tijdschrift voor Nieuwste Geschiedenis*, 31 (2001) 3-4, 621-647.

Shane, Leslie. *Letters of Herbert Cardinal Vaughan to Lady Herbert of Lea, 1867 to 1903*. London: Burns and Oates, 1942.

Shaw, Pauline J. *Elizabeth Hayes. Pioneer Franciscan Journalist*. Leominster: Gracewing Publishers, 2009.

Showalter, Elaine. "Literary Criticism". *Signs*, 1 (1975), 435-460.

Showalter, Elaine. "Feminist Criticism in the Wilderness". *Critical Inquiry*, 8 (1981) 2, 179-205.

Showalter, Elaine. "Florence Nightingale's Feminist Complaint: Suggestions for Thought". *Signs*, 6 (1981), 395-412.

Showalter, Elaine. "Introduction - The Rise of Gender". In: Elaine Showalter (ed.). *Speaking of Gender*. New York: Routledge, 1989, 1-13.

Simon, Aloïs. *Le Cardinal Sterckx et son temps (1792-1867)*. Wetteren: Scaldis, 1950, 2 vol.

Simon, Aloïs. *Lettres de Pecci (1843-1846)*. Brussels: Institut Historique Belge de Rome, 1959.

Simon, Aloïs. *Instructions aux nonces de Bruxelles (1835-1889)*. Brussels: Institut Historique Belge de Rome, 1961.

Simon, Aloïs. "Villermont (Antoine-Charles Hennequin de)". In: *Biographie Nationale*. Brussels: Académie Royale de Belgique, 1961-1962, XXXI, 713-715.

Simon, Maurice. "L'enseignement du catéchisme en Belgique francophone". In: Raymond Brodeur and Brigitte Caulier (eds.). *Enseigner le catéchisme: autorités et instructions: XVIe-XXe siècles*. Paris: Cerf, 1997, 234-249.

Smith, Bonnie G. *Ladies of the Leisure Class: the Bourgeoises of Northern France in the Nineteenth Century*. Princeton: Princeton University Press, 1981.

Smith, Bonne G. *Changing Lives: Women in European History since 1700*. Lexington: Heath, 1989.

Smith, James M. *Ireland's Magdalen Laundries and the Nation's Architecture of Containment*. Notre Dame: University of Notre-Dame Press, 2007.

Smyth, Elizabeth M. (ed.). *Changing Habits: Women's Religious Orders in Canada*. Toronto: Novalis, 2007.

Snauwaert, Livia and De Wilde, Peter. *Het kasteel van Wissekerke te Bazel*. Ghent: Provinciebestuur Oost-Vlaanderen, 2003.

Sohn-Kronthaler, Michaela; Hopfgartner, Willibald and Zahner, Paul (eds.). *Zwischen Gebet, Reform und Sozialem Dienst. Franziskanisch inspirierte Frauen in den Umbrüchen ihrer Zeit*. Vienna: Tyrolia-Verlag, 2015.

Sperber, Jonathan. *Popular Catholicism in Nineteenth-Century Germany*. Princeton: Princeton University Press, 1984.

Sprows Cummings, Kathleen. *New Women of the Old Faith: Gender and American Catholicism in the Progressive Era*. Chapel Hill: The University of North Carolina Press, 2009.

Stevens, Fred. "Les associations religieuses en Belgique pendant le 19e siècle". In: Jan De Maeyer, Sofie Leplae, and Joachim Schmiedl (eds.). *Religious Institutes in Western Europe in the 19th and 20th Centuries. Historiography, Research and Legal Position*. Leuven: Leuven University Press, 2004, 185-203.

Steverlynck, Carine. "La traite des Blanches et la prostitution enfantine en Belgique. 1800-1950". *Paedagogica Historica*, 29 (1993) 3, 779-820.

Stockman, René. *Liefde in actie: tweehonderd jaar Broeders van Liefde*. Leuven: Davidsfonds, 2006.

Stogdon, Kate. "A Journey with Thérèse Couderc: Inspiration, Liability or Possibility for Change?". *Feminist Theology*, 16 (2008) 2, 211-229.

Stogdon, Kate. "Expressions of Self-Surrender in Nineteenth-Century France: the Case of Thérèse Couderc (1805-1885)". In: Laurence Lux Sterrit and Carmen Mangion (eds.). *Gender, Catholicism and Spirituality. Women and the Roman Catholic Church in Britain and Europe, 1200-1900*. Basingstoke: Palgrave-Macmillan, 2011, 149-164.

Strobbe, Karel and Suenens, Kristien. *Zusters Kindsheid Jesu 1835-2010*. Leuven/Oostakker: KADOC/Zusters Kindsheid Jesu, 2010.

Stynen, Ludo. *Rosalie en Virginie: leven en werk van de gezusters Loveling*. Tielt: Lannoo, 1997.

Suau, Pierre. *La mère Marie de Jésus Émilie d'Oultremont baronne d'Hooghvorst (1818-1878), fondatrice de la Société de Marie Réparatrice*. Rome: Desclée, 1905.

Suenens, Kristien. "Het proces De Buck (1864-1868). Een erfenisproces als inzet van het klerikaal-liberale conflict in België". *Trajecta*, 14 (2005) 1, 3-24.

Suenens, Kristien. "L'École du Grand Chrétien. Een bekend retraitehuis ca. 1840-ca.1965". In: Johan Decavele et al. (eds.). *De oude abdij van Drongen: elf eeuwen geschiedenis*. Drongen: Oude Abdij, 2006, 373-393.

Suenens, Kristien. "Dominica Van der Stichele en de dominicanessen van Brugge". *Dominicaans Leven. Tijdschrift van de Vlaamse Dominicaanse familie*, 64 (2007) 4, 7-14.

Suenens, Kristien. "Apostolische actie en spirituele passie. Negentiende-eeuwse vrouwelijke congregatiestichteressen en hun zoektocht naar een spirituele identiteit". *Trajecta*, 17 (2009) 3, 243-262.

Suenens, Kristien. "'Pères spirituels' en 'Dames illusionnées': Pater Jean-Baptiste Boone sj, de Brusselse jezuïeten en het Institut de l'Adoration Perpétuelle du Saint Sacrement (1846-1871)". In: Alain Deneef and Xavier Rousseaux (eds.). *Quatre siècles de présence jésuite à Bruxelles. Vier eeuwen jezuïeten te Brussel*. Leuven: Jesuitica/KADOC, 2012, 433-448.

Suenens, Kristien. "Glorieux. Een sociaal bewogen priester in een bewogen tijd (1825-1852)". *Trajecta*, 23 (2014) 1, 65-89.

Suenens, Kristien. "Jésuites et congrégations féminines en Belgique (ca. 1850-ca. 1880): rencontres, influences et confits". In: Silvia Mostaccio et al. (eds.). *Échelles de pouvoir, rapports de genre. Femmes, jésuites et le modèle ignatien dans le long XIXe siècle*. Louvain-la-Neuve: Presses Universitaire de Louvain, 2014, 249-270.

Suenens, Kristien and De Staercke, Anneleen. *Eén van hart en één van ziel: geschiedenis van de Gasthuiszusters-Augustinessen van Lier 1130-2005*. Lier/Leuven: H. Hartziekenhuis/KADOC, 2005.

Suenens, Kristien and Kwanten, Godfried. "Zusters voor de klas. Archief Annonciaden Huldenberg". *KADOC Nieuwsbrief*, (2013) 2, 4-9.

Suenens, Kristien and Marcélis, Anne-Dolorès. "Vrouwelijke religieuze instituten in België in de negentiende en twintigste eeuw. Een historiografisch overzicht". *Belgisch Tijdschrift voor Filologie en Geschiedenis*, 86 (2008) 3-4, 841-864.

Tagliaferri, Maurizio. *Anna de Meeûs. Fondatrice delle Religiose dell'Eucarestia: cenni biografici*. Rome: Religiose dell'Eucaristia, 1995.

Terwecoren, Edouard. *Salazar ou la chapelle expiatoire du Très-Saint Sacrement de miracle, à Bruxelles*. Brussels: Goemaere, 1852.

Thompson, Margaret. "Women, Feminism, and the New Religious History: Catholic Sisters as a Case Study". In: Philip R. Vandermeer and Robert P. Swierenga (eds.). *Belief and Behavior: Essays in the New Religious History*. New Brunswick: Rutgers University Press, 1991, 136-162.

Thonissen, Jean-Joseph. *Vie du comte Ferdinand de Meeûs*. Leuven: Peeters, 1863.

Tihon, André. "Les religieuses en Belgique du XVIIIe au XXe siècle. Approche statistique". *Belgisch Tijdschrift voor Nieuwste Geschiedenis*, 7 (1976) 1-2, 1-54.

Tihon, André. "Dieu dans les mandements de carême des archevêques de Malines (1803-1926)". In: *Qu'est-ce que Dieu? Philosophie/ Théologie. Hommage à l'abbé Daniel Coppieters de Gibson (1929-1983)*. Brussels: Facultés universitaires Saint-Louis, 1985, 651-684.

Timmermans, Ruth. *Het Convent van Bethlehem: een half millennium vrouwelijke spiritualiteit en bedrijvigheid*. Duffel/Leuven: Convent van Bethlehem/KADOC, 2000.

Torcivia, Mario. "Il Can. F. Russo (1829-1890). Le *Sacramentine* (1888-1896) e la presenza a Palermo delle Religiose della Adorazione Perpetua (1896-1912)". *Syntaxis*, 29 (2011) 3, 139-174.

Torfs, Lodewijk. *Nieuwe geschiedenis van Antwerpen of Schets van de beginsels en gebeurtenissen dezer stad, alsmede van de opkomst harer instellingen en gestichten*. Antwerp: Buschmann, 1862-1865, 2 vol.

T'Serstevens, Patricia. *Le recrutement et l'origine sociale des Sœurs de Notre-Dame et des Sœurs de Sainte-Marie au XIXe siècle*. Unpublished master thesis, Université Catholique de Louvain, 1972.

Turin, Yvonne. *Femmes et religieuses au XIXe siècle: le féminisme en religion*. Paris: Nouvelle Cité, 1989.

Tyck, Charles. *Notices historiques sur les congrégations et communautés religieuses et les instituts de missionnaires du XIXe siècle*. Leuven: Peeters, 1892.

Tyssens, Jeffrey and Witte, Els. *De vrijzinnige traditie in België: van getolereerde tegencultuur tot erkende levensbeschouwing*. Brussels: VUBPress, 1996.

Un'anima Eucaristica: Biografia della Ven. Madre Geltrude Comensoli. Bergamo: s.n., 1981.

Van Biervliet, Melanie. *De l'éducation dans les pensionnats de demoiselles*. Tournai: Casterman, 1863.

Van Cauwenberge, Sabine. "Femmes artistes en Belgique au XIXe siècle". *Sextant*, 12 (1999), 7-35.

Vandenberghe, Gerd. *De opvang en zorg voor 'arme wezen' in België in de negentiende eeuw. De casus van de Zuid-Oost-Vlaamse stad Ronse (1800-1894)*. Unpublished master thesis, Universiteit Gent, 2012.

Vandenbussche, Liselotte. *Het veld der verbeelding. Vrijzinnige vrouwen in Vlaamse literaire en algemeen-culturele tijdschriften*. Ghent: Koninklijke Academie voor Nederlandse Taal- en Letterkunde, 2008.

Vandenbussche, Liselotte et al. "Virginie Loveling (1836-1923) as a Cultural Mediator: From Translating Klaus Groth to Manipulating Charles Darwin". In: Petra Broomans (ed.). *From Darwin to Weil: Women as Transmitters of Ideas*. Groningen: Barkhuis, 2009, 47-71.

Vandenbussche, Liselotte. "Peripheral autonomy/mutual sympathy? Women translators in Flanders, 1870-1914". In: Petra Broomans and Sandra van Voorst (eds.). *Rethinking Cultural Transfer and Transmission: Reflections and New Perspectives*. Groningen: Barkhuis, 2012, 93-117.

Van den Eeckhout, Patricia. "Brussels". In: Martin Daunton (ed.). *Housing the workers. 1850-1914*. Leicester: Leicester University Press, 1990, 67-106.

Van de Perre, Stijn. "Catholic Fundraising to Educate the Poor. The History of the Société Civile du Crédit de la Charité (1855-1878)". In: Christoph De Spiegeleer (ed.). *The Civilising Offensive. Social and Educational Reform in 19th-century Belgium*. Berlin/Boston: De Gruyter, 2019, 62-81.

Van de Putte, Bart. *Partnerkeuze in de 19de eeuw: klasse, geografische afkomst, romantiek en de vorming van sociale groepen op de huwelijksmarkt*. Leuven: Leuven University Press, 2005.

Vanderputten, Steven. "Reformatorische lichamelijkheid en geconditioneerde emoties van twee religieuze vrouwen omstreeks het jaar 1000". *Tijdschrift voor Geschiedenis*, 126 (2013) 4, 466-479.

Vanderputten, Steven. *Dark Age Nunneries: The Ambiguous Identity of Female Monasticism, 800-1050*. Ithaca, Cornell University Press, 2018.

Vanderstraeten, Raf and Preneel, Marij. *175 jaar Zusters der Christelijke Scholen Vorselaar (1820-1995)*. Vorselaar/Leuven: Zusters der Christelijke Scholen/KADOC, 1996.

Van Dijck, Maarten. "From Workhouse to Convent. The Sisters of Saint Vincent and Public Charity in Eeklo, 1830-1900". In: Maarten Van Dijck and Jan De Maeyer (eds.). *The Economics of Providence. Management, Finances and Patrimony of Religious Orders and Congregations in Europe, 1773-c.1930*. Leuven: Leuven University Press, 2013, 159-84.

Van Dijck, Maarten and De Maeyer, Jan (eds.). *The Economics of Providence. Management, Finances and Patrimony of Religious Orders and Congregations in Europe, 1773-c.1930*. Leuven: Leuven University Press, 2013.

Van Dijck, Maarten and Suenens, Kristien. "La Belgique charitable: Charity by Catholic Congregations in Rural West Flanders, 1830-1880". In: Inga Brandes and Katrin Marx-Jaskulski (eds.). *Armenfürsorge und Wohltätigkeit. Ländliche Gesellschaften in Europa, 1850-1930. Poor Relief and Charity. Rural Societies in Europe, 1850-1930*. Frankfurt a.M.: Peter Lang, 2008, 153-185.

Van Drenth, Annemieke and De Haan, Francisca. *The Rise of Caring Power: Elizabeth Fry and Josephine Butler in Britain and the Netherlands*. Amsterdam: Amsterdam University Press, 1999.

Van Gemert, Lie. "A Witty Pioneer of Realism: Jeanette Delcroix". In: Lia Van Gemert et al. (eds.). *Women's Writing from the Low Countries 1200-1875. A Bilingual Anthology*. Amsterdam: Amsterdam University Press, 2010, 548-557.

Van Heijst, Annelies. *Zusters, vrouwen van de wereld: aktieve religieuzen en haar emancipatie*. Amsterdam: SUA, 1985.

Van Heijst, Annelies. "Het passie-paradigma: zorg om eeuwig leven". In: Marjet Derks, José Eijt and Marit Monteiro (eds.). *Sterven voor de wereld. Een religieus ideaal in meervoud*. Hilversum: Verloren, 1997, 17-33.

Van Heijst, Annelies. *Models of Charitable Care: Catholic Nuns and Children in their Care in Amsterdam, 1852-2002*. Leiden: Brill, 2008.

Van Heijst, Annelies and Derks, Marjet. "Godsvrucht en gender: naar een geschiedschrijving in meervoud". In: Annelies van Heijst and Marjet Derks (eds.). *Terra incognita. Historisch onderzoek naar katholicisme en vrouwelijkheid*. Kampen: Kok, 1994, 7-38.

Van Heijst, Annelies; Derks, Marjet, and Monteiro, Marit. *Ex Caritate: kloosterleven, apostolaat en liefdewerken van actieve vrouwelijke religieuzen in Nederland in de 19^e en 20^e eeuw*. Hilversum: Verloren, 2010.

Van Hove, Erik; Daems, Herman and Knops, Nicole. *Van Mariadal tot MPI Oosterlo: Hoe een pensionaat uitgroeide tot een netwerk van zorg en onderwijs voor personen met een verstandelijke handicap*. Geel: MPI Oosterlo vzw, 2012.

Van Isacker, Karel. *Werkelijk en wettelijk land: de katholieke opinie tegenover de rechterzijde 1863-1884*. Antwerp: Standaard, 1955.

Van Loon, Tina. "Opvattingen, hulpverlening en wetgeving ten aanzien van prostitutie in België". *Ethiek en Maatschappij*, 13 (2010) 1, 104-126.

Van Kalken, Frans. *Commotions populaires en Belgique (1834-1902)*. Brussels: Lebègue, 1936.

Van Molle, Leen. *Katholieken en landbouw: landbouwpolitiek in België, 1884-1914*. Leuven: Leuven University Press, 1989.

Van Molle, Leen. *Ieder voor allen. De Belgische Boerenbond 1890-1990*. Leuven: Leuven University Press, 1990.

Van Molle, Leen. "Zakenvrouwen of vrouwenzaken? Een historiografische zoektocht". In: Leen Van Molle and Peter Heyrman (eds.). *Vrouwenzaken-zakenvrouwen: facetten van vrouwelijk zelfstandig ondernemerschap in Vlaanderen, 1800-2000*. Ghent: Provinciebestuur Oost-Vlaanderen, 2001, 17-39.

Van Molle, Leen. "De nieuwe vrouwenbeweging in Vlaanderen. Een andere lezing". *Belgisch Tijdschrift voor Nieuwste Geschiedenis*, 34 (2004) 3, 359-397.

Van Molle, Leen. "Constance Teichmann (1824-1896)". In: Éliane Gubin et al. (eds.). *Dictionnaire des femmes belges. XIXe et XXe siècles*. Brussels: Éditions Racine, 2006, 524-525.

Van Molle, Leen. "Comparing Religious Perspectives on Social Reform. An introduction". In: Leen Van Molle (ed.). *Charity and Social Welfare*. Leuven: Leuven University Press, 2017, 7-33.

Van Molle, Leen and Jacques, Catherine. "De verpleegkundigen: grenzeloos vrouwelijk". In: Jan De Maeyer (ed.). *Er is leven voor de dood. Tweehonderd jaar gezondheidszorg in Vlaanderen*. Kapellen: Pelckmans, 1991, 203-213.

Van Osselaer, Tine. "Reform of Piety in the Southern Netherlands/Belgium". In: Anders Jarlert (ed.). *Piety and Modernity*. Leuven: Leuven University Press, 2012, 101-123.

Van Osselaer, Tine. "Sensitive but Sane: Male Visionaries and Their Emotional Display in Interwar Belgium". *BMGN – Low Countries Historical* Review, 127 (2012) 1, 127-149.

Van Osselaer, Tine. *The Pious Sex: Catholic Constructions of Masculinity and Femininity in Belgium, c. 1800–1940*. Leuven: Leuven University Press, 2013.

Van Osselaer, Tine. "Religion, Family and Domesticity in Nineteenth and Twentieth Centuries. An Introduction". In: Tine Van Osselaer and Patrick Pasture (eds.). *Christian Homes: Religion, Family and Domesticity in the 19th and 20th Centuries*. Leuven: Leuven University Press, 2014, 7-25.

Van Osselaer, Tine. "Introduction". In: Tine Van Osselaer, Henk De Smaele and Kaat Wils (eds.). *Sign or Symptom? Exceptional Corporeal Phenomena in Religion and Medicine in the Nineteenth and Twentieth Centuries*. Leuven: Leuven University Press, 2017, 7-21.

Van Osselaer, Tine. "The 'Affair of the Photographs': Controlling the Public Image of a Nineteenth-Century Stigmatic". *Journal of Ecclesiastical History*, 68 (2017) 4, 784-806.

Van Osselaer, Tine and Buerman, Thomas. "Feminization Thesis: A Survey of International Historiography and a Probing of Belgian Grounds". *Revue d'Histoire Ecclésiastique*, 103 (2008) 2, 497-544.

Vanpaemel, Geert. "Laissons aux hommes les recherches savantes. Les femmes dans l'histoire des sciences du 19ᵉ siècle". *Sextant*, 13-14 (2000), 179-187.

Van Praag, Philip. "Émilie Claeys 1855-1943". *Tijdschrift voor Sociale Geschiedenis*, 11 (1978) 2, 177-196.

Van San, Piet. *Het onderwijs en de scholen in Overijse in de negentiende eeuw*. Leuven: Acco, 2007.

Van Vugt, Joos. *Broeders in de katholieke beweging: de werkzaamheden van vijf Nederlandse onderwijscongregaties van broeders en fraters, 1840-1970*. Nijmegen: KDC/KSC, 1994.

Vastiau, Michel. "De bewoners van het klooster in de 'Grote Sleutel' te Alsemberg". *En het dorp zal duren... Trimestrieel Tijdschrift van het Heemkundig Genootschap 'van Witthem' Beersel*, 14 (2012) 53, 23-72.

Veestraeten, Erika. *De wezenzorg in de openbare instellingen van de stad Antwerpen 1870-1914*. Unpublished master thesis, KU Leuven, 1994.

Venard, Jacques. *Les eudistes au XXe siècle*. Paris: Médiaspaul, 2008.

Venarde, Bruce L. *Women's Monasticism and Medieval Society: Nunneries in France and England, 890-1215*. Ithaca: Cornell University Press, 1997.

Verschaffel, Tom. "Vrouwenrollen in de vaderlandse drama's van het negentiende-eeuwse België". *De Negentiende Eeuw*, 24 (2000) 1, 33-51.

Verschuere, Antonellus. *Hoe zij groeide ..: de Congregatie der Zusters van den Heiligen Vincentius a Paulo van Opwijk, 1847-1947*. Mechelen: St. Franciscusdrukkerij, 1947.

Verwilghen, Michel. *Le mythe d'Argenteuil: demeure d'un couple royal*. Brussels: Racine, 2006.

Viaene, Vincent. *Belgium and the Holy See from Gregory XVI to Pius IX (1831-1859): Catholic Revival, Society and Politics in 19th-Century Europe*. Leuven: Leuven University Press, 2001.

Viaene, Vincent. "The Roman Question. Catholic Mobilisation and Papal Diplomacy during the Pontificate of Pius IX". In: Emiel Lamberts (ed.). *The Black International. The Holy See and Militant Catholicism in Europe*. Leuven: Leuven University Press, 2002, 135-143.

Viaene, Vincent. "Introduction: Reality and Image in the Pontificate of Leo XIII". In: Vincent Viaene (ed.). *The Papacy and the New World Order: Vatican Diplomacy, Catholic Opinion and International Politics at the Time of Leo XIII, 1878-1903*. Leuven: Leuven University Press, 2005, 9-29.

Viaene, Vincent. "Katholisches Reveil und ultramontane Pietät in Belgien (1815-1860)". In: Gisela Fleckenstein and Joachim Schmiedl (eds.). *Ultramontanismus. Tendenzen der Forschung*. Paderborn: Bonifatius, 2005, 111-134.

Viaene, Vincent. "The Second Sex and the First Estate. The Dames de St.-André between the Bishop of Tournai (Belgium) and Rome in the 19th Century". *Journal of Ecclesiastical History*, 59 (2008) 3, 447-474.

Viaene, Vincent. "De ontplooiing van een 'vrije' kerk (1830-1883)". In: Jan De Maeyer et al. (eds.). *Het aartsbisdom Mechelen-Brussel. 450 jaar geschiedenis*. Antwerp: Halewijn, 2009, II, 35-99.

Viaene, Vincent. "Nineteenth-Century Catholic Internationalism and Its Predecessors". In: Abigail Green and Vincent Viaene (eds.). *Religious Internationals in the Modern World*. Basingstoke: Palgrave MacMillan, 2012, 82-110.

Viaene, Vincent. "A Pope's Dilemma. Temporal Power and Moral Authority in the History of the Modern Vatican". In: Jan De Maeyer and Vincent Viaene (eds.). *World Views and Worldly Wisdom: Religion, Ideology and Politics, 1750-2000*. Leuven: Leuven University Press, 2016, 245-255.

Vial, Paul. "Jaricot, Marie-Pauline". In: *Dictionnaire de spiritualité ascétique et mystique, doctrine et histoire*. Paris: Beauchesne, 1974, VIII, 170-171.

Vie de la révérende mère Marie Claire de Jésus, co-fondatrice et deuxième supérieure générale de l'Institut des Sœurs de Sainte-Marie. Namur: Godenne, 1895.

Vints, Luc. "Komt en haalt ons, wij zijn met te velen die hier verlangende staan: de Belgische katholieke missiebeweging in de negentiende eeuw ten tijde van Gezelle". In: *Reizen in den geest: de boekenwereld van Guido Gezelle*. Bruges: Stadsbestuur Brugge, 1999, 33-47.

Vloeberghs, Charles (Madame). *La Belgique Charitable*. Brussels: Dewit, 1904.

Vloeberghs, Charles (Madame). *Belgique Enseignante*. Brussels: Dewit, 1905.

Voets, Bertus. *Bewaar het toevertrouwde pand: het verhaal van het bisdom Haarlem*. Hilversum: Gooi en Sticht, 1981.

Wall, Barbra M. *Unlikely Entrepreneurs: Catholic Sisters and the Hospital Marketplace, 1865-1925*. Columbus: Ohio State University Press, 2005.

Walsh, Barbara. *Roman Catholic Nuns in England and Wales 1800-1937: A Social History*. Dublin: Irish Academic Press, 2002.

Wang, Ping-Yuan. "Neither ex officio nor ex gratia: The Brussels Visitandines' Discourses of Authority and the Collective Will, 1668-99". In: Veerle Fraeters and Imke de Gier (eds.). *Mulieres Religiosae. Shaping Female Spiritual Authority in the Medieval and Early Modern Periods*. Turnhout: Brepols, 2014, 265-285.

Wautrecht, Rodolphe and Pandor, Pierre. *La Hulpe de la préhistoire à nos jours*. La Hulpe: P. Pandor, 1970.

Weber, Alison. *Teresa of Avila and the Rhetoric of Femininity*. Princeton: Princeton University Press, 1990.

Weemaes, Richard. *In het spoor van Anna Piers. 300 jaar meisjesonderwijs in Beveren, 1698-1998*. Beveren: s.n., 1998.

Wenner, Francis. "Théodelinde Dubouché". *Dictionnaire de spiritualité ascétique et mystique, doctrine et histoire*. Paris: Beauchesne, 1954, XVIII-XIX, 1743-1745.

Werner, Yvonne Maria (ed.). *Nuns and Sisters in the Nordic Countries after the Reformation: A Female Counter-Culture in Modern Society*. Uppsala: Swedish Institute of Missionary Research, 2004.

Werner, Yvonne M. (ed.). *Christian Masculinity: Men and Religion in Northern Europe in the 19th and 20th Centuries*. Leuven: Leuven University Press, 2011.

Wiertz, Wendy. "Une femme complète. La Comtesse Marie de Villermont (1848-1925)". *Le Parchemin*, 82 (2017) 430, 289-308.

Wiertz, Wendy. *Adellijk & Artistiek. Amateurkunstenaressen met blauw bloed in België (1806-1914)*. Unpublished PhD thesis, KU Leuven, 2018.

Willems, Loes. *Marie Baers (1883-1859): de constructie van een vrouwbeeld ten opzichte van een manbeeld. Genderdiscours in de Belgische katholieke zuil*. Unpublished master thesis, Universiteit Gent, 2011.

Wils, Kaat. "Science, an Ally of Feminism? Isabelle Gatti de Gamond on Women and Science". *Belgisch Tijdschrift voor Filologie en Geschiedenis*, 77 (1999) 2, 416-439.

Wils, Kaat. "Inleiding". In: Kaat Wils (ed.). *Het lichaam m/v*. Leuven: Leuven University Press, 2001, 7-23.

Wils, Lode. "België in de negentiende eeuw: religieus, politiek en sociaal". In: Emmanuel Gerard (ed.). *De christelijke arbeidersbeweging in België*. Leuven: Universitaire Pers Leuven, 1991, I, 18-55.

Wirth, Morand. *Don Bosco et les Salésiens: cent cinquante ans d'histoire*. Turin: Elle Di Ci, 1970.

Witte, Els. "The Battle for Monasteries, Cemeteries and Schools: Belgium". In: Christopher Clark and Wolfram Kaiser (eds.). *Culture Wars: Secular-Catholic Conflict in Nineteenth-Century Europe*. Cambridge: Cambridge University Press, 2003, 102-128.

Wouters, Wilfried. *Broeders in het kunstonderwijs: de Sint-Lucasscholen in België 1866-1966*. Unpublished PhD thesis, KU Leuven, 2011.

Wynants, Paul. *Religieuses 1801-1975. Vol I. Belgique – Luxembourg – Maastricht – Vaals*. Namur: Facultés Universitaires Notre-Dame de la Paix, 1981.

Wynants, Paul. *Les Sœurs de la Providence de Champion et leurs écoles 1833-1914*. Namur: Presses universitaires de Namur, 1984.

Wynants, Paul. "Le gouvernement des instituts féminins de vie active au 19e siècle en Belgique". In: Luc Courtois, Jean Pirotte, and Françoise Rosart (eds.). *Femmes et pouvoirs: flux et reflux de l'émancipation féminine depuis un siècle*. Louvain-la-Neuve/Brussels: Collège Erasme/Nauwelaerts, 1992, 81-100.

Wynants, Paul and Hanoteau, Marie-Emilie. "La condition féminine des religieuses de vie active en Belgique francophone (19e-20e siècles)". In: Luc Courtois, Jean Pirotte, and Françoise Rosart (eds.). *Femmes des années 80. Un siècle de condition féminine en Belgique (1889-1989)*. Louvain-la-Neuve: Academia, 1989, 145-150.

Wynants, Paul and Paret, Martine. "Les religieuses de vie active en Belgique et aux Pays-Bas, 19e-20e siècles". *Revue d'Histoire Ecclésiastique*, 95 (2000) 3, 238-256.

Yernault, Jean-Pierre. "Deux grands 'guérisseurs' de la région: la sœur Marie-Rose Carouy (1851-1923) et l'abbé Auguste Marie Ghislain Reveillon (1912-1989)". *Bulletin trimestriel du Cercle royal d'Histoire et d'Archéologie d'Ath*, 10 (2003) 213, 49-78.

INDEX OF NAMES

Auchard de Saint-Laurent, Jean-Louis 148
Auchard de Saint-Laurent, Louisa 148-149, 152-153, 155, 157, 215

Baesen, Gabriëlle 191, 221-222
Bailly, Emmanuel 59
Barat, Sophie 40, 45, 50-51, 58, 61, 68, 110, 154, 159, 177, 273, 315
Barnabo, Allesandro 305-306
Beckx, Petrus 191-192, 300, 305
Bel, Jeanne-Françoise 133
Belpaire, Marie Elisabeth 229, 242, 273
Bergen, Jan 327
Berlaymont, Julie 140
Bernaud, Marie du Sacré-Cœur 245-246
Bethune, Jean-Baptiste 224, 232, 274, 311
Bethune, Marie-Antoinette 232
Billiart, Julie 20, 50, 58, 68, 77, 109, 154, 159, 176, 312-313, 315
Bizzarri, Giuseppe Andrea 190, 295
Blin de Bourdon, Françoise 20, 58, 154, 176
Boccali, Gabriel 306
Boch, Anna 229
Bogaerts, Petrus 9, 94, 98-99, 127-128, 130, 136-138, 152-153, 167, 172, 179, 182, 229, 231, 234-235, 256, 291
Bonzel, Theresia 106, 108, 113
Boone, Jean-Baptiste 62, 66-67, 79-80, 83-84, 86, 89-90, 93, 118, 125, 132, 135-136, 140-142, 158, 164-165, 171, 173, 177-178, 182, 190-193, 208, 210 212, 271, 294, 297-299, 319-320, 335, 338
Borromeo, Charles 77
Bossaert, Frederic 224
Bracq, Henri 222, 227, 294
Busine, Edouard 116, 118, 129, 131, 133, 148, 168

Capri, Giovanni 304
Carless, Louisa > Auchard de Saint-Laurent, Louisa
Carouy, Marie-Rose 261
Cattani, Giacomo 268, 292, 294, 298, 302
Cawet, Félicité 208
Chaillot, Ludovic 192, 294-295, 297-300, 334

Charlotte (Princess) 133
Chateaubriand, François René de 59
Chevalier, Jean-Baptiste 138, 143-144, 227, 241, 290, 293
Cogels, Caroline 122, 142, 147, 155-156, 188
Comensoli, Gertrude 106, 111
Connelly, Cornelia 57, 86, 181
Cornet, Antoinette 21, 29, 33-35, 43-47, 69-70, 73, 76, 99-101, 109-110, 112, 114, 124, 126, 137-138, 143-144, 150, 154-157, 163, 169-172, 176-177, 180, 182, 184, 186, 199-200, 203-204, 206-208, 214, 218-219, 226-230, 233-234, 236, 238, 240-243, 253-254, 260, 267, 272-273, 277-278, 280-281, 283, 285, 289-291, 293, 309, 315-317, 331, 333-339
Cornet, Omer 69
Couderc, Thérèse 79, 86, 248
Crombeen, Joanna Francisca 326

d'Alzon, Emmanuel 132
d'Arenberg, Eléonore-Ursule 237, 304, 321
d'Avenas, Aimée de Guillin 40, 43, 45, 58, 61, 81
Davis, Emily 27
de Bar, Cathérine 106
De Beukelaer, Coleta (Vincent) 168, 196, 199-200, 205-206, 252-253, 280, 325
de Bruyn, Henri 249
De Buck, Victor 136, 141, 191, 193
Dechamps, Adolphe 132
Dechamps, Victor 29, 115, 130-134, 136, 138-139, 142, 157-159, 167, 169, 173, 177, 179, 183-184, 187, 196, 209, 215-217, 225-226, 231, 247, 253, 267, 270, 287-294, 296, 298-299, 302-304, 310, 317-318, 334-335, 337-338
de Chantal, Jeanne-Françoise 117-118
de Chantal, Marie 160
de Cicé, Adelaïede 48, 58, 178
de Clorivière, Pierre-Joseph 178
de Courballay, Caroline 305-306
de Courtebourne (Marquise) 233
De Decker, Benedictus 154
de Dorlodot, Marie 225, 232, 236-237
de Gamond, Zoé 56, 242

de Guerin, Eugénie 154
de Haerne, Désiré 83
de Hase, Almain 233-234
de Hemptinne, Joseph 12, 151, 220-222, 224, 228
de Hemptinne, Marie 151, 221
de Hemptinne, Paul 222
Dehon, Leon 132
de Jonghe d'Ardoye, Zoé 122, 156, 275
De Keyser, Nicaise 54, 265
de la Bouillerie, François-Alexandre 81-82, 104
de Lamennais, Felicité 164-165
de la Serna, Pierre-Ferdinand 142-143, 304
Delcourt, Joachim 158
Delebecque, Louis Joseph 140
Delehaye, Josse 228
Delehaye, Laurent 229
Delehaye, Ludovica 229-230, 232, 234-235
Delehaye, Pauline 228-229
Del Marmol, Antoine 225, 237
Deluil-Martiny, Marie 133
Delvigne-Gérard, Adèle 151, 214-215
de Marillac, Louise 117
de Mauroy 89
de Meeûs, Anatole 150
de Meeûs, Anna 21, 29-30, 33-35, 42-47, 53-56, 58, 61-68, 73-74, 76, 79-86, 89-93, 104-105, 107-109, 111, 113-118, 122, 125-126, 132, 135-136, 139-143, 146-151, 153-161, 164, 166, 171-175, 177-178, 181-182, 184-185, 187-193, 200, 208-216, 220-225, 228-229, 232, 234, 240-241, 244-245, 247-253, 257, 265-268, 271, 274-275, 277-279, 281, 283-286, 293-306, 309, 318-324, 331-337, 339-340
de Meeûs, Ferdinand 43, 54, 63-64, 88, 91, 129, 192, 222
de Meeûs, Henri 224-225
de Meeûs, Idalie 222
de Meeûs, Marie-Hortense 150
de Mérode, François-Xavier 89, 192, 302
De Molder, Felix 235, 255-256, 277, 292-293, 299
de Montaignac de Chauvance, Louise-Thérèse 82
de Montalembert, Charles 193
de Montpellier, Théodore 213, 224-225, 275, 294, 298, 300
de Namur d'Helzée, Louise 150
de Nédonchel, Mathilde 89, 108, 266-267
de Robertsart, Juliette 67, 229
de Robiano, Elisabeth 48, 150
de Robiano, Eugène 150
de Robiano, Eugénie 150, 155, 257, 281
de Robiano, Léopoldine 122, 146-147, 150, 153, 156, 188, 192, 318
de Robiano, Victor 82, 150
de Robiano, Victorine 150
de Rodriguez, Alphonso 112
de Saint-Martin, Eve 285

de San, Anna (sister Des Anges) 155, 157, 207, 236, 291
Desbille, Justine 20, 58, 77, 153, 312
Desmaissières y López, Micaela 65, 104, 107, 111, 315, 324
Desmanet de Biesme, Julie 82, 122, 155-156, 188, 275, 297-298, 340
De Smedt, Maria-Anna 47
de Tomasz de Bossière, Clarisse 268
Devenise, Jean 72-73
de Vialar, Emilie 154, 193
de Villermont, Charles 89-90, 139, 229, 310
de Villermont, Marie 229
d'Hoogvorst > van der Linden d'Hoogvorst
Dierckx, Marie-Joseph 326-327
Donche, Lodewijk 314
d'Oultremont, Emilie 107, 109, 128, 153, 185, 188, 209, 211-212, 267, 333
Draveman, Fanny 242, 255
Dubouché, Théodelinde 79, 106-107, 132, 173, 324
du Bourg, Camille 68, 133, 139
Ducpétiaux, Edouard 96, 229
Dupanloup, Felix 78, 257

Escherich, Joannes 303-304
Eymard, Pierre-Julien 132, 247, 268

Fage, Antoinette 151
Ferrari, Luigi 192
Flasselaerts, Albertine 214-215, 237
Fontaine, Thérèse 71-72, 155, 170
Francis de Sales 118, 131, 136, 174
Fullerton, Georgiana 68, 228-229

Gatti de Gamond, Isabelle 242-243
Geefs, Fanny 55, 314
Glorieux, Stefaan 175
Goethals, Paul 267
Gonella, Matteo 88
Gonthyn, Pauline 222, 232
Goossens, Petrus 310-311, 317
Gravez, Théodore 214-215, 226, 237

Havenith, Charles 231
Havenith-Fuchs, Adelaïde 229, 231, 234-235, 260
Hayes, Elizabeth 149, 336, 338
Haze, Marie-Thérèse 46, 115, 128, 312, 315
Heger, Constantin 56
Helleputte, Joris 311
Helsen, Amand 72
Herbert, Elizabeth 228-229, 251-252
Hoola van Nooten, Bertha 86

Ignatius 132

Javouhey, Anne-Marie 86

Jennesseaux, Pierre 177
Joseph II 59
Juliana of Cornillon 117, 134, 139, 318

Kestre, Fanny 21, 29-30, 33-35, 43-47, 53, 61-63, 65, 67-68, 73, 76-81, 83, 86-90, 102-103, 107-109, 111-117, 125-126, 128-134, 136, 138-140, 148-151, 154, 158-160, 167-169, 171-175, 183-187, 189, 196, 200, 208-209, 214-216, 225-226, 229, 232, 234, 236-237, 239-241, 246-249, 257-258, 265-268, 270, 277-282, 284-285, 293, 296, 304, 308-315, 324, 331-340
Kestre, Félicie 53, 151
Kestre, Louis 53, 67
Kestre, Marie 53
Kestre, Sidonie 67-68, 73, 152, 160, 279
Knight, Mary Clare 106-107
Kockerols, Jean 129-131, 133, 268, 294
Kohrsch, Anna Bella 130

Labouré, Cathérine 115-116
Lacordaire, Jean Baptiste 65
Lagae, Agatha 126
Lagasse, Maria 208
Lalieu-Gérard, Alix 214-215, 278, 311
Lambertz, Joannes 314
Lammens, Jules 220-222, 224
Lammens, Marie 232
Lammens, Mina 160, 188, 220, 224, 232
Lamotte, Clara 326
Lateau, Louise 133
Lauwers, Henriette 185
Lauwers, Jean-Baptiste 170
Leclercq, Angelique 53
Legrelle, Aloysius 124, 144, 177, 183-184, 207, 226-227, 256, 281, 291-293, 334, 338
Leirens, Cécile 209
Lejeune, Paulin 323
Lenferna de Laresle, Marie-Augustine (Caroline) 109, 302
Leo XIII 54, 250-251, 253, 257-258, 305-307, 319-321, 337
Leopold II 323
Liguori, Alphonsus 111, 118, 131
Looijaard, Jan 157
Loos, Antoinette 72
Loveling, Rosalie 87, 93, 314
Loveling, Virginie 87, 93, 273

Maartens, Wilhelmina 208
MacCarthy, Nicholas Tuite 272-273
Maes, Fanny-Joseph 158, 160, 212
Mallet, Gabriël 313
Malou, Jean-Baptist 189, 300
Manning, Henry Edward 250-252
Marie-Claire de Jésus (sister) 313, 319

Marx, Karl 75
Maus-Poncelet, Marie-Barde 131
Milleret, Marie-Eugénie 106, 132
Minsart, Nicolas 314
Miron, Jacques 272-273
Mizet (Parish priest of Sougné) 254
Momm, Adelheid 260

Nolet de Brauwere van Steeland, Ivan 317

Oeyen, Thérèse 275-277
Ozanam, Frédéric 59

Papeians de Morchoven, Emma 321
Parent, Zoé 56
Paridaens, Cicercule 46, 48, 61, 177, 312, 319, 326
Patrizi, Constantino 305-306
Pauwels, Ernest 325
Pecci, Vincenzo > Leo XIII
Pététot, Pierre 215, 246-247, 250
Pieraerts, Constant 152
Pieraerts, Hortense 152-153
Pisani de la Gaude, Charles 58
Pius IX 88-89, 122, 132, 134, 169, 193, 197, 213, 245, 266, 295, 300, 305, 312
Pius X 109, 321
Pladys, Eugène 318
Poodts, Sylvie 155, 157
Potter, Mary 307
Prout, Elizabeth 159

Quaglia, Angelo 303

Rogiers, Louise 232-233
Roothaan, Jan 136, 176, 191

Sacré, Petrus J.F. 242
Schellekens, Antonia 275
Scheppers, Victor 175
Scheys, Elisabeth 77
Schoofs, Philippe 130, 144-145, 172, 179-182, 203, 265, 291-292
Schouppe, François-Xavier 284, 299
Serruys, Caroline 249
Serruys, Léonce 249
Serweytens, Annette 126, 174
Snickers, Petrus, 304
Sohy,Philippe 280
Sterckx, Engelbertus 58-59, 70, 72-73, 79-80, 83-84, 86-87, 90, 99-101, 133-134, 140-141, 156, 158-159, 162-171, 175, 177-179, 183, 186-187, 189, 191, 250, 288

Taylor, Fanny 149, 181, 196, 199, 252, 336, 338
Teichmann, Constance 47-48, 51, 60-61, 65, 149, 151, 242, 340

Teichmann-Cooppal, Marie-Antoinette 47, 61, 97
Telghuys, Hendrik 46-47
Telghuys, Isabella 47, 54
Telghuys, Wilhelmina 9-10, 21, 29, 33-35, 46-47, 49, 53-54, 60-61, 65-66, 73, 75-76, 94-99, 109-114, 117, 124-128, 136-138, 143-145, 149, 151-155, 167-168, 171-172, 175, 179-182, 184, 196, 200, 203-206, 208, 214, 226, 227-232, 234-236, 240-242, 252-256, 258-266, 273, 275-284, 291-293, 309, 324-327, 331-337, 339-340
Teresa of Avila 116-117, 138, 212, 330
Triest, Petrus-Jozef 154

Van Achter, Felix 131-132
Van Biervliet, Melanie 243-244, 273, 280
van Caloen, Louis 94
Van Celst, Helena 97, 153
Van Celst, Sophie 153
Van Crombrugghe, Clara 232-233
Vanderhaegen, Augustine 156-157
van der Linden d'Hooghvorst, Marie-Thérèse 82, 86, 142, 211
Van de Stichele, Dominica 118
Van Diest, Isala 273
Van Hoylant, Joannes 72-73
Van Langermeersch, Jeroom 319-320
Vannutelli, Vincenzo 306
van Outryve-d'Ydewalle, Emilie 232, 234, 251
Van Roey, Jozef Ernest 322-324
Vaughan, Herbert 251, 336
Verbeke, Charles 239
Verest, Jules 326
Verhaegen, Arthur 12, 224
Verhelle, Agathe 20
Verhoustraeten, Ludovic 80, 129, 133
Verlaine, Marguerite 315, 317
Vermeersch, Zénobie 149
Veuillot, Louis 67
Vezeri, Teresa 301
Vilain XIIII, Alfred 227
Vilain XIIII, Charles 227
Vilain XIIII, Marie 144, 218, 226-228, 233-234, 236, 253, 290, 337, 340
Vilain XIIII, Philippe 227
Vincent de Sales 117
Vitteleschi, Salvatore Nobili 300
Voirin, Marie-Xavier 128

Ward, Mary 57
Willems, Marie-Aloysia 280
Wilmer, Gerardus 249-250, 267, 303-304
Winnen, Jean-Phlippe 185-186
Wiseman, Nicholas 128
Woolf, Virginia 30, 125
Wüllenweber, Thérèse von 212-213

COLOPHON

FINAL EDITING
Luc Vints

COPY EDITING
Lieve Claes

LAY-OUT
Alexis Vermeylen

KADOC
Documentation and Research Center on Religion, Culture and Society
Vlamingenstraat 39
B - 3000 Leuven
www.kadoc.kuleuven.be

Leuven University Press
Minderbroedersstraat 4
B - 3000 Leuven
www.lup.be

COLOPHON